BRADFORD'S
CROSSWORD
SOLVER'S
LISTS

Collins

HarperCollins Publishers
Westerhill Road
Bishopbriggs
Glasgow
G64 2QT
Great Britain

Second Edition 2008

Reprint 10 9 8 7 6 5 4 3 2 1 0

© HarperCollins Publishers 2004
Some of the lists in this book have
been adapted from material in
*Collins Bradford's Crossword Solver's
Dictionary*, © Anne R. Bradford, 2003

ISBN 978-0-00-728086-5

Collins® is a registered trademark of
HarperCollins Publishers Limited

www.collinslanguage.com

A catalogue record for this book is
available from the British Library

Technical Production Coordination
by Thomas Callan
Typeset by Wordcraft, Glasgow

Printed by LEGO Spa, Lavis (Trento),
Italy

EDITOR
Helen Hucker

CONSULTANT EDITOR
Anne R. Bradford

Note

Preface

Since the *Bradford's Crossword Solver's Dictionary* was first published in 1986, it has proved to be an invaluable aid for countless cruciverbalists. Compiled as a daily task since 1957 by Anne R. Bradford, a true crossword lover and an active member of the Crossword Club who still solves around 20 crosswords a week, the book has gone from strength to strength over a number of editions, offering the user over 200,000 crossword solutions as well as advice on solving cryptic clues. The latest edition has proved to be the most successful and popular yet.

Now, the **Bradford's Crossword Lists** offers all crossword solvers the essential companion to the *Bradford's Crossword Solver's Dictionary*. It provides hundreds of word lists covering a wide range of subjects, to help with solving tricky crossword clues.

This brand-new addition to the Bradford's crossword series has been compiled from the Collins thesaurus database, with additional material and advice from Anne Bradford, and gives useful word lists on hundreds of subjects, from **Artists**, **Birds**, and **Collectors** to **Winds**, **Worms**, and **Zoology**. Where the entry consists of a straight list of vocabulary on a given subject – for example at **Fish** – the lists are arranged by number of letters and then alphabetically, so that you can spot the word you need to complete your grid quickly. Where an entry includes additional useful information – for example, at **Capitals**, where both the capital and its country are shown – the list is arranged in columns to allow you to find the relevant material which you need to solve your clue. The book therefore provides both vocabulary lists and encyclopedic information – both of which are invaluable for crossword solving.

Solving crossword clues

Crossword puzzles tend to be basically 'quick' or 'cryptic'. A 'quick' crossword usually relies on a one or two-word clue which is a simple definition of the answer required. As has been stated, many words have different meanings, so that the clue 'ball' could equally well lead to the answer 'sphere', 'orb' or 'dance'. The way to solve 'quick' crosswords is to press on until probable answers begin to interlink, which is a good sign that you are on the right track.

'Cryptic' crosswords are another matter. Here the clue usually consists of a basic definition, given at either the beginning or end of the clue, together with one or more definitions of parts of the answer. Here are some examples taken from alltime favourites recorded over the years:

1. *'Tradesman who bursts into tears'* (**Stationer**)

   Tradesman is a definition of stationer. Bursts is cleverly used as an indication of an anagram, which into tears is of stationer.

2. *'Sunday school tune'* (**Strain**)

   Here Sunday is used to define its abbreviation S, school is a synonym for train, and put together they give strain, which is a synonym of tune.

3. *'Result for everyone when head gets at bottom'* (**Ache**) (used as a 'down' clue)

   This is what is known as an '& lit' clue, meaning that the setter has hit on a happy composition which could literally be true. Everyone here is a synonym for each, move the head (first letter) of the word to the bottom, and the answer is revealed, the whole clue being the definition of the answer in this case.

4. *'Tin out East'* (**Sen**)

   In this example, tin, implying 'money', requires its chemical symbol Sn to go out(side) East, or its abbreviation, E, the whole clue being a definition of a currency (sen) used in the East.

5. *'Information given to communist in return for sex'* (**Gender**)

   Information can be defined as gen; communist is almost always red, in return indicates 'reversed', leading to gen-der, a synonym for sex.

6. *'Row about no enclosure of this with sardines'* (**Tin-opener**)

   Row is a synonym for tier, about indicates 'surrounding', no enclosure can be no pen, leading to ti-no pen-er, and another '& lit' clue.

7. 'Cake-sandwiches-meat, at Uncle Sam's party' (Clambake)

   Meat here is lamb, sandwiches is used as a verb, so we have C-lamb-ake, which is a kind of party in America. Uncle Sam or US is often used to indicate America.

8. 'Initially passionate meeting of boy and girl could result in it' (Pregnancy)

   Initially is usually a sign of a first letter, in this case 'p' for passionate + Reg (a boy) and Nancy (a girl), and another clever '& lit'.

With 'cryptic' clues the solver needs to try to analyse the parts to see what he or she is looking for – which word or words can be the straight definition, and which refer to the parts or hint at anagrams or other subterfuges. Whilst it would be unrealistic to claim total infallibility, practice has shown that in most crosswords some 90% of the answers are to be found in this work.

Anne R. Bradford

How to use the book

This book gives useful vocabulary lists and information on hundreds of subjects which are likely to come up as part of crossword clues. The lists are arranged alphabetically by subject, so finding the one you want is as quick and easy as looking up a dictionary. A full table of the lists and the pages on which they appear is also given at the front of the book.

Where the entry consists of a straightforward list of words relevant to a given subject, such as **Pigs**, **Pasta**, or **Birds**, the words are arranged by length, with all three-letter words grouped together in alphabetical order, then all four-letter words, then all five-letter words, and so on.

Where an entry includes additional useful information – for example at **US States**, where not only the name of each state is shown, but also its **abbreviation**, **zip code**, **nickname**, and **capital** – the list is arranged in columns to allow you to find the relevant information you need to solve your clue. The book thus provides both vocabulary and encyclopaedic information, set out in whichever way will be most helpful to the user.

Lists such as **Artists** and **Composers**, which consist of people's names, are arranged by length of the surname, or whichever part of the name the person is best known by, and then alphabetically within each length group. First names and other more 'optional' elements, such as nicknames and initials, are shown after the main part of the name, in italics. You can therefore find the person you are looking for straight away, and then choose the part of their name which is relevant to your crossword solution.

Cross-references are also included wherever appropriate at the ends of entries, so that if you happen to be looking up, for example, the entry for **Animals**, you can see straight away that there are also related lists at **Amphibians**, **Birds**, **Insects**, and so on, which may provide further useful information to help you solve your clue. The cross-references are introduced by the line 'See also:' and each is preceded by the symbol ➤ with the cross-referenced list's title shown in bold type.

About the Author

Anne Bradford's love of words began to make itself evident even in her schooldays, when, as Head Girl of her school, she instituted a novel punishment – instead of making rulebreakers write lines, she had them write out pages from a dictionary, on the grounds that this was a more useful exercise. Little did she know this was soon to be her own daily routine!

In time, crosswords became a magnificent obsession for Anne. All lovers of crosswords can understand the irresistible lure of solving them, but Anne's interest went much deeper than most people's, and when she stopped work in 1957 to have her first child, she found herself starting to note down answers to particularly tricky clues as an aid to memory, in case she should come across them again in another puzzle. It was from this simple beginning that this crossword dictionary evolved.

Over the space of 25 years, Anne continued to build on her collection of solutions, analysing every crossword clue as she solved it and adding it to her steadily growing bank of entries. This unique body of material eventually reached such proportions that she had the idea of offering it to her fellow crossword-solvers as a reference book, and since then, the book has gone from strength to strength, providing valuable help to countless cruciverbalists over a number of editions.

Anne Bradford continues to devote time each day to solving crosswords, averaging some 20 a week – both quick and cryptic – and still avidly collects new solutions for her Crossword Solver's Dictionary at a rate of around 150 a week, compiling each solution by hand (without the use of a computer!) This latest edition therefore includes much new material, gleaned by a true crossword lover who not only solves crosswords but, as an active member of the Crossword Club, can offer the user an insight into the mind of a cunning crossword compiler.

The Crossword Club

If you are interested in crosswords, you might like to consider joining the Crossword Club. Membership is open to all who enjoy tackling challenging crosswords and who appreciate the finer points of clue-writing and grid construction. The Club's magazine, Crossword, contains two prize puzzles each month. A sample issue and full details are available on request.

The Crossword Club
Coombe Farm
Awbridge
Romsey, Hants.
SO51 0HN
UK

email: bh@thecrosswordclub.co.uk
website address: www.crosswordclub.demon.co.uk

Contents

A

C

D

E

F

G

H

I

M

N

O

P

Q

R

S

T

Y

Z

A

Abbreviations

CLASSIFIED ADVERTISEMENTS

Abbreviation	Meaning
AMC *or* amc	All mod cons
Deps	Deposit
Exc *or* excl	Excluding
F/f	Furnished flat
GCH	Gas central heating
Inc *or* incl	Including
Pcm	Per calendar month
Pw	Per week

LONELY HEARTS COLUMN ABBREVIATIONS

Abbreviation	Meaning
GSOH	Good sense of humour
GWM	Gay white male
LTR	Long term relationship
NS or N/S	Non-smoker
SOH	Sense of humour
SWF	Single white female
VGSOH	Very good sense of humour
WLTM	Would like to meet
WSOH	Weird *or* wicked sense of humour

OTHER ABBREVIATIONS

1 letter:

A	L	W
B	M	X
C	N	Y
D	O	Z
E	P	**2 letters:**
F	Q	AA
G	R	Aa
H	S	AB
I	T	A/C
K	U	AC
	V	A/c

Abbreviations

Ac	Bo	D/A
AD	Bp	DA
Ae	B/R	DB
A/F	BR	DC
AF	Br	DD
Af	B/S	DE
AG	BS	D/F
AH	BT	DF
AI	Bt	DG
AK	BV	Dg
AL	B/W	DI
A/M	BW	DJ
AM	Bx	DM
Am	Bz	D/O
AN	C/A	DO
A/O	CA	Do
AO	Ca	D/P
AP	CB	DP
AQ	Cb	DR
Aq	CC	Dr
AR	Cc	DS
Ar	CD	DU
AS	C/d	Du
AT	Cd	DV
At	CE	D/W
AU	CF	Ea
AV	C/f	EC
Av	Cf	Ed
A-v	CG	EE
AZ	Cg	Ee
Az	CH	Eg
BA	Ch	EI
BB	CI	EN
BC	CJ	Eo
B/D	CM	EP
BD	C/N	Ep
Bd	CO	EQ
B/E	C/o	Eq
BE	Co	ER
Bé	CP	ET
B/F	Cp	EU
BJ	CQ	EV
Bk	CR	Ex
B/L	Cr	Ez
BL	CS	FA
Bl	CT	Fa
BM	Ct	FC
Bm	CU	Fc
Bn	Cu	FD
B/O	CV	FI
BO	CW	FL

Fl	HT	Ky
FM	Ht	LA
Fm	HV	La
FO	HW	Lb
Fo	Ia	L/C
Fp	IC	LC
Fr	I/c	Lc
Fs	ID	LD
FT	Id	Ld
Ft	IE	LE
Fv	Ie	LF
FX	IF	LG
GA	IG	Lg
Ga	IL	LH
GB	IM	Lh
Gb	IN	LI
GC	In	LJ
GG	I/O	LL
GI	IP	Ll
Gi	IQ	Ln
Gk	Iq	LO
GM	IR	L/P
GO	Ir	LP
GP	Is	LT
GQ	IT	Lt
Gr	It	LU
GS	IU	LV
GT	Iv	Lv
Gu	JA	LW
Gv	JC	MA
Ha	JD	MB
HC	JJ	Mb
Hd	JP	MC
HE	Jr	MD
HF	Jt	Md
Hf	KB	ME
HG	Kb	Me
Hg	KC	MF
HH	Kc	Mf
HI	KD	MG
HJ	KE	MI
HK	KG	Mi
HL	Kg	Mk
HM	Kn	ML
HO	KP	MM
Ho	Kr	Mm
HP	KS	MN
HQ	KT	MO
HR	Kt	Mo
Hr	KV	MP
HS	KW	Mp

Abbreviations

MR	OM	QR
MS	ON	Qr
MT	OP	QS
Mt	Op	Qs
MU	OR	Qt
MV	OS	Qv
Mv	OT	Qy
MW	OU	RA
MX	Oz	RC
MY	PA	Rc
NA	Pa	RD
N/a	PB	Rd
NB	P/C	RE
Nb	PC	RF
NC	Pc	Rf
ND	PD	RH
Nd	Pd	Rh
NE	PE	RI
N/F	Pf	RL
NF	PG	RM
NG	Pg	Rm
NH	Ph	RN
NI	PI	RP
NJ	PK	RQ
NL	Pk	RR
Nl	PL	RS
NM	Pl	RT
Nm	PM	Rt
No	Pm	RU
NP	PN	RV
Np	PO	Rv
Nr	PP	RW
NS	Pp	SA
Ns	PQ	Sa
NT	Pq	Sb
NV	PR	SC
NY	Pr	Sc
NZ	PS	SD
OB	Ps	Sd
Ob	PT	SF
OC	Pt	Sf
O/c	PW	SG
OD	PX	Sg
OE	QB	SI
Oe	QC	SJ
OF	Qe	SK
OG	QF	Sk
Og	Ql	S/L
OH	QM	SL
OJ	Qm	Sl
OK	Qn	SM

SO	VL	ACA
SP	Vl	ACC
Sp	VO	Acc
Sq	Vo	ACM
Sr	VP	ACT
SS	VR	ACW
St	VS	ADC
SU	Vs	ADD
SV	Vt	ADH
Sv	Vv	Adj
SW	VW	Adm
Sw	WA	ADO
TA	WB	Adv
TB	Wb	AEA
Tb	WC	AEC
TC	Wc	Aet
TD	WD	AEW
TG	Wd	AFB
Tg	Wf	AFC
TM	Wg	Afg
TN	WI	AFK
Tr	WK	AFL
TT	Wk	AFM
TU	WO	AFN
TV	W/o	Afp
TX	WP	AFV
UA	WR	AGC
UC	Wt	AGM
Uc	WV	AGN
UK	WY	AGR
UN	Xn	Agr
UP	XO	Agt
UR	Xt	AHQ
U/S	YC	AIA
US	Yd	AID
Us	Yr	AIF
UT	YT	AIH
UU	ZB	AIM
UV		AIR
VA	**3 letters:**	AIS
Va	AAA	AJA
VB	AAM	AJC
Vb	AAP	Aka
VD	ABA	Ala
Vd	ABC	Alb
VF	ABH	Ald
VG	Abl	ALF
Vg	ABM	Alg
VI	Abp	Alk
Vi	ABS	ALP
VJ	ABV	ALS

5

Abbreviations

ALU	Ave	BNA
AMA	AVM	BNP
AMF	Avn	BOD
AMM	AWA	Bol
AMP	AWS	BOT
Amp	AWU	Bot
Amt	AZT	BPC
AMU	BAF	BPE
Amu	BAK	Bpi
ANA	BAL	BPR
ANC	BAR	Bps
ANU	Bar	Bpt
ANZ	BBC	BRB
AOB	BBL	BRE
AOC	BBQ	Bro
AOH	BBS	BRT
AOR	BCA	BSB
APB	BCC	BSC
APR	BCD	BSc
Apr	BCE	BSE
APT	BCF	BSF
Apt	BCG	BSI
ARA	BCh	BSL
ARC	BCL	Bs/L
Arg	BCS	Bsl
Ark	BDA	BSP
Arm	Bde	BSS
Arr	Bdl	BST
ART	BDS	BSW
ARV	Bds	BTG
ASA	BEA	BTh
ASB	BEd	Btl
ASL	BEF	BTU
Asl	BEM	Btu
ASM	BeV	BTW
AST	BFA	Bty
ASW	BFI	BUF
ATB	BFN	Bul
ATC	BHP	Bur
ATK	Bhp	BVA
ATM	Bid	BVM
Atm	BIM	BWD
ATN	BIS	BWG
ATP	Bkg	BWR
ATV	Bks	BWV
AUC	BLL	CAA
Aug	BMA	CAB
AUS	BMI	CAE
Aus	BMJ	CAF
AUT	BMR	CAI
AVC	BMX	CAL

Cal	CIE	CRO
CAM	Cie	CRP
Can	Cif	CRT
CAP	CIM	CSA
Cap	CIO	CSB
CAR	Cir	CSC
CAS	CIS	Csc
CAT	CIT	CSE
Cat	Cit	CSF
CAV	CJA	CSM
CAW	CJD	CSR
CBC	CLC	CSS
CBD	CMG	CST
CBE	Cml	CSV
CBI	CMV	CTC
CBR	CNA	Ctn
CBS	CND	CTO
CBT	CNG	CTR
Ccc	CNN	Cts
CCD	CNR	CTU
CCF	CNS	CTV
CCJ	CoA	CVA
CDC	COD	CVO
CDE	COI	CVS
Cdf	Col	CWA
Cdn	Com	Cwo
CDR	Con	CWS
Cdr	COO	Cwt
CDT	CoO	CWU
CDU	COP	CYA
CDV	Cor	CYF
CER	COS	DAB
CET	Cos	Dak
CFB	Cot	Dan
CFC	COV	DAP
CFD	Coy	DAR
CFE	CPA	DAT
Cfi	CPD	Dat
CFL	Cpd	DBE
CFS	CPI	Dbh
CGI	Cpi	DBS
CGM	Cpl	DCB
CGS	CPO	DCC
CGT	CPR	DCF
ChB	CPS	DCL
ChE	Cps	DCM
Chg	CPU	DDR
ChM	CQB	DDS
CIA	CRE	Deb
CIB	CRI	Dec
CID	CRM	Def

Abbreviations

Deg	DSS	EOC
Del	DST	Eom
Dem	DTI	EPA
Den	DTL	EPG
Dep	DTP	Eph
DES	DT's	EPO
DET	DTT	EPP
DFC	Dur	EPR
DFM	DVD	Eps
DHA	DVM	EPZ
DHB	DVT	EQC
DHS	DWP	ERA
Din	Dwt	Erf
Dip	EAS	ERM
Dir	EBS	ERO
DIY	EBU	ERS
DLL	EBV	ESA
DLR	ECB	ESB
Dlr	ECG	Esd
DMA	ECR	ESL
DMD	ECS	ESN
DMF	ECT	ESO
DMK	EDC	ESP
DMS	EDI	Esq
DMs	EDM	ESR
DMT	EDT	EST
DMZ	EEA	Est
DNR	EEC	Esu
DNS	EEG	ETA
DOA	EFA	Etc
DOC	EFL	ETD
Doc	EGM	ETF
DOD	EHF	Eth
DOE	EHO	Ety
DoH	EHV	EVA
Dol	EIA	EWO
DOM	EIB	Exc
Dom	EKG	Exr
Doz	ELF	Ext
DPB	ELT	FAA
DPH	Emf	FAB
Dpi	EMS	FAI
DPM	EMU	FAO
DPP	Emu	FAQ
Dpt	EMV	Faq
DPW	Enc	FAS
DSC	ENG	FBA
DSc	Eng	FBI
DSM	ENO	FBL
DSO	Ens	FBW
Dsp	ENT	FCA

FCC	GCE	Heb
FCO	GCF	Her
FDA	GDP	HEU
Fdm	GDR	HEW
FDP	Gds	HGH
FDR	Gen	Hgt
Feb	Ger	HGV
Fec	GeT	Hhd
Fed	GeV	HIE
Fem	GHB	HIH
FET	GHQ	HIM
Ffa	GIS	HIV
FIA	GLA	HJS
Fig	GLC	HMG
Fin	Gld	HMI
Fla	GMB	HMS
Fld	GMC	HNC
FMD	Gmc	HND
FMS	GMO	Hon
Fob	GMT	Hos
FoC	GNC	HPV
FoE	GNP	HRE
Fol	Gns	HRH
For	GOC	HRT
FPA	GOM	HSE
FPO	GOP	HSH
Fps	Gov	HSM
FRG	GPI	HST
Fri	GPO	Hts
Frl	GPS	HUD
FRS	GPU	HWM
Frt	GRF	Hyp
FSA	Gro	IAA
FSB	GSM	IAF
FSH	Gsm	IAP
Fth	GSR	IAS
Ft-l	GST	IBA
Fur	GTC	IBF
FWD	Gtd	ICA
Fwd	GUM	ICC
FYI	Gyn	ICE
FZS	HAA	Ice
GAA	Hab	ICI
GAI	HAC	ICJ
GAL	Hag	ICS
Gal	HBC	ICT
GBE	HBM	ICU
GBH	HCF	IDA
GBS	HCG	Ida
GCA	Hcp	IDB
GCB	HDL	IDC

Abbreviations

IDD	ITA	Lam
IDN	Ita	LAN
IDP	ITC	Lat
IEA	ITN	LBD
IEE	ITO	Lbf
IFA	ITU	LBJ
IFC	ITV	LBO
IFF	IUD	LBV
IFP	IUS	Lbw
IFR	IVF	LCD
IFS	IVR	Lcd
IGC	IWC	LCJ
IGM	IWW	LCL
IGY	JAG	Lcm
IHC	Jam	Ldg
Iid	Jan	LDL
IJC	JAP	LDR
Ill	Jap	LDS
ILO	Jas	LEA
ILR	JCD	LED
ILS	JCL	LEO
ILU	JCR	Lev
IMF	JCS	LGV
IMO	Jer	Lhd
Imp	JFK	Lib
IMS	JIT	Liq
Inc	Jnd	Lit
IND	Jnr	LLB
Ind	Jon	LLD
INF	JSA	LLM
INS	JSD	LMS
Ins	JUD	LNG
IOC	Jud	LOL
IOM	Jul	Loq
IOW	Jun	LPG
IPA	JWV	LPO
IPO	Kan	LPS
IRA	KBE	LRT
IRC	KCB	LSD
IRD	Kčs	LSE
Ire	Ken	LSI
IRL	KeV	LSO
IRM	KIT	LSZ
IRO	KKK	LTA
IRS	Knt	Ltd
IRW	Kph	LTR
ISA	KRL	LUV
ISD	KWh	Lux
Isl	KZN	LVP
ISM	Lab	Lwl
ISP	LAC	LWM

MAC	MLF	MVP
Mac	MLG	MVS
Mag	MLR	Nah
Maj	MMC	NAI
Mal	Mmf	NAS
Mar	MMM	Nat
Mat	MMP	NAV
Max	MMV	NBA
MBA	MNA	NBC
MBE	MOB	NBG
MBO	MoC	NCC
MCB	MOD	NCM
MCC	Mod	NCO
MCG	MOH	NCP
MCh	MOI	NDE
MCP	Mol	NDP
MCS	Mon	NDT
MDF	MOR	NEB
MDR	Mor	NEC
MDS	MOS	NEG
MEC	MOT	Neg
MEd	MPC	Neh
Med	MPG	NEP
MEP	Mpg	Nev
Mer	Mph	NFA
Met	MPP	NFB
Mex	MPS	NFL
MEZ	MPV	NFS
MFA	MRA	NFT
Mfd	MRC	NFU
Mfg	MRE	NGA
MFH	MRI	NGC
Mfr	MRM	NGF
MGB	MRP	NGk
Mgr	Msb	NGL
MHA	MSC	NGO
MHC	MSc	NHI
MHD	MSD	NHL
MHG	MSF	NHS
MHR	MSG	NIC
MIA	MSI	NII
Mic	Msl	NLC
Mid	MSM	NLF
Mil	MSP	NLS
Min	MSS	NLW
MIP	MST	NMR
MIT	Mtg	NNP
Mkt	MTV	NOI
MLA	Mus	Nom
MLC	MVD	Nos
MLD	MVO	Nov

Abbreviations

NPA	OHG	PFI
NPC	Ohv	PGA
NPD	OIC	PGD
NPL	OLG	PGR
NPV	OMM	PHC
NQA	OMS	PhD
NRA	ONC	PHS
NRC	OND	PID
NRL	Ono	P-i-n
NRN	ONS	Pkg
NRT	Ont	Pkt
NRV	ONZ	PKU
NSB	OPC	PLA
NSF	Ops	Plc
NSG	Org	PLO
NSU	OSA	PLP
NSW	OSB	PLR
Nth	OSD	PLU
NTO	OSF	PMG
NTP	OSI	PMI
NTS	OST	PMS
NUJ	OTC	PMT
NUM	OTE	PNI
Num	OTT	POB
NUR	Ozs	POD
NUS	PAC	POE
NUT	Pac	POL
NVQ	Pal	Pol
NWT	Pan	POM
NYC	Par	POP
NZC	PAU	Pop
NZE	PAX	POS
NZR	PBX	Pos
OAP	PCB	POW
OAS	PCC	Ppd
OAU	Pcm	PPE
Obb	PCP	Ppm
OBE	PCR	PPP
Obj	Pct	Ppr
Obs	PCV	PPS
OCD	PDA	PRB
OCR	Pdl	Prn
OCS	Pdq	PRO
Oct	PDR	PRP
ODA	PEI	Prs
ODI	Pen	PRT
OED	PEP	PRW
OEM	PER	Psf
OFM	PET	PSG
OFS	Pet	Psi
OFT	Pfa	PSK

PSL	RCM	RRP
PSS	RCN	RSA
PST	RCO	RSC
PSV	RCP	RSG
PTA	RCS	RSI
Pte	RCT	RSJ
Ptg	Rct	RSL
PTN	RDA	RSM
PTO	RDC	RSV
Pts	RDS	RTA
Pty	RDX	RTC
Pub	Ref	RTE
PVA	Reg	RTF
PVC	Rel	RTR
PVR	REM	RTT
PVS	Rep	RUC
Pvt	Res	RUG
PWA	Rev	Rwd
PWR	RFC	Rwy
Pwt	RGB	SAC
QCA	RGN	SAD
QCD	RGS	SAE
QED	Rgt	Sae
QEF	RHA	SAm
QFD	Rhd	Sam
Qld	RHG	SAR
QMC	RHS	SAS
QMG	RIA	SAT
QMS	RIC	SAW
QMV	RIP	SBA
Qqv	Rit	SBE
QSM	Rly	SBS
QSO	RMA	SBU
Qto	RME	ScD
QTS	Rmm	SCE
Qty	RMS	SCG
Que	Rms	Sch
RAC	RMT	Sci
Rad	RNR	SCM
RAE	RNZ	SCP
RAF	ROC	SCR
RAM	Rom	Scr
Ram	Rot	SDI
RAN	RPC	SDP
RAR	RPG	SEC
RAS	RPI	Sec
RBE	Rpm	SEN
RCA	RPS	Sen
RCD	Rps	Seq
Rcd	Rpt	SFA
RCL	RPV	SFO

Abbreviations

SFW	SSM	TLS
Sgd	SSN	TMI
Sgt	SSP	TMT
SHA	Ssp	TMV
SHF	SSR	Tng
SHM	SST	Tob
SIB	Sta	Tox
Sig	STC	TPI
SIN	STD	Tpr
Sin	Std	TQM
SIS	Ste	TRC
SIT	Stg	TRH
SJA	Sth	Trs
SJC	Stk	TSB
SJD	STP	TSE
Skt	Str	TSH
SLD	STV	TSO
Sld	Sub	Tsp
SLR	Suf	TTA
SMD	Sun	TTL
SMP	Sup	TUC
SMS	SUV	TUF
SMV	SVQ	TVM
SNG	Syn	TVP
SNP	Syr	TVR
Snr	TAB	TXT
Sob	Tab	Typ
Soc	TAC	UAE
SOE	TAI	UAM
Sol	Tan	UAR
Som	Tbc	UAV
SOP	Tbs	UBR
Sop	TBT	UCL
SPA	TCM	UCT
SpA	Tdc	UDA
SPD	Tdm	UDC
SPF	TES	UDI
Spp	Tex	UDR
SPR	TGV	UFO
Spt	ThB	UGC
SQA	ThD	UHF
SQL	THI	UHT
Sqn	THX	Ukr
Sqq	TIA	Ult
SRA	Tid	UNA
Sra	Tim	UNO
SRN	TIR	UPC
SRO	Tit	UPI
SSB	TKO	URC
SSC	TLA	URL
SSD	TLC	Uru

USA	WEA	AECL
USB	Wed	AFTN
USM	Wef	AICC
USN	WEU	Alas
USO	WFF	ALCM
USP	Whf	Alta
USS	WHO	AMDG
USW	Whr	Amer
UTC	Wig	Anat
UV-A	Wis	Anim
UV-B	WLM	Anon
UVF	WMD	ANSI
UWT	Wmk	AOCB
VAD	WMO	AONB
VAR	WOF	Apoc
Var	WOW	APRA
VAT	WPA	Arch
Vat	WPB	ARCM
VCR	WPC	ARCS
VDC	Wpm	Ariz
VDT	WST	ARSM
VDU	WTC	Asap
Ven	WTG	ASDE
Vet	WTO	ASIO
VGA	W Va	Assn
VHF	WVS	ASSR
VHS	WWF	Asst
VIP	WWI	ASTM
VIR	WWW	Astr
Vis	Wyo	At no
Viz	XUV	A to J
VLA	YBA	Attn
VLF	YHA	Atty
VMD	Yrs	At wt
VMI	YTS	AUEW
Voc	ZCC	Aust
Vol	ZPG	Avdp
VPL		AWRE
VRI	**4 letters:**	BAOR
Vsb	ACCA	Bapt
VSO	ACCC	Bart
VTR	ACER	BBBC
WAN	ACGI	BBFC
War	ACII	BCAR
WBA	ACLU	BCNU
WBC	Actg	BCNZ
WBO	ACTT	BCom
WBU	ACTU	Beds
WCC	ADFA	Belg
WDA	ADHD	BEng
WDM	Advt	BFPO

Abbreviations

Biog	C of I	Econ
Biol	C of S	ECSC
Bkcy	Colo	Ecua
Bkpt	Comr	EFIS
Bldg	Cong	EFTS
BLit	Conj	Encl
Blvd	Conn	ENEA
BMus	Cons	Engr
BNFL	Coop	Epis
BOAC	Corp	EPNS
Braz	CPAG	ERCP
BRCS	CPRE	ERDF
Brig	CPSA	ESRC
Brit	CPSU	Esth
Bros	CPVE	Et al
BSSc	CQSW	Exec
Bulg	CRAC	Exod
BYOB	Cres	Exor
CABE	Crim	Ezek
Camb	Crit	FACE
Cant	CSCE	FAHA
Caps	CSYS	Fath
Capt	DATV	Fcap
Card	DBib	FCCA
CART	DBMS	FCII
CATV	DCMG	F Eng
CBSO	DCMS	FIDE
CCEA	DCVO	Fl dr
CCMA	DDSc	Flem
CCRC	Decd	Fl oz
CCTA	DEng	FMCG
CCTV	Dent	FMRI
CDNA	Dept	Foll
Cdre	DETR	FONE
CEGB	Deut	FRCM
CEng	DfEE	FRCO
CGBR	DFID	FRCP
Chap	DHSS	FRCS
Chem	Diag	FRGS
Ches	Dial	FRPS
Chin	Diam	FRSC
CICA	DMAC	Ft-lb
CIFE	DMSO	FWIW
CIGS	DMus	GAIN
C in C	DOCG	Gall
Cllr	DTLR	GCHQ
Cmdr	DVLA	GCMG
CMEA	Ebor	GCSE
CNAA	EBRD	GCVO
CNAR	Eccl	Gdns
C of E	Ecol	Genl

Geod	Incl	MDMA
Geog	INLA	Meth
Geol	INRI	Mich
Geom	Inst	MICR
Glos	Intl	MIHL
GmbH	Intr	Minn
GMTA	IOOF	Misc
GnRH	IPCC	Miss
GNVQ	IRAS	MMDS
Govt	IRBM	MmHg
GPMU	ISBN	MMus
GPRS	ISDN	Mont
Grad	ISSN	MPLA
Gram	ISSP	MRBM
Gr wt	Isth	MRCA
GSOH	Ital	MRIA
GSVQ	IUCD	MRNA
Guat	Josh	MRSA
Guin	Junc	MRSC
HAND	Junr	Msgr
Hdbk	JurD	MTBE
HDTV	Kcal	MTBF
HFEA	KCMG	MTNG
HFMD	KCVO	MusB
Hind	KISS	MusD
HMAS	KStJ	MusM
HMCS	LACW	MVDI
HMSO	LAIA	MVSc
Hond	Lb tr	Myth
HSRC	L/Cpl	NAHT
HTLV	Lgth	NAIC
HTML	LH-RH	Natl
HTTP	Ling	NCCL
Hung	Lith	NCEA
IAAF	LMVD	NCIS
IAEA	Long	NCVO
IARU	LRSC	Nebr
Ibid	LTNS	NEDC
IBRD	LTSA	NERC
ICAO	Luth	Neth
ICBM	LVAD	Neut
ICSH	Macc	NFWI
ICTZ	MAgr	NIHE
IDDM	MAOI	NKGB
IFAD	Marq	NKVD
IGBP	Masc	Norm
IKBS	Mass	Norw
ILEA	Math	NRMA
IMCO	Matt	Nt wt
IMHO	MCom	NYSE
Inbd	MCPS	NZEF

Abbreviations

NZEI	Prob	RRNA
NZLR	Proc	RRSP
NZMA	Prod	RSGB
NZOM	Prof	RSNO
NZPA	Prog	RSNZ
NZRN	Pron	RSPB
NZSE	Prot	RSVP
NZSO	Prov	RUOK
Obad	Prox	Russ
Obdt	PSBR	SABC
OCAM	Psia	SABS
OECD	Psid	SACC
OEEC	Psig	SACP
OHMS	PSIS	SAfr
Okla	PSNI	Sans
Oreg	PSTN	SARS
Orig	PTFE	Sask
Orth	PTSD	SATB
OSCE	Quad	SAYE
Oxon	Quot	SCID
PABX	RAAF	Scot
Part	RACQ	SCQF
Pass	RAEC	S Dak
Patd	Rall	SDLP
Path	RAMC	SDRs
PAYE	RAOC	Secy
Payt	RASC	SEED
PCOS	RAVC	SEPA
PDSA	RCAF	Sept
Penn	RCMP	Seqq
Perf	Rcpt	SGML
Peta	RCVS	Shpt
Phar	Recd	SIDS
Phil	Rect	Sing
PHLS	Regd	SIPS
Phon	Regt	SLBM
PHSE	Rept	SLCM
Phys	Retd	SLSC
Pizz	Revd	SNCF
Plur	RFID	SOHF
PNdB	RFLP	Span
Port	RIBA	SPCK
Poss	RICS	Spec
POST	RNAS	Sp gr
PPTA	RNIB	Sp ht
Pred	RNID	SPQR
Pref	RNLI	Srta
Prem	RNVR	SSHA
Prep	RNZN	SSRI
Pres	ROFL	SSSI
Priv	Ronz	SSTA

Stat	V Rev	CITES
Stbd	VSOP	CMIIW
Stge	Vulg	Comdg
Stir	Wash	Comdr
STUC	WFTU	Comdt
Subj	Wisd	Const
Suff	Wkly	Contd
Supt	WKND	Cosec
Surg	WLTM	Cotan
Surv	WRAC	Cryst
Suth	WRAF	CSIRO
SVGA	WRNS	Cwlth
SWFF	Wrnt	Denom
SWOT	WRVS	DipAD
SYHA	WSSD	DipEd
TATT	WWII	DLitt
TAVR	XLNT	DPhil
TCAS	Xnty	Epiph
Tech	YMCA	Epist
Temp	YMHA	Equiv
Tenn	Yugo	Et seq
Terr	YWCA	Ex div
TGWU	YWHA	Ex lib
TIGR	ZAMS	Ex off
TPWS	Zech	Exptl
Trig	Zeph	FASSA
T-RNA	Zool	FRACP
TTFN		FRACS
TTYL	**5 letters:**	FRCVS
Tues	A'asia	FRICS
Turk	Accel	Front
TVEI	Aeron	FRSNZ
TVNZ	AFAIK	FYROM
TVRO	AFNOR	Genit
UKCC	AMICE	Gloss
ULCC	AMIEE	GMDSS
Unit	Archd	H and c
Univ	Assoc	Hants
UPVC	BArch	Hdqrs
USAF	Barit	Herts
USSR	BBSRC	Horol
V aux	BECTU	ICFTU
VCJD	Berks	Ichth
VDQS	BLitt	IMarE
Vers	BPhil	IMinE
Vert	Bucks	IMunE
Visc	Calif	Incog
VLBI	Cambs	Indef
VLCC	CCANZ	Indic
VLSI	Chron	Indiv
Vols	Cifci	Infin

Abbreviations

In mem
Inorg
Inter
Intro
Irreg
Kbyte
Lancs
Leics
Lieut
Lincs
LittB
LittD
L'pool
Lt Cdr
Lt Col
Lt Gen
Lt Gov
Maced
Madag
Manuf
MArch
March
Maths
Mbyte
MEcon
Metal
Middx
MLitt
Moham
Mol wt
Morph
MPhil
MTech
Mt Rev
Mycol
NAACP
Navig
NIDDM
NLLST
Nottm
Notts
NSAID
NSPCC
NZCER
NZRFU
OFris
Op cit
PAGAD
Paren
PPARC
Presb

Propr
Pseud
RAFVR
R and R
Réaum
Ref Ch
Repub
RNWMP
RNZAF
RSFSR
RSPCA
Rt Hon
SAARC
SARFU
Sergt
SGHWR
SHEEP
SMATV
SQUID
Stacc
Subst
Suffr
Switz
Synop
Theol
Theos
Thess
Thurs
Topog
TRALI
Trans
Treas
UKAEA
UNHCR
V and A
Venez
Visct
WAAAF
Warks
Westm
Whsle
Wilts
Worcs
WRAAC
WRAAF
WRANS
Yorks

6 letters:
AARNet
Abbrev

AFL-CIO
AFRAeS
A into G
Am-dram
Approx
Arccos
Archbp
Archit
Arcsin
Arctan
Astrol
Att Gen
Attrib
BPharm
Cantab
CertEd
Colloq
Com Ver
Confed
Covers
DipCom
DipMet
EBITDA
Eccles
Ecclus
Geneal
GOC-in-C
Hon Sec
IChemE
Illust
IMechE
IMNSHO
Imperf
Imp gal
Interj
IONARC
Lib Dem
Loc cit
Maj Gen
MIMinE
MIMunE
NATFHE
Nem con
Neurol
Non seq
Northd
NZEFIP
Obstet
Pat Off
Petrog
Petrol

Philem
Philol
Philos
Photog
Prelim
QARANC
Rev Ver
ROFLOL
Rt Revd
Sgt Maj
Sociol
S of Sol
Sqn Ldr
Staffs
UNCTAD
Ut dict

7 letters:
AFSLAET
Anthrop
Austral
Auth Ver
Bibliog
Brig Gen
Cantuar

Co Derry
Contrib
Decresc
Embryol
Entomol
E Sussex
Intrans
Lexicog
Mineral
New Test
Nol pros
Non pros
Oceanog
Old Test
OTPOTSS
Pat pend
P/E ratio
Physiol
Psychol
Reg prof
Rom Cath
Technol
TE score
Verb sap

8 letters:
AMIChemE
AMIMechE
Archaeol
Co Durham
In loc cit
Meteorol
Ornithol
TCA cycle

9 letters:
Bacteriol
Northants
Pharmacol

10 letters:
Cur adv vult
DipChemEng
Ophthalmol
Palaeontol
Psychoanal

11 letters:
IYKWIMAITYD

Acids

SPECIFIC ACIDS

2 letters:
PH

3 letters:
DNA
HCL
RNA

4 letters:
Dopa
Uric

5 letters:
Auric
Boric
Caro's
L-dopa
Malic
Mucic
Oleic
Orcin

Trona

6 letters:
Acetic
Adipic
Bromic
Capric
Cholic
Citric
Cyanic
Erucic
Formic
Gallic
Lactic
Lauric
Leucin
Lipoic
Maleic
Niacin
Nitric

Oxalic
Pectic
Phenol
Picric
Quinic
Sialic
Sorbic
Tannic
Tiglic
Valine

7 letters:
Abietic
Alginic
Benzoic
Butyric
Caproic
Cerotic
Chloric
Chromic

Acids

Creatin
Ellagic
Ferulic
Folacin
Fumaric
Fusidic
Guanine
Malonic
Meconic
Muramic
Nitrous
Orcinol
Prussic
Pteroic
Pyruvic
Racemic
Sebacic
Selenic
Silicic
Stannic
Stearic
Suberic
Terebic
Titanic
Valeric
Xanthic
Xylonic

8 letters:
Abscisic
Ascorbic
Aspartic
Butanoic
Caprylic
Carbamic
Carbolic
Carbonic
Chlorous
Cinnamic
Creatine
Cresylic
Crotonic
Cyclamic
Decanoic
Ethanoic
Fulminic
Glutamic
Glyceric
Glycolic
Guanylic
Hexanoic

Hippuric
Itaconic
Linoleic
Lysergic
Manganic
Muriatic
Myristic
Nonanoic
Palmitic
Phthalic
Rhodanic
Succinic
Tantalic
Tartaric
Telluric
Tungstic
Tyrosine
Valproic

9 letters:
Aqua-regia
Citydylic
Dichromic
Hydrazoic
Hydriodic
Isocyanic
Linolenic
Methanoic
Nalidixic
Nicotinic
Panthenic
Pentanoic
Propanoic
Propenoic
Pyroboric
Saccharic
Salicylic
Sassolite
Selenious
Sulphonic
Sulphuric

10 letters:
Aquafortis
Asparagine
Barbituric
Citrulline
Dithionous
Dodecanoic
Glucoronic
Glutaminic
Hyaluronic

Methionine
Pelargonic
Perchloric
Phosphoric
Proprionic
Pyrogallic
Ricinoleic
Sulphurous
Thiocyanic
Tryptophan

11 letters:
Arachidonic
Decanedioic
Ethanedioic
Ferricyanic
Ferrocyanic
Gibberellic
Hydnocarpic
Hydrobromic
Methacrylic
Octanedioic
Pantothenic
Permanganic
Phosphorous
Ribonucleic
Sarcolactic
Taurocholic

12 letters:
Aminobenzoic
Chloroacetic
Hydrochloric
Hydrofluoric
Hypochlorous
Indoleacetic
Persulphuric
Phenylalanin
Polyadenalic
Prostacyclin
Pyroligneous
Spiraeic acid
Terephthalic

13 letters:
Galactosamine
Glacial acetic
Heptadecanoic
Indolebutyric
Phenylalanine
Platinocyanic
Prostaglandin

Pyrosulphuric
Thiosulphuric

14 letters:
Hypophosphoric
Metaphosphoric

Polyphosphoric
Pyrophosphoric

15 letters:
Hypophosphorous
Orthophosphoric

Trichloroacetic

16 letters:
Deoxyribonucleic
Para-aminobenzoic

TYPES OF ACID

4 letters:
Acyl
Pyro

5 letters:
Amide
Amino
Fatty
Folic
Iodic

Lewis
Osmic

7 letters:
Dibasic
Mineral
Nucleic
Peracid

8 letters:
Periodic

9 letters:
Polybasic

10 letters:
Carboxylic

12 letters:
Dicarboxylic

14 letters:
Polycarboxylic

AMINO ACIDS

6 letters:
Lysine
Serine

7 letters:
Alanine
Cystine
Glycine
Leucine

Proline

8 letters:
Arginine

9 letters:
Ethionine
Glutamine
Histidine
Ornithine

Threonine

10 letters:
Citrulline
Isoleucine

16 letters:
Triiodothyronine

Actaeon's hounds

4 letters:
Agre
Alce
Nape

5 letters:
Aello
Arcas
Lacon
Ladon
Thous

6 letters:
Canace
Dromas
Lachne
Lebros
Leucon
Sticte

Theron
Tigris

7 letters:
Asbolus
Cyprius
Dorceus
Harpyia
Hylaeus
Laelaps
Lycisce

8 letters:
Agriodus
Arethusa
Harpalus
Hylactor
Melampus
Melaneus

Oribasus
Poemenis
Pterelas

9 letters:
Pamphagus

10 letters:
Ichnobates
Theridamas

11 letters:
Nebrophonus

12 letters:
Melanchaetes

13 letters:
Oresistrophus

Actors

MALE

3 letters:
Lee, *Bruce*
Lee, *Christopher*
Rey, *Fernando*

4 letters:
Cook, *Peter*
Dean, *James*
Depp, *Johnny*
Ford, *Harrison*
Hope, *Bob*
Hurt, *John*
Kean, *Edmund*
Peck, *Gregory*
Penn, *Sean*
Roth, *Tim*
Shaw, *Glen Byam*
Tati, *Jacques*
Wood, *Elijah*

5 letters:
Allen, *Woody*
Bates, *Alan*
Boyer, *Charles*
Brody, *Adrien*
Caine, *Michael*
Flynn, *Errol*
Fonda, *Henry*
Gabin, *Jean*
Gable, *Clark*
Grant, *Cary*
Hanks, *Tom*
Hardy, *Oliver*
Irons, *Jeremy*
Jones, *Tommy Lee*
Kelly, *Gene*
Lloyd, *Harold*
Mason, *James*
Miles, *Bernard*
Mills, *John*
Moore, *Dudley*
Neill, *Sam*
Niven, *David*
Quinn, *Anthony*
Tracy, *Spencer*
Wayne, *John*

6 letters:
Beatty, *Warren*
Bogart, *Humphrey*
Brando, *Marlon*
Brooks, *Mel*
Burton, *Richard*
Cagney, *James*
Callow, *Simon*
Carrey, *Jim*
Cleese, *John*
Cooper, *Chris*
Cooper, *Gary*
Coward, *Noel*
Cruise, *Tom*
De Niro, *Robert*
De Sica, *Vittorio*
Dexter, *John*
Fields, *WC*
Finney, *Albert*
Gibson, *Mel*
Howard, *Leslie*
Howard, *Trevor*
Hudson, *Rock*
Irving, *Henry*
Jacobi, *Derek*
Jolson, *Al*
Keaton, *Buster*
Keitel, *Harvey*
Kemble, *John*
Laurel, *Stan*
Lugosi, *Bela*
Massey, *Raymond*
Morley, *Robert*
Neeson, *Liam*
Newman, *Paul*
Oldman, *Gary*
O'Toole, *Peter*
Pacino, *Al*
Quayle, *Anthony*
Reagan, *Ronald*
Spacey, *Kevin*
Welles, *Orson*
Willis, *Bruce*

7 letters:
Astaire, *Fred*
Bennett, *Alan*

Bogarde, *Dirk*
Branagh, *Kenneth*
Burbage, *Richard*
Carlyle, *Robert*
Chaplin, *Charlie*
Clooney, *George*
Connery, *Sean*
Costner, *Kevin*
Douglas, *Kirk*
Douglas, *Michael*
Freeman, *Morgan*
Garrick, *David*
Gielgud, *John*
Hackman, *Gene*
Hoffman, *Dustin*
Hopkins, *Anthony*
Hordern, *Michael*
Karloff, *Boris*
McQueen, *Steve*
Mitchum, *Robert*
Olivier, *Laurence*
Redford, *Robert*
Robbins, *Tim*
Robeson, *Paul*
Sellers, *Peter*
Shepard, *Sam*
Stewart, *James*
Ustinov, *Peter*

8 letters:
Barrault, *Jean-Louis*
Belmondo, *Jean-Paul*
Crawford, *Michael*
Day-Lewis, *Daniel*
DiCaprio, *Leonardo*
Eastwood, *Clint*
Guinness, *Alec*
Harrison, *Rex*
Kingsley, *Ben*
Laughton, *Charles*
Macready, *William*
McGregor, *Ewan*
McKellen, *Ian*
Redgrave, *Michael*
Robinson, *Edward G*

Scofield, *Paul*
Stallone, *Sylvester*
Travolta, *John*
Von Sydow, *Max*

9 letters:
Barrymore, *John*
Chevalier, *Maurice*
Depardieu, *Gerard*
Fairbanks,
 Douglas Jr
Fairbanks,
 Douglas Snr

FEMALE
3 letters:
Bow, *Clara*

4 letters:
Cruz, *Penelope*
Gish, *Lillian*
Hawn, *Goldie*
Qing, *Jian*
West, *Mae*

5 letters:
Brice, *Fanny*
Close, *Glenn*
Davis, *Bette*
Davis, *Geena*
Davis, *Judy*
Dench, *Judi*
Evans, *Edith*
Fonda, *Jane*
Garbo, *Greta*
Kelly, *Grace*
Lange, *Jessica*
Leigh, *Vivien*
Lenya, *Lotte*
Lopez, *Jennifer*
Loren, *Sophia*
Smith, *Maggie*
Stone, *Sharon*
Terry, *Ellen*
Welch, *Raquel*

6 letters:
Arnaud, *Yvonne*
Bardot, *Brigitte*
Foster, *Jodie*
Harlow, *Jean*
Hiller, *Wendy*

Humphries, *Barry*
Lancaster, *Burt*
Nicholson, *Jack*
Pleasence, *Donald*
Radcliffe, *Daniel*
Valentino, *Rudolph*

10 letters:
Richardson, *Ralph*
Sutherland, *Donald*

11 letters:
Mastroianni,
 Marcello

Hunter, *Holly*
Keaton, *Diane*
Kemble, *Fanny*
Kidman, *Nicole*
Mirren, *Helen*
Monroe, *Marilyn*
Moreau, *Jeanne*
Robson, *Flora*
Rogers, *Ginger*
Seyrig, *Delphine*
Spacek, *Sissy*
Streep, *Meryl*
Suzman, *Janet*
Taylor, *Elizabeth*
Temple, *Shirley*
Theron, *Charlize*
Weaver, *Sigourney*

7 letters:
Andrews, *Julie*
Bergman, *Ingrid*
Binoche, *Juliette*
Colbert, *Claudette*
Deneuve, *Catherine*
Dunaway, *Faye*
Gardner, *Ava*
Garland, *Judy*
Hepburn, *Audrey*
Hepburn, *Katharine*
Huppert, *Isabelle*
Jackson, *Glenda*
McKenna, *Siobhan*
Roberts, *Julia*
Siddons, *Sarah*
Walters, *Julie*
Winslet, *Kate*

Weissmuller,
 Johnny

12 letters:
Attenborough,
 Richard
Stanislavsky,
 Konstantin

14 letters:
Schwarzenegger,
 Arnold

8 letters:
Ashcroft, *Peggy*
Bankhead, *Tallulah*
Crawford, *Joan*
Dietrich, *Marlene*
Grenfell, *Joyce*
Knightly, *Keira*
Lawrence, *Gertrude*
Lockwood, *Margaret*
MacLaine, *Shirley*
Mercouri, *Melina*
Minnelli, *Liza*
Pfeiffer, *Michelle*
Pickford, *Mary*
Redgrave, *Vanessa*
Sarandon, *Susan*
Signoret, *Simone*
Thompson, *Emma*
Whitelaw, *Billie*

9 letters:
Bernhardt, *Sarah*
Blanchett, *Cate*
Plowright, *Joan*
Streisand, *Barbra*
Thorndike, *Sybil*
Zellweger, *Renée*
Zeta-Jones, *Catherine*

10 letters:
Rutherford,
 Margaret
Woffington, *Peg*

12 letters:
Bonham Carter,
 Helena

Affection, terms of

3 letters:
Pet

4 letters:
Babe
Baby
Bean
Dear
Doll
Lamb
Love
Star

5 letters:
Angel
Babes
Goose
Honey
Kitty
Lover
Petal
Puppy
Sugar

Tiger
Toots

6 letters:
Flower
Kitten
Muppet
Poppet
Sweets
Weasel

7 letters:
Beloved
Chicken
Darling
Dearest
Dear one
Pet lamb
Pumpkin
Treacle

8 letters:
Kitty cat
Little 'un

Loved one
Munchkin
Precious
Princess
Pussycat
Treasure
Truelove

9 letters:
Bunnykins
Dearheart
Little one
Pepperpot

10 letters:
Honey bunny
Sweetheart
Sweetie pie

11 letters:
Fluffy bunny

12 letters:
Chicken bunny

Agriculturalists

4 letters:
Coke, *Thomas William*
Tull, *Jethro*

5 letters:
Lawes, *Sir John Bennet*
Young, *Arthur*

6 letters:
Carver, *George Washington*

7 letters:
Borlaug, *Norman Ernest*

Burbank, *Luther*

8 letters:
Bakewell, *Robert*

9 letters:
McCormick, *Cyrus Hall*

12 letters:
Boussingault, *Jean-Baptiste Joseph*

Agricultural terms

2 letters:
EE

3 letters:
Agr
Bed
Box

BST
CAP
Cot
Cow
Cut
Dag
Dip

Dry
End
Ewe
Fan
Hay
Hoe
Hog

Hut
Kye
Lea
Ley
Mob
Mow
NFU
Pen
Pig
Pug
Ram
RAS
Rig
Run
Rye
Set
Sow
Sty
Tag
Ted
Teg
Tup
Van
Win

4 letters:
Bail
Bale
Balk
Barn
Beam
Bone
Boss
Bull
Byre
Calf
Chip
Clip
Cock
Comb
Come
Coop
Corn
Cote
Crib
Crop
Cull
Disc
Dogy
Drag
Dump

Dung
Duty
Fall
Farm
Feed
Fire
Foal
Fold
Frib
Gang
Grow
Hack
Ha-ha
Hame
Heel
Herd
Hind
Hops
IFAD
Lair
Lamb
Land
Leaf
Lime
List
Loan
Mare
Marl
Mash
Meal
Milk
Muck
Oast
Oats
Pest
Plow
Poll
Pook
Rabi
Rape
Raze
Rean
Reap
Rear
Reen
Rich
Rick
Ring
Salt
Seed
Shaw

Shed
Show
Sick
Silo
Slop
Soil
Sole
Sour
Span
Spit
Spud
Stub
Till
Toun
Turn
Unit
Wain
Walk
Wisp
Yard
Yeld
Yoke

5 letters:
Baler
Bench
Board
Bogle
Brake
Cadet
Calve
Capon
Carry
Cavie
Chaff
Chalk
Check
Churn
Chute
Clamp
Clear
Cling
Close
Cocky
Colon
Cover
Crawl
Croft
Dairy
Daych
Dogie

Agricultural terms

Dress
Drift
Drill
Drove
Field
Flail
Flake
Flush
Force
Frame
Frost
Fruit
Glean
Grain
Grass
Graze
Grist
Haunt
Heart
Hedge
Hodge
Horse
Hough
Hovel
Jembe
Kraal
Lands
Lease
Levee
Lodge
Milch
Mulch
Oxbow
Paddy
Plaas
Plant
Poley
Punch
Quern
Quick
Raise
Ranch
Range
Rodeo
Rogue
Rural
Share
Sheaf
Shear
Sheep
Shoat

Shock
Shook
Shote
Singe
Sloot
Spell
Stack
Stale
Stall
Stand
Stile
Stirk
Stock
Stook
Store
Straw
Strip
Swath
Swede
Sweep
Swill
Tally
Tilth
Tolly
Trash
Tribe
Truck
Wheat

6 letters:
Animal
Apiary
Arable
Bail up
Barley
Barren
Barrow
Barton
Binder
Candle
Cattle
Cereal
Cheque
Clutch
Colter
Corral
Cotton
Cowboy
Cowman
Cowpat
Cradle

Cratch
Crutch
Culler
Cut out
Dobbin
Drover
Duster
Eatage
Enrich
Ensile
Fallow
Farmed
Farmer
Farrow
Fatten
Feeder
Fleece
Fodder
Foison
Forage
Furrow
Garner
Gavage
Grange
Grease
Greasy
Grieve
Harrow
Haw-haw
Haymow
Heeler
Heifer
Hen run
Herder
Hockey
Hogget
Hopper
Hummel
Hurdle
Incult
Kharif
Lea-rig
Linhay
Lister
Litter
Manger
Manure
Meadow
Mealie
Mellow
Middle

Mielie
Milker
Mistal
Moshav
Muster
Pakahi
Parity
Pastor
Pigpen
Pigsty
Pleugh
Plough
Porker
Rancho
Ratoon
Reaper
Reddle
Ringer
Ripple
Roller
Ruddle
Run off
Runway
Scythe
Seeder
Shamba
Shears
Shed up
Sheepo
Sheuch
Shorts
Sickle
Silage
Smudge
Spider
Spread
Stable
Stitch
Stover
Summer
Swathe
Take up
Tar boy
Tedder
Thrash
Thresh
Titman
Vinery
Winnow
Winter
Zoo doo

7 letters:
Breaker
Break in
Breeder
Bucolic
Calving
Chamber
Combine
Compost
Conacre
Contact
Coulter
Cowbell
Cowherd
Cowshed
Crofter
Cropper
Culture
Daglock
Dockage
Drummer
Earmark
Exhaust
Farming
Fatling
Feedbag
Feedlot
Fertile
Florist
Foaling
Freshen
Fruiter
Granary
Grazier
Grazing
Grow bag
Haggard
Harvest
Haycock
Hayfork
Hayrick
Hayseed
Hencoop
Hennery
Herbage
Hogwash
Infield
Kolkhoz
Lairage
Lambing
Lay down

Lazy bed
Machair
Milkman
Milling
Multure
Nest box
Nest egg
Nitrate
Nitrify
Oil cake
Orchard
Organic
Paddock
Pannage
Parlour
Pasture
Piggery
Pinfold
Planter
Pork pig
Poultry
Poverty
Prairie
Predial
Produce
Pruning
Rattoon
Reaping
Rearing
Reclaim
Round up
Scarify
Shedder
Shed out
Show day
Skirter
Sleeper
Soilage
Sovkhoz
Sprayer
Staddle
Station
Stubble
Subsoil
Swidden
Swipple
Tankage
Tillage
Topsoil
Tractor
Tumbrel

Agricultural terms

Turbary
Upgrade
Vintage
Wigging
Windrow
Wrangle
Wrestle
Yarding

8 letters:
Abattoir
Agrarian
Agrestal
Agrology
Agronomy
Apiarian
Apiarist
Barnyard
Bone meal
Butchery
Caponize
Cash crop
Checkrow
Chin ball
Churning
Cockatoo
Cockerel
Corncrib
Cornhusk
Cow cocky
Creamery
Crofting
Dairying
Dairyman
Dieldrin
Ditching
Domestic
Drainage
Dressing
Elevator
Empty cow
Ensilage
Farm hand
Farmland
Farmyard
Fishmeal
Flushing
Foremilk
Forestry
Fruitage
Fumatory

Generous
Geoponic
Goatherd
Hacienda
Handfeed
Hatchery
Haymaker
Haystack
Haywagon
Headland
Henhouse
Herdsman
Home farm
Hot fence
Huntaway
Irrigate
Lamb down
Land girl
Land-poor
Landside
Loosebox
Marginal
Maverick
Milkmaid
Moorburn
Mowburnt
Muckrake
Muirburn
Muleteer
Outfield
Overcrop
Pastoral
Perchery
Pharming
Pigswill
Plant out
Plougher
Poundage
Praedial
Preserve
Property
Quickset
Richness
Root crop
Rotation
Seed corn
Seminary
Set-aside
Shambles
Shed hand
Sheep-dip

Shepherd
Shieling
Soil bank
Spreader
Stabling
Stampede
Steading
Stockman
Stubbled
Swanherd
Sweatbox
Systemic
Thresher
Top-dress
Town milk
Two-tooth
Unbolted
Vineyard
Vintager
Voorskot
Watering
Wayleggo
Wool clip
Woolshed
Workfolk
Wrangler
Zamindar
Zemindar

9 letters:
Aftermath
Agterskot
Beastings
Beestings
Bell sheep
Bellyband
Biestings
Biosafety
Breakaway
Broadcast
Bunkhouse
Butterfat
Canebrake
Cane piece
Catalogue
Catch crop
Cattleman
Cleanskin
Cornfield
Corn shock
Corn shuck

Cornstalk
Cover crop
Cultivate
Dairymaid
Dead stock
Depasture
Dog tucker
Enclosure
Expellers
Extensive
Farmstead
Fertilize
Field corn
Field tile
Flystrike
Free-range
Geoponics
Gleanings
Grassland
Hand glass
Hand-piece
Hard wheat
Harvester
Haymaking
Home-grown
Homestead
Hop-picker
Husbandry
Intensive
Intercrop
Livestock
Moldboard
Mole drain
No-tillage
Overgraze
Overstock
Pasturage
Pesticide
Phosphate
Pitchfork
Ploughboy
Ploughing
Ploughman
Poulterer
Provender
Rangeland
Rice field
Rotary hoe
Rotovator
Scarifier
Scourings

Seed drill
Sharecrop
Shearling
Sheepcote
Sheepfold
Sheep race
Sheepwalk
Shrinkage
Side-dress
Slaughter
Soft wheat
Stall-feed
Stock unit
Stock whip
Stockyard
Sundowner
Sunk fence
Swineherd
Tea garden
Thrashing
Threshing
Ventilate
Vernalize
Water-sick
Winnowing
Wool table
Zamindari

10 letters:
Apiculture
Aviculture
Battery hen
Bull tongue
Cattle-cake
Cattle-grid
Cattle prod
Cattle-stop
Corn circle
Corn-picker
Cotton belt
Cotton cake
Cottonseed
Cowfeteria
Crop circle
Crutchings
Cultivable
Cultivated
Cultivator
Deep-litter
Disc harrow
Disc plough

Dry farming
Energy crop
Fertilizer
Fire blight
Fumatorium
Gang plough
Hamshackle
Harvesting
Harvestman
Heading dog
Herd tester
Husbandman
Impregnate
Irrigation
Land reform
Ley farming
Mouldboard
Nitro-chalk
Plantation
Poultryman
Quernstone
Rouseabout
Roustabout
Seed potato
Self-feeder
Semination
Showground
Stockhorse
Stockroute
Stump ranch
Turkey nest
Underdrain
Ungrateful
Unimproved
Virgin soil
Wine grower
Winterfeed
Wool cheque
Woolgrower

11 letters:
Agriculture
Agrobiology
Aquaculture
Aquiculture
Catching pen
Chamberhand
Compostable
Crop-dusting
Cultivation
Dogleg fence

Agricultural terms

Estate agent
Extractions
Factory farm
Full-mouthed
Green manure
Harvest home
Head station
Hedge laying
Hobby farmer
Hydroponics
Insecticide
Latifundium
Mariculture
Milking shed
Monoculture
Mule skinner
Pastoralist
Ploughshare
Ploughstaff
Pomiculture
Reclamation
Sericulture
Sharefarmer
Share-milker
Stock saddle
Subirrigate
Submarginal
Tank farming
Tattie-bogle
Top dressing
Vinedresser
Viniculture
Viticulture
Water meadow
Windlestraw
Winter wheat
Zero grazing

12 letters:
Agribusiness
Agricultural
Agrochemical
Agroforestry

Break feeding
Broiler house
Citriculture
Cotton picker
Crop rotation
Cutting horse
Double-dumped
Forcing house
Furfuraceous
Market garden
Mixed farming
Muck spreader
Rotary plough
Sharecropper
Shearing gang
Shearing shed
Sheep station
Slash-and-burn
Slaughterman
Smallholding
Staddlestone
Strong-eye dog
Taranaki gate
Ten-acre block
Tenant farmer
Transhumance
Trash farming
Uncultivated

13 letters:
Anthropophyte
Double digging
Freezing works
Middlebreaker
Pumice country
Sheepshearing
Strip cropping
Stubble-jumper
Thremmatology

14 letters:
Cottonseed meal
Holding paddock

Milking machine
Slaughterhouse
Terminator seed

15 letters:
Animal husbandry
Butterfat cheque
Cooperative farm
Gentleman-farmer
Green revolution
Market gardening
Nonagricultural
Stump-jump
  plough

16 letters:
Combine harvester
Contour ploughing
Rabbit-proof fence
Sacrifice paddock
Soil conservation
Threshing machine

17 letters:
Aerial top dressing
Potassium chloride
Soldier settlement

18 letters:
Subsistence
farming

19 letters:
Bovine
  somatotrophin
Shifting
  cultivation

20 letters:
Stock and station
  agent

24 letters:
Common
Agricultural
  Policy

Aircraft

TYPES OF AIRCRAFT

3 letters:
Jet
MIG
SST

4 letters:
Moth
STOL
VTOL
Wing

5 letters:
Avion
Blimp
Camel
Comet
Drone
Gotha
Jumbo
Rigid
Stuka
Taube

6 letters:
Auster
Bomber
Canard
Chaser
Fokker
Galaxy
Glider
Hunter
Mirage
Ramjet
Tanker
Tri-jet

7 letters:
Airship
Aviette
Balloon
Biplane
Chopper
Fighter
Harrier
Heinkel
Jump jet
Parasol

Penguin
Propjet
Sopwith
Trident

8 letters:
Aerodyne
Aerostat
Airliner
Autogiro
Autogyro
Brabazon
Concorde
Gyrodyne
Jetliner
Jet plane
Jumbo jet
Mosquito
Oerlikon
Scramjet
Seaplane
Skiplane
Spitfire
Triplane
Turbofan
Turbojet
Viscount
Warplane
Zeppelin

9 letters:
Amphibian
Autoflare
Coleopter
Cyclogiro
Delta-wing
Dirigible
Doodlebug
Fixed-wing
Freighter
Hurricane
Lancaster
Liberator
Microlite
Monoplane
Orthopter
Rotaplane

Sailplane
Semi-rigid
Swept-wing
Swing-wing
Taxiplane
Turboprop

10 letters:
Dive bomber
Flying boat
Flying wing
Hang-glider
Helicopter
Microlight
Multiplane
Tankbuster

11 letters:
Intercepter
Interceptor
Lifting body
Ornithopter
Turboramjet

12 letters:
Night fighter
Sopwith Camel
Stealth plane
Stratotanker
Troop carrier

13 letters:
Convertaplane
Convertiplane
Convertoplane
Fighter-bomber
Hot-air balloon
Light aircraft
Messerschmitt
Stealth bomber
Stratocruiser

16 letters:
Gas-filled balloon

17 letters:
Helicopter gunship

Aircraft

AIRCRAFT PARTS

3 letters:
Fin
Pod
Tab

4 letters:
Body
Cowl
Flap
Hold
Horn
Keel
Nose
Slat
Tail
Wing

5 letters:
Cabin
Pylon
Rotor
Waist

6 letters:
Basket
Canopy
Elevon
Engine
Galley
Pusher
Ramjet
Rudder
Turret

7 letters:
Aileron
Airlock
Athodyd
Blister
Bomb bay
Capsule
Chassis
Cockpit
Cowling
Fairing

Gondola
Jet pipe
Nacelle
Spinner
Spoiler
Trim tab
Winglet
Wing tip

8 letters:
Aerofoil
Airframe
Air scoop
Airscrew
Anti-icer
Arrester
Black box
Bulkhead
Drop tank
Elevator
Fuel tank
Fuselage
Heat sink
Joystick
Longeron
Pulsejet
Tailskid

9 letters:
Air-intake
Altimeter
Astrodome
Autopilot
Bombsight
Clamshell
Dashboard
Empennage
Engine pod
Jet engine
Main plane
Nose wheel
Pitot tube
Propeller
Tailplane

Tail wheel

10 letters:
Astrohatch
Cantilever
Flight deck
Hydroplane
Launch shoe
Stabilizer

11 letters:
Afterburner
Horn balance
Landing gear
Slinger ring

12 letters:
Control stick
Ejection seat
Inclinometer
Landing light
Ramjet engine
Trailing edge

13 letters:
Aerostructure
All-flying tail
Control column
Launching shoe
Undercarriage

14 letters:
Flight recorder

15 letters:
Instrument panel

16 letters:
Aerometeorograph

17 letters:
Artificial horizon

18 letters:
Auxiliary power
   unit

Airline flight codes

Code	Airline
AA	American Airlines
AC	Air Canada
AF	Air France
AH	Air Algerie
AI	Air India
AJ	Air Belgium
AM	Aeromexico
AQ	Aloha Airlines (Hawaii)
AR	Aerolineas Argentinas
AY	Finnair
AZ	Alitalia
BA	British Airways
BD	British Midland
BY	Britannia Airways
CA	Air China
CO	Continental Airlines
CP	Canadian Airlines International
CT	Air Sofia
CU	Cubana
CY	Cyprus Airways
DA	Air Georgia
DI	Deutsche BA
DL	Delta Airlines
DX	Danish Air Transport
EI	Aer Lingus
EK	Emirates
FE	Royal Khmer Airlines
FI	Icelandair
FR	Ryanair
GF	Gulf Air
GH	Ghana Airways
GM	Air Slovakia
HA	Hawaiian Airlines
IB	Iberia
IC	Indian Airlines
IL	Istanbul Airways
IR	Iran Air
JA	Air Bosnia
JE	Manx Airlines
JG	Air Greece
JL	Japan Airlines
JM	Air Jamaica
JU	JAT (Yugoslavia)
KL	KLM
KQ	Kenya Airways
KU	Kuwait Airways
LG	Luxair

Airline flight codes

Code	Airline
LH	Lufthansa
LV	Albanian Airlines
LY	El Al
MA	Malev (Hungary)
MS	Egyptair
NG	Lauda Air (Austria)
NH	All Nippon Airlines
NV	Northwest Territorial Airways (Canada)
NW	Northwest Airlines (USA)
NY	Air Iceland
NZ	Air New Zealand
OA	Olympic Airlines (Greece)
OG	Go
OK	Czech Airlines
OS	Austrian Airlines
OU	Croatia Airlines
OV	Estonian Air
PC	Fiji Air
PK	Pakistan International Airlines
PS	Ukraine International Airlines
QF	Qantas
QR	Qatar Airways
QS	Tatra Air (Slovakia)
QU	Uganda Airlines
QZ	Zambia Airways
RG	Varig (Brazil)
RM	Air Moldova
RO	Tarom (Romania)
RR	Royal Air Force
SA	South African Airways
SK	SAS (Scandinavian Airlines, Sweden)
SN	Sabena Belgian World Airlines
SQ	Singapore Airlines
SR	Swissair
SU	Aeroflot (Russia)
TE	Lithuanian Airlines
TK	Turkish Airlines
TP	TAP Air Portugal
TT	Air Lithuania
TW	TWA (USA)
UA	United Airlines (USA)
UK	KLM UK
UL	Sri Lankan Airlines
UM	Air Zimbabwe
US	USAir
VS	Virgin Atlantic Airways
WN	Southwest Airlines (USA)
WT	Nigeria Airways
WX	Cityjet (Ireland)
ZB	Monarch Airlines (UK)

Airports

3 letters:
JFK
Lod

4 letters:
Dyce
Faro
Lydd
Orly
Sfax
Wick

5 letters:
Logan
Luton
McCoy
O'Hare

6 letters:
Dulles
Gander
Gerona
Lympne

7 letters:
Ataturk
Dalaman
Entebbe
Gatwick
Kennedy
Kerkyra
Lincoln
Shannon

8 letters:
Beauvais
Ciampino
G Marconi
Heathrow
Idlewild
Keflavik
McCarran
Mohamed V
Schiphol
Stansted

9 letters:
Ben Gurion
Charleroi
Fiumicino
Jose Marti
Marco Polo
Peninsula
Prestwick
Queen Alia
Turnhouse

10 letters:
Hellenikon
King Khaled
Louis Botha
Reina Sofia
Will Rogers

11 letters:
Ninoy Aquino

12 letters:
Benito Juarez
Chiang Kai She
Indira Gandhi
Jomo Kenyatta
Norman Manley
Papola Casale
Queen Beatrix
Santos Dumont
Simon Bolivar

13 letters:
Grantley Adams
King Abdul Aziz

14 letters:
Galileo Galilei
Lester B Pearson
Luis Munoz Marin

15 letters:
Charles De Gaulle
General Mitchell
Leonardo da Vinci
Murtala
  Muhammed
Sir Seretse Khama

17 letters:
Cristoforo Colombo
Houari
  Boumedienne

Alcohols

4 letters:
Diol

5 letters:
Cetyl
Ethal
Ethyl
Meths
Nerol

6 letters:
Cresol
Lauryl
Mescal

Phytol
Propyl
Sterol

7 letters:
Borneol
Choline
Ethanol
Mannite
Xylitol

8 letters:
Acrolein
Aldehyde

Catechol
Farnesol
Fusel-oil
Geraniol
Glycerin
Inositol
Linalool
Mannitol
Methanol
Sorbitol

9 letters:
Glycerine
Isopropyl

37

Algae

Mercaptan

11 letters:
Cholesterol

Citronellol
Sphingosine

Algae

3 letters:
Red

4 letters:
Kelp

5 letters:
Brown
Dulse
Fucus
Green
Jelly
Laver
Wrack

6 letters:
Desmid
Diatom
Fucoid
Lichen
Nostoc
Volvox

7 letters:
Euglena
Isokont
Oarweed

Seaweed
Valonia

8 letters:
Anabaena
Carageen
Conferva
Gulfweed
Plankton
Pleuston
Rockweed
Sargasso
Sea wrack
Ulothrix

9 letters:
Carrageen
Chlorella
Irish moss
Prokaryon
Sargassum
Sea tangle
Spirogyra
Star-jelly
Stonewort

10 letters:
Carragheen
Sea lettuce

11 letters:
Blanketweed
Iceland moss
Protococcus

12 letters:
Bladderwrack
Heterocontae
Reindeer moss
Ulotrichales
Zooxanthella

13 letters:
Blackfish weed
Phytoplankton

14 letters:
Dinoflagellate

16 letters:
Neptune's
   necklace

Alkalis

5 letters:
Borax

6 letters:
Betane
Emetin
Harmin
Potash

7 letters:
Brucine
Codeine
Emetine
Harmine
Narceen

Quinine
Tropine

8 letters:
Harmalin
Hyoscine
Lobeline
Narceine
Nicotine
Piperine
Thebaine
Veratrin

9 letters:
Bebeerine

Berberine
Capsaicin
Ephedrine
Gelsemine
Guanidine
Harmaline
Reserpine
Rhoeadine
Sparteine
Veratrine
Yohimbine

10 letters:
Colchicine
Papaverine

11 letters:
Apomorphine
Gelseminine

Scopolamine
Theobromine
Vinblastine

Vincristine

12 letters:
Theophylline

Alloys

5 letters:
Brass
Invar®
Monel
Potin
Steel
Terne

6 letters:
Albata
Alnico®
Billon
Bronze
Cermet
Chrome
Latten
Magnox
Marmem
Occamy
Oreide
Ormolu
Oroide
Pewter
Tambac
Tombac
Tombak

7 letters:
Amalgam
Babbitt
Chromel
Nimonic
Nitinol
Paktong

Platina
Shakudo
Similor
Spelter
Tutenag

8 letters:
Electron
Electrum
Gunmetal
Kamacite
Manganin®
Nichrome®
Orichalc
Stellite®
Zircaloy
Zircoloy

9 letters:
Bell metal
Duralumin®
Magnalium
Permalloy
Pinchbeck
Platinoid
Shibuichi
Type metal
White gold
Zircalloy

10 letters:
Bell bronze
Constantan
Misch metal

Nicrosilal
Osmiridium
Soft solder

11 letters:
Babbit metal
Cupronickel
Ferronickel
Monell metal

12 letters:
Ferrosilicon
Nickel silver
Nimonic alloy

13 letters:
Brazing solder
Ferrochromium
Magnolia metal
Platiniridium
Speculum metal

14 letters:
Britannia metal
Ferromanganese
Phosphor bronze
Sterling silver

15 letters:
Ferromolybdenum

24 letters:
Austenitic
  stainless steel

Alphabets

RELATED VOCABULARY

3 letters:
ITA

4 letters:
Kana

Ogam

5 letters:
Cufic
Kanji

Kufic
Latin
Ogham
Roman

Alphabets

6 letters:
Brahmi
Glagol
Hangul
Nagari
Pinyin
Romaji

7 letters:
Braille
Futhark
Futhorc
Futhork

Glossic
Grantha
Linear A
Linear B
Pangram

8 letters:
Cyrillic
Hiragana
Katakana
Logogram
Phonetic

9 letters:
Logograph
Syllabary

10 letters:
Devanagari
Estrangelo
Glagolitic
Lexigraphy

11 letters:
Estranghelo

ARABIC ALPHABET

Alif
Bā
Tā
Thā
Jīm
Ḥā
Khā
Dāl
Dhāl
Rā
Zā

Sīn
Shīn
Ṣād
Ḍād
Ṭā
Ẓā
'Ain
Ghain
Fā
Qāf
Kāf

Lām
Mīm
Nūn
Hā
Wāw
Yā

GREEK ALPHABET

Alpha
Beta
Chi
Delta
Epsilon
Eta
Gamma
Iota
Kappa

Lambda
Mu
Nu
Omega
Omicron
Phi
Pi
Psi
Rho

Sigma
Tau
Theta
Upsilon
Xi
Zeta

HEBREW ALPHABET

Aleph
Ayin
Ain
Beth
Daleth
Daled
Gimel
He
Heth
Cheth
Kaph

Koph
Qoph
Lamed
Lamedh
Mem
Nun
Pe
Resh
Sadhe
Sade
Tsade

Samekh
Shin
Sin
Tav
Taw
Teth
Vav
Waw
Yod
Yodh
Zayin

Amercian and British equivalences

COMMUNICATIONS CODE WORDS FOR THE ALPHABET

Alpha	Juliet	Sierra
Bravo	Kilo	Tango
Charlie	Lima	Uniform
Delta	Mike	Victor
Echo	November	Whiskey
Foxtrot	Oscar	X-Ray
Golf	Papa	Yankee
Hotel	Quebec	Zulu
India	Romeo	

American and British equivalences

British	American
Aeroplane	Airplane
American football	Football
Antenatal	Prenatal
Aubergine	Egg plant
Autumn	Fall
Bad-tempered	Mean
Banknote	Bill
Bat	Paddle
Benefit	Welfare
Bin *or* dustbin	Trashcan
Biscuit	Cookie
Black pudding	Blood sausage
Blinds	Shades
Bonnet	Hood
Boot	Trunk
Braces	Retainer
Braces	Suspenders
Breve	Double whole note
Broad bean	Fava bean
Building society	Savings and loan
Burgle	Burglarize
Candy floss	Cotton candy
Car	Automobile
Car park	Parking lot
Chemist	Drug store
Chips	French fries
Clothes peg	Clothes pin
Coffin	Casket
Condom	Rubber
Cornflour	Corn starch
Cot	Crib
Courgette	Zucchini
Crisps	Chips *or* potato chips
Crossroads	Intersection

41

Amercian and British equivalences

British	American
Crotchet	Quarter note
Current account	Checking account
Curtains	Drapes
Cutlery	Flatware *or* silverware
CV	Résumé
Dialing code	Area code
Dinner jacket	Tuxedo
Double cream	Heavy cream
Drapery	Dry goods
Draughts	Checkers
Drawing pin	Thumb tack
Dressing gown	Robe
Dummy	Pacifier *or* soother
Engaged tone	Busy signal
Estate agent	Realtor
Estate car	Station wagon
Fire lighter	Fire starter
First floor	Second floor
Flat	Apartment
Flick knife	Switch blade
Football	Soccer
Foyer	Lobby
Fringe	Bangs
Garden	Yard
Gear lever	Stick shift
Goose pimples	Goose bumps
Ground floor	First floor
Hair grip	Bobby pin
Hairpin bend	Switchback
Handbag	Purse
Hessian	Burlap
High street	Main street
Holiday	Vacation
Indicator	Blinker
Invigilator	Proctor
Ironmonger	Hardware store
Jam	Jelly
Janitor	Caretaker
Lawyer	Attorney
Lift	Elevator
Mangetout	Snowpea
Mate	Friend
Merry-go-round	Carousel
Methylated spirits	Denatured alcohol
Mince	Ground beef
Minim	Half note
Nappy	Diaper
Neat	Straight
Noughts and crosses	Tick-tack-toe
Nursery	Kindergarten

Amercian and British equivalences

British	American
Off licence	Liquor store
Paraffin	Kerosene
Pavement	Sidewalk
Pepper	Bell pepper
Petrol	Gas *or* gasoline
Pissed	Drunk
Plait	Braid
Plasterboard	Dry lining
Plot	Lot
Porridge	Oatmeal
Postcode	Zip code
Postman	Mail man
Pub *or* public house	Bar
Public school	Private school
Purse	Pocketbook
Pushchair	Stroller
Quaver	Eighth note
Quilt *or* eiderdown	Comforter
Railway	Railroad
Receptionist	Desk clerk
Reverse charge	Collect
Ring road	Beltway
Roll *or* bap	Bun
Rubber	Eraser
Rubbish	Trash *or* garbage
See-saw	Teeter-totter
Semibreve	Whole note
Semi-detached	Duplex
Semiquaver	Sixteenth note
Shop	Store
Silencer	Muffler
Skip	Dumpster
Skirting board	Baseboard
Sleeper	Tie
Slowcoach	Slowpoke
Soft drink	Soda
Spanner	Wrench
Spring onion *or* salad onion	Scallion
State school	Public school
Stream	Creek
Surgical spirit	Rubbing alcohol
Sweet	Candy
Tap	Faucet
Tarmac	Asphalt
Telegram	Wire
Thread	Cotton
Tights	Pantihose
Timber	Lumber
Torch	Flashlight
Town centre	Downtown

American football terms

British	American
Trainers	Sneakers
Tram	Streetcar
Trousers	Pants
Turn up	Cuff
VAT	Sales tax
Vest	Undershirt
Waistcoast	Vest
Windscreen	Windshield

American football teams

11 letters:
New York Jets
St Louis Rams

12 letters:
Buffalo Bills
Chicago Bears
Detroit Lions

13 letters:
Dallas Cowboys
Denver Broncos
Houston Texans
Miami Dolphins
New York Giants

14 letters:
Atlanta Falcons
Oakland Raiders

15 letters:
Baltimore Ravens
Cleveland Browns
Green Bay Packers
Seattle Seahawks

Tennessee Titans

16 letters:
Arizona Cardinals
Carolina Panthers
Kansas City Chiefs
Minnesota Vikings
New Orleans Saints
San Diego Chargers

17 letters:
Cincinnati Bengals
Indianapolis Colts

18 letters:
New England Patriots
Philadelphia Eagles
Pittsburgh Steelers
Tampa Bay Buccaneers
Washington Redskins

19 letters:
Jacksonville Jaguars

23 letters:
San Francisco Forty-niners

Amphibians

3 letters:
Eft
Olm

4 letters:
Frog
Hyla
Newt
Pipa
Rana

Toad

5 letters:
Anura
Guana
Siren
Snake

6 letters:
Desman
Hassar

7 letters:
Axolotl
Crapaud
Proteus
Tadpole
Urodela
Urodele

8 letters:
Bullfrog

Caecilia
Cane toad
Congo eel
Mud puppy
Tree frog
Urodelan

9 letters:
Ambystoma
Caecilian
Hairy frog

Salientia

10 letters:
Amblystoma
Batrachian
Hellbender
Natterjack
Salamander

11 letters:
Goliath frog

Midwife toad
Surinam toad

16 letters:
Brown-striped frog

18 letters:
Queensland cane
 toad

Ancient cities

2 letters:
Ur

3 letters:
Bam

4 letters:
Coba
Rome
Susa
Troy
Tula
Tyre
Uruk

5 letters:
Aksum
Argos
Bosra
Copán
Hatra
Huari
Kabah
Khiva
Labna
Mitla
Moche
Nemea
Petra
Sayil
Shloh
Tegea
Tikal
Tultm
Uxmal

6 letters:
Athens
Byblos
Delphi
Jabneh
Jamnia
Megara
Napata
Nippur
Sardis
Sikyon
Sparta
Thebes
Ugarit
Xlapak

7 letters:
Antioch
Babylon
Bukhara
Cahokia
Corinth
Eleusis
El Tajin
Ephesos
Ephesus
Mayapan
Miletus
Mycenae
Mykenae
Nineveh
Olympia
Pompeii
Samaria
Sybaris

8 letters:
Carthage
Cihuatán
Damascus
Palenque
Pergamon
Pergamum
Sigiriya
Tashkent
Thysdrus

9 letters:
Byzantium
Perepolis
Samarkand
Sukhothai

10 letters:
Alexandria
Carchemish
Heliopolis
Hierapolis

11 letters:
Chichén Itzá
Machu Picchu
Polonnaruwa

12 letters:
Anuradhapura

13 letters:
Halicarnassus

14 letters:
Constantinople

Angels

ANGELS

5 letters:
Ariel
Uriel

6 letters:
Abdiel
Arioch
Azrael
Belial
Rimmon

Uzziel

7 letters:
Asmadai
Gabriel
Israfel
Lucifer
Michael
Raphael
Zadkiel

Zephiel

8 letters:
Apollyon
Ithuriel

9 letters:
Beelzebub

10 letters:
Adramelech

ANGELIC ORDERS

6 letters:
Angels
Powers

7 letters:
Thrones
Virtues

8 letters:
Cherubim

Seraphim

9 letters:
Dominions

10 letters:
Archangels
Princedoms

11 letters:
Dominations

14 letters:
Principalities

Animals

RELATED WORDS

Animal	**Related adjective**
Ant	Formic
Ass	Asinine
Bear	Ursine
Bee	Apian
Bird	Avian *or* ornithic
Bull	Taurine
Cat	Feline
Crab	Cancroid
Crow	Corvine
Deer	Cervine
Dog	Canine
Dove	Columbine
Eagle	Aquiline
Elephant	Elephantine
Falcon	Falconine
Fish	Piscine *or* ichthyoid
Fowl	Gallinaceous

Animal	Related adjective
Fox	Vulpine
Goat	Caprine *or* hircine
Goose	Anserine *or* anserous
Gull	Larine
Hare	Leporine
Hawk	Accipitrine
Horse	Equine
Lion	Leonine
Lynx	Lyncean
Mite *or* tick	Acaroid
Monkey	Simian
Ox	Bovine
Parrot	Psittacine
Peacock	Pavonine
Pig	Porcine
Puffin	Alcidine
Seal	Phocine
Sheep	Ovine
Snake	Serpentine, anguine, ophidian, *or* colubrine
Swallow	Hirundine
Wasp	Vespine
Wolf	Lupine

COLLECTIVE ANIMALS

Animal	Collective noun
Antelopes	Herd
Apes	Shrewdness
Asses	Pace *or* herd
Badgers	Cete
Bears	Sloth
Bees	Swarm *or* grist
Birds	Flock, congregation, flight, *or* volery
Bitterns	Sedge *or* siege
Boars	Sounder
Bucks	Brace *or* lease
Buffaloes	Herd
Capercailzies	Tok
Cats	Clowder
Cattle	Drove *or* herd
Choughs	Chattering
Colts	Rag
Coots	Covert
Cranes	Herd, sedge, *or* siege
Crows	Murder
Cubs	Litter
Curlews	Herd
Curs	Cowardice
Deer	Herd

Animals

Animal	Collective noun
Dolphins	School
Doves	Flight *or* dule
Ducks	Paddling *or* team
Dunlins	Flight
Elk	Gang
Fish	Shoal, draught, haul, run, *or* catch
Flies	Swarm *or* grist
Foxes	Skulk
Geese	Gaggle *or* skein
Giraffes	Herd
Gnats	Swarm *or* cloud
Goats	Herd *or* tribe
Goldfinches	Charm
Grouse	Brood, covey, *or* pack
Gulls	Colony
Hares	Down *or* husk
Hawks	Cast
Hens	Brood
Herons	Sedge *or* siege
Herrings	Shoal *or* glean
Hounds	Pack, mute, *or* cry
Insects	Swarm
Kangaroos	Troop
Kittens	Kindle
Lapwings	Desert
Larks	Exaltation
Leopards	Leap
Lions	Pride *or* troop
Mallards	Sord *or* sute
Mares	Stud
Martens	Richesse
Moles	Labour
Monkeys	Troop
Mules	Barren
Nightingales	Watch
Owls	Parliament
Oxen	Yoke, drove, team, *or* herd
Partridges	Covey
Peacocks	Muster
Pheasants	Nye *or* nide
Pigeons	Flock *or* flight
Pigs	Litter
Plovers	Stand *or* wing
Pochards	Flight, rush, bunch, *or* knob
Ponies	Herd
Porpoises	School *or* gam
Poultry	Run
Pups	Litter
Quails	Bevy
Rabbits	Nest

Animal	Collective noun
Racehorses	Field *or* string
Ravens	Unkindness
Roes	Bevy
Rooks	Building *or* clamour
Ruffs	Hill
Seals	Herd *or* pod
Sheep	Flock
Sheldrakes	Dopping
Snipe	Walk *or* wisp
Sparrows	Host
Starlings	Murmuration
Swallows	Flight
Swans	Herd *or* bevy
Swifts	Flock
Swine	Herd, sounder, *or* dryft
Teal	Bunch, knob, *or* spring
Whales	School, gam, *or* run
Whelps	Litter
Whiting	Pod
Wigeon	Bunch, company, knob, *or* flight
Wildfowl	Plump, sord, *or* sute
Wolves	Pack, rout, *or* herd
Woodcocks	Fall

HABITATIONS

Animal	Habitation
Ant	Ant hill *or* formicary
Badger	Set *or* sett
Beaver	Lodge
Bee	Hive *or* apiary
Bird	Nest
Eagle	Aerie *or* eyrie
Fish	Redd
Fox	Earth
Otter	Holt
Pig	Sty
Puffin	Puffinry
Rabbit	Warren
Rook	Rookery
Seal	Sealery
Squirrel	Drey *or* dray
Termite	Termitarium
Wasp	Vespiary *or* bike

MALE ANIMALS

Animal	Male
Ass	Jack
Bird	Cock
Cat	Tom

Animals

Animal	Male
Deer	Hart *or* stag
Donkey	Jack
Duck	Drake
Elephant	Bull
Falcon	Tercel *or* tiercel
Ferret	Hob
Fowl	Cock
Fox	Dog
Goat	Billy *or* buck
Goose	Gander
Hare	Buck
Horse	Stallion
Kangaroo	Buck *or* old man
Lobster	Cock
Ox	Bull
Peafowl	Peacock
Pig	Boar
Rabbit	Buck
Reindeer	Buck
Ruff	Ruff
Sheep	Ram *or* tup
Swan	Cob
Weasel	Whittret
Whale	Bull

FEMALE ANIMALS

Animal	Female
Ass	Jenny
Bird	Hen
Cat	Queen
Deer	Doe *or* hind
Dog	Bitch
Donkey	Jenny
Elephant	Cow
Ferret	Gill *or* jill
Fowl	Hen
Fox	Vixen
Goat	Nanny
Hare	Doe
Horse	Mare
Leopard	Leopardess
Lion	Lioness
Lobster	Hen
Mink	Sow
Ox	Cow
Peafowl	Peahen
Pig	Sow
Rabbit	Doe
Ruff	Reeve
Sheep	Ewe

Animal	Female
Swan	Pen
Tiger	Tigress
Whale	Cow
Wolf	Bitch
Wren	Jenny

YOUNG ANIMALS

Animal	Young
Bear	Cub
Bird	Chick, fledgling, fledgeling, *or* nestling
Butterfly	Caterpillar, chrysalis, *or* chrysalid
Cat	Kitten
Cod	Codling
Deer	Fawn
Dog	Pup *or* puppy
Duck	Duckling
Eagle	Eaglet
Eel	Elver *or* grig
Elephant	Calf
Falcon	Eyas
Ferret	Kit
Fish	Fry *or* fingerling
Fox	Kit *or* cub
Frog	Tadpole
Goat	Kid *or* yeanling
Goose	Gosling
Hare	Leveret
Herring	Alevin, brit, *or* sparling
Horse	Foal, colt, *or* filly
Kangaroo	Joey
Lion	Cub
Moth	Caterpillar
Owl	Owlet
Ox	Calf
Pig	Piglet
Pigeon	Squab
Salmon	Alevin, grilse, parr, *or* smolt
Seal	Pup
Sheep	Lamb *or* yeanling
Sprat	Brit
Swan	Cygnet
Tiger	Cub
Toad	Tadpole
Whale	Calf
Wolf	Cub *or* whelp

See also:

➤ **Amphibians** ➤ **Anteaters** ➤ **Antelopes** ➤ **Birds**
➤ **Dinosaurs** ➤ **Fish** ➤ **Insects** ➤ **Invertebrates**
➤ **Mammals, extinct** ➤ **Parasites** ➤ **Reptiles**

Anniversaries

Anniversaries

Year	Traditional	Modern
1st	Paper	Clocks
2nd	Cotton	China
3rd	Leather	Crystal or glass
4th	Linen or silk	Electrical appliances
5th	Wood	Silverware
6th	Iron	Wood
7th	Wool or copper	Desk sets
8th	Bronze	Linen or lace
9th	Pottery or china	Leather
10th	Tin or aluminium	Diamond jewellery
11th	Steel	Fashion jewellery or accessories
12th	Silk	Pearls or coloured gems
13th	Lace	Textile or furs
14th	Ivory	Gold jewellery
15th	Crystal	Watches
20th	China	Platinum
25th	Silver	Sterling silver
30th	Pearl	Diamond
35th	Coral or jade	Jade
40th	Ruby	Ruby
45th	Sapphire	Sapphire
50th	Gold	Gold
55th	Emerald	Emerald
60th	Diamond	Diamond

Anteaters and other edentates

2 letters:
Ai

5 letters:
Sloth

6 letters:
Numbat

7 letters:
Echidna

Tamandu

8 letters:
Aardvark
Anteater
Pangolin
Tamandua

9 letters:
Armadillo

13 letters:
Scaly anteater
Spiny anteater

14 letters:
Banded anteater
Lesser anteater

Antelopes

3 letters:
Elk
Gnu
Kob

4 letters:
Kudu
Oryx
Puku
Suni

Thar
Topi

5 letters:
Addax

Bongo
Bubal
Eland
Goral
Kaama
Nagor
Nyala
Oribi
Sable
Saiga
Sasin
Serow
Takin

6 letters:
Dikdik
Duiker
Duyker
Dzeren
Impala
Inyala
Koodoo
Lechwe
Nilgai
Nilgau

Ourebi
Pallah
Pygarg
Reebok
Rhebok

7 letters:
Blaubok
Blesbok
Bloubok
Bubalis
Chamois
Chikara
Gazelle
Gemsbok
Gerenuk
Grysbok
Kongoni
Madoqua
Nylghau
Sassaby
Stembok

8 letters:
Bluebuck

Bontebok
Bushbuck
Hartbees
Pale-buck
Reedbuck
Steenbok
Stemback
Tsessebe

9 letters:
Blackbuck
Prongbuck
Pronghorn
Sitatunga
Situtunga
Steinbock
Tragelaph
Waterbuck

10 letters:
Hartebeest
Wildebeest

12 letters:
Klipspringer

Antibiotics

7 letters:
Opsonin

8 letters:
Colistin
Neomycin
Nystatin

9 letters:
Kanamycin
Mitomycin
Oxacillin
Polymixin
Rifamycin

10 letters:
Bacitracin

Gentamicin
Gramicidin
Lincomycin
Rifampicin
Terramycin®
Tyrocidine

11 letters:
Actinomycin
Cloxacillin
Doxorubicin
Doxycycline
Interleukin
Methicillin
Tyrothricin

12 letters:
Erythromycin
Griseofulvin
Streptomycin
Tetracycline

13 letters:
Cephalosporin
Spectinomycin

14 letters:
Streptothricin

15 letters:
Oxytetracycline

Antiques

3 letters:
Bow
FSA

4 letters:
Adam
Buhl

5 letters:
Bulla
Curio

Ants, bees and wasps

Inlay
Relic
Resto
Spode
Style
Tudor

6 letters:
Boulle
Branks
Bureau
Bygone
Flacon
Gothic
Period
Rococo
Sconce
Settle

7 letters:
Antique
Baroque
Charger
Curiosa
Diptych
Dresser
Gadroon
Godroon
Kiwiana
Netsuke
Regency
Snuffer

Tallboy

8 letters:
Baluster
Coalport
Ephemera
Jacobean
Snuffbox

9 letters:
Antiquary
Antiquate
Bed warmer
Davenport
Fleurette
George III
Marquetry
Porcelain
Queen Anne
Washstand

10 letters:
Art Nouveau
Bellarmine
Blue willow
Escritoire
Escutcheon
Four-poster
Secretaire
Victoriana

11 letters:
Antiquarian

Antiquities
Chinoiserie
Chippendale
Collectable
Cromwellian
Hepplewhite
Museum piece
Period piece
Renaissance

12 letters:
Apostle spoon
Elgin marbles
Gateleg table
Sanction mark
Welsh dresser

13 letters:
Drop-leaf table
Early Georgian
Fiddle pattern
Neo-classicism

14 letters:
Collector's item
William and Mary

15 letters:
English Heritage

Ants, bees and wasps

3 letters:
Ant
Bee

4 letters:
Wasp

5 letters:
Emmet
Minga

7 letters:
Army ant
Blue ant
Bull ant

Bull Joe
Hive bee
Termite
Wood ant

8 letters:
Gall wasp
Honey ant
Honeybee
Horntail
Kootchar
Mason bee
Sand wasp
Slave ant

White ant
Wood wasp

9 letters:
Amazon ant
Bumblebee
Cuckoo bee
Driver ant
Humblebee
Killer bee
Mason wasp
Mining bee
Mud dauber
Native bee

Sirex wasp
Velvet ant

10 letters:
Bulldog ant
Digger wasp
Flower wasp
Pharaoh ant

11 letters:
Honeypot ant

Sugarbag fly

12 letters:
Carpenter bee
Cicada hunter
Ichneumon fly
Legionary ant
Policeman fly
Ruby-tail wasp
Yellow jacket

13 letters:
Ichneumon wasp
Leafcutter ant
Leafcutter bee

17 letters:
Spider-hunting
  wasp

Apocalypse, Four Horsemen of

Colour	Represents
White	Christ
Red	War
Black	Famine
Pale	Death

Apostles

4 letters:
John
Jude

5 letters:
James (the Great)
James (the Less)
Peter

Simon

6 letters:
Andrew
Philip
Thomas

7 letters:
Matthew

8 letters:
Matthias

11 letters:
Bartholomew

Apparatus

4 letters:
Loom

5 letters:
Churn
Davis
Golgi
Kipp's
Proto®
Still
Tromp
Tuner

6 letters:
Graith
Retort
Rounce

Tackle
Trompe

7 letters:
Alembic
Caisson
Coherer
Exciter
Skimmer
Snorkel
Tokamak

8 letters:
Critical
Cryostat
Digester
Gasogene

Gazogene
Injector
Jacquard
Lease-rod
Multi-gym
Pulmotor®
Resistor
Scrubber
Substage
Tackling
Telecine
Teleseme
Ventouse

9 letters:
Appliance

Apples

Aspirator
Autoclave
Chemostat
Clinostat
Condenser
Cosmotron
Equipment
Gyroscope
Hodoscope
Holophote
Hygrostat
Incubator
Kymograph
Photostat®
Phytotron
Potometer
Projector
Slide rest
Tellurian
Tellurion

10 letters:
Commutator
Eprouvette
Eudiometer
Heliograph
Helioscope
Hydrophone
Inspirator

Mimeograph
Nephoscope
Nitrometer
Oxygenator
Percolator
Phonometer
Photophone
Radiosonde
Respirator
Rotisserie
Soundboard
Spirophore
Steriliser
Switchgear
Thermopile

11 letters:
Alkalimeter
Calorimeter
Colorimeter
Microreader
Pasteuriser
Plate-warmer
Replenisher
Stellarator
Teleprinter
Transformer
Transmitter

12 letters:
Ebullioscope
Effusiometer
Electrograph
Electroscope
Installation
Oscillograph
Respirometer
Resuscitator
Sphygmograph
Whip-and-derry

13 letters:
Defibrillator
Electrophorus
Hemocytometer
Kipp generator
Life-preserver
Plumber's snake
Scintiscanner

14 letters:
Plethysmograph

16 letters:
Wheatstone bridge

17 letters:
Wheatstone's
  bridge

Apples

4 letters:
Crab
Fuji
John
Lobo
Love
Pome
Snow

5 letters:
Pyrus
Sugar
Thorn

6 letters:
Balsam
Biffin
Codlin

Elstar
Empire
Idared
Mammee
Medlar
Pippin
Pomace
Pomroy
Rennet
Russet
Sunset

7 letters:
Baldwin
Bramley
Codling
Costard
Custard

Pomeroy
Ribston
Ruddock
Spartan
Sturmer
Winesap

8 letters:
Braeburn
Greening
Jonagold
Jonathan
Jonathon
Pearmain
Pink Lady
Reinette
Ribstone
Sweeting

9 letters:
Alligator
Charlotte
Crab apple
Discovery
Grenadier
Jenneting
Nonpareil
Quarenden
Quarender
Redstreak
Royal Gala

10 letters:
Quarantine
Quarrender
Red Ellison

Sops-in-wine

11 letters:
Charles Ross
Granny Smith
James Grieve
Leather-coat
Quarrington

12 letters:
Greensleeves
Laxton Superb
Prince Albert
Red Delicious

13 letters:
Lord Lambourne
Seek-no-further

14 letters:
Blenheim Orange
Egremont Russet
Rosemary Russet

15 letters:
Golden Delicious

16 letters:
Cox's orange pippin

17 letters:
Worcester
 Pearmain

Archaeology

ARCHAEOLOGICAL PERIODS

6 letters:
Ice age
La Tène
Minoan

7 letters:
Azilian
Iron Age

8 letters:
Asturian
Helladic

9 letters:
Acheulean

Acheulian
Bronze Age
Levallois
Mycenaean
Neolithic
Solutrean

10 letters:
Eneolithic
Gravettian
Mesolithic
Mousterian

11 letters:
Aurignacian

Magdalenian
New Stone Age
Old Stone Age

12 letters:
Chalcolithic
Levalloisian
Palaeolithic

13 letters:
Neo-Babylonian
Old Babylonian

15 letters:
Châtelperronian

ARCHAEOLOGICAL TERMS

4 letters:
Celt
Cist
Core
Kist

5 letters:
Baulk
Blade
Burin
Cairn

Flake
Flint
Henge
Mound
Pylon
Stela
Stele

6 letters:
Arcade
Barrow

Bogman
Cirque
Dolmen
Eolith
Larnax
Vallum

7 letters:
Callais
Caveman
Hogback

Ley line
Neolith
Obelisk
Patella
Retouch
Sondage
Tumulus

8 letters:
Bifacial
Cartouch
Cromlech
Graffito
Hillfort
Megalith
Palmette

Palstave
Tribrach

9 letters:
Acropolis
Alignment
Bracteate
Cartouche
Earthwork
Hut circle
Microlith

10 letters:
Souterrain

11 letters:
Clovis point

Cross-dating
Stone circle

12 letters:
Robber trench
Stratigraphy

15 letters:
Archeomagnetism

16 letters:
Archaeomagnetism

17 letters:
Radiocarbon
 dating

Archbishops of Canterbury

3 letters:
Oda

4 letters:
Lang, *Cosmo*
Laud, *William*
Pole, *Reginald*
Rich, *Edmund*
Tait, *Archibald*
Wake, *William*

5 letters:
Abbot, *George*
Carey, *George*
Deane, *Henry*
Islip, *Simon*
Juxon, *William*
Kempe, *John*
Moore, *John*
Serio, *Sigeric*

6 letters:
Anselm
Becket, *Thomas à*
Benson, *Edward*
Coggan, *Frederick*
Fisher, *Geoffrey*
Howley, *William*
Hutton, *Matthew*
Justus
Lyfing
Mepham, *Simon*

Morton, *John*
Offord, *John*
Parker, *Matthew*
Pecham, *John*
Potter, *John*
Ramsey, *Arthur*
Robert *of Jumieges*
Runcie, *Robert*
Secker, *Thomas*
Sumner, *John*
Sutton, *Charles*
Temple, *Frederick*
Temple, *William*
Walden, *Roger*
Walter, *Hubert*
Warham, *William*

7 letters:
Aelfric
Arundel, *Thomas*
Baldwin
Cranmer, *Thomas*
Dunstan
Eadsige
Grindal, *Edmund*
Herring, *Thomas*
Langham, *Simon*
Langton, *Stephen*
Le Grant, *Richard*
Longley, *Charles*
Nothelm

Richard *of Dover*
Sheldon, *Gilbert*
Stigand
Sudbury, *Simon*
Tatwine
Tenison, *Thomas*
William *of Corbeil*
Wulfred

8 letters:
Aelfheah
Aelfsige
Bancroft, *Richard*
Boniface *of Savoy*
Ceolnoth
Chichele, *Henry*
Davidson, *Randall*
D'Escures, *Ralph*
Honorius
Lanfranc
Mellitus
Plegmund
Reynolds, *Walter*
Sancroft, *William*
Stafford, *John*
Theobald *of Bec*
Whitgift, *John*
Williams
Wulfhelm

9 letters:
Aethelgar

Aethelred
Augustine
Breguwine
Courtenay, *William*
Deusdedit
Feologild
Kilwardby, *Robert*
Stratford, *John*
Theodorus

Tillotson, *John*

10 letters:
Aethelhelm
Aethelnoth
Beorhthelm
Bourgchier, *Thomas*
Cornwallis,
  Frederick
Cuthbeorht

Jaenbeorht
Laurentius
Whittlesey, *William*
Winchelsey, *Robert*

11 letters:
Aethelheard
Beorhtweald
Bradwardine

Arches

3 letters:
Gee

4 letters:
Keel
Ogee
Skew

5 letters:
Acute
Hance
Ogive
Roman
Vault

6 letters:
Gothic

Haunch
Lancet
Lierne
Marble
Norman
Portal
Soffit
Trajan

7 letters:
Pointed
Squinch

8 letters:
Cross-rib
Intrados

9 letters:
Admiralty
Arblaster
Archivolt
Ctesiphon
Horseshoe
Triumphal

10 letters:
Proscenium

11 letters:
Counterfort

Architecture

ARCHITECTURAL STYLES

5 letters:
Doric
Ionic
Roman
Saxon
Tudor

6 letters:
Empire
Gothic
Norman
Rococo
Tuscan

7 letters:
Art Deco
Baroque
Bauhaus
Moderne
Moorish
Morisco
Mudéjar
Regency
Saracen

8 letters:
Colonial
Georgian

Jacobean

9 letters:
Brutalist
Byzantine
Classical
Composite
Decorated
Edwardian
Mannerist
Modernist
Palladian
Queen-Anne
Victorian

Architecture

10 letters:
Art Nouveau
Corinthian
Federation
Louis Seize
Romanesque
Transition

11 letters:
Elizabethan
Louis Quinze
Louis Treize

Renaissance

12 letters:
Early English
Greek Revival
New brutalist
Transitional

13 letters:
Functionalism
Gothic Revival
Louis Quatorze

Neoclassicist
Perpendicular
Postmodernist

14 letters:
Churrigueresco
Early Christian

15 letters:
Churrigueresque

18 letters:
International Style

ARCHITECTURAL TERMS

3 letters:
Hip

4 letters:
Drum
Naos
Rise

5 letters:
Giant
Order
Shaft
Shell
Stria

6 letters:
Filler
Florid
Fluted
Hipped
Invert
Lierne
Lintel
Listed
Loggia
Member
Module
Return
Rhythm
Soffit
Spring
Storey
String
Summer

7 letters:
Abuttal
Astylar

Bolster
Bracket
Castled
Engaged
Galilee
Profile
Rampant
Respond
Stilted
Subbase
Surbase

8 letters:
Abutment
Colossal
Cradling
Diastyle
Diminish
Dipteral
Foliated
Galleria
King post
Lanceted
Moresque
Postiche
Prostyle
Shafting
Stringer
Tail beam
Trabeate
Tympanic

9 letters:
Composite
Crenelate
Discharge
Elevation
Eurhythmy

Floor plan
Floreated
Floriated
Foliation
Hexastyle
Hypostyle
Imbricate
Pulvinate
Queen post
Rendering
Rusticate
Springing
Stylobate
Tailpiece
Trabeated

10 letters:
Cloistered
Crenellate
Flamboyant
Ground plan
Imbricated
Joggle post
Polychromy
Pulvinated
Sexpartite
Summer tree

11 letters:
Castellated
Cinquecento
Denticulate
Fenestrated
High-pitched
Orientation

12 letters:
String course

13 letters:
Architectonic
Architectural
Springing line
Supercolumnar

14 letters:
Architectonics
Springing point

15 letters:
Underpitch vault

17 letters:
Intercolumniation
Ribbon
  development

ARCHITECTURAL FEATURES

3 letters:
Bow
Cap
Die
Ell
Fan
Rib
Web

4 letters:
Anta
Apse
Arch
Balk
Band
Base
Bead
Beak
Case
Cove
Cusp
Cyma
Dado
Drip
Foil
Jube
Naos
Neck
Ogee
Pace
Pier
Quad
Reed
Sill
Stoa
Term
Tore
Xyst

5 letters:
Aisle
Ancon
Apsis

Arris
Atlas
Attic
Cella
Cheek
Choir
Coign
Conch
Congé
Crown
Doors
Facet
Facia
Gable
Garth
Glyph
Groin
Gutta
Hance
Helix
Label
Newel
Niche
Ogive
Oriel
Ovolo
Patio
Porch
Pylon
Quirk
Quoin
Ridge
Shaft
Spire
Splay
Stela
Stele
Stria
Table
Talon
Tenia
Thumb

Torus
Truss
Vault
Verge

6 letters:
Abacus
Ancone
Arcade
Atrium
Baguet
Belfry
Bezant
Billet
Binder
Breast
Broach
Byzant
Canopy
Casing
Cellar
Coffer
Coigne
Column
Concha
Corbel
Cordon
Corona
Coving
Crenel
Cullis
Cupola
Dentil
Ectype
Exedra
Facade
Facial
Fascia
Fillet
Finial
Flèche
Frieze
Garret

Architecture

Gazebo
Gradin
Griffe
Grotto
Haunch
Hipped
Impost
Lacuna
Leaded
Listel
Loggia
Louvre
Metope
Mutule
Offset
Perron
Piazza
Pillar
Plinth
Podium
Portal
Reglet
Relief
Return
Reveal
Rosace
Scotia
Screen
Soffit
Squint
Summer
Taenia
Trophy
Turret
Tympan
Volute

7 letters:

Acroter
Annulet
Antefix
Apteral
Balcony
Bezzant
Bracket
Caisson
Calotte
Capital
Cavetto
Ceiling
Channel

Chaplet
Chevron
Corbeil
Cornice
Crochet
Crocket
Cushion
Echinus
Entasis
Fantail
Fascial
Festoon
Fluting
Footing
Frustum
Gadroon
Gallery
Gambrel
Godroon
Hip roof
Landing
Lantern
Lucarne
Mansard
Meander
Minaret
Mullion
Narthex
Necking
Obelisk
Parapet
Pendant
Perpend
Portico
Postern
Reeding
Respond
Rosette
Rotunda
Roundel
Squinch
Steeple
Strigil
Tambour
Telamon
Tracery
Trefoil
Tribune
Trumeau
Veranda

8 letters:

Acanthus
Accolade
Apophyge
Arcature
Astragal
Atlantes
Baguette
Baluster
Banderol
Bannerol
Basement
Buttress
Caryatid
Casement
Chapiter
Cloister
Crenelle
Cresting
Crossing
Crow step
Curb roof
Cymatium
Dancette
Dogtooth
Extrados
Fanlight
Fenestra
Gable end
Gargoyle
Gorgerin
Headwork
Imperial
Intrados
Keystone
Moulding
Ogee arch
Pedestal
Pediment
Pinnacle
Platform
Predella
Semidome
Shafting
Skew arch
Skylight
Spandrel
Spandril
Springer
Tellamon
Terminal

Terminus
Transept
Traverse
Triglyph
Tympanum
Verandah
Vignette

9 letters:
Anthemion
Archivolt
Arcuation
Baldachin
Banderole
Bay window
Bilection
Bolection
Bow window
Cartouche
Choir loft
Colonnade
Corbeille
Decastyle
Dripstone
Embrasure
Footstall
Gatehouse
Headstone
Helicline
Hood mould
Hypophyge
Medallion
Modillion
Onion dome
Penthouse
Peristyle
Poppyhead
Roman arch
Strap work
Stylobate

Triforium

10 letters:
Ambulatory
Arc-boutant
Architrave
Ballflower
Belt course
Cantilever
Cinquefoil
Clerestory
Corbel step
Corbie-step
Egg and dart
Fan tracery
Fenestella
Gothic arch
Hagioscope
Lancet arch
Norman arch
Propylaeum
Quadrangle
Quatrefoil
Rose window
Saddleback
Saddle roof
Sash window
Scrollwork
Stereobate
Wagon vault
Water table

11 letters:
Amphistylar
Barge couple
Barge course
Barrel vault
Bed moulding
Bottom house
Brattishing
Columbarium

Corbie gable
Curtail step
Curtain wall
Cuspidation
Entablature
Gable window
Half landing
Oeil-de-boeuf
Oriel window
Tunnel vault

12 letters:
Articulation
Columniation
Egg and anchor
Egg and tongue
Frontispiece
Lancet window
Palm vaulting
Porte-cochere
Quarter round
String course

13 letters:
Amphiprostyle
Compass window
French windows
Machicolation

14 letters:
Catherine wheel
Flying buttress
Straining piece

15 letters:
Underpitch vault

16 letters:
Long-and-short
work

17 letters:
Whispering gallery

ARCHITECTS

3 letters:
Oud, *Jacobus Johann Pieter*
Pei, *I(eoh) M(ing)*

4 letters:
Adam, *James*
Adam, *Robert*
Adam, *William*

Kahn, *Louis I(sadore)*
Kent, *William*
Loos, *Adolf*
Nash, *John*
Shaw, *Richard Norman*
Webb, *Aston*
Webb, *Philip*
Wood, *John*

Architecture

Wren, *Christopher*

5 letters:
Aalto, *Alvar*
Baker, *Herbert*
Barry, *Charles*
Bryce, *David*
Dance, *George*
Doshi, *Balkrishna Vithaldas*
Dudok, *Willem Marinus*
Engel, *Johann Carl Ludwig*
Gaudí, *Antonio*
Gibbs, *James*
Gilly, *Friedrich*
Horta, *Victor*
Jones, *Inigo*
Levau, *Louis*
Moore, *Charles Willard*
Nervi, *Pier Luigi*
Pugin, *Augustus (Welby Northmore)*
Scott, *George Gilbert*
Scott, *Giles Gilbert*
Soane, *John*
Tange, *Kenzo*
Terry, *(John) Quinlan*
Utzon, *Jorn*
Wyatt, *James*

6 letters:
Boulle, *Etienne-Louis*
Breuer, *Marcel Lajos*
Burton, *Decimus*
Casson, *Hugh (Maxwell)*
Coates, *Wells Wintemute*
Foster, *Norman*
Fuller, *(Richard) Buckminster*
Geddes, *Patrick*
Giotto *(di Bondone)*
Howard, *Ebenezer*
Lasdun, *Denys*
Ledoux, *Claude Nicolas*
Lescot, *Pierre*
Nissen, *Godber*
Paxton, *Joseph*
Perret, *Auguste*
Pisano, *Andrea*
Pisano, *Nicola*
Pollio, *Marcus Vitruvius*
Repton, *Humphrey*
Rogers, *Richard*
Romano, *Giulio*

Scopas
Serlio, *Sebastiano*
Smirke, *Robert*
Spence, *Basil (Unwin)*
Street, *George Edmund*
Stuart, *James*
Vasari, *Giorgio*
Voysey, *Charles (Francis Annesley)*
Wagner, *Otto*
Wright, *Frank Lloyd*

7 letters:
Alberti, *Leon Battista*
Asplund, *Erik Gunnar*
Behrens, *Peter*
Berlage, *Hendrick Petrus*
Bernini, *Gian Lorenzo*
Burnham, *David Hudson*
Candela, *Felix*
Columbo, *David*
Da Vinci, *Leonardo*
De l'Orme, *Philibert*
Gabriel, *Ange-Jacques*
Garnier, *Tony (Antoine)*
Gibberd, *Frederick*
Gilbert, *Cass*
Gropius, *Walter*
Guarini, *Guarino*
Holland, *Henry*
Ictinus
Imhotep
Johnson, *Philip Cortelyou*
Lethaby, *William Richard*
Lorimer, *Robert Stodart*
Lutyens, *Edwin*
Maderna, *Carlo*
Maderno, *Carlo*
Mansart, *François*
Mansart, *Jules Hardouin*
Neumann, *Johann Balthasar*
Orcagna *(Andrea di Cionne)*
Peruzzi, *Baldassare Tommaso*
Poelzig, *Hans*
Raphael
Renwick, *James*
Thomson, *Alexander (Greek)*
Venturi, *Robert*
Vignola, *Giacomo*

8 letters:
Bramante, *Donato*
Chambers, *William*

Daedalus
De Brosse, *Salomon*
Di Cambio, *Arnolfo*
Erickson, *Arthur Charles*
Hamilton, *Thomas*
Hoffmann, *Josef*
Jacobsen, *Arne*
Niemeyer, *Oscar*
Palladio, *Andrea*
Piranesi, *Giambattista*
Playfair, *William Henry*
Rietveld, *Gerrit Thomas*
Saarinen, *Eero*
Schinkel, *Karl Friederich*
Smythson, *Robert*
Sottsass, *Ettore Jr*
Soufflot, *Jacques Germain*
Stirling, *James*
Sullivan, *Louis (Henri)*
Vanbrugh, *John*
Yamasaki, *Minoru*

9 letters:
Anthemias *of Tralles*
Bartholdi, *Frédéric August*
Borromini, *Francesco*
Cockerell, *Charles Robert*
Da Cortona, *Pietro*
Da Cortona, *Pietro Berrettini*
Da Vignola, *Giacomo Barozzi*
Di Giorgio, *Francesco*
Haussmann, *Georges Eugene*
Hawksmoor, *Nicholas*
Labrouste, *(Pierre Francois) Henri*

Mackmurdo, *Arthur Heygate*
Macquarie, *Lachlan*
Sansovino, *Jacopo*
Van Campen, *Jacob*
Vitruvius
Von Erlach, *Johann Bernhard Fischer*

10 letters:
Chermayeff, *Serge*
Mackintosh, *Charles Rennie*
Mendelsohn, *Eric*
Michelozzo
Sanmicheli, *Michele*
Trophonius
Van der Rohe, *Ludwig Mies*
Van de Velde, *Henry*
Waterhouse, *Alfred*

11 letters:
Abercrombie, *(Leslie) Patrick*
Butterfield, *William*
Callicrates
Churriguera, *Don Jose*
De Cuvillies, *Francois*
Le Corbusier
Van Doesburg, *Theo*

12 letters:
Brunelleschi, *Filippo*
Michelangelo
Viollet-le-Duc, *Eugène Emmanuel*

14 letters:
Von Hildebrandt, *Johann Lukas*

Armour

4 letters:
Cush
Jack
Mail
Tace
Umbo

5 letters:
Armet
Bevor
Cuish
Culet
Curat

Fauld
Jupon
Nasal
Petta
Tasse
Visor
Vizor

6 letters:
Beaver
Byrnie
Camail
Corium

Couter
Crinet
Cuisse
Curiet
Gorget
Greave
Gusset
Helmet
Jamber
Poleyn
Secret
Taslet

Tasset
Thorax
Tonlet
Tuille
Voider

7 letters:
Ailette
Basinet
Besagew
Brasset
Buckler
Casspir
Corslet
Cuirass
Hauberk
Jambart
Jambeau
Lamboys
Panoply
Placcat

Placket
Poitrel
Roundel
Sabaton
Ventail

8 letters:
Barbette
Bascinet
Chaffron
Chamfron
Chanfron
Chausses
Corselet
Gauntlet
Jazerant
Pauldron
Pavloron
Plastron
Pouldron
Solleret

Spaudler
Vambrace

9 letters:
Chamfrain
Garniture
Habergeon
Jesserant
Lance rest
Nosepiece
Sword belt
Vantbrass

10 letters:
Brigandine
Cataphract
Coat-of-mail

11 letters:
Breastplate
Genouillère
Mentonnière

Art

ART STYLES AND MOVEMENTS

2 letters:
Op

3 letters:
Pop

4 letters:
Clip
Dada
Deco
Fine
Kano

5 letters:
Cobra
Dedal
Nabis
Tatum
Virtu

6 letters:
Bonsai
Brücke
Cubism
Daedal
Gothic

Kitsch
Rococo
Trouvé
Ukiyo-e

7 letters:
Art Deco
Baroque
Bauhaus
Dadaism
Daedale
De Stijl
Fauvism
Flemish
Kinetic
Minimal
Montage
New Wave
Norwich
Nouveau
Optical
Orphism
Plastic
Realism
Relievo

Sienese
Tachism
Trivium

8 letters:
Abstract
Futurism
Mandorla
Nazarene
Tachisme
Trecento

9 letters:
Mannerism
Modernism
Primitive
Still-life
Symbolism
Tenebrism
Toreutics
Vorticism

10 letters:
Arte Povera
Art Nouveau
Bloomsbury

Classicism
Commercial
Conceptual
Decorative
Jugendstil
Naturalism
Postmodern
Quadratura
Quadrivium
Romanesque
Surrealism
Synthetism

11 letters:
Chiaroscuro
Divisionism
Performance
Perigordian

ART EQUIPMENT

Pointillism
Psychedelic
Romanticism
Suprematism
Synchronism
Trompe l'oeil

12 letters:
Clair-obscure
Clare-obscure
Neoclassical

13 letters:
Expressionism
Impressionism
Impressionist
Neoclassicism
Neoplasticism

Postmodernism
Pre-Raphaelite

14 letters:
Abstractionism
Barbizon School
Constructivism
Der Blaue Reiter

16 letters:
Neoimpressionism

17 letters:
Postimpressionism

21 letters:
Abstract
　expressionism

ART EQUIPMENT

3 letters:
Ink

5 letters:
Brush
Chalk
Easel
Glaze
Paint

6 letters:
Canvas
Crayon
Ground
Pastel

Pencil

7 letters:
Acrylic
Palette
Spatula
Varnish

8 letters:
Airbrush
Charcoal
Fixative
Oil paint
Paintbox
Spray gun

9 letters:
Lay figure

10 letters:
Linseed oil
Paintbrush
Sketchbook

11 letters:
Watercolour

12 letters:
Drawing paper
Palette knife

Arthurian legend

CHARACTERS IN ARTHURIAN LEGEND

4 letters:
Bors

5 letters:
Nimue

6 letters:
Arthur
Elaine
Gawain
Merlin
Modred

7 letters:
Caradoc
Galahad
Gawayne
Igraine
Launfal
Tristan
Viviane

8 letters:
Bedivere

Lancelot
Parsifal
Perceval
Tristram

11 letters:
Morgan Le Fay

14 letters:
Gareth of Orkney
Launcelot du Lac
Uther Pendragon

Artists

16 letters:
The Lady of the
Lake

PLACES IN ARTHURIAN LEGEND

6 letters:
Avalon

Camelot

9 letters:
Lyonnesse

7 letters:
Astolat

8 letters:
Tintagel

11 letters:
Glastonbury

Artists

3 letters:
Arp, *Hans*
Arp, *Jean*
Cox, *David*
Dou, *Gerrit*
Fry, *Roger*
Gui, *Xia*
Nay, *Ernst Wilhelm*
Ray, *Man*

4 letters:
Bell, *Vanessa*
Boyd, *Arthur*
Caro, *Anthony*
Cuyp, *Aelbert*
Dadd, *Richard*
Dalí, *Salvador*
Doré, *Gustave*
Dufy, *Raoul*
Etty, *William*
Gabo, *Naum*
Gill, *Eric*
Goya (y Lucientes), *Francisco
José de*
Gris, *Juan*
Gros, *Antoine Jean*
Hals, *Frans*
Hunt, *William Holman*
John, *Augustus*
John, *Gwen*
Klee, *Paul*
Kuei, *Hsia*
Kuyp, *Aelbert*
Lely, *Peter*
Marc, *Franz*
Miró, *Joan*
Nash, *Paul*

Opie, *John*
Phiz *(Hablot Knigh Browne)*
Reni, *Guido*
Rosa, *Salvator*
West, *Benjamin*
Zorn, *Anders*

5 letters:
Aiken, *John MacDonald*
Appel, *Karel*
Bacon, *Francis*
Bakst, *Leon Nikolayevich*
Beuys, *Joseph*
Blake, *Peter*
Blake, *William*
Bosch, *Hieronymus*
Brown, *Ford Madox*
Burra, *Edward*
Corot, *Jean Baptiste Camille*
Crane, *Walter*
Crome, *John*
Danby, *Francis*
David, *Jacques Louis*
Degas, *Hilaire Germain Edgar*
Denis, *Maurice*
Dulac, *Pierre Charles*
Dürer, *Albrecht*
Ensor, *James*
Ernst, *Max*
Freud, *Lucian*
Gorky, *Arshile*
Grant, *Duncan*
Greco, *El*
Grosz, *George*
Hirst, *Damien*
Hoare, *William*
Homer, *Winslow*

Hooch, *Pieter de*
Johns, *Jasper*
Kitaj, *Ron B(rooks)*
Klimt, *Gustav*
Kline, *Franz*
Leech, *John*
Léger, *Fernand*
Lewis, *Wyndham*
Lippi, *Filippino*
Lotto, *Lorenzo*
Lowry, *L(awrence) S(tephen)*
Manet, *Edouard*
Monet, *Claude Oscar*
Moore, *Henry*
Morse, *Samuel Finley Breese*
Moses, *Grandma*
Munch, *Edvard*
Myron
Nolan, *Sidney*
Nolde, *Emil*
Orpen, *Sir William*
Oudry, *Jean Baptiste*
Pilon, *Germain*
Piper, *John*
Puget, *Pierre*
Redon, *Odilon*
Riley, *Bridget*
Rodin, *Auguste*
Runge, *Philipp Otto*
Seago, *Edward*
Shahn, *Ben*
Sloan, *John*
Smith, *David*
Steen, *Jan*
Steer, *Philip Wilson*
Stoss, *Veit*
Tatum, *Mary*
Watts, *George Frederick*
Zumbo, *Gaetano Giulio*

6 letters:

Albers, *Josef*
Andrei, *Rublev*
Andrei, *Rublyov*
Benton, *Thomas Hart*
Boudin, *Eugène*
Braque, *Georges*
Buffet, *Bernard*
Butler, *Reg*
Calder, *Alexander*
Callot, *Jacques*

Campin, *Robert*
Canova, *Antonio*
Clouet, *François*
Clouet, *Jean*
Copley, *John*
Coypel, *Antoine*
De Goya, *Francisco*
Derain, *André*
De Wint, *Peter*
Dobell, *William*
D'Orsay, *Count Alfred Guillaum Gabriel*
Eakins, *Thomas*
Fuseli, *Henry*
Gérard, *François*
Giotto *(di Bondone)*
Greuze, *Jean Baptiste*
Guardi, *Francesco*
Haydon, *Benjamin Robert*
Hopper, *Edward*
Houdon, *Jean Antoine*
Ingres, *Jean Auguste Dominique*
Knight, *Laura*
Lebrun, *Charles*
Le Nain, *Antoine*
Le Nain, *Louis*
Le Nain, *Mathieu*
Mabuse, *Jan*
Martin, *John*
Massys, *Quentin*
Millet, *Jean François*
Moreau, *Gustave*
Morris, *William*
Newman, *Barnett*
O'Keefe, *Georgia*
Orozco, *José Clemente*
Palmer, *Samuel*
Pisano, *Andrea*
Pisano, *Giovanni*
Pisano, *Nicola*
Potter, *Paulus*
Ramsay, *Allan*
Renoir, *Pierre Auguste*
Ribera, *Jusepe de*
Rivera, *Diego*
Romano, *Giulio*
Romney, *George*
Rothko, *Mark*
Rubens, *Peter Paul*
Scopas
Sendak, *Maurice*

Artists

Sesshu, *Toyo*
Seurat, *Georges*
Signac, *Paul*
Sisley, *Alfred*
Sluter, *Claus*
Stubbs, *George*
Tanguy, *Yves*
Tatlin, *Vladimir*
Tissot, *James Jacques Joseph*
Titian
Turner, *J(oseph) M(allord) W(illiam)*
Vasari, *Giorgio*
Villon, *Jacques*
Warhol, *Andy*
Wilson, *Richard*
Wright, *Joseph*
Zeuxis

7 letters:

Alberti, *Leon Battista*
Allston, *Washington*
Apelles
Audubon, *John James*
Balthus *(Balthasar Klossowski de Rola)*
Bellini, *Giovanni*
Bernini, *Gian Lorenzo*
Bomberg, *David*
Bonheur, *Rosa*
Bonnard, *Pierre*
Borglum, *Gutzon*
Boucher, *Francois*
Brassaï, *Gyula*
Bruegel, *Jan*
Bruegel, *Pieter*
Cassatt, *Mary*
Cellini, *Benvenuto*
Cézanne, *Paul*
Chagall, *Marc*
Chardin, *Jean-Baptiste Siméon*
Cimabue, *Giovanni*
Collier, *John*
Courbet, *Gustave*
Cranach, *Lucas*
Daumier, *Honoré*
Da Vinci, *Leonardo*
De Hooch, *Pieter*
De Hoogh, *Pieter*
Delvaux, *Paul*
Duchamp, *Marcel*

Epstein, *Jacob*
Flaxman, *John*
Fouquet, *Jean*
Gauguin, *Paul*
Gibbons, *Grinling*
Hobbema, *Meindert*
Hockney, *David*
Hofmann, *Hans*
Hogarth, *William*
Hokusai, *Katsushika*
Holbein, *Hans*
Hoppner, *John*
Kneller, *Godfrey*
Kossoff, *Leon*
Lindsay, *Norman Alfred William*
Lorrain, *Claude*
Maillol, *Aristide*
Martini, *Simone*
Matisse, *Henri*
Memlinc, *Hans*
Memling, *Hans*
Millais, *John Everett*
Morisot, *Berthe*
Morland, *George*
Murillo, *Bartolomé Esteban*
Nattier, *Jean Marc*
Orcagna, *Andrea di Cionne*
Pasmore, *Victor*
Patinir, *Joachim*
Peruzzi, *Baldassare*
Pevsner, *Antoine*
Phidias
Picabia, *Francis*
Picasso, *Pablo*
Pigalle, *Jean Baptiste*
Pissaro, *Camille*
Pollock, *Jackson*
Poussin, *Nicolas*
Proesch, *Gilbert*
Prud'hon, *Pierre Paul*
Rackham, *Arthur*
Raeburn, *Henry*
Raphael
Rouault, *Geroges*
Sargent, *John Singer*
Schiele, *Egon*
Sickert, *Walter Richard*
Soutine, *Chaim*
Spencer, *Stanley*
Teniers, *David*
Tiepolo, *Giambattista*

Uccello, *Paolo*
Utamaro, *Kitigawa*
Utrillo, *Maurice*
Van Dyck, *Anthony*
Van Eyck, *Jan*
Van Gogh, *Vincent*
Van Rijn, *Rembrandt Harmensz*
Vecchio, *Palma*
Vermeer, *Jan*
Watteau, *Jean Antoine*
Zeuxian
Zoffany, *Johann*

8 letters:
Angelico, *Fra*
Annigoni, *Pietro*
Auerbach, *Frank*
Beckmann, *Max*
Boccioni, *Umberto*
Bramante, *Donato*
Brancusi, *Constantin*
Breughel, *Jan*
Breughel, *Pieter*
Bronzino, *Agnolo*
Brueghel, *Jan*
Brueghel, *Pieter*
Carracci, *Agostino*
Carracci, *Annibale*
Carracci, *Ludovico*
Chadwick, *Lynn*
Daubigny, *Charles François*
De La Tour, *Georges*
Delaunay, *Robert*
De Ribera, *José*
Di Cosimo, *Piero*
Di Duccio, *Agostino*
Drysdale, *George Russell*
Dubuffet, *Jean*
Eastlake, *Sir Charles Lock*
Ghiberti, *Lorenzo*
González, *Julio*
Hamilton, *Richard*
Jongkind, *Johan Barthold*
Jordaens, *Jacob*
Kirchner, *Ernst Ludwig*
Landseer, *Edwin*
Lawrence, *Thomas*
Leighton, *Frederic*
Leonardo
Lipchitz, *Jacques*
Lysippus

Magritte, *René*
Malevich, *Kasimir Severinovich*
Mantegna, *Andrea*
Masaccio *(Thomasso Giovanni di Simone Guidi)*
Mondrian, *Piet*
Munnings, *Alfred*
Nevinson, *Christopher Richard Wynne*
Paolozzi, *Eduardo*
Passmore, *George*
Patenier, *Joachim*
Perugino, *Pietro*
Piranesi, *Giambattista*
Pissarro, *Camille*
Pontormo, *Jacopo Carucci*
Reynolds, *Joshua*
Rossetti, *Dante Gabriel*
Rousseau, *Henri Julien*
Rousseau, *Théodore*
Ter Borch, *Gerard*
Topolski, *Feliks*
Van Goyen, *Jan*
Vasarely, *Victor*
Veronese, *Paolo*
Whistler, *James Abbott McNeill*
Zurbarán, *Francisco*

9 letters:
Altdorfer, *Albrecht*
Bartholdi, *Frédéric August*
Beardsley, *Aubrey Vincent*
Bonington, *Richard Parkes*
Canaletto *(Giovanni Antonio Canal)*
Carpaccio, *Vittore*
Cavallini, *Pietro*
Constable, *John*
Correggio, *Antonio Allegri da*
Da Cortona, *Pietro*
Da Messina, *Antonello*
De Chirico, *Giorgio*
De Kooning, *Willem*
Delacroix, *Eugène*
Delaroche, *Paul*
Donatello *(Donato di Betto Bardi)*
Feininger, *Lyonel*
Fragonard, *Jean Honoré*
Friedrich, *Caspar David*
Géricault, *Théodore*

Artists

Giorgione, *Giorgio Barbarelli*
Grünewald, *Isaak*
Hiroshige, *Ando*
Kandinsky, *Wassily*
Kauffmann, *Angelica*
Kokoschka, *Oscar*
Kuniyoshi, *Utagawa*
Lehmbruck, *Wilhelm*
Mestrovic, *Ivan*
Nicholson, *Ben*
Nollekens, *Joseph*
Oldenburg, *Claes*
Pisanello
Rembrandt *(Rembrandt Harmensz van Rijn)*
Rodchenko, *Alexander Mikhailovich*
Roubiliac, *Louis-François*
Roubillac, *Louis-François*
Siqueiros, *David Alfaro*
Thornhill, *James*
Velázquez, *Diego Rodríguez de Silva y*

10 letters:
Alma-Tadema, *Lawrence*
Archipenko, *Aleksandr Porfiryevich*
Arcimboldo, *Giuseppe*
Bonnington, *Richard Parkes*
Botticelli, *Sandro*
Buonarroti, *Michelangelo*
Burne-Jones, *Edward*
Da Corregio, *Antonio Allegri*
Da Fabriano, *Gentile*
De Vlaminck, *Maurice*
Giacometti, *Alberto*
Guillaumin, *Armand*
Mackintosh, *Charles Rennie*
Michelozzo, *Michelozzi*
Modigliani, *Amedeo*
Moholy-Nagy, *László*
Polyclitus
Polygnotus
Praxiteles
Rowlandson, *Thomas*
Schongauer, *Martin*
Schwitters, *Kurt*
Signorelli, *Luca*
Sutherland, *Graham*
Tintoretto, *Jacopo*

Van der Goes, *Hugo*
Van de Velde, *Adriaen*
Van de Velde, *Willem*

11 letters:
Bartolommeo, *Fra*
Callimachus
De Chavannes, *Pierre Puvis*
Del Barbiere, *Domenico*
Della Robbia, *Andrea*
Della Robbia, *Luca*
Domenichino *(Domenico Zampien)*
Ghirlandaio, *Domenico*
Giambologna *(Jean de Boulogne)*
Terbrugghen, *Hendrik*
Thorvaldsen, *Bertel*
Van Ruisdael, *Jacob*
Van Ruysdael, *Salomen*
Vigée-Lebrun, *Élisabeth*

12 letters:
Da Caravaggio, *Michelangelo Merisi*
De Champaigne, *Philippe*
Della Quercia, *Jacopa*
Fantin-Latour, *Henri*
Gainsborough, *Thomas*
Lichtenstein, *Roy*
Michelangelo *(Michelagniolo di Lodovico Buonarriti)*
Parmigianino *(Girolano Francesco Maria Mazzola)*
Pinturicchio *(Bernardino di Betto)*
Rauschenberg, *Robert*
Van der Weyden, *Rogier*
Winterhalter, *Franz Xaver*

13 letters:
Del Pollaiuolo, *Antonio*
Del Pollaiuolo, *Piero*
Del Verrocchio, *Andrea*
Di Buoninsegna, *Duccio*
Messerschmidt, *Franz Xavier*

14 letters:
Da Castelfranco, *Giorgione*
Della Francesca, *Piero*
Gaudier-Brzeska, *Henri*

16 letters:
Gilbert and George

17 letters:
De Toulouse-Lautrec, *Henri Marie Raymond*

Asteroids

4 letters:
Eros
Juno

5 letters:
Ceres

6 letters:
Hermes
Pallas

8 letters:
Hesperia

Phaethon

Astrology terms

2 letters:
MC

3 letters:
Air

4 letters:
Cusp
Fire

5 letters:
Earth
Fixed
House
Stars
Trine
Water

6 letters:
Aspect
Square
Zodiac

7 letters:
Element
Mutable
Sun sign

8 letters:
Cardinal
Quintile
Star sign

9 letters:
Ascendant

Ascendent
Horoscope
Midheaven

10 letters:
Birthchart
Descendant
Descendent
Opposition

11 letters:
Conjunction
Satellitium

12 letters:
Ruling planet

Astronomers

4 letters:
Hale, *Alan*
Oort, *Jan*

5 letters:
Brahe, *Tycho*
Encke, *Johann Franz*
Hoyle, *Sir Fred(erick)*
Jeans, *Sir James Hopwood*
Meton
Reber, *Grote*
Roche, *Edouard*

6 letters:
Bessel, *Friedrich Wilhelm*
Halley, *Edmund*

Hewish, *Antony*
Hubble, *Edwin*
Kepler, *Johannes*
Lovell, *Sir (Alfred Charles)
  Bernard*

7 letters:
Bradley, *James*
Cassini, *Giovanni*
Celsius, *Anders*
Eudoxus
Galileo, *Galilei*
Huggins, *Sir William*
Khayyam, *Omar*
Laplace, *Pierre Simon de*
Lockyer, *Sir Joseph Norman*

Astronomy terms

Ptolemy *(Claudius Ptolemaeus)*

8 letters:
Almagest
Callipic
Herschel, *Caroline*
Herschel, *William*

9 letters:
Eddington, *Sir Arthur*
Flamsteed, *John*
Leverrier, *Urbain Jean Joseph*
Sosigenes

10 letters:
Copernicus, *Nicolas*
Hipparchus
Tycho Brahe

11 letters:
Aristarchus

12 letters:
Eratosthenes

13 letters:
Schwarzschild, *Karl*

Astronomy terms

3 letters:
Jet
Ray

4 letters:
Apse
Coma
Cusp
Limb
Mass
Node
Nova
Pole
Ring
Star
Tide

5 letters:
Apsis
Basin
Burst
Comet
Crust
Dwarf
Epoch
Flare
Giant
Lunar
Maria
Nadir
Orbit
Quiet
Rupes
Saros
Solar

Space
Spray
Train

6 letters:
Albedo
Aurora
Bolide
Colure
Corona
Cosmic
Crater
Ejecta
Facula
Galaxy
Merger
Meteor
Nebula
Octant
Plages
Quasar
Rising
Spinar
Syzygy
Zenith

7 letters:
Apapsis
Apolune
Appulse
Aureola
Aureole
Azimuth
Cluster
Ellipse

Equator
Equinox
Farside
Inertia
Ingress
New moon
Nucleus
Perigee
Plerion
Primary
Quarter
Radiant
Sextile
Spicule
Stellar
Sunspot

8 letters:
Aerolite
Altitude
Analemma
Aphelion
Asteroid
Cislunar
Crescent
Dynamics
Emersion
Evection
Filament
Fireball
Loadstar
Lodestar
Mass loss
Meridian
Nearside

Northing
Nutation
Parallax
Red giant
Regolith
Rotation
Solstice
Southing
Spherule
Universe

9 letters:
Aerospace
Anthelion
Black drop
Black hole
Chondrite
Collapsar
Companion
Cosmogony
Cosmology
Eccentric
Ecosphere
Ephemeris
Exosphere
Flocculus
Immersion
Light year
Magnitude
Meteorite
Meteoroid
Moonquake
Obliquity
Percentre
Periapsis
Planetary
Planetoid
Polar axis
Protostar
Ring plain
Satellite
Secondary
Shell star
Spacetime
Star cloud
Supernova
Variation
White hole

10 letters:
Achondrite
Aerosphere

Almacantar
Almucantar
Astrobleme
Atmosphere
Barycentre
Binary star
Brown dwarf
Elongation
Extinction
Inequality
Insolation
Ionosphere
Luminosity
Mesosphere
Metal ratio
Oblateness
Opposition
Periastron
Perihelion
Precession
Prominence
Quadrature
Revolution
Supergiant
Terminator
Tidal force
Triple star
White dwarf

11 letters:
Apocynthion
Chemosphere
Circumlunar
Circumpolar
Circumsolar
Colour index
Conjunction
Culmination
Evolved star
Gravitation
Heliosphere
Inclination
Inner planet
Major planet
Metallicity
Meteor storm
Missing mass
Neutron star
Observatory
Occultation
Open cluster

Outer planet
Photosphere
Protogalaxy
Protoplanet
Radio source
Retardation
Singularity
Solar system
Stellar wind
Troposphere

12 letters:
Asteroid belt
Chromosphere
Interstellar
Lunar eclipse
Mass transfer
Meteor shower
Multiple star
Planetesimal
Plasmasphere
Proper motion
Sidereal time
Solar eclipse
Spectral type
Sunspot cycle
Supercluster
Telluric line
Thermosphere
Tidal capture
Total eclipse
Tropical year
Variable star

13 letters:
Blue straggler
Circumstellar
Constellation
Magnetosphere
Moving cluster
Red supergiant
Scintillation
Seyfert galaxy
Solar constant
Solar spectrum
Spectral class
Sublunar point
Subsolar point
Symbiotic star
Synodic period
Tidal friction
Universal time

Athletic events

14 letters:
Annular eclipse
Aurora borealis
Escape velocity
Galactic centre
Inferior planet
Interplanetary
Molecular cloud
Northern lights
Partial eclipse
Reciprocal mass
Southern lights
Superior planet
Total magnitude
Vertical circle
Zenith distance

15 letters:
Aurora australis
Cepheid variable
Galactic equator
Meridian passage
Meteoroid stream
Nucleosynthesis
Orbital elements
Orbital velocity
Planetary system
Ptolemaic system
Strömgren sphere
Substellar point

Visual magnitude

16 letters:
Coordinate system
Copernican system
Galactic rotation
Naked singularity
Penumbral eclipse
Stellar evolution
Stellar structure

17 letters:
Physical libration
Pulsating universe
Pulsating variable
Shepherd satellite
Terrestrial planet

18 letters:
Chandrasekhar
  limit
Heliocentric
  system
North celestial
  pole
Northern
  hemisphere
North polar
  distance
Planetary
  alignment

Quasi-stellar
  object
South celestial
  pole
Southern
  hemisphere
South polar
  distance
Velocity dispersion

19 letters:
Cataclysmic
  variable
Oscillating
  universe
Schwarzschild
  radius

20 letters:
Effective
  temperature

23 letters:
Transient lunar
  phenomena

24 letters:
Precession of the
  equinoxes

See also:
➤ **Asteroids** ➤ **Atmosphere, layers of** ➤ **Comets** ➤ **Galaxies**
➤ **Meteor showers** ➤ **Planets** ➤ **Satellites**
➤ **Stars and constellations**

Athletic events

5 letters:
Relay

6 letters:
Discus
Hammer

7 letters:
Hurdles
Javelin
Shot put
Walking

8 letters:
High jump
Long jump
Marathon

9 letters:
Decathlon
Pole vault
Triathlon

10 letters:
Heptathlon

Pentathlon
Triple jump

12 letters:
Half marathon
Orienteering
Steeplechase

19 letters:
Cross-country
  running

Atmosphere, layers of

10 letters:
Ionosphere
Mesosphere
Ozone layer

11 letters:
Ozonosphere
Troposphere

12 letters:
Stratosphere
Thermosphere

Aviation terms

3 letters:
SBA
Yaw

4 letters:
Bank
Bunt
Crab
Dive
Gate
Hunt
Loop
Mach
Rake
Roll
Spin
Taxi
Trim

5 letters:
Ditch
Glide
Pilot
Pitch
Stack
Stall

6 letters:
Cruise
Drogue
Redeye
Reheat
Runway

7 letters:
Air miss
Airside
Batsman
Ceiling
Copilot
Feather
Landing

Loading
Overfly
Takeoff
Taxiway
Yaw axis

8 letters:
Airspeed
Anhedral
Approach
Attitude
Clearway
Dihedral
Flameout
In-flight
Landside
Nose dive
Roll axis
Sideslip
Snap roll
Subsonic
Tailspin
Wide-body
Wingover

9 letters:
Autopilot
Chandelle
Crash-dive
Crash-land
Fly-by-wire
Immelmann
Navigator
Overshoot
Pitch axis
Power dive
Sonic boom

10 letters:
Aerobatics
Barrel roll
Bird strike

Flight path
Shockstall
Supersonic
Undershoot

11 letters:
Air corridor
Groundspeed
Vapour trail
Victory roll

12 letters:
Approach path
Autorotation
Belly landing
Boarding pass
Redeye flight
Sound barrier

13 letters:
Charter flight
Contact flight
Head-up display
Immelmann turn

14 letters:
Automatic pilot
Holding pattern
Pancake landing

15 letters:
Scheduled flight

17 letters:
Air traffic control

20 letters:
Standard beam
  approach

23 letters:
Flight
  management
  systems

B

Back words

2 letters:
Ah / Ha
Am / Ma
At / Ta
Eh / He
Em / Me
Er / Re
Ha / Ah
He / Eh
Ho / Oh
Ma / Am
Me / Em
Mp / Pm
No / On
Oh / Ho
On / No
Pm / Mp
Re / Er
Ta / At

3 letters:
And / Dna
Are / Era
Bad / Dab
Bag / Gab
Ban / Nab
Bat / Tab
Ben / Neb
Bid / Dib
Big / Gib
Bin / Nib
Bog / Gob
Boy / Yob
Bud / Dub
Bun / Nub
Bus / Sub
But / Tub
Cam / Mac
Cor / Roc
Dab / Bad

Dag / Gad
Dal / Lad
Dam / Mad
Dew / Wed
Dib / Bid
Dim / Mid
Dna / And
Dog / God
Doh / Hod
Don / Nod
Dot / Tod
Dub / Bud
Eel / Lee
Era / Are
Gab / Bag
Gad / Dag
Gal / Lag
Gas / Sag
Gel / Leg
Gib / Big
Git / Tig
Gob / Bog
God / Dog
Got / Tog
Gum / Mug
Gut / Tug
Hay / Yah
Hod / Doh
Jar / Raj
Lad / Dal
Lag / Gal
Lap / Pal
Lee / Eel
Leg / Gel
Mac / Cam
Mad / Dam
Map / Pam
May / Yam
Mid / Dim
Mug / Gum

Nab / Ban
Nap / Pan
Neb / Ben
Net / Ten
Nib / Bin
Nip / Pin
Nit / Tin
Nod / Don
Not / Ton
Now / Won
Nub / Bun
Owt / Two
Pal / Lap
Pam / Map
Pan / Nap
Par / Rap
Pat / Tap
Pay / Yap
Per / Rep
Pin / Nip
Pit / Tip
Pot / Top
Pus / Sup
Put / Tup
Raj / Jar
Rap / Par
Rat / Tar
Raw / War
Rep / Per
Roc / Cor
Rot / Tor
Sag / Gas
Saw / Was
Sub / Bus
Sup / Pus
Tab / Bat
Tap / Pat
Tar / Rat
Ten / Net
Tig / Git

Tin / Nit
Tip / Pit
Tod / Dot
Tog / Got
Ton / Not
Top / Pot
Tor / Rot
Tub / But
Tug / Gut
Tup / Put
Two / Owt
War / Raw
Was / Saw
Way / Yaw
Wed / Dew
Won / Now
Yah / Hay
Yam / May
Yap / Pay
Yaw / Way
Yob / Boy

4 letters:
Abut / Tuba
Agas / Saga
Ajar / Raja
Auks / Skua
Avid / Diva
Bard / Drab
Bats / Stab
Bird / Drib
Bonk / Knob
Brag / Garb
Buns / Snub
Burg / Grub
Buts / Stub
Cram / Marc
Dart / Trad
Deem / Meed
Deep / Peed
Deer / Reed
Deus / Sued
Dial / Laid
Diva / Avid
Doom / Mood
Door / Rood
Drab / Bard
Draw / Ward
Dray / Yard
Drib / Bird
Dual / Laud

Edam / Made
Edit / Tide
Emir / Rime
Emit / Time
Ergo / Ogre
Et al / La te
Evil / Live
Flog / Golf
Flow / Wolf
Gals / Slag
Garb / Brag
Girt / Trig
Gnat / Tang
Gnus / Sung
Golf / Flog
Grub / Burg
Gulp / Plug
Gums / Smug
Guns / Snug
Hoop / Pooh
Keel / Leek
Keep / Peek
Knob / Bonk
Laid / Dial
Lair / Rial
Late / Etal
Laud / Dual
Leek / Keel
Leer / Reel
Liar / Rail
Live / Evil
Loop / Pool
Loot / Tool
Macs / Scam
Made / Edam
Maps / Spam
Marc / Cram
Mart / Tram
Maws / Swam
Meed / Deem
Meet / Teem
Mood / Doom
Moor / Room
Naps / Span
Nets / Sten
Nips / Spin
Nuts / Stun
Ogre / Ergo
Pals / Slap
Pans / Snap
Part / Trap

Paws / Swap
Peed / Deep
Peek / Keep
Pees / Seep
Pets / Step
Pins / Snip
Plug / Gulp
Pooh / Hoop
Pool / Loop
Pots / Stop
Prat / Tarp
Rail / Liar
Raja / Ajar
Raps / Spar
Rats / Star
Reed / Deer
Reel / Leer
Rial / Lair
Rime / Emir
Rood / Door
Room / Moor
Saga / Agas
Saps / Spas
Scam / Macs
Seep / Pees
Skua / Auks
Slag / Gals
Slap / Pals
Smug / Gums
Snap / Pans
Snip / Pins
Snot / Tons
Snub / Buns
Snug / Guns
Spam / Maps
Span / Naps
Spar / Raps
Spas / Saps
Spat / Taps
Spin / Nips
Spit / Tips
Spot / Tops
Stab / Bats
Star / Rats
Sten / Nets
Step / Pets
Stew / Wets
Stop / Pots
Stub / Buts
Stun / Nuts
Sued / Deus

Back words

Sung / Gnus
Swam / Maws
Swap / Paws
Sway / Yaws
Swot / Tows
Tang / Gnat
Taps / Spat
Tarp / Prat
Teem / Meet
Tide / Edit
Time / Emit
Tips / Spit
Tons / Snot
Tool / Loot
Tops / Spot
Tort / Trot
Tows / Swot
Trad / Dart
Tram / Mart
Trap / Part
Trig / Girt
Trot / Tort
Tuba / Abut
Ward / Draw
Wets / Stew
Wolf / Flow
Yard / Dray
Yaws / Sway

5 letters:

Debut / Tubed
Decaf / Faced
Decal / Laced
Deeps / Speed
Denim / Mined
Devil / Lived
Draws / Sward
Faced / Decaf
Fires / Serif
Keels / Sleek
Knits / Stink
Laced / Decal
Lager / Regal
Leper / Repel
Lever / Revel
Lived / Devil
Loops / Spool
Loots / Stool
Mined / Denim

Nonet / Tenon
Pacer / Recap
Parts / Strap
Pools / Sloop
Ports / Strop
Rebut / Tuber
Recap / Pacer
Regal / Lager
Remit / Timer
Repel / Leper
Revel / Lever
Rones / Senor
Señor / Roñes
Serif / Fires
Sleek / Keels
Sloop / Pools
Smart / Trams
Snaps / Spans
Snips / Spins
Spans / Snaps
Speed / Deeps
Spins / Snips
Spool / Loops
Spots / Stops
Sprat / Tarps
Stink / Knits
Stool / Loots
Stops / Spots
Stows / Swots
Strap / Parts
Straw / Warts
Strop / Ports
Sward / Draws
Swots / Stows
Tarps / Sprat
Tenon / Nonet
Timer / Remit
Trams / Smart
Tubed / Debut
Tuber / Rebut
Warts / Straw

6 letters:

Denier / Reined
Diaper / Repaid
Drawer / Reward
Looter / Retool
Pilfer / Reflip
Pupils / Slipup

Recaps / Spacer
Redraw / Warder
Reflip / Pilfer
Reflow / Wolfer
Reined / Denier
Reknit / Tinker
Rennet / Tenner
Repaid / Diaper
Retool / Looter
Reward / Drawer
Sleets / Steels
Slipup / Pupils
Sloops / Spools
Snoops / Spoons
Spacer / Recaps
Spools / Sloops
Spoons / Snoops
Sports / Strops
Steels / Sleets
Strops / Sports
Tenner / Rennet
Tinker / Reknit
Warder / Redraw
Wolfer / Reflow

7 letters:

Amaroid / Diorama
Deifier / Reified
Deliver / Reviled
Dessert / Tressed
Diorama / Amaroid
Gateman /
  Nametag
Nametag /
  Gateman
Reified / Deifier
Reknits / Stinker
Reviled / Deliver
Stinker / Reknits
Tressed / Dessert

8 letters:

Desserts / Stressed
Redrawer /
  Rewarder
Rewarder /
  Redrawer
Stressed / Desserts

Bacteria

4 letters:
MRSA

5 letters:
Cocci
Staph
Strep

6 letters:
Aerobe

Vibrio

7 letters:
Bacilli
Lysogen

8 letters:
Listeria
Pathogen
Spirilla

10 letters:
Salmonella

11 letters:
Pasteurella

13 letters:
Streptococcus

Bags

3 letters:
Bum
Cod
Ice
Net
Sea
Tea

4 letters:
Body
Caba
Cool
Dime
Grip
Poke
Port
Sack
Tote

5 letters:
Amaut
Amowt
Bulse
Cabas
Dilli
Dilly
Ditty
Doggy
Jelly
Jiffy®
Nunny
Pikau
Pouch

Purse
Scrip
Water

6 letters:
Bergen
Carpet
Clutch
Duffel
Kitbag
Oxford
Sachet
Saddle
Sponge
Tucker
Valise
Vanity
Wallet

7 letters:
Alforja
Carrier
Daypack
Dorothy
Handbag
Holdall
Satchel
Shopper
Sporran
Weekend
Workbag

8 letters:
Backpack

Carryall
Crumenal
Knapsack
Pochette
Reticule
Ridicule
Rucksack
Shoulder
Sleeping
Suitcase
Survival

9 letters:
Briefcase
Carpetbag
Gladstone
Haversack
Overnight
Saddlebag
Vanity box

10 letters:
Diplomatic
Portmantle
Portmantua
Sabretache
Vanity case

11 letters:
Portmanteau

Ballets

Ballets

5 letters:
Manon
Rodeo

6 letters:
Bolero
Carmen
Façade
Ondine
Onegin
Parade

7 letters:
Giselle
Masques
Orpheus

8 letters:
Coppélia
Firebird
Les Noces
Serenade

Swan Lake

9 letters:
Les Biches
Spartacus

10 letters:
Cinderella
La Bayadère
Nutcracker
Petroushka

11 letters:
Billy the Kid

12 letters:
Les Sylphides
Rite of Spring
Scheherazade

14 letters:
Romeo and Juliet

Sleeping Beauty

16 letters:
Enigma Variations
La Fille mal gardée

17 letters:
Appalachian Spring

18 letters:
L'après-midi d'un
faune

19 letters:
La Boutique
Fantasque

20 letters:
Midsummer
Night's Dream

Ballet steps and terms

3 letters:
Pas

4 letters:
Jeté
Plié

5 letters:
Adage
Battu
Brisé
Coupé
Decor
Passé
Tombé

6 letters:
Adagio
Aplomb
Ballon
Chassé
Croisé
Dégagé
Ecarté
En l'air

Failli
Ouvert
Pointe
Relevé

7 letters:
Allegro
Allongé
Balancé
Ciseaux
Déboulé
Échappé
Emboîté
Soutenu
Turn-out

8 letters:
Absolute
Abstract
Assemblé
Attitude
Ballonné
Ballotté
Batterie

Cabriole
Demi-plié
En dedans
En dehors
En pointe
Figurant
Glissade
Pas coupé
Romantic
Sickling
Sur place
Temps lié
Toe-dance

9 letters:
Arabesque
Ballerina
Battement
Classical
Cou-de-pied
Détournée
Développée
Elevation
Entrechat

Pas de chat
Pas de deux
Pirouette
Raccourci
Temps levé
Variation

10 letters:
Changement
Demi-pointe
En couronne
Foudroyant
Grand écart
Grande plié
Pas ciseaux
Pas de brisé
Pas échappé
Soubresaut
Tour en l'air

11 letters:
Ballet blanc
Contretemps
Pas ballotté
Pas de bourée
Pas de chassé

Ports de bras
Rond de jambe
Terre à terre

12 letters:
Ballet de cour
Croisé devant
Enchaînement
Gargouillade

13 letters:
Ballet d'action
En tire-bouchon
Pas de sissonne
Temps de cuisse
Temps de flèche

14 letters:
Benesh notation
Croisé derrière
Entrée de ballet
Premier danseur
Prima ballerina
Temps de poisson
Temps dévelopée

15 letters:
Cecchetti method

16 letters:
Pas de bourée
 couru
Première danseuse
Stepanov notation
Von Laban
 notation

17 letters:
Changement de
 pieds
Fouetté en
 tournant

21 letters:
Défilé de corps de
 ballet

22 letters:
Prima ballerina
 assoluta

Ball games

4 letters:
Golf

5 letters:
Fives

6 letters:
Boules
Hockey
Soccer
Squash
Tennis

7 letters:
Bowling
Croquet
Hurling
Netball
Pinball

Pyramid
Snooker

8 letters:
Baseball
Football
Goalball
Handball
Korfball
Lacrosse
Pushball
Rounders
Subbuteo®

9 letters:
Badminton
Bagatelle
Billiards
Crazy golf

Paintball
Punchball

10 letters:
Volleyball

11 letters:
Bumble-puppy

12 letters:
Bar billiards

15 letters:
Australian Rules
Pocket billiards

16 letters:
American football
Canadian football
Piggy in the middle

Baseball teams

Baseball teams

11 letters:
Chicago Cubs
New York Mets

12 letters:
Boston Red Sox
Texas Rangers
Tampa Bay Rays

13 letters:
Anaheim Angels
Atlanta Braves
Detroit Tigers
Houston Astros

14 letters:
Cincinnati Reds
Florida Marlins
Minnesota Twins
New York Yankees
San Diego Padres

15 letters:
Chicago White Sox
Colorado Rockies
Seattle Mariners

Toronto Blue Jays

16 letters:
Baltimore Orioles
Cleveland Indians
Kansas City Royals
Los Angeles Angels
Milwaukee Brewers
Oakland Athletics
St Louis Cardinals

17 letters:
Los Angeles Dodgers
Pittsburgh Pirates
Tampa Bay Devil Rays

18 letters:
San Francisco Giants

19 letters:
Arizona Diamondbacks
Washington Nationals

20 letters:
Philadelphia Phillies

Basketball teams

8 letters:
Utah Jazz

9 letters:
Miami Heat

11 letters:
Phoenix Suns

12 letters:
Atlanta Hawks
Chicago Bulls
Orlando Magic

13 letters:
Boston Celtics
Denver Nuggets
Indiana Pacers
New Jersey Nets
New York Knicks

14 letters:
Detroit Pistons
Houston Rockets
Milwaukee Bucks
Toronto Raptors

15 letters:
Dallas Mavericks
Sacramento Kings
San Antonio Spurs

16 letters:
Charlotte Bobcats
Los Angeles Lakers
Memphis Grizzlies

17 letters:
New Orleans Hornets
Philadelphia 76ers
Washington Wizards

18 letters:
Cleveland Cavaliers
Los Angeles Clippers
Seattle SuperSonics

19 letters:
Golden State Warriors

20 letters:
Portland Trail Blazers

21 letters:
Minnesota Timberwolves

Bats

5 letters:
Fruit

6 letters:
Kalong

7 letters:
Noctule
Vampire

8 letters:
Serotine

9 letters:
Flying fox
Horseshoe

10 letters:
Hammerhead

11 letters:
Barbastelle
Pipistrelle

12 letters:
False vampire

13 letters:
Insectivorous

Battles

Battle	Year
Aboukir Bay *or* Abukir Bay	1798
Actium	31 BC
Agincourt	1415
Alamo	1836
Arnhem	1944
Atlantic	1939–45
Austerlitz	1805
Balaklava *or* Balaclava	1854
Bannockburn	1314
Barnet	1471
Bautzen	1813
Belleau Wood	1918
Blenheim	1704
Borodino	1812
Bosworth Field	1485
Boyne	1690
Britain	1940
Bulge	1944–45
Bull Run	1861;1862
Bunker Hill	1775
Cannae	216 BC
Crécy	1346
Culloden	1746
Dien Bien Phu	1954
Edgehill	1642
El Alamein	1942
Falkirk	1298; 1746

Battles

Battle	Year
Flodden	1513
Gettysburg	1863
Guadalcanal	1942–3
Hastings	1066
Hohenlinden	1800
Imphal	1944
Inkerman	1854
Issus	333 BC
Jemappes	1792
Jena	1806
Killiecrankie	1689
Kursk	1943
Ladysmith	1899–1900
Le Cateau	1914
Leipzig	1813
Lepanto	1571
Leyte Gulf	1944
Little Bighorn	1876
Lützen	1632
Manassas	1861; 1862
Mantinea *or* Mantineia	418 BC; 362 BC
Marathon	490 BC
Marengo	1800
Marston Moor	1644
Missionary Ridge	1863
Naseby	1645
Navarino	425 BC
Omdurman	1898
Passchendaele	1917
Philippi	42 BC
Plains of Abraham	1759
Plassey	1757
Plataea	479 BC
Poltava	1709
Prestonpans	1745
Pydna	168 BC
Quatre Bras	1815
Ramillies	1706
Roncesvalles	778
Sadowa *or* Sadová	1866
Saint-Mihiel	1918
Salamis	480 BC
Sedgemoor	1685
Sempach	1386
Shiloh	1862
Shipka Pass	1877–78
Somme	1916; 1918
Stalingrad	1941–42
Stamford Bridge	1066
Stirling Bridge	1297

Battle	Year
Tannenberg	1410; 1914
Tewkesbury	1471
Thermopylae	480 BC
Tobruk	1941; 1942
Trafalgar	1805
Trenton	1776
Verdun	1916
Vitoria	1813
Wagram	1809
Waterloo	1815
Ypres	1914; 1915; 1917; 1918
Zama	202 BC

Bays

2 letters:
MA

3 letters:
Ise

4 letters:
Pigs
Vigo
Wick

5 letters:
Algoa
Bonny
Byron
Casco
Dvina
False
Fleet
Fundy
Glace
Green
Hawke
Herne
Horse
James
Korea
Milne
Omura
Osaka
Shark
Sligo
Suvla
Table
Tampa
Tokyo
Urado

6 letters:
Abukir
Ariake
Baffin
Bantry
Bengal
Biscay
Botany
Broken
Callao
Colwyn
Daphne
Dublin
Galway
Golden
Hawke's
Hudson
Jervis
Lobito
Manila
Mobile
Newark
Tasman
Toyama
Tralee
Ungava
Vyborg
Walvis

7 letters:
Aboukir
Cape Cod
Delagoa
Delogoa
Dundalk
Florida
Jiazhou
Montego
Moreton
New York
Pegasus
Poverty
Setúbal
Swansea
Thunder
Walfish
Whitley

8 letters:
Biscayne
Buzzards
Cardigan
Delaware
Georgian
Hangzhou
Quiberon
San Pedro
Santiago

9 letters:
Bay of Acre
Bay of Pigs
Bombetoka
Discovery
Encounter
Famagusta
Frobisher

Beans and other pulses

Guanabara
Inhambane
Kuskokwim
Magdalena
Morecambe
St Austell

10 letters:
Bay of Cádiz
Bay of Fundy
Bay of Vlorë
Caernarvon
Carmarthen
Chesapeake
Cienfuegos

Guantánamo
Lützow-Holm

11 letters:
Bay of Bengal
Bay of Biscay
Bay of Gdansk
Bay of Naples
Bay of Plenty
Port Phillip

12 letters:
Bay of Kaválla
Narragansett
San Francisco

13 letters:
Bay of Campeche
Bay of St Michel
Corpus Christi
Massachusetts
Passamaquoddy

14 letters:
Bay of Gibraltar

16 letters:
Bay of Trincomalee

18 letters:
Bay of Espírito
  Santo

Beans and other pulses

3 letters:
Red

4 letters:
Dhal
Gram
Lima
Mung
Navy
Soya

5 letters:
Black
Bobby
Broad
Field
Green
Pinto

6 letters:
Adsuki

Adzuki
Butter
French
Kidney
Lentil
Runner
String

7 letters:
Haricot
Snow pea

8 letters:
Borlotti
Chick pea
Garbanzo
Split pea

9 letters:
Black-eyed
Cannelini

Flageolet
Mangetout
Petit pois
Pigeon pea
Puy lentil
Red kidney
Red lentil

11 letters:
Green lentil

12 letters:
Black-eyed pea
Marrowfat pea
Sugar snap pea

17 letters:
Continental lentil

Beds

3 letters:
Air
Box
Cot
Day
Mat

4 letters:
Bunk
Camp
Cott
Crib
Kang
Lilo®

Loft
Sofa
Twin

5 letters:
Berth
Couch

Divan
Field
Futon
Water

6 letters:
Cradle
Double
Litter
Murphy
Pallet
Put-u-up
Single
Sleigh

7 letters:
Amenity

Charpoy
Feather
Folding
Hammock
Trestle
Truckle
Trundle

8 letters:
Apple-pie
Bassinet
Captain's
Carrycot
Foldaway
Hospital
King-size
Mattress

Platform

9 letters:
Couchette
King-sized
Paillasse
Palliasse
Queen-size
Shake down
Stretcher

10 letters:
Four-poster
Queen-sized

11 letters:
Procrustean

Beetles

3 letters:
Bee
Dor
May
Oil

4 letters:
Bark
Cane
Dorr
Dung
Flea
Gold
Huhu
June
King
Leaf
Mall
Maul
Pill
Rose
Rove
Stag

5 letters:
Bacon
Black
Click
Clock
Jewel
Roach

Snout
Tiger
Water

6 letters:
Batler
Carpet
Chafer
Diving
Dor-fly
Elater
Gregor
Ground
Hammer
Larder
Mallet
May bug
Museum
Potato
Scarab
Sexton
Sledge
Spider
Weevil

7 letters:
Asiatic
Blister
Burying
Cabinet
Cadelle

Carrion
Elytron
Elytrum
Firefly
Goldbug
Goliath
Hop-flea
Hornbug
June bug
Ladybug
Leather
Skelter
Soldier
Vedalia

8 letters:
Ambrosia
Bum-clock
Cardinal
Colorado
Curculio
Darkling
Glow-worm
Hercules
Japanese
Ladybird
Longhorn
Māori bug
Scarabee
Skipjack
Snapping

Tortoise
Wireworm

9 letters:
Buprestus
Cantharis
Carpet bug
Christmas
Cockroach
Furniture
Goldsmith
Kekerengu
Longicorn
Pea weevil
Pinchbuck

Scavenger
Timberman
Tumble-bug
Whirligig
Woodborer

10 letters:
Bean weevil
Boll weevil
Bombardier
Churchyard
Cockchafer
Deathwatch
Dumbledore
Long-horned

Rhinoceros
Rose chafer
Spanish fly
Turnip-flea

11 letters:
Bloody-nosed
Typographer

12 letters:
Buzzard-clock
Sledge-hammer

16 letters:
Devil's coach-
  horse

Bets and betting systems

3 letters:
Win

4 letters:
Ante
Flag
Back
Tote

5 letters:
Heinz
Place

6 letters:
Chance
Double
Lucky 7
Parlay
Patent
Single
Treble
Trixie
Yankee

7 letters:
A cheval
Each-way

Goliath
Lucky 15
Lucky 31
Lucky 63
Rounder
Tricast

8 letters:
Antepost
Canadian
Forecast
Perfecta
Quinella
Trifecta

9 letters:
Asian line
Goal crazy
Quadrella
Scorecast
Super flag
Union Jack
Up-and-down

10 letters:
Martingale

Parimutuel
Roundabout
Round Robin
Superfecta
Super Heinz

11 letters:
Accumulator
Super Yankee

12 letters:
Correct score
Podium finish
Treble chance

16 letters:
Race dual forecast
Reversed forecast

18 letters:
Combination
  tricast

19 letters:
Combination
  forecast

Bible

BOOKS OF THE BIBLE: OLD TESTAMENT

3 letters:
Job

4 letters:
Amos
Ezra
Joel
Ruth

5 letters:
Hosea
Jonah
Kings
Micah
Nahum

6 letters:
Daniel
Esther

Exodus
Haggai
Isaiah
Joshua
Judges
Psalms
Samuel

7 letters:
Ezekiel
Genesis
Malachi
Numbers
Obadiah

8 letters:
Habakkuk
Jeremiah
Nehemiah

Proverbs

9 letters:
Leviticus
Zechariah
Zephaniah

10 letters:
Chronicles

11 letters:
Deuteronomy

12 letters:
Ecclesiastes
Lamentations

13 letters:
Song of Solomon

BOOKS OF THE BIBLE: NEW TESTAMENT

4 letters:
Acts
John
Jude
Luke
Mark

5 letters:
James
Peter
Titus

6 letters:
Romans

7 letters:
Hebrews
Matthew
Timothy

8 letters:
Philemon

9 letters:
Ephesians

Galatians

10 letters:
Colossians
Revelation

11 letters:
Corinthians
Philippians

13 letters:
Thessalonians

BOOKS OF THE BIBLE: APOCRYPHA

5 letters:
Tobit

6 letters:
Baruch
Esdras
Judith
Wisdom

8 letters:
Manasseh

9 letters:
Maccabees

14 letters:
Ecclesiasticus
Song of the Three

16 letters:
Daniel and
    Susanna

20 letters:
Daniel, Bel and the
    Snake

Bible

CHARACTERS IN THE BIBLE

3 letters:
Dan
Eve
Gad
Ham
Job
Lot

4 letters:
Abel
Adam
Ahab
Amos
Boaz
Cain
Cush
Enos
Esau
Ezra
Jael
Jehu
Joab
Joel
John
Jude
Kush
Leah
Levi
Luke
Mark
Mary
Noah
Paul
Ruth
Saul
Seth
Shem

5 letters:
Aaron
Ammon
Asher
David
Dinah
Dives
Elias
Enoch
Hagar
Herod

Hiram
Hosea
Isaac
Jacob
James
Jesse
Jonah
Jonas
Jubal
Judah
Laban
Magus
Micah
Moses
Nahum
Naomi
Peter
Sarah
Simon
Tobit
Uriah

6 letters:
Andrew
Balaam
Baruch
Belial
Caspar
Daniel
Dorcas
Elijah
Elisha
Esther
Gideon
Gilead
Haggai
Hannah
Isaiah
Jephte
Jethro
Joseph
Joshua
Josiah
Judith
Martha
Midian
Miriam
Naboth
Nathan

Nimrod
Philip
Rachel
Reuben
Salome
Samson
Samuel
Simeon
Thomas
Zilpah

7 letters:
Abigail
Abraham
Absalom
Ananias
Deborah
Delilah
Ephraim
Ezekiel
Gabriel
Goliath
Ishmael
Japheth
Jezebel
Lazarus
Malachi
Matthew
Meshach
Obadiah
Rebecca
Solomon
Susanna
Thadeus
Zachary
Zebedee
Zebulun

8 letters:
Abednego
Barabbas
Benjamin
Caiaphas
Habakkuk
Hezekiah
Issachar
Jephthah
Jeremiah
Jeroboam

Jonathan
Lot's wife
Manasseh
Matthias
Melchior
Mordecai
Naphtali
Nehemiah
Potiphar
Shadrach
Thaddeus
Zedekiah

9 letters:
Ahasuerus
Balthazar
Bathsheba
Beelzebub
Boanerges

Nabonidus
Nathanael
Nicodemus
Tubal-cain
Zachariah
Zacharias
Zechariah
Zephaniah

10 letters:
Achitophel
Ahithophel
Belshazzar
Holofernes
Methuselah
Virgin Mary

11 letters:
Bartholomew
Gog and Magog

Jehoshaphat
Jesus Christ
Melchizedek
Prodigal Son

12 letters:
Melchisedech
Queen of Sheba

13 letters:
Good Samaritan
Judas Iscariot
Mary Magdalene

14 letters:
John the Baptist
Nebuchadnezzar
Nebuchadrezzar
Tetragrammaton
Whore of Babylon

PLACE NAMES IN THE BIBLE

2 letters:
On

4 letters:
Aram
Cana
Eden
Gath
Gaza
Moab

5 letters:
Babel
Horeb
Judah
Judea
Ophir
Sodom

6 letters:
Ararat
Bashan
Canaan

Goshen
Judaea
Shiloh
Shinar
Tadmor
Tophet

7 letters:
Antioch
Calvary
Galilee
Gehenna
Jericho
Samaria
Shittim
Topheth

8 letters:
Aceldama
Bethesda
Golgotha
Gomorrah

Gomorrha
Nazareth

9 letters:
Arimathea
Bethlehem
Capernaum
Jerusalem
Land of Nod

10 letters:
Arimathaea
Gethsemane
Wilderness

12 letters:
Garden of Eden
Rabbath Ammon

18 letters:
Land of milk and
  honey

Bicycles

TYPES OF BIBLE

2 letters:
AV
NT
OT
RV

3 letters:
RSV

4 letters:
Whig

5 letters:
Douai
Douay
Itala

6 letters:
Family
Geneva
Gideon
Gospel

Italic
Missal
Tanach
Targum
Wyclif
Zurich

7 letters:
Bamberg
Cranmer
Hexapla
Mazarin
Midrash
Peshito
Psalter
Tyndale
Vulgate

8 letters:
Cromwell
Mazarine

Peshitta
Peshitto
Polyglot
Wycliffe

9 letters:
Apocrypha
Coverdale
King James
Taverners

10 letters:
Pentateuch
Septuagint

12 letters:
Antilegomena

14 letters:
Revised Version

16 letters:
King James version

Bicycles

BICYCLE PARTS

4 letters:
Bell

5 letters:
Pedal
Wheel

6 letters:
Saddle

7 letters:
Pannier

Rat-trap

8 letters:
Crossbar
Mudguard

9 letters:
Kickstand
Saddlebag

10 letters:
Handlebars

Mileometer
Stabilizer

11 letters:
Bicycle pump

12 letters:
Bicycle chain

TYPES OF BICYCLE

3 letters:
BMX

6 letters:
Tandem

7 letters:
Bicycle
Chopper

8 letters:
Roadster

9 letters:
Autocycle

10 letters:
Boneshaker
Fairy cycle

Velocipede

12 letters:
Exercise bike
Mountain bike

13 letters:
Penny-farthing

Biochemists

3 letters:
Dam, *Henrik Carl Peter*

4 letters:
Cori, *Carl Ferdinand*
Cori, *Gerti*
Funk, *Casimir*
Funk, *Kazimierz*
Katz, *Bernard*

5 letters:
Bloch, *Konrad Emil*
Boyer, *Herbert*
Cohen, *Stanley*
Doisy, *Edward Adelbert*
Krebs, *Sir Hans Adolf*
Monod, *Jaques Lucien*
Moore, *Stanford*
Ochoa, *Severo*
Stein, *William H(oward)*
Synge, *Richard*

6 letters:
Beadle, *George Wells*
De Duve, *Christian*
Domagk, *Gerhard*
Florey, *Sir Howard Walter*
Holley, *Robert W(illiam)*
Martin, *Archer*
Mullis, *Kary Banks*
Oparin, *Alexandr*
Porter, *Rodney Robert*

Sanger, *Frederick*
Sumner, *James B(atcheller)*

7 letters:
Buchner, *Eduard*
Edelman, *Gerald M(aurice)*
Fleming, *Sir Alexander*
Gilbert, *Walter*
Hopkins, *Sir Frederick Gowland*
Kendrew, *John C(owdery)*
Khorana, *Har Gobind*
Macleod, *John James Richard*
Rodbell, *Martin*
Stanley, *Wendell Meredith*
Waksman, *Selman Abraham*
Warburg, *Otto Heinrich*

8 letters:
Anfinsen, *Christian Boehmer*
Chargaff, *Erwin*
Kornberg, *Arthur*
Meyerhof, *Otto Fritz*
Northrop, *John H(oward)*

9 letters:
Bergstrom, *Sune K(arl)*
Butenandt, *Adolf Friedrich Johann*
Ferdinand, *Max Perutz*
Nirenberg, *Marshall W(arren)*

10 letters:
Samuelsson, *Bengt*

Biology

BRANCHES OF BIOLOGY

6 letters:
Botany

7 letters:
Ecology
Zoology

8 letters:
Biometry
Cytology
Genetics

Taxonomy

9 letters:
Histology

10 letters:
Biophysics
Biostatics
Morphology
Organology
Somatology

Teratology

11 letters:
Aerobiology
Agrobiology
Biodynamics
Cryobiology

12 letters:
Astrobiology
Bacteriology

Biology

Biochemistry
Biogeography
Cytogenetics
Microbiology
Oceanography
Organography
Parasitology

Photobiology
Radiobiology
Sociobiology
Stoichiology

13 letters:
Actinobiology

Chronobiology
Palaeontology
Photodynamics

BIOLOGY TERMS

3 letters:
DNA
Egg
RNA

4 letters:
Bone
Cell
Gene
Ovum
Root
Seed
Skin
Soil

5 letters:
Blood
Class
Clone
Fruit
Genus
Gland
Gonad
Order
Organ
Sperm
Spore
Virus

6 letters:
Albino
Allele
Dorsal
Embryo
Enzyme
Family
Flower
Foetus
Fossil
Fungus
Gamete
Growth
Hybrid

Muscle
Phylum
Pollen
Zygote

7 letters:
Aerobic
Biomass
Diploid
Haploid
Hormone
Kingdom
Meiosis
Mitosis
Nucleus
Osmosis
Progeny
Protein
Puberty
Species
Ventral
Vitamin

8 letters:
Anterior
Bacteria
Division
Dominant
Heredity
Mutation
Parasite
Pathogen
Pectoral
Predator
Ribosome
Skeleton

9 letters:
Anaerobic
Cytoplasm
Diffusion
Digestion
Ecosystem

Epidermis
Evolution
Excretion
Food chain
Gestation
Life cycle
Ovulation
Pollution
Posterior
Pregnancy
Recessive
Symbiosis

10 letters:
Chromosome
Conception
Copulation
Krebs cycle
Metabolism
Protoplasm
Vertebrate
Viviparous

11 letters:
Allelomorph
Blood vessel
Circulation
Codominance
Cold-blooded
Environment
Germination
Inheritance
Pollination
Propagation
Respiration
Warm-blooded
X-chromosome
Y-chromosome

12 letters:
Assimilation
Fermentation
Invertebrate

Menstruation
Reproduction
Spermatozoon

13 letters:
Agglutination
Binary fission
Fertilization
Hermaphrodite
Metamorphosis
Nitrogen cycle
Translocation
Transpiration

14 letters:
Photosynthesis

BIOLOGISTS

3 letters:
May, *Robert McCredie*
Orr, *John Boyd*

4 letters:
Berg, *Paul*
Koch, *Robert*

5 letters:
Crick, *Francis Harry Compton*
Krebs, *Hans Adolf*

6 letters:
Beadle, *George Well*
Carrel, *Alexis*
Carson, *Rachel*
Claude, *Albert*
Darwin, *Charles (Robert)*
Harvey, *William*
Huxley, *Andrew Fielding*
Huxley, *Julian*
Huxley, *Thomas Henry*
Mendel, *Gregor*
Morgan, *Thomas Hunt*

Poikilothermic

16 letters:
Natural selection

17 letters:
Circulatory system
Ribose nucleic acid

18 letters:
Sexual reproduction

19 letters:
Asexual reproduction

20 letters:
Deoxyribonucleic acid

Watson, *James Dewey*

7 letters:
Fleming, *Alexander*
Haeckel, *Ernst Heinrich*
Pasteur, *Louis*

8 letters:
Delbrück, *Max*
Dulbecco, *Renato*
Franklin, *Rosalind*
Linnaeus
Von Linné, *Carl*

9 letters:
Baltimore, *David*
Von Haller, *Albrecht*

10 letters:
Denisovich, *Trofim*
Dobzhansky, *Theodosius*

14 letters:
Van Leeuwenhoek, *Anton*

See also:
➤ **Bacteria** ➤ **Enzymes** ➤ **Hormones** ➤ **Membranes**
➤ **Proteins** ➤ **Sugars**

Birds

2 letters:
Ka

3 letters:
Ani
Auk
Boo
Cob
Emu
Fum
Jay
Kae
Kea
Maw
Mew
Nun
Oil
Owl
Pea
Pie
Ree
Roc
Ruc
Tit
Tui

4 letters:
Barb
Chat
Cirl
Cobb
Coly
Coot
Crax
Crow
Dove
Emeu
Erne
Eyas
Fung
Gled
Guan
Guga
Gull
Hawk
Hern
Huma
Ibis
Iynx

Jynx
Kagu
Kaka
Kite
Kiwi
Knot
Koel
Kora
Lark
Loon
Lory
Lyre
Mina
Monk
Myna
Otis
Pavo
Pawn
Pern
Piet
Pink
Pown
Pyot
Rail
Rhea
Roch
Rook
Ruff
Runt
Ruru
Rype
Shag
Smee
Sora
Swan
Taha
Tara
Teal
Tern
Tody
Tuli
Weka
Whio
Whip
Wren
Xema
Yale
Yite

5 letters:
Agami
Ardea
Ariel
Bennu
Booby
Bosun
Capon
Chook
Colin
Colly
Cooee
Crake
Crane
Diver
Egret
Finch
Fleet
Galah
Galar
Glede
Goose
Goura
Grebe
Heron
Hobby
Homer
Isaac
Junco
Kight
Liver
Lowan
Macaw
Madge
Manch
Mavis
Merle
Micky
Mimus
Mohua
Monal
Mulga
Murre
Mynah
Nandu
Nelly
Noddy
Ousel

Ouzel
Ox-eye
Peggy
Pekan
Pewit
Picus
Piper
Pipit
Pitta
Poaka
Poker
Potoo
Prion
Quail
Quest
Quist
Raven
Reeve
Rifle
Robin
Rotch
Ryper
Saker
Scape
Scart
Scaup
Scops
Scray
Scrub
Serin
Shama
Sitta
Skart
Snipe
Solan
Soree
Spink
Sprug
Squab
Stare
Stilt
Stint
Stork
Sugar
Swift
Sylph
Terek
Tewit
Topaz
Twite
Umber

Umbre
Urubu
Veery
Vireo
Wader
Whaup
Widow
Wonga
Yaffa

6 letters:
Amazon
Aquila
Avocet
Avoset
Bantam
Barbet
Bishop
Bittor
Bittur
Bonxie
Boubou
Brolga
Bulbul
Canary
Chough
Chukar
Condor
Conure
Corbie
Coucal
Cuckoo
Culver
Curlew
Cushat
Darter
Dikkop
Dipper
Drongo
Duiker
Dunlin
Duyker
Elanet
Evejar
Falcon
Fulmar
Gambet
Gander
Gannet
Garuda
Gentle

Gentoo
Gillar
Go-away
Godwit
Gooney
Goslet
Grakle
Grouse
Hagden
Hagdon
Haglet
Hermit
Hoopoe
Houdan
Jabiru
Jaçana
Jaegar
Jaeger
Kakapo
Karoro
Kereru
Kokako
Kotare
Kotuku
Lahore
Lanner
Leipoa
Linnet
Lintie
Locust
Loriot
Lourie
Lungie
Magpie
Martin
Menura
Merlin
Merops
Missel
Mistle
Monaul
Mopoke
Mossie
Motmot
Musket
Nandoo
Oriole
Osprey
Parrot
Parson
Pavone

Birds

Peahen
Peewee
Peewit
Pernis
Petrel
Phoebe
Pigeon
Pipipi
Plover
Pouter
Progne
Puffin
Pukeko
Pullet
Queest
Quelea
Quoist
Redcap
Reeler
Roller
Scamel
Scarth
Scaury
Scraye
Sea-cob
Sea-mew
Seapie
Shrike
Simara
Simorg
Simurg
Siskin
Skarth
Smeath
Soland
Sorage
Strich
Sultan
Sylvia
Tailor
Takahe
Tarcel
Tassel
Tauhou
Tewhit
Thrush
Tom-tit
Toucan
Towhee
Trogon
Turaco

Turbit
Tyrant
Tystie
Verdin
Wading
Walker
Waxeye
Weaver
Whidah
Whydah
Willet
Woosel
Yaffle
Ynambu
Yucker
Zoozoo

7 letters:
Amokura
Anhinga
Antbird
Apostle
Apteryx
Axebird
Babbler
Bécasse
Bittern
Bittour
Blighty
Bluecap
Blue-eye
Blue jay
Bluetit
Boobook
Bullbat
Bunting
Buphaga
Bushtit
Bustard
Buzzard
Cacique
Cariama
Catbird
Chewink
Chicken
Coal tit
Coletit
Colibri
Corella
Cotinga
Courlan

Courser
Cowbird
Creeper
Crombec
Cropper
Cumulet
Diamond
Dinorus
Dottrel
Dovekie
Dunnock
Emu-wren
Fantail
Fern-owl
Fig-bird
Finfoot
Flicker
Frigate
Gobbler
Goburra
Gorcrow
Goshawk
Grackle
Grallae
Hacklet
Hadedah
Hagbolt
Hagdown
Halcyon
Hemipod
Hoatzin
Humming
Ice-bird
Jacamar
Jackdaw
Jacobin
Kahawai
Kamichi
Kestrel
Killdee
Kinglet
Lapwing
Leghorn
Limpkin
Manakin
Marabou
Maribou
Martlet
Mesites
Minivet
Mudlark

Ortolan
Oscires
Ostrich
Pandion
Peacock
Peafowl
Pelican
Penguin
Phoenix
Pickmaw
Piculet
Pinnock
Pintado
Pintail
Pochard
Pockard
Poe-bird
Poy-bird
Quetzal
Rainbow
Rasores
Redpoll
Redwing
Regulus
Rooster
Rosella
Rotchie
Ruddock
Sakeret
Sawbill
Scooper
Scourie
Sea-mell
Seriema
Simurgh
Sirgang
Sitella
Skimmer
Skylark
Snow-cap
Soldier
Spadger
Sparrow
Squacco
Staniel
Stinker
Sturnus
Sunbird
Swallow
Tanager
Tarrock

Tattler
Teacher
Teuchat
Tiercel
Tinamou
Titanis
Titlark
Titling
Tokahea
Totanus
Touraco
Tumbler
Tweeter
Vulture
Vulturn
Wagtail
Warbler
Waxbill
Waxwing
Whooper
Widgeon
Wimbrel
Witwall
Wood hen
Woosell
Wren-tit
Wrybill
Wryneck
Yang-win

8 letters:
Aasvogel
Accentor
Adjutant
Aigrette
Alcatras
Altrices
Amadavat
Aquiline
Arapunga
Avadavat
Barnacle
Bee-eater
Bellbird
Blackcap
Bluebird
Blue duck
Blue-wing
Boatbill
Boattail
Bobolink

Bobwhite
Buln-buln
Bush wren
Capuchin
Caracara
Cardinal
Cargoose
Cheewink
Chirn-owl
Cockatoo
Coquette
Curassow
Dabchick
Didapper
Dip-chick
Dobchick
Dotterel
Estridge
Fauvette
Fernbird
Firebird
Fish-hawk
Flamingo
Gambetta
Gang-gang
Garefowl
Garganey
Great tit
Greenlet
Grosbeak
Guacharo
Hackbolt
Hangbird
Hangnest
Hawfinch
Hazelhen
Hemipode
Hernshaw
Hill myna
Hoactzin
Hornbill
Kakariki
Killdeer
Kingbird
Kiskadee
Koromako
Landrail
Lanneret
Laverock
Longspur
Lorikeet

Birds

Lovebird
Lyrebird
Magotpie
Makomako
Māori hen
Marsh tit
Megapode
Mire-drum
Miromiro
Morepork
Murrelet
Nightjar
Nuthatch
Ovenbird
Oxpecker
Paradise
Parakeet
Peetweet
Percolin
Petchary
Pheasant
Philomel
Pihoihoi
Podargus
Poorwill
Puffbird
Quarrian
Quarrion
Rainbird
Rallidae
Redshank
Redstart
Reedbird
Reedling
Reed-wren
Ricebird
Rifleman
Ringdove
Ringtail
Riroriro
Rock dove
Sandpeep
Scolopar
Screamer
Shake-bag
Shoebill
Silktail
Skua-gull
Snowbird
Stanniel
Starling

Struthio
Surfbird
Swiftlet
Tantalus
Tapacolo
Tapaculo
Teru-tero
Thrasher
Thresher
Throstle
Tick-bird
Titmouse
Tom-noddy
Toucanet
Tragopan
Trembler
Troopial
Troupial
Umbrella
Umbrette
Water-hen
Weka rail
Wheatear
Whimbrel
Whinchat
Whitecap
White-eye
Woodchat
Woodcock
Wood ibis
Woodlark
Woodwale
Yoldring

9 letters:
Accipiter
Aepyornis
Albatross
Aylesbury
Baldicoot
Baltimore
Beccaccia
Beccafico
Bergander
Blackbird
Blackcock
Blackhead
Blackpoll
Bowerbird
Brambling
Broadbill

Brown duck
Brown kiwi
Bullfinch
Campanero
Cassowary
Chaffinch
Chatterer
Chickadee
Coachwhip
Cockateel
Cockatiel
Cormorant
Corncrake
Crocodile
Crossbill
Currawong
Cushie-doo
Dowitcher
Estreldid
Fieldfare
Fig-pecker
Firecrest
Fledgling
Francolin
Friarbird
Frogmouth
Gallinule
Gerfalcon
Gier-eagle
Goldcrest
Goldfinch
Goosander
Grassquit
Green leek
Grenadier
Guillemot
Happy Jack
Helldiver
Heronshaw
Icteridae
Impundulu
Jacksnipe
Kittiwake
Lintwhite
Mallemuck
Merganser
Mistletoe
Mollymawk
Mousebird
Nighthawk
Nutjobber

Olive-back
Ossifraga
Ossifrage
Pardalote
Parrakeet
Partridge
Peaseweep
Peregrine
Phalarope
Pictarnie
Pied goose
Policeman
Porphyrio
Ptarmigan
Razorbill
Redbreast
Red grouse
Riflebird
Ring ouzel
Rosy finch
Salangane
Sandpiper
Sapsucker
Scansores
Sea-turtle
Secretary
Seedeater
Sheldrake
Shoveller
Silvereye
Skunk-bird
Snakebird
Solitaire
Spoonbill
Standgale
Stock dove
Stonechat
Storm-cock
Swart-back
Swordbill
Talegalla
Thickhead
Thick-knee
Thornbill
Trochilus
Trumpeter
Turnstone
Volucrine
Water rail
Willow tit
Wind-hover

Xanthoura

10 letters:
Aberdevine
Banded rail
Bearded tit
Bell magpie
Bishopbird
Black robin
Bluebreast
Blue grouse
Bluethroat
Brain-fever
Bubbly-jock
Budgerigar
Bush canary
Bush shrike
Butter-bump
Cape pigeon
Chiffchaff
Crested tit
Demoiselle
Dickcissel
Didunculus
Dollarbird
Ember-goose
Eyas-musket
Flycatcher
Fringillid
Goatsucker
Gobemouche
Grassfinch
Greenfinch
Greenshank
Guinea fowl
Hen harrier
Honeyeater
Honey guide
Hooded crow
Jungle fowl
Kingfisher
Kookaburra
Magpie lark
Marsh-robin
Meadowlark
Night heron
Noisy miner
Nutcracker
Pettichaps
Pettychaps
Piwakawaka

Pratincole
Quaker-bird
Racket-tail
Rafter-bird
Regent-bird
Rhampastos
Rhinoceros
Roadrunner
Rockhopper
Rock pigeon
Saddleback
Saddlebill
Sage grouse
Sanderling
Sandgrouse
Sand martin
Scandaroon
Shearwater
Sheathbill
Sicklebill
Silverbill
Snowy egret
Song thrush
Spatchcock
Stone-snipe
Sun bittern
Tailorbird
Tanagridae
Tree-runner
Tropicbird
Turtledove
Water crake
Water ouzel
Wattlebird
Weaverbird
Whisky-jack
Whisky-john
White heron
Wild turkey
Wonga-wonga
Woodpecker
Wood pigeon
Yaffingale
Yellowlegs
Yellowtail
Yellowyite
Zebra finch

11 letters:
Black cuckoo
Black grouse

Birds

Bokmakierie
Bristlebird
Butcherbird
Button quail
Cape sparrow
Carrion crow
Coppersmith
Corn bunting
Gnatcatcher
Grallatores
Green plover
Grey warbler
Happy family
Honeysucker
House martin
Hummingbird
Java sparrow
King penguin
Leatherhead
Lily-trotter
Magpie goose
Meadow pipit
Mockingbird
Moss-bluiter
Moss-cheeper
Nightingale
Pied wagtail
Plain turkey
Plantcutter
Pyrrhuloxia
Reed bunting
Reed warbler
Scissortail
Snow bunting
Song sparrow
Stone curlew
Storm petrel
Stymphalian
Tawny pippit
Thunderbird
Titipounamu
Tree creeper
Tree sparrow
Wall creeper
Water thrush
Whitethroat
Wonga pigeon
Woodcreeper
Woodswallow
Wood warbler

Yellow-ammer
Zebra parrot

12 letters:
Bronze-pigeon
Brown creeper
Bustard quail
Capercaillie
Capercailzie
Chimney swift
Cliff swallow
Collared dove
Cuckoo-shrike
Drongo-cuckoo
Drongo-shrike
Flower-pecker
Golden oriole
Hedge sparrow
Homing pigeon
Honey creeper
House sparrow
Marsh harrier
Missel thrush
Mistle thrush
Mosquito hawk
Mountain duck
Mourning dove
Murray magpie
Painted finch
Pallid cuckoo
Paradise duck
Peppershrike
Piping shrike
Plains turkey
Putangitangi
Ring-dotterel
Ringed plover
Ruffed grouse
Sage-thrasher
Sedge warbler
Serpent-eater
Spotted crake
Standard-wing
Stonechatter
Stormy petrel
Throstle-cock
Whippoorwill
Willow grouse
Willy wagtail
Yellowhammer
Yellow-yowley

13 letters:
Bushman's clock
Chaparral cock
Cock-of-the-rock
Crow blackbird
Gouldian finch
Long-tailed tit
Major Mitchell
Numidian crane
Oyster-catcher
Pipiwharauroa
Plantain-eater
Settler's clock
Swamp pheasant
Topknot pigeon
Whistling duck
White cockatoo
Whooping crane
Willow warbler

14 letters:
Banded dotterel
Bird of paradise
Chimney swallow
Cockatoo-parrot
Emperor penguin
Manx shearwater
Noisy friarbird
Ortolan bunting
Pheasant coucal
Pie-billed grebe
Ringneck parrot
Robin redbreast
Satin bowerbird
Scarlet tanager
Superb blue wren
Superb lyrebird
Tawny frogmouth
Woodchat shrike

15 letters:
American ostrich
Australian crane
Baltimore oriole
Blackbacked gull
Blue-wattled crow
Boat-billed heron
Cape Barren goose
Chipping sparrow
Chuck-will's-
  widow

Demoiselle crane
Green woodpecker
Laughing jackass
Native companion
Purple gallinule
Rainbow lorikeet
Red-backed shrike
Regent bowerbird
Shining starling

16 letters:
Black-fronted tern
Californian quail
Cardinal grosbeak
Loggerhead shrike
Metallic starling
New Zealand
  pigeon
Piping crow-shrike

EXTINCT BIRDS

3 letters:
Moa

4 letters:
Dodo
Huia

6 letters:
Piopio

Regent honeyeater
Spotted sandpiper
White-fronted tern

17 letters:
Great crested grebe
Pectoral sandpiper
Port Lincoln parrot
Spotted flycatcher

18 letters:
Bronze-winged
  cuckoo
Great northern
  diver
Grey-crowned
  babbler
Red-backed
  sandpiper

8 letters:
Great auk
Notornis

9 letters:
Solitaire

11 letters:
Archaeornis

Red-legged
  partridge
Ring-necked
  pheasant

19 letters:
Leadbeater's
  cockatoo
Purple-breasted
  finch

20 letters:
Great brown
  kingfisher
Yellowtail
  kingfisher

22 letters:
Sulphur-crested
  cockatoo

Ichthyornis

13 letters:
Archaeopteryx

15 letters:
Passenger pigeon

See also:
➤ **Ducks** ➤ **Fowl** ➤ **Hawks** ➤ **Prey, birds of**
➤ **Sea birds**

Birthstones

Month	Stone
January	Garnet
February	Amethyst
March	Aquamarine, Bloodstone
April	Diamond
May	Emerald
June	Pearl, Alexandrite, Moonstone
July	Ruby
August	Peridot, Sardonyx
September	Sapphire
October	Opal, Tourmaline
November	Topaz
December	Turquoise, Zircon

Biscuits

Biscuits

3 letters:
Nut
Sea
Tea

4 letters:
Farl
Kiss
Rusk
Soda
Tack

5 letters:
Marie
Matzo
Pilot
Ship's
Wafer
Water

6 letters:
Cookie
Empire
Oliver
Parkin
Perkin

7 letters:
Bannock
Bourbon

Cracker
Fairing
Oatcake
Osborne
Pig's ear
Pretzel
Ratafia
Rich tea
Tararua

8 letters:
Captain's
Charcoal
Cracknel
Flapjack
Hardtack
Macaroon
Mattress
Poppadom
Poppadum
Zwieback

9 letters:
Abernethy
Dandyfunk
Digestive
Garibaldi
Ginger nut
Jaffa cake®

Lebkuchen
Petit four
Shortcake
Sweetmeal

10 letters:
Bath Oliver
Brandy snap
Butterbake
Crispbread
Dunderfunk
Florentine
Ginger snap
Love letter
Shortbread

12 letters:
Caramel wafer
Cream cracker
Langue de chat

13 letters:
Graham cracker

14 letters:
Gingerbread man

18 letters:
Chocolate digestive

Black and white shades

3 letters:
Ash
Jet

4 letters:
Grey
Iron

5 letters:
Black
Cream
Ebony
Ivory
Pearl

Putty
Raven
Sable
Slate
Stone
White

6 letters:
Pewter
Silver

8 letters:
Charcoal
Eggshell

Gunmetal
Off-white
Platinum

9 letters:
Steel grey

10 letters:
Pitch-black

11 letters:
Oyster white

Blemishes

3 letters:
Zit

4 letters:
Boil
Mole
Scab
Scar
Spot
Wart

5 letters:
Stain

6 letters:
Callus
Naevus
Pimple

7 letters:
Freckle
Pustule
Verruca

8 letters:
Pockmark

9 letters:
Birthmark
Blackhead
Carbuncle
Whitehead

12 letters:
Dicoloration

14 letters:
Strawberry mark

Blood cells

9 letters:
Haemocyte
Leucocyte
Macrocyte
Microcyte
Polymorph

10 letters:
Lymphocyte

11 letters:
Erythrocyte
Poikilocyte

12 letters:
Reticulocyte

24 letters:
Phagocytic white
 blood cell

Blue, shades of

3 letters:
Sky

4 letters:
Aqua
Bice
Cyan
Navy
Nile
Saxe
Teal

5 letters:
Azure
Clear
Perse
Royal
Saxon
Slate
Steel

6 letters:
Berlin
Cantab
Cobalt
Indigo
Oxford
Petrol
Pewter
Powder
Saxony
Welkin

7 letters:
Celeste
Duck-egg
Gentian
Nattier
Peacock
Watchet

8 letters:
Bleuâtre
Caesious
Cerulean
Eggshell
Electric
Lavender
Mazarine
Midnight
Prussian
Sapphire
Stafford
Wedgwood®

9 letters:
Cambridge
Germander
Robin's egg
Turquoise

Board games

10 letters:	Heliotrope	Lapis lazuli
Aquamarine	Periwinkle	Ultramarine
Copenhagen		
Cornflower	**11 letters:**	
	Clair de lune	

Board games

2 letters:
Go

3 letters:
I-go

4 letters:
Ludo

5 letters:
Chess
Halma

6 letters:
Cluedo®

7 letters:
Reversi

8 letters:
Chequers
Draughts
Monopoly®
Scrabble®

9 letters:
Acey-deucy
Bagatelle
Parcheesi®
Solitaire

10 letters:
Backgammon
Kriegspiel
Speed chess

11 letters:
Fox and geese

14 letters:
Lightning chess
Nine men's morris
Shove-halfpenny

15 letters:
Chinese chequers

16 letters:
Snakes and ladders

Boats and ships

1 letter:
Q

2 letters:
MY
PT
VJ

3 letters:
Ark
Cat
Cog
Cot
Dow
Gig
Hoy
MTB
Red
Tub
Tug

4 letters:
Argo

Bark
Brig
Buss
Cock
Dhow
Dory
Duck
Grab
Junk
Koff
Maxi
Nina
Pink
Pont
Pram
Prau
Proa
Punt
Raft
Ro-ro
Saic
Scow

Snow
Tall
Tern
Trow
Yawl
Zulu

5 letters:
Aviso
Barge
Broke
Camel
Canal
Canoe
Coble
Coper
Crare
Dandy
Dingy
Drake
E-boat
Ferry

Funny
Jolly
Kayak
Ketch
Laker
Liner
Moses
Oiler
Pinky
Pinto
Prore
Púcán
Razee
Sabot
Scoot
Screw
Scull
Shell
Skiff
Sloop
Swamp
Tramp
U-boat
Umiak
Whiff
Xebec
Yacht
Zabra
Zebec

6 letters:

Argosy
Banker
Barque
Bateau
Bawley
Beagle
Bethel
Bireme
Boatel
Borley
Bounty
Caïque
Carack
Carvel
Castle
Coaler
Cobble
Cooper
Crayer
Cutter

Decker
Dingey
Dinghy
Dogger
Droger
Dromon
Drover
Dugout
Flotel
Frigot
Galiot
Galley
Gay-you
Hooker
Jigger
Launch
Lorcha
Lugger
Masula
Narrow
Nuggar
Oomiak
Packet
Pedalo
Pequod
Pinkie
Pirate
Pitpan
Pulwar
Puteli
Randan
Rowing
Sampan
Sandal
Schuit
Schuyt
Sealer
Settee
Slaver
Tanker
Tartan
Tender
Tonner
Torpid
Trader
Whaler
Wherry
Zebeck

7 letters:

Airboat

Belfast
Bidarka
Bumboat
Capital
Caravel
Carrack
Carract
Carrect
Catboat
Clipper
Coaster
Collier
Coracle
Counter
Crabber
Cruiser
Currach
Curragh
Dredger
Drifter
Drogher
Dromond
Factory
Felucca
Fishing
Floatel
Flyboat
Foyboat
Frigate
Gabbard
Gabbart
Galleas
Galleon
Galliot
Galloon
Geordie
Gondola
Gunboat
Jet-boat
Jetfoil
Liberty
Lymphad
Man o' war
Masoola
Mistico
Monitor
Mudscow
Oomiack
Patamar
Pelican
Pinnace

Boats and ships

Piragua
Pirogue
Polacca
Polacre
Pontoon
Revenge
Rowboat
Sailing
Scooter
Shallop
Sharpie
Steamer
Stew-can
Tartane
Titanic
Torpedo
Towboat
Trawler
Trireme
Tugboat
Vedette
Victory
Vidette
Warship

8 letters:
Acapulco
Bilander
Billyboy
Cabotage
Cockboat
Corocore
Corocoro
Corvette
Dahabieh
Faldboat
Faltboat
Fireboat
Flatboat
Foldboat
Galleass
Galliass
Gallivat
Hoveller
Ice yacht
Indiaman
Ironclad
Keelboat
Lifeboat
Longboat
Longship

Mackinaw
Man-of-war
Mary Rose
Masoolah
Merchant
Monohull
Outboard
Pinafore
Sailboat
Savannah
Schooner
Shanghai
Showboat
Skipjack
Surfboat
Trimaran

9 letters:
Auxiliary
Bucentaur
Catamaran
Cutty Sark
Dahabeeah
Dahabiyah
Dahabiyeh
Destroyer
Dromedary
First-rate
Freighter
Frigatoon
Houseboat
Hydrofoil
Klondiker
Klondyker
Lapstrake
Lapstreak
Leviathan
Lightship
Mayflower
Minelayer
Monoxylon
Motorboat
Multihull
Outrigger
Oysterman
Peter-boat
Powerboat
Shear-hulk
Sheer-hulk
Speedboat
Steamboat

Steamship
Submarine
Troopship
Vaporetto
Whale-back
Whaleboat

10 letters:
Bathyscape
Bathyscaph
Battleship
Bermuda rig
Brigantine
Cockleboat
Golden Hind
Hydroplane
Icebreaker
Knockabout
Minehunter
Motor yacht
Paddleboat
Quadrireme
Santa Maria
Trekschuit
Triaconter
Windjammer

11 letters:
Barquantine
Barquentine
Bathyscaphe
Bellerophon
Berthon-boat
Bulk carrier
Cockleshell
Dreadnaught
Dreadnought
Merchantman
Minesweeper
Penteconter
Quinquereme
Sidewheeler
Skidbladnir
Submersible
Supertanker
Threedecker
Three-master
Weathership

12 letters:
Cabin cruiser
Fore-and-after

Great Eastern
Landing craft
Marie Celeste
Motor torpedo
Square-rigger
Stern-wheeler

13 letters:
Battlecruiser

See also:
➤ **Ships, parts of**

Paddle steamer
Revenue cutter
Ship of the line

14 letters:
Ocean greyhound
Vaucluse junior

15 letters:
Aircraft carrier

Destroyer escort

16 letters:
Pocket battleship

20 letters:
Torpedo-boat
destroyer

Body, parts of

Part of the body	Technical name	Related adjective
Abdomen	—	Abdominal
Adenoids	Pharyngeal tonsil	Adenoid *or* adenoidal
Alimentary canal	—	—
Ankle	Talus	—
Anus	—	Anal
Appendix	Vermiform appendix	Appendicular
Arm	Brachium	Brachial
Armpit	Axilla	Axillary
Artery	—	Arterial
Back	—	Dorsal
Belly	Venter	Ventral
Bladder	Urinary bladder	Vesical
Blood	—	Haemal, haemic, *or* haematic
Bone	Os	Osseous, osteal, *or* osteoid
Brain	Encephalon	Cerebral
Breast	—	—
Buttocks	Nates	Natal *or* gluteal
Caecum	—	Caecal
Calf	—	—
Capillary	—	Capillary
Cervix	—	Cervical
Cheek	Gena	Genal
Chest	—	Pectoral
Chin	—	Genial *or* mental
Clitoris	—	Clitoral
Colon	—	Colonic
Duodenum	—	Duodenal
Ear	—	Aural
Elbow	—	—
Epiglottis	—	Epiglottal

Body, parts of

Part of the body	Technical name	Related adjective
External ear	Auricle *or* pinna	—
Eye	—	Ocular *or* ophthalmic
Eyebrow	—	Superciliary
Eyelash	Cilium	Ciliary
Eyelid	—	Palpebral
Fallopian tube	Oviduct	Oviducal *or* oviductal
Finger	—	Digital
Fingernail	—	Ungual *or* ungular
Fist	—	—
Follicle	—	Follicular
Fontanelle *or* fontanel	—	—
Foot	Pes	Pedal
Forearm	—	Cubital
Forehead	—	Frontal
Foreskin	Prepuce	Preputial
Gall bladder	—	—
Gland	—	Adenoid
Glottis	—	Glottic
Groin	—	Inguinal
Gullet	Oesophagus	Oesophageal
Gum	Gingiva	Gingival
Hair	—	—
Half-moon	Lunula *or* lunule	—
Hamstring	—	Popliteal
Hand	Manus	Manual
Hard palate	—	—
Head	Caput	Capital
Heart	—	Cardiac
Heel	—	—
Hip	—	—
Ileum	—	Ileac *or* ileal
Inner ear *or* internal ear	Labyrinth	—
Instep	—	—
Intestine	—	Alvine
Jaw	—	Gnathic *or* gnathal
Jejunum	—	Jejunal
Jugular vein	—	—
Kidney	—	Renal *or* nephritic
Knee	Genu	Genicular
Knuckle	—	—
Labia majora	—	Labial
Labia minora	—	Labial
Large intestine	—	—
Leg	Crus	Crural
Lip	—	Labial
Liver	—	Hepatic

Part of the body	Technical name	Related adjective
Loin	Lumbus	Lumbar
Lung	—	Pulmonary
Lymph cell	Lymphocyte	—
Lymph node	—	—
Midriff	Diaphragm	—
Mons pubis	—	—
Mons veneris	—	—
Mouth	—	Stomatic
Nape	Nucha	Nuchal
Navel or omphalos	Umbilicus	Umbilical
Neck	Cervix	Cervical
Nerve	—	Neural
Nerve cell	Neuron or neurone	Neuronic
Nipple or teat	Mamilla or papilla	Mamillary
Nose	—	Nasal
Nostril	Naris	Narial or narine
Occiput	—	Occipital
Ovary	—	Ovarian
Pancreas	—	Pancreatic
Penis	—	Penile
Pharynx	—	Pharyngeal
Pubes	—	Pubic
Rectum	—	Rectal
Red blood cell	Erythrocyte	Erythrocytic
Ribcage	—	—
Scalp	—	—
Scrotum	—	Scrotal
Shin	—	—
Shoulder	—	—
Side	—	—
Skin	Cutis	Cutaneous
Small intestine	—	—
Soft palate	—	—
Sole	—	Plantar
Spleen	—	Lienal or splenetic
Stomach	—	Gastric
Tear duct	Lacrimal duct	—
Temple	—	Temporal
Tendon	—	—
Testicle	—	Testicular
Thigh	—	Femoral or crural
Thorax	—	Thoracic
Throat	—	Guttural, gular, or jugular
Thumb	Pollex	Pollical
Toe	—	—
Toenail	—	Ungual or ungular

Bombs

Part of the body	Technical name	Related adjective
Tongue	Lingua	Lingual *or* glottic
Tonsil	—	Tonsillar *or* tonsillary
Torso	—	—
Transverse colon	—	—
Trunk	—	—
Umbilical cord	Umbilicus	—
Ureter	—	Ureteral *or* ureteric
Urethra	—	Urethral
Vagina	—	Vaginal
Vein	Vena	Venous
Vocal cords	Glottis	Glottal
Voice box	Larynx	Laryngeal
Vulva	—	Vulval, vulvar, *or* vulvate
Waist	—	—
White blood cell	Leucocyte	Leucocytic
Windpipe	Trachea	Tracheal *or* tracheate
Womb	Uterus	Uterine
Wrist	Carpus	—

See also:
➤ **Blood cells** ➤ **Bodily humours** ➤ **Bones**
➤ **Brain, parts of** ➤ **Ear, parts of**
➤ **Eye** ➤ **Glands** ➤ **Heart, part of** ➤ **Membranes**
➤ **Muscles** ➤ **Nerves** ➤ **Organs**
➤ **Teeth** ➤ **Veins**

Bombs

4 letters:
Atom
Nail

5 letters:
A-bomb
Mills

6 letters:
Fusion
Petrol

7 letters:
Cluster

Grenade
Neutron
Nuclear
Plastic

8 letters:
Bouncing
Hydrogen

10 letters:
Incendiary

11 letters:
Blockbuster

Depth charge
Hand grenade
Stun grenade

15 letters:
Molotov cocktail

16 letters:
Bangalore torpedo

Bones

Bone	Nontechnical names
Astragalus	Anklebone
Calcaneus	Heel bone
Carpal	Wrist
Carpus	Wrist
Centrum	—
Clavicle	Collarbone
Coccyx	—
Costa	Rib
Cranium	Brainpan
Cuboid	—
Ethmoid	—
Femur	Thighbone
Fibula	—
Frontal bone	—
Hallux	—
Humerus	Funny
Hyoid	—
Ilium	—
Incus	Anvil
Innominate bone	Hipbone
Ischium	—
Malar	Cheek
Malleus	Hammer
Mandible	Lower jawbone
Mastoid	—
Maxilla	Upper jawbone
Metacarpal	—
Metatarsal	—
Metatarsus	—
Nasal	Nose
Occipital bone	—
Parietal bone	—
Patella	Kneecap
Pelvis	—
Phalanx	—
Pubis	—
Radius	—
Rib	—
Sacrum	—
Scapula	Shoulder blade
Skull	—
Sphenoid	—
Spinal column *or* spine	Backbone
Stapes	Stirrup
Sternum	Breastbone
Talus	Anklebone
Tarsal	—

Bone	Nontechnical names
Tarsus	—
Temporal bone	—
Tibia	Shinbone
Trapezium	—
Ulna	—
Vertebra	—
Vertebral column	Backbone
Zygomatic bone	Cheekbone

Books

TYPES OF BOOK

3 letters:
Log

4 letters:
A to Z
Hymn
Road
Song

5 letters:
Album
Atlas
Bible
Comic
Diary
Novel
Score

6 letters:
Annual
Gradus
Jotter
Ledger
Manual
Missal
Phrase
Prayer
Primer
Reader

7 letters:
Almanac
Anatomy
Bibelot
Cookery
Grammar
Journal

Lexicon
Logbook
Novella
Ordinal
Peerage
Psalter
Service
Speller
Statute
Who's who

8 letters:
Armorial
Baedeker
Bestiary
Breviary
Brochure
Casebook
Copybook
Exercise
Grimoire
Handbook
Notebook
Register
Textbook
Wordbook
Workbook
Yearbook

9 letters:
Anthology
Biography
Catalogue
Catechism
Companion
Directory

Formulary
Gazetteer
Guidebook
Monograph
Novelette
Reference
Scrapbook
Storybook
Thesaurus
Vade mecum

10 letters:
Compendium
Dictionary
Lectionary
Miscellany
Prospectus
Sketchbook

11 letters:
Coffee-table
Commonplace
Concordance

12 letters:
Confessional
Dispensatory
Encyclopedia
Graphic novel

13 letters:
Autobiography
Encyclopaedia
Pharmacopoeia

18 letters:
Telephone directory

PARTS OF A BOOK

4 letters:
Back
Leaf
Page
Tail

5 letters:
Blurb
Cover
Folio
Index
Plate
Proem
Recto
Spine
Verso

6 letters:
Errata
Gutter
Margin
Rubric

7 letters:
Binding
Chapter
Flyleaf
Preface
Prelims
Wrapper

8 letters:
Addendum
Appendix
Contents
Endpaper
Epigraph
Epilogue
Fore-edge
Foreword
Glossary
Prologue
Slipcase

9 letters:
Afterword

Half-title
Interleaf
Title page

10 letters:
Back matter
Corrigenda
Dedication
Dust jacket
Postscript

11 letters:
Front matter
Running head

12 letters:
Bibliography
Frontispiece
Illustration
Introduction
Prolegomenon

15 letters:
Acknowledgments

Botany

BRANCHES OF BOTANY

8 letters:
Algology
Bryology
Mycology

9 letters:
Carpology

10 letters:
Dendrology
Floristics

11 letters:
Agrostology
Astrobotany
Ethnobotany
Phytography
Pteridology

12 letters:
Archeobotany
Palaeobotany
Phytogenesis

13 letters:
Archaeobotany

14 letters:
Phytogeography
Phytopathology

17 letters:
Palaeoethnobotany

BOTANY TERMS

3 letters:
Key
Nut
Sap

4 letters:
Axil
Axis

Bulb
Corm
Leaf
Pith
Root
Seed
Stem

5 letters:
Auxin
Berry
Calyx
Fruit
Hilum
Ovary
Ovule

Botany

Sepal
Shoot
Spore
Stoma
Style
Testa
Tuber
Xylem

6 letters:
Anther
Carpel
Corona
Cortex
Flower
Lamina
Legume
Phloem
Pistil
Pollen
Raceme
Runner
Spadix
Stamen
Stigma
Stolon

7 letters:
Cambium
Corolla
Cuticle
Plumule
Radicle
Rhizome

Root cap
Rosette
Seed pod
Tropism

8 letters:
Filament
Lenticel
Meristem
Root hair
Seedcase

9 letters:
Cotyledon
Epidermis
Foliation
Guard cell
Gynaecium
Mesophyll
Micropyle
Operculum

10 letters:
Abscission
Androecium
Geotropism
Integument
Receptacle
Root nodule
Seed vessel
Sporangium

11 letters:
Androgynous
Archegonium

Chlorophyll
Chloroplast
Dicotyledon
Germination
Pollination
Seed capsule

12 letters:
Hydrotropism
Phototropism

13 letters:
Inflorescence
Monocotyledon
Translocation
Transpiration

14 letters:
Nastic movement
Photosynthesis
Vascular bundle

15 letters:
Self-pollination
Spongy mesophyll
Wind pollination

16 letters:
Cross-pollination

17 letters:
Insect pollination
Palisade mesophyll

22 letters:
Vegetative
 reproduction

BOTANISTS

3 letters:
Ray, *John*

5 letters:
Banks, *Joseph*
Brown, *Robert*

6 letters:
Carver, *George Washington*
Darwin, *Charles (Robert)*
Hooker, *Joseph Dalton*
Hooker, *William Jackson*
Mendel, *Gregor Johann*

7 letters:
Bellamy, *David (James)*
De Vries, *Hugo*
Eichler, *August Wilhelm*

8 letters:
Linnaeus
Von Linné, *Carl*

10 letters:
De Candolle, *Auguste Pyrame*
Tradescant, *John*

See also:
- ➤ **Algae** ➤ **Ferns** ➤ **Fungi** ➤ **Grasses** ➤ **Lilies**
- ➤ **Mosses** ➤ **Palms** ➤ **Plants** ➤ **Sea-weeds** ➤ **Shrubs**
- ➤ **Trees**

Bottles

5 letters:
Flask
Gourd
Phial
Water

6 letters:
Carboy
Caster
Flacon
Flagon
Lagena

Nansen
Stubby
Woulfe

7 letters:
Ampulla
Feeding

8 letters:
Decanter
Demijohn
Half-jack
Hot-water

Screw top

9 letters:
Miniature

10 letters:
Pycnometer
Soda siphon

11 letters:
Marie-Jeanne
Vinaigrette

Boxes

4 letters:
Case
Coin
Deed
Nest
Poor
Wine

5 letters:
Bulla
Chest
Ditty
Glory
Glove
Grass
Music
Trunk

6 letters:
Ballot

Carton
Casket
Coffer
Coffin
Hatbox
Haybox
Pounce
Saggar
Vanity
Window

7 letters:
Bandbox
Caisson
Cracket
Honesty
Keister
Pillbox
Pouncet

Saltbox
Sandbox
Soapbox

8 letters:
Dispatch
Matchbox
Paintbox
Solander

9 letters:
Cartouche
Papeterie
Strongbox
Tinderbox

10 letters:
Desiccator

11 letters:
Packing case

Boxing weights

Weight	Amateur	Professional
Light flyweight	48 kg	49 kg
Flyweight	51 kg	51 kg

Brain, parts of

Weight	Amateur	Professional
Bantamweight	54 kg	53.5 kg
Featherweight	57 kg	57 kg
Junior lightweight	—	59 kg
Lightweight	60 kg	61 kg
Light welterweight	63.5 kg	63.5 kg
Welterweight	67 kg	66.6 kg
Light middleweight	71 kg	70 kg
Middleweight	75 kg	72.5 kg
Light heavyweight	81 kg	79 kg
Cruiserweight	—	88.5 kg
Heavyweight	91 kg	+88.5 kg
Superheavyweight	+91 kg	—

Brain, parts of

6 letters:
Vermis

8 letters:
Amygdala
Cerebrum
Meninges
Midbrain
Thalamus

9 letters:
Brainstem

10 letters:
Afterbrain
Broca's area
Cerebellum
Grey matter
Pineal body

11 letters:
Frontal lobe
Hippocampus
Pons Varolli
White matter

12 letters:
Diencephalon
Hypothalamus
Infundibulum
Limbic system
Optic chiasma
Parietal lobe
Temporal lobe

13 letters:
Central sulcus
Choroid plexus
Mamillary body

Occipital lobe
Wernicke's area

14 letters:
Cerebral cortex
Corpus callosum
Myelencephalon
Pituitary gland
Substantia alba
Third ventricle

15 letters:
Fourth ventricle

16 letters:
Cerebral aqueduct
Medulla oblongata

18 letters:
Cerebrospinal fluid

Breads

3 letters:
Bap
Bun
Cob
Nan
Pan
Rye

4 letters:
Corn
Loaf
Naan

Puri
Roll
Roti
Soda

5 letters:
Bagel
Black
Brown
Matza
Matzo
Pitta

Plain
Plait
White

6 letters:
Beigel
Coburg
Damper
French
Gluten
Hallah
Indian

Matzah
Matzoh
Muffin

7 letters:
Bloomer
Brioche
Buttery
Challah
Chapati
Granary®
Long tin
Paratha
Stollen
Wheaten

8 letters:
Baguette
Barm cake

Chapatti
Ciabatta
Corn pone
Focaccia
Poppadom
Poppadum
Quartern
Split tin
Tortilla

9 letters:
Barmbrack
Batch loaf
Croissant
Farmhouse
Fruit loaf
Schnecken
Sourdough

Square tin
Wholemeal

10 letters:
Billy-bread
Bridge roll
Johnny cake
Unleavened
Whole-wheat

11 letters:
Cottage loaf
French stick

12 letters:
Griddlebread
Half-quartern
Pumpernickel

Bridges

BRIDGES

4 letters:
Skye
Tyne

5 letters:
Tower

6 letters:
Humber
London
Rialto
Severn

7 letters:
Rainbow

TYPES OF BRIDGE

4 letters:
Deck
Snow
Turn

5 letters:
Pivot
Swing
Truss

6 letters:
Bailey

8 letters:
Brooklyn
Waterloo

9 letters:
Forth Road
Halfpenny

10 letters:
Golden Gate
Millennium
Oakland Bay

11 letters:
Westminster

7 letters:
Balance
Bascule
Clapper
Flyover
Pontoon
Viaduct

8 letters:
Aqueduct

9 letters:
Box-girder

12 letters:
Forth Railway

13 letters:
Bridge of Sighs
Sydney Harbour

17 letters:
Clifton Suspension

19 letters:
Gateshead
  Millennium

10 letters:
Cantilever
Drawbridge
Footbridge
Suspension

11 letters:
Cable-stayed

12 letters:
Counterpoise

British forces

RANKS OF THE ARMY/ROYAL MARINES

5 letters:
Major

6 letters:
Marine

7 letters:
Captain
Colonel
General
Private

8 letters:
Corporal

Sergeant

9 letters:
Brigadier

10 letters:
Lieutenant

12 letters:
Field Marshal
Major General
Officer Cadet

13 letters:
Lance Corporal

Staff Sergeant

14 letters:
Colour Sergeant
Warrant Officer

17 letters:
Lieutenant Colonel
Lieutenant General

RANKS OF THE ROYAL NAVY

7 letters:
Admiral
Captain

9 letters:
Commander
Commodore

10 letters:
Able Rating
Lieutenant

Midshipman

11 letters:
Leading Rate
Rear Admiral
Vice Admiral

12 letters:
Petty Officer

13 letters:
Sub-Lieutenant

14 letters:
Warrant Officer

17 letters:
Admiral of the
  Fleet
Chief Petty Officer

19 letters:
Lieutenant
  Commander

RANKS OF THE ROYAL AIR FORCE

10 letters:
Air Marshal

12 letters:
Air Commodore
Group Captain

13 letters:
Flying Officer
Wing Commander

14 letters:
Air Vice-Marshal
Squadron Leader

15 letters:
Air Chief Marshal
Marshal of the
  RAF

16 letters:
Flight Lieutenant

Brown, shades of

3 letters:
Bay
Dun
Tan

4 letters:
Buff
Drab
Ecru

Fawn
Fusc
Rust
Sand

Sore
Teak

5 letters:
Abram
Amber
Beige
Camel
Cocoa
Cream
Hazel
Henna
Khaki
Liver
Mocha
Mousy
Sable
Sepia
Soare
Taupe
Tawny
Tenné
Umber

6 letters:
Almond
Auburn

Bisque
Bistre
Bronze
Burnet
Coffee
Copper
Fallow
Ginger
Nutmeg
Rufous
Russet
Sienna
Sorrel
Walnut

7 letters:
Biscuit
Brindle
Caramel
Caromel
Filemot
Fulvous
Fuscous
Neutral
Oatmeal
Oxblood
Vandyke

8 letters:
Brunette
Chestnut
Cinnabar
Cinnamon
Mahogany
Mushroom
Nutbrown
Philamot

9 letters:
Butternut
Chocolate
Seal brown

10 letters:
Burnt umber
Café au lait
Coromandel
Terracotta
Testaceous

11 letters:
Burnt sienna

13 letters:
Tortoiseshell

Buddhism

3 letters:
Zen

4 letters:
Jodo
Soto

5 letters:
Foism
Geluk
Kagyü
Sakya

6 letters:
Rinjai
Tendai

7 letters:
Lamaism
Nyingma

8 letters:
Hinayana
Mahayana
Nichiren

9 letters:
Theravada
Vajrayana

10 letters:
Soka Gakkai

16 letters:
Pure Land
 Buddhism

Bugs

4 letters:
Lace

5 letters:
Māori
Mealy

Stink
Water

6 letters:
Bedbug
Chinch

Cicada
Cicala
Damsel
Debris
Shield

Buildings and monuments

7 letters:
Kissing
Spittle

9 letters:
Harlequin

10 letters:
Froghopper
Leaf-hopper
Pond-skater

11 letters:
Water skater

12 letters:
Water boatman
Water strider

13 letters:
Spittle insect
Water scorpion

Buildings and monuments

5 letters:
Kaaba

6 letters:
Big Ben
Louvre
Masada

7 letters:
Beehive
Knossos
Kremlin
Lateran
Vatican

8 letters:
Alhambra
Barbican
Cenotaph
Monument
Pentagon
Taj Mahal

9 letters:
Charminar
Hermitage

10 letters:
White House

11 letters:
Eiffel Tower
Scone Palace

12 letters:
Althorp House
Mansion House

13 letters:
Arc de Triomphe
Crystal Palace
Elysées Palace
Forbidden City
Holyroodhouse
Lambeth Palace
Longleat House
Nelson's Column
Tower of London

14 letters:
Admiralty House
Blenheim Palace

15 letters:
Angel of the North
Edinburgh Castle

16 letters:
Buckingham Palace

Cleopatra's Needle
Kensington Palace
Westminster
  Abbey

17 letters:
Saint James's
  Palace

18 letters:
Hampton Court
  Palace
Houses of
  Parliament
Leaning Tower of
  Pisa
Palace of
  Versailles

19 letters:
Empire State
  Building

Businesspeople

4 letters:
Benz, *Karl Friedrich*
Bond, *Alan*
Boot, *Sir Jesse*
Cook, *Thomas*
Ford, *Henry*
Jobs, *Steven Paul*
Mond, *Sir Robert Ludwig*
Shah, *Eddy*

Tate, *Sir Henry*

5 letters:
Astor, *Lord John Jacob*
Dawes, *Charles Gates*
Dyson, *James*
Flynt, *Larry*
Forte, *Lord Charles*
Frick, *Henry Clay*
Gates, *Bill*

Butterflies and moths

Getty, *Jean Paul*
Grade, *Michael*
Heinz, *Henry John*
Honda, *Soichiro*
Jones, *Digby*
Krupp, *Friedrich*
Laker, *Sir Freddie*
Lyons, *Sir Joseph*
Marks, *Lord Simon*
Rolls, *Charles Stewart*
Royce, *Sir Henry*
Sieff, *Lord Israel*
Sugar, *Alan*
Zeiss, *Carl*

6 letters:
Ashley, *Laura*
Austin, *Lord Herbert*
Boeing, *William Edward*
Butlin, *Billy*
Conran, *Sir Terence*
Cunard, *Sir Samuel*
Dunlop, *John Boyd*
Farmer, *Sir Tom*
Hammer, *Armand*
Hanson, *Lord James*
Hilton, *Conrad Nicholson*
Hoover, *William Henry*
Hughes, *Howard*
Hulton, *Sir Edward*
Lipton, *Sir Thomas*
Morris, *William Richard*
 (Viscount Nuffield)
Ogilvy, *David*
Packer, *Kerry*
Ratner, *Gerald Irving*
Turner, *Ted*
Warner, *Harold*

7 letters:
Agnelli, *Giovanni*

Barclay, *Robert*
Branson, *Sir Richard*
Bugatti, *Ettore*
Burrell, *Sir William*
Cadbury, *George*
Citroën, *André Gustave*
Douglas, *Donald*
Kennedy, *Joseph Patrick*
Maxwell, *Robert*
Murdoch, *Rupert*
Onassis, *Aristotle*
Roddick, *Dame Anita Lucia*
Tiffany, *Charles Lewis*

8 letters:
Birdseye, *Clarence*
Carnegie, *Andrew*
Christie, *James*
Guinness, *Sir Benjamin Lee*
Michelin, *André*
Olivetti, *Adriano*
Pulitzer, *Joseph*
Rowntree, *Joseph*
Sinclair, *Sir Clive*
Southeby, *John*
Zaharoff, *Sir Basil*

9 letters:
Firestone, *Harvey Samuel*
Sainsbury, *Lord Aan*
Selfridge, *Harry Gordon*
Woolworth, *Frank Winfield*

10 letters:
Rothschild, *Meyer Amschel*
Vanderbilt, *Cornelius*

11 letters:
Beaverbrook, *Lord Max*
Harvey-Jones, *Sir John Henry*
Rockefeller, *John Davison*

Butterflies and moths

2 letters:
Io

3 letters:
Bag
Bee
Fox

Nun
Owl
Wax

4 letters:
Arch
Bell

Blue
Goat
Hawk
Leaf
Luna
Meal
Puss

Butterflies and moths

Wave

Winter
Yellow

Vapourer
Wainscot

5 letters:
Argus
Atlas
Brown
Comma
Eggar
Egger
Flour
Ghost
Gipsy
Grass
Gypsy
Heath
House
Owlet
Snout
Swift
Thorn
Tiger
Tinea
Umber
White
Y-moth

6 letters:
Antler
Apollo
Bogong
Bugong
Burnet
Carpet
Codlin
Copper
Dagger
Ermine
Herald
Kitten
Lackey
Lappet
Lichen
Magpie
Morpho
Muslin
Noctua
Pieris
Psyche
Sphinx
Thecla
Turnip
Veneer

7 letters:
Abraxas
Bagworm
Buff-tip
Cabbage
Clothes
Codling
Drinker
Emperor
Festoon
Hook-tip
Kallima
Leopard
Lobster
Monarch
Noctuid
Old lady
Peacock
Pug-moth
Ringlet
Silver-Y
Skipper
Stamper
Sulphur
Thistle
Tortrix
Tussock
Unicorn
Vanessa
Zygaena

8 letters:
Bobowler
Bombycid
Cardinal
Cecropia
Cinnabar
Dart-moth
Geometer
Goldtail
Grayling
Hesperid
Oak-egger
Peppered
Saturnia
Silkworm
Sphingid
Tapestry
Tineidae

9 letters:
Arctiidae
Brimstone
Brown-tail
Carpenter
Clearwing
Cleopatra
Geometrid
Honeycomb
Notodonta
Orange-tip
Pyralidae
Saturniid
Scavenger
Underwing
Wall brown

10 letters:
Common blue
Death's-head
Fritillary
Gate-keeper
Hairstreak
Large white
Leafroller
Polyphemus
Privet hawk
Red admiral
Silverspot
Small white
Yellowtail

11 letters:
Diamondback
Hummingbird
Large copper
Meadow brown
Painted lady
Swallowtail

12 letters:
Cabbage white
Cactoblastis
Kentish glory
Lymantriidae
Marbled white
Red underwing
Sallow-kitten
Speckled wood

Butterflies and moths

White admiral

13 letters:
Clouded yellow
Mother-of-pearl
Mother Shipton
Mourning cloak

Processionary
Purple emperor

14 letters:
Two-tailed pasha

15 letters:
Yellow underwing

16 letters:
Camberwell beauty
Clifden nonpareil
Tiger swallowtail

C

3 letters:
Bun
Nut
Oil
Pan
Set

4 letters:
Baba
Farl
Kueh
Pone
Puff
Puri
Rock
Roti
Rout
Rusk
Slab
Soul
Tart

5 letters:
Angel
Babka
Cream
Donut
Fairy
Farle
Fudge
Genoa
Lardy
Latke
Layer
Poori
Pound
Rosti
Scone
Sushi
Tansy

Tipsy
Torte
Wafer

6 letters:
Almond
Carrot
Cherry
Coburg
Cotton
Dainty
Dundee
Eccles
Eclair
Gateau
Girdle
Hockey
Johnny
Jumbal
Jumble
Kuchen
Marble
Muffin
Parkin
Simnel
Sponge
Tablet
Waffle
Wonder
Yumyum

7 letters:
Baklava
Banbury
Bannock
Brioche
Brownie
Carcake
Chapati
Chupati

Coconut
Cruller
Crumpet
Cupcake
Fritter
Galette
Jannock
Jumbles
Kruller
Linseed
Madeira
Oatmeal
Pancake
Paratha
Pavlova
Pikelet
Pomfret
Ratafia
Rum baba
Savarin
Stollen
Teacake
Vetkoek
Wedding

8 letters:
Agnus dei
Birthday
Black bun
Chapatti
Chillada
Chupatty
Doughnut
Dumpling
Flapjack
Macaroon
Meringue
Mince pie
Napoleon
Pandowdy

Calendars

Sandwich
Seedcake
Teabread
Tortilla
Turnover

9 letters:
Angel food
Barmbrack
Buckwheat
Chocolate
Christmas
Chupattie
Clapbread
Cream puff
Croquette
Drop scone
Fruitcake
Kuglehopf
Lamington
Madeleine
Panettone

Petit four
Puftaloon
Queencake
Sally Lunn
Swiss roll

10 letters:
Battenberg
Battenburg
Coffee kiss
Devil's food
Frangipane
Frangipani
Koeksister
Ladyfinger
Pontefract
Puftaloona
Religieuse
Upside-down

11 letters:
Gingerbread

Hot cross bun
Linzer torte
Profiterole
Sachertorte

12 letters:
Bakewell tart
Danish pastry
French pastry
Maid of honour
Millefeuille
Singing hinny
Sponge finger

13 letters:
Genoese sponge

14 letters:
Selkirk bannock
Victoria sponge

17 letters:
Black forest gateau

Calendars

4 letters:
Maya

5 letters:
Bahá'í
Hindu
Lunar
Roman
Solar

6 letters:
Coptic

Fiscal
Hebrew
Jewish
Julian

7 letters:
Chinese
Iranian
Islamic
Persian
Tibetan

8 letters:
Japanese

9 letters:
Arbitrary
Gregorian
Lunisolar
Malayalam

19 letters:
French Revolution

Cameras

CAMERA PARTS
6 letters:
Tripod

7 letters:
Hot shoe
Shutter

8 letters:
Flash gun
Lens hood

Sprocket
Zoom lens

9 letters:
Amplifier
Macro lens

10 letters:
Autowinder
Viewfinder

12 letters:
Synchroflash

13 letters:
Accessory shoe

Canals

TYPES OF CAMERA

3 letters:
Box

4 letters:
Cine

6 letters:
Candid
Reflex
Webcam

7 letters:
Brownie

Compact
Digital
Pinhole
Process

8 letters:
Polaroid

9 letters:
Automatic
Camcorder
Miniature
Steadicam

10 letters:
Programmed

12 letters:
Subminiature

Canals

3 letters:
Suo

4 letters:
Erie
Göta
Kiel
Suez

5 letters:
Grand

6 letters:
Moscow
Panama
Twente

7 letters:
Corinth

Welland

8 letters:
Berezina

9 letters:
Champlain

10 letters:
Caledonian
Grand Union
Mittelland
Rhine-Herne

11 letters:
Bridgewater
Canal du Midi
Dortmund-Ems
Houston Ship

12 letters:
Canal do Norte

14 letters:
Manchester Ship

17 letters:
Canal de São
  Gonçalo
New York State
  Barge

Capes

3 letters:
Cod
Hoe
May
Ras

4 letters:
Fear
Hogh
Horn
Naze
Race
Roca

Scaw
Skaw

5 letters:
Byron
Canso
North
Parry
Sable
Sandy
Verde
Wrath

6 letters:
Helles
Lizard
Reinga
Sontag
Ushant

7 letters:
Agulhas
Comorin
Delgado
Leeuwin
Matapan

Runaway
Western

8 letters:
Farewell
Flattery
Good Hope
Hatteras

Palatine

9 letters:
Canaveral
Dungeness
Guardafui
Lindesnes
Southwest

St Vincent
Trafalgar

10 letters:
Finisterre

11 letters:
Fairweather

Capitals

Capital	Country, region, state, etc
Abidjan	Ivory Coast
Abu Dhabi	United Arab Emirates
Abuja	Nigeria
Accra	Ghana
Acra	Hunger
Addis Ababa	Ethiopia
Adelaide	South Australia
Agana	Guam
Albany	New York (state capital)
Algiers	Algeria
Amman	Jordan
Amsterdam	Netherlands
Andorra la Vella	Andorra
Ankara	Turkey
Annapolis	Maryland
Antananarivo	Madagascar
Antioch	Ancient Syria
Apia	Samoa
Ashkhabad	Turkmenistan
Asmara	Eritrea
Astana	Kazakhstan
Asunción	Paraguay
Athens	Greece
Atlanta	Georgia
Austin	Texas
Baghdad	Iraq
Baku	Azerbaijan
Bamako	Mali
Bandar Seri Begawan	Brunei
Bangalore	Karnataka
Bangkok	Thailand
Bangui	Central African Republic
Banjul	Gambia
Barnaul	Altai
Basseterre	St. Kitts and Nevis
Bastia	Corsica
Baton Rouge	Louisiana
Beijing *or* Peking	People's Republic of China

Capitals

Capital	Country, region, state, etc
Beirut *or* Beyrouth	Lebanon
Belfast	Northern Ireland
Belgrade	Yugoslavia (Serbia and Montenegro)
Belmopan	Belize
Berlin	Germany
Berne	Switzerland
Bishkek	Kyrgyzstan
Bissau	Guinea-Bissau
Bloemfontein	Judicial capital of South Africa
Bogotá	Colombia
Bonn	Federal Republic of Germany (formerly)
Brasília	Brazil
Bratislava	Slovakia
Brazzaville	Congo (Republic of)
Bridgetown	Barbados
Brisbane	Queensland
Brno	Moravia
Bruges	West Flanders
Brussels	Belgium
Bucharest	Romania
Budapest	Hungary
Buenos Aires	Argentina
Bujumbura	Burundi
Caen	Basse-Normandie
Cagliari	Sardinia
Cairo	Egypt
Calcutta	West Bengal
Cali	Valley of the Cauca, Colombia
Canberra	Australia
Cape Town	Legislative capital of South Africa
Caracas	Venezuela
Cardiff	Wales
Cartagena	Bolivar
Castries	St. Lucia
Cayenne	French Guiana
Charleston	West Virginia
Colombo	Sri Lanka
Conakry *or* Konakry	Guinea
Copenhagen	Denmark
Cordoba	Cordoba
Dakar	Senegal
Damascus	Syria
Darwin	Northern Territory, Australia
Delhi	India
Dhaka *or* Dacca	Bangladesh
Dili	East Timor

Capital	Country, region, state, etc
Djibouti *or* Jibouti	Djibouti *or* Jibouti
Dodoma	Tanzania
Doha	Qatar
Douglas	Isle of Man
Dublin	Republic of Ireland
Dushanbe	Tajikistan
Edinburgh	Scotland
Enugu	Enugu
Faro	The Algarve
Fongafale	Tuvalu
Fort-de-France	Martinique
Freetown	Sierra Leone
Funafuti	Tuvalu
Funchal	Madeira
Gaborone	Botswana
Georgetown	Guyana
Guatemala City	Guatemala
Hanoi	Vietnam
Harare	Zimbabwe
Havana	Cuba
Helsinki	Finland
Heraklion *or* Eraklion	Crete
Hobart	Tasmania
Honiara	Solomon Islands
Honolulu	Hawaii
Ibadan	Oyo State, Nigeria
Ipoh	Perak
Islamabad	Pakistan
Istanbul *or* Constantinople	Turkey (formerly)
Jakarta *or* Djakarta	Indonesia
Jerusalem	Israel
Jos	Plateau (central Nigeria)
Kabul	Afghanistan
Kampala	Uganda
Karachi	Sind
Katmandu *or* Kathmandu	Nepal
Khartoum *or* Khartum	Sudan
Kiel	Schleswig-Holstein
Kiev	Ukraine
Kigali	Rwanda
Kingston	Jamaica
Kingstown	St. Vincent and the Grenadines
Kinshasa	Congo (Democratic Republic of)
Kirkwall	Orkney Islands
Kishinev	Moldova
Kobe	Honshu
Koror	Palau
Kuala Lumpur	Malaysia
Kuwait	Kuwait
Lagos	Nigeria (formerly)

Capitals

Capital	Country, region, state, etc
La Paz	Administrative capital of Bolivia
Lassa *or* Lhasa	Tibet
Leningrad, St Petersburg, *or* Petrograd	Russia (formerly)
Libreville	Gabon
Lilongwe	Malawi
Lima	Peru
Lisbon	Portugal
Little Rock	Arkansas
Ljubljana	Slovenia
Lomé	Togo
London	United Kingdom
Luanda	Angola
Lusaka	Zambia
Luxembourg	Luxembourg
Madrid	Spain
Majuro	Marshall Islands
Malabo	Equatorial Guinea
Malé	Maldives
Managua	Nicaragua
Manama	Bahrain
Manila	Philippines
Maputo	Mozambique
Maseru	Lesotho
Mathura	Braj Bhoomi
Mbabane	Swaziland
Memphis	Egypt, Old Kingdom
Mexico City	Mexico
Minsk	Belarus
Mogadishu	Somalia
Monaco-Ville	Monaco
Monrovia	Liberia
Montevideo	Uruguay
Moroni	Comoros
Moscow	Russia
Muscat	Oman
Nairobi	Kenya
Nashville	Tennessee
Nassau	Bahamas
Ndjamena	Chad
Niamey	Niger
Nicosia	Cyprus
Nineveh	Ancient Assyrian empire
Nouakchott	Mauritania
Nuku'alofa	Tonga
Nuuk	Greenland
Olympia	Washington state
Oslo	Norway
Ottawa	Canada
Ouagadougou	Burkina-Faso

Capital	Country, region, state, etc
Palermo	Sicily
Palikir	Micronesia
Panama City	Panama
Pandemonium *or* Pandaemonium	Hell
Paramaribo	Suriname
Paris	France
Persepolis	Ancient Persia
Phnom Penh	Cambodia
Pishpek	Kirghizia
Port-au-Prince	Haiti
Port Louis	Mauritius
Port Moresby	Papua New Guinea
Port of Spain	Trinidad and Tobago
Porto Novo	Benin
Port Vila	Vanuatu
Prague	Czech Republic
Praia	Cape Verde
Pretoria	Administrative capital of South Africa
Pristina	Kosovo (Federal Republic of Yugoslavia)
Providence	Rhode Island
Pyongyang	North Korea
Quito	Ecuador
Rabat	Morocco
Reykjavik	Iceland
Riga	Latvia
Rio	Rio de Janeiro
Rio Branco	Acre
Riyadh	Saudi Arabia
Rome	Italy
Roseau	Dominica
Samarkand	Mongol Empire (14th century)
San'a'	Yemen
San José	Costa Rica
San Juan	Puerto Rico
San Marino	San Marino
San Salvador	El Salvador
Santiago	Chile
Santo Domingo	Dominican Republic
São Tomé	São Tomé and Principe
Sarajevo	Bosnia and Herzegovina
Sendai	Tohoku
Seoul	South Korea
Singapore	Singapore
Skopje	Macedonia
Sofia	Bulgaria
Sokoto	Sokoto
St. George's	Grenada
St. John's	Antigua and Barbuda

Capitals

Capital	Country, region, state, etc
Stockholm	Sweden
Stuttgart	Baden-Württemberg
Sucré	Legislative and judicial capital of Bolivia
Susa	Ancient Persia (Achaemenid dynasty)
Suva	Fiji
Taipei	Taiwan
Tallinn	Estonia
Tarawa	Kiribati
Tashkent	Uzbekistan
Tbilisi	Georgia
Tegucigalpa	Honduras
Tehran or Teheran	Iran
Tel Aviv	Israel
Thebes	Ancient Egypt (18th dynasty)
Thimphu or Thimbu	Bhutan
Tirana	Albania
Tokyo	Japan
Topeka	Kansas
Trebizond	Trebizond
Tripoli	Libya
Tunis	Tunisia
Ufa	Bashkiria
Ulan Bator	Mongolia
Vaduz	Liechtenstein
Valladolid	Castilla-Léon
Valletta	Malta
Vatican City	Vatican City
Victoria	Seychelles
Vienna	Austria
Vientiane	Laos
Vilnius	Lithuania
Warsaw	Poland
Washington DC	United States of America
Wellington	New Zealand
Windhoek	Namibia
Winnipeg	Manitoba
Xanthus	Ancient Lycia
Xian	Shaanxi
Yamoussoukro	Côte d'Ivoire
Yangon (Rangoon)	Myanmar (Burma)
Yaoundé or Yaunde	Cameroon
Yaren	Nauru
Yerevan	Armenia
Zagreb	Croatia

Caps

3 letters:
Mob
Taj
Tam

4 letters:
Blue
Caul
Coif
Cope
Cowl
Flat
Kepi

5 letters:
Beret
Chaco
Chape
Cloth
Kippa
Mutch
Pagri
Quoif
Shako
Toque
Tuque
Turk's

6 letters:
Abacot
Amorce
Barret
Berret
Biggin
Blakey
Calpac
Chapka
Cornet

Czapka
Dunce's
Forage
Gandhi
Granny
Jockey
Juliet
Kalpak
Kipput
Kiss-me
Morion
Pileus
Pinner
Square
Toorie

7 letters:
Bathing
Bellhop
Bendigo
Biretta
Bycoket
Calotte
Calpack
Chapeau
Chechia
Fatigue
Grannie
Kippoth
Liberty
Monteer
Montero
Morrion
Newsboy

8 letters:
Balmoral

Baseball
Capeline
Chaperon
Garrison
Havelock
Monmouth
Phrygian
Puggaree
Schapska
Skullcap
Stocking
Thinking
Trencher
Yarmulka
Yarmulke
Zuchetto

9 letters:
Balaclava
Glengarry
Trenchard

10 letters:
Cockernony
Kilmarnock

11 letters:
Bonnet-rouge
Deerstalker
Kiss-me-quick
Mortar-board
Tam-o'-shanter

12 letters:
Cheese-cutter
Davy Crockett

Cards

CARD GAMES

3 letters:
Loo
Nap

4 letters:
Faro
Skat

Snap
Solo

5 letters:
Cinch
Monte
Ombre

Poker
Rummy
Stops
Whist

6 letters:
Boston

Cards

Bridge
Casino
Chemmy
Écarté
Euchre
Hearts
Piquet
Quinze
Switch

7 letters:
Bezique
Canasta
Cooncan
Old maid
Pinocle
Pontoon
Seven up

8 letters:
Baccarat

Canfield
Conquian
Cribbage
Gin rummy
Napoleon
Patience
Penuchle
Penuckle
Pinochle
Slapjack

9 letters:
Blackjack
Solo whist
Spoilfive
Stud poker

10 letters:
Strip poker

11 letters:
Five hundred

Rouge et noir

12 letters:
Rubber bridge

13 letters:
Auction bridge
Happy families

14 letters:
Contract bridge

15 letters:
Duplicate bridge

16 letters:
Trente et quarante

17 letters:
Beggar-my-
neighbour

BRIDGE TERMS

4 letters:
East
Ruff
Slam
West

5 letters:
Dummy
North
South
Trick

Trump

6 letters:
Double
Rubber

7 letters:
Finesse
No-trump

8 letters:
Contract

Redouble

9 letters:
Grand slam
Singleton
Small slam

10 letters:
Little slam
Vulnerable
Yarborough

POKER TERMS

3 letters:
See
Shy

4 letters:
Ante
Pair

5 letters:
Flush
Raise

8 letters:
Showdown
Stand pat
Straddle
Straight

9 letters:
Full house

10 letters:
Royal flush

13 letters:
Straight flush

OTHER CARD TERMS

3 letters:
Ace
Cut

4 letters:
Deal
Deck

Hand
Jack
King

Suit
Trey
Wild

5 letters:
Clubs
Deuce

Joker
Knave
Queen

6 letters:
Hearts
Revoke

Spades

8 letters:
Diamonds
Face card

9 letters:
Court card

Carnivores

3 letters:
Cat
Dog
Fox

4 letters:
Bear
Coon
Eyra
Lion
Lynx
Mink
Puma
Wolf

5 letters:
Civet
Dhole
Dingo
Genet
Hyena
Otter
Ounce
Panda
Potto
Rasse
Ratel
Sable
Skunk
Stoat
Tayra
Tiger
Zibet

6 letters:
Badger
Bobcat
Chetah
Corsac
Cougar
Coyote
Ermine

Fennec
Ferret
Grison
Hyaena
Jackal
Jaguar
Kit fox
Margay
Marten
Nanook
Ocelot
Racoon
Red fox
Serval
Teledu
Weasel

7 letters:
Caracal
Cheetah
Genette
Glutton
Grey fox
Grizzly
Leopard
Linsang
Meerkat
Panther
Polecat
Raccoon
Rooikat
Sun bear
Zorilla
Zorille

8 letters:
Aardwolf
Carcajou
Grey wolf
Kinkajou
Kolinsky

Mongoose
Sea otter
Swift fox
Tiger cat
Warrigal
Zibeline

9 letters:
Arctic fox
Binturong
Black bear
Brown bear
Cacomixle
Catamount
Hog badger
Honey bear
Ichneumon
Native dog
Palm civet
Polar bear
Silver fox
Sloth bear
Wolverine

10 letters:
Cacomistle
Desert lynx
Giant panda
Jaguarondi
Jaguarundi
Kodiak bear
Otter shrew
Pine marten
Prairie dog
Raccoon dog
Strandwolf
Timber wolf

11 letters:
Grizzly bear
Prairie wolf
Snow leopard

Carpets and rugs

Stone marten
Sweet marten

12 letters:
Catamountain
Cat-o'-mountain

See also:
➤ **Cats** ➤ **Dogs**

Cinnamon bear
Mountain lion
Spotted hyena

13 letters:
Hognosed skunk

Laughing hyena

Carpets and rugs

5 letters:
Kilim

6 letters:
Durrie
Kirman
Numdah
Wilton

7 letters:
Ingrain

8 letters:
Aubusson
Chenille

9 letters:
Axminster
Broadloom
Flat-woven

10 letters:
Bukhara rug

Persian rug

12 letters:
Turkey carpet

13 letters:
Kidderminster
Persian carpet

14 letters:
Brussels carpet

Carriages and carts

3 letters:
Cab
Car
Fly
Gig
Rig

4 letters:
Bier
Cart
Chay
Coch
Drag
Ekka
Pung
Rath
Shay
Sled
Trap
Wain

5 letters:
Bandy
Brake
Buggy

Coach
Coupé
Ratha
Sulky
Tonga
Wagon

6 letters:
Berlin
Britka
Calash
Chaise
Charet
Dennet
Do-si-do
Drosky
Fiacre
Gharry
Go-cart
Hansom
Herdic
Landau
Limber
Pochay

Randem
Remise
Sledge
Spider
Surrey
Tandem
Troika
Whisky

7 letters:
Berline
Britska
Britzka
Calèche
Cariole
Caroche
Chariot
Chassis
Dogcart
Dos-a-dos
Droshky
Growler
Norimon
Phaeton

Tilbury
Vetture
Vis-à-vis
Voiture
Whiskey

8 letters:
Barouche
Brougham
Cape cart
Carriage
Carriole
Carryall
Clarence
Curricle
Equipage
Pochaise
Quadriga
Rickshaw

Rockaway
Sociable
Stanhope
Tarantas
Victoria

9 letters:
Britschka
Buckboard
Cabriolet
Gladstone
Horseless
Jaunty car
Landaulet
Tarantass
Wagonette
Whirligig

10 letters:
Four-in-hand

Post chaise
Stagecoach
Tim-whiskey

11 letters:
Hurly-hacket
Jaunting car

12 letters:
Covered wagon

13 letters:
Désobligeante
Spider phaeton

14 letters:
Conestoga wagon

15 letters:
Prairie schooner

Cars

TYPES OF CAR

2 letters:
BL
GT
MG
RR
VW

3 letters:
Cab
Elf

4 letters:
Audi
Biza
Drag
Fiat
Ford
Kart
Lada
Limo
Merc
Mini
Opel
Tank

5 letters:
Astra

Buick
Coupé
Panda
Prowl
Racer
Rolls
Sedan
Skoda
Squad
Stock
Turbo

6 letters:
Beetle
Bubble
Bumper
Dodgem®
Estate
Hearse
Hot-rod
Lancia
Morris
Patrol
Ragtop
Roller
Sports

Tourer

7 letters:
Bugatti
Company
Cortina
Daimler
Formula
Hardtop
Hillman
Lagonda
Sunbeam
Veteran
Vintage

8 letters:
Cadillac
Dragster
Drophead
Fastback
Mercedes
Roadster

9 letters:
Cabriolet
Hatchback
Landaulet

Cars

Landrover
Limousine
Notchback
Two-seater

CAR PARTS

3 letters:
Fan
Top

4 letters:
Axle
Body
Boot
Bulb
Coil
Cowl
Door
Fuse
Gear
Hood
Horn
Jack
Lock
Plug
Roof
Seat
Sump
Tank
Trim
Tyre
Wing

5 letters:
Brake
Choke
Crank
Light
Pedal
Valve
Wheel

6 letters:
Air bag
Big end
Bonnet
Bumper
Clutch
Engine
Fascia
Fender

10 letters:
Subcompact

11 letters:
Convertible

Gasket
Grille
Heater
Hubcap
Piston
Points
Towbar
Window

7 letters:
Ammeter
Ashtray
Battery
Bearing
Chassis
Exhaust
Fan belt
Fog lamp
Fuse box
Gearbox
Hard top
Mud flap
Oil pump
Soft top
Springs
Starter
Sunroof
Wing nut

8 letters:
Brake pad
Camshaft
Cylinder
Demister
Dipstick
Flywheel
Foglight
Headrest
Ignition
Manifold
Odometer
Radiator
Seat belt
Silencer
Sprocket

Stretch-limo

12 letters:
Station wagon
Three-wheeler

Tailgate
Tailpipe
Wheel nut

9 letters:
Crankcase
Dashboard
Fuel gauge
Gear lever
Gearshift
Generator
Handbrake
Headlight
Indicator
Little end
Milometer
Oil filter
Petrol cap
Radius arm
Rear light
Sidelight
Taillight
Wheel trim

10 letters:
Alternator
Brake light
Bucket seat
Crankshaft
Disc brakes
Door handle
Driveshaft
Mileometer
Petrol tank
Safety belt
Spare wheel
Suspension
Torsion bar
Wheel brace
Windscreen
Wing mirror

11 letters:
Accelerator
Anti-roll bar

Cars

Carburettor
Distributor
Hazard light
Luggage rack
Numberplate
Parcel shelf
Petrol gauge
Speedometer

12 letters:
Cylinder head
Parking light
Sunshine roof

Transmission

13 letters:
Connecting rod
Passenger seat
Shock absorber
Steering wheel

14 letters:
Automatic choke
Childproof lock
Convertible top
Distributor cap
Radiator grille

Rear-view mirror
Reversing light
Steering column
Universal joint

15 letters:
Windscreen wiper

16 letters:
Glove compartment
Oil-pressure gauge

18 letters:
Catalytic converter

INTERNATIONAL CAR REGISTRATION LETTERS

Letter(s)	Country	Letter(s)	Country
A	Austria	EAU	Uganda
ADN	Yemen	EC	Ecuador
AFG	Afghanistan	ES	El Salvador
AL	Albania	ET	Egypt
AND	Andorra	ETH	Ethiopia
AUS	Australia	EW	Estonia
B	Belgium	F	France
BD	Bangladesh	FIN	Finland
BDS	Barbados	FJI	Fiji
BG	Bulgaria	FL	Liechtenstein
BH	Belize	FR	Faeroe Islands
BR	Brazil	GB	United Kingdom
BRN	Bahrain	GBA	Alderney
BRU	Brunei	GBG	Guernsey
BS	Bahamas	GBJ	Jersey
BUR	Myanmar	GBM	Isle of Man
C	Cuba	GBZ	Gibraltar
CDN	Canada	GCA	Guatemala
CH	Switzerland	GH	Ghana
CI	Côte d'Ivoire	GR	Greece
CL	Sri Lanka	GUY	Guyana
CO	Colombia	H	Hungary
CR	Costa Rica	HK	Hong Kong
CY	Cyprus	HKJ	Jordan
CZ	Czech Republic	HR	Croatia
D	Germany	I	Italy
DK	Denmark	IL	Israel
DOM	Dominican Republic	IND	India
		IR	Iran
DY	Benin	IRL	Republic of Ireland
DZ	Algeria		
E	Spain	IRQ	Iraq
EAK	Kenya	IS	Iceland
EAT	Tanzania	J	Japan

Cars

Letter(s)	Country	Letter(s)	Country
JA	Jamaica	RMM	Mali
K	Cambodia	RO	Romania
KWT	Kuwait	ROK	South Korea
L	Luxembourg	ROU	Uruguay
LAO	Laos	RP	Philippines
LAR	Libya	RSM	San Marino
LB	Liberia	RU	Burundi
LS	Lesotho	RUS	Russian Federation
LT	Lithuania	RWA	Rwanda
LV	Latvia	S	Sweden
M	Malta	SD	Swaziland
MA	Morocco	SGP	Singapore
MAL	Malaysia	SK	Slovakia
MC	Monaco	SME	Surinam
MEX	Mexico	SN	Senegal
MS	Mauritius	SWA	Namibia
MW	Malawi	SY	Seychelles
N	Norway	SYR	Syria
NA	Netherlands Antilles	T	Thailand
		TG	Togo
NIC	Nicaragua	TN	Tunisia
NL	Netherlands	TR	Turkey
NZ	New Zealand	TT	Trindad and Tobago
OMAN	Oman		
P	Portugal	USA	United States of America
PA	Panama		
PE	Peru	V	Vatican City
PK	Pakistan	VN	Vietnam
PL	Poland	WAG	Gambia
PNG	Papua New Guinea	WAL	Sierra Leone
		WAN	Nigeria
PY	Paraguay	WD	Dominica
RA	Argentina	WG	Grenada
RB	Botswana	WL	St. Lucia
RC	Taiwan	WS	Western Samoa
RCA	Central African Republic	WV	St. Vincent and the Grenadines
RCB	Congo Republic		
RCH	Chile	YU	Yugoslavia
RH	Haiti	YV	Venezuela
RI	Indonesia	Z	Zambia
RIM	Mauritania	ZA	South Africa
RL	Lebanon	ZRE	Zaire
RM	Madagascar	ZW	Zimbabwe

Cartoon characters

3 letters:
Doc
Ren
Tom

4 letters:
Dino
Kyle
Stan

5 letters:
Bambi
Bluto
Dopey
Dumbo
Goofy
Happy
Itchy
Jerry
Kenny
Pluto
Snowy

6 letters:
Bam-Bam
Boo-Boo
Grumpy
Krusty
Popeye
Shaggy
Sleepy
Sneezy

Stimpy
Tigger
Tintin
Top Cat

7 letters:
Bashful
Cartman
Muttley
Pebbles
Swee' Pea

8 letters:
Olive Oyl
Scratchy
Yogi Bear

9 letters:
Betty Boop
Daffy Duck
Elmer Fudd
Scooby-Doo
Sylvester
Tweety-Pie

10 letters:
Donald Duck
Roadrunner

11 letters:
Bart Simpson
Betty Rubble
Lisa Simpson

Mickey Mouse
Minnie Mouse
Ned Flanders
Sideshow Bob
Wile E Coyote
Yosemite Sam

12 letters:
Barney Rubble
Homer Simpson
Marge Simpson

13 letters:
Dick Dastardly
Maggie Simpson
Officer Dibble
The Hooded Claw
Winnie the Pooh

14 letters:
Foghorn Leghorn
Fred Flintstone
Speedy Gonzalez

15 letters:
Penelope Pitstop
Wilma Flintstone

19 letters:
Groundskeeper
  Willie

Cases

3 letters:
Box
Pod

4 letters:
Aril
Beer
Bere
Etui
Flan
Grip
Hull
Husk
Port

5 letters:
Ascus
Blimp
Burse
Calyx
Chase
Crate
Crust
Etwee
Frame
Ocrea
Theca
Trunk
Volva

6 letters:
Basket
Chitin
Cocoon
Locket
Lorica
Manche
Ochrea
Penner
Quiver
Sheath
Telium
Valise
Walise

Castles

Wallet

7 letters:
Cabinet
Capsule
Compact
Elytron
Hanaper
Hold-all
Humidor
Keister
Nacelle
Sheathe
Six-pack
Sporran
Wardian

8 letters:
Bundwall
Canister
Cartouch
Cellaret
Dispatch
Flapjack
Indusium
Nutshell
Scabbard
Tantalus
Tea-chest
Vasculum

9 letters:
Cartouche

Cartridge
Chrysalis
Croustade
Housewife
Papeterie

10 letters:
Canterbury
Phylactery
Sabretache

12 letters:
Plummer-block

Castles

3 letters:
Man

4 letters:
Cheb
Drum
More
Rait
Trim

5 letters:
Aydon
Blois
Cabra
Cahir
Conwy
Corfe
Dinan
Hever
Leeds
Spain
Torún
Vaduz

6 letters:
Brodie
Dublin
Durham
Farney
Forfar
Glamis
Kilkea
Ludlow

Raglan
Rithes
Stuart

7 letters:
Amboise
Arundel
Ashford
Barnard
Beeston
Belvoir
Blarney
Braemar
Calzean
Canossa
Chillon
Colditz
Crathes
Culzean
Despair
Harlech
Lincoln
Otranto
Schloss
Skipton
St Mawes
Warwick
Windsor

8 letters:
Balmoral
Balvenie

Bamburgh
Bastille
Berkeley
Bunraity
Carbonek
Darnaway
Doubting
Egremont
Elephant
Elsinore
Kilkenny
Killaghy
Leamaneh
Malahide
Malperdy
Monmouth
Pembroke
Portlick
Rackrent
Richmond
Stirling
Stokesay
Taymouth
Tintagel
Urquhart
Wartburg

9 letters:
Beaumaris
Dangerous
Dunnottar
Dunsinane

Edinburgh
Esterháza
Inverness
Kilravock
Lancaster
Leicester
Pendennis
Restormel
Sherborne
Trausnitz
Vincennes

10 letters:
Caernarfon
Caerphilly
Carmarthen

Heidelberg
Kenilworth
Launceston
Pontefract

11 letters:
Aberystwyth
Carisbrooke
Eilean Donan
Gormenghast
Scarborough

12 letters:
Berkhamstead
Caerlaverock
Château-Raoul
Dunstaffnage

Fotheringhay
Herstmonceux
Rock of Cashel

13 letters:
Ballindalloch
Carrickfergus

14 letters:
Ashby de la Zouch

16 letters:
Berwick-upon-
  Tweed

Cathedrals in the UK

3 letters:
Ely

4 letters:
Peel

5 letters:
Derby
Isles
Leeds
Ripon
Truro
Wells

6 letters:
Bangor
Brecon
Dundee
Durham
Exeter
Oxford

7 letters:
Arundel
Bristol
Cardiff
Chester
Clifton
Dornoch
Glasgow
Lincoln
Newport
Norwich

Salford
St Asaph
St John's
St Mary's
St Paul's
Swansea
Wrexham

8 letters:
Aberdeen
Bradford
Carlisle
Coventry
Hereford
Llandaff
Plymouth
St Albans
St Davids

9 letters:
Blackburn
Brentwood
Edinburgh
Guilford
Inverness
Lancaster
Leicester
Lichfield
Liverpool
Newcastle
Rochester
Salisbury

Sheffield
Southwark
St Andrews
Wakefield
Worcester

10 letters:
Birmingham
Canterbury
Chelmsford
Chichester
Gloucester
Manchester
Nottingham
Portsmouth
Shrewsbury
Winchester

11 letters:
Northampton
Westminster
York Minster

12 letters:
Christ Church
Peterborough

13 letters:
Middlesbrough
St Edmundsbury

16 letters:
Southwell Minster

Cats

BREEDS OF CAT

3 letters:
Rex

4 letters:
Manx

5 letters:
Tabby

6 letters:
Angora
Havana

7 letters:
Burmese
Persian
Ragdoll
Siamese
Turkish

9 letters:
Himalayan
Maine Coon

10 letters:
Abyssinian

11 letters:
Colourpoint
Russian blue

13 letters:
Bengal leopard
Tortoiseshell

FAMOUS CATS

3 letters:
Tom

4 letters:
Bast
Jinx

5 letters:
Bucky
Felix
Fritz
Hodge
Salem

6 letters:
Arthur
Bastet
Ginger

Huckle
Muessa
Selima
Top Cat

7 letters:
Bagpuss
Lucifer
Slipper

8 letters:
Garfield
Lady Jane
Scratchy
Snowball

9 letters:
Mehitabel

Mistigris
Thomasina
Tobermory

10 letters:
Grizabella
Heathcliff

11 letters:
Bombalurina
Cat in the Hat
Cheshire Cat
Mungojerrie
Puss-in-Boots
Snagglepuss

13 letters:
Fat Freddy's Cat

Cattle and other artiodactyls

2 letters:
Ox
Zo

3 letters:
Cow
Dzo
Elk
Gnu
Goa
Kob
Pig
Yak
Zho

4 letters:
Axis
Boar
Bull
Deer
Gaur
Goat
Ibex
Kudu
Oont
Oryx
Pudu
Sika

Stag
Tahr
Thar
Zebu

5 letters:
Addax
Argal
Ariel
Bison
Bongo
Bubal
Camel
Eland

Cattle and other artiodactyls

Gayal
Goral
Izard
Jacob
Llama
Moose
Nagor
Nyala
Okapi
Oribi
Saiga
Serow
Sheep
Takin

6 letters:
Alpaca
Aoudad
Argali
Bharal
Chital
Dik-dik
Duiker
Duyker
Impala
Koodoo
Nilgai
Reebok
Rhebok
Sambar
Sambur
Vicuña
Wapiti

7 letters:
Alpacca
Blaubok
Blesbok
Brocket
Bubalis
Buffalo
Bushpig
Carabao
Caracul

Caribou
Chamois
Gazelle
Gemsbok
Gerenuk
Giraffe
Grysbok
Guanaco
Jumbuck
Karakul
Kongoni
Kouprey
Markhor
Mouflon
Muntjac
Muntjak
Nilghau
Nylghau
Peccary
Red deer
Roe deer
Sassaby
Wart hog
Water ox

8 letters:
Antelope
Babirusa
Boer goat
Bontebok
Boschbok
Bushbuck
Markhoor
Moufflon
Mule deer
Musk deer
Reedbuck
Reindeer
Steenbok
Wild boar

9 letters:
Blacktail
Dromedary

Hartbeest
Marshbuck
Mouse deer
Pronghorn
Razorback
Springbok
Waterbuck

10 letters:
Camelopard
Chevrotain
Hartebeest
Jacob sheep
Wildebeest

11 letters:
Barking deer
Cape buffalo
Kashmir goat

12 letters:
Hippopotamus
Klipspringer
Mountain goat
Water buffalo

13 letters:
Bactrian camel
Sable antelope

14 letters:
Père David's deer

15 letters:
White-tailed deer

16 letters:
Chinese water deer

17 letters:
Harnessed
  antelope
Rocky Mountain
  goat

See also:
➤ **Cows** ➤ **Pigs** ➤ **Sheep**

Cattle, breeds of

4 letters:
Aver
Gyal
Neat
Nout
Nowt
Soum
Sowm
Stot

5 letters:
Devon
Heard
Kerry
Kraal
Kyloe
Luing
Owsen
Store

6 letters:
Ankole
Catalo
Dexter
Durham
Jersey
Rother
Sussex

7 letters:
Brahman
Cattalo

Kouprey
Lairage
Lincoln
Red Poll

8 letters:
Alderney
Ayrshire
Charbray
Friesian
Galloway
Gelbvieh
Guernsey
Hereford
Highland
Holstein
Limousin
Longhorn
Normandy

9 letters:
Charolais
Friesland
Illawarra
Red Polled
Shorthorn
Simmental
Teeswater

10 letters:
Africander
Brown Swiss

Piemontese
Simmenthal
Welsh black

11 letters:
Chillingham

12 letters:
Norwegian Red

13 letters:
Aberdeen Angus
Texas longhorn

14 letters:
Belted Galloway
Santa Gertrudis

16 letters:
Blonde d'Aquitaine
Holstein Friesian
Meuse-Rhine-
  Ijssel

18 letters:
Illawarra shorthorn

Chairs

3 letters:
Pew
Tub

4 letters:
Bath
Camp
Cane
Club
Deck
Easy
Form
Pouf
Wing

5 letters:
Bench
Sedan
Stool
Súgán
Swing

6 letters:
Barrel
Basket
Bosun's
Carver
Corner
Curule
Dining

Estate
Garden
Jampan
Morris
Pouffe
Rocker
Settle
Swivel
Throne

7 letters:
Beanbag
Berbice
Bergère
Dos-à-dos

Champagne bottles

Folding
Guérite
Hassock
Jampani
Lounger
Ottoman
Rocking
Windsor

8 letters:
Armchair
Bar stool
Bentwood
Birthing
Campaign
Captain's
Cathedra
Electric

Fauteuil
Jampanee
Recliner
Straight
Wainscot

9 letters:
Banquette
Butterfly
Director's
Highchair
Opsitbank
Reclining

10 letters:
Bucket seat
Fiddle-back
Ladder-back

Music stool
Piano stool
Wheelchair
Window seat

11 letters:
Gestatorial

12 letters:
Milking stool

13 letters:
Shooting stick
Windsor rocker

14 letters:
Platform rocker

Champagne bottles

Bottle	Capacity
Magnum	2 bottles
Jeroboam	2 magnums
Rehoboam	3 magnums
Methuselah	4 magnums
Salmanazar	6 magnums
Balthazar	8 magnums
Nebuchadnezzar	10 magnums

Channels

3 letters:
Fox

5 letters:
North

6 letters:
Queen's

7 letters:
Bristol

English
Yucatán

8 letters:
Spithead

9 letters:
St George's

10 letters:
Mozambique

11 letters:
Solway Firth

12 letters:
Saint George's

14 letters:
Molucca Passage

Cheeses

3 letters:
Ewe
Fet
Oka
Pot

4 letters:
Blue
Brie
Curd
Edam
Feta

Goat
Hard
Skyr
Tofu
Yarg

151

Chefs

5 letters:
Caboc
Cream
Derby
Esrom
Fynbo
Goats'
Gouda
Islay
Kenno
Quark
Samsø

6 letters:
Cantal
Chèvre
Damson
Dunlop
Ermite
Junket
Orkney
Romano
Tilsit

7 letters:
Boursin
Chaumes
Cheddar
Chessel
Cottage
Crowdie
Fontina
Gjetost
Gruyère
Havarti
Kebbock
Kebbuck
Limburg
Munster
Mycella
Ricotta

Sapsago
Stilton®

8 letters:
American
Bel Paese
Blue vein
Cheshire
Emmental
Halloumi
Huntsman
Muenster
Parmesan
Pecorino
Raclette
Taleggio
Tornegus
Vacherin
Vignotte

9 letters:
Amsterdam
Appenzell
Blue Vinny
Camembert
Emmenthal
Ilchester
Jarlsberg®
Killarney
Leicester
Limburger
Lymeswold®
Mousetrap
Port-Salut
Provolone
Reblochon
Roquefort
Sage Derby
Saint Agur

10 letters:
Blue Vinney

Bonchester
Caerphilly
Cambazolla
Canestrato
Danish blue
Dolcelatte
Emmentaler
Gloucester
Gorgonzola
Lanark Blue
Lancashire
Mascarpone
Mozzarella
Neufchâtel
Red Windsor
Stracchino

11 letters:
Blue Stilton
Coulommiers
Dunsyre Blue
Emmenthaler
Ribblesdale
Wensleydale

12 letters:
Bavarian blue
Bleu de Bresse
Caciocavallo
Fromage frais
Monterey jack
Red Leicester

13 letters:
Bleu d'Auvergne

14 letters:
Blue Shropshire

16 letters:
Double Gloucester

Chefs

3 letters:
Hom, *Kenneth*

4 letters:
Diat, *Louis*
Gray, *Rose*
Kerr, *Graham*

Puck, *Wolfgang*
Roux, *Albert*
Roux, *Michel*
Spry, *Constance*

5 letters:
Beard, *James*

Blanc, *Raymond*
David, *Elizabeth*
Floyd, *Keith*
Leith, *Prue*
Nairn, *Nick*
Sardi, *Vincent*

Chemical elements

Smith, *Delia*
Soyer, *Alexis*
Stein, *Rick*
White, *Marco Pierre*

6 letters:
Mrs Beeton
Bocuse, *Paul*
Elliot, *Rose*
Farmer, *Fannie*
Lawson, *Nigella*
Oliver, *Jamie*
Patten, *Marguerite*
Ramsay, *Gordon*
Rhodes, *Gary*
Slater, *Nigel*

7 letters:
Cradock, *Fanny*
Grigson, *Jane*
Jaffrey, *Madhur*

8 letters:
Grossman, *Loyd*
Harriott, *Ainsley*
Mosimann, *Anton*
Paterson, *Jennifer*

9 letters:
Carluccio, *Antonio*
Claiborne, *Craig*
Delmonico, *Lorenzo*
Escoffier, *Auguste*
McCartney, *Linda*

Prudhomme, *Paul*

10 letters:
Blumenthal, *Heston*

13 letters:
Dickson-Wright,
  Clarissa

15 letters:
Worrall-
  Thompson,
  Anthony

21 letters:
Fearnley-
  Whittingstall,
  Hugh

Chemical elements

Chemical element	Symbol	Atomic number
Hydrogen	H	1
Helium	He	2
Lithium	Li	3
Beryllium	Be	4
Boron	B	5
Carbon	C	6
Nitrogen	N	7
Oxygen	O	8
Fluorine	F	9
Neon	Ne	10
Sodium	Na	11
Magnesium	Mg	12
Aluminium *or* aluminum	Al	13
Silicon	Si	14
Phosphorus	P	15
Sulphur *or* sulfur	S	16
Chlorine	Cl	17
Argon	Ar	18
Potassium	K	19
Calcium	Ca	20
Scandium	Sc	21
Titanium	Ti	22
Vanadium	V	23
Chromium	Cr	24
Manganese	Mn	25
Iron	Fe	26
Cobalt	Co	27
Nickel	Ni	28
Copper	Cu	29

Chemical elements

Chemical element	Symbol	Atomic number
Zinc	Zn	30
Gallium	Ga	31
Germanium	Ge	32
Arsenic	As	33
Selenium	Se	34
Bromine	Br	35
Krypton	Kr	36
Rubidium	Rb	37
Strontium	Sr	38
Yttrium	Y	39
Zirconium	Zr	40
Niobium	Nb	41
Molybdenum	Mo	42
Technetium	Tc	43
Ruthenium	Ru	44
Rhodium	Rh	45
Palladium	Pd	46
Silver	Ag	47
Cadmium	Cd	48
Indium	In	49
Tin	Sn	50
Antimony	Sb	51
Tellurium	Te	52
Iodine	I	53
Xenon	Xe	54
Caesium *or* cesium	Cs	55
Barium	Ba	56
Lanthanum	La	57
Cerium	Ce	58
Praseodymium	Pr	59
Neodymium	Nd	60
Promethium	Pm	61
Samarium	Sm	62
Europium	Eu	63
Gadolinium	Gd	64
Terbium	Tb	65
Dysprosium	Dy	66
Holmium	Ho	67
Erbium	Er	68
Thulium	Tm	69
Ytterbium	Yb	70
Lutetium *or* lutecium	Lu	71
Hafnium	Hf	72
Tantalum	Ta	73
Tungsten *or* wolfram	W	74
Rhenium	Re	75
Osmium	Os	76
Iridium	Ir	77
Platinum	Pt	78
Gold	Au	79

Chemical element	Symbol	Atomic number
Mercury	Hg	80
Thallium	Tl	81
Lead	Pb	82
Bismuth	Bi	83
Polonium	Po	84
Astatine	At	85
Radon	Rn	86
Francium	Fr	87
Radium	Ra	88
Actinium	Ac	89
Thorium	Th	90
Protactinium	Pa	91
Uranium	U	92
Neptunium	Np	93
Plutonium	Pu	94
Americium	Am	95
Curium	Cm	96
Berkelium	Bk	97
Californium	Cf	98
Einsteinium	Es	99
Fermium	Fm	100
Mendelevium	Md	101
Nobelium	No	102
Lawrencium	Lr	103
Rutherfordium	Rf	104
Dubnium	Db	105
Seaborgium	Sg	106
Bohrium	Bh	107
Hassium	Hs	108
Meitnerium	Mt	109
Darmstadtium	Ds	110
Roentgenium	Rg	111

Chemistry

BRANCHES OF CHEMISTRY

7 letters:
Nuclear
Organic
Zymurgy

8 letters:
Chemurgy
Kinetics
Physical

9 letters:
Inorganic

10 letters:
Analytical

12 letters:
Biochemistry
Geochemistry
Zoochemistry

13 letters:
Cytochemistry
Stoichiometry

14 letters:
Astrochemistry
Histochemistry
Neurochemistry
Petrochemistry
Phonochemistry
Photochemistry
Phytochemistry
Radiochemistry

15 letters:
Immunochemistry

Chemistry

Stereochemistry
Thermochemistry

Magnetochemistry

CHEMISTRY TERMS

2 letters:
PH

3 letters:
Fat
Gas
Ion
Oil
Ore

4 letters:
Acid
Atom
Base
Bond
Foam
Fuel
Mole
Salt
Soap

5 letters:
Alloy
Anion
Anode
Chain
Ester
Ether
Inert
Metal
Solid
Sugar

6 letters:
Alkali
Alkane
Cation
Dilute
Fusion
Isomer
Liquid
Proton

7 letters:
Alcohol
Cathode
Crystal

Element
Fission
Formula
Halogen
Isotope
Mineral
Mixture
Monomer
Neutral
Neutron
Nucleus
Organic
Plastic
Polymer
Reagent
Soluble
Solvent
Valency

8 letters:
Analysis
Catalyst
Compound
Electron
Emulsion
Equation
Inert gas
Molarity
Molecule
Noble gas
Nonmetal
Reaction
Solution

9 letters:
Allotrope
Amino acid
Corrosion
Diffusion
Electrode
Fatty acid
Inorganic
Insoluble
Ionic bond
Metalloid
Oxidation

Reduction
Saturated
Synthesis

10 letters:
Atomic mass
Combustion
Hydrolysis
Ionization
Lanthanide
Litmus test
Suspension

11 letters:
Alkali metal
Evaporation
Hydrocarbon
Precipitate
Sublimation
Unsaturated

12 letters:
Atomic number
Boiling point
Carbohydrate
Concentrated
Condensation
Covalent bond
Distillation
Electrolysis
Fermentation
Melting point

13 letters:
Chain reaction
Periodic table
Radioactivity
Redox reaction

14 letters:
Brownian motion
Chromatography
Electrovalency
Saponification

15 letters:
Crystallization

Transition metal

16 letters:

Rare-earth

element

17 letters:
Van der Waals
forces

18 letters:
Alkaline earth

metal

20 letters:
Substitution
reaction

CHEMISTS

4 letters:
Auer, *Karl*
Caro, *Heinrich*
Davy, *Humphrey*
Hall, *Charles Martin*
Hill, *Archibald Vivian*
Kipp, *Petrus Jacobus*
Mond, *Ludwig*
Swan, *Joseph Wilson*
Todd, *Alexander Robert*
Urey, *Harold Clayton*

5 letters:
Abney, *William*
Adams, *Roger*
Aston, *Francis William*
Baumé, *Antoine*
Black, *James (Whyte)*
Black, *Joseph*
Bosch, *Carl*
Boyle, *Robert*
Brown, *Herbert Charles*
Curie, *Marie*
Curie, *Pierre*
Dakin, *Henry*
Debye, *Peter Joseph Wilhelm*
Dewar, *James*
Dumas, *Jean-Baptiste André*
Eigen, *Manfred*
Ernst, *Richard Robert*
Haber, *Fritz*
Henry, *William*
Hooke, *Robert*
Libby, *Willard Frank*
Nobel, *Alfred Bernhard*
Prout, *William*
Soddy, *Frederick*

6 letters:
Barton, *Derek*
Brandt, *Georg*
Bunsen, *Robert Wilhelm*
Calvin, *Melvin*

Carver, *Geroge Washington*
Dalton, *John*
Draper, *John William*
Liebig, *Justus*
Morley, *Edward Williams*
Müller, *Paul Hermann*
Mullis, *Kary Banks*
Nernst, *Walther Hermann*
Perutz, *Max Ferdinand*
Porter, *George*
Proust, *Joseph Louis*
Ramsay, *William*
Schiff, *Hugo*
Solvay, *Ernest*
Tizard, *Henry*
Werner, *Alfred*
Wöhler, *Friedrich*
Woulfe, *Peter*

7 letters:
Abelson, *Philip*
Andrews, *Thomas*
Bergius, *Friedrich (Karl Rudolph)*
Buchner, *Eduard*
Castner, *Hamilton Young*
Crookes, *William*
Faraday, *Michael*
Fischer, *Emil Hermann*
Fischer, *Ernst Otto*
Fischer, *Hans*
Gadolin, *Johan*
Gomberg, *Moses*
Guthrie, *Samuel*
Hodgkin, *Dorothy Crowfoot*
Leblanc, *Nicolas*
Macadam, *John*
Ostwald, *Wilhelm*
Pasteur, *Louis*
Pauling, *Linus Carl*
Piccard, *Jean Félix*
Scheele, *Karl Wilhelm*
Seaborg, *Glenn Theodore*

Chess pieces

Von Babo, *Lambert*
Warburg, *Otto Heinrich*
Ziegler, *Carl*

8 letters:
Beckmann, *Ernst Otto*
Grignard, *Victor*
Langmuir, *Irving*
Mulliken, *Robert Sanderson*
Newlands, *John Alexander*
Sabatier, *Paul*
Silliman, *Benjamin*
Smithson, *James*
Sorensen, *Soren Peter Lauritz*
Van't Hoff, *Jacobus Hendricus*
Woodward, *R(obert) B(urns)*

9 letters:
Arrhenius, *Svante August*
Butenandt, *Adolf Frederick Johann*
Cavendish, *Henry*
Cornforth, *John Warcup*

Gay-Lussac, *Joseph Louis*
Lavoisier, *Antoine Laurent*
Pelletier, *Pierre Joseph*
Priestley, *Joseph*
Prigogine, *Ilya*
Von Baeyer, *Johann Friedrich Wilhelm Adolf*
Von Hevesy, *George*
Zsigmondy, *Richard Adolf*

10 letters:
Chardonnet, *(Louis Marie) Hilaire Bernigaud*
Erlenmeyer, *Emil*
Mendeleyev, *Dmitri Ivanovich*
Van Helmont, *Jean Baptiste*

13 letters:
Von Stradonitz, *(Friedrich) August Kekulé*

25 letters:
Von Nagyrapolt Szent-Gyorgyi, *Albert*

See also:
➤ **Acids** ➤ **Alcohols** ➤ **Alkalis** ➤ **Alloys** ➤ **Chemical elements** ➤ **Compounds** ➤ **Crystals** ➤ **Hydrocarbons** ➤ **Minerals** ➤ **Molecules** ➤ **Ores** ➤ **Salts** ➤ **Silicas and Silicates** ➤ **Subatomic particles** ➤ **Sugars**

Chess pieces

Piece	Abbreviation
Bishop	B
King	K
King's bishop	KB
King's knight	KN
King's rook	KR
Knight	N
Pawn	P
Queen	Q
Queen's bishop	QB
Queen's knight	QN
Queen's rook	QR

Chess players

UNDISPUTED WORLD CHAMPIONS

Chess player	Term title held	Country
Wilhelm Steinitz	1886–94	Austria
Emanuel Lasker	1894–1921	Germany
José Raúl Capablanca	1921–27	Cuba
Alexander Alekhine	1927–35, 1937–46	Soviet Union
Max Euwe	1935–37	Netherlands
Mikhail Botvinnik	1948–57, 1958–60, 1961–63	Soviet Union
Vasily Smyslov	1957–58	Soviet Union
Mikhail Tal	1960–61	Latvia
Tigran Petrosian	1963–69	Soviet Union
Boris Spassky	1969–72	Soviet Union
Robert Fischer	1972–75	United States
Anatoly Karpov	1975–85	Soviet Union
Garry Kasparov	1985–1993	Soviet Union/Russia
Vladimir Kramnik	2006–2007	Russia
Viswanathan Anand	2007–	India

FIDE WORLD CHAMPIONS

Chess player	Term title held	Country
Anatoly Karpov	1993–99	Russia
Alexander Khalifman	1999–2000	Russia
Viswanathan Anand	2000–2002	India
Ruslan Ponomariov	2002–2004	Ukraine
Rustam Kasimdzhanov	2004–2005	Usbekistan
Veselin Topalov	2005–2006	Bulgaria

CLASSICAL WORLD CHAMPIONS

Chess player	Term title held	Country
Garry Kasparov	1993–2000	Russia
Vladimir Kramnik	2000–2006	Russia

Chinaware

4 letters:	Hizen	7 letters:
Goss	Imari	Crackle
Ming	Seric	Dresden
Waly	Spode®	Limoges
Ware	Wally	Meissen

5 letters:	6 letters:	8 letters:
Delft	Kaolin	Coalport
Derby	Minton	Eggshell

Etrurian
Wedgwood®

9 letters:
Cameoware
Porcelain

10 letters:
Rockingham
Willowware

Christian denominations and sects

5 letters:
Amish

7 letters:
Mormons

9 letters:
Adventism
Calvinism
Methodism
Quakerism
Shakerism

10 letters:
Anabaptism

11 letters:
Anglicanism
Catholicism
Lutheranism

12 letters:
Coptic Church
Unitarianism

13 letters:
Baptist Church
Protestantism
Salvation Army

14 letters:
Evangelicalism
Maronite Church
Moravian Church
Orthodox Church

Pentecostalism

15 letters:
Byzantine Church
Episcopal Church
Latter-day Saints
Presbyterianism

16 letters:
Christian Science
Plymouth Brethren
Roman Catholicism
Society of Friends

17 letters:
Congregationalism
Jehovah's Witnesses
Unification Church

18 letters:
Christadelphianism
New Jerusalem Church

19 letters:
Dutch Reformed Church
Greek Orthodox Church
Seventh-Day Adventism

20 letters:
United Reformed Church

21 letters:
Eastern Orthodox Church
Russian Orthodox Church

Cinema and television

2 letters:
TV

3 letters:
Act
BBC
Cue
Fan

ITV
Set

4 letters:
Cast
Crew
Film
Hero

Mike
Part
Play
Plot
Role
Shot
Show
Star

Unit

5 letters:
Actor
Cable
Drama
Enact
Extra
Flick
Movie
Odeon
Oscar
Radio
Scene
Telly
Video

6 letters:
Camera
Ceefax
Cinema
Comedy
Critic
Make up
Movies
Rushes
Screen
Script
Serial
Series
Sit com
Studio
Talkie
TV show

7 letters:
Actress
Cartoon
Compere
Feature
Film set
Flicker
Heroine
Musical
Network
Perform
Phone-in
Pop star
Portray
Present
Produce
Sponsor

Tragedy
Trailer

8 letters:
Audience
Bioscope
Chat show
Cinerama
Comedian
Director
Festival
Film crew
Film star
Fruit pie
Newsreel
Pictures
Premiere
Producer
Quiz show
Tape deck
Telecast
Telefilm

9 letters:
Blue movie
Broadcast
Cameraman
Character
Direction
Entertain
Exhibitor
Fillm club
Film actor
Film extra
Film-strip
Flash-back
Goggle-box
Guest star
Interview
Movie-goer
Movie show
Movie star
Performer
Photoplay
Programme
Projector
Recording
Rehearsal
Soap opera
Spectacle
Title role
Voice-over

10 letters:
Commercial
Crowd scene
Home-movies
Horror film
Horse opera
Microphone
Movie actor
Needle time
Newscaster
Newsreader
On location
Performing
Production
Screenplay
Silent film
Television
The critics

11 letters:
Broadcaster
Credit title
Documentary
Echo chamber
Entertainer
Feature film
Performance
Picture show
Radio caster
Sound effect
Talking film
Technicolor

12 letters:
Academy award
Cinéma vérité
Clapperboard
Film festival
Picture house
Scriptwriter
Show business
Silver screen

13 letters:
Chinese puzzle
Cinematograph
Cine projector
Clapperboards
Continuity man
Entertainment
Global village
Motion picture

Cities

Nouvelle Vague
Picture palace
Tape recording
Telerecording
Television set
Videocassette
Video recorder

14 letters:
Cinematography
Closed circuits
Continuity girl
Feature picture
Features editor

Moving pictures
Question master
Supporting cast
Supporting film
Supporting part
Supporting role
Television play
Third Programme

15 letters:
Animated cartoon
Cable television
Cinematographer
Cinematographic

Documentary film
French subtitles
Peak viewing time
Situation comedy
Slapstick comedy
Spot advertising

Cities

4 letters:
Baku
Bari
Bonn
Brno
Cork
Gifu
Giza
Graz
Homs
Hull
Ipoh
Kano
Kiel
Kiev
Kobe
Lima
Lodz
Nice
Omsk
Oran
Oslo
Riga
Rome

5 letters:
Accra
Adana
Amman
Basle
Basra
Belem
Berne
Bursa

Cairo
Chiba
Dacca
Davao
Delhi
Essen
Genoa
Gorky
Haifa
Halle
Hanoi
Izmir
Kabul
Kazan
Kyoto
Lagos
La Paz
Leeds
Lyons
Malmo
Mecca
Miami
Milan
Mosul
Omaha
Osaka
Padua
Paris
Patna
Perth
Poona
Quito
Rabat

Sakai
Seoul
Sofia
Surat
Tampa
Tokyo
Tomsk
Tunis
Turin

6 letters:
Aachen
Abadan
Aleppo
Ankara
Asmara
Athens
Austin
Baroda
Beirut
Berlin
Bilbao
Bochum
Bogota
Bombay
Boston
Bremen
Cracow
Dallas
Dayton
Denver
Dublin
Dundee
Durban

El Paso
Frunze
Fukoka
Fushun
Gdansk
Geneva
Harbin
Havana
Ibadan
Indore
Jaipur
Kanpur
Kansas
Khulna
Kumasi
Lahore
Lisbon
London
Luanda
Lübeck
Lusaka
Madras
Madrid
Magpur
Málaga
Malang
Manila
Mexico
Moscow
Multan
Munich
Mysore
Nantes
Naples
Newark
Odessa
Oporto
Ottawa
Oxford
Panama
Peking
Penang
Poznan
Prague
Puebla
Quebec
Santos
Shiraz
St Paul
Sydney
Tabriz

Taipei
Talinn
Toledo
Venice
Verona
Vienna
Warsaw
Zagreb
Zürich

7 letters:
Abidjan
Algiers
Antwerp
Atlanta
Baghdad
Bangkok
Barnaul
Belfast
Bologna
Brescia
Bristol
Buffalo
Caracas
Cardiff
Chengtu
Chicago
Cologne
Colombo
Córdoba
Corunna
Detroit
Donetsk
Dresden
Firenze
Foochow
Glasgow
Gwalior
Hamburg
Hanover
Houston
Irkutsk
Isfahan
Jakarta
Kalinin
Karachi
Kharkov
Kowloon
Kwangju
La Plata
Leipzig

Lucknow
Managua
Memphis
Messina
Mombasa
Nairobi
Nanking
New York
Oakland
Palermo
Phoenix
Rangoon
Rosario
San Jose
San Juan
Santa Fe
Sapporo
Saratov
Seattle
Seville
Soochow
Stettin
St Louis
Taranto
Tbilisi
Teheran
Tel Aviv
Toronto
Trieste
Tripoli
Utrecht

8 letters:
Aberdeen
Adelaide
Amritsar
Auckland
Augsburg
Belgrade
Bordeaux
Bradford
Brasilia
Brisbane
Brussels
Budapest
Bulawayo
Cagliari
Calcutta
Campinas
Canberra
Capetown

Cities

Columbus
Coventry
Curitiba
Damascus
Dortmund
Duisborg
Edmonton
Florence
Gorlovka
Hague, The
Haiphong
Hamilton
Hangchow
Helsinki
Honolulu
Istanbul
Katmandu
Katowice
Khartoum
Kingston
Kinshasa
Kumamoto
Kweiyang
Mandalay
Mannheim
Montreal
Murmansk
Nagasaki
Oklahoma
Peshawar
Plymouth
Portland
Port Said
Pretoria
Pyongang
Richmond
Salonika
Salt Lake
San Diego
Santiago
Sao Paulo
Sarajevo
Shanghai
Sholapur
Srinagar
Tashkent
Tientsin
Toulouse
Winnipeg
Yokohama

9 letters:
Ahmedabad
Allahabad
Amagasaki
Amsterdam
Archangel
Asahikawa
Astrakhan
Baltimore
Bangalore
Barcelona
Brunswick
Bucharest
Cambridge
Cartagena
Chengchow
Chihuahua
Cleveland
Des Moines
Edinburgh
Fort Worth
Frankfurt
Guatemala
Guayaquil
Hamamatsu
Hiroshima
Hyderabad
Jerusalem
Karlsruhe
Krasnodar
Krivoi Rog
Kuibyshev
Kwangchow
Las Palmas
Leicester
Leningrad
Liverpool
Magdeburg
Maracaibo
Marrakesh
Melbourne
Milwaukee
Nuremberg
Reykjavik
Rotterdam
Salisbury
Samarkand
Saragossa
Sheffield
Singapore
Stockholm

Stuttgart
Vancouver
Volgograd
Wuppertal

10 letters:
Addis Ababa
Alexandria
Baton Rouge
Birmingham
Bratislava
Canterbury
Casablanca
Chittagong
Cincinnati
Coimbatore
Copenhagen
Düsseldorf
Gothenburg
Jamshedpur
Los Angeles
Louisville
Manchester
Marseilles
Monte Video
New Orleans
Nottingham
Pittsburgh
Portsmouth
Rawalpindi
Sacramento
San Antonio
Strasbourg
Sunderland
Sverdlovsk
Tananarive
Valparaiso
Washington
Wellington

11 letters:
Baranquilla
Braunshweig
Buenos Aires
Chelyabinsk
Dar-es-Salaam
Guadalajara
Kuala Lumpur
Mar del Plata
Novosibirsk
Pondicherry
Rostov-on-Don

San Salvador
Southampton
Vladivostok

12 letters:
Barquisimeto
Bloemfontein
Indianapolis
Jacksonville
Johannesburg

Magnitogorsk
Philadelphia
Port-au-Prince
Rio de Janeiro
San Francisco
Santo Domingo
Stoke-on-Trent

13 letters:
Gelsenkirchen

Karl-Marx-Stadt
Port Elizabeth
Shihkiachwang
Wolverhampton

14 letters:
Dnepropetrovsk

Clothing

ARTICLES OF CLOTHING

3 letters:
Aba
Alb
Tie

4 letters:
Abba
Body
Bubu
Coat
Gown
Haik
Hose
Izar
Kilt
Muff
Rami
Robe
Sari
Sash
Shoe
Slop
Sock
Toga
Vest
Wrap

5 letters:
Abaya
Ao dai
Apron
Burka
Burqa
Cardy
Chaps
Cimar

Cotta
Dress
Ephod
Fanon
Frock
Gilet
Glove
Ihram
Jupon
Kanga
Kanzu
Levis
Pilch
Plaid
Ramée
Ramie
Ruana
Saree
Shawl
Shift
Shirt
Smock
Stola
Stole
Tanga
Thong
Tunic

6 letters:
Barrow
Basque
Bikini
Blouse
Bodice
Bolero
Boubou

Braces
Caftan
Cardie
Chador
Chimer
Cilice
Coatee
Cossie
Dirndl
Dolman
Exomis
Garter
Halter
Jacket
Jerkin
Jersey
Jibbah
Jubbah
Jumper
Kaftan
Kameez
Kaross
Khanga
Kimono
Kittel
Mantle
Mitten
Peplos
Rochet
Sarong
Serape
Shorts
Skivvy
Tabard
Tallit

Clothing

Tights
Trunks
T-shirt
Zephyr

7 letters:
Baldric
Blouson
Bourkha
Burnous
Bustier
Busuuti
Catsuit
Chapeau
Chuddah
Chuddar
Chudder
Costume
Dashiki
Djibbah
Doublet
Exomion
Hauberk
Leotard
Maillot
Manteau
Necktie
Nightie
Overall
Pajamas
Paletot
Pallium
Partlet
Pelisse
Pyjamas
Rompers
Shalwar
Singlet
Soutane

Sporran
Surcoat
Sweater
Tank top
Tunicle
Unitard
Wrapper
Yashmac
Yashmak

8 letters:
Bathrobe
Bodysuit
Cardigan
Chasuble
Chausses
Codpiece
Dalmatic
Galluses
Gambeson
Himation
Jump suit
Negligée
Overcoat
Pashmina
Peignoir
Pelerine
Pullover
Scapular
Surplice
Swimsuit
Tee shirt

9 letters:
Cover-slut
Dungarees
Housecoat
Loincloth
Mandilion

Mandylion
Nightgown
Overskirt
Pantihose
Pantyhose
Sanbenito
Waistcoat

10 letters:
Chaparajos
Chaparejos
Cote-hardie
Cummerbund
Jeistiecor
Kummerbund
Nightdress
Nightshirt
Oversleeve
Salopettes
Suspenders

11 letters:
Bathing suit
Bib and brace
Breechcloth
Dreadnought

12 letters:
Body stocking
Dressing gown
Undergarment

14 letters:
Bathing costume
Swimming trunks

15 letters:
Swimming
  costume

PARTS OF CLOTHING

3 letters:
Arm
Hem
Leg

4 letters:
Cuff
Hood
Seam

Tail
Yoke

5 letters:
Dicky
Jabot
Lapel
Train
Waist

6 letters:
Armlet
Bodice
Collar
Gusset
Lining
Pocket
Sleeve

7 letters:
Armhole
Flounce
Hemline

8 letters:
Neckline

Shoulder

9 letters:
Epaulette
Waistline

10 letters:
Buttonhole

11 letters:
Patch pocket
Shawl collar

TYPES OF CLOTHING

4 letters:
Hose

5 letters:
Mufti
Slops

6 letters:
Armour
Civies
Livery
Samfoo

7 letters:
Civvies
Hosiery
Uniform
Weepers

8 letters:
Black tie
Fatigues
Froufrou

Knitwear
Lingerie
Neckwear
Skivvies
Swimwear
White tie

9 letters:
Beachwear
Clericals
Coveralls
Long-coats
Millinery
Nightwear
Sackcloth
Separates
Underwear

10 letters:
Canonicals
Fancy dress
Sportswear

11 letters:
Baby clothes
Coordinates
Long clothes
Underthings
Widow's weeds

12 letters:
Evening dress
Morning dress
Nightclothes
Overgarments

13 letters:
Academic dress
Highland dress
Undergarments

16 letters:
Swaddling clothes

See also:
➤ **Caps** ➤ **Coats and Cloaks** ➤ **Dresses** ➤ **Hats**
➤ **Hoods** ➤ **Jackets** ➤ **Scarves** ➤ **Shirts** ➤ **Shoes and Boots** ➤ **Skirts** ➤ **Socks and Tights** ➤ **Suits** ➤ **Sweaters** ➤ **Ties and Cravats** ➤ **Trousers and Shorts** ➤ **Underwear**

Clouds

3 letters:
Fog

4 letters:
Haze
Mist

5 letters:
Storm

6 letters:
Cirrus

Nimbus

7 letters:
Cumulus
Strat(o)us

8 letters:
Water-dog
Woolpack

9 letters:
Goat's hair

Mare's tail

11 letters:
Altocumulus
Altostratus
False cirrus
Thunderhead

12 letters:
Cirrocumulus
Cirrostratus

Clubs

Cumulonimbus
Nimbostratus

13 letters:
Fractocumulus

Fractostratus
Stratocumulus

Clubs

3 letters:
RAC

4 letters:
Bath
Golf

5 letters:
Disco
Slate
Youth

6 letters:
Brook's
Cotton
Drones
Guards
Jockey
Kitcat
Monday
Reform
Rotary
Savage
Savile

White's

7 letters:
Adelphi
Almack's
Boodles
Carlton
Cavalry
Country
Garrick
Hampden
Jacobin
Kiwanis
Leander
Variety

8 letters:
Atheneum
Hell-fire
Rotarian

9 letters:
Athenaeum
Beefsteak

10 letters:
Crockford's
Devonshire
Landsdowne
Oddfellows
Travellers

11 letters:
Army and Navy
Caterpillar
Discotheque

12 letters:
Conservative

13 letters:
Junior Carlton
Thatched House

14 letters:
Constitutional
United Services

15 letters:
National Liberal

Clubs and bats

3 letters:
Bat

4 letters:
Cosh
Kiri
Mace
Maul
Mell
Mere
Meri
Patu
Polt

5 letters:
Basto

Lathi
Waddy

6 letters:
Alpeen
Cudgel
Kierie
Priest

7 letters:
Bourdon

8 letters:
Bludgeon
Shillala
Trunnion

9 letters:
Blackjack
Knobstick
Truncheon

10 letters:
Knobkerrie
Nightstick
Nulla-nulla
Shillelagh

12 letters:
Quarterstaff

13 letters:
Life preserver

Coats and cloaks

3 letters:
Aba
Box
Car
Fur
Mac
Top

4 letters:
Abba
Capa
Cape
Cope
Hair
Hood
Jack
Jump
Mack
Polo
Rail
Sack
Seal
Tail
Tent
Toga
Warm
Wool

5 letters:
Abaya
Acton
Amice
Dress
Frock
Grego
Jelab
Jemmy
Jupon
Lammy
Loden
Manta
Palla
Parka
Pilch
Sagum
Tails

6 letters:
Abolla

Achkan
Afghan
Anarak
Anorak
Capote
Chimer
Coatee
Covert
Dolman
Domino
Duffel
Duster
Fleece
Fun fur
Jacket
Jerkin
Joseph
Kaross
Lammie
Mantle
Parkee
Peplum
Poncho
Raglan
Riding
Tippet
Trench
Tuxedo
Ulster
Vestry
Visite

7 letters:
Admiral
Burnous
Cassock
Chimere
Chlamys
Chuddah
Chuddar
Crombie®
Cutaway
Galabea
Galabia
Hacking
Jellaba
Manteel
Mantlet

Matinee
Morning
Mozetta
Paenula
Paletot
Pallium
Peacoat
Pelisse
Posteen
Rocklay
Rokelay
Sarafan
Slicker
Snorkel
Spencer
Surcoat
Surtout
Swagger
Topcoat
Zamarra
Zamarro

8 letters:
Barathea
Bathrobe
Benjamin
Burberry®
Burnoose
Burnouse
Capuchin
Cardinal
Chasuble
Djellaba
Galabieh
Gambeson
Hall-robe
Haqueton
Himation
Jellabah
Jodhpuri
Mackinaw
Mantelet
Mantilla
Overcoat
Peignoir
Poshteen
Raincoat
Revestry

Coins

Scapular
Sherwani
Taglioni
Tailcoat
Vestiary

9 letters:
Balmacaan
Caracalla
Chlamydes
Coat dress
Djellabah
Gabardine
Gaberdine
Gallabeah
Greatcoat
Hacqueton
Housecoat
Inverness

Macintosh
Newmarket
Opera hood
Pea jacket
Petersham
Redingote
Sheepskin
Sou'wester
Undercoat

10 letters:
Fearnaught
Fearnought
Gallabiyah
Gallabiyeh
Mackintosh
Opera cloak
Roquelaure
Ulsterette

Waterproof
Windjammer
Wrap-rascal

11 letters:
Dreadnaught
Dreadnought
Swallowtail

12 letters:
Chesterfield
Dressing gown
Mousquetaire
Paludamentum
Prince Albert

13 letters:
Swallow-tailed

Coins

1 letter:
D

2 letters:
As
DM
Kr
Rd
Xu

3 letters:
Ban
Bar
Bob
Cob
Dam
Ecu
Fen
Fil
Fin
Flu
Hao
Jun
Kip
Lat
Lei
Lek
Leu
Lev

Lew
Mil
Mna
Moy
Ore
Pul
Pya
Red
Sen
Sol
Som
Sou
Won
Yen
Zuz

4 letters:
Anna
Baht
Bani
Birr
Buck
Cedi
Cent
Chon
Dibs
Dime
Doit
Dong

Dram
Duro
Euro
Fiat
Fils
Inti
Jack
Jane
Jiao
Kina
Kobo
Kuna
Kyat
Lari
Lion
Lira
Loti
Maik
Mark
Merk
Mina
Obol
Para
Paul
Peag
Peni
Peso
Pice

Coins

Pula
Puli
Punt
Rand
Real
Reis
Rial
Riel
Rock
Ryal
Sene
Slog
Spur
Tael
Taka
Tala
Toea
Vatu
Yuan
Zack

5 letters:
Agora
Angel
Asper
Aurar
Baiza
Bekah
Belga
Bodle
Broad
Brown
Butat
Butut
Chiao
Colon
Conto
Crore
Crown
Daric
Dibbs
Dinar
Dobra
Ducat
Eagle
Eyrir
Franc
Fugio
Gerah
Groat
Grosz

Haler
Krona
Krone
Kroon
Kurus
Laari
Laree
Leone
Liard
Litas
Livre
Louis
Lyart
Maile
Manat
Maneh
Mohur
Mongo
Mopus
Naira
Nakfa
Ngwee
Noble
Obang
Oscar
Paisa
Paolo
Pence
Pengo
Penie
Penni
Penny
Plack
Pound
Razoo
Rider
Royal
Ruble
Rupee
Sceat
Scudo
Scute
Semis
Sente
Shand
Soldo
Souon
Sucre
Sycee
Tenge
Thebe

Tical
Ticky
Tolar
Toman
Tyiyn
Zaire
Zimbi
Zloty

6 letters:
Aureus
Balboa
Bawbee
Bender
Bezant
Boddle
Byzant
Canary
Centas
Copeck
Couter
Dalasi
Danace
Deaner
Décime
Denier
Derham
Dirham
Dirhem
Dodkin
Dollar
Double
Drachm
Ekuele
Escudo
Filler
Florin
Forint
Gilder
Gourde
Guinea
Gulden
Halala
Heller
Hryvna
Jitney
Kobang
Koruna
Kroner
Kroona
Kwacha

Coins

Kwanza
Lepton
Likuta
Loonie
Makuta
Mancus
Markka
Mawpus
Pa'anga
Pagoda
Pataca
Pennia
Peseta
Pesewa
Qintar
Rappen
Rouble
Rupiah
Santum
Satang
Sceatt
Seniti
Sequin
Shekel
Sickle
Siglos
Stater
Stiver
Stotin
Talent
Tanner
Tester
Teston
Thaler
Tickey
Toonie
Tugrik
Turner
Vellon
Wakiki

7 letters:
Afghani
Austral
Bolivar
Cardecu
Carolus
Centavo
Chetrum
Cordoba

Crusado
Drachma
Ekpwele
Guarani
Guilder
Hryvnya
Jacobus
Joannes
Kreuzer
Lemoira
Metical
Millime
Milreis
Moidore
Ostmark
Ouguiya
Patrick
Piastre
Piefort
Pistole
Pollard
Quarter
Quetzal
Ringgit
Ruddock
Rufiyaa
Sextans
Solidus
Spanker
Tambala
Testoon
Testril
Thrimsa
Thrymsa
Tughrik
Unicorn
Xerafin

8 letters:
Brockage
Cardecue
Cruzeiro
Denarius
Doubloon
Ducatoon
Emalengi
Farthing
Groschen
Johannes
Kreutzer

Llangeni
Louis d'or
Maravedi
Millieme
Napoleon
Ngultrum
Picayune
Pistolet
Planchet
Portague
Portigue
Quadrans
Rigmarie
Semuncia
Sesterce
Shilling
Skilling
Solidare
Stotinka
Xeraphin
Zecchino

9 letters:
Boliviano
Britannia
Centesimo
Dandiprat
Dandyprat
Didrachma
Dupondius
Luckpenny
Pistareen
Rennminbi
Rix-dollar
Rose noble
Schilling
Sovereign
Spur-royal
Yellowboy
Zwanziger

10 letters:
Broadpiece
Chervonets
Krugerrand
Portcullis
Reichsmark

11 letters:
Deutschmark
Sword-dollar

Tetradrachm

12 letters:
Antoninianus

13 letters:
Rennminbi yuan

18 letters:
Maria Theresa
 dollar

Collective nouns

Noun	Collective noun
Actors	Company
Aldermen	Bench, guzzle
Bakers	Tabernacle
Bishops	Bench
Critics	Shrivel
Directors	Board
Eggs	Clutch
Flowers	Bouquet
Inventions	Budget
Judges	Bench
People	Audience, crowd, congregation, horde, mob
Poems	Garland
Policemen	Posse
Prisoners	Gang
Remedies	Rabble
Rumours	Nest
Sailors	Crew
Ships	Fleet
Stories	Anthology
Thieves	Gang
Workmen	Gang

See also:
➤ **Animals**

Collectors and enthusiasts

Collector/Enthusiast	Object
Ailurophile	Cats
Arctophile	Teddy bears
Audiophile	High-fidelity sound reproduction
Automobilist	Cars
Bibliophile	Books
Brolliologist	Umbrellas
Campanologist	Bell-ringing
Cartophilist	Cigarette cards
Cruciverbalist	Crosswords
Deltiologist	Picture postcards

Colleges

Collector/Enthusiast	Object
Discophile	Gramophone records
Fusilatelist	Phonecards
Herbalist	Herbs
Lepidopterist	Moths and butterflies
Medallist	Medals
Numismatist	Coins
Oenophile	Wine
Paranumismatist	Coin-like objects
Philatelist	Stamps
Phillumenist	Matchbox labels
Phraseologist	Phrases
Scripophile	Share certificates
Vexillologist	Flags
Zoophile	Animals

Colleges

3 letters:
New

4 letters:
City
Dana
Eton
Fife
Iona
Reed
Snow
Taft
York

5 letters:
Bates
Chase
Clare
Green
Jesus
Keble
King's
Oriel
Peace
Ripon
Salem
Smith
Union
Wells

6 letters:
Bethel
Boston
Darwin

Durham
Exeter
Geneva
Girton
Gordon
Hebrew
Ithaca
Merton
Queen's
Selwyn
Thomas
Vassar
Wadham

7 letters:
Amherst
Aquinas
Balliol
Barnard
Bedford
Bermuda
Bowdoin
Chatham
Christ's
Concord
Cornell
Cypress
Douglas
Downing
Emerson
Erskine
Kellogg
Linacre

Lincoln
New Hall
Newnham
St Anne's
St Cross
St Hugh's
St John's
St Paul's
Trinity
Wolfson

8 letters:
All Souls
Bryn Mawr
Carleton
Columbia
Emmanuel
Findhorn
Hamilton
Hastings
Hertford
Homerton
Illinois
Imperial
Lewisham
Longwood
Magdalen
Meredith
Monmouth
National
Nuffield
Pembroke
Robinson

St Hilda's
St Peter's

9 letters:
Brasenose
Churchill
Clare Hall
Claremont
Gateshead
Guildford
Hampshire
Haverford
Kalamazoo
Lafayette
Magdalene
Manhattan
Mansfield
Newcastle
St Antony's
St Edmund's
Templeton

Wellesley
Worcester

10 letters:
Chesapeake
Goldsmith's
Greyfriars
Heidelberg
Hughes Hall
Huntingdon
Middlebury
Paul Smith's
Peterhouse
Somerville
St Stephen's
University
Washington

11 letters:
Blackfriars
Campion Hall
Fitzwilliam

King Alfred's
Regent's Park
Springfield
Trinity Hall

12 letters:
Christ Church
Sidney Sussex
St Benet's Hall
St Catharine's
St Catherine's
St Edmund Hall
Wycliffe Hall

13 letters:
Corpus Christi
Lucy Cavendish

16 letters:
Gonville and Caius
Harris Manchester
Lady Margaret Hall

See also:
➤ **Academic degrees** ➤ **Education terms** ➤ **Ivy League universities** ➤ **Oxbridge colleges** ➤ **Schools**

Colours

3 letters:
Jet
Red
Tan

4 letters:
Anil
Blue
Ecru
Fawn
Gold
Grey
Iris
Jade
Navy
Onyx
Opal
Pink
Plum
Puce
Rose
Ruby
Rust

Sand
Sage

5 letters:
Amber
Beige
Black
Brown
Cocoa
Coral
Cream
Ebony
Green
Hazel
Henna
Ivory
Khaki
Lemon
Lilac
Mauve
Ochre
Olive
Peach

Pearl
Sepia
Slate
Taupe
Topaz
Umber
White

6 letters:
Auburn
Blonde
Bottle
Bronze
Canary
Cerise
Cherry
Claret
Cobalt
Copper
Indigo
Maroon
Orange
Purple

Comedians

Russet
Salmon
Silver
Violet
Walnut
Yellow

7 letters:
Apricot
Avocado
Biscuit
Caramel
Crimson
Emerald
Fuchsia
Gentian
Magenta

Mustard
Saffron
Scarlet

8 letters:
Burgundy
Charcoal
Chestnut
Cinnamon
Eau de nil
Lavender
Magnolia
Mahogany
Sapphire
Viridian

9 letters:
Aubergine

Chocolate
Pistachio
Tangerine
Turquoise
Vermilion

10 letters:
Aquamarine
Chartreuse
Cobalt blue
Terracotta

11 letters:
Burnt sienna
Lemon yellow
Ultramarine

Comedians

3 letters:
Dee, *Jack*
Fry, *Stephen*
Ray, *Ted*
Wax, *Ruby*

4 letters:
Ali G
Ball, *Lucille*
Barr, *Roseanne*
Cook, *Peter*
Dodd, *Ken*
Hill, *Benny*
Hill, *Harry*
Hope, *Bob*
Hudd, *Roy*
Idle, *Eric*
Marx, *Chico*
Marx, *Groucho*
Marx, *Harpo*
Marx, *Zeppo*
Sims, *Joan*
Took, *Barry*
Wall, *Max*
Wise, *Ernie*
Wood, *Victoria*

5 letters:
Abbot, *Russ*
Allen, *Dave*
Allen, *Woody*

Askey, *Arthur*
Benny, *Jack*
Borge, *Victor*
Brand, *Jo*
Bruce, *Lenny*
Burns, *George*
Chase, *Chevy*
Cohen, *Sacha Baron*
Cosby, *Bill*
Drake, *Charlie*
Elton, *Ben*
Emery, *Dick*
Goons, *The*
Hardy, *Jeremy*
Hardy, *Oliver*
Henry, *Lenny*
Hicks, *Bill*
Horne, *Kenneth*
James, *Sidney*
Jones, *Griff Rhys*
Jones, *Spike*
Jones, *Terry*
Leary, *Denis*
Lewis, *Jerry*
Lloyd, *Harold*
Moore, *Dudley*
Myers, *Mike*
Oddie, *Bill*
Palin, *Michael*

Pryor, *Richard*
Robey, *Sir George*
Sayle, *Alexei*
Smith, *Linda*
Smith, *Mel*
Starr, *Freddie*
Sykes, *Eric*
Worth, *Harry*

6 letters:
Abbott, *Bud*
Bailey, *Bill*
Barker, *Ronnie*
Carrey, *Jim*
Cleese, *John*
Coogan, *Steve*
Cooper, *Tommy*
Dawson, *Les*
De Vito, *Danny*
Fields, *W(illiam) C(laude)*
French, *Dawn*
Garden, *Graeme*
Howerd, *Frankie*
Izzard, *Eddie*
Junkin, *John*
Keaton, *Buster*
Laurel, *Stan*
Laurie, *Hugh*
Lehrer, *Tom*

Comets

Martin, *Steve*
Mayall, *Rik*
Merton, *Paul*
Murphy, *Eddie*
Proops, *Greg*
Reeves, *Vic*
Ullman, *Tracey*
Wisdom, *Norman*

7 letters:
Aykroyd, *Dan*
Baddiel, *David*
Belushi, *John*
Bentine, *Michael*
Bremner, *Rory*
Carrott, *Jasper*
Chaplin, *Charlie*
Chapman, *Graham*
Charles, *Craig*
Corbett, *Ronnie*
Crystal, *Billy*
Edwards, *Jimmy*
Enfield, *Harry*
Everett, *Kenny*
Feldman, *Marty*
Gervais, *Ricky*
Goodman, *John*

Grammer, *Kelsey*
Hancock, *Tony*
Handley, *Tommy*
Jacques, *Hattie*
Manning, *Bernard*
Matthau, *Walter*
Newhart, *Bob*
Rushton, *Willie*
Secombe, *Harry*
Sellers, *Peter*
Tarbuck, *Jimmy*
Toksvig, *Sandi*
Ustinov, *Sir Peter*

8 letters:
Coltrane, *Robbie*
Connolly, *Billy*
Costello, *Lou*
Goldberg, *Whoopi*
Groening, *Matt*
Milligan, *Spike*
Mortimer, *Bob*
Sadowitz, *Jerry*
Saunders, *Jennifer*
Seinfeld, *Jerry*
Sessions, *John*
Williams, *Kenneth*

Williams, *Robin*

9 letters:
Edmondson, *Adrian*
Humphries, *Barry*
Monkhouse, *Bob*
Morecambe, *Eric*
Whitfield, *June*

10 letters:
Pete and Dud
Stephenson,
  Pamela
Whitehouse, *Paul*

11 letters:
Monty Python
Terry-Thomas

12 letters:
Brooke-Taylor, *Tim*

14 letters:
Rowan and Martin

15 letters:
The Marx Brothers
The Three Stooges

Comets

4 letters:
Wild
West

8 letters:
Borrelly
Hale-Bopp
Kohoutek
McNaught

9 letters:
Hyakutake
Ikeya-Seki
Oort cloud

11 letters:
Swift-Tuttle

12 letters:
Halley's Comet

13 letters:
Shoemaker-Levy

19 letters:
Schwassmann-
  Wachmann

Commonwealth members

4 letters:
Fiji

5 letters:
Ghana
India
Kenya

Malta
Nauru
Samoa
Tonga

6 letters:
Belize

Brunei
Canada
Cyprus
Guyana
Malawi
Tuvalu
Uganda

Communications

Zambia

7 letters:
Grenada
Jamaica
Lesotho
Namibia
Nigeria
St Lucia
Vanuatu

8 letters:
Barbados
Botswana
Cameroon
Dominica
Kiribati
Malaysia
Maldives
Pakistan

Sri Lanka
Tanzania
Zimbabwe

9 letters:
Australia
Mauritius
Singapore
Swaziland
The Gambia

10 letters:
Bangladesh
Mozambique
New Zealand
Seychelles
The Bahamas

11 letters:
Sierra Leone
South Africa

13 letters:
United Kingdom

14 letters:
Papua New
  Guinea
Solomon Islands

15 letters:
St Kitts and Nevis

17 letters:
Antigua and
Barbuda
Trinidad and
  Tobago

25 letters:
St Vincent and
  The Grenadines

Communications

2 letters:
IT
PA

3 letters:
BCD
Cue
Dah
Dit
Dot
DVD
FAQ
Fax
FTP
IAP
ICT
ISP
LAN
Net
Out
TMT
URL
WAN
WAP
Web
XML

4 letters:
Alfa
Byte
CCTA
Code
Dash
Data
E-CRM
E-FIT
HTML
Java
Link
Mail
Mast
Over
Page
SGML
Site
Spam
WiFi
Worm

5 letters:
Bleep
Carry
Comms
Crier

Datum
DOVAP
Email
Flame
GMDSS
Inbox
Media
Modem
Pager
Radar
Radio
Stamp
Telex
Virus

6 letters:
Aerial
Browse
Cipher
Codify
Convey
Decode
Direct
Encode
Letter
Mayday
Medium

Nettie
Newbie
Outbox
Return
Server
Trojan
Usenet

7 letters:
Bleeper
Browser
Courier
Decrypt
DEW line
Digital
Dossier
En clair
Encrypt
Entropy
Evernet
E-wallet
Lurking
Message
Meta tag
Nethead
Netizen
Network
Tapping
Webcast
Web page
Website

8 letters:
Anti-site
Blocking
Boob tube
Chatroom
Codeword
Computer
Coverage
Data bank
Database
Decipher
Diaphone
Dispatch
Disperse
E-address
Envelope
E-payment
Ethernet
Firewall
Internet

Intranet
Listen in
Minidish
New media
Postmark
Register
Registry
Semaphor
Wireless

9 letters:
Aldis lamp
Bandwidth
Bluetooth
Broadband
Cybercafé
Digital TV
Direction
Directory
E-commerce
Facsimile
Frequency
Hypertext
Mass media
Morse code
Paperless
Royal Mail
Satellite
Snail mail
Telephone
Time-stamp

10 letters:
Beam aerial
Come across
Correspond
Dead letter
Degenerate
Fax machine
JavaScript
Media event
Memorandum
Multimedia
Netiquette
Silicon Fen
Ticker tape
Ultrafiche
Undirected

11 letters:
Address book
Chain letter

Communicate
Cryptograph
Dactylology
Mailing list
Mobile phone
Safe surfing
Silicon Glen

12 letters:
Cause célèbre
Conversation
Cryptography
Email address
Registration
Silicon Alley
Silver surfer

13 letters:
Bandspreading
Communication
Communicative
Correspondent
Cryptanalysis
Dead letter box
Dispatch rider
Online banking
Rural delivery
Satellite dish
Silicon Valley

14 letters:
Conversational
Correspondence
Electronic mail
Registered post

16 letters:
Recorded delivery

17 letters:
Branch instruction
Desktop
  publishing
General Post
  Office

18 letters:
Bottom-up
  processing
Exclusive OR
  circuit
Wireless
  networking

Compass and cardinal points

Compass and cardinal points

COMPASS POINTS

Name	Abbreviation
North	N
North by East	N by E
North North East	NNE
North East by North	NE by N
North East	NE
North East by East	NE by E
East North East	ENE
East by North	E by N
East	E
East by South	E by S
East South East	ESE
South East by East	SE by E
South East	SE
South East by South	SE by S
South South East	SSE
South by East	S by E
South	S
South by West	S by W
South South West	SSW
South West by South	SW by S
South West	SW
South West by West	SW by W
West South West	WSW
West by South	W by S
West	W
West by North	W by N
West North West	WNW
North West by West	NW by W
North West	NW
North West by North	NW by N
North North West	NNW
North by West	N by W

CARDINAL POINTS

Name	Related adjective
North	Arctic or boreal
East	Oriental
South	Meridional or austral
West	Occidental or hesperidan

Composers

CLASSICAL COMPOSERS

3 letters:
Bax, *Arnold*

4 letters:
Adam, *Adolphe*
Arne, *Thomas*
Bach, *Carl Philipp Emanuel*
Bach, *Johann Christian*
Bach, *Johann Christoph Friedrich*
Bach, *Johann Sebastian*
Bach, *Wilhelm Friedemann*
Berg, *Alban*
Blow, *John*
Bull, *John*
Byrd, *William*
Cage, *John*
Dima, *Gheorghe*
Ives, *Charles*
Lalo, *Édouard*
Nono, *Luigi*
Orff, *Carl*
Pärt, *Arvo*
Peri, *Jacopo*
Raff, *Joachim*
Ward, *David*
Weir, *Judith*
Wolf, *Hugo*

5 letters:
Adams, *John*
Alwyn, *William*
Auber, *Daniel François Espirit*
Auric, *Georges*
Balfe, *Michael William*
Berio, *Luciano*
Biber, *Heinrich*
Bizet, *Georges*
Bliss, *Arthur*
Bloch, *Ernest*
Boito, *Arrigo*
Boyce, *William*
Brian, *Havergal*
Bruch, *Max*
Crumb, *George*
D'Indy, *Vincent*
Dukas, *Paul*
Dupré, *Marcel*

Dutch, *Jan Pieterszoon Sweelinck*
Elgar, *Edward*
Fauré, *Gabriel*
Field, *John*
Finzi, *Gerald*
Glass, *Philip*
Gluck, *Christoph Willibald*
Grieg, *Edvard*
Harty, *Sir (Herbert) Hamilton*
Haydn, *Franz Joseph*
Haydn, *Michael*
Henze, *Hans Werner*
Holst, *Gustav*
Ibert, *Jacques*
Jones, *Daniel*
Lawes, *Henry*
Lawes, *William*
Lehár, *Franz*
Liszt, *Franz*
Lloyd, *George*
Locke, *Matthew*
Loewe, *Karl*
Lully, *Jean Baptiste*
Nyman, *Michael*
Ogdon, *John*
Parry, *Hubert*
Prout, *Ebenezer*
Ravel, *Maurice*
Reger, *Max*
Reich, *Steve*
Rieti, *Vittorio*
Rossi, *Luigi*
Satie, *Erik*
Smyth, *Ethel*
Sousa, *John Philip*
Suppe, *Franz von*
Tosti, *Francesco Paolo*
Verdi, *Giuseppi*
Watts, *Isaac*

6 letters:
Alfven, *Hugo*
Arnold, *Malcolm*
Azione
Barber, *Samuel*
Bartók, *Béla*

Composers

Boulez, *Pierre*
Brahms, *Johannes*
Bridge, *Frank*
Burney, *Charles*
Busoni, *Ferruccioni*
Carter, *Eliot*
Carver, *Robert*
Casals, *Pablo*
Chopin, *Frédéric*
Clarke, *Jeremiah*
Coates, *Eric*
Czerny, *Karl*
Davies, *Peter Maxwell*
Delius, *Frederick*
Doráti, *Antal*
Duparc, *Henri*
Dvořák, *Antonín*
Enesco, *Georges*
Farmer, *John*
Flotow, *Friedrich Freiherr von*
Franck, *César*
German, *Sir Edward*
Glière, *Reinhold*
Glinka, *Mikhail Ivanovich*
Gounod, *Charles François*
Gurney, *Ivor*
Halévy, *Fromental*
Handel, *George Frederick*
Harris, *Roy*
Hummel, *Johann Nepomuk*
Joplin, *Scott*
Kodály, *Zoltán*
Lassus, *Orlandus*
Ligeti, *György*
Mahler, *Gustav*
Martin, *Frank*
Mingus, *Charles*
Morley, *Thomas*
Mozart, *Leopold*
Mozart, *Wolfgang Amadeus*
Ogolon
Rameau, *Jean Philippe*
Rubbra, *Edmund*
Schütz, *Heinrich*
Straus, *Oscar*
Tallis, *Thomas*
Thomas, *Ambroise*
Varèse, *Edgar*
Varèse, *Edgard*
Wagner, *Richard*
Walton, *William*

Webern, *Anton*

7 letters:
Albéniz, *Isaac*
Allegri, *Gregorio*
Antheil, *George*
Bantock, *Granville*
Bellini, *Vincenzo*
Bennett, *Richard Rodney*
Berlioz, *Hector*
Berners, *Gerald*
Borodin, *Aleksandr Porfirevich*
Britten, *Benjamin*
Brubeck, *Dave (David Warren)*
Copland, *Aaron*
Corelli, *Arcangelo*
Debussy, *Claude*
De Falla, *Manuel*
Delibes, *Léo*
De Lisle, *Claude Joseph Rouget*
Des Prés, *Josquin*
Di Lasso, *Orlando*
Dowland, *John*
Duruflé, *Maurice*
Gibbons, *Orlando*
Górecki, *Henryk*
Ireland, *John*
Janáček, *Leoš*
Joachim, *Joseph*
Knussen, *Oliver*
Krommer, *Franz*
Kubelik, *Raphael*
Lambert, *Constant*
Lutyens, *Elisabeth*
Martinů, *Bohuslav*
Menotti, *Gian Carlo*
Milhaud, *Darius*
Nicolai, *Carl Otto Ehrenfried*
Nielsen, *Carl*
Poulenc, *Francis*
Puccini, *Giacomo*
Purcell, *Henry*
Purnell, *Alton*
Quilter, *Roger*
Rodrigo, *Joaquín*
Romberg, *Sigmund*
Rossini, *Gioacchino Antonio*
Roussel, *Albert*
Salieri, *Antonio*
Schuman, *William*

Simpson, *Robert*
Smetana, *Bedřich*
Stainer, *John*
Strauss, *Johann*
Strauss, *Richard*
Tartini, *Giuseppe*
Tavener, *John*
Thomson, *Virgil*
Tippett, *Michael*
Vivaldi, *Antonio*
Warlock, *Peter*
Weelkes, *Thomas*
Wellesz, *Egon*
Xenakis, *Yannis*

8 letters:

Alaleona, *Domenico*
Albinoni, *Tomaso*
Benjamin, *Arthur*
Berkeley, *Lennox*
Bonporti, *Francesco Antonio*
Bruckner, *Anton*
Chabrier, *Emmanuel*
Chausson, *Ernest*
Cimarosa, *Domenico*
Couperin, *François*
De Lassus, *Roland*
Gabrieli, *Andrea*
Gabrieli, *Giovanni*
Gershwin, *George*
Gesualdo, *Carlo*
Glazunov, *Aleksandr
  Konstantinovich*
Goossens, *Eugene*
Grainger, *Percy*
Granados, *Enrique*
Holliger, *Heinz*
Honegger, *Arthur*
Korngold, *Erich*
Kreutzer, *Conradin*
Maconchy, *Elizabeth*
Marcello, *Benedetto*
Marenzio, *Luca*
Martland, *Steve*
Mascagni, *Pietro*
Massenet, *Jules Émile Frédéric*
Messager, *André*
Messiaen, *Olivier*
Musgrave, *Thea*
Ockeghem, *Johannes*
Paganini, *Niccolò*

Panufnik, *Andrzej*
Respighi, *Ottorino*
Schnabel, *Artur*
Schubert, *Franz*
Schumann, *Clara*
Schumann, *Robert*
Scriabin, *Aleksandr Nikolayvich*
Sessions, *Roger*
Sibelius, *Jean*
Stanford, *Charles*
Taverner, *John*
Telemann, *Georg Philipp*
Von Weber, *Carl Maria*

9 letters:

Balakirev, *Mily Alexeyevich*
Bernstein, *Leonard*
Bocherini, *Luigi*
Boulanger, *Nadia*
Broughton, *Bruce*
Buxtehude, *Dietrich*
Carpenter, *John Alden*
Chaminade, *Cecile*
Cherubini, *Luigi*
De Machaut, *Guillaume*
Donizetti, *Gaetano*
Dunstable, *John*
Dutilleux, *Henri*
Ginastera, *Alberto*
Hildegard *of Bingen*
Hindemith, *Paul*
Klemperer, *Otto*
MacMillan, *James*
Meyerbeer, *Giacomo*
Offenbach, *Jacques*
Pachelbel, *Johann*
Pergolesi, *Giovanni Battista*
Prokofiev, *Sergei Sergeyevich*
Scarlatti, *Alessandro*
Scarlatti, *Domenico*
Schnittke, *Alfred*
Takemitsu, *Toru*
Tortelier, *Paul*
Von Flotow, *Friedrich*
Whitehead, *Gillian*
Zemlinsky, *Alexander*

10 letters:

Birtwistle, *Harrison*
Canteloube, *Joseph*
De Victoria, *Tomás Luis*
Monteverdi, *Claudio*

Composers

Mussorgsky, *Modest Petrovich*
Paderewski, *Ignace Jan*
Palestrina, *Giovanni Pierluigi da*
Penderecki, *Krzystof*
Ponchielli, *Amilcare*
Praetorius, *Michael*
Rawsthorne, *Alan*
Rubinstein, *Anton Grigorevich*
Saint-Saëns, *Camille*
Schoenberg, *Arnold*
Sculthorpe, *Peter*
Stravinsky, *Igor Fyodorovich*
Villa-Lobos, *Heitor*
Williamson, *Malcolm*

11 letters:
Butterworth, *George*
Charpentier, *Gustave*
Charpentier, *Marc-Antoine*
Frescobaldi, *Girolamo*
Fürtwangler, *Wilhelm*
Humperdinck, *Englebert*
Leoncavallo, *Ruggiero*
Lutosławski, *Witold*
Mendelssohn, *Fanny*
Mendelssohn, *Felix*

Rachmaninov, *Sergei Vassilievich*
Stockhausen, *Karlheinz*
Szymanowski, *Karol*
Tchaikovsky, *Pyotr Ilyich*
Theodorakis, *Mikis*
Von Dohnányi, *Ernst*
Wolf-Ferrari, *Ermanno*

12 letters:
Dallapiccola, *Luigi*
Khachaturian, *Aram Ilich*
Rostropovich, *Mstislav Leopoldovich*
Shostakovich, *Dmitri Dmitriyevich*
Van Beethoven, *Ludwig*

14 letters:
Jaques-Dalcroze, *Émile*
Rimsky-Korsakov, *Nikolai Andreyevich*

15 letters:
Coleridge-Taylor, *Samuel*
Vaughan Williams, *Ralph*

POPULAR COMPOSERS, SONGWRITERS, AND LYRICISTS

4 letters:
Baez, *Joan*
Bart, *Lionel*
Brel, *Jacques*
Cahn, *Sammy*
Duke, *Vernon*
Hart, *Lorenz*
John, *Elton*
Kern, *Jerome (David)*
King, *Carole*
Mann, *Barry*
Monk, *Thelonious (Sphere)*
Rice, *Tim*
Webb, *Jimmy*
Weil, *Cynthia*

5 letters:
Arlen, *Harold*
Barry, *John*
Bowie, *David*
Brown, *Nacio Herb*
Cohan, *George*
Cohen, *Leonard*

Dixon, *Willie*
Dylan, *Bob*
Handy, *W(illiam) C(hristopher)*
Jarre, *Maurice*
Jobim, *Antonio Carlos*
Loewe, *Frederick*
Pomus, *Doc*
Shore, *Howard*
Simon, *Paul*
Styne, *Jule*
Waits, *Tom*
Weill, *Kurt*

6 letters:
Berlin, *Irving*
Coward, *Noel*
Dozier, *Lamont*
Foster, *Stephen*
Goffin, *Gerry*
Herman, *Jerry*
Jagger, *Mick*
Lehrer, *Tom*
Lennon, *John*

Lerner, *Alan Jay*
Lieber, *Jerry*
McColl, *Ewan*
McColl, *Kirsty*
McHugh, *Jimmy*
Nelson, *Willie*
Porter, *Cole*
Strong, *Barrett*
Warren, *Harry*
Wilson, *Brian*

7 letters:
Gilbert, *W(illiam) S(chwenck)*
Guthrie, *Woody*
Holland, *Brian*
Holland, *Eddie*
Johnson, *Robert*
Loesser, *Frank*
Mancini, *Henry*
Manilow, *Barry*
Novello, *Ivor*
Rodgers, *Richard*
Romberg, *Sigmund*
Stoller, *Mike*
Youmans, *Vincent*

8 letters:
Gershwin, *George*
Hamlisch, *Marvin*
Mitchell, *Joni*

Morrison, *Van*
Richards, *Keith*
Robinson, *William 'Smokey'*
Sondheim, *Stephen*
Sullivan, *Arthur*
Williams, *Hank*
Williams, *John*

9 letters:
Bacharach, *Burt*
Bernstein, *Leonard*
Ellington, *Duke*
Goldsmith, *Jerry*
Ledbetter, *Huddie 'Leadbelly'*
McCartney, *Paul*
Strayhorn, *Billy*
Toussaint, *Allen*
Van Heusen, *Johnny*
Whitfield, *Norman*

10 letters:
Carmichael, *Hoagy*
Goldenthal, *Elliot*
Livingston, *Jay*

11 letters:
Hammerstein, *Oscar*
Lloyd-Webber, *Andrew*

13 letters:
Kristofferson, *Kris*

Compounds

3 letters:
Azo

4 letters:
Alum
EDTA
Enol
Haem
Heme
TEPP
Urea

5 letters:
Allyl
Amide
Amino
Azide
Azine

Azole
Diazo
Diene
Dimer
Diode
Erbia
Ester
Furan
Halon
Imide
Imine
Lipid
Olein
Oxide
Oxime
Potin
Pyran

Sarin
Tabun
Thiol
Trona
Vinyl

6 letters:
Acetal
Alkane
Alkene
Arsine
Baryta
Borane
Calque
Cetane
Chrome
Cresol
Epimer

Compounds

Fluate
Glycol
Halide
Haloid
Hexene
Isatin
Isomer
Ketone
Lithia
Niello
Phenol
Pinene
Potash
Purine
Pyrone
Retene
Silane
Speiss
Tartar
Tetryl
Thymol
Triene
Trimer
Uranyl

7 letters:
Acetone
Acridin
Aglycon
Ammonia
Benzene
Betaine
Bromide
Caliche
Calomel
Camphor
Carbide
Chelate
Choline
Cinerin
Creatin
Cumarin
Cyanide
Diamine
Diazine
Diazole
Dioxide
Dvandva
Epoxide
Erinite
Ethanol

Eugenol
Fenuron
Flavone
Hormone
Hydrate
Hydride
Indican
Indoxyl
Lactate
Menthol
Metamer
Monomer
Nitrite
Oxazine
Peptone
Polymer
Protein
Quassia
Quinoid
Quinone
Realgar
Skatole
Steroid
Sulfide
Syncarp
Taurine
Terpene
Toluene
Tritide
Uridine
Wolfram

8 letters:
Acridine
Aglycone
Aldehyde
Alizarin
Arginine
Butyrate
Catenane
Chloride
Chromene
Coenzyme
Coumarin
Creatine
Cyanogen
Datolite
Dieldrin
Dopamine
Farnesol
Fluoride

Glycogen
Hydroxyl
Indoform
Isologue
Ketoxime
Lecithin
Massicot
Melamine
Monoxide
Pentosan
Peroxide
Piperine
Ptomaine
Pyrazole
Rock-alum
Rotenone
Selenate
Silicide
Siloxane
Sodamide
Stilbene
Sulphide
Sulphone
Tautomer
Tetroxid
Thiazide
Thiazine
Thiazole
Thiotepa
Thiourea
Titanate
Triazine
Triazole
Trilling
Tyramine
Urethane
Xanthate
Xanthine
Zirconia

9 letters:
Aflatoxin
Alicyclic
Aliphatic
Anhydride
Biguanide
Carbazole
Carnitine
Cellulose
Cementite
Cortisone

Deuteride
Dipeptide
Disulfram
Endorshin
Ferrocene
Flavanone
Glycoside
Guanosine
Haematein
Histamine
Hydrazide
Hydroxide
Imidazole
Impsonite
Ionophore
Monoamine
Pentoxide
Phenoxide
Pheromone
Phosphide
Piperonal
Polyamine
Porphyrin
Qinghaosu
Quercetus
Quinoline
Serotonin
Tetroxide

Veratrine

10 letters:
Amphoteric
Argyrodite
Dimethoate
Disulphide
Enkephalin
Isocyanate
Lumisterol
Mercaptide
Nucleoside
Phenocaine
Picrotoxin
Piperazine
Piperidine
Propionate
Putrescine
Tatpurusha
Thimerosal
Tocopherol

11 letters:
Acetanilide
Amphetamine
Coprosterol
Dimercaprol
Electrolyte
Fluorescein

Computer games

Ghitathione
Hydrocarbon
Neostigmine
Sesquioxide

12 letters:
Carbohydrate
Formaldehyde
Haematoxylin
Hydroquinone
Permanganate
Polyurethane
Triglyceride
Trimethadine

13 letters:
Catecholamine
Cycloheximide
Isoproterenol
Metronidazole
Nortriptyline
Trinucleotide

14 letters:
Oxyhaemoglobin
Polycarboxylic
Polyunsaturate
Trohalomethane

Computer games

Computer games

3 letters:
Jak

4 letters:
Doom
Halo

6 letters:
Driver
Far Cry

7 letters:
RockMan
Top Spin

8 letters:
Half-Life
Max Payne
Ragnarok
Star Wars
Warcraft

Xenosaga

9 letters:
Ace Combat
Bejeweled
Guild Wars
Homeworld
Spy Hunter

10 letters:
Call of Duty
Dragon Fire
Fight Night
Fire Emblem
Primal Rage
Redemption
Terminator

11 letters:
Ghost Master

Ninja Gaiden

12 letters:
Age of Wonders
Apocalyptica
City of Heroes
Return to Arms
Viewtiful Joe

13 letters:
Rise of Nations

14 letters:
Ace Yeti Trapper
Ancient Empires
Backyard Skater
Beyond Divinity
Grand Theft Auto
Massive Assault
Prince of Persia

Computers

Computers

COMPUTER PARTS

COMPUTER TERMS

2 letters:
AI
I/O
IT
PC

3 letters:
Bit
Bpi
Bug
Bus
CAD
CAE
CAI
CAL
CAM
CAT
CBT
CIM
COL
COM
DAC
DMA
DOS®
Dpi
DTP
FAT
FTP
Gif
ICL
IDE
Job
LAN
OCR
OEM
PDA
Pdf
RAM
ROM
Run
SAM
USB
WAN
WAP
XML

4 letters:
ADSL
Area

Bomb
Boot
Byte
Cast
CISC
Code
Data
Dump
Echo
Edit
Exit
File
Flag
Gate
Giga-
GIGO
Host
HTML
Icon
IKBS
ISDN
Jpeg
Kilo-
Load
Loop
Mega-
Menu
Midi
Mpeg
Node
Open
PROM
RISC
SCSI
SGML
Sort
UNIX®
WIMP
Word
Worm

5 letters:
Array
ASCII
Brain
CD-Rom
Clock
Crash
Cyber

Cycle
Datel®
Digit
Earom
E-mail
Eniac
EPROM
ERNIE
Field
Flops
Fuzzy
Input
JANET
Key in
Log in
Macro
Micro
Patch
Pixel
Queue
Rerun
Reset
Sense
Stack
Store
Tally
Tower
Virus
Voxel
Warez

6 letters:
Access
Analog
Applet
Backup
Buffer
Bundle
Busbar
CADCAM
CADMAT
Caster
Cookie
Cursor
Device
Driver
Duplex
Earcon
EBCDIC

Computers

Editor
EEPROM
Figure
Hacker
Holmes
Hot key
Infect
Kludge
Laptop
Legacy
Linker
Log out
Module
Online
OR gate
Output
Packet
Parser
Prompt
Read in
Reboot
Record
Scroll
Server
Sprite
String
SWITCH
Syntax
System
TAURUS
Toggle
Uptime
Window
Wizard

7 letters:
ActiveX
Address
AND gate
Capture
Chipset
Clip art
Command
Corrupt
Counter
Databus
Default
Desktop
Digital
Freenet
Gateway

Install
Keyword
Lapheld
Manager
Measure
Network
NOR gate
NOT gate
Numlock
Offline
Package
Palette
Palmtop
Pointer
Power up
Process
Program
Read out
Routine
Run time
Time out
Utility
Vaccine
WYSIWIG
Wysiwyg

8 letters:
Analogue
Assemble
Autosave
Backbone
Beta-test
Black box
Calculus
Checksum
Chiphead
Compiler
Constant
Data bank
Database
Digitize
Document
Download
Downsize
Down time
Emulator
Estimate
Extranet
Fail-safe
Filename
Firewall

FireWire
Firmware
Freeware
Function
Gigabyte
Graphics
Hard card
Hard copy
Hardware
Idle time
Internet
Intranet
Kilobyte
Language
Liveware
Location
Megabyte
Morphing
NAND gate
Optimize
Overflow
Password
Platform
Portable
Printout
Protocol
Pushdown
Realtime
Reckoner
Skinning
Software
TALISMAN
Terabyte
Terminal
Topology
Tristate
Variable
Wild card

9 letters:
Algorithm
Alpha-test
Assembler
Authoring
Bandwidth
Bluetooth
Bootstrap
Broadband
Bus master
Calculate
Character

Co-routine
Cybercafé
Cyberpunk
Debugging
Directory
Dithering
Dot matrix
Ecommerce
Flowchart
Groupware
Handshake
Hard-wired
Hypertext
Interface
Interrupt
Logic bomb
Mainframe
Multi-user
Parameter
Power down
Procedure
Processor
Retrieval
Shareware
Smart card
Statement
Tetrabyte
Trackball
Underflow
User group

10 letters:
3D graphics
Access time
Address bus
Compatible
Core memory
Cyberspace
Encryption
Fileserver
Hypermedia
Initialize
Integrator
Linked list
Main memory
Menu-driven
Patch board
Programmer
README file
Robustness
Scratchpad

Stand-alone
Subroutine
Throughput
Transcribe
Translator
Transputer
Voice input
Webcasting

11 letters:
Antialising
Base address
Binary digit
Bits per inch
Cache memory
Clickstream
Computerate
Computerize
Concordance
Cut and paste
Cybernetics
Data capture
Dots per inch
File manager
Function key
Help screens
Input device
Input/output
Instruction
Interactive
Interpreter
Machine code
Mail bombing
Multiaccess
NAND circuit
Parity check
Screensaver
Spreadsheet
Superserver
Systems disk
Time sharing
Trackerball
Work station

12 letters:
Architecture
Backing store
Digital fount
Disassembler
Dumb terminal
Error message
Expert system

Global search
Housekeeping
Logic circuit
Minicomputer
Mobile device
Remote access
Reserved word
Search engine
Shell program
Telesoftware
World Wide Web

13 letters:
Audio response
Bulletin board
Configuration
Data structure
Decision table
Escape routine
Expansion slot
Memory mapping
Microcomputer
Multi-threaded
Neurocomputer
Object program
Query language
Queuing theory
Source program
Storage device
Supercomputer
Turnkey system
Virtual memory
Voice response
Word processor

14 letters:
Binary notation
Communications
Condition codes
Cross assembler
Data processing
Data protection
Digital imaging
Digital mapping
Document reader
Electronic mail
Hybrid computer
Magnetic bubble
Microprocessor
Neural computer
Number-cruncher
Plug compatible

Computers

Read only memory
Source document
Teleprocessing
Text processing
User-defined key
Virtual address
Virtual reality
Virtual storage
Volatile memory
Web development

15 letters:
Absolute address
Archival storage
Automatic repeat
Batch processing
Command language
Computer science
Control commands
Digital computer
Fifth-generation
Machine learning
Machine readable
Operating system
Packet-switching
Palmtop computer
Storage capacity
Store and forward
Systems analysis

16 letters:
Analogue computer
Assembly language
Computer graphics
Digital watermark
Distributed logic
Electronic office
Hand-held computer
Image enhancement
Interactive video
Local area network
Logic programming
Low-level language
Multiprogramming
Notebook computer
Personal computer
Program generator
Program statement
Sequential access
Serial processing
Voice recognition

17 letters:
Branch instruction
Desktop publishing
Development system
Front-end processor
High-level language
Speech recognition
Top-down processing
Visual programming

18 letters:
Application program
Bottom-up processing
Database management
Direct memory access
Exclusive OR circuit
Incremental plotter
Machine translation
Parallel processing
Random access memory
Real-time processing
Serial access memory

19 letters:
Computer-aided design
Computer typesetting
Direct-access storage
Disk operating system®
Hexadecimal notation
Incremental recorder
Intelligent terminal
Polymorphic function
Programming language
Random-access storage
Software engineering

20 letters:
Computer aided trading
Computer conferencing
Concurrent processing
Dataflow architecture
Electronic publishing
File transfer protocol
Restricted users group

21 letters:
Computer-aided learning
Computer-aided teaching
Computer-based training
Decision support system
Information technology

22 letters:
Artificial intelligence
Graphical user interface

23 letters:
Computer-aided management

24 letters:
Computer-aided engineering
Computer-aided instruction
Computer-aided manufacture
Computer-assisted learning
Computer input on microfilm

25 letters:
Distributed array processor
Windows icons menus pointers

26 letters:
Programmable read only memory

28 letters:
Random Instruction Set Computer

29 letters:
Complex instruction set computer
Computer integrated manufacture
Original equipment manufacturer
Reduced instruction set computer
Small Computer Systems Interface

31 letters:
Intelligent knowledge-based system

32 letters:
Floating-point operations per second

33 letters:
Computer-aided design and manufacture

34 letters:
Electronic flight information systems

41 letters:
Extended binary-coded decimal-interchange code

COMPUTER SCIENTISTS

4 letters:
Cray, *Seymour*

5 letters:
Aiken, *Howard*
Gates, *Bill*

6 letters:
Eckert, *John Presper*

Turing, *Alan Mathison*

7 letters:
Babbage, *Charles*
Mauchly, *John W.*

8 letters:
Lovelace, *Ada (Countess of)*
Sinclair, *Clive*

Confectionery

Confectionery

3 letters:
Gem
Gum

4 letters:
Jube
Kiss
Mint
Rock

5 letters:
Candy
Dolly
Fudge
Halva
Lolly
Taffy

6 letters:
Bonbon
Button
Cachou
Comfit
Confit
Dainty
Dragée
Halvah
Humbug
Jujube
Nougat
Sorbet
Sundae
Tablet

Toffee

7 letters:
Brittle
Caramel
Fondant
Gumdrop
Halavah
Lozenge
Panocha
Praline
Sherbet
Truffle

8 letters:
Acid drop
All-sorts
Bull's eye
Licorice
Lollipop
Marzipan
Noisette
Pastille
Peardrop
Scroggin
Stickjaw

9 letters:
Blackball
Chocolate
Fruit drop
Jelly baby
Jelly bean

Lemon drop
Liquorice
Marchpane

10 letters:
Brandyball
Candyfloss
Chewing gum
Coconut ice
Gob-stopper
Nanaimo bar
Peppermint
Pick and mix
Soft-centre

11 letters:
Barley sugar
Boiled sweet
Marshmallow
Toffee apple

12 letters:
Burnt-almonds
Butterscotch

13 letters:
Fruit pastille

14 letters:
Turkish delight

20 letters:
Hundreds and
  thousands

Containers for liquids

3 letters:
Can
Jar
Jug

Keg
Tin

4 letters:
Cask

Tube

5 letters:
Flask
Gourd

Tinny

6 letters:
Barrel
Bottle
Carafe
Carton
Coldie
Firkin
Flagon
Magnum
Stubby

7 letters:
Amphora

Ampulla
Pitcher
Polypin

8 letters:
Decanter
Hogshead
Jeroboam
Rehoboam
Screw-top
Tantalus

9 letters:
Balthazar
Miniature

10 letters:
Half-bottle
Methuselah
Salmanazar

14 letters:
Nebuchadnezzar

Continents

4 letters:
Asia

6 letters:
Africa
Europe

9 letters:
Australia

10 letters:
Antarctica

12 letters:
North America
South America

Cookery

GENERAL COOKERY TERMS

3 letters:
Fry
Ice

4 letters:
Bake
Bard
Boil
Chef
Cook
Dice
Ghee
Jerk
Lard
Luau
Mash
Mask
Meze
Rise
Roux

Soup
Stew
Whip

5 letters:
Au jus
Barde
Baste
Broth
Cured
Dough
Farci
Flour
Fumet
Glacé
Glaze
Grate
Gravy
Grill
Icing

Knead
Ladle
Offal
Paste
Poach
Purée
Roast
Sauce
Sauté
Steam
Stock
Sweat
Tikka
Yeast

6 letters:
Au lait
Barbie
Batter
Blanch

Cookery

Braise
Coddle
Commis
Corned
Creole
Entrée
Fajita
Fillet
Flambé
Fondue
Goujon
Lardon
Leaven
Mornay
Panada
Potage
Ragout
Season
Sippet
Smoked

7 letters:
À la king
À la mode
Caterer
Cobbler
Cuisine
Curried
Custard
Garnish
Giblets
Goulash
Lardoon
Liaison
Marengo
Marmite
Newburg
Parboil

Rissole
Roulade
Supreme
Timbale
Topping

8 letters:
Au gratin
Barbecue
Browning
Chasseur
Colander
Consommé
Cookbook
Dressing
En croute
Gelatine
Julienne
Marinade
Marinate
Meunière
Mirepoix
Scramble
Tandoori
Teriyaki
Unsmoked

9 letters:
Antipasto
Au naturel
Blackened
Carbonado
Casserole
Char-grill
Cook-chill
Entremets
Fricassee
Lyonnaise
Macedoine

Oven-ready
Salipicon
Tenderize
Undressed
Wholemeal

10 letters:
Caramelise
Jardinière
Médaillons
Medallions
Parmentier
Provençale
Rijstaffel
Royal icing
Stroganoff
Unleavened
Wholewheat

11 letters:
Chafing dish
Cookery book
En brochette
Graham flour
Hors d'oeuvre

12 letters:
Boil-in-the-bag
Confectioner
Sweet-and-sour

13 letters:
Silver service

14 letters:
Cuisine minceur
Wholemeal flour

15 letters:
Nouvelle cuisine

CUISINES AND COOKING STYLES

4 letters:
Ital
Thai

5 letters:
Balti
Greek
Halal
Tapas
Vegan

6 letters:
French
Indian
Kosher
Tex-Mex

7 letters:
Chinese
Italian
Mexican
Seafood

Sichuan
Turkish

8 letters:
Fast food
Japanese
Szechuan

9 letters:
Cantonese
Caribbean

Malaysian
Provençal

10 letters:
Cordon bleu
Indonesian
Vegetarian

11 letters:
Californian

Home cooking

12 letters:
Haute cuisine

13 letters:
Gutbürgerlich
International
Mediterranean

14 letters:
Cuisine minceur

15 letters:
Nouvelle cuisine

Counties

ENGLISH COUNTIES

4 letters:
Kent

5 letters:
Devon
Essex

6 letters:
Dorset
Durham
Surrey

7 letters:
Bristol
Cumbria
Norfolk
Rutland
Suffolk

8 letters:
Cheshire
Cornwall
Somerset

9 letters:
Berkshire

Hampshire
Wiltshire

10 letters:
Derbyshire
East Sussex
Lancashire
Merseyside
Shropshire
West Sussex

11 letters:
Isle of Wight
Oxfordshire
Tyne and Wear

12 letters:
Bedfordshire
Lincolnshire
Warwickshire
West Midlands

13 letters:
Greater London
Herefordshire
Hertfordshire

Staffordshire
West Yorkshire

14 letters:
Cambridgeshire
Leicestershire
Northumberland
North Yorkshire
South Yorkshire
Worcestershire

15 letters:
Buckinghamshire
Gloucestershire
Nottinghamshire

16 letters:
Northamptonshire

17 letters:
Greater
  Manchester

21 letters:
East Riding of
  Yorkshire

FORMER ENGLISH COUNTIES

4 letters:
Kent

5 letters:
Devon
Essex

6 letters:
Dorset
Durham

Surrey

7 letters:
Norfolk
Rutland

8 letters:
Cheshire
Cornwall
Somerset

9 letters:
Berkshire
Hampshire
Wiltshire

10 letters:
Cumberland
Derbyshire
East Sussex

Counties

Lancashire
Shropshire
West Sussex

11 letters:
East Suffolk
Oxfordshire
Westmorland
West Suffolk

12 letters:
Bedfordshire
Lincolnshire
Warwickshire

13 letters:
East Yorkshire
Greater London
Herefordshire
Hertfordshire
Staffordshire
West Yorkshire

14 letters:
Leicestershire
Northumberland
North Yorkshire
Worcestershire

15 letters:
Buckinghamshire
Gloucestershire
Nottinghamshire

16 letters:
Northamptonshire

25 letters:
Huntingdon and
  Peterborough

26 letters:
Cambridgeshire
  and Isle of Ely

SCOTTISH COUNTIES

4 letters:
Fife

5 letters:
Angus
Moray

6 letters:
Orkney

7 letters:
Falkirk

8 letters:
Highland
Shetland
Stirling

10 letters:
Dundee City
Eilean Siar
Inverclyde
Midlothian

11 letters:
East Lothian
Glasgow City
West Lothian

12 letters:
Aberdeen City

East Ayrshire
Renfrewshire
Western Isles

13 letters:
Aberdeenshire
Argyll and Bute
North Ayrshire
South Ayrshire

15 letters:
City of Edinburgh
Perth and Kinross
Scottish Borders

16 letters:
Clackmannanshire
East Renfrewshire
North Lanarkshire
South Lanarkshire

18 letters:
East Dunbartonshire
West Dunbartonshire

19 letters:
Dumfries and Galloway

FORMER SCOTTISH COUNTIES

4 letters:
Bute
Fife

5 letters:
Angus
Banff
Moray
Nairn

6 letters:
Argyll
Dundee
Orkney

7 letters:
Glasgow
Kinross

8 letters:
Aberdeen
Ayrshire
Roxburgh
Shetland

9 letters:
Caithness
Edinburgh

10 letters:
Banffshire
Kincardine
Midlothian
Nairnshire

4 letters: (Perthshire column)
Perthshire
Sutherland

11 letters:
East Lothian
Lanarkshire
West Lothian

12 letters:
Berwickshire
Kinross-shire
Peeblesshire
Renfrewshire
Selkirkshire
Wigtownshire

13 letters:
Aberdeenshire
Dumfriesshire
Roxburghshire
Stirlingshire

14 letters:
Dunbartonshire
Inverness-shire

15 letters:
Kincardineshire
Ross and Cromarty

16 letters:
Clackmannanshire

18 letters:
Kirkcudbrightshire

WELSH COUNTIES (POST-1998)

5 letters:
Conwy
Powys

7 letters:
Cardiff
Gwynedd
Newport
Swansea
Torfaen
Wrexham

8 letters:
Anglesey
Bridgend

10 letters:
Caerphilly
Ceredigion
Flintshire

12 letters:
Blaenau Gwent
Denbighshire

13 letters:
Merthyr Tydfil
Monmouthshire
Pembrokeshire

15 letters:
Carmarthenshire

Countries

Neath Port Talbot
Vale of Glamorgan

16 letters:
Rhondda, Cynon, Taff

FORMER WELSH COUNTIES

5 letters:
Clwyd
Dyfed
Gwent
Powys

7 letters:
Gwynedd

12 letters:
Mid Glamorgan

13 letters:
West Glamorgan

14 letters:
South Glamorgan

NORTHERN IRISH COUNTIES

4 letters:
Down

6 letters:
Antrim

Armagh
Tyrone

9 letters:
Fermanagh

11 letters:

Londonderry

REPUBLIC OF IRELAND COUNTIES

4 letters:
Cork
Mayo

5 letters:
Cavan
Clare
Kerry
Laois
Louth
Meath
Sligo

6 letters:
Carlow
Dublin
Galway
Offaly

7 letters:
Donegal
Kildare
Leitrim
Wexford
Wicklow

8 letters:
Kilkenny
Limerick
Longford
Monaghan

9 letters:
Roscommon
Tipperary
Waterford
Westmeath

Countries

4 letters:
Chad
Cuba
Fiji
Iran
Iraq
Laos
Mali
Oman
Peru
Togo

5 letters:
Belau

Benin
Chile
Congo
Egypt
Gabon
Ghana
Haiti
India
Italy
Japan
Kenya
Libya
Malta
Nauru

Nepal
Niger
Qatar
Samoa
Spain
Sudan
Syria
Tonga
Wales
Yemen

6 letters:
Angola
Belize

Bhutan
Brazil
Brunei
Canada
Cyprus
France
Gambia
Greece
Guinea
Guyana
Israel
Jordan
Kuwait
Latvia
Malawi
Mexico
Monaco
Norway
Panama
Poland
Russia
Rwanda
Serbia
Sweden
Taiwan
Turkey
Tuvalu
Uganda
Zambia

7 letters:
Albania
Algeria
Andorra
Armenia
Austria
Bahamas
Bahrain
Belarus
Belgium
Bolivia
Burundi
Comoros
Croatia
Denmark
Ecuador
England
Eritrea
Estonia
Finland
Georgia

Germany
Grenada
Hungary
Iceland
Jamaica
Lebanon
Lesotho
Liberia
Moldova
Morocco
Myanmar
Namibia
Nigeria
Romania
Senegal
Somalia
St Lucia
Surinam
Tunisia
Ukraine
Uruguay
Vanuatu
Vietnam

8 letters:
Barbados
Botswana
Bulgaria
Cambodia
Cameroon
Colombia
Djibouti
Dominica
Ethiopia
Honduras
Kiribati
Malaysia
Mongolia
Pakistan
Paraguay
Portugal
Scotland
Slovakia
Slovenia
Sri Lanka
Tanzania
Thailand
Zimbabwe

9 letters:
Argentina
Australia

Cape Verde
Costa Rica
East Timor
Greenland
Guatemala
Indonesia
Kirghizia
Lithuania
Macedonia
Mauritius
Nicaragua
San Marino
Singapore
Swaziland
Venezuela

10 letters:
Azerbaijan
Bangladesh
El Salvador
Kazakhstan
Luxembourg
Madagascar
Mauritania
Micronesia
Montenegro
Mozambique
New Zealand
North Korea
Puerto Rico
Seychelles
South Korea
Tajikistan
Uzbekistan
Yugoslavia

11 letters:
Afghanistan
Burkina-Faso
Côte d'Ivoire
Netherlands
Philippines
Saudi Arabia
Sierra Leone
South Africa
Switzerland
Vatican City

12 letters:
Guinea-Bissau
Turkmenistan

Cows

13 letters:
American Samoa
Czech Republic
Liechtenstein
United Kingdom

14 letters:
Papua New Guinea
Solomon Islands

15 letters:
Marshall Islands
Northern Ireland
St Kitts and Nevis

16 letters:
Equatorial Guinea

17 letters:
Antigua and
 Barbuda
Dominican
 Republic
Republic of Ireland
Trinidad and
 Tobago

18 letters:
Republic of
 Maldives
São Tomé and
 Principe
United Arab
 Emirates

20 letters:
Bosnia and
 Herzegovina

21 letters:
United States of
 America

22 letters:
Central African
 Republic
People's Republic
 of China

25 letters:
St Vincent and the
 Grenadines

See also:
➤ **Commonwealth members** ➤ **Dependencies**
➤ **European Union** ➤ **Republics**

Cows

2 letters:
Zo

3 letters:
Dun
Zho

4 letters:
Zebu

5 letters:
Colly
Kyloe
Milch
Mooly

Muley
Stirk

6 letters:
Crummy
Dexter
Heifer
Jersey
Mulley
Rother

7 letters:
Kouprey
Redpoll

8 letters:
Alderney
Galloway
Guernsey
Hereford

9 letters:
Charolais
Red Sindhi
Simmental
Teeswater

11 letters:
Rother-beast

See also:
➤ **Cattle**

Crafts

5 letters:
Batik

6 letters:
Sewing

7 letters:
Crochet
Macramé
Pottery
Weaving

8 letters:
Basketry
Ceramics
Knitting
Knotwork

Quilling
Quilting
Spinning
Tapestry

9 letters:
Decoupage
Patchwork

10 letters:
Crewelwork
Embroidery
Raffia work
Sugarcraft
Wickerwork

11 letters:
Calligraphy

Cloisonnage
Dressmaking
Needlepoint

12 letters:
Basket-making

15 letters:
Flower arranging

Cricketers

3 letters:
Dev, *Kapil*
Fry, *C(harles) B(urgess)*
Lee, *Brett*
May, *Peter*

4 letters:
Ames, *Leslie*
Bird, *Harold 'Dicky'*
Boon, *David*
Hick, *Graham*
Khan, *Imran*
Lara, *Brian*
Lock, *Tony*
Snow, *John*
Vaas, *Chaminda*

5 letters:
Croft, *Colin*
Evans, *Godfrey*
Gooch, *Graham*
Gough, *Darren*
Gower, *David*
Grace, *W(illiam) G(ilbert)*
Greig, *Tony*
Hobbs, *Sir Jack*
Knott, *Alan*
Laker, *Jim*
Lloyd, *Clive Hubert*
Marsh, *Rodney*
Patil, *Sandeep Madhusuda*
Singh, *Harbhajan*
Smith, *M(ichael) J(ohn) K(night)*
Tyson, *Frank*
Walsh, *Courtney*
Warne, *Shane*
Waugh, *Mark*
Waugh, *Steve*

6 letters:
Akhtar, *Shoaib*
Bailey, *Trevor*
Barnes, *Sydney*
Benaud, *Richie*
Bishan, *Bedi*
Border, *Allan*
Botham, *Ian*
Cronje, *Hansie*
Dexter, *Ted*
Donald, *Allan*
Dravid, *Rahul*
Flower, *Andrew*
Garner, *Joel*
Hadlee, *Sir Richard*
Hayden, *Matthew*
Haynes, *Desmond*
Hutton, *Sir Len*
Kallis, *Jacques*
Kambli, *Vinod*
Kumble, *Anil*
Laxman, *V(angipurappu)
  V(enkata) S(ai)*
Lillee, *Dennis*
Loader, *Peter*
Mankad, *Mulvantrai Himatlal
  'Vinoo'*
McCabe, *Stanley*
Olonga, *Henry*
Rhodes, *Jonty*
Sehwag, *Virender*
Sobers, *Sir Garfield*
Styris, *Scott*
Thorpe, *Graham*
Turner, *Glenn*
Wardle, *Johnny*
Weekes, *Sir Everton*
Younis, *Waqar*

Cricket terms

7 letters:
Ambrose, *Curtly*
Boycott, *Geoffrey*
Bradman, *Sir Donald*
Compton, *Denis*
Cowdrey, *Sir Colin*
Fleming, *Stephen*
Ganguly, *Saurav*
Ganguly, *Sourav*
Gatting, *Mike*
Hammond, *Walter*
Hussein, *Nasser*
Jardine, *Douglas*
Larwood, *Harold*
McGrath, *Glenn*
Miandad, *Javed*
O'Reilly, *Bill*
Pollock, *Shaun*
Ponting, *Ricky*
Srinath, *Javagal*
Statham, *Brian*
Stewart, *Alec*
Thomson, *Jeffrey*
Trueman, *Fred*
Tufnell, *Phil*
Umrigar, *Pahelam Ratanji*
Vaughan, *Michael*
Wadekar, *Ajit Laxman*
Walcott, *Sir Clyde*
Worrell, *Sir Frank*

8 letters:
Amarnath, *Lala*
Amarnath, *Mohinder*
Amarnath, *Surinder*
Atherton, *Mike*
Brearley, *Michael*
Chappell, *Greg*
Chappell, *Ian*

Gavaskar, *Sunil*
Flintoff, *Andrew (Freddie)*
Graveney, *Tom*
Houghton, *Dave*
Lindwall, *Ray*
Marshall, *Malcolm*
Mohammad, *Hanif*
Richards, *Viv*

9 letters:
D'Oliveira, *Basil Lewis*
Gilchrist, *Adam*
Gillespie, *Jason*
Greenidge, *Gordon*
Manjrekar, *Sanjay Vijay*
Pieterson, *Kevin*
Ranatunga, *Arjuna*
Sutcliffe, *Herbert*
Tendulkar, *Sachin*
Underwood, *Derek*

10 letters:
Azharuddin, *Mohammed*
Barrington, *Ken*
Greatbatch, *Mark*
Jayasuriya, *Sanath*
Vengsarkar, *Dilip Balwant*

11 letters:
Heyhoe-Flint, *Rachel*
Trescothick, *Marcus*

12 letters:
Inzamam-ul-Haq
Muralitharan, *Muttiah*
Ranjitsinhji, *K(umar) S(hri)*

13 letters:
Chandrasekhar, *Bhagwat Subramaniam*

Cricket terms

2 letters:
In

3 letters:
Bat
Bye
Cut
Out

Pad
Run
Six

4 letters:
Bail
Ball
Bowl

Duck
Edge
Four
Hook
Over
Pull
Seam
Slip

Spin
Wide

5 letters:
Ashes
Catch
Drive
Extra
Glide
Gully
Mid on
Pitch
Stump
Sweep
Swing
Umpie

6 letters:
Appeal
Bowled
Bowler
Bumper
Caught
Covers
Crease
Glance
Googly
Leg bye
Long on
Maiden
Mid off

No ball
On side
Opener
Run out
Single
Umpire
Wicket
Yorker

7 letters:
Batsman
Bouncer
Century
Declare
Fielder
Fine leg
Innings
Leg side
Leg slip
Long leg
Long off
Off side
Stumped

8 letters:
Boundary
Chinaman
Follow on
Full toss
Leg break
Off break

Short leg
Third man

9 letters:
Fieldsman
Hit wicket
Mid wicket
Square leg
Test match

10 letters:
Cover point
Extra cover
Fast bowler
Maiden over
Silly mid on
Twelfth man

11 letters:
Silly mid off

12 letters:
Wicketkeeper

13 letters:
Nightwatchman

14 letters:
Opening batsman

15 letters:
Leg before wicket

Crime terms

2 letters:
Do
Go

3 letters:
Job
Rap
Sin

4 letters:
Abet
Gaol
Heat
Jail
Life
Rape
View

5 letters:
Admit
Alibi
Arson
Atone
Bribe
Caper
Cough
Crime
Do for
Fraud
Guilt
Panel
Remit
Steal
Sting

Theft
Thief

6 letters:
Acquit
Bigamy
Charge
Commit
Degree
Detect
Exposé
Felony
Finger
Guilty
Hijack
Incest
Indict

Crime terms

Infect
Murder
Piracy
Punish
Record
Turn in
Verbal
Wanted

7 letters:
Assault
Battery
Bribery
Burglar
Confess
Convict
Cover-up
Find out
Forgery
Impeach
Larceny
Mugging
Offence
Penance
Pentito
Perjury
Robbery
Soldier
Treason
Villain

8 letters:
Acqittal
Barratry
Burglary
Conspire
Criminal
Homicide
Infamous
Innocent
Litigate
Murderer
Offender
Penology
Poaching
Prisoner
Sabotage

Thriller
Tu quoque
War crime

9 letters:
Accessory
Admission
Blackmail
Blasphemy
Criminate
Desertion
Detective
Extortion
Guiltless
Hate crime
Implicate
Innocence
Inside job
Penal code
Pilfering
Principal
Red-handed
Terrorism
Vandalism
Whodunnit
Wrongdoer

10 letters:
Accomplice
Accusation
Bail bandit
Commission
Commitment
Conspiracy
Conviction
Corruption
Cybercrime
Delinquent
Entrapment
Indictable
Indictment
Kidnapping
Litigation
Misconduct
Perpetrate
Petty theft
Punishment

Recidivism

11 letters:
Conspirator
Criminology
Delinquency
Hooliganism
Incriminate
Infanticide
Investigate
Law-and-order
Lawlessness
Premeditate

12 letters:
Death penalty
Denunciation
Embezzlement
Extraditable
Life sentence
Manslaughter
Misadventure
Misdemeanour

13 letters:
Drug smuggling
Housebreaking
Identity theft
Premeditation
Reinvestigate
Transgression

15 letters:
Computer hacking
Crime passionnel
Victimless crime

16 letters:
Bill of indictment
Private detective

17 letters:
Capital punishment

19 letters:
Justifiable homicide

20 letters:
Identification
  parade

Crime writers

3 letters:
Poe, *Edgar Allan*

4 letters:
Vine, *Barbara*

5 letters:
Block, *Lawrence*
Doyle, *Arthur Conan*
James, *P(hyllis) D(orothy)*

6 letters:
Rankin, *Ian*
Sayers, *Dorothy L(eigh)*

7 letters:
Bateman, *Colin*
Grisham, *John*
Hiaasen, *Carl*
Rendell, *Ruth*
Simenon, *Georges (Joseph Christian)*

Wallace, *Edgar (Richard Horatio)*

8 letters:
Chandler, *Raymond*
Christie, *Dame Agatha (Mary Clarissa)*
Connelly, *Michael*
Connolly, *John*
Cornwell, *Patricia*

9 letters:
Brookmyre, *Christopher*
Highsmith, *Patricia*

10 letters:
Wiesenthal, *Simon*

Critics

4 letters:
Frye, *Northrop*
Ross, *Jonathan*
Said, *Edward*
Self, *Will*
Shaw, *George Bernard*

5 letters:
Bloom, *Harold*
Booth, *Wayne*
Burke, *Kenneth*
Carey, *John*
De Man, *Paul*
Greer, *Bonnie*
Greer, *Germaine*
Hegel, *Georg W(ilhelm) F(riedrich)*
Lodge, *David (John)*
Plato
Ronay, *Egon*
Tynan, *Kenneth*
Weber, *Max*
Woolf, *(Adeline) Virginia*

6 letters:
Barker, *Harley Granville*
Berlin, *Isaiah*
Bhabha, *Homi K.*
Brooks, *Cleanth*
Clarke, *Oz*
Horace
Lawson, *Mark*
Leavis, *F(rank) R(aymond)*
Milnes, *Rodney*
Morley, *Paul*
Norman, *Barry*
Norman, *Emma*
Orwell, *George*
Parker, *Dorothy*
Paulin, *Tom*
Ruskin, *John*
Sartre, *Jean-Paul*
Sewell, *Brian*
Sontag, *Susan*

7 letters:
Bakhtin, *Mikhail*
Barthes, *Roland*

Crosses

Carlyle, *Thomas*
Chomsky, *Noam*
Derrida, *Jacques*
Forster, *E(dward) M(organ)*
Goolden, *Jilly*
Kermode, *Frank*
Nabokov, *Vladimir (Vladimirovich)*

8 letters:
Benjamin, *Walter*
Bradbury, *Malcolm*
Eagleton, *Terry*
Foucault, *Michel*
Longinus
Plotinus

Sedgwick, *Eve Kosofsky*

9 letters:
Aristotle
Showalter, *Elaine*
Winterson, *Jeanette*

10 letters:
De Beauvoir, *Simone*
Greenblatt, *Stephen*
Lewis-Smith, *Victor*

11 letters:
Bogdanovich, *Peter*

12 letters:
Wittgenstein, *Ludwig*

Crosses

3 letters:
Red
Tau

4 letters:
Ankh
Crux
Iona
Iron
Rood
Tree

5 letters:
Fiery
Greek
Latin
Papal
Pommé
Rouen

6 letters:
Ansate
Barbée
Botone
Celtic
Chiasm
Fitché
Fleury
Fylfot
Geneva
George

Graded (Calvary)
Moline
Pattée
Potent
Raguly
Trefly

7 letters:
Botonne
Calvary
Chiasma
Eleanor
Maltese
Patonce
Potence
Rarulée
Saltier
Saltire

8 letters:
Cercelée
Crosslet
Crucifix
Globical
Holy rood
Lorraine
Military
Millvine
Pectoral
Quadrate
Southern

St Peter's
Svastika
Swastika
Victoria

9 letters:
Encolpion
Jerusalem
St Andrew's
St George's

10 letters:
Canterbury
Clover-leaf
Crux ansata
St Anthony's

11 letters:
Constantine
Patriarchal

12 letters:
Pattée formée

13 letters:
Cross crosslet

14 letters:
Archiepiscopal

15 letters:
Russian Orthodox

Crustaceans

4 letters:
Crab
Craw

5 letters:
Koura
Krill
Prawn

6 letters:
Cyprid
Cypris
Isopod
Marron
Scampi
Scampo
Shrimp
Slater

7 letters:
Camaron
Copepod
Cyclops
Decapod
Foot-jaw
Gribble
Lobster
Macrura
Squilla

8 letters:
Amphipod

Barnacle
Cirriped
Cirripid
Crawfish
Crayfish
Cumacean
Decapoda
King crab
Land crab
Nauplius
Pagurian
Sand flea
Scorpion

9 letters:
Beach flea
Cirripede
Euphausia
Fishlouse
King prawn
Langouste
Ostracoda
Phyllopod
Schizopod
Sea spider
Water flea
Woodlouse

10 letters:
Brachyuran
Cladoceran

Hermit crab
Oyster crab
Robber crab
Sand hopper
Sand shrimp
Spider crab
Stomatopod

11 letters:
Langoustine
Rock lobster

12 letters:
Branchiopoda
Entomostraca
Spiny lobster

13 letters:
Goose barnacle
Horseshoe crab
Malacostracan
Norway lobster
Opossum shrimp
Rhizocephalan
Soft-shell crab

14 letters:
Dublin Bay prawn

16 letters:
Freshwater shrimp

Crystals

4 letters:
Lead
Rock
Spar

5 letters:
Beryl
Druse
Glass
Macle
Nicol
Prism
Purin

6 letters:
Liquid
Purine
Quartz

7 letters:
Baccara
Cumarin
Epitaxy

8 letters:
Baccarat
Coumarin
Dendrite

Jarosite
Melamine
Pinacoid
Pinakoid
Sorbitol
Trichite
Trilling

9 letters:
Hemitrope
Love-arrow
Rubicelle
Snowflake
Xenocryst

Cupboards and cabinets

10 letters:
Phenocryst
Rhinestone

Watch-glass

12 letters:
Enantiomorph

15 letters:
Allotriomorphic

Cupboards and cabinets

4 letters:
Safe

5 letters:
Ambry
Chest
Press
Shelf
Stand

6 letters:
Buffet
Bureau
Closet
Dooket
Drawer
Larder
Locker

Lowboy
Pantry

7 letters:
Armoire
Cabinet
Commode
Console
Dresser

Cups and other drinking vessels

3 letters:
Cup
Mug
Nut
Pot
Tig
Tot
Tyg

4 letters:
Dish
Horn

5 letters:
Calix
Cruse
Cylix
Glass
Hanap
Kylix
Tazza

6 letters:
Beaker
Copita
Cotyle
Fingan
Finjan
Goblet
Loving
Noggin
Porrón
Quaich
Rhyton
Tassie

7 letters:
Canteen
Chalice
Cyathus
Scyphus
Stirrup
Tankard

Tea-dish
Tumbler

8 letters:
Pannikin
Schooner
Tantalus
Tastevin

9 letters:
Cantharus
Demitasse
Moustache

10 letters:
Monstrance

11 letters:
Water bottle

14 letters:
Champagne flute

Cups and trophies

2 letters:
FA

4 letters:
UEFA

5 letters:
Davis
Fairs
Rider
Ryder

World

8 letters:
America's
Calcutta
European

Étagère
Highboy
Tallboy
Vitrine
Whatnot

8 letters:
Bookcase
Cellaret
Credenza
Wardrobe

9 letters:
Garderobe
Sideboard

10 letters:
Canterbury
Chiffonier

11 letters:
Chiffonnier

12 letters:
Chest-on-chest

Clothes-press
Welsh dresser

13 letters:
Court cupboard
Credence table
Filing cabinet
Medicine chest

14 letters:
Chest of drawers
Coolgardie safe

Currencies

Country	Currency
Afghanistan	Afghani
Albania	Lek
Algeria	Algerian dinar
Andorra	Euro
Angola	Kwanza
Antigua and Barbuda	East Caribbean dollar
Argentina	Peso
Armenia	Dram
Australia	Australian dollar
Austria	Euro
Azerbaijan	Manat
Bahamas	Bahamian dollar
Bahrain	Dinar
Bangladesh	Taka
Barbados	Barbados dollar
Belarus	Rouble
Belgium	Euro
Belize	Belize dollar
Benin	CFA franc
Bhutan	Ngultrum
Bolivia	Boliviano
Bosnia-Herzegovina	Convertible marka
Botswana	Pula
Brazil	Real
Brunei	Brunei dollar
Bulgaria	Lev
Burkina-Faso	CFA franc
Burundi	Burundi franc
Cambodia	Riel
Cameroon	CFA franc
Canada	Canadian dollar
Cape Verde	Escudo
Central African Republic	CFA franc
Chad	CFA franc

Currencies

Country	Currency
Chile	Peso
China	Yuan
Colombia	Peso
Comoros	Comorian franc
Congo (Democratic Republic of)	Congolese franc
Congo (Republic of)	CFA franc
Costa Rica	Cólon
Côte d'Ivoire	CFA franc
Croatia	Kuna
Cuba	Peso
Cyprus	Pound
Czech Republic	Koruna
Denmark	Krone
Djibouti	Djibouti franc
Dominica	East Caribbean dollar
Dominican Republic	Peso
East Timor	US dollar
Ecuador	US dollar
Egypt	Pound
El Salvador	Cólon
Equatorial Guinea	CFA franc
Eritrea	Nakfa
Estonia	Kroon
Ethiopia	Birr
Fiji	Fiji dollar
Finland	Euro
France	Euro
French Guiana	French franc
Gabon	CFA franc
Gambia	Dalasi
Germany	Euro
Ghana	Cedi
Greece	Euro
Greenland	Danish krone
Grenada	East Caribbean dollar
Guatemala	Quetzal
Guinea	Guinea franc
Guinea-Bissau	CFA franc
Guyana	Guyana dollar
Haiti	Gourde
Honduras	Lempira
Hungary	Forint
Iceland	Krona
India	Rupee
Indonesia	Rupiah
Iran	Rial
Iraq	Dinar
Ireland (Republic of)	Euro
Israel	Shekel
Italy	Euro

Country	Currency
Jamaica	Jamaican dollar
Japan	Yen
Jordan	Dinar
Kazakhstan	Tenge
Kenya	Shilling
Kirghizia	Som
Kiribati	Australian dollar
Kosovo	Dinar; euro
Kuwait	Dinar
Kyrgyzstan	Som
Laos	Kip
Latvia	Lat
Lebanon	Pound
Lesotho	Loti
Liberia	Liberian dollar
Libya	Dinar
Liechtenstein	Swiss franc
Lithuania	Litas
Luxembourg	Euro
Macedonia	Denar
Madagascar	Malagasy franc
Malawi	Kwacha
Malaysia	Ringgit
Maldives (Republic of)	Rufiyaa
Mali	CFA franc
Malta	Lira
Marshall Islands	U.S. dollar
Mauritania	Ouguiya
Mauritius	Rupee
Mexico	Peso
Micronesia	U.S. dollar
Moldova	Leu
Monaco	French franc
Mongolia	Tugrik
Montenegro	Euro
Montserrat	East Caribbean dollar
Morocco	Dirham
Mozambique	Metical
Myanmar	Kyat
Namibia	Namibian dollar
Nauru	Australian dollar
Nepal	Rupee
Netherlands	Euro
New Zealand	New Zealand dollar
Nicaragua	Córdoba
Niger	CFA franc
Nigeria	Naira
North Korea	Won
Norway	Krone
Oman	Rial

Currencies

Country	Currency
Pakistan	Rupee
Palau	U.S. dollar
Panama	Balboa
Papua New Guinea	Kina
Paraguay	Guarani
Peru	New sol
Philippines	Philippine peso
Poland	Zloty
Portugal	Euro
Qatar	Riyal
Romania	Leu
Russia	Rouble
Rwanda	Rwanda franc
St. Kitts and Nevis	East Caribbean dollar
St. Lucia	East Caribbean dollar
St. Vincent and the Grenadines	East Caribbean dollar
Samoa	Tala
San Marino	Euro
São Tomé and Principe	Dobra
Saudi Arabia	Riyal
Senegal	CFA franc
Seychelles	Rupee
Sierra Leone	Leone
Singapore	Singapore dollar
Slovakia	Koruna
Slovenia	Tolar
Solomon Islands	Solomon Islands dollar
Somalia	Shilling
South Africa	Rand
South Korea	Won
Spain	Euro
Sri Lanka	Rupee
Sudan	Dinar
Surinam	Guilder
Swaziland	Lilangeni
Sweden	Krona
Switzerland	Swiss franc
Syria	Pound
Taiwan	Taiwan dollar
Tajikistan	Somoni
Tanzania	Shilling
Thailand	Baht
Togo	CFA franc
Tonga	Pa'anga
Trinidad and Tobago	Trinidad and Tobago dollar
Tunisia	Dinar
Turkey	Turkish lira
Turkmenistan	Manat
Tuvalu	Australian dollar
Uganda	Shilling

Country	Currency
Ukraine	Hryvna
United Arab Emirates	Dirham
United Kingdom	Pound sterling
United States of America	U.S. dollar
Uruguay	Peso
Uzbekistan	Sum
Vanuatu	Vatu
Vatican City	Euro
Venezuela	Bolívar
Vietnam	Dong
Yemen	Riyal
Yugoslavia (Serbia)	Dinar
Zambia	Kwacha
Zimbabwe	Zimbabwe dollar

Curries

4 letters:
Dhal
Phal

5 letters:
Balti
Bhuna
Kofta
Korma
Tikka

6 letters:
Achari

Bhoona
Chasni
Karahi
Madras
Masala
Pathia

7 letters:
Biryani
Dhansak
Dopiaza
Jaipuri

Nentara
Pasanda
Red thai

8 letters:
Jalfrezi
Tandoori
Vindaloo

9 letters:
Green thai
Mussalman
Rogan josh

Cutting tools

3 letters:
Axe
Bit
Saw

4 letters:
Adze
Sawn

5 letters:
Dicer
Lance
Mower

6 letters:
Carver

Chisel
Grater
Jigsaw
Padsaw
Ripsaw
Scythe
Shaver
Shears
Sickle

7 letters:
Chopper
Cleaver
Coulter
Handsaw

Scissor

8 letters:
Engraver

9 letters:
Secateurs

11 letters:
Ploughshare

D

Dams

4 letters:
Guri
Hume
Pati

5 letters:
Aswan
Nurek
Rogun

6 letters:
Hoover
Inguri
Itaipu

Kariba
Vaiont

7 letters:
Benmore

8 letters:
Chapetón

9 letters:
Aswan High

10 letters:
Glen Canyon

11 letters:
Grand Coulee
Three Gorges

13 letters:
Grande Dixence
Vishvesvaraya

16 letters:
Syncrude Tailings

Dance

DANCES

3 letters:
Fan
Gig
Hay
Hey
Ice
Jig
Lap
Pas
Poi
Sun
Tap
Toe
War

4 letters:
Alma
Ball
Barn
Bump
Clog

Dump
Fado
Folk
Foot
Frug
Giga
Go-go
Haka
Hora
Hula
Jive
Jota
Juba
Juke
Kolo
Lion
Mosh
Nach
Pogo
Polo

Reel
Shag
Slam
Spin
Stag
Step
Taxi
Trip

5 letters:
Belly
Bogle
Brawl
Break
Caper
Carol
Ceroc®
Conga
Disco
Dolin
Fling

Furry
Galop
Ghost
Gigue
Gopak
Horah
Limbo
Loure
Mambo
Mooch
Natch
Paspy
Pavan
Paven
Pavin
Polka
Raver
Round
Rumba
Salsa
Samba
Shake
Skank
Snake
Stomp
Strut
Sword
Tango
Twist
Valse
Vogue
Volta
Waltz
Whirl

6 letters:
Almain
Apache
Ballet
Bolero
Boogie
Boston
Branle
Canary
Cancan
Cha-cha
Do-si-do
Fading
Floral
German
Gigolo

Hustle
Jump-up
Kathak
Lavolt
Maenad
Maxixe
Minuet
Morris
Nautch
Oberek
Pavane
Petipa
Redowa
Shimmy
Spring
Square
Trophe
Valeta
Veleta
Zapata

7 letters:
Baladin
Ballant
Beguine
Bourrée
Bransle
Brantle
Calypso
Cantico
Capuera
Carioca
Coranto
Cossack
Country
Courant
Csardas
Czardas
Farruca
Forlana
Foxtrot
Furlana
Gavotte
Halling
Hetaera
Hetaira
Hoedown
Lambada
Lancers
Ländler
Lavolta

Macaber
Macabre
Mazurka
Moresco
Morisco
Morrice
Moshing
Musette
Old-time
One-step
Pericon
Planxty
Polacca
Pyrrhic
Ridotto
Romaika
Roundel
Roundle
Sardana
Sashaya
Saunter
Shuffle
St Vitus
Tanagra
Tordion
Trenise
Two-step
Ziganka

8 letters:
Baladine
Ballroom
Bayadère
Boogaloo
Bunny hug
Cachucha
Cakewalk
Canticoy
Capoeira
Chaconne
Corybant
Coryphee
Cotillon
Courante
Egg-dance
Excuse-me
Fandango
Flamenco
Flip-flop
Galliard
Habanera

Dance

Hay-de-guy
Haymaker
Heythrop
Hoolican
Hornpipe
Hula-hula
Irish jig
Joncanoe
Junkanoo
Kantikoy
Kazachok
Kazatzka
Lindy hop
Macarena
Marinera
Matachin
Medicine
Merengue
Murciana
Orchesis
Pierette
Rigadoon
Rigaudon
Robotics
Ronggeng
Saraband
Snowball
Soft-shoe
Trippant
Trucking
Vogueing

9 letters:
Allemande
Ballabile
Bergamask
Bergomask
Bossa nova
Breakdown
Butterfly
Caballero
Cha-cha-cha
Cotillion
Ecossaise

Eightsome
Farandole
Formation
Gallopade
Hoolachan
Jitterbug
Kathakali
Malagueña
Pas de deux
Paso doble
Passepied
Paul Jones
Polonaise
Poussette
Quadrille
Quickstep
Ring-shout
Roundelay
Siciliano
Sink-a-pace
Tambourin
Tripudium
Variation
Zapateado

10 letters:
Antimasque
Carmagnole
Charleston
Cinque-pace
Corroboree
Gay Gordons
Hay-de-guise
Hay-de-guyes
Hey-de-guise
Hokey cokey
Nautch-girl
Passamezzo
Petronella
Saltarello
Seguidilla
Sicilienne
Sinke-a-pace
Strathspey

Tarantella
Trenchmore
Tripudiate
Turkey trot
Tyrolienne

11 letters:
Antistrophe
Black bottom
Body popping
Buck and wing
Contradance
Contredanse
Cracovienne
Lambeth walk
Palais glide
Passacaglia
Pastourelle
Schottische
Shimmy-shake
Terpsichore
Varsovienne

12 letters:
Bharat Natyam
Labanotation
Passemeasure
Passy-measure
Robot dancing
Saltatorious
Virginia reel

13 letters:
Eightsome reel
Highland fling

14 letters:
Jack-in-the-green
Strip the willow

18 letters:
Sir Roger de
Coverley

20 letters:
Dashing White
Sergeant

GENERAL DANCE STEPS AND TERMS

3 letters:
Pas
Set

4 letters:
Time

5 letters:
Glide
Score
Steps

6 letters:
Chassé
Dosido
In step

Phrase
Rhythm

7 letters:
Pas seul
Routine
Shuffle

8 letters:
Keep step
Sequence
Slip step

9 letters:
Out of step
Promenade

10 letters:
Grand chain
Pigeonwing

11 letters:
Comprimario
Pas de basque
Progressive

12 letters:
Choreography

See also:
➤ **Ballets** ➤ **Ballet steps and terms**

Degrees

Degree	Abbreviation
Bachelor of Agriculture	BAgr
Bachelor of Arts	BA
Bachelor of Commerce	BCom
Bachelor of Dental Surgery	BDS
Bachelor of Divinity	BD
Bachelor of Education	BEd
Bachelor of Engineering	BEng
Bachelor of Law	BL
Bachelor of Laws	LLB
Bachelor of Letters	BLitt
Bachelor of Medicine	BM *or* MB
Bachelor of Music	BMus, MusB, *or* MusBac
Bachelor of Pharmacy	BPharm
Bachelor of Philosophy	BPhil
Bachelor of Science	BSc
Bachelor of Surgery	BS
Diploma in Education	DipEd
Doctor of Dental Surgery *or* Science	DDS *or* DDSc
Doctor of Divinity	DD
Doctor of Laws	LLD
Doctor of Letters *or* Literature	DLitt *or* LittD
Doctor of Medicine	MD
Doctor of Music	DMus, MusD, *or* MusDoc
Doctor of Philosophy	PhD
Higher National Certificate	HNC
Higher National Diploma	HND

Dependencies

Degree	Abbreviation
Master of Arts	MA
Master of Education	MEd
Master of Laws	LLM
Master of Letters	MLitt
Master of Music	MMus
Master of Philosophy	MPhil
Master of Science	MSc
Master of Surgery	MCh
Master of Technology	MTech
Ordinary National Certificate	ONC
Ordinary National Diploma	OND

Dependencies

4 letters:
Guam
Niue

5 letters:
Aruba
Macau (S.A.R.)
Undof

6 letters:
Jersey

7 letters:
Bermuda
Mayotte
Reunion
Tokelau

8 letters:
Anguilla
Guernsey
Hong Kong (S.A.R.)
Jan Mayen
Svalbard
West Bank

9 letters:
Aksai Chin
East Timor
Gaza Strip
Gibraltar
Greenland
Isle of Man
Wake Atoll

10 letters:
Antarctica
Guadeloupe
Martinique
Montserrat
Puerto Rico

11 letters:
Baker Island
Cook Islands
Kingman Reef
Saint Helena

12 letters:
Bouvet Island
Cocos Islands
Europa Island
Faroe Islands
French Guiana
Golan Heights
Jarvis Island
New Caledonia
Palmyra Atoll

13 letters:
American Samoa
Bassas da India
Cayman Islands
Howland Island
Islas Malvinas
Johnston Atoll
Midway Islands
Navassa Island
Norfolk Island

Virgin Islands
Western Sahara

14 letters:
Keeling Islands
Paracel Islands
Spratly Islands
Tromelin Island

15 letters:
Christmas Island
Coral Sea Islands
Falkland Islands
French Polynesia
Glorioso Islands
Pitcairn Islands
Wallisand Futuna

16 letters:
Clipperton Island
Juan de Nova
   Island

19 letters:
Netherlands
   Antilles

20 letters:
British Virgin
   Islands

21 letters:
Turks and Caicos
   Islands

22 letters:
Northern Mariana Islands
Saint Pierre and Miquelon

24 letters:
Ashmore and Cartier Islands

27 letters:
British Indian Ocean Territory

29 letters:
Heard Island and McDonald
 Islands

31 letters:
French Southern and Antarctic
 Lands

38 letters:
South Georgia and the South
 Sandwich Islands

Deserts

4 letters:
Gobi
Thar

6 letters:
Gibson
Libyan
Mohave
Mojave
Nubian
Sahara

7 letters:
Arabian
Atacama
Kara Kum

8 letters:
Kalahari
Kyzyl Kum

9 letters:
Dasht-e-Lut
Dasht-i-Lut

10 letters:
Great Sandy
Rub'al Khali

11 letters:
Death Valley

13 letters:
Great Victoria

15 letters:
Taklimakan Shama

Desserts and sweet dishes

3 letters:
Ice
Pav
Pud

4 letters:
Duff
Eve's
Fool
Milk
Plum
Rice
Sago
Suet
Tart
Whip

5 letters:
Black
Bombe
Coupe

Crème
Crêpe
Hasty
Jello
Jelly
Kulfi
Pease
Slump
Sweet
Tansy
Torte

6 letters:
Afters
Blintz
Gâteau
Haggis
Junket
Kissel
Mousse
Panada

Pashka
Queen's
Sorbet
Sowens
Sponge
Stodge
Summer
Sundae
Trifle
Yogurt

7 letters:
Cabinet
Caramel
Cassata
Cobbler
College
Compote
Crumble
Custard
Dessert

Detectives

Fondant
Fritter
Furmety
Furmity
Panocha
Parfait
Pavlova
Popover
Pudding
Sabayon
Soufflé
Spumone
Spumoni
Steamed
Strudel
Tapioca
Tartlet

8 letters:
Bavarois
Cocktail
Dumpling
Flummery
Fromenty
Fruit cup
Frumenty
Furmenty
Ice cream
Pandowdy
Plum duff
Roly-poly
Semolina

Sillabub
Stickjaw
Syllabub
Tiramisu
Vacherin
Water ice

9 letters:
Charlotte
Christmas
Cranachan
Shortcake
White hass
Yorkshire

10 letters:
Blancmange
Brown Betty
Cheesecake
Fruit salad
Nesselrode
Peach Melba
Shoofly pie
White hause
White hawse
Zabaglione

11 letters:
Athole Brose
Atholl Brose
Baked Alaska
Banana split
Crème brûlée

Easter-ledge
Spotted dick
Tutti-frutti

12 letters:
Butterscotch
Crème caramel
Crêpe suzette
Île Flottante

13 letters:
Bavarian cream
Marrons glacés

14 letters:
Bread and butter
Charlotte russe

15 letters:
Clootie dumpling

16 letters:
Death by chocolate

17 letters:
Black Forest gateau
Mississippi mud
  pie

18 letters:
Knickerbocker
  glory
Neapolitan ice
  cream

Detectives

7 letters:
Maigret
Taggart

8 letters:
Ironside
Sam Spade

9 letters:
Dick Tracy
Donald Lam
Joe Friday
Lew Archer
Nancy Drew
Nero Wolfe

10 letters:
Jane Marple
Mike Hammer
Paul Temple
Perry Mason

11 letters:
Charlie Chan
Ellery Queen
Father Brown
Jim Bergerac
Jim Rockford
Lord Peter Wimsey
Travis McGee

12 letters:
Sergeant Cuff
Simon Templar

13 letters:
Albert Campion
C Auguste Dupin
Hercule Poirot
Jonathan Creek
Kinky Friedman
Philip Marlowe

14 letters:
Brother Cadfael
Charlie Resnick

Inspector Morse
Inspector Rebus
Sherlock Holmes

15 letters:
Eddie Shoestring
Inspector Bucket
Lieutenant Kojak

16 letters:
Inspector Wexford

17 letters:
Inspector Clouseau
Inspector Lestrade
Lieutenant
 Columbo

Marcus Didius
Falco

19 letters:
Commissario
 Brunetti

Devils and demons

4 letters:
Beng

5 letters:
Hades
Iblis
Satan

6 letters:
Belial
Mammon
Plutus

7 letters:
Abaddon

Bheliar
Clootie
Gehenna
Lucifer
Mastema
Old Nick
Sammael
Shaitan

8 letters:
Apollyon
Baphomet
Diabolos
Diabolus

9 letters:
Beelzebub
Old Cloots

10 letters:
Demogorgon
Lord of Lies
Malebolgia

14 letters:
Mephistopheles

Dialects

2 letters:
Wu

3 letters:
Eye
Min
Twi

4 letters:
Burr
Erse
Manx
Norn
Pedi
Taal
Tyke

5 letters:
Attic
Doric
Eldin
Eolic
Ionic

Joual
Koine
Ladin
Scots

6 letters:
Aeolic
Basuto
Gascon
Khalka
Mackem
Norman
Parsee
Patois
Scouse
Syriac
Tuscan

7 letters:
Arcadic
Brummie
Chicano

Cockney
Estuary
Geechee
Geordie
Jockney
Konkani
Lallands
Prakrit
Riffian
Romansh
Yealdon

8 letters:
Friulian
Hegelian
Pitmatic
Romansch
Yenglish
Yinglish

9 letters:
Alemannic

Diarists

Castillian
Landsmaal
Langue d'oc
Low German
Potteries

10 letters:
Franconian
Langue d'oil
Langue d'oui

11 letters:
Appalachian
Langobardic
Maltenglish

12 letters:
Gallo-Romance
Old Icelandic

14 letters:
Hiberno-English

Old North French

19 letters:
Black Country
  English

21 letters:
Received
  Pronunciation

Diarists

3 letters:
Nin, *Anaïs*

4 letters:
Gide, *André (Paul Guillaume)*

5 letters:
Frank, *Anne*
Pepys, *Samuel*

6 letters:
Burney, *Fanny*
Evelyn, *John*

7 letters:
Kilvert, *Francis*

8 letters:
Fielding, *Helen (Bridget Jones)*

Townsend, *Sue (Adrian Mole)*

9 letters:
Delafield, *E M*
Grossmith, *George and Weedon*
  (Charles Pooter)

10 letters:
Wordsworth, *Dorothy*

11 letters:
Rivers-Moore, *Marion*

12 letters:
Bashkirtseff, *Marie*

Dinosaurs

8 letters:
Allosaur
Mosasaur
Stegodon
Theropod

9 letters:
Apatosaur
Hadrosaur
Iguanodon
Oviraptor
Pterosaur
Stegodont
Stegosaur
Trachodon

10 letters:
Allosaurus
Ankylosaur
Brontosaur
Ceratosaur
Dimetrodon
Diplodocus
Dromiosaur
Elasmosaur
Iguanodont
Megalosaur
Mosasaurus
Plesiosaur
Pteranodon
Titanosaur

11 letters:
Apatosaurus
Atlantosaur
Brachiosaur
Dolichosaur
Hadrosaurus
Ichthyosaur
Pterodactyl
Stegosaurus
Triceratops
Tyrannosaur

12 letters:
Ankylosaurus
Brontosaurus
Ceratosaurus

Dromiosaurus
Elasmosaurus
Megalosaurus
Plesiosaurus
Titanosaurus

Velociraptor

13 letters:
Atlantosaurus
Brachiosaurus
Compsognathus

Dolichosaurus
Ichthyosaurus
Protoceratops
Tyrannosaurus

Directors

3 letters:
Lee, *Ang*
Lee, *Spike*
Ray, *Satyajit*
Woo, *John*

4 letters:
Coen, *Ethan*
Coen, *Joel*
Ford, *John*
Hall, *Peter*
Hill, *George Roy*
Lang, *Fritz*
Lean, *David*
Penn, *Arthur*
Reed, *Carol*
Roeg, *Nicholas*
Tati, *Jacques*
Weir, *Peter*
Wise, *Robert*

5 letters:
Allen, *Woody*
Brook, *Peter*
Capra, *Frank*
Carné, *Marcel*
Clair, *René*
Dante, *Joe*
Demme, *Johnathan*
Gance, *Abel*
Hawks, *Howard*
Ivory, *James*
Kaige, *Chen*
Kazan, *Elia*
Leigh, *Mike*
Leone, *Sergio*
Loach, *Ken*
Lucas, *George*
Lumet, *Sidney*
Lynch, *David*
Malle, *Louis*
Pabst, *G(eorge) W(ilhelm)*

Reitz, *Edgar*
Roach, *Hal*
Scott, *Ridley*
Stone, *Oliver*
Vadim, *Roger*
Wajda, *Andrei*
Yimou, *Zhang*

6 letters:
Altman, *Robert*
Badham, *John*
Beatty, *Warren*
Besson, *Luc*
Brooks, *Mel*
Buñuel, *Luis*
Burton, *Tim*
Corman, *Roger*
Cuarón, *Alfonso*
Curtiz, *Michael*
De Sica, *Vittoria*
Donner, *Richard*
Forbes, *Bryan*
Forman, *Milös*
Frears, *Stephen*
Godard, *Jean-Luc*
Guitry, *Sacha*
Haneke, *Michael*
Herzog, *Werner*
Huston, *John*
Jarman, *Derek*
Jordan, *Neil*
Kasdan, *Lawrence*
Keaton, *Buster*
Landis, *John*
Lester, *Richard*
Méliès, *Georges*
Mendes, *Sam*
Miller, *George*
Miller, *Jonathon Wolfe*
Ophüls, *Max*
Pagnol, *Marcel*

Directors

Parker, *Alan*
Powell, *Michael*
Reiner, *Carl*
Reiner, *Rob*
Renoir, *Jean*
Rohmer, *Eric*
Romero, *George*
Siegel, *Don*
Welles, *Orson*
Wilder, *Billy*
Winner, *Michael*

7 letters:
Aldrich, *Robert*
Asquith, *Anthony*
Bergman, *Ingmar*
Boorman, *John*
Bresson, *Robert*
Cameron, *James*
Campion, *Jane*
Chabrol, *Claude*
Cocteau, *Jean*
Coppola, *Francis Ford*
De Mille, *Cecil B(lount)*
De Palma, *Brian*
Edwards, *Blake*
Fellini, *Federico*
Fleming, *Victor*
Forsyth, *Bill*
Gilliam, *Terry*
Jackson, *Peter*
Kaufman, *Philip*
Kubrick, *Stanley*
McBride, *Jim*
Nichols, *Mike*
Olivier, *Laurence*
Pollack, *Sydney*
Puttnam, *David*
Redford, *Robert*
Resnais, *Alain*
Ritchie, *Guy*
Robbins, *Tim*
Russell, *Ken*
Sturges, *Preston*
Van Sant, *Gus*
Wenders, *Wim*

8 letters:
Anderson, *Lindsay*
Anderson, *Wes*
Columbus, *Christopher*
Eastwood, *Clint*

Friedkin, *William*
Grierson, *John*
Griffith, *D(avid) W(ark)*
Kurosawa, *Akira*
Levinson, *Barry*
Merchant, *Ismail*
Minnelli, *Vincente*
Pasolini, *Pier Paolo*
Polanski, *Roman*
Pudovkin, *Vsevolod*
Scorsese, *Martin*
Truffaut, *François*
Visconti, *Luchino*
Von Trier, *Lars*
Zemeckis, *Robert*

9 letters:
Almódovar, *Pedro*
Antonioni, *Michelangelo*
Armstrong, *Gillian*
Carpenter, *John*
Dovzhenko, *Aleksandr Petrovitch*
Greenaway, *Peter*
Hitchcock, *Alfred*
Minghella, *Anthony*
Mizoguchi, *Kenji*
Peckinpah, *Sam*
Preminger, *Otto*
Spielberg, *Steven*
Stevenson, *Robert*
Tarantino, *Quentin*
Tarkovsky, *Andrei*
Tavernier, *Bertrand*
Zinnemann, *Fred*

10 letters:
Bertolucci, *Bernardo*
Cronenberg, *David*
Eisenstein, *Sergei Mikhailovich*
Fassbinder, *Rainer Werner*
Kieslowski, *Krzysztof*
Mankiewicz, *Joseph*
Rossellini, *Roberto*
Soderbergh, *Steven*
Zeffirelli, *Franco*

11 letters:
Bogdanovich, *Peter*
Mackendrick, *Alexander*
Pressburger, *Emeric*
Riefenstahl, *Leni*
Schlesinger, *John*

Von Stroheim, *Erich*   Von Sternberg, *Joseph*

12 letters:
Attenborough, *Richard*

Disciples

4 letters:
John
Jude

5 letters:
James (*the Great*)
James (*the Less*)
Judas

Peter
Simon

6 letters:
Andrew
Philip
Thomas

7 letters:
Matthew

11 letters:
Bartholomew

Diseases

2 letters:
CD
ME
MS
TB
VD

3 letters:
ALD
BSE
CFS
Flu
Gid
Haw
Pip
Pox
Rot
TSE
Wog

4 letters:
Acne
Ague
AIDS
Boba
Bots
Bunt
Clap
Cold
Conk
Gout
Kuru
Loco

Lues
Lyme
Roup
Scab
Yaws

5 letters:
Bang's
Brand
Braxy
Ebola
Edema
Ergot
Favus
Gapes
Lupus
Lurgi
Lurgy
Mesel
Mumps
Ngana
Palsy
Pinta
Polio
Pott's
Sprue
Surra
Tinea
Weil's

6 letters:
Anbury
Angina

Asthma
Blight
Blotch
Cancer
Canker
Caries
Chagas'
Chorea
Cowpox
Crohn's
Cruels
Dartre
Dengue
Dropsy
Eczema
Farcin
Goitre
Grapes
Graves'
Heaves
Herpes
Income
Iritis
Johne's
Lampas
Mad cow
Meazel
Mildew
Morbus
Nagana
Oedema
Otitis

Diseases

Paget's
Q fever
Quinsy
Rabies
Sapego
Scurvy
Spavin
Still's
Sweeny
Thrush
Typhus
Ulitis
Urosis
Warble
Zoster

7 letters:
Anthrax
Apraxia
Ascites
Bright's
British
Bulimia
Caisson
Cholera
Coeliac
Colitis
Crewels
Dourine
Earache
Founder
Glue ear
Hansen's
Hard pad
Hydatid
Icterus
Lampers
Leprosy
Lockjaw
Lumbago
Maidism
Malaria
Marburg
Measles
Megrims
Mooneye
Moor-ill
Murrain
Myiasis
Pébrine
Pinkeye

Porrigo
Prurigo
Purples
Purpura
Quittor
Ratbite
Rickets
Roaring
Rosette
Rubella
Scabies
Scrapie
Sequela
Serpigo
Sitfast
Sycosis
Tetanus
Tetters
Typhoid
Uraemia
Uveitis
Variola
Wilson's

8 letters:
Addison's
Alastrim
Anorexia
Aortitis
Beriberi
Blackleg
Bornholm
Bull nose
Bursitis
Carditis
Clubroot
Coxalgia
Cushing's
Cynanche
Cystitis
Diabetes
Dutch elm
Economo's
Epilepsy
Ergotism
Fishskin
Fowl pest
Glanders
Glaucoma
Grand mal
Gummosis

Hidrosis
Hodgkin's
Hookworm
Impetigo
Jaundice
Kala-azar
Loose-cut
Lumpy jaw
Lymphoma
Mastitis
Menière's
Minamata
Myopathy
Myxedema
Osteitis
Pellagra
Petit mal
Phthisis
Phytosis
Pleurisy
Progeria
Pullorum
Rachitis
Raynaud's
Red water
Rhinitis
Ringbone
Ringworm
Rose-rash
Sciatica
Scrofula
Seedy toe
Shingles
Smallpox
Staggers
Suppeago
Swayback
Swinepox
Syphilis
Tay-Sachs
Toe crack
Trachoma
Trembles
Venereal
Vincent's
Vulvitis
Windgall
Zoonosis

9 letters:
Acariasis

Arthritis
Bilharzia
Brown lung
Calenture
Chancroid
Chin cough
Chloracne
Chlorosis
Christmas
Cirrhosis
Dhobi itch
Diarrhoea
Diathesis
Distemper
Dysentery
Emphysema
Enteritis
Exanthema
Gastritis
Glossitis
Gonorrhea
Hepatitis
Idiopathy
Influenza
Ixodiasis
Kawasaki's
Laminitis
Lathyrism
Leucaemia
Leukaemia
Loose smut
Malanders
Milk fever
Myxoedema
Nephritis
Nephrosis
Newcastle
Pellagrin
Pemphigus
Phlebitis
Pneumonia
Porphyria
Psoriasis
Pyorrhoea
Retinitis
Sand crack
Sapraemia
Scratches
Siderosis
Silicosis
Sinusitis

Splenitis
Strangles
Sunstroke
Synovitis
Tarantism
Tick fever
Trichosis
Tularemia
Urticaria
Vaginitis
Vagotonia
Varicosis
Varioloid
Whistling

10 letters:
Absinthism
Acromegaly
Alcoholism
Alzheimer's
Amoebiasis
Asbestosis
Ascariasis
Autoimmune
Babesiosis
Bagassosis
Bell's palsy
Black Death
Broken wind
Bronchitis
Byssinosis
Cellulitis
Chickenpox
Common cold
Dandy-fever
Dermatitis
Diphtheria
Ebola virus
Erysipelas
Fibrositis
Filariasis
Framboesia
Gingivitis
Gonorrhoea
Heartwater
Hemophilia
Hepatitis A
Hepatitis B
Hog cholera
Ichthyosis
Impaludism

Laryngitis
Lassa fever
Leuchaemia
Limber-neck
Lou Gehrig's
Louping ill
Mallanders
Mallenders
Meningitis
Moniliasis
Muscardine
Narcolepsy
Neuropathy
Ornithosis
Parkinson's
Pityriasis
Rinderpest
Salmonella
Scarlatina
Scleriasis
Seborrhoea
Shell shock
Springhalt
Stomatitis
Stringhalt
Swamp fever
Swine fever
Texas fever
Tularaemia
Urethritis
Valvulitis

11 letters:
Anthracosis
Brittle-bone
Brucellosis
Cardiopathy
Consumption
Dead fingers
Farmer's lung
Green monkey
Haemophilia
Hebephrenia
Huntington's
Hypothermia
Jungle fever
Kwashiorkor
Listeriosis
Myxomatosis
Parasitosis
Pharyngitis

Diseases

Psittacosis
Rickettsial
Salpingitis
Scleroderma
Scrub typhus
Septicaemia
Spina bifida
Spondylitis
Thoroughpin
Tonsillitis
Trench fever
Trench mouth
Trichinosis
Utriculitis
Yellow fever

12 letters:
Aeroneurosis
Anaplasmosis
Appendicitis
Athlete's foot
Avitaminosis
Bilharziasis
Bilharziosis
Black measles
Bush sickness
Constipation
Cor pulmonale
Encephalitis
Endocarditis
Enterobiasis
Fascioliasis
Finger and toe
Foot-and-mouth
Furunculosis
Gallsickness
Herpes zoster
Hoof-and-mouth
Legionnaire's
Milk sickness
Molybdenosis
Motor neurone
Osteomalacia
Osteoporosis
Pericarditis
Quarter crack
Ratbite fever
Sarcomatosis
Scarlet fever
Schizothymia
Sclerodermia

Shaking palsy
Sheep measles
Splenomegaly
Spotted fever
Thalassaemia
Tuberculosis
Typhoid fever
Uncinariasis

13 letters:
Actinomycosis
Blind staggers
Bronchiolitis
Bubonic plague
Elephantiasis
Enterocolitis
Genital herpes
German measles
Greensickness
Herpes simplex
Labyrinthitis
Leichmaniasis
Leishmaniasis
Leishmaniosis
Leptospirosis
Lupus vulgaris
Moon blindness
Non-A hepatitis
Non-B hepatitis
Osteomyelitis
Poliomyelitis
Polycythaemia
Reye's syndrome
Salmonellosis
Schizophrenia
Serum sickness
Syringomyelia
Toxoplasmosis
Tsutsugamushi
Undulant fever
Whooping cough

14 letters:
Bulimia nervosa
Cardiomyopathy
Coal miner's lung
Conjunctivitis
Cystic fibrosis
Diverticulitis
Encephalopathy
Glandular fever
Histoplasmosis

Hypothyroidism
Kaposi's sarcoma
Leucodystrophy
Onchocerciasis
Osteoarthritis
Pneumoconiosis
Relapsing fever
Rheumatic fever
Senile dementia
Spirochaetosis
Sporotrichosis
Swine vesicular
Trichomoniasis
Trichophytosis
Variola porcina
Vincent's angina
Vulvovaginitis

15 letters:
Agranulocytosis
Ancylostomiasis
Ankylostomiasis
Anorexia nervosa
Atherosclerosis
Blackwater fever
Burkitt lymphoma
Double pneumonia
Equine distemper
Gastroenteritis
Pleuropneumonia
Schistosomiasis
Strongyloidosis
Sydenham's chorea
Trypanosomiasis

16 letters:
Actinodermatitis
Anchylostomiasis
Arteriosclerosis
Bronchopneumonia
Burkitt's lymphoma
Creutzfeldt-Jakob
Erythroblastosis
Ménière's
  syndrome
Myasthenia gravis
Paratyphoid fever
Saint Vitus's dance
Sleeping sickness
Strongyloidiasis
Sweating sickness
Tourette syndrome

17 letters:
Encephalomyelitis
Haemoglobinopathy
Huntington's chorea
Multiple sclerosis
Muscular dystrophy
Osteitis deformans
Presenile dementia
Radiation sickness
Sickle-cell anaemia

18 letters:
Cerebellar syndrome
Coccidioidomycosis
Exophthalmic goitre
Glomerulonephritis
Lupus erythematosus
Pelvic inflammatory
Toxic shock syndrome

19 letters:
Infectious hepatitis
Korsakoff's psychosis
Non-Hodgkin's lymphoma
Rheumatoid arthritis

20 letters:
Adrenoleukodystrophy
Carpal tunnel syndrome
Necrotising fasciitis

21 letters:
Decompression sickness

22 letters:
Chronic fatigue syndrome

23 letters:
Bacillary white diarrhoea
Equine infectious anaemia
Infectious mononucleosis

24 letters:
Myalgic encephalomyelitis

25 letters:
Rocky Mountain spotted fever
Seasonal affective disorder

30 letters:
Bovine spongiform
  encephalopathy

Dishes

3 letters:
Fry
Pan
Pie
Poi

4 letters:
Dent
Flan
Fool
Hash
Lanx
Mess
Olla
Paté
Puri
Soba
Soss
Soup
Stew
Taco
Tofu
Udon

5 letters:
Balti
Belle
Bhaji
Bitok
Brawn
Brose
Broth
Champ
Chips
Crêpe
Curry
Cutie
Daube
Dolma
Fry-up
Gomer
Grits
Kasha
Kebab
Kibbe
Knish
Kofta

Korma
Laksa
Maror
Paten
Patin
Patty
Pilaf
Pilao
Pilau
Pilaw
Pilow
Pizza
Poori
Quorn®
Raita
Ramen
Roast
Rojak
Salad
Salmi
Sango
Satay
Sushi

Dishes

Tamal
Thali
Tikka
Toast

6 letters:
Apollo
Bharta
Blintz
Bredie
Bridie
Burgoo
Canapé
Coddle
Cook-up
Croute
Cuscus
Entrée
Faggot
Fondue
Haggis
Hotpot
Houmus
Hummus
Humous
Kimchi
Kishke
Laggen
Laggin
Luggie
Mousse
Muesli
Nachos
Omelet
Paella
Pakora
Panada
Patera
Patine
Pilaff
Pirogi
Pot pie
Quiche
Ragout
Salmis
Samosa
Sanger
Sarmie
Scampi
Scouse
Sowans

Sowens
Subgum
Tagine
Tamale
Tsamba
Won ton

7 letters:
Biriani
Bobotie
Bouchée
Burrito
Calzone
Ceviche
Chafing
Charger
Cocotte
Comport
Compote
Crowdie
Crubeen
Crumble
Custard
Cuvette
Dariole
Dhansak
Dopiaza
Egg roll
Epergne
Fajitas
Falafel
Fel-a-fel
Flasket
Foo yong
Foo Yung
Friture
Goulash
Grav lax
Lasagne
Mousaka
Navarin
Padella
Polenta
Pottage
Poutine
Ramekin
Rarebit
Ravioli
Risotto
Rissole
Roulade

Sashimi
Scallop
Seviche
Skirlie
Sosatie
Soufflé
Stir-fry
Stottie
Stovies
Tartlet
Tempura
Terrine
Timbale
Tostada

8 letters:
Brandade
Caponata
Chop suey
Chow mein
Consommé
Coolamon
Coq au vin
Coquille
Couscous
Crostini
Dolmades
Entremes
Escargot
Feijoada
Fish cake
Gado-gado
Halloumi
Kedgeree
Keftedes
Kickshaw
Kouskous
Kreplach
Kromesky
Matelote
Mazarine
Meat loaf
Mirepoix
Moussaka
Omelette
Pandowdy
Pannikin
Pastrami
Pirozhki
Porridge
Pot-au-feu

Dishes

Pot roast
Quenelle
Raclette
Ramequin
Salpicon
Sandwich
Shashlik
Sillabub
Souvlaki
Steak pie
Sukiyaki
Syllabub
Teriyaki
Tomalley
Tortilla
Tsatsiki
Tzatziki
Yakimono
Yakitori

9 letters:
Carbonara
Casserole
Cassoulet
Compotier
Croquette
Curry puff
Egg-fo-yang
Enchilada
Entremets
Forcemeat
Fricassee
Galantine
Game chips
Gravad lax
Guacamole
Hamburger
Howtowdie
Irish stew
Jambalaya
Lobscouse
Madrilène
Manicotti
Matelotte
Mutton pie
Osso bucco
Pastitsio
Pepper pot
Reistafel
Rijstafel

Schnitzel
Scotch egg
Scotch pie
Shashlick
Souvlakia
Succotash
Surf √n' turf
Tyropitta
Vol-au-vent

10 letters:
Avgolemono
Baked beans
Blanquette
Bombay duck
Bruschetta
Cacciatore
Cottage pie
Coulibiaca
Couscousou
Doner kebab
Egg-foo-yung
Fish finger
Fish supper
Hotchpotch
Jugged hare
Koulibiaca
Laver bread
Minestrone
Mixed grill
Nasi goreng
Parmigiana
Provencale
Quesadilla
Red pudding
Rijsttafel
Salmagundi
Salmagundy
Sauerkraut
Scaloppine
Scaloppini
Shish kebab
Smørrebrød
Spitchcock
Spring roll
Stroganoff
Vegeburger

11 letters:
Buck-rarebit
Caesar salad

Chicken Kiev
Clam chowder
Cock-a-leekie
Corn chowder
Cullen skink
Frankfurter
French toast
Fritto misto
Gefilte fish
Hominy grits
Olla podrida
Palm-oil chop
Ratatouille
Saltimbocca
Sauerbraten
Sausage roll
Scotch broth
Smorgasbord
Spanakopita
Spanish rice
Spanokopita
Suet pudding
Vichyssoise
Welsh rabbit

12 letters:
Cheeseburger
Club sandwich
Cockie-leekie
Cornish pasty
Eggs Benedict
Fish and chips
Forfar bridie
Gefüllte fish
Mulligatawny
Open sandwich
Pease pudding
Prawn cracker
Shepherd's pie
Steak tartare
Taramasalata
Veggieburger
Waldorf salad
Welsh rarebit
White pudding

13 letters:
Prairie oyster
Rumbledethump
Salade niçoise
Scrambled eggs

Divination

Toad-in-the-hole

14 letters:
Beef bourguinon
Beef stroganoff
Chilli con carne
Lobster Newburg
Macaroni cheese
Mock turtle soup
Quiche lorraine
Rumbledethumps

15 letters:
Bubble and squeak
Ploughman's
  lunch

16 letters:
Blanquette de veau
Boeuf bourguignon
Lancashire hotpot
Lobster thermidor
Yorkshire pudding

17 letters:
Angels-on-
  horseback
Cauliflower cheese
Devils-on-
  horseback
Steak-and-kidney
  pie

21 letters:
Steak-and-kidney
  pudding

Divination

METHODS OF DIVINATION

4 letters:
Dice

5 letters:
Runes
Tarot

6 letters:
I Ching

7 letters:
Dowsing
Scrying

9 letters:
Astrology
Palmistry
Sortilege
Tea leaves

10 letters:
Numerology

12 letters:
Clairvoyance

13 letters:
Crystal gazing

MEANS OF DIVINATION

Name	Object used
Ailuromancy	Cats
Alphitomancy	Wheat *or* barley cakes
Arachnomancy	Spiders
Astragalomancy	Dice
Bibliomancy	Passages from books
Cartomancy	Cards
Catoptromancy	Mirror
Ceromancy	Melted wax
Chiromancy	Hands
Cleidomancy	Suspended key
Crithomancy	Freshly baked bread
Cromniomancy	Onions
Crystallomancy	Crystal ball
Dactylomancy	Suspended ring
Geomancy	Earth, sand, *or* dust
Hippomancy	Horses
Hydromancy	Water
Lampadomancy	Oil lamps
Lithomancy	Precious stones
Lychnomancy	Flames of wax candles
Molybdomancy	Molten lead

Name	Object used
Necromancy	The dead
Oneiromancy	Dreams
Ornithomancy	Birds
Pegomancy	Sacred pool
Pyromancy	Fire *or* flames
Radiesthesia	Pendulum
Rhabdomancy	Rod *or* wand
Sciomancy	Ghosts
Tasseography	Tea leaves
Theomancy	God
Tyromancy	Cheese

Dogs

3 letters:
Cur
Lab
Pom
Pug

4 letters:
Barb
Bush
Chow
Dane
Kuri
Peke
Puli
Stag
Tosa

5 letters:
Akita
Alans
Apsos
Boxer
Brach
Cairn
Coach
Corgi
Husky
Spitz
Spoor

6 letters:
Afghan
Bandog
Barbet
Beagle
Blanch

Borzoi
Briard
Chenet
Cocker
Collie
Eskimo
Goorie
Kelpie
Messan
Pariah
Poodle
Pye-dog
Saluki
Scotch
Setter
Shough
Sleuth
Talbot
Teckel
Vizsla
Westie
Yorkie

7 letters:
Basenji
Boerbul
Bouvier
Brachet
Bulldog
Courser
Griffon
Harrier
Lurcher
Maltese
Maremma

Mastiff
Mongrel
Pointer
Prairie
Raccoon
Samoyed
Sapling
Scottie
Shar-Pei
Sheltie
Shih-tzu
Showghe
Spaniel
Terrier
Volpino
Whippet

8 letters:
Aardwolf
Aberdeen
Airedale
Alsatian
Blenheim
Bratchet
Carriage
Chow-chow
Doberman
Elkhound
Foxhound
Huntaway
Keeshond
Komondor
Labrador
Landseer
Malamute

Dogs

Malemute
Papillon
Pekinese
Pembroke
Pinscher
Samoyede
Scottish
Sealyham
Springer
Warragal
Warrigal

9 letters:
Buckhound
Chihuahua
Coonhound
Dachshund
Dalmatian
Deerhound
Gazehound
Great Dane
Greyhound
Kerry blue
Lhasa apso
Pekingese
Red setter
Retriever
Schnauzer
Staghound
St. Bernard
Wolfhound

10 letters:
Bedlington
Bloodhound
Blue cattle
Blue heeler
Bruxellois
Fox terrier
Otterhound
Pomeranian
Rottweiler
Schipperke
Tripehound
Weimaraner
Welsh corgi

11 letters:
Afghan hound
Basset hound
Bichon Frise
Bull mastiff

Bull terrier
Irish setter
Jack Russell
Rough collie
Skye terrier
Sydney silky

12 letters:
Belvoir hound
Border collie
Cairn terrier
Field spaniel
Gordon setter
Irish terrier
Japanese tosa
Newfoundland
Saint Bernard
Water spaniel
Welsh terrier
West Highland

13 letters:
Affenpinscher
Alpine spaniel
Bearded collie
Border terrier
Boston terrier
Cocker spaniel
Dandie Dinmont
English setter
French bulldog
Scotch terrier
Sussex spaniel

14 letters:
Clumber spaniel
Egyptian basset
German shepherd
Irish wolfhound
Norfolk terrier
Norwich terrier
Pit bull terrier

15 letters:
Aberdeen terrier
Airedale terrier
Alaskan malamute
Blenheim spaniel
Blue Gascon
  hound
Cuban bloodhound
Golden retriever

Highland terrier
Japanese spaniel
Lakeland terrier
Mexican hairless
Sealyham terrier
Springer spaniel

16 letters:
Australian cattle
Doberman
  pinscher
Italian greyhound
Kerry blue terrier
Persian greyhound
Pyrenean
  mountain
Russian wolfhound
Shetland sheepdog
Yorkshire terrier

17 letters:
Australian terrier
Bedlington terrier
Dobermann-
  pinscher
Irish water spaniel
Labrador retriever
Manchester terrier
Norwegian
  elkhound
Wire-haired terrier

18 letters:
Black-and-tan
  terrier
Jack Russell
  terrier
King Charles
  spaniel
Old English
  sheepdog
Rhodesian
  ridgeback

20 letters:
Dandie Dinmont
  terrier
Queensland blue
  heeler

22 letters:
American pit bull
  terrier

Australian silky
  terrier
Norfolk springer
  spaniel

24 letters:
Staffordshire bull
  terrier
West Highland
  white terrier

Drama

2 letters:
No

3 letters:
Noh

5 letters:
Farce

6 letters:
Comedy
Kabuki
Sitcom
Sketch

7 letters:
Tragedy

8 letters:
Jacobean

9 letters:
Kathakali
Melodrama
Soap opera

10 letters:
Shadow play

11 letters:
Kitchen sink
Mystery play
Passion play
Tragicomedy

12 letters:
Costume drama
Costume piece
Grand Guignol
Morality play

13 letters:
Street theatre

14 letters:
Revenge tragedy

15 letters:
Comedy of
  manners

Situation comedy

16 letters:
Commedia
  dell'arte
Theatre of cruelty

17 letters:
Restoration
  Comedy

18 letters:
Theatre of the
  absurd

Dramatists

2 letters:
Fo, *Dario*

3 letters:
Fry, *Christopher Harris*
Gay, *John*
Kyd, *Thomas*

4 letters:
Amos, *Robert*
Bond, *Edward*
Ford, *John*
Gray, *Oriel*
Hare, *David*
Inge, *William Motter*
Lyly, *John*

Shaw, *George Bernard*

5 letters:
Albee, *Edward (Franklin)*
Behan, *Brendan*
Eliot, *T(homas) S(tearns)*
Esson, *Louis*
Friel, *Brian*
Genet, *Jean*
Gogol, *Nikolai Vasilievich*
Havel, *Václav*
Hayes, *Alfred*
Ibsen, *Henrik*
Lorca, *Federico García*
Mamet, *David*
Odets, *Clifford*

Dramatists

Orton, *Joe*
Otway, *Thomas*
Synge, *(Edmund) J(ohn) M(illington)*
Udall, *Nicholas*
Wilde, *Oscar (Fingal O'Flahertie Wills)*
Yeats, *W(illiam) B(utler)*

6 letters:

Adamov, *Arthur*
Beynon, *Richard*
Brecht, *Bertolt (Eugen Friedrich)*
Bridie, *James (Osborne Henry Mavor)*
Brieux, *Eugene*
Coward, *Noël (Pierce)*
Dekker, *Thomas*
De Vega, *Lope*
Dryden, *John*
Goethe, *Johann Wolfgang von*
Greene, *Robert*
Hebbel, *(Christian) Friedrich*
Hewett, *Dorthy*
Howard, *Sidney*
Jonson, *Ben(jamin)*
Kaiser, *George*
Lawler, *Ray*
Miller, *Arthur*
Oakley, *Barry*
O'Casey, *Sean*
O'Neill, *Eugene (Gladstone)*
Pinero, *Arthur Wing*
Pinter, *Harold*
Porter, *Hal*
Racine, *Jean (Baptiste)*
Sartre, *Jean-Paul*
Seneca, *Lucius Annaeus*
Wilder, *Thornton*

7 letters:

Anouilh, *Jean*
Beckett, *Samuel (Barclay)*
Chapman, *George*
Chekhov, *Anton Pavlovich*
Gilbert, *W(illiam) S(chwenk)*
Goldoni, *Carlo*
Heywood, *Thomas*
Hibberd, *Jack*
Ionesco, *Eugène*
Kushner, *Tony*
Marlowe, *Christopher*

Marston, *John*
Molière
Osborne, *John*
Patrick, *John*
Plautus, *Titus Maccius*
Pushkin, *Aleksander Sergeyevich*
Romeril, *John*
Rostand, *Edmond*
Russell, *Willy*
Seymour, *Alan*
Shaffer, *Peter*
Shepard, *Sam*
Soyinka, *Wole*
Terence
Webster, *John*

8 letters:

Beaumont, *Francis*
Congreve, *William*
Fletcher, *John*
Lochhead, *Liz*
Menander
Rattigan, *Terence (Mervyn)*
Schiller, *Johann Christoph Friedrich von*
Shadwell, *Thomas*
Sheridan, *Richard Brinsley*
Sherwood, *Robert*
Stoppard, *Tom*
Vanbrugh, *Sir John*
Wedekind, *Frank*
Williams, *Tennessee*
Wycherly, *William*

9 letters:

Aeschylus
Ayckbourn, *Alan*
Bleasdale, *Alan*
Corneille, *Pierre*
De la Barca, *Pedro Calderón*
Euripides
Giraudoux, *(Hippolyte) Jean*
Goldsmith, *Oliver*
Hauptmann, *Gerhart Johann Robert*
Massinger, *Philip*
Middleton, *Thomas*
Sackville, *Thomas*
Sophocles

10 letters:

Drinkwater, *John*

Galsworthy, *John*
Pirandello, *Luigi*
Strindberg, *August*
Williamson, *David Keith*

11 letters:
Maeterlinck, *Count Maurice*
Shakespeare, *William*

12 letters:
Aristophanes
Beaumarchais, *Pierre Augustin*
  Caron de

14 letters:
De Beaumarchais, *Pierre*
  Augustin Caron

Dresses

4 letters:
Coat
Midi
Sack
Sari

5 letters:
Burka
Pinny
Saree
Shift
Tunic

6 letters:
Caftan
Chiton
Dirndl
Jumper
Kaftan
Kimono
Mantua
Muu-muu

Nighty
Sheath

7 letters:
Busuuti
Chemise
Gymslip
Nightie
Sweater
Tea gown
Wedding

8 letters:
Ballgown
Cocktail
Negligée
Peignoir
Pinafore
Sundress

9 letters:
Cheongsam

Maxidress
Minidress
Nightgown
Nightrobe
Overdress

10 letters:
Microdress
Nightdress
Nightshirt
Shirtdress
Shirtwaist

11 letters:
Riding habit

12 letters:
Shirtwaister

13 letters:
Button-through
Mother Hubbard

Drinks

2 letters:
It

3 letters:
Ale
Ava
Cha
Cup
Dão
Dop
Gin
Ice
IPA
Keg

Kir
Mum
Nog
Pop
Rum
Rye
Tea
Vin

4 letters:
Arak
Asti
Beef
Bock

Brut
Bull
Bush
Cava
Coke®
Cola
Corn
Dram
Flip
Gavi
Grog
Herb
Hock
Java

Drinks

Kava
Kola
Korn
Kvas
Malt
Marc
Maté
Mead
Mild
Milk
Mint
Nipa
Nogg
Ouzo
Palm
Pils
Port
Purl
Raki
Rosé
Rosy
Sack
Saké
Saki
Sekt
Soda
Soma
Sour
Sura
Tent
Tutu
Yill

5 letters:
Anise
Anjou
Assam
Bingo
Black
Blend
Bohea
Bombo
Brown
Bumbo
China
Cider
Cocoa
Congo
Crème
Crush
Cyder

Decaf
Fitou
Float
Fruit
Glogg
Grain
Grass
Green
Guest
Haoma
Heavy
Hogan
Hooch
Hyson
Irish
Juice
Julep
Kefir
Kirsh
Kvass
Lager
Latte
Ledum
Lemon
Light
Lirac
Mâcon
Mauby
Meath
Medoc
Meths
Mirin
Mobby
Mocha
Mosel
Mulse
Nappy
Negus
Noyau
Pekoe
Pepsi®
Perry
Pinot
Plain
Polly
Pombe
Punch
Quass
Rakee
Rhine
Rioja

Roero
Rueda
Rully
Rummy
Salop
Senna
Shake
Shrub
Sixty
Sling
Soave
Stout
Straw
Syrah
Tavel
Tizer®
Toddy
Tokay
Tonic
Twist
Yerba
Vimto®
Vodka
Water
Wheat
White
Xeres

6 letters:
Arrack
Atomic
Bandol
Barley
Barolo
Barsac
Beaune
Bishop
Bovril®
Brandy
Burton
Busera
Cahors
Canary
Carema
Cassis
Caudle
Cauker
Ceylon
Chaser
Claret
Coffee

Cognac
Congou
Cooler
Cooper
Crusta
Doctor
Eggnog
Eighty
Enzian
Export
Frappé
Gaelic
Gibson
Gimlet
Ginger
Glayva®
Grappa
Graves
Gueuze
Herbal
Indian
Kaffir
Kahlua
Kenyan
Kephir
Kirsch
Kölsch
Koumis
Kumiss
Kümmel
Lambic
Lisbon
Málaga
Malibu®
Meathe
Merlot
Mescal
Midori
Mocker
Mojito
Muscat
Nectar
Nobbie
Oolong
Oulong
Orgasm
Orgeat
Pastis
Pernod®
Poitín
Porter

Posset
Poteen
Pulque
Quincy
Redeye
Ribena®
Rickey
Samshu
Saumur
Scotch
Shandy
Sherry
Shiraz
Squash
Stingo
Strega
Taffia
Tisane
Tokaji
Waragi
Whisky
Yaqona
Zombie
Zythum

7 letters:
Absinth
Akvavit
Alcopop
Alicant
Amarone
Amoroso
Aquavit
Arabica
Auslese
Bacardi®
Banyuls
Bastard
Bellini
Bitters
Blended
Bourbon
Bucelas
Campari®
Catawba
Chablis
Chanoyu
Chianti
Chinese
Cinzano®
Cobbler

Collins
Cordial
Cowslip
Curaçao
Curaçoa
Daquiri
Dark rum
Draught
Eggflip
Eiswein
Essence
Fendant
Fleurie
Fustian
Gaillac
Guarana
Gunfire
Herb tea
Hokonui
Instant
Italian
Jasmine
Koumiss
Koumyss
Lapsang
Limeade
Liqueur
Madeira
Malmsey
Margaux
Marsala
Martini®
Mineral
Moselle
Negroni
Oenomel
Oloroso
Orvieto
Pale ale
Palinka
Parrina
Perrier®
Persico
Pilsner
Pink gin
Pomerol
Pommard
Ratafee
Ratafia
Real ale
Red-root

Drinks

Retsina
Rhenish
Robusta
Rooibos
Russian
Sambuca
Sangria
Sazerac
Schnaps
Scrumpy
Seltzer
Seventy
Shebean
Shebeen
Sherbet
Sherris
Shnapps
Shooter
Sidecar
Slammer
Sloe gin
Special
Stengah
Stinger
Swizzle
Tequila
Tio Pepe®
Turkish
Twankay
Vouvray

8 letters:
Absinthe
Advocaat
Aleberry
Amaretto
Ambrosia
Anisette
Apéritif
Armagnac
Bairrada
Bergerac
Bordeaux
Brouilly
Brown ale
Bucellas
Bullshot
Burgundy
Cabernet
Café noir
Calvados

Camomile
Champers
Charneco
Ciderkin
Coca-Cola®
Cocktail
Cold duck
Condrieu
Daiquiri
Dog's nose
Drambuie®
Dubonnet®
Earl Grey
Eau de vie
Espresso
Espumoso
Essencia
Faugères
Frascati
Fruit tea
Galliano®
Geropiga
Gigondas
Gin sling
Gluhwein
Highball
Hollands
Home brew
Hydromel
Iron brew
Jerepigo
Jurançon
Kabinett
Labrador
Lemonade
Lemon tea
Light ale
Lucozade®
Mahogany
Malvasia
Malvesie
Montilla
Muscadel
Muscadet
Muscatel
Palm wine
Paraguay
Pauillac
Persicot
Pilsener
Pink lady

Pinotage
Pradikat
Prunelle
Red biddy
Resinata
Resinate
Rice beer
Rice wine
Riesling
Root beer
Sambucca
Sancerre
Sangaree
Sauterne
Schnapps
Sillabub
Skokiaan
Smoothie
Snowball
Souchong
Sour mash
Spätlese
Spremuta
Spritzer
Spumante
Switchel
Syllabub
Tequilla
Tia Maria®
Trappist
Verdelho
Vermouth
White rum
Witblitz

9 letters:
Alexander
Americano
Applejack
Aqua vitae
Ayahuasco
Bacharach
Badminton
Bardolino
Bourgogne
Bourgueil
Brazilian
Buck's fizz
Chamomile
Champagne
Chocolate

Christmas
Claret cup
Cointreau®
Colombian
Corbières
Côte Rôtie
Cream soda
Cuba libre
Falernian
Firewater
Framboise
Fumé Blanc
Gattinara
Gingerade
Ginger ale
Gladstone
Grenadine
Gunpowder
Hard cider
Hermitage
Hippocras
Hoccamore
Lambrusco
Lambswool
Languedoc
Macchiato
Malvoisie
Manhattan
Margarita
Meersault
Metheglin
Meursault
Milk punch
Milk shake
Milk stout
Minervois
Mint julep
Mirabelle
Muscadine
Nor'wester
Orangeade
Pinot noir
Rauchbier
Rusty Nail
Sauternes
Sauvignon
Slivovitz
Snakebite
Soda water
St Emilion
Sundowner

Tarragona
Triple sec
Van der Hum
Weissbier
Whisky mac
White lady
Zinfandel

10 letters:
Apple juice
Barbaresco
Barley wine
Beaujolais
Bloody Mary
Bull's Blood
Buttermilk
Café au lait
Cappuccino
Chambertin
Chardonnay
Chartreuse®
Constantia
Costa Rican
Darjeeling
Dry martini
Elderberry
Frangelico
Fruit juice
Genevrette
Ginger beer
Ginger wine
Hochheimer
Hogan-mogen
Lolly water
Malt liquor
Manzanilla
Maraschino
Mochaccino
Montrachet
Moscow Mule
Mulled wine
Peter-see-me
Piesporter
Piña colada
Pousse-café
Rosé d'Anjou
Russian tea
Saint-Véran
Shandygaff
Single malt
Spruce beer

Sweet stout
Tom Collins
Valdepeñas
Vatted malt
Verdicchio
Vichy water
Vinho Verde
Weizenbier

11 letters:
Aguardiente
Amontillado
Apple brandy
Barley water
Benedictine
Bitter lemon
Black and tan
Black velvet
Boiler-maker
Continental
Crusted port
Egri Bikaver
Frappuccino
French roast
Half-and-half
Irish coffee
Kirshwasser
Lemon squash
Lime cordial
Monbazillac
Niersteiner
Orange juice
Orange pekoe
Pinot Grigio
Pouilly-Fumé
Post-and-rail
Rosso Cònero
Rüdesheimer
Saint-Julien
Screwdriver
Scuppernong
Skinny latte
Soapolallie
Steinberger
Tomato juice
Yerba de Maté
Whiskey sour

12 letters:
Asti Spumante
Barbera d'Albi
Barbera d'Asti

Drinks

Bière de Garde
Black Russian
Blue mountain
Cherry brandy
Christmas ale
Colheita Port
Côtes du Rhône
Crème de cacao
Gaelic coffee
Grand Marnier®
Hot chocolate
Humpty-dumpty
Ice-cream soda
India Pale Ale
Irish whiskey
Johannisberg
Kirschwasser
Liqueur Tokay
Marcobrunner
Mineral water
Moscato d'Asti
Old-fashioned
Perrier water®
Saint-Émilion
Saint-Estèphe
Sarsaparilla
Seltzer water
Tome-and-Jerry
Valpolicella
Vin ordinaire
Vosne-Romanée

13 letters:
Amendoa Amarga
Blanc de blancs
Crème de menthe
Decaffeinated
Eau des creoles
Entre-Deux-Mers
Liebfraumilch
Liqueur Muscat
Long Island Tea
Mâcon-Villages
Peach schnapps
Pessac-Léognan
Planter's punch
Pouilly-Fousse
Pouilly-Fuissé
Prairie oyster
Sixty shilling

14 letters:
Crémant d'Alsace
Crémant de Loire
Eighty shilling
Elderberry wine
French vermouth
Gewürztraminer
Herbal infusion
Johannisberger
John Barleycorn
Quarts de Chaume
Singapore sling
Tokay-Pinot Gris
Veuve Jacquolot

15 letters:
Alcohol-free beer
Applejack brandy
Brandy Alexander
Cask-conditioned
Crozes-Hermitage
Grange Hermitage
Grapefruit juice
Italian vermouth
Lachryma Christi
Lapsang Souchong
Salice Salentino
Seventy shilling
Southern Comfort®

16 letters:
Gevrey-Chambertin
Harvey Wallbanger
Non-alcoholic beer

17 letters:
Bailey's Irish Cream®
Beaujolais nouveau
Bereich Bernkastel
Bottle-conditioned
Cabernet Sauvignon
Nuits-Saint-Georges
Peppermint cordial

18 letters:
Blanquette de Limoux
Cask-conditioned ale
Coteaux du Tricastin
Teroldego Rotaliano

19 letters:
Dandelion and burdock

Drugs and drug terms

Drugs and drug terms

Drugs and drug terms

Wafer

6 letters:
Amulet
Amytal®
Ativan®
Bombed
Bromal
Bummer
Burned
Charas
Cocain
Cook up
Curare
Curari
Dealer
Dosage
Downer
Dragée
Dry out
Elixir
Emetic
Get off
Heroin
Hooked
Inulin
Ipecac
Jack up
Joypop
Junkie
Kaolin
Liquor
Loaded
Make it
Mescla
Monkey
Mummia
Nod out
Normal
Number
Opiate
Peyote
Pituri
Popper
Prozac®
Pusher
Reefer
Remedy
Saloop
Skin up
Spaced

Spirit
Spliff
Squill
Step on
Stoned
Sulpha
Turn on
Valium®
Viagra®
Wasted
Weight
Zonked

7 letters:
Anodyne
Araroba
Argyrol®
Aspirin
Atabrin
Atebrin®
Atropin
Blocker
Botanic
Calomel
Cardiac
Cascara
Charlie
Chillum
Churrus
Cocaine
Codeine
Crank up
Damiana
Dapsone
Ecbolic
Ecstasy
Errhine
Ethical
Eucaine
Exhaust
Extract
Guarana
Hashish
Hemagog
Hemlock
Henbane
Hepatic
Hophead
Hyped up
Hypnone
Insulin

Jellies
Kaoline
Librium®
Linctus
Metopon
Miltown®
Mixture
Mogadon®
Morphia
Nervine
Patulin
Pep pill
Pessary
Placebo
Pothead
Quinine
Reactor
Rhatany
Salicin
Seconal®
Shoot up
Skin-pop
Smashed
Steroid
Styptic
Suramin
Swacked
Synergy
Tetanic
Topical
Trional
Turpeth
Vehicle
Veronal®
Vinegar
Wrecked

8 letters:
Acidhead
Adjuvant
Antabuse®
Antidote
Aromatic
Atabrine®
Ataraxic
Atropine
Autacoid
Bacterin
Banthine
Barbital
Benadryl®

Bioassay
Blockade
Caffeine
Cannabis
Cinchona
Cohobate
Comedown
Cortisol
Curarine
Designer
Diazepam
Diuretic
Emulsion
Endermic
Ephedrin
Excitant
External
Fentanyl
Freebase
Goofball
Hyoscine
Hypnotic
Inhalant
Ketamine
Krameria
Laetrile
Laudanum
Laxative
Lenitive
Mainline
Mersalyl
Mescalin
Methadon
Miticide
Moonrock
Morphine
Naloxone
Narcotic
Nembutal®
Neomycin
Nepenthe
Nicotine
Nystatin
Opium den
Overdose
Oxytocic
Pectoral
Positive
Psilocin
Pulmonic
Reaction

Relaxant
Retrovir®
Rifampin
Roborant
Salicine
Santonin
Scammony
Scopolia
Sedative
Serevent®
Snowball
Spansule
Specific
Switch on
Terebene
Tetronal
Thiazide
Tincture
Tolerant
Valerian
Vesicant
Viricide
Wormseed
Zerumbet

9 letters:
Acyclovir
Addiction
Addictive
Analeptic
Analgesic
Angel dust
Anovulant
Antrycide
Arsenical
Ataractic
Attenuant
Augmentin
Azedarach
Barbitone
Berberine
Biguanide
Botanical
Bring down
Busulphan
Calmative
Captopril
Carbachol
Cathartic
Cisplatin
Clozapine

Corticoid
Cortisone
Crackhead
Cyclizine
Cytotoxin
Decoction
Demulcent
Digitalis
Dramamine®
Electuary
Ephedrine
Excipient
Expellant
Expellent
Febrifuge
Foscarnet
Frusemide
Galenical
Glycoside
Goa powder
Hemagogue
Ibuprofen
Inotropic
Iprindole
Isoniazid
Jaborandi
Lorazepam
Magistral
Marihuana
Marijuana
Menstruum
Mepacrine
Merbromin
Mercurial
Mescaline
Methadone
Mydriasis
Novocaine®
Nux vomica
Officinal
Oleoresin
Paludrine®
Paregoric
Pethidine
Phenytoin
Practolol
Purgative
Quercetin
Quercitin
Quinidine
Quinquina

Drugs and drug terms

Reserpine
Resolvent
Revulsive
Safflower
Scopoline
Senna leaf
Senna pods
Sensitise
Sensitize
Signature
Smackhead
Soporific
Spaced out
Speedball
Stimulant
Strung out
Sudorific
Synergism
Synergist
Tamoxifen
Temazepam
Teniacide
Teniafuge
Totaquine
Tricyclic
Trinitrum
Verapamil
Vermifuge
Vulnerary
Wych hazel
Yohimbine

10 letters:
Abirritant
Absorption
Acetanilid
Agrypnotic
Alterative
Amantadine
Ampicillin
Anesthetic
Antagonist
Antibiotic
Antiemetic
Antimonial
Antipyrine
Anxiolytic
Astringent
Atracurium
Bacitracin
Belladonna

Benzedrine®
Benzocaine
Biological
Bufotenine
Chalybeate
Cholagogue
Cimetedine
Cimetidine
Cinchonine
Clofibrate
Clomiphene
Cold turkey
Colestipol
Confection
Connection
Convulsant
Dependency
Depressant
Disulfiram
Ergotamine
Ethambutol
Euphoriant
Formestane
Get through
Haemagogue
Helminthic
Hemostatic
Hypodermic
Imipramine
Indapamide
Isoniazide
Ivermectin
Lethal dose
Long-acting
Medication
Mefloquine
Meperidine
Methyldopa
Mickey Finn
Nalbuphine
Nifedipine
Nitrazepam
Painkiller
Palliative
Papaverine
Parenteral
Penicillin
Pentaquine
Phenacaine
Phenacetin
Phenformin

Potash alum
Potentiate
Prednisone
Preventive
Primaquine
Probenecid
Psilocybin
Quinacrine
Rifampicin
Salbutamol
Selegiline
Side effect
Space cadet
Speedfreak
Spermicide
Stramonium
Sucralfate
Taeniacide
Taeniafuge
Terramycin®
Thiouracil
Unofficial
Vesicatory
Witch hazel
Withdrawal
Ziduvudine

11 letters:
Acetanilide
Acriflavine
Adiaphorous
Allopurinol
Aminobutene
Amphetamine
Amyl nitrite
Anaesthetic
Antifebrile
Antimycotic
Antipyretic
Antitussive
Aphrodisiac
Apomorphine
Barbiturate
Beta-blocker
Bitter aloes
Bupivacaine
Cantharides
Carbimazole
Carminative
Chloroquine
Chrysarobin

Cinnarizine
Clenbuterol
Clindamycin
Contrayerva
Deserpidine
Diamorphine
Diaphoretic
Distalgesic
Embrocation
Emmenagogue
Expectorant
Fluconazole
Gemfibrozil
Haemostatic
Haloperidol
Hyoscyamine
Ipecacuanha
Ipratropium
Isoxsuprine
Laughing gas
Magic bullet
Masticatory
Meprobamate
Neuroleptic
Nikethamide
Paracetamol
Paraldehyde
Pentamidine
Pentazocine
Pravastatin
Propranolol
Proprietary
Psychedelic
Psychodelic
Purple heart
Restorative
Sanguinaria
Scopolamine
Sensitivity
Short-acting
Succedaneum
Suppository
Suppurative
Thalidomide
Theobromine
Tolbutamide
Tous-les-mois
Trituration
Tropomyosin
Tumefacient
Vasodilator

Vinblastine
Vincristine

12 letters:
ACE inhibitor
Alexipharmic
Alpha-blocker
Anthelmintic
Antimalarial
Antiperiodic
Arsphenamine
Azathioprine
Chlorambucil
Control group
Cyclopropane
Cyclosporin-A
Decongestant
False saffron
Fluidextract
Fluphenazine
Glue-sniffing
Gonadotropin
Guanethidine
Hallucinogen
Idiosyncrasy
Incompatible
Indomethacin
Intoxicating
Mecamylamine
Methaqualone
Methotrexate
Mifepristone
Nitrous oxide
Perphenazine
Physotigmine
Prednisolone
Prescription
Promethazine
Prophylactic
Psychoactive
Radio mimetic
Recreational
Solvent abuse
Sorbefacient
Spermatocide
Streptomycin
Stupefacient
Tetracycline
Tranquilizer
Trimethoprim
Venepuncture

Venipuncture

13 letters:
Abortifacient
Amitriptyline
Anaphrodisiac
Anthelminthic
Antihistamine
Antispasmodic
Carbamazepine
Contraceptive
Co-trimoxazole
Depressomotor
Knockout drops
Magic mushroom
Materia medica
Mind-expanding
Penicillamine
Phencyclidine
Phenothiazine
Pyrimethamine
Sulphadiazine
Sympatholytic
Tachyphylaxis
Thiabendazole
Tranquilliser
Tranquillizer
Triamcinolone
Vasoinhibitor
Vinca alkaloid

14 letters:
Anticonvulsant
Antidepressant
Antimetabolite
Antiphlogistic
Bendrofluozide
Benzodiazepine
Bronchodilator
Butyrhophenone
Cascara sagrada
Chlorothiazide
Chlorpromazine
Chlorpropamide
Chlorthalidone
Contraindicate
Dimenhydrinate
Flucloxacillin
Hydrocortisone
Hypersensitive
Mean lethal dose
Mercaptopurine

Ducks

Norethisterone
Over-the-counter
Pentobarbitone
Phenacyclidine
Phenobarbitone
Phenylbutazone
Rochelle powder
Seidlitz powder
Sulfamethazine
Sulphadimidine
Sulphanilamide
Sulphathiozole
Sulphisoxazole

15 letters:
Acetophenetidin
Alkylating agent
Anticholinergic
Bioavailability
Chloramphenicol
Dinitrogen oxide
Local anesthetic
Methamphetamine
Phenolphthalein
Psychotomimetic
Seidlitz powders
Shooting gallery
Sodium Pentothal®
Sympathomimetic
Vasoconstrictor

16 letters:
Anti-inflammatory
Blow someone's mind
Chemoprophylaxis
Chlordiazepoxide
Hypodermic needle
Local anaesthetic

See also:
➤ **Antibiotics**

Median lethal dose
Thiopental sodium

17 letters:
Calcium antagonist
Chlortetracycline

28 letters:
Nonsteroidal anti-
  inflammatory
Dextroamphetamine
Diethyltryptamine
General anesthetic
Hypodermic syringe
Immunosuppressive
Minimum lethal dose
Pentylenetetrazol
Thiopentone sodium

18 letters:
Dimethyltryptamine
General anaesthetic
Intermediate-acting
Withdrawal symptoms

19 letters:
Acetylsalicylic acid
Sodium pentabarbital

20 letters:
Pentobarbitone sodium

21 letters:
Procaine hydrochloride

23 letters:
Meperidene hydrochloride

24 letters:
Lysergic acid diethylamide

Ducks

4 letters:
Blue
Musk
Smee
Smew
Sord

Surf
Teal
Wood

5 letters:
Eider
Ruddy

Scaup

6 letters:
Garrot
Hareld
Herald
Runner

Scoter
Smeath
Smeeth
Tufted
Wigeon

7 letters:
Flapper
Gadwall
Mallard
Muscovy
Pintail
Pochard
Spatula
Widgeon

8 letters:
Bald-pate

Garganey
Mandarin
Oldsquaw
Paradise
Shelduck
Shoveler

9 letters:
Aylesbury
Bargander
Bergander
Golden-eye
Goosander
Greenhead
Harlequin
Sheldduck
Shoveller

Sprigtail
Whistling

10 letters:
Bufflehead
Canvasback
Long-tailed
Shieldrake
Surfscoter

11 letters:
Ferruginous

12 letters:
Velvet scoter

Dwarfs

3 letters:
Doc

5 letters:
Dopey

Happy

6 letters:
Grumpy
Sleepy

Sneezy

7 letters:
Bashful

Dyes

3 letters:
Azo
Vat

4 letters:
Anil
Chay
Choy
Ikat
Kohl
Wald
Weld
Woad
Wold

5 letters:
Batik
Chaya
Chica
Congo
Eosin
Grain

Henna
Shaya
Sumac
Woald

6 letters:
Archil
Battik
Cobalt
Corkir
Crotal
Direct
Flavin
Fustic
Fustoc
Gambir
Indigo
Kamala
Kermes
Korkir
Madder

Orcein
Orchel
Orchil
Raddle
Sumach
Tannin
Tie-dye

7 letters:
Alkanet
Camwood
Crocein
Crottle
Cudbear
Engrain
Flavine
Fuchsin
Gambier
Indican
Indoxyl
Indulin

Dyes

Magenta
Mauvein
Para-red
Puccoon
Sunfast
Valonia

8 letters:
Catechin
Cinnabar
Fuchsine
Indamine
Induline
Mauveine
Nigrosin
Orchella
Purpurin
Pyronine
Safranin
Stone-rag

Stone-raw
Turnsole
Xanthium
Xylidine

9 letters:
Cochineal
Envermeil
Indirubin
Myrobalan
Nigrosine
Phthalein
Primuline
Quinoline
Rhodamine
Rosanilin
Safranine

10 letters:
Anthracene

Azobenzine
Carthamine
Quercitron
Resorcinol
Rosaniline
Tartrazine
Tropaeolin

11 letters:
Incarnadine

13 letters:
Anthraquinone
Canthaxanthin

14 letters:
Dinitrobenzene

15 letters:
Phenolphthalein

See also:
➤ **Pigments**

E

Ear, parts of

5 letters:
Ancus
Incus
Pinna

6 letters:
Meatus
Stapes
Tragus

7 letters:
Cochlea
Eardrum
Ear lobe
Malleus
Saccule

Utricle

8 letters:
Tympanum

10 letters:
Oval window

11 letters:
Round window

12 letters:
Organ of Corti

13 letters:
Auditory canal
Auditory nerve

14 letters:
Eustachian tube

16 letters:
Tympanic
membrane

18 letters:
Semicircular canals

21 letters:
External auditory
canal

Earth's crust

4 letters:
Sial
Sima

7 letters:
Oceanic

8 letters:
Basement

11 letters:
Continental
Lithosphere
Lower mantle
Upper mantle

13 letters:
Asthenosphere

14 letters:
Transition zone

24 letters:
Mohorovicíc
discontinuity

Eating habits

Food	**Name of habit**
Fellow humans	Anthropophagic *or* anthropophagous
Bees	Apivorous
Other members of the same species	Cannibalistic
Meat	Carnivorous
Fruit	Carpophagous, frugivorous, *or* fruitarian
Dead and rotting flesh	Carrion
Dung	Coprophagous

Ecclesiastical terms

Food	Name of habit
Earth	Geophagous
Plants	Herbivorous
Wood	Hylophagous
Insects	Insectivorous
Mud	Limivorous
Large pieces of food	Macrophagous
Only one food	Monophagous
Fungi	Mycetophagous
Ants	Myrmecophagous
Nectar	Nectarivorous
Nuts	Nucivorous
Meat and plants	Omnivorous
Raw food	Omophagic *or* omophagous
Fish	Piscivorous
Gods	Theophagous
No animal products	Vegan
No flesh	Vegetarian
Animals	Zoophagous

Ecclesiastical terms

1 letter:
R
S
V
X
Y

2 letters:
BV
CE
DG
DV
HC
MS
PB
PP
RR
Sr
SS
St
VG
VW
Xn
XP
Xt

3 letters:
Abp
Alb

BVM
Cup
Dip
Fra
God
IDN
IHS
Lay
LDS
Mgr
Nun
Par
Pie
Pit
Pix
Pye
Pyx
Rev
See
Sta
STD
Ste
Sun
Use
Ven
Vow
WCC
Zen

4 letters:
Abbé
Alms
Ambo
Amen
Apse
Bans
Bapt
Beat
Bell
Cell
Chap
C of E
Cope
Cowl
Crib
Cure
Dame
Dean
Dove
Ebor
Eccl
Fall
Fold
Font
Hadg
Hajj
Halo

Holy
Host
Hymn
Idol
Kirk
Laic
Lent
Mass
Monk
None
Pall
Revd
Rite
Rood
Rule
Sain
Seal
Sext
Sign
Sion
Slip
Suff
Text
Veil
V Rev
Wake
Whit
Xmas
Xnty
YMCA
Yule
YWCA
Zion

5 letters:
Abbey
Abbot
Agape
Allah
Altar
Ambry
Amice
Amish
Angel
Banns
Bedel
Bible
Bless
Canon
Carol
Catho

Cense
Chant
Choir
Clerk
Close
Cloth
Credo
Creed
Cross
Cruet
Crypt
Curse
Deify
Deism
Deist
Deity
Demon
Denom
Devil
Dirge
Dogma
Dowry
Druid
Elder
Elect
Epiph
Exeat
Faith
Flock
Friar
Frock
Glebe
Glory
Godly
Grace
Hindu
Hours
House
Islam
Jesus
Jewry
Karma
Koran
Laity
Laver
Maker
Manna
Manse
Matin
Miter
Mitre

Mt Rev
Myrrh
Nones
Offer
Order
Padre
Pagan
Papal
Paten
Patin
Pietà
Piety
Plate
Prior
Psalm
Pyxis
Rabbi
Saint
Satan
Stall
Stole
Stoop
Stoup
Suffr
Synod
Teind
Tithe
Title
Trump
Vigil
Wafer

6 letters:
Abbacy
Abbess
Advent
Almuce
Anoint
Anthem
Archbp
Assume
Aumbry
Austin
Beadle
Bishop
Cantor
Censer
Chapel
Cherub
Chrism
Christ

Ecclesiastical terms

Church
Clergy
Cleric
Coming
Common
Crèche
Curacy
Curate
Curtal
Deacon
Devout
Divine
Dossal
Dragon
Easter
Eparch
Exarch
Exodus
Father
Ferial
Friary
Fundie
Gloria
Gnosis
God man
Godson
Gospel
Gradin
Hallow
Harrow
Heaven
Hebrew
Heresy
Homily
Housel
Hymnal
Impose
Intone
Israel
Jesuit
Jewish
Judaic
Lavabo
Lector
Legend
Lenten
Lesson
Litany
Living
Marian
Martyr

Matins
Maundy
Mormon
Mosaic
Moslem
Mosque
Mother
Muslim
Novice
Nuncio
Oblate
Octave
Office
Old man
Ordain
Orders
Papacy
Papism
Papist
Parish
Parson
Pastor
Patron
Paynim
Person
Postil
Prayer
Preach
Priest
Priory
Proper
Pulpit
Purify
Purple
Quaker
Redeem
Revert
Ritual
Rosary
Rt Revd
Rubric
Sacral
Sacred
Schism
Season
Secret
Sermon
Server
Sexton
Shiite
Shinto

Shrine
Shroud
Simony
Sinful
Sinner
Sister
Solemn
Stigma
Sufism
Sunday
Suttee
Talmud
Tantra
Taoism
Te Deum
Temple
Theism
Tippet
Tongue
Venite
Verger
Vesper
Vestal
Vestry
Virgin
Votary
Warden

7 letters:

Aaronic
Acolyte
Agrapha
Ampulla
Anagoge
Apostle
Article
Ascetic
Asperse
Atheism
Atheist
Bahaism
Bambino
Baptism
Baptist
Baptize
Benison
Blessed
Brother
Canonry
Cantuar
Cassock

Cenacle
Chalice
Chancel
Chantry
Chapter
Chrisom
Classis
Cluniac
Collate
Collect
College
Commune
Confess
Confirm
Conform
Convent
Council
Counsel
Crosier
Crozier
Deanery
Decanal
Defrock
Deified
Devotee
Diocese
Dissent
Dominie
Element
Epistle
Eremite
Errancy
Evangel
Evil One
Expiate
Frontal
Genesis
Gentile
Glorify
Gnostic
Godhead
Godhood
Halidom
Hassock
Heathen
Holy day
Holy Joe
Hosanna
Idolize
Immerse

Incense
Infulae
Inspire
Introit
Jainism
Jehovah
Judaism
Kenosis
Kerygma
Kirkman
Labarum
Lady Day
Laicize
Liturgy
Low Mass
Lustral
Madonna
Maniple
Martyry
Mattins
Maurist
Messiah
Minster
Miracle
Mission
Monkery
Monkish
Mortify
Mourner
Movable
Mystery
Notitia
Nunhood
Nunnery
Old Nick
Oratory
Ordinal
Our Lady
Parlour
Paschal
Pauline
Peccant
Penance
Pietism
Pilgrim
Pontiff
Prebend
Prelacy
Prelate
Present

Primacy
Primate
Profane
Prophet
Proverb
Provide
Puritan
Ramadan
Recluse
Rectory
Regular
Reredos
Respond
Retable
Revival
Sabbath
Sacring
Sanctum
Sanctus
Saviour
Secular
Sedilia
Service
Species
Sponsor
Spousal
Station
Stylite
Tantric
Titulus
Tribune
Trinity
Unction
Unfrock
Vatican
Vespers
Whitsun
Worship
Xmas Day
Yule log
Zionism

8 letters:
Abbatial
Ablution
Advowson
Affusion
Agnus Dei
Alleluia
Altar boy
Anathema

Ecclesiastical terms

Anglican
Antiphon
Beadsman
Bedesman
Benefice
Brownist
Buddhism
Buddhist
Canonist
Canonize
Canon law
Canticle
Cathedra
Catholic
Celibacy
Cellarer
Cenobite
Chancery
Chapelry
Chaplain
Charisma
Chasuble
Cherubim
Choirboy
Christen
Ciborium
Clerical
Cloister
Coenacle
Colloquy
Creation
Crucifix
Deaconry
Dedicate
Devotion
Diaconal
Dies Irae
Diocesan
Diriment
Disciple
Disfrock
Docetism
Doxology
Druidess
Druidism
Ecce Homo
Ecclesia
Emmanuel
Empyrean
Epiphany
Epistler

Evensong
Expiable
Faithful
Footpace
Fraction
Frontlet
Galilean
Gallican
Godchild
God's acre
Godsquad
Guardian
Hail Mary
Hallowed
Heavenly
Hierarch
Hieratic
High Mass
Holiness
Holy City
Holy Land
Holy rood
Holy Week
Hymn book
Immanent
Immanuel
Jacobite
Jubilate
Lavatory
Libellee
Lord's Day
Lustrate
Lutheran
Man of God
Maronite
Marriage
Menology
Ministry
Miserere
Mohammed
Monachal
Monastic
Monition
Monkhood
Nativity
Oblation
Offering
Ordinand
Ordinary
Orthodox
Paradise

Parament
Parclose
Pastoral
Pelagian
Penitent
Pericope
Piacular
Postlude
Priestly
Prophesy
Province
Psalmody
Redeemer
Registry
Response
Reverend
Rigorism
Rogation
Sacristy
Sanctify
Sanctity
Sarum use
Scapular
Sentence
Separate
Silenced
Simoniac
Sinecure
Son of God
Suffrage
Superior
Tantrism
Tertiary
Thurible
Thurifer
Tithable
Traditor
Transept
Unchurch
Unhallow
Veronica
Versicle
Vesperal
Vestment
Viaticum
Vicarage
Vicarial

9 letters:
Adoration
Alleluiah

Allelujah
Ambrosian
Antiphony
Apostolic
Archangel
Aspersion
Augustine
Avoidance
Baptistry
Beelzebub
Bishopric
Blasphemy
Born-again
Calvinism
Calvinist
Candlemas
Canonical
Cantorial
Capitular
Catechism
Catechize
Cathedral
Celebrant
Celestial
Christian
Christmas
Churchman
City of God
Claustral
Clergyman
Clericals
Cloistral
Coadjutor
Coenobite
Collation
Collative
Collegium
Comforter
Commendam
Communion
Conciliar
Confessor
Confirmed
Dalai Lama
Damnation
Deaconess
Dei gratia
Diaconate
Dimissory
Directory
Discalced

Dissenter
Dog collar
Dominical
Easter Day
Ecumenism
Epiclesis
Episcopal
Establish
Eucharist
Exarchate
Expectant
Expiation
Expiatory
Formalism
Formulary
Godfather
Godmother
Godparent
Gospeller
Graveyard
Hagiarchy
Halloween
Hallowmas
Hermitage
Hierarchy
High altar
Holocaust
Holy Ghost
Holy Grail
Holy water
Homiletic
Immersion
Impeccant
Incensory
Incumbent
Institute
Interdict
Jerusalem
Last rites
Lay sister
Libellant
Liturgics
Liturgist
Love feast
Low Sunday
Martinmas
Martyrdom
Mercy seat
Methodism
Methodist
Millenary

Miscreant
Missioner
Monastery
Mortal sin
Novitiate
Obedience
Offertory
Officiant
Officiate
Our Father
Out sister
Paraclete
Parochial
Parsonage
Pastorate
Patriarch
Patrimony
Patristic
Patrology
Patroness
Pentecost
Perdition
Pluralism
Plurality
Pluralize
Polyptych
Precentor
Preceptor
Predicant
Prelatism
Presbyter
Proselyte
Provision
Quakerism
Recession
Reconcile
Reconvert
Reformism
Religieux
Religious
Reliquary
Remission
Ritualism
Ritualize
Rubrician
Rural dean
Sacrament
Sacrarium
Sacrifice
Sacrilege
Sacristan

Ecclesiastical terms

Saint's day
Salvation
Sanctuary
Scientist
Seneschal
Shintoism
Solemnize
Spiritual
Succentor
Succursal
Suffragan
Surrogate
Sutteeism
Synagogue
Testament
Tradition
Translate
Venerable
Venial sin
Vestryman
Vicariate
Yom Kippur

10 letters:
Act of faith
Allhallows
Altar cloth
Amen corner
Antinomian
Antiphonal
Apostolate
Archbishop
Archdeacon
Archpriest
Asceticism
Ascription
Assumption
Athanasian
Bar mitzvah
Benedicite
Benedictus
Canonicals
Canonicate
Canonicity
Canto fermo
Catechumen
Ceremonial
Chancellor
Childermas
Churchgoer
Circumcise

Cloistered
Conference
Confessant
Confession
Confirmand
Conformist
Conformity
Connection
Consecrate
Consistory
Conventual
Dedication
Deo gratias
Deo volente
Devotional
Discipline
Ecumenical
Enthusiasm
Enthusiast
Episcopacy
Episcopate
Evangelism
Evangelist
Evangelize
Fellowship
Fenestella
Free Church
Gnosticize
Good Friday
Gospel oath
Hagiolatry
Halleluiah
Hallelujah
Hierocracy
High Church
High Priest
Holy Family
Holy orders
Holy Spirit
Homiletics
Horologium
House group
House of God
Idolatrize
Impanation
Impeccable
Insufflate
Intinction
Invitatory
Invocation
Irreligion

Lammastide
Last Supper
Lay brother
Lectionary
Limitarian
Liturgical
Lord's table
Magnificat
Metropolis
Millennium
Miscreance
Misericord
Missionary
Mother's Day
Ordination
Palm Sunday
Pancake Day
Pilgrimage
Pontifical
Prayer book
Preachment
Prebendary
Presbytery
Priesthood
Profession
Protestant
Providence
Provincial
Puritanism
Religieuse
Requiescat
Reredorter
Responsory
Retrochoir
Reunionist
Revelation
Revivalism
Revivalist
Sacerdotal
Sacrosanct
Sanctified
Sanctitude
Scriptures
Secularize
Sexagesima
Shrovetide
Sisterhood
Solifidian
Subreption
Subsellium
Superaltar

Tabernacle
Twelfth Day
Unhallowed
Unhouseled
Versicular
Vigil light
Visitation
Whit Monday
Whit Sunday

11 letters:
All Souls' Day
Antependium
Antiphonary
Archdiocese
Aspersorium
Augustinian
Benediction
Beneficiary
Blasphemous
Book of hours
Brotherhood
Calefactory
Cardinalate
Catholicism
Celtic cross
Christening
Christingle
Churchwoman
Clericalism
Cockleshell
Coessential
Commandment
Communicant
Communicate
Contemplate
Conventicle
Convocation
Crucifixion
Evangelical
Externalism
Gloria Patri
Glossolalia
Goddaughter
Hare Krishna
House church
Immanentism
Impropriate
Incarnation
Incorporeal
Independent

Institution
Irreligious
Jesus Christ
Judgment Day
Lord of Hosts
Lord's Prayer
Lord's Supper
Martyrology
Millenarian
Monasticism
Monseigneur
Mother of God
Oecumenical
Parish clerk
Parishioner
Paschal Lamb
Passiontide
Passion Week
Patron saint
Pelagianism
Pentecostal
Preparation
Priestcraft
Prodigal Son
Proselytize
Protomartyr
Purificator
Rastafarian
Recessional
Ritualistic
Sabbatarian
Sacramental
Sanctus bell
Scriptorium
Stabat Mater
Sursum corda
Temporality
Thaumaturge
Twelfthtide
Whitsuntide
Year of grace
Zen Buddhism

12 letters:
Advent Sunday
All Saints' Day
Anathematize
Annunciation
Apostolic See
Archdeaconry
Ascension Day

Ash Wednesday
Body of Christ
Chapel of ease
Chapterhouse
Christmas Day
Christmas Eve
Churchwarden
Circuit rider
Concelebrate
Confessional
Confirmation
Confucianism
Congregation
Deconsecrate
Disestablish
Dispensation
Ecclesiastic
Ecclesiology
Eleanor Cross
Episcopalian
Episcopalism
Good Shepherd
Heteroousian
Holy Saturday
Holy Thursday
Immersionism
Independency
Intercession
Judgement Day
Kyrie eleison
Last Judgment
Messeigneurs
Metropolitan
Ministration
Most Reverend
New Testament
Non-Christian
Obedientiary
Old Testament
Palingenesis
Patriarchate
Presbyterian
Presentation
Presentative
Procathedral
Processional
Providential
Quadragesima
Real presence
Residentiary
Rogation Days

Ecclesiastical terms

Satisfaction
Satisfactory
Septuagesima
Spirituality
Spiritualize
Spy Wednesday
Subapostolic
Subscription
Sunday school
Superhumeral
Thanksgiving
Traducianism
Twelfth Night
Very Reverend
Vicar general
Well dressing
Winding sheet

13 letters:
Allhallowtide
Apostles' Creed
Archbishopric
Archidiaconal
Ascensiontide
Autocephalous
Baptism of fire
Burnt offering
Canonical hour
Contemplation
Contemplative
Corpus Christi
Credence table
Day of Judgment
Divine service
Ecclesiolatry
Excommunicate
Gift of tongues
Glorification
Holy Communion
Incardination
Last Judgement
Mater dolorosa
Metrical psalm
Mortification
Nonpractising
Passion Sunday

Premillennial
Protestantism
Quadragesimal
Quinquagesima
Right Reverend
Roman Catholic
Sacerdotalism
Salvation Army
Sanctuary lamp
Shrove Tuesday
Spoiled priest
Trinity Sunday
Unconsecrated

14 letters:
Archidiaconate
Archiepiscopal
Article of faith
Day of Judgement
Ecclesiastical
Exclaustration
Extracanonical
Fundamentalism
Gregorian chant
Indifferentism
Intercommunion
Maundy Thursday
Millenarianism
Orthodox Church
Parish register
Peculiar people
Pontifical Mass
Rastafarianism
Recording Angel
Reverend Mother
Sacramentalism
Sacramentarian
Territorialism

15 letters:
Act of contrition
Archiepiscopate
Athanasian Creed
Church of England
Dominical letter
Ecclesiasticism

Excommunication
Father confessor
General Assembly
Jehovah's Witness
Mothering Sunday
Presbyterianism
Ten
  Commandments

16 letters:
Apostolic Fathers
Blessed Sacrament
Church of Scotland
Patriarchal cross
Premillennialism
Prince of Darkness
Saint Swithin's Day
Sustentation fund

17 letters:
Communion of
  saints
Established Church
Saint Andrew's
  Cross
Speaking in
  tongues

18 letters:
College of Cardinals
Establishmentarian
Stations of the
  Cross

19 letters:
Gloria in Excelsis
Deo

22 letters:
World Council of
Churches

27 letters:
Ecclesiastical
  Commissioners
Purification of the
  Virgin Mary

Economics

BRANCHES OF ECONOMICS

7 letters:
Welfare

10 letters:
Agronomics
Industrial

11 letters:
Cliometrics

12 letters:
Econometrics

14 letters:
Macroeconomics
Microeconomics

15 letters:
Economic history

ECONOMICS TERMS

2 letters:
HP

3 letters:
Bid
GDP
GNP
Pay
PEP
Tax
UBR
VAT

4 letters:
Bank
Boom
Cash
Debt
Duty
Hire
Loan
MCAs
Mint
PAYE
PSBR
Rent
Shop
Wage

5 letters:
Asset
Lease
Money
Price
Sales
Share
Slump
Stock
Trade

Trust
Yield

6 letters:
Barter
Budget
Cartel
Credit
Demand
Export
Import
Income
Labour
Lender
Market
Merger
Patent
Picket
Profit
Retail
Salary
Saving
Supply
Tariff
Wealth

7 letters:
Autarky
Boycott
Capital
Dumping
Duopoly
Embargo
Finance
Freight
Funding
Hedging
Holding
Invoice

Lockout
Payroll
Pension
Premium
Revenue
Subsidy
Surplus
Synergy
Trustee
Utility

8 letters:
Base rate
Capacity
Consumer
Currency
Discount
Dividend
Earnings
Employee
Employer
Exchange
Freeport
Hoarding
Hot money
Interest
Junk bond
Monopoly
Mortgage
Offshore
Overtime
Producer
Recovery
Supplier
Takeover
Taxation
Tax haven
Training

Economics

9 letters:
Commodity
Deflation
Franchise
Free rider
Free trade
Income tax
Insurance
Liability
Liquidity
Means test
Mediation
Middleman
Net profit
Oligopoly
Overheads
Piecework
Portfolio
Rationing
Recession
Recycling
Reflation
Trademark
Unit trust

10 letters:
Automation
Bankruptcy
Bear market
Bull market
Capitalism
Closed shop
Commission
Depression
Divestment
Employment
Fiscal drag
Fiscal year
Fixed costs
Forfaiting
Game theory
Green money
Insolvency
Investment
Monetarism
Pawnbroker
Production
Redundancy
Share issue
Tax evasion
Trade union

Wholesaler

11 letters:
Arbitration
Capital good
Central bank
Competition
Consumption
Cooperative
Corporation
Devaluation
Durable good
Expenditure
Fixed assets
Foreclosure
Gross profit
Index-linked
Indirect tax
Intangibles
Legal tender
Liquid asset
Liquidation
Money supply
Overheating
Overmanning
Pension fund
Poverty trap
Premium bond
Public works
Pump priming
Revaluation
Savings bank
Self service
Shareholder
Share market
Shop steward
Social costs
Speculation
Stagflation
Stockbroker
Stock market
Stop-go cycle
Transaction
Underwriter

12 letters:
Balance sheet
Black economy
Bridging loan
Buyer's market
Clearing bank
Common market

Consumer good
Cost of living
Customs union
Depreciation
Deregulation
Discount rate
Disinflation
Dutch disease
Earned income
Entrepreneur
Exchange rate
Fiscal policy
Five-Year Plan
Gold standard
Hard currency
Hire purchase
Human capital
Interest rate
Joint venture
Labour market
Laisser faire
Laissez faire
Mercantilism
Merchant bank
Mixed economy
Moonlighting
National debt
Pay-as-you-earn
Productivity
Profit margin
Rent controls
Risk analysis
Soft currency
Stock control
Tax avoidance
Terms of trade
Trade barrier
Unemployment
Welfare state

13 letters:
Budget deficit
Business cycle
Credit squeeze
Discount house
Financial year
Free trade area
Free trade zone
Futures market
Income support
Invisible hand

Listed company
Market failure
Multinational
Primary sector
Privatization
Profitability
Profit sharing
Protectionism
Public finance
Public utility
Ratchet effect
Seller's market
Sequestration
Service sector
Stock exchange
Unit of account
Value-added tax
Variable costs
Wage restraint

14 letters:
Balanced budget
Balance of trade
Barriers to exit
Command economy
Commercial bank
Corporation tax
Credit controls
Current account
Deposit account
Disequilibrium
Economic growth
Economic policy
Fringe benefits
Full employment
Gains from trade
Government bond
Hyperinflation
Infrastructure
Inheritance tax
Mass production
Monetary policy
National income
Nondurable good
Planned economy
Public interest
Quality control
Regional policy
Self-employment
Simple interest
Specialization

Tangible assets
Unearned income
Venture capital
Working capital

15 letters:
Barriers to entry
Building society
Diversification
Fixed investment
Friendly society
Marginal revenue
Marginal utility
Nationalization
National product
Per capita income
Private property
Purchasing power
Rationalization
Self-sufficiency
Share price index

16 letters:
Demand management
Disposable income
Division of labour
Economies of scale
Industrial estate
Industrial policy
Industrial sector
Instalment credit
Intangible assets
Invisible balance
Management buy-out
Medium of exchange
Retail price index
Standard of living

17 letters:
Balance of payments
Chamber of Commerce
Cost effectiveness
Cost-push inflation
Economic sanctions
Free-market economy
Gilt-edged security
Industrial dispute
International debt
Joint-stock company
Private enterprise
Public expenditure
Subsidiary company

Economics

18 letters:
Diminishing returns
Environmental audit
Import restrictions
Inflationary spiral
Perfect competition
Personal equity plan
Socio-economic group
Trade-weighted index

19 letters:
Cost-benefit analysis
Deindustrialization
Demand-pull inflation
Industrial relations
Labour theory of value
Macroeconomic policy
Microeconomic policy
Progressive taxation
Stabilization policy
Supply-side economics
Unemployment benefit
Uniform business rate
Vertical integration
Worker participation

20 letters:
Collective bargaining
Comparative advantage
Greenfield investment
Gross domestic product
Gross national product
Imperfect competition
Information agreement
Profit-and-loss account
Rational expectations
Residual unemployment
Seasonal unemployment

21 letters:
Foreign exchange market

Forward exchange market
Horizontal integration
International reserves
Polluter pays principle
Voluntary unemployment

22 letters:
Conspicuous consumption
Institutional investors
Prices and incomes policy
Recommended retail price
Research and development
Structural unemployment

23 letters:
Fixed exchange-rate system
Foreign exchange controls

25 letters:
Intellectual property right
Natural rate of unemployment
Public-sector debt repayment
Restrictive labour practice

26 letters:
Floating exchange-rate system

27 letters:
Medium-term financial strategy
Monetary compensatory
amounts

28 letters:
International competitiveness

30 letters:
National insurance
contributions

32 letters:
Public-sector borrowing
requirement

ECONOMICS SCHOOLS AND THEORIES

7 letters:
Chicago
Marxism

8 letters:
Austrian

9 letters:
Classical

10 letters:
Monetarism

11 letters:
Physiocrats
Reaganomics
Rogernomics
Thatcherism

12 letters:
Keynesianism
Mercantilism
Neoclassical

13 letters:
NeoKeynesians

ECONOMISTS

4 letters:
Hume, *David*
Marx, *Karl*
Mill, *James*
Mill, *John Stuart*
Ward, *Dame Barbara (Mary)*
Webb, *Sidney*
West, *Arthur Lewis*

5 letters:
Passy, *Frédéric*
Smith, *Adam*
Weber, *Max*

6 letters:
Angell, *Norman*
Bright, *John*
Cobden, *Richard*
Delors, *Jacques*
Frisch, *Ragnar*
George, *Henry*
Jevons, *William Stanley*
Keynes, *John Maynard*
Laffer, *Arthur*
Monnet, *Jean*
Pareto, *Vilfredo*
Turgot, *Anne Robert Jacques*
Veblen, *Thorstein*

7 letters:
Bagehot, *Walter*

Cournot, *Augustin*
D' Oresme, *Nicole*
Douglas, *C(lifford) H(ugh)*
Kuznets, *Simon*
Leacock, *Stephen Butler*
Malthus, *Thomas Robert*
Quesnay, *François*
Ricardo, *David*
Toynbee, *Arnold*
Wootton, *Barbara (Frances)*

8 letters:
Beccaria, *Cesare Bonesana*
Friedman, *Milton*
Mansholt, *Sicco Leendert*
Marshall, *Alfred*
Phillips, *A(lban) W(illiam) H(ousego)*
Von Hayek, *Friedrich August*

9 letters:
Beveridge, *William Henry*
Galbraith, *J(ohn) K(enneth)*
Tinbergen, *Jan*

10 letters:
De Sismondi, *Jean Charles Léonard Simonde*
Papandreou, *Andreas (George)*
Schumacher, *Ernst Friedrich*
Schumpeter, *Joseph*

Education terms

2 letters:
UE

3 letters:
COP
Don
Dux
GCE
GPS
Jig
LMS
ONC
PTA
SCE
Set
Wag

4 letters:
Co-ed
CPVE
Crib
Dean
Exam
Fail
GCSE
Gown
Hall
Hood
Mich
Pass
Pipe
SATS

Term
Test
Year

5 letters:
Class
Dunce
Entry
Essay
Expel
Flunk
Gaudy
Grade
Grant
Hooky
House

Education terms

Lines
Lycée
Mitch
Mocks
Pandy
Resit
Shell
Sizar
Stage
Tutee
Tutor
Union

6 letters:
A level
Alumna
Bedder
Binary
Bursar
Campus
Credit
Degree
Docent
Fellow
Ferule
Greats
Higher
Honors
Hookey
Incept
Infant
Junior
Master
Matric
O grade
O level
Pedant
Porter
Reader
Recess
Rector
Regent
Remove
Report
Second
Senate
Senior
Stream
Thesis
Truant
Warden

7 letters:
Adviser
Advisor
Alumnus
Banding
Battels
Boarder
Bursary
Crammer
Deanery
Dominie
Donnish
Dropout
Educate
Faculty
Federal
Fresher
Honours
Janitor
Lecture
Marking
Midterm
Prefect
Prelims
Primers
Proctor
Provost
Seminar
Session
Subject
Teach-in
Tuition

8 letters:
A bursary
Academic
Accredit
Aegrotat
B bursary
Comedown
Commoner
Delegacy
Dunce cap
Emeritus
Exercise
External
Freshman
Graduand
Graduate
Headship
Homework

Internal
Key stage
Lecturer
Manciple
Mistress
Parietal
Redbrick
Remedial
Semester
Send down
Sorority
Transfer
Tutorial
Wrangler

9 letters:
Assistant
Associate
Bubs grade
Bursarial
Catalogue
Catchment
Classmate
Classroom
Collegial
Collegian
Detention
Education
Extension
Gymnasium
Moderator
Muck-up day
Principal
Professor
Reception
Registrar
Rusticate
Schoolman
Sixth form
Sophomore
Speech day
Sports day
Statement
Trimester

10 letters:
Assignment
Bursarship
Chancellor
Collegiate
Coursework
Curricular

Curriculum
Department
Easter term
Eleven-plus
Exhibition
Extramural
Fellowship
Graded post
Graduation
Grant-in-aid
Headmaster
High school
Hilary term
Imposition
Instructor
Intramural
Invigilate
Prepositor
Prospectus
Readership
Recreation
Sabbatical
Scholastic
Schoolmarm
Supervisor
Transcript
Unstreamed

11 letters:
Coeducation
Convocation
Educational
Examination
Housefather
Housemaster
Housemother
In residence
Invigilator
Lower school
Matriculate
Trinity term
Upper school

12 letters:
Accumulation
Chapterhouse
Commencement
Congregation
Core subjects
Dissertation
Exhibitioner
Headmistress

Open learning
Postgraduate
Privatdocent
Schoolleaver
Schoolmaster
Self-educated
Subprincipal

13 letters:
Advanced level
Baccalaureate
Boarding house
Cuisenaire rod®
Full professor
Lowerclassman
Matriculation
Mature student
Ordinary grade
Ordinary level
Professoriate
Schoolteacher
Standard Grade
Summa cum laude
Undergraduate

14 letters:
Common Entrance
Family grouping
Headmastership
Liaison officer
Michaelmas term
Sandwich course
Schoolmistress
Student teacher
Tutorial system
Vice chancellor

15 letters:
Advisory teacher
Cross-curricular
Extracurricular
Grant-maintained
Hall of residence
Interscholastic
Refresher course
Regius professor
Tertiary bursary

16 letters:
Campus university
Further education
Headmistress-ship

Electronics terms

Junior common room
Middle common room
Senior common room
Sixth-form college
Vertical grouping

17 letters:
Level of attainment
Literae humaniores
Local examinations
School Certificate
Visiting professor

18 letters:
Great Public Schools
National Curriculum
Punishment exercise
University entrance

19 letters:
Conductive education
Record of achievement
Summative assessment

20 letters:
Continuous assessment

23 letters:
Nuffield teaching project
Standard assessment tasks

24 letters:
Certificate of Proficiency
Local management of schools
Parent teacher association

27 letters:
Ordinary National Certificate

29 letters:
General Certificate of Education
University entrance
  examination

30 letters:
Scottish Certificate of
  Education

35 letters:
Certificate of Pre-vocational
  Education

38 letters:
General Certificate of Secondary
  Education

Electronics terms

3 letters:
Bar
Bus
CCD
Eye
Key
LCD
LED
Pad

4 letters:
Bell
Bulb
Card
Chip
Coil
Cord
Dial
Disc
Duct
Flex
Fuse

Gate
Gobo
Jack
Lead
Lobe
Loop
Mike
Neon
Plug
Port
Slug
Tube
Wire

5 letters:
Array
Balun
Cable
Choke
Clock
Coder
Diode

Donor
Drain
Latch
Maser
Mixer
Motor
Plate
Shunt
Spool
Tuner
Valve
Wafer
Wiper

6 letters:
Aerial
Bridge
Buffer
Busbar
Button
Buzzer
Bypass

Electronics terms

Carbon
Driver
Feeder
Heater
Mosaic
Needle
Outlet
Phasor
Pick-up
Radome
Scaler
Screen
Sensor
Sheath
Sleeve
Slicer
Socket
Stator
Stylus
Switch
Triode
Woofer

7 letters:
Acetate
Adaptor
Antenna
Battery
Bimorph
Booster
Breaker
Bushing
Capstan
Charger
Chassis
Chopper
Clipper
Console
Counter
Coupler
Crystal
Display
Divider
Element
Emitter
Exciter
Excitor
Fuse box
Gyrator
Harness
Igniter

Krytron
Limiter
Mag tape
Monitor
Negator
Pentode
Reactor
Scanner
Speaker
Tetrode
Tone arm
Trimmer
Tweeter

8 letters:
Acceptor
Black box
Detector
Diffuser
Digitron
Envelope
Expander
Filament
Heat sink
Ignitron
Inverter
Live wire
Magic eye
Neon lamp
Orthicon
Radiator
Receiver
Recorder
Repeater
Resistor
Rheostat
Sleeving
Slip ring
Solenoid
Varactor
Varistor
Vibrator

9 letters:
Amplifier
Autometer
Autotimer
Bolometer
Call alarm
Capacitor
Cartridge
Choke coil

Component
Condenser
Conductor
Contactor
Delay line
Drift tube
Dummy load
Dynamotor
Equalizer
Flame lamp
Fluxmeter
Hygristor
Image tube
Kinescope
Labyrinth
Leyden jar
Light bulb
Magnetron
Metal tape
Microchip
Nixie tube
Optophone
Phono plug
Phototube
Pilot lamp
Plugboard
Plumbicon
Power pack
Rectifier
Reflector
Resnatron
Resonator
Sequencer
Spark coil
Tesla coil
Thyratron
Thyristor
Turntable
Voltmeter
Wattmeter

10 letters:
Acorn valve
Alternator
Banana plug
Breadboard
Camera tube
Chrome tape
Commutator
Comparator
Compressor

Electronics terms

Controller
Coulometer
Esaki diode
Goniometer
Harmonizer
Hydrophone
LCD display
LED display
Microphone
Mimic panel
Moving coil
Multimeter
NOT circuit
Oscillator
Patch board
Photodiode
P-n junction
Push button
Radio valve
Reproducer
Rhumbatron
Screen grid
Servomotor
Shadow mask
Sodium lamp
Solar panel
Stabilizer
Suppressor
Switchgear
Thermistor
Time switch
Transducer
Transistor
Trip switch
Vacuum tube
Variometer
Voltameter
Wander plug
Welding rod
Zener diode

11 letters:
Anticathode
Autochanger
Cat's whisker
Cold cathode
Electric eye
Faraday cage
Interrupter
Junction box
Knife switch

Loading coil
Loudspeaker
Microswitch
Motherboard
NAND circuit
Open circuit
Picture tube
Ring circuit
Silicon chip
Space heater
Storage tube
Strobe tuner
Switchboard
Tickler coil
Transformer
Tunnel diode
Voltammeter

12 letters:
Bow collector
Circuit board
Coaxial cable
Electrometer
Electron tube
Friction tape
Magnetic tape
Microcircuit
Oscillograph
Oscilloscope
Preamplifier
Squirrel cage
Standard cell
Toggle switch

13 letters:
Crystal pick-up
Discharge tube
Discriminator
Electric motor
Image orthicon
Induction coil
Low-pass filter
Mercury switch
Multivibrator
Potentiometer
Quartz crystal
Record-changer
Rhombic aerial
Ripple control
Semiconductor
Tumbler switch

14 letters:
Band-pass filter
Circuit breaker
Heating element
High-pass filter
Image converter
Induction motor
Long-wire aerial
Magnetic pick-up
Magnetic stripe
Mesh connection
Motor generator
Noise generator
Peltier element
Power amplifier
Printed circuit
Schmitt trigger
Servomechanism
Star connection
Television tube
Trickle charger
Turbogenerator
Universal motor
Voltage divider

15 letters:
Alloyed junction
Autotransformer
Bleeder resistor
Bridge rectifier
Cavity resonator
Class-A amplifier
Class-B amplifier
Class-C amplifier
Crystal detector
Drift transistor
Electric circuit
Local oscillator
Majority carrier
Minority carrier
Phototransistor
Shuttle armature
Signal generator
Thermionic valve

16 letters:
Carbon microphone
Gas-discharge tube
Image intensifier
Potential divider
Ribbon microphone
Silicon rectifier

Smoothing circuit
Sodium-vapour lamp
Spark transmitter
Spectrum analyser
Synchronous motor
Transmission line

17 letters:
Crystal microphone
Electrostatic lens
Equivalent circuit
Full-wave rectifier
Ground-plane aerial
Integrated circuit
Lightning arrester
Photoelectric cell

18 letters:
Dynatron oscillator
Electronic ignition
I-type semiconductor
Junction transistor
Light-emitting diode
Lightning conductor
Travelling-wave tube

19 letters:
Epitaxial transistor

Parametric amplifier
Parametric equalizer
Pulse height analyser
Seven-segment display

20 letters:
Liquid-crystal display
Multichannel analyser
Operational amplifier
Relaxation oscillator
Synchronous converter

21 letters:
Electric-discharge lamp
Field-effect transistor
Residual current device

22 letters:
Electrostatic generator
Intrinsic semiconductor

24 letters:
Analogue-digital converter

26 letters:
Silicon-controlled rectifier

32 letters:
Steam-generating heavy-water
   reactor

Embroidery stitches

3 letters:
Fly

4 letters:
Back
Barb
Coil
Fern
Post
Rice
Stem

5 letters:
Briar
Catch
Chain
Coral
Cross
Daisy
Greek

Satin
Split

6 letters:
Basque
Beaded
Berlin
Cast on
Cretan
Crewel
Damask
Eyelet
Ladder
Scroll

7 letters:
Berwick
Blanket
Bullion
Chevron

Chinese
Convent
Feather
Kloster
Outline
Plaited
Running
Russian
Sampler
Sham Hem

8 letters:
Pekinese
Scottish
Wheatear

9 letters:
Arrowhead
Crow's-foot
Lazy Daisy

Open Chain
Quilt Knot

10 letters:
Buttonhole
Casalguidi
French Knot
German Knot
Portuguese
Roman Chain
Whipped Fly

11 letters:
Caterpillar
Double Cross
Herringbone
Montenegrin
Renaissance
Ribbed Wheel

Threaded Fly
Whipped Back
Whipped Stem
Zigzag Chain

12 letters:
Ghiordes Knot
Russian Cross
Twisted Chain
Whipped Chain

13 letters:
Buttonhole Bar
Closed Feather
Porto Rico rose

14 letters:
Crossed corners
Feathered Chain

Whipped Running

15 letters:
Buttonhole Wheel
Threaded Running

16 letters:
Closed Buttonhole

17 letters:
Crossed
 Buttonhole
Threaded
 Arrowhead
Woven Spider's
 Wheel

18 letters:
Twisted Lattice
 Band

Emperors

TITLES OF EMPERORS

3 letters:
Imp
Rex

4 letters:
Inca
King
Tsar

5 letters:
Kesar
Mpret
Negus
Rosco
Ruler
Shang
Tenno

6 letters:
Kaiser
Keasar
Mikado
Purple
Sultan

9 letters:
Sovereign

FAMOUS EMPERORS

3 letters:
Leo

4 letters:
John
Ming
Nero
Otho
Otto
Pu-yi
Wu Di

5 letters:
Akbar
Asoka

Babur
Gaius
Henry
Jimmu
Kesar
Meiji
Negus
Nerva
Pedro
Rosco
Shang
Tenno
Titus

6 letters:
Caesar
George
Joseph
Kaiser
Keaser
Trajan
Valens
Yong Lo

7 letters:
Akihito
Charles
Francis

Gratian
Hadrian
Leopold
Lothair
Menelik
Severus
William

8 letters:
Agramant
Augustan
Augustus
Caligula
Claudius
Commodus
Hirohito
Matthias
Napoleon
Octavian
Qian Long
Theodore
Tiberius
Valerian
Xuan Zong

9 letters:
Agramante
Atahualpa
Aurangzeb
Bonaparte
Caracalla
Diomitian
Ferdinand
Frederick
Heraclius
Justinian
Montezuma
Shah Jahan
Vespasian
Vitellius

10 letters:
Barbarossa
Dessalines
Diocletian
Franz Josef
Kublai Khan
Maximilian
Theodosius
Theophilus

Wenceslaus

11 letters:
Charlemagne
Constantine
Genghis Khan
Valentinian

13 letters:
Akbar the Great
Antoninus Pius
Haile Selassie
Peter the Great

16 letters:
Germanicus
Caesar

17 letters:
Napoleon
Bonaparte
Ras Tafari
Makonnen

19 letters:
Frederick
Barbarossa

Engineering, types of

5 letters:
Civil
Naval

6 letters:
Mining

7 letters:
Genetic
Nuclear
Process
Traffic

8 letters:
Chemical
Military
Sanitary

9 letters:
Aerospace

10 letters:
Automotive
Electrical
Ergonomics
Hydraulics
Mechanical
Production
Structural

11 letters:
Electronics
Geotechnics

12 letters:
Aerodynamics

Aeronautical
Agricultural
Astronautics
Cosmonautics
Mechatronics

13 letters:
Computer-aided
Environmental
Fluid dynamics

14 letters:
Bioengineering

Entertainment

TYPES OF ENTERTAINMENT

3 letters:
Gig

4 letters:
Agon
Ball
Fair
Fête
Film
Gala
Play
Rave
Show

5 letters:
Dance
Farce
Feast
Gaudy
Levee
Magic
Opera
Party
Revue
Rodeo

6 letters:
Ballet
Circus
Comedy
Kermis
Masque
Review
Soiree

7 letters:
Airshow
Banquet
Busking
Cabaret
Ceilidh
Charade

Concert
Ice show
Karaoke
Kirmess
Musical
Reading
Recital
Ridotto
Tragedy
Variety
Waltzer

8 letters:
All-dayer
Après-ski
Aquashow
Carnival
Cotillon
Juggling
Operetta
Road show
Sideshow
Singsong
Zarzuela

9 letters:
Conjuring
Cotillion
Fireworks
Floor show
Light show
Melodrama
Music hall
Pantomime
Raree show
Reception
Slide show
Video game

10 letters:
Acrobatics

Aerobatics
All-nighter
Antimasque
Escapology
Exhibition
Masked ball
Puppet show
Recitation
Shadow play
Striptease
Vaudeville
Whist drive

11 letters:
Bear-baiting
Fashion show
Funambulism
Galanty show
Garden party
Slot machine
Wall of death

12 letters:
Bullfighting
Cockfighting
Minstrel show
Pyrotechnics
Son et lumière

13 letters:
Burlesque show
Street theatre
Ventriloquism

14 letters:
Warehouse party

16 letters:
Tightrope-walking

18 letters:
Command
  performance

Entertainment

TYPES OF ENTERTAINER

4 letters:
Diva
Fool

5 letters:
Actor
Clown
Mimic

6 letters:
Artist
Busker
Dancer
Guiser
Jester
Mummer
Singer

7 letters:
Acrobat
Actress
Artiste
Auguste
Juggler
Trouper
Tumbler

8 letters:
Comedian
Conjurer
Funnyman

Gracioso
Jongleur
Magician
Minstrel
Musician
Show girl
Stripper

9 letters:
Fire eater
Harlequin
Lion tamer
Performer
Puppeteer
Raconteur
Strongman
Tragedian

10 letters:
Chorus girl
Comedienne
Go-go dancer
Prima donna
Ringmaster
Unicyclist

11 letters:
Equilibrist
Funambulist
Illusionist

Merry-andrew
Stripteaser
Tragedienne

12 letters:
Circus artist
Escapologist
Exotic dancer
Impersonator
Organ-grinder
Snake charmer
Vaudevillian

13 letters:
Bareback rider
Contortionist
Impressionist
Trapeze artist
Ventriloquist

14 letters:
Prima ballerina
Sword swallower

15 letters:
Strolling player
Tightrope walker

17 letters:
Quick-change
  artist

PLACES OF ENTERTAINMENT

3 letters:
Zoo

4 letters:
Hall
Lido

5 letters:
Arena
Disco

6 letters:
Big top
Cinema
Circus
Museum

7 letters:
Funfair
Gallery

Marquee
Niterie
Stadium
Theatre

8 letters:
Ballroom
Carnival
Coliseum
Waxworks

9 letters:
Bandstand
Bingo hall
Colosseum
Dance hall
Music hall
Nightclub
Nightspot

10 letters:
Auditorium
Fairground
Opera house
Social club
Vaudeville

11 letters:
Concert hall

12 letters:
Amphitheatre

13 letters:
Leisure centre

15 letters:
Amusement
  arcade

Enzymes

Enzymes

3 letters:
ACE

5 letters:
Lyase
Lysin
Renin

6 letters:
Cytase
Kinase
Ligase
Lipase
Mutase
Papain
Pepsin
Rennin
Urease
Zymase

7 letters:
Amylase
Apyrase
Casease
Cyclase
Enolase
Erepsin
Guanase
Hydrase
Inulase
Lactase
Maltase
Oxidase
Pectase
Pepsine
Plasmin
Ptyalin
Trypsin

8 letters:
Aldolase
Arginase
Bromelin
Catalase
Diastase
Elastase
Esterase
Lysozyme
Nuclease
Permease
Protease
Steapsin
Thrombin

9 letters:
Amylopsin
Autolysin
Bromelain
Cathepsin
Cellulase
Deaminase
Hydrolase
Invertase
Isomerase
Oxygenase
Reductase
Sulfatase
Trehalase
Urokinase

10 letters:
Allosteric
Kallikrein
Luciferase
Peroxidase
Polymerase

Proteinase
Saccharase
Subtilisin
Sulphatase
Tyrosinase

11 letters:
Carboxylase
Chymopapain
Collagenase
Dipeptidase
Histaminase
Phosphatase
Restriction
Transferase

12 letters:
Asparaginase
Carbohydrase
Chymotrypsin
Enterokinase
Fibrinolysin
Flavoprotein
Ribonuclease
Transaminase

13 letters:
Decarboxylase
Oxdoreductase
Streptokinase
Transcriptase

14 letters:
Cholinesterase
Pectinesterase
Streptodornase
Thromboplastin

Equestrianism

EQUESTRIAN EVENTS AND SPORTS

4 letters:
Hunt
Oaks
Polo

5 letters:
Ascot
Derby
Joust

Plate

7 letters:
Classic
Jump-off

Meeting

8 letters:
Dressage
Eventing
Gymkhana
Races, the

9 letters:
Badminton
Cavalcade
Puissance

10 letters:
Picnic race

Saint Leger
Sweepstake

11 letters:
Buckjumping
Horse racing
Race meeting
Showjumping
Sweepstakes

12 letters:
Claiming race
Point-to-point
Steeplechase

13 letters:
Grand National
Harness racing
Kentucky Derby
Nursery stakes

16 letters:
Three-day eventing

18 letters:
One Thousand
  Guineas
Two Thousand
  Guineas

CLASSIC ENGLISH HORSE RACES

Race	Course	Distance
One Thousand Guineas (fillies)	Newmarket	One mile
Two Thousand Guineas (colts)	Newmarket	One mile
Derby (colts)	Epsom	One and a half miles
The Oaks (fillies)	Epsom	One and a half miles
St. Leger (colts and fillies)	Doncaster	One and three quarter miles

HORSE RACING TERMS

3 letters:
Nap

4 letters:
Away
Card
Colt
Draw
Flat
Gate
Head
Neck
Pole
Post
Turf
Wire

5 letters:
Break
Chase
Fence
Filly
Going
Handy
Pacer
Place

Plate
Sweat
Track

6 letters:
Boring
Chaser
Come in
Course
Faller
Finish
Flight
Hurdle
Impost
Jockey
Length
Maiden
Novice
Plater
Scurry
Stakes
Stayer

7 letters:
Also-ran
Classic

Each way
Furlong
Meeting
Paddock
Roughie
Scratch
Starter
Steward
Stretch
Sweat up
Trainer
Weigh in

8 letters:
Dead heat
Distance
Handicap
Hurdling
Milepost
Race card
Straight
Ticktack
Unplaced
Walkover
Yearling

European Union

TYPES OF JUMP

European Union

Year joined	Member Country
1958	Belgium
1958	France
1958	Germany
1958	Italy
1958	Luxembourg
1958	The Netherlands
1973	Denmark
1973	Republic of Ireland
1973	United Kingdom
1981	Greece
1986	Portugal
1986	Spain
1995	Finland
1995	Sweden
1995	Austria
2004	Cyprus

Year joined	Member Country
2004	Czech Republic
2004	Estonia
2004	Hungary
2004	Latvia
2004	Lithuania
2004	Malta
2004	Poland
2004	Slovakia
2004	Slovenia
2007	Bulgaria
2007	Romania

Explorers

4 letters:

Byrd, *Richard E*	1888–1957	US
Cook, *Captain James*	1728–79	British
Dias, *Bartolomeu*	c. 1450–1500	Portuguese
Diaz, *Bartolomeu*	c. 1450–1500	Portuguese
Eyre, *Edward John*	1815–1901	British
Gama, *Vasco da*	c. 1469–1524	Portuguese
Hume, *Hamilton*	1797–1873	Australian
Park, *Mungo*	1771–c.1806	Scottish
Polo, *Marco*	c. 1254–1324	Venetian
Ross, *Sir James Clark*	1800–62	British
Soto, *Hernando de*	c. 1496–1542	Spanish

5 letters:

Baker, *Sir Samuel White*	1821–93	British
Barth, *Heinrich*	1821–65	German
Boone, *Daniel*	1735–1820	US
Bruce, *James*	1730–94	British
Burke, *Robert O'Hara*	1820–61	Irish
Cabot, *John (Giovanni Caboto)*	c. 1450–c.1500	Italian
Fuchs, *Sir Vivian*	1908–99	British
Laird, *Macgregor*	1808–61	Scottish
Oates, *Lawrence Edwards Grace*	1880–1912	British
Peary, *Robert Edwin*	1856–1920	US
Scott, *Robert Falcon*	1868–1912	British
Speke, *John Hanning*	1827–64	British
Sturt, *Charles*	1795–1869	British

6 letters:

Baffin, *William*	1584–1622	English
Balboa, *Vasco Núñez de*	c.1475–1517	Spanish
Bering, *Vitus*	1681–1741	Danish
Brazza, *Pierre Paul François Camille Savorgnan de*	1852–1905	French
Brooke, *Sir James*	1803–68	British

Explorers

Burton, *Sir Richard*	1821–90	British
Cortés, *Hernán(do)*	1485–1547	Spanish
Nansen, *Fridtjof*	1861–1930	Norwegian
Ralegh, *Sir Walter*	1554–1618	British
Stuart, *John McDouall*	1815–66	Scottish
Tasman, *Abel*	1603–c.1659	Dutch

7 letters:

Barents, *Willem*	c. 1550–97	Dutch
Cartier, *Jacques*	1491–1557	French
Córdoba, *Francisco Hernández de*	d. 1517 or 1526	Spanish
Covilhã, *Pêro da*	c. 1460–after 1526	Portuguese
Dampier, *William*	1652–1715	English
Fiennes, *Sir Ranulph*	1944–	British
Frémont, *John C*	1813–90	US
Hillary, *Sir Edmund*	1919–2008	New Zealand
La Salle, *Robert Cavalier, Sieur de*	1643–87	French
McClure, *Sir Robert John le Mesurier*	1807–73	Irish
Raleigh, *Sir Walter*	1554–1618	British
Stanley, *Sir Henry Morton*	1841–1904	British
Wilkins, *Sir George Hubert*	1888–1958	British
Wrangel, *Ferdinand Petrovich, Baron von*	1794–1870	Russian

8 letters:

Amundsen, *Roald*	1872–1928	Norwegian
Barentsz, *Willem*	c. 1550–97	Dutch
Columbus, *Christopher*	1451–1506	Italian
Cousteau, *Jacques Yves*	1910–97	French
Flinders, *Matthew*	1774–1814	English
Franklin, *Sir John*	1786–1847	British
Humboldt, *Alexander von*	1769–1859	German
Magellan, *Ferdinand*	1480–1521	Portuguese
Marchand, *Jean Baptiste*	1863–1934	French
Vespucci, *Amerigo*	1454–1512	Italian

9 letters:

Champlain, *Samuel de*	1567–1635	French
Frobisher, *Sir Martin*	c. 1535–94	English
Iberville, *Pierre le Moyne, Sieur d'*	1661–1706	French–Canadian
Leichardt, *Ludwig*	1813–48	German
Marquette, *Jacques*	1637–75	French
Mungo Park	1771–c.1806	Scottish
Rasmussen, *Knud Johan Victor*	1879–1933	Danish
Vancouver, *George*	1757–98	English

10 letters:

Erik the Red	late 10th Century	Norwegian

Shackleton, *Sir Ernest Henry*	1874–1922	British

11 letters:

Livingstone, *David*	1813–73	Scottish
Ponce de Leon, *Juan*	1460–1521	Spanish
Vasco da Gama	c. 1469–1524	Portuguese

12 letters:

Leif Eriksson	11th Century	Icelandic

14 letters:

Bellingshausen, *Fabian Gottlieb, Baron von*	1778–1852	Russian

Explosives

2 letters:
HE

3 letters:
Cap
SAM
TNT

4 letters:
Mine

5 letters:
Agene
Jelly
Petar

6 letters:
Amatol
Dualin
Petard
Semtex®
Tetryl

Tonite
Trotyl

7 letters:
Ammonal
Cordite
Dunnite
Grenade
Warhead

8 letters:
Cheddite
Fireball
Firedamp
Firework
Landmine
Melinite
Roburite
Xyloidin

9 letters:
Gelignite

Guncotton
Gunpowder
Xyloidine

10 letters:
Aquafortis
Euchlorine

11 letters:
Firecracker

12 letters:
Thunderflash

14 letters:
Nitroglycerine

15 letters:
Trinitrobenzene

16 letters:
Bangalore torpedo

Eye

PARTS OF THE EYE

3 letters:
Rod

4 letters:
Cone
Iris
Lens

5 letters:
Fovea
Pupil

6 letters:
Cornea
Retina

Sclera

7 letters:
Choroid
Eyeball

8 letters:
Chorioid

Eye

9 letters:
Blind spot

10 letters:
Optic nerve

11 letters:
Ciliary body

Conjunctiva

12 letters:
Ocular muscle
Vitreous body

13 letters:
Aqueous humour

14 letters:
Retinal vessels
Vitreous humour

18 letters:
Suspensory
  ligament

AFFLICTIONS OF THE EYE

6 letters:
Iritis
Miosis
Myosis
Nebula
Xeroma

7 letters:
Leucoma
Scotoma
Thylose
Tylosis
Wall-eye

8 letters:
Cataract
Coloboma
Diplopia
Glaucoma

Hemiopia
Synechia
Thylosis
Trachoma

9 letters:
Amblyopia
Ametropia
Ceratitis
Entropion
Keratitis
Lippitude
Micropsia
Nystagmus
Retinitis
Scotomata

10 letters:
Asthenopia

Nyctalopia
Presbyopia
Stigmatism
Strabismus
Teichopsia
Tritanopia

11 letters:
Aniseikonia
Astigmatism
Hemeralopia
Hemianopsia

12 letters:
Exophthalmus

13 letters:
Anisomatropia
Hypermetropia
Xerophthalmia

F

Fabrics

3 letters:
Abb
Fur
Net
Rep
Say
Web

4 letters:
Aida
Baft
Ciré
Cord
Doek
Drab
Duck
Felt
Fent
Gair
Haik
Harn
Huck
Hyke
Ikat
Jean
Kelt
Knit
Lace
Lamé
Lawn
Leno
Line
Mull
Nude
Puke
Rund
Shag
Silk
Slop
Sulu

Tick
Wool

5 letters:
Atlas
Baize
Batik
Beige
Binca
Budge
Chino
Crape
Crash
Crepe
Denim
Dobby
Drill
Duroy
Fanon
Foulé
Frisé
Gauze
Gunny
Haick
Honan
Jaspe
Kanga
Kente
Khadi
Khaki
Kikoi
Linen
Lisle
Llama
Loden
Lurex®
Lycra®
Moiré
Mongo
Mungo

Ninon
Orlon®
Panne
Perse
Piqué
Plaid
Plush
Poult
Rayon
Satin
Scrim
Serge
Slops
Stuff
Stupe
Surah
Surat
Surge
Tabby
Tamin
Tammy
Terry
Tibet
Toile
Towel
Tulle
Tweed
Tweel
Twill
Union
Voile
Wigan

6 letters:
Aertex®
Alpaca
Angora
Armure
Barège
Battik

Fabrics

Beaver
Bouclé
Broche
Burlap
Burnet
Burrel
Byssus
Caddis
Calico
Camlet
Camlot
Canvas
Chintz
Cilice
Cloqué
Coburg
Cotton
Coutil
Crepon
Cubica
Cyprus
Dacron®
Damask
Devoré
Dimity
Domett
Dossal
Dossel
Dowlas
Dralon®
Duffel
Duffle
Dupion
Durrie
Etamin
Faille
Fannel
Fleece
Frieze
Gloria
Greige
Gurrah
Haique
Harden
Herden
Hodden
Humhum
Hurden
Jersey
Kersey
Khanga

Kincob
Lampas
Madras
Medley
Melton
Merino
Mohair
Mongoe
Moreen
Muslin
Nankin
Oxford
Pongee
Poplin
Rateen
Ratine
Runner
Russel
Russet
Samite
Satara
Sateen
Saxony
Sendal
Shalli
Sherpa
Shoddy
Sindon
Soneri
Stroud
Tamine
Tartan
Thibet
Tricot
Tussah
Tusser
Velour
Velure
Velvet
Vicuna
Wadmal
Wincey
Winsey

7 letters:
Abattre
Acrilan®
Alepine
Baracan
Batiste
Brocade

Bunting
Cabbage
Cambric
Camelot
Challie
Challis
Cheviot
Chiffon
Crombie
Cypress
Delaine
Dhurrie
Doeskin
Dornick
Drabbet
Drapery
Droguet
Drugget
Duvetyn
Etamine
Façonné
Fannell
Fishnet
Flannel
Foulard
Fustian
Galatea
Genappe
Gingham
Gore-Tex®
Grogram
Hessian
Holland
Hopsack
Jaconet
Jamdani
Khaddar
Kitenge
Leather
Lockram
Marabou
Mockado
Nankeen
Oilskin
Organza
Orleans
Ottoman
Paisley
Percale
Rabanna
Raploch

Raschel
Ratteen
Rattine
Sacking
Sagathy
Satinet
Schappe
Silesia
Sinamay
Spandex
Stammel
Suiting
Tabaret
Tabinet
Taffeta
Ticking
Tiffany
Tussore
Veiling
Velours
Viyella®
Wadmaal
Webbing
Woolsey
Worsted
Zanella

8 letters:
Algerine
American
Armozeen
Armozine
Arresine
Bagheera
Barathea
Barracan
Bayadere
Bird's-eye
Bobbinet
Brocatel
Buckskin
Cameline
Cashmere
Casimere
Celanese
Chambray
Chamelot
Chenille
Ciclaton
Corduroy
Corporal

Coteline
Coutille
Cretonne
Diamanté
Drabette
Duchesse
Dungaree
Duvetine
Duvetyne
Eolienne
Gambroon
Gossamer
Homespun
Jacquard
Jeanette
Lambskin
Lava-lava
Lustring
Mackinaw
Mantling
Marcella
Marocain
Mazarine
Moleskin
Moquette
Nainsook
Organdie
Osnaburg
Paduasoy
Pashmina
Prunella
Prunelle
Prunello
Rodevore
Sarcenet
Sarsenet
Shabrack
Shalloon
Shantung
Sheeting
Shirting
Sicilian
Spun silk
Swanskin
Tabbinet
Tarlatan
Terylene®
Toilinet
Whipcord
Wild silk
Zibeline

9 letters:
Balzarine
Bengaline
Bombasine
Bombazine
Calamanco
Cassimere
Cerecloth
Charmeuse®
Ciclatoun
Corporale
Cottonade
Crepoline
Crimplene®
Crinoline
Evenweave
Farandine
Filoselle
Folk weave
Gaberdine
Georgette
Grenadine
Grosgrain
Haircloth
Horsehair
Huckaback
Indiennes
Levantine
Mandylion
Marseille
Matelassé
Messaline
Nun's cloth
Organzine
Paramatta
Penistone
Percaline
Persienne
Petersham
Piña cloth
Polyester
Ravenduck
Sailcloth
Satinette
Sharkskin
Silkaline
Stockinet
Swan's-down
Tarpaulin
Towelling
Tricotine

Fates

Velveteen
Wire gauze
Worcester
Zibelline

10 letters:
Balbriggan
Broadcloth
Brocatelle
Candlewick
Farrandine
Fearnaught
Fearnought
Ferrandine
Florentine
India print
Kerseymere
Lutestring
Marseilles
Monk's cloth
Mousseline
Needlecord
Parramatta

Peau de soie
Polycotton
Ravensduck
Seersucker
Shabracque
Sicilienne
Tattersall
Toilinette
Tuftaffeta
Winceyette

11 letters:
Abercrombie
Cheesecloth
Cloth of gold
Covert cloth
Dotted Swiss
Drap-de-berry
Dreadnought
Hammercloth
Harris Tweed®
Interfacing
Kendal green

Marquisette
Poult-de-soie
Sempiternum
Stockinette
Stretch knit
Swiss muslin

12 letters:
Brilliantine
Cavalry twill
Crepe de chine
Donegal tweed
Leather-cloth
Slipper satin

13 letters:
Cotton flannel
Gros de Londres
Jacquard weave
Linsey-woolsey

14 letters:
Paisley pattern

See also:
➤ **Materials** ➤ **Silks**

Fates

6 letters:
Clotho

7 letters:
Atropos

8 letters:
Lachesis

Fencing terms

4 letters:
Mask
Volt

5 letters:
Carte
Feint
Guard
Parry
Piste
Prime
Reach

Sabre
Sixte
Terce
Touch

6 letters:
Bracer
Octave
Parade
Quarte
Quinte
Tierce

Touché

7 letters:
Seconde
Septime

9 letters:
Backsword
Repechage

11 letters:
Singlestick

Ferns

3 letters:
Oak

4 letters:
Hard
Lady
Male
Tara
Tree

5 letters:
Beech
Cycad
Filmy
Grape
Marsh
Ponga
Punga
Royal
Sword

6 letters:
Azolla
Meadow
Nardoo
Pteris
Shield
Silver

7 letters:
Bladder
Bracken
Buckler
Cyathea
Elkhorn
Filices
Isoetes
Osmunda
Parsley
Polypod
Walking
Wall rue
Woodsia

8 letters:
Adiantum
Aspidium
Barometz
Bungwall
Ceterach
Cinnamon
Fishbone
Marsilea
Marsilia
Moonwort
Mosquito
Mulewort

Pillwort
Rachilla
Schizaea
Staghorn

9 letters:
Asparagus
Asplenium
Bird's nest
Cryptogam
Dicksonia
Filicales
Rock brake

10 letters:
Maidenhair
Pepperwort
Spleenwort
Venus's-hair

11 letters:
Hart's-tongue
Nephrolepis

12 letters:
Adder's-tongue
Ophioglossum

13 letters:
Scolopendrium

Festivals

3 letters:
Mod
Tet

4 letters:
Feis
Gaff
Holi
Mela
Noel
Obon
Puja
Utas
Yule

5 letters:
Doseh

Druid
Hosay
Litha
Mabon
Miraj
Pasch
Pesah
Pooja
Purim
Seder
Vesak
Wesak

6 letters:
Adonia
Ashura
Bairam

Dewali
Divali
Diwali
Easter
Eostra
Fringe
Hosein
Imbolc
Lammas
Ostara
Pardon
Pesach
Pongal
Poojah
Shrove
Yomtov

Fibres

7 letters:
Al Hijra
Baisaki
Beltane
Gregory
Harvest
Holy-ale
Kermess
Kermiss
Kirmess
Lady-day
Lemural
Lemuria
Matsuri
Palilia
Potlach
Samhain
Vinalia

8 letters:
Al Hijrah
Baisakhi
Bayreuth
Biennale
Cerealia
Chanukah
Dassehra
Dionysia

Encaenia
Epiphany
Hanukkah
Hock-tide
Id-al-fitr
Panegyry
Passover
Shabuath
Shavuath
Yuletide

9 letters:
Aldeburgh
Candlemas
Chanukkah
Church-ale
Crouchmas
Hallowmas
Navaratra
Navaratri
Pentecost
Thargelia
Up-Helly-Aa

10 letters:
Ambarvalia
Childermas
Eisteddfod

Lughnasadh
Lupercalia
Merry-night
Michaelmas
Quirinalia
Saturnalia
Semi-double
Shrovetide
Terminalia
Visitation

11 letters:
Anthesteria

12 letters:
All Saints' Day
Circumcision
Lailat-ul-Qadr
Lesser Bairam
Panathenaean
Rosh Hashanah
Simchat Torah
Thesmophoria

13 letters:
Corpus Christi
Laylat-al-Miraj

Fibres

3 letters:
Tow

4 letters:
Bass
Bast
Coir
Flax
Hemp
Herl
Jute
Noil
Pita
Pons
Pulu
Rami
Rhea

5 letters:
Abaca

Buaze
Bwazi
Istle
Ixtle
Kapok
Kenaf
Noils
Nylon
Orlon®
Ramee
Viver
Watap

6 letters:
Aramid
Arghan
Cotton
Cuscus
Dralon®

Kevlar®
Kittul
Strick

7 letters:
Acrilan®
Acrylic
Cantala
Filasse
Funicle
Gore-Tex®
Monofil
Pontine
Tampico
Whisker

8 letters:
Elastane
Henequen
Henequin

Monomode
Peduncle
Piassaba
Piassava

Sunn-hemp
Toquilla

9 letters:
Courtelle®

11 letters:
Monkey-grass

Figures of speech

5 letters:
Irony

6 letters:
Aporia
Climax
Simile
Tmesis
Zeugma

7 letters:
Analogy
Kenning
Litotes
Meiosis
Sarcasm

8 letters:
Allusion
Anaphora
Chiasmus
Emphasis
Metaphor
Metonymy
Oxymoron
Pleonasm

9 letters:
Apophasis
Hendiadys
Hypallage
Hyperbole
Inversion
Prolepsis
Syllepsis

10 letters:
Anastrophe
Antithesis
Apostrophe
Epanaphora
Gemination
Hyperbaton
Paralipsis
Repetition
Spoonerism
Synecdoche

11 letters:
Anacoluthia
Anadiplosis
Antiphrasis
Antonomasia

Aposiopesis
Catachresis
Exclamation
Malapropism
Paraleipsis
Parenthesis
Periphrasis
Prosopopeia

12 letters:
Alliteration
Epanorthosis
Onomatopoeia
Polysyndeton
Prosopopoeia

14 letters:
Circumlocution

15 letters:
Personification

16 letters:
Hysteron proteron

18 letters:
Rhetorical
  question

Film and television

1 letter:
A
U

2 letters:
AA
PG

3 letters:
BFI
CGI
Cut
Dub

Pan
SFX
Zap

4 letters:
BBFC
Boom
Edit
Emmy
Grip
HDTV
IMAX
Sync

TiVo

5 letters:
Anime
BAFTA
Cameo
Frame
Oscar
Short
Weepy

6 letters:
Action

Fireworks

Biopic
B movie
Co-star
Editor
Gaffer
Razzie
Repeat
Romcom
X-rated

7 letters:
Animate
Backlot
Betacam
Cable TV
Credits
Fleapit
Footage
Key grip
Prequel
Ratings
Trailer
Western
Zapping

8 letters:
Actioner
Art house
Britpack
Game show
Long shot
Stuntman
Subtitle
Talk show
Typecast

9 letters:
Animation

Big screen
Bollywood
Celluloid
Cinematic
Digital TV
Docu-drama
Flashback
Footprint
Hollywood
LCD screen
Reality TV
Road movie
Satellite
Set-top box
Stop-frame

10 letters:
Access card
Adult movie
Blue screen
Body double
Chick flick
Flat screen
Home cinema
Neorealism
Screen test
Slow motion
Snuff movie
Soundtrack
Stop-motion
Storyboard
Video nasty
Widescreen

11 letters:
Channel-surf
Chapter stop
Cinemascope

Cliffhanger
Freeze-frame
Reality show
Satellite TV
Small screen
Synthespian

12 letters:
Animatronics
Cinematheque
Plasma screen
Screenwriter
Slasher movie
Sneak preview

13 letters:
Interactive TV
Motion capture
Remote control
Satellite dish

14 letters:
Channel-surfing
Postproduction
Shooting script
Special effects

16 letters:
Spaghetti western

17 letters:
Digital television

19 letters:
Satellite
   television

21 letters:
Interactive
   television

Fireworks

3 letters:
SIB

4 letters:
Cake
Mine
Pioy

5 letters:
Gerbe
Peeoy

Pioye
Squib
Wheel

6 letters:
Banger
Fizgig
Maroon
Petard
Rocket

7 letters:
Cracker
Serpent

8 letters:
Fountain
Pinwheel
Sparkler

9 letters:
Girandole

Skyrocket
Whizzbang

10 letters:
Cherry bomb

11 letters:
Bengal light
Roman candle
Tourbillion

14 letters:
Catherine wheel

First names

BOYS

3 letters:	**4 letters:**	
Abe	Abel	Jock
Alf	Abie	John
Ali	Adam	José
Ben	Alan	Josh
Bob	Aldo	Juan
Dan	Amos	Karl
Don	Andy	Kurt
Ger	Avis	Leon
Gus	Bart	Luca
Guy	Bert	Luke
Ian	Bill	Marc
Jan	Carl	Mark
Jim	Chad	Matt
Joe	Clem	Mick
Kim	Dave	Mike
Len	Dick	Muir
Leo	Dirk	Neal
Luc	Drew	Neil
Max	Duke	Nick
Nat	Earl	Noel
Ned	Egon	Olaf
Nye	Eric	Otto
Ray	Evan	Owen
Reg	Ewan	Paco
Rex	Fred	Paul
Roy	Gene	Pepe
Sam	Gert	Pete
Sid	Gwyn	Phil
Tam	Hans	Raul
Ted	Hugh	Rémy
Tim	Hugo	Rene
Tom	Iain	Rhys
Val	Ivan	Rick
Vic	Ivor	Rolf
Viv	Jack	Rory
Wal	Jake	Ross
Wim	Jean	Rudi
	Jeff	Ryan
		Sa'id

First names

Saul
Sean
Stan
Theo
Toby
Tony
Walt
Will
Yves

5 letters:
Aaron
Abdul
Adolf
Ahmed
Aidan
Alain
Alfie
Algie
Alvin
André
Angus
Anton
Artur
Barry
Basil
Benny
Bernd
Bobby
Boris
Brian
Bruce
Bruno
Caleb
Carlo
Cecil
Celio
Chris
Cliff
Clive
Colin
Cyril
Cyrus
Danny
Darby
D'Arcy
David
Davie
Denis
Derek
Diego

Dodie
Dylan
Eamon
Eddie
Edgar
Elias
Eliot
Ellis
Elmer
Émile
Enoch
Ernie
Ernst
Errol
Felix
Frank
Franz
Fritz
Garry
Garth
Gavin
Geoff
Georg
Giles
Guido
Harry
Hasan
Heinz
Henri
Henry
Hiram
Inigo
Jacky
Jacob
Jaime
Jakob
Jamal
James
Jamie
Jason
Jerry
Jesse
Jesús
Jimmy
Jorge
Jules
Keith
Kevin
Klaus
Lance
Lenny

Lewis
Lloyd
Louis
Luigi
Manny
Marco
Mario
Marty
Miles
Moses
Myles
Niall
Nicky
Nigel
Orson
Oscar
Pablo
Paddy
Paolo
Pedro
Perce
Percy
Perry
Peter
Piero
Ralph
Robin
Rodge
Roger
Romeo
Rufus
Serge
Simon
Steve
Tariq
Terry
Tomás
Vijay
Vince
Wayne

6 letters:
Adrian
Adrien
Albert
Aldous
Alexis
Alfred
Andrés
Andrew
Antony

Archie
Arnaud
Arnold
Arthur
Arturo
Aubrey
Austin
Aylwin
Barney
Benoît
Billie
Calvin
Carlos
Caspar
Cedric
Claude
Connor
Conrad
Damian
Daniel
Darsey
Deepak
Dermot
Didier
Dieter
Donald
Dougal
Dudley
Dugald
Duncan
Dustin
Dwight
Edmund
Edward
Egbert
Enrico
Ernest
Esmond
Eugene
Fergus
Gareth
Gaston
George
Gerald
Gideon
Gilles
Gordon
Graham
Gregor
Hamish
Harold

Harvey
Hector
Helmut
Hilary
Horace
Howard
Hubert
Hugues
Hunter
Ingram
Irving
Isaiah
Israel
Jackie
Jasper
Javier
Jeremy
Jerome
Johann
Joseph
Joshua
Josiah
Julian
Julien
Julius
Jürgen
Justin
Kenelm
Larrie
Laurie
Leslie
Lester
Lionel
Lucius
Ludwig
Luther
Magnus
Mahmud
Manuel
Marcel
Marcus
Marius
Martin
Melvin
Melvyn
Merlin
Mervyn
Michel
Mickey
Miguel
Murray

Nathan
Norman
Norris
Oliver
Osbert
Oswald
Petrus
Philip
Pierre
Rainer
Rashid
Reuben
Robert
Rodney
Roland
Ronald
Rupert
Samuel
Sanjiv
Selwyn
Sergio
Sidney
Stefan
Steven
Stuart
Sydney
Thomas
Trevor
Ulrich
Victor
Vikram
Vivian
Wallis
Walter
Warner
Warren
Werner
Wesley
Wilbur
Willie
Willis
Xavier
Yasser
Yehudi

7 letters:
Abraham
Alberto
Alfonso
Alfredo
Alister

First names

Ambrose
Andreas
Anthony
Antoine
Antonio
Baldwin
Barnaby
Bernard
Bertram
Brendan
Cameron
Carlton
Charles
Charlie
Clement
Clemmie
Desmond
Diarmid
Dominic
Douglas
Ebeneza
Edmondo
Edoardo
Édouard
Emanuel
Erasmus
Estéban
Étienne
Ezekiel
Fabrice
Filippo
Francis
Gabriel
Geordie
Georges
Geraint
Gerhard
Giacomo
Gilbert
Giorgio
Godfrey
Gregory
Herbert
Horatio
Ibrahim
Jacques
Jeffrey
Joachim
Joaquin
Kenneth
Lachlan

Laurent
Leonard
Leopold
Lindsey
Lorenzo
Luciano
Malcolm
Matthew
Maurice
Maxwell
Michael
Montagu
Murdoch
Mustafa
Neville
Nicolas
Norbert
Obadiah
Olivier
Pascual
Patrice
Patrick
Placido
Quentin
Raphael
Raymond
Richard
Rodrigo
Rolando
Rudolph
Rudyard
Russell
Sigmund
Solomon
Spencer
Stanley
Stefano
Stephan
Stephen
Stewart
Terence
Thibaut
Thierry
Timothy
Umberto
Valerie
Vaughan
Vincent
Wallace
Wilfred
Wilhelm

William
Windsor
Winston
Wyndham
Youssef

8 letters:
Abdullah
Alasdair
Alastair
Aloysius
Augustus
Benedict
Benjamin
Bernabas
Bernardo
Bertrand
Charlton
Clarence
Claudius
Clifford
Consuelo
Cuthbert
Dietrich
Emmanuel
Fabrizio
Farquhar
Fernando
François
Geoffrey
Giovanni
Giuliano
Giuseppe
Heinrich
Hercules
Humphrey
Johannes
Jonathan
Lancelot
Laurence
Lawrence
Leonardo
Llewelyn
Marcello
Matthias
Matthieu
Montague
Morrison
Mortimer
Muhammed
Nicholas

Octavius
Odysseus
Percival
Philippe
Reginald
Roderick
Salvador
Santiago
Sherlock
Silvanus
Sinclair
Somerset
Stéphane
Theodore
Timothée
Wolfgang

9 letters:
Alejandro
Alexander
Alexandre
Alphonsus
Archibald
Augustine
Christian
Cornelius
Dominique
Ethelbert
Ferdinand
Francesco
Frederick
Friedrich
Gottfried
Grégroire

Guillaume
Marmaduke
Nathaniel
Peregrine
Sebastian
Sébastien
Siegfried
Sylvester

10 letters:
Alessandro
Christophe
Maximilian
Montgomery

11 letters:
Bartholomew
Christopher

GIRLS

3 letters:
Ada
Amy
Ana
Ann
Bab
Bea
Bel
Dot
Ena
Eva
Eve
Fay
Flo
Gay
Ger
Ina
Isa
Jan
Joy
Kay
Kim
Kit
Liz
Lyn
May
Meg
Nan
Net
Pam
Pat

Peg
Pen
Pip
Pru
Rae
Sal
Sis
Sue
Tam
Una
Ute
Val
Zoe

4 letters:
Alba
Ally
Alma
Anke
Anna
Anne
Babs
Bess
Beth
Cara
Ciss
Cleo
Dawn
Dora
Edna
Ella

Elma
Elsa
Emma
Enid
Gail
Gill
Gina
Gita
Gwen
Hope
Inge
Iona
Iris
Jane
Jean
Jess
Jill
Joan
Judy
June
Kate
Leah
Lena
Lily
Lisa
Lois
Lola
Lucy
Lynn
Mary
Maud

First names

Myra
Nell
Nina
Nita
Olga
Oona
Rene
Rita
Romy
Rosa
Rose
Ruby
Ruth
Sara
Tess
Tina
Vera
Zara

5 letters:
Abbie
Adele
Aggie
Agnes
Ailie
Ailsa
Alice
Aline
Anita
Annie
April
Avril
Beata
Becca
Bella
Berry
Beryl
Betsy
Betty
Biddy
Carla
Carol
Cathy
Celia
Chloe
Chris
Clara
Clare
Coral
Corin
Daisy

D'Arcy
Delia
Diana
Diane
Dilys
Dinah
Dolly
Donna
Doris
Edith
Edwin
Effie
Elise
Eliza
Ellen
Ellis
Elsie
Emily
Ethel
Faith
Fanny
Fiona
Fleur
Flora
Freda
Gerda
Ginny
Grace
Greta
Hazel
Heidi
Helen
Helga
Hetty
Hilda
Honor
Irene
Isaac
Jacky
Janet
Janey
Jayne
Jenny
Jesse
Josie
Joyce
Julie
Karen
Katja
Kitty
Laura

Laure
Leila
Leona
Libby
Liese
Linda
Lindy
Lorna
Lotte
Lucia
Luisa
Lydia
Lynne
Mabel
Madge
Maeve
Magda
Mamie
Marge
Margo
Maria
Marie
Marta
Marty
Maude
Mavis
Merle
Milly
Mitzi
Moira
Molly
Morag
Moray
Morna
Myrna
Nancy
Nanny
Naomi
Nelly
Netty
Nicky
Nicol
Norma
Patty
Paula
Pearl
Peggy
Penny
Polly
Renée
Rhoda

Rhona
Sadie
Sally
Sandy
Sarah
Sofia
Sonia
Sonja
Susan
Susie
Sybil
Tania
Tanya
Tatum
Thora
Tilly
Tracy
Vicky
Viola
Wanda
Wendy

6 letters:
Agatha
Aileen
Alexis
Alicia
Alison
Althea
Amanda
Amelia
Amélie
Andrea
Angela
Arabel
Arline
Astrid
Athene
Audrey
Aurora
Bertha
Bianca
Billie
Blaise
Brenda
Bryony
Carmen
Carole
Carrie
Cécile
Céline

Cherry
Cheryl
Claire
Concha
Daphne
Davina
Debbie
Denise
Dianne
Doreen
Dulcie
Easter
Edwina
Eileen
Eilidh
Elaine
Elinor
Elisha
Elodie
Elvira
Emilia
Esther
Eunice
Evadne
Evelyn
Fatima
Gertie
Gladys
Gloria
Gretel
Gwenda
Hannah
Hattie
Hélène
Hester
Hilary
Imogen
Indira
Ingrid
Isabel
Isobel
Isolde
Jackie
Jamila
Janice
Jeanne
Jemima
Jessie
Joanna
Joanne
Judith

Juliet
Kirsty
Krista
Lesley
Lilian
Lolita
Lottie
Louisa
Louise
Madhur
Maggie
Maisie
Marcia
Margie
Marian
Marina
Marion
Martha
Maxine
Minnie
Miriam
Monica
Morgan
Morrie
Morris
Morven
Muriel
Myrtle
Nadine
Nessie
Nettie
Nicola
Nicole
Noelle
Odette
Oonagh
Oriana
Paloma
Pamela
Petula
Phoebe
Rachel
Raquel
Regina
Renata
Robina
Rowena
Roxana
Sabina
Sabine
Salome

First names

Sandra
Selina
Serena
Sharon
Sheena
Sheila
Silvia
Simone
Sophia
Sophie
Stella
Sylvia
Tamsin
Thelma
Tricia
Trixie
Trudie
Ulrike
Ursula
Verity
Violet
Vivian
Winnie
Yvette
Yvonne

7 letters:
Abigail
Adriana
Alfreda
Annabel
Annette
Antonia
Ariadne
Aurelia
Barbara
Belinda
Bernice
Bettina
Blanche
Bridget
Bronwen
Camilla
Camille
Candida
Carolyn
Cecilia
Celeste
Chantal
Charity
Charlie

Chrissy
Christy
Clarice
Claudia
Colette
Corinna
Corinne
Cynthia
Deborah
Deirdre
Dolores
Dorothy
Eleanor
Elspeth
Estella
Eugenia
Fenella
Florrie
Flossie
Frances
Gertrud
Gillian
Giselle
Gwyneth
Harriet
Heather
Isadora
Jessica
Jocelyn
Josette
Juliana
Justine
Katrina
Kirstie
Kristin
Lavinia
Leonora
Letitia
Lillian
Lindsey
Linette
Lucille
Lucinda
Manuela
Margery
Marilyn
Martina
Martine
Matilda
Maureen
Melanie

Melissa
Mildred
Mirabel
Miranda
Modesty
Myfanwy
Natalie
Natasha
Ophelia
Ottilie
Pauline
Perdita
Petrina
Phyllis
Queenie
Rebecca
Roberta
Rosalie
Sabrina
Shelagh
Shelley
Shirley
Siobahn
Susanna
Suzanne
Theresa
Valerie
Vanessa
Yolande

8 letters:
Adrienne
Angeline
Arabella
Beatrice
Beverley
Brigitta
Brigitte
Carlotta
Carolina
Caroline
Cathleen
Catriona
Charmian
Claribel
Clarissa
Claudine
Clemence
Collette
Conchita
Consuela

Cordelia
Cressida
Danielle
Dominica
Dorothea
Drusilla
Euphemia
Felicity
Florence
Francine
Georgina
Gertrude
Hermione
Isabelle
Iseabail
Jeanette
Jeannine
Jennifer
Juliette
Kathleen
Lorraine
Madeline
Magdalen
Marcella
Margaret
Marianne
Marigold
Marjorie
Mercedes
Meredith
Michaela
Michelle
Patience
Patricia
Penelope
Perpetua

Primrose
Prudence
Prunella
Rosalind
Rosamund
Rosemary
Samantha
Scarlett
Theodora
Veronica
Victoria
Violette
Virginia
Virginie
Winifred

9 letters:
Alejandra
Alexandra
Anastasia
Anastasie
Annabella
Cassandra
Catherina
Catherine
Charlotte
Christina
Christine
Constance
Elizabeth
Esmerelda
Francesca
Françoise
Gabrielle
Genevieve
Geraldine
Gwendolyn

Henrietta
Jacquetta
Josephine
Katharine
Madeleine
Magdalene
Millicent
Mirabelle
Nicolette
Phillippa
Priscilla
Rosabella
Sempronia
Seraphina
Stephanie
Veronique

10 letters:
Alessandra
Antoinette
Christabel
Christelle
Christiana
Christiane
Clementine
Concepción
Emmanuelle
Jacqueline
Lieselotte
Margherita
Marguerite
Petronella
Wilhelmina

11 letters:
Bernadettte
Constantine

Fish

2 letters:
Ai
Id

3 letters:
Aua
Ayu
Bar
Bib
But
Cat

Cod
Cow
Dab
Dib
Dog
Eel
Gar
Ged
Hag
Ice

Ide
Koi
Lax
Lob
Par
Pod
Ray
Rig
Sar
Tai

Fish

Top

4 letters:
Bass
Blay
Bley
Brim
Brit
Butt
Carp
Cero
Chad
Char
Chub
Chum
Coho
Cray
Cusk
Dace
Dare
Dart
Dory
Fugu
Gade
Goby
Gump
Hake
Harl
Hoki
Huso
Huss
Jack
Kelt
Keta
Lant
Leaf
Ling
Luce
Lump
Maid
Maze
Moki
Mort
Opah
Orfe
Parr
Peal
Peel
Pike
Pogy
Pope

Pout
Raun
Rawn
Rigg
Rudd
Ruff
Scad
Scar
Scat
Scup
Seer
Seir
Shad
Sild
Slip
Snig
Sole
Star
Tope
Trot
Tuna
Tusk
Woof

5 letters:
Ablet
Ahuru
Allis
Angel
Apode
Barra
Basse
Betta
Bleak
Bream
Brill
Bully
Capon
Charr
Cisco
Clown
Cobia
Cohoe
Coley
Cuddy
Danio
Dorad
Doras
Doree
Dorse
Elops

Elver
Fluke
Gadus
Gibel
Grunt
Guppy
Jewie
Jurel
Koaea
Laker
Lance
Loach
Lythe
Maise
Maize
Manta
Masus
Mease
Molly
Moray
Murre
Murry
Nerka
Padle
Perai
Perca
Perch
Pilot
Piper
Pirai
Platy
Pogge
Porae
Porgy
Powan
Prawn
Roach
Roker
Ruffe
Saith
Sargo
Saury
Scrod
Sewen
Sewin
Shark
Sheat
Skate
Slope
Smelt
Snoek

Snook
Solen
Speck
Sprat
Sprod
Tench
Tetra
Toado
Togue
Torsk
Trout
Tunny
Umber
Wahoo
Whiff
Wirra
Witch
Yabby
Zebra

6 letters:
Alevin
Allice
Anabas
Angler
Araara
Archer
Ballan
Barbel
Belone
Beluga
Bigeye
Blenny
Bonito
Bounce
Bowfin
Braise
Braize
Bumalo
Burbot
Callop
Caplin
Caranx
Caribe
Cheven
Clupea
Cockle
Comber
Conger
Conner
Cottus

Cudden
Cuddie
Cuddin
Cunner
Cuttle
Darter
Dentex
Diodon
Dipnoi
Discus
Doctor
Dorado
Dun-cow
Finnac
Finnan
Flying
Fogash
Fumado
Gadoid
Garvie
Gilgie
Goramy
Grilse
Groper
Gulper
Gunnel
Gurami
Gurnet
Haddie
Hapuka
Hapuku
Hassar
Inanga
Jerker
Jilgie
Kelpie
Kipper
Kokopu
Labrus
Lancet
Launce
Lizard
Louvar
Lunker
Mad Tom
Mahsir
Maomao
Marari
Marlin
Meagre
Medaka

Medusa
Megrim
Milter
Minnow
Morgay
Mudcat
Mullet
Murena
Nerite
Nigger
Oyster
Paddle
Paidle
Pakoko
Parore
Parrot
Patiki
Pholas
Pillie
Piraña
Piraya
Plaice
Podley
Pollan
Porgie
Puffer
Rawaru
Red cod
Redfin
Remora
Robalo
Roughy
Runner
Saithe
Salmon
Samlet
Samson
Sander
Sardel
Sargus
Sauger
Saurel
Scampi
Sea-bat
Sea-owl
Seeder
Serran
Shanny
Sheath
Shiner
Skelly

Fish

Sparid
Sucker
Tailor
Tarpon
Tautog
Toitoi
Tomcod
Trygon
Turbot
Twaite
Ulicon
Ulikon
Vendis
Weever
Wirrah
Wrasse
Yabbie
Zander
Zingel

7 letters:
Alewife
Anchovy
Anemone
Asterid
Azurine
Batfish
Beardie
Bellows
Bergylt
Bloater
Bluecap
Blue cod
Boxfish
Brassie
Buffalo
Bummalo
Cabezon
Capelin
Catfish
Cavalla
Cavally
Ceviche
Cichlid
Codfish
Copepod
Cowfish
Crappie
Croaker
Crucian
Crusian

Cutlass
Dogfish
Eelfare
Eelpout
Escolar
Findram
Finnack
Finnock
Flattie
Garfish
Garpike
Garvock
Geelbek
Gemfish
Goldeye
Gourami
Grouper
Growler
Grunion
Gudgeon
Gurnard
Gwiniad
Gwyniad
Haddock
Hagdown
Hagfish
Halibut
Herling
Herring
Hirling
Hogfish
Homelyn
Houting
Ichthys
Inconnu
Javelin
Jewfish
Kahawai
Keeling
Koi carp
Kokanee
Lampern
Lamprey
Lampuki
Lantern
Lingcod
Lobster
Lyomeri
Mahseer
Medacca
Merling

Mojarra
Mooneye
Morwong
Mudfish
Muraena
Oarfish
Old-wife
Oolakan
Opaleye
Osseter
Oulakan
Oulicon
Panchax
Pandora
Pegasus
Pigfish
Pinfish
Piranha
Pollack
Pollock
Pomfret
Pompano
Ragfish
Rasbora
Ratfish
Rat-tail
Redfish
Rock cod
Rorqual
Sand dab
Sand eel
Sardine
Sawfish
Scalare
Scallop
Sculpin
Sea bass
Sea-cock
Sea-dace
Sea-moth
Sea-pike
Sea-star
Sea-wife
Sillock
Skegger
Skipper
Sleeper
Snapper
Sockeye
Sparoid
Speldin

Sterlet
Sunfish
Surgeon
Teleost
Tiddler
Tilapia
Titling
Torgoch
Torpedo
Ulichon
Vendace
Walleye
Warehou
Whipray
Whiting
Wide-gab

8 letters:
Albacore
Anableps
Arapaima
Asteroid
Atherine
Ballahoo
Bay trout
Billfish
Black cod
Blind eel
Bloodfin
Blowfish
Blueback
Bluefish
Bluegill
Blue moki
Blue nose
Boarfish
Bonefish
Brisling
Bullhead
Bullhorn
Cabezone
Cabrilla
Cardinal
Cavefish
Characid
Characin
Chimaera
Climbing
Coalfish
Corkwing
Cucumber

Cyprinid
Dealfish
Devil ray
Dragonet
Drumfish
Eagle-ray
Escallop
Eulachon
Fallfish
Fighting
Filefish
Flatfish
Flathead
Flounder
Four-eyed
Four-eyes
Frogfish
Ganoidei
Gillaroo
Gilthead
Goatfish
Gobiidae
Goldfish
Graining
Grayling
Hackbolt
Hairtail
Halfbeak
Hard-head
Holostei
Hornbeak
Hornpout
Jackfish
John Dory
Kabeljou
Kelpfish
Killfish
Kingfish
Kingklip
Kukukuma
Lionfish
Luderick
Lumpfish
Lungfish
Mackerel
Mahi-mahi
Mangrove
Manta ray
Mata Hari
Menhaden
Milkfish

Monkfish
Moonfish
Mulloway
Nannygai
Nennigai
Nine-eyes
Oulachon
Paradise
Patutuki
Pickerel
Pilchard
Pipefish
Pirarucu
Redbelly
Red bream
Rock bass
Rock-cook
Rockfish
Rockling
Roncador
Rosefish
Saibling
Sailfish
Saltfish
Sardelle
Scabbard
Sciaenid
Scorpion
Scuppaug
Sea bream
Sea-devil
Sea horse
Sea-lemon
Sea perch
Sea raven
Sea robin
Sea snail
Sea trout
Sergeant
Serranus
Skipjack
Smear-dab
Snake-eel
Sparling
Stenlock
Stingray
Stonecat
Sturgeon
Tarakihi
Tarwhine
Teraglin

Fish

Terakihi
Tilefish
Toadfish
Trevalla
Trevally
Tropical
Tubenose
Tullibee
Weakfish
Whitling
Wobegong
Wolffish
Wollamai
Wollomai

9 letters:
Alfonsino
Amberjack
Anabantid
Anchoveta
Angelfish
Argentine
Barracuda
Black bass
Blackfish
Blindfish
Bony bream
Bull trout
Butterfly
Cascadura
Ceratodus
Chaetodon
Chavender
Clingfish
Clupeidae
Coregonus
Coryphene
Devilfish
Gaspereau
Glassfish
Globefish
Goldfinny
Goldsinny
Golomynka
Goosefish
Greenbone
Greenling
Grenadier
Haberdine
Hornyhead
Hottentot

Houndfish
Ichthyoid
Jacksmelt
Jewelfish
Kabeljouw
Killifish
Labyrinth
Lamper eel
Latimeria
Lemon sole
Menominee
Mudhopper
Neon tetra
Pikeperch
Placoderm
Porbeagle
Porcupine
Quillback
Red mullet
Red salmon
Roussette
Sand lance
Scaldfish
Schnapper
Scorpaena
Selachian
Shubunkin
Siluridae
Slickhead
Snailfish
Snakehead
Snipefish
Solenette
Spadefish
Spearfish
Speldring
Stargazer
Steelhead
Steenbras
Stingaree
Stockfish
Stone bass
Stonefish
Surfperch
Surmullet
Swellfish
Swordfish
Swordtail
Thornback
Threadfin
Tittlebat

Tommy ruff
Topminnow
Trachinus
Troutfish
Trunkfish
Whitebait
White-bass
Whitefish
Wobbegong
Wobbygong
Wreckfish
Yellowfin

10 letters:
Archerfish
Barracoota
Barracouta
Barramunda
Barramundi
Bitterling
Black bream
Black perch
Bombay duck
Bottlehead
Brook trout
Brown trout
Butterfish
Candlefish
Cockabully
Coelacanth
Coral trout
Cornetfish
Cyclostome
Damselfish
Demoiselle
Dollarfish
Etheostoma
Fingerling
Flutemouth
Giant perch
Groundling
Guitarfish
Horned pout
King salmon
Lumpsucker
Māori chief
Maskalonge
Maskanonge
Maskinonge
Midshipman
Mirror carp

Mossbunker
Mudskipper
Needlefish
Nurse-hound
Ouananiche
Paddlefish
Pakirikiri
Parrotfish
Pearl perch
Rabbitfish
Red emperor
Red snapper
Ribbonfish
Rock salmon
Rudderfish
Scopelidae
Sea lamprey
Sea-poacher
Sea-surgeon
Serrasalmo
Sheepshead
Shovelnose
Silverfish
Silverside
Springfish
Squeteague
Teleostome
Titarakura
Tommy rough
Tripletail
Yellow jack
Yellowtail

11 letters:
Bluefin tuna
Chondrostei
Dolly Varden
Electric eel
Golden perch
Istiophorus
Lake herring
Lepidosiren
Maskallonge
Moorish idol
Murray perch

Muskellunge
Ostracoderm
Oxyrhynchus
Plagiostome
Pumpkinseed
Salmon trout
Scolopendra
Sea scorpion
Seventy-four
Silver belly
Silversides
Sleeper goby
Smooth hound
Soldierfish
Stickleback
Stone roller
Surgeonfish
Triggerfish
Trumpetfish
Whiting pout
Yellow-belly

12 letters:
Baggie minnow
Ballan-wrasse
Elasmobranch
Father lasher
Heterosomata
Histiophorus
Mangrove Jack
Miller's thumb
Mouthbreeder
Native salmon
Orange roughy
Ox-eye herring
Plectognathi
Rainbow trout
River lamprey
Silver salmon
Skipjack tuna
Squirrelfish
Walleyed pike
Yarra herring

13 letters:
Armed bullhead

Black kingfish
Black rockfish
Brown bullhead
Chinook salmon
Climbing perch
Flying gurnard
Horse mackerel
Leatherjacket
Northern porgy
Quinnat salmon
Sailor's choice
Sergeant Baker
Sergeant major
Speckled trout

14 letters:
Largemouth bass
Orange chromide
School mackerel
Smallmouth bass

15 letters:
Crossopterygian
Freshwater bream
Siamese fighting
Spanish mackerel
Spotted mackerel

16 letters:
Australian salmon

17 letters:
Queensland
halibut

18 letters:
Queensland
kingfish
Queensland
lungfish

19 letters:
Queensland
trumpeter

22 letters:
Short-spined sea
scorpion

See also:
➤ **Seafood** ➤ **Sharks**

Flags

7 letters:
Saltire

8 letters:
Lone Star
Old Glory
Swastika

9 letters:
Betsy Ross
Blue Peter
Maple Leaf
Red Dragon
Red Duster
Rising Sun
Tricolore
Tricolour

Union Jack

10 letters:
Blue Ensign
Bonnie Blue
Jolly Roger
Lonely Star
Single Star

11 letters:
Golden Arrow
White Duster

12 letters:
Federal Cross
Herring Salad
Stars and Bars

13 letters:
Southern Cross

14 letters:
Flag of the South

15 letters:
Cross of St George
Hammer and
 Sickle
Stainless Banner
Stars and Stripes

18 letters:
Skull and
 crossbones

Flies

3 letters:
Bee
Bot
Fly
Fox

4 letters:
Bulb
Bush
Cleg
Deer
Dung
Frit
Gnat
Horn
Moth
Pium
Zimb

5 letters:
Alder
Aphid
Aphis
Baker
Black
Brize
Crane
Drake
Drone

Flesh
Fruit
Hover
Musca
Nymph
Onion
Sedge
Snake
Snipe
Zebub

6 letters:
Blowie
Botfly
Breese
Breeze
Caddis
Carrot
Dayfly
Dragon
Gadfly
Mayfly
Medfly
Motuca
Mutuca
Needle
Pomace
Robber
Stable

Thrips
Tipula
Tsetse
Tzetze
Warble
Willow

7 letters:
Antlion
Beetfly
Blowfly
Brommer
Bushfly
Chalcid
Cluster
Diptera
Gallfly
Grannom
Harvest
Hessian
Lantern
Mangold
Sandfly
Spanish
Tabanid
Tachina
Vinegar
Watchet

8 letters:
Assassin
Bedstead
Blackfly
Dutchman
Glossina
Greenfly
Horsefly
Housefly
Lacewing
Mosquito
Ox-warble
Scorpion
Simulium
Stonefly
Whitefly

9 letters:
Bean aphid
Bee killer
Blue-arsed
Damselfly

Dobsonfly
Dragonfly
Greenhead
Homoptera
Ichneumon
Jock Scott
Sciaridae
Screwworm
Syrphidae

10 letters:
Bluebottle
Cecidomyia
Drosophila
Plant louse
Silverhorn

11 letters:
Apple blight
Buffalo gnat
Greenbottle
Plecopteran

12 letters:
Cheesehopper
Green blowfly
Jenny-spinner
Trichopteran

13 letters:
Cheese skipper
Daddy-longlegs

14 letters:
American blight

15 letters:
Welshman's
  button

18 letters:
Mediterranean
  fruit

19 letters:
Devil's darning-
  needle

Flowers

4 letters:
Aloe
Arum
Cyme
Disa
Flag
Gold
Gool
Gule
Irid
Iris
Lily
Pink
Rose

5 letters:
Agave
Aster
Brook
Bugle
Camas
Daisy
Enemy
Hosta
Lotus

Lupin
Oxlip
Padma
Pansy
Peony
Phlox
Poppy
Stock
Tansy
Toran
Tulip
Umbel
Yulan

6 letters:
Acacia
Adonis
Arabis
Azalea
Betony
Cactus
Camash
Camass
Corymb
Crants

Crocus
Dahlia
Gollan
Henbit
Madder
Maguey
Mallow
Nuphar
Onagra
Orchid
Paeony
Pompom
Pompon
Protea
Safety
Scilla
Sesame
Silene
Smilax
Spadix
Tassel
Torana
Vernal
Violet
Yarrow

Flowers

Zinnia

7 letters:
Aconite
Alyssum
Anemone
Arbutus
Astilbe
Begonia
Bugloss
Burdock
Campion
Cowslip
Dog rose
Freesia
Fumaria
Gentian
Gilt-cup
Glacier
Godetia
Golland
Gowland
Hemlock
Ipomoea
Jasmine
Jonquil
Kikumon
Lobelia
Melilot
Petunia
Picotee
Primula
Quamash
Ragweed
Rampion
Saffron
Sulphur
Verbena

8 letters:
Abutilon
Acanthus
Amaranth
Argemone
Asphodel
Aubretia
Aubrieta
Bignonia
Bindi-eye
Bluebell
Camellia

Camomile
Carolina
Clematis
Cyclamen
Daffodil
Floscule
Foxglove
Gardenia
Geranium
Gillyvor
Glory-pea
Harebell
Hepatica
Hibiscus
Hyacinth
Kok-sagyz
Larkspur
Lavender
Magnolia
Mandrake
Marigold
Marjoram
Myosotis
Oleander
Oxtongue
Primrose
Samphire
Scabious
Snowdrop
Stapelia
Sweet pea
Trollius
Tuberose
Turnsole
Valerian
Wisteria
Woodbine

9 letters:
Amaryllis
Aubrietia
Bald-money
Belamoure
Buttercup
Calendula
Carnation
Celandine
Chamomile
Clianthus
Columbine
Dandelion

Desert pea
Digitalis
Edelweiss
Eglantine
Gessamine
Gladiolus
Groundsel
Hellebore
Hollyhock
Hydrangea
Jessamine
Melampode
Monkshood
Narcissus
Pimpernel
Pre-vernal
Rudbeckia
Santonica
Saxifrage
Speedwell
Strobilus
Sunflower
Tiger lily
Water lily

10 letters:
Aspidistra
Bellamoure
Busy Lizzie
Cornflower
Coronation
Delphinium
Gypsophila
Heart's-ease
Heliotrope
Immortelle
Marguerite
Nasturtium
Oxeye daisy
Pentstemon
Poinsettia
Snapdragon
Stavesacre
Sweetbrier
Tibouchine
Touch-me-not
Wallflower
Willowherb

11 letters:
Bog asphodel

Bur-marigold
Cotoneaster
Forget-me-not
Gilliflower
Gillyflower
Guelder-rose
London pride
Loose-strife
Meadowsweet
Ragged robin
Wintergreen
Wood anemone

12 letters:
Hortus siccus

See also:
➤ **Lilies**

Morning-glory
None-so-pretty
Old man's beard
Sweet william
Tradescantia

13 letters:
African violet
Babe-in-a-cradle
Bougainvillea
Chrysanthemum
Grape hyacinth
Passionflower

14 letters:
Black-eyed Susan

Cardinal flower
Cooktown orchid
Love-in-idleness

15 letters:
Christmas cactus
Lily of the valley
Michaelmas daisy
Sturt's desert pea

16 letters:
Deadly nightshade
Love-lies-bleeding
Scarlet pimpernel

Football

TERMS USED IN (ASSOCIATION) FOOTBALL

2 letters:
FA

3 letters:
Bar
Cap
Net
Nil
SFA

4 letters:
Back
FIFA
Foul
Goal
Half
Mark
Pass
Post
Save
Shot
Trap
UEFA
Wall
Wing

5 letters:
Cross
Derby
Dummy

6 letters:
Corner
Cut out
Goalie
Lay off
Nutmeg
One-two
Onside
Square
Tackle
Winger

7 letters:
Booking
Bye kick
Caution
Dribble
Forward
Goal net
Kick off
Offside

Own goal
Penalty
Playoff
Red card
Referee
Striker
Sweeper
Throw in

8 letters:
Crossbar
Defender
Free kick
Fullback
Full time
Goal area
Goal kick
Goalpost
Halfback
Half time
Handball
Left back
Linesman
Long ball
Midfield

Football

Pass-back
Reserves
Route One
Spot kick
Transfer
Wall pass

9 letters:
Aggregate
Breakaway
Clearance
Extra time
Finishing
Inswinger
Non-league
Promotion
Right back
Score draw
Target man
Touchline

10 letters:
Ballplayer

Ballwinner
Catenaccio
Centre half
Corner kick
Goalkeeper
Injury time
Inside left
Midfielder
Penalty box
Relegation
Sending-off
Six-yard box
Substitute
Yellow card

11 letters:
Half way line
Inside right
Offside trap
Ordering-off
Outside left
Penalty area
Penalty kick

Penalty spot
Six-yard line

12 letters:
Centre circle
Outside right
Stoppage time

13 letters:
Centre forward
International
Sliding tackle
Total football

14 letters:
Aggregate score
Direct free kick

15 letters:
Penalty shoot-out

16 letters:
Indirect free kick
Professional foul

TERMS USED IN AUSTRALIAN RULES FOOTBALL

3 letters:
AFL

4 letters:
Goal
Mark
Rove
Ruck

5 letters:
Flank
Footy
Point
Rover

6 letters:
Behind
Rub out
Stanza

7 letters:
Quarter

Throw in

8 letters:
Boundary
Eighteen, the
Follower
Free kick
Guernsey
Half-back
Handball
Shepherd
Stab kick

9 letters:
Ruckrover
Scrimmage

10 letters:
Back pocket
Behind line
Behind post

Goal umpire
Shirt front

11 letters:
Aussie Rules
Field umpire
Half-forward
Interchange

12 letters:
Twentieth man

13 letters:
Forward pocket
Nineteenth man

14 letters:
Aerial ping-pong

24 letters:
Australian Football
  League

TERMS USED IN AMERICAN FOOTBALL

3 letters:
Run

4 letters:
Down
Line
Pass
Play
Punt
Rush
Sack
Snap

5 letters:
Blitz
Block
Guard

6 letters:
Center
Kicker
Punter
Safety
Tackle

7 letters:
Defense
End zone
Lineman
Offense
Pigskin
Shotgun

8 letters:
Complete
Football
Fullback
Gridiron
Halfback
Overtime
Tight end
Turnover

9 letters:
Backfield
Field goal
Scrimmage
Secondary
Super Bowl

Touchback
Touchdown

10 letters:
Cornerback
Incomplete
Line backer
Point after

11 letters:
Quarterback
Running back
Special team

12 letters:
Defensive end
Interception
Wide receiver

13 letters:
Defensive back

15 letters:
Line of scrimmage

Football clubs

EUROPEAN FOOTBALL CLUBS

4 letters:
Ajax
Genk
Lyon
Roma

5 letters:
Lazio
Parma

6 letters:
Brugge
Lierse
Monaco

7 letters:
AC Milan

Beveren
Brondby
FC Porto
Hamburg

8 letters:
Besiktas
Juventus
Valencia

9 letters:
AEK Athens
Barcelona
Celta Vigo
Feyenoord
Stuttgart
Villareal

10 letters:
Anderlecht
Dynamo Kiev
Heerenveen
Inter Milan
Olympiacos
Real Madrid

11 letters:
Ferencvaros
Galatasaray
Rapid Vienna
RCD Mallorca

12 letters:
Bayern Munich
Dinamo Zagreb

Football clubs

PSV Eindhoven
Real Sociedad
Sparta Prague

13 letters:
Austria Vienna
Panathenaikos

14 letters:
Paris St Germain

15 letters:
Lokomotiv
  Moscow
Red Star Belgrade
Steaua Bucharest

16 letters:
Borussia
  Dortmund

Partizan Belgrade

17 letters:
Deportivo La
  Coruna

18 letters:
Olympique
  Marseille

UK FOOTBALL CLUBS

Club	Nickname	Ground
Aberdeen	Dons	Pittodrie
Arsenal	Gunners	Highbury
Aston Villa	Villa	Villa Park
Birmingham City	Blues	St Andrews
Blackburn Rovers	Rovers	Ewood Park
Bolton	Trotters	Reebok Stadium
Bradford	Bantams	Valley Parade
Bristol City	Robins	Ashton Gate
Burnley	Clarets	Turf Moor
Cardiff	Bluebirds	Ninian Park
Celtic	Celts, Hoops	Parkhead
Charlton	Addicks	The Valley
Chelsea	Pensioners	Stamford Bridge
Coventry City	Sky Blues	Highfield Road
Crewe	Railwaymen	Gresty Road
Crystal Palace	Glaziers	Gogg Lane
Derby County	Rams	Pride Park
Dundee	Dark Blues	Dens Park
Dundee United	Tangerines	Tannadice
Dunfermline Athletic	Pars	East End Park
Everton	Toffee Men	Goodison Park
Fulham	Cottagers	Craven Cottage
Gillingham	Gills	Prestfield Stadium
Hearts	Jambos, Jam Tarts	Gorgie Road
Hibernian	Hibs, Hibees	Easter Road
Inverness Caledonian Thistle	Caley, The Jags	East Longman
Ipswich	Blues	Portman Road
Kilmarnock	The Killies	Rugby Park
Leeds United	United	Elland Road
Leicester City	Filberts	Filbert Street
Leyton Orient	Orient	Brisbane Road
Liverpool	Reds	Anfield
Livingston	Thistle,Wee Jags	West London Courier
Manchester City	City	Maine Road
Manchester United	Reds, Red Devils	Old Trafford
Middlesbrough	Boro	Riverside Stadium
Millwall	Lions	The Den

Club	Nickname	Ground
Motherwell	Steelmen, Well	Fir Park
Newcastle	Magpies, Toon	St James Park
Norwich	Canaries	Carrow Road
Nottingham Forest	Forest	City Ground
Partick Thistle	Jags	Firhill
Peterborough	Posh	London Road
Portsmouth	Pompey	Fratton Park
Preston	Lilywhites	Deepdale
Queen of the South	The Doonhamers	Palmerston Park
Queen's Park Rangers	QPR	Loftus Road
Rangers	Gers, The Blues	Ibrox
Reading	Royals, Biscuitmen	Madejski Stadium
Rotherham	Merry Millers	Millmoor
St Johnstone	The Saints	McDiarmid Park
St Mirren	The Buddies	Love Street
Sheffield United	Blades	Bramall Lane
Sheffield Wednesday	Owls	Hillsborough
Southampton	Saints	The Dell
Stenhousemuir	The Warriors	Ochilview Park
Stoke	Potteries	Britannia Stadium
Sunderland	Rokerites	Stadium of Light
Tottenham Hotspur	Spurs	White Hart Lane
Tranmere Rovers	Rovers	Prenton Park
Walsall	Saddlers	Bescot Stadium
Watford	Hornets	Vicarage Road
West Bromwich Albion	Throstles, Raggies	The Hawthorns
West Ham	Hammers	Upton Park
Wigan	Latics	JJB Stadium
Wimbledon	Dons	Selhurst Park
Wolverhampton Wanderers	Wolves	Molineux

Footballers

3 letters:
Law, *Dennis*

4 letters:
Ball, *Alan*
Best, *George*
Cacá
Dean, *Dixie*
Didi
Duff, *Damien*
Figo, *Luis*
Gray, *Eddie*
Hunt, *Roger*
Owen, *Michael*

Pele
Repp, *Johnny*
Rush, *Ian*
Zoff, *Dizo*

5 letters:
Adams, *Tony*
Banks, *Gordon*
Giggs, *Ryan*
Giles, *John*
Greig, *John*
Henry, *Thierry*
Hurst, *Geoff*
Messi, *Lionel*

Footballers

Moore, *Bobby*
Pires, *Robert*
Rossi, *Paulo*

6 letters:
Agathe, *Didier*
Baggio, *Roberto*
Barnes, *John*
Baxter, *Jim*
Bowles, *Stan*
Cooper, *Davie*
Crespo, *Hernan*
Cruyff, *Johann*
Finney, *Tom*
Ginola, *David*
Graham, *George*
Gullit, *Ruud*
Hansen, *Alan*
Heskey, *Emil*
Hoddle, *Glen*
Horton, *Jim*
Keegan, *Kevin*
Lawton, *Tommy*
Mackay, *Dave*
McNeil, *Billy*
McStay, *Paul*
Muller, *Gerd*
Puskas, *Ferenc*
Robson, *Brian*
Rooney, *Wayne*
Seaman, *David*
Stiles, *Nobby*
St John, *Ian*
Viduka, *Mark*
Vieira, *Patrick*
Wright, *Billy*
Wright, *Ian*
Yashin, *Lev*
Zidane, *Zinedine*

7 letters:
Alberto, *Carlos*
Beckham, *David*
Bremner, *Billy*
Cantona, *Eric*
Charles, *Joun*
DiCanio, *Paulo*
Eusebio
Francis, *Trevor*
Gemmell, *Archie*
Gemmell, *Tommy*
Gilzean, *Alan*

Greaves, *Jimmy*
Larsson, *Henrik*
Lineker, *Gary*
Lorimer, *Peter*
Mannion, *Wilf*
McCoist, *Ally*
Platini, *Michel*
Rivaldo
Ronaldo
Ronaldo, *Cristiano*
Scholes, *Paul*
Shearer, *Alan*
Shilton, *Peter*
Souness, *Graeme*
Toshack, *John*
Waddell, *Willie*

8 letters:
Bergkamp, *Dennis*
Charlton, *Bobby*
Charlton, *Jack*
Dalglish, *Kenny*
Fontaine, *Just*
Heighway, *Steve*
Jennings, *Pat*
Johnston, *Willie*
Maradona, *Diego*
Matthaus, *Lothar*
Socrates

9 letters:
Archibald, *Steve*
Cannavaro, *Fabio*
Collymore, *Stan*
DiStefano, *Alfredo*
Gascoigne, *Paul*
Henderson, *Willie*
Jairzinho
Johnstone, *Jimmy*
Klinsmann, *Jurgen*
Lofthouse, *Nat*
Van Basten, *Marco*

10 letters:
Battistuta, *Gabriel*
Djourkaeff, *Youri*
McClintock, *Frank*
Ronaldinho
Schillacci, *Toto*

11 letters:
Beckenbauer, *Franz*

12 letters:
Blanchflower, *Danny*

13 letters:
Van Nistelrooy, *Ruud*

Foreign words and phrases

3 letters:
Ami
Jeu
Mot

4 letters:
À bas
Abbé
Doge
Gene
In re
Lied
Vivo

5 letters:
Ab ovo
Addio
À deux
Ad hoc
Adios
Ad lib
Ad rem
Adsum
À gogo
Aidos
Apage
Arras
Assai
Buffo
Ca ira
Canto
Corno
Desto
Dolce
Domus
École
Étude
Grave
Largo
Lento
Lycée
Mores
Obiit
Per se
Plaza
Pleno

Reich
Salle
Segno
Segue
Sordo
Tacet
Torte
Tutti
Usine

6 letters:
Abattu
Abrege
Agrege
Allons
Aperçu
À terre
Aubade
Au fait
Au fond
Avanti
Avenir
Bel air
Bêtise
Bon mot
Bon ton
Cortes
Crible
Da capo
Dégagé
Déja vu
De jure
Der Tag
Emptor
En fête
Fi donc
Flèche
Giusto
Grazia
Ibidem
In vivo
Legato
Lieder
Maison
Mañana

Nobile
Ottava
Palais
Posada
Presto
Rubato
Sempre
Subito
Tenuto
Torero
Troppo
Vivace

7 letters:
Acharne
Ad astra
Ad finem
Ad litem
À droite
Ad vivum
Affaire
Affiche
Agaçant
À gauche
Agitato
À jamais
À la mode
Alcaide
Alcalde
Al conto
Altesse
Animato
A priori
À quatre
Attacca
Au mieux
Auslese
Bas bleu
Battuta
Berceau
Bonjour
Bonsoir
Bourrée
Bravura
Calando

Foreign words and phrases

Cantina
Canzona
Canzone
Caramba
Chambre
Chanson
Château
Chez moi
Clavier
Codetta
Comedia
Con brio
Con moto
Couloir
Cui bono
D'accord
Danseur
Ébauche
En prise
En route
Ex aequo
Fagotto
Farceur
Fermata
Friture
Furioso
Gestalt
Giocoso
Gouache
Haut ton
Ich dien
In utero
In vacuo
In vitro
Ländler
Laus Deo
Märchen
Morceau
Morendo
Palazzo
Pas seul
Peccavi
Pension
Pesante
Piacere
Plafond
Pomposo
Pro rata
Qui vive
Ragazza
Rathaus

Rigsdag
Riksdag
Rondeau
Rondino
Rosalio
Roulade
Schloss
Sine die
Sordino
Sub rosa
Tant pis
Vibrato

8 letters:

Abat jour
Abat-voix
Ad summum
Agaçerie
Agrément
À la carte
Alta moda
Apéritif
A piacere
Après ski
À quoi bon
Au gratin
Au revoir
Autobahn
Aux armes
À volonté
Banlieue
Bel canto
Bien-être
Bona fide
Bout-rime
Chez nous
Col legno
Con amore
Con fuoco
Coryphée
Cum laude
Dal segno
Danseuse
Déjeuner
Démarche
Deus vult
Dies irae
Distrait
Doloroso
Duettino
Enceinte

Entresol
Estancia
Et cetera
Excerpta
Ex gratia
Faubourg
Fine Gael
Gendarme
Grand mal
Hacienda
Hic jacet
Idée fixe
Leggiero
Maestoso
Maggiore
Mala fide
Mal de mer
Mandamus
Mea culpa
Moderato
Mon repos
Mot juste
Ostinato
Par avion
Parlando
Parlante
Pro forma
Raisonné
Rara avis
Ripiendo
Ritenuto
Sayonara
Scordato
Semplice
Serenata
Sobranje
Spianato
Staccato
Sub poena
Trouvère
Una corda
Vorspiel

9 letters:

À bon droit
Aborigine
A cappella
Ad hominem
Ad libitum
Ad nauseam
Ad valorem

A fortiori
Alla breve
Alma mater
Âme perdue
Anschluss
Antipasto
À outrance
Arc-en-ciel
Aria buffa
Assez bien
Au courant
Au naturel
Au secours
Ausgleich
Autopista
Autoroute
Bal masque
Beaux arts
Beaux yeux
Bel esprit
Belle amie
Ben venuto
Bête noire
Bon marché
Bon vivant
Bon viveur
Bon voyage
Bundesrat
Bundestag
Buona sera
Cantabile
Carpe diem
Cauchemar
Cave canem
Centumvir
Coup d'état
Das heisst
Dei gratia
De rigueur
Dolce vita
En famille
En passant
Et tu, Brute
Flute-a-bec
Folketing
Gemütlich
Glissando
Grandioso
Grand prix
Haut monde
Inter alia

Ipse dixit
Ipso facto
Landsting
Leitmotiv
Mardi Gras
Meden agan
Mezza voce
Nisi prius
Obbligato
Objet d'art
Pari passu
Pas de deux
Passepied
Per capita
Per contra
Petit four
Piacevole
Piangendo
Politburo
Pro patria
Pro re nata
Ricercare
Rus in urbe
Scherzoso
Sforzando
Siciliana
Sine prole
Smerzando
Solfeggio
Sostenuto
Sotto voce
Spiritoso
Sub judice
Sub specie
Succès fou
Tant mieux
Taoiseach
Tête-à-tête
Tout à fait
Tout court
Vers libre
Volkslied
Vox humana

10 letters:

À bon marché
Absente reo
Ad absurdum
Ad vizandum
Affettuoso
Aficionado

Alla Franca
Allargando
All tedesca
Anno Domini
Art nouveau
Au pis aller
Autostrada
Avant garde
Bar mitzvah
Bêche-de-mer
Ben trovato
Billet doux
Bon appetit
Buon giorno
Café au lait
Camino real
Canto fermo
Canzonetta
Certiorari
Cinquepace
Confiserie
Con sordini
Con spirito
Cordon bleu
Danke schön
Deo gratias
Deo volente
Dernier cri
Eisteddfod
Feuilleton
Fianna Fáil
Forte piano
Gesundheit
In excelsis
In extremis
Jardinière
Jus commune
Jus gentium
Lebensraum
Magnum opus
Mezzo forte
Mezzo piano
Nom-de-plume
Opera buffa
Ottava rima
Perdendosi
Pied-à-terre
Plat du jour
Ponticello
Prima facie
Prix unique

Foreign words and phrases

Pro hac vice
Quid pro quo
Recitativo
Ritardando
Ritornelle
Ritornello
Scherzando
Scordatura
Seguidilla
Semper idem
Sens unique
Sine qua non
Stringendo
Sui generis
Table d'hôte
Terra firma
Thé dansant
Tiergarten
Tout de même
Tremolando
Ultra vires
Urbi et orbi
Villanella

11 letters:
Accelerando
Ad infinitum
Aetatis suae
Aide-mémoire
Allez-vous en
Alto-relievo
Amor patriae
Amour-propre
À nos moutons
A posteriori
Arcades ambo
Arrivederci
Au contraire
Avec plaisir
À votre santé
Belle époque
Bien entendu
Bonne bouche
Boutonnière
Capriccioso
Carte du jour
Cavo-relievo
Che sera sera
Comme il faut
Concertante
Contra punto

Contredanse
Coram populo
Crème brûlée
Dail Eireann
Decrescendo
Degringoler
De haut en bas
De profundis
Ex hypothesi
Ex post facto
Femme fatale
Fieri facias
Fin de siècle
Fritto misto
Hasta mañana
In medias res
In principio
Lèse majesté
Lignum vitae
Litterateur
Mise en scène
Motu proprio
Musica ficta
Ne plus ultra
Nihil obstat
Nom de guerre
Nous verrons
Obiter dicta
Objet trouvé
Opera bouffe
Papier-mâché
Pas de quatre
Pax vobiscum
Politbureau
Raison d'être
Rellentando
Savoir-faire
Schottische
Smörgasbord
Summum bonum
Tempo giusto
Tempus fugit
Tertium quid
Tout le monde
Und so weiter
Vivacissimo

12 letters:
Acciaccatura
Amicus curiae
Ancien régime

Ante meridiem
Appassionata
Appoggiatura
À quatre mains
Arrière-garde
Ave atque vale
Ballon d'essai
Basso-relievo
Buenas noches
Carte blanche
Cause célèbre
Caveat emptor
Compos mentis
Concertstück
Conseil d'état
Contra mundum
Crème caramel
Degringolade
Donnerwetter
Doppelganger
Eppur si muove
Experto crede
Fait accompli
Ferae naturae
Feu d'artifice
Force majeure
Gesellschaft
Glockenspiel
Habeas corpus
Hasta la vista
Haute couture
Homme du monde
Honoris causa
Hors concours
Hors de combat
Hors d'oeuvres
Hotel de ville
Laissez-faire
Lapsus calami
Lite pendente
Mezzo-relievo
Modus vivendi
Obiter dictum
Opéra comique
Piobaireachd
Pollice verso
Pons asinorum
Porte-cochère
Porte-monnaie
Quelque chose
Rien ne va plus

Salle à manger
Sauve qui peut
S'il vous plait
Terminus a quo
Zigeunerlied

13 letters:
Ab urbe condita
Aggiornamento
À la bonne heure
À propos de rien
Ariston metron
Arrière pensée
Avant-gardiste
Avis au lecteur
Basso profondo
Champs Élysées
Cogito ergo sum
Corps de ballet
Corpus delicti
Couleur de rose
Crème de menthe
Croix de guerre
Cum grano salis
Deux ex machina
Éminence grise
Exempli gratia
Ex proprio motu
Faites vos jeux
Fête champêtre
Force de frappe

In vino veritas
Laissez-passer
Lapsus linguae
Magna cum laude
Mirabile dictu
Modus operandi
Multum in parvo
Nolens vivendi
Noli-me-tangere
Nolle prosequi
Nouvelle Vague
Nulli secundus
Palais de danse
Poisson d'avril
Quartier latin
Schadenfreude
Succès d'estime
Summa cum laude
Très au sérieux

14 letters:
A minori ad majus
Annus mirabilis
Auf Wiedersehen
Bureau de change
Ceteris paribus
Crème de la crème
Deuxième Bureau
Dis aliter visum
Divide et impera
Dolce far niente

Double entendre
Ejusdem generis
Enfant terrible
Et in Arcadia ego
Facile princeps
Hapax legomenon
Homme d'affaires
In loco parentis
Ipsissima verba
Maxima cum laude
Ne obliviscaris
Obiit sine prole
Petit bourgeois
Terminus ad quem
Terra incognita
Tertius gaudens
Valet de chambre

15 letters:
Ad misericordiam
Amende honorable
À propos de bottes
Argumentum ad
   rem
Cherchez la femme
Cordon sanitaire
Crime passionnel
Gaudeamus igitur
Mutatis mutandis
Persona non grata
Rem acu tetigisti

Fossils

5 letters:
Amber

6 letters:
Eozoon
Olenus

7 letters:
Exuviae
Ichnite
Zoolite

8 letters:
Ammonite
Baculite
Blastoid
Calamite
Conchite

Conodont
Eohippus
Mosasaur
Pliosaur
Ram's horn
Scaphite
Solenite
Volulite
Volutite
Wood-opal

9 letters:
Belemnite
Buccinite
Ceratodus
Chondrite
Cordaites

Encrinite
Goniatite
Ichnolite
Miliolite
Muscalite
Nummulite
Ostracite
Patellite
Phytolite
Serpulite
Stigmaria
Strombite
Tellinite
Trilobite
Turbinate
Turrilite

Fowl

10 letters:
Blastoidea
Eurypterus
Graptolite
Lingulella
Mosasauros
Orthoceras
Osteolepis
Plesiosaur
Pliohippus
Pterygotus

Sigillaria
Snakestone

11 letters:
Gongiatites
Ichthyolite
Ostracoderm

12 letters:
Pythonomorph
Sinanthropus
Stromatolite

Uintatherium

13 letters:
Titanotherium
Zinganthropus

14 letters:
Conchyliaceous

15 letters:
Ichthyodurolite

Fowl

3 letters:
Cob
Hen
Ree

4 letters:
Cock
Coot
Duck
Gnow
Kora
Nene
Smew
Swan
Teal

5 letters:
Capon
Chock
Chook
Eider
Ember
Goose
Layer
Quail
Reeve
Rumpy
Scaup
Solan

6 letters:
Ancona
Bantam
Boiler
Brahma

Cochin
Eirack
Guinea
Houdan
Jungle
Pullet
Rumkin
Sitter
Sultan
Sussex
Tappit
Turkey
Wigeon

7 letters:
Campine
Chicken
Dorking
Gadwall
Greylag
Hamburg
Leghorn
Mallard
Minorca
Moorhen
Partlet
Pintado
Pintail
Pochard
Poulard
Redhead
Rooster
Sawbill
Sea duck

Sumatra
Whooper
Widgeon

8 letters:
Baldpate
Blue duck
Cockerel
Hamburgh
Langshan
Marsh hen
Megapode
Musk duck
Mute swan
Pheasant
Screamer
Shelduck
Shoveler
Wood duck

9 letters:
Black swan
Blue goose
Eider duck
Faverolle
Goldeneye
Goosander
Merganser
Orpington
Partridge
Pertelote
Ruddy duck
Scaup duck
Snow goose
Welsummer

Wyandotte

10 letters:
Andalusian
Australorp
Bufflehead
Burrow-duck
Canvasback
Chittagong
Mallee fowl
Spatchcock
Spitchcock

11 letters:
Bewick's swan

Brissle-cock
Brush turkey
Canada goose
Magpie goose
Muscovy duck
Scrub turkey
Whooper swan

12 letters:
Greylag goose
Mandarin duck
New Hampshire
Paradise duck
Plymouth Rock

Velvet scoter

13 letters:
Barnacle goose
Buff Orpington
Harlequin duck
Trumpeter swan
Whistling swan

14 letters:
American wigeon
Rhode Island Red

Fruits

3 letters:
Fig
Haw
Hep
Hip
Hop
Jak

4 letters:
Akee
Bael
Bito
Date
Gage
Gean
Jack
Kaki
Kiwi
Lime
Pear
Pepo
Plum
Pome
Sloe
Sorb
Star
Tuna
UGLI®

5 letters:
Anana
Anona
Apple
Assai

Berry
Bread
Choko
Gourd
Grape
Guava
Jaffa
Lemon
Lichi
Lotus
Mango
Melon
Nancy
Naras
Nashi
Nelis
Olive
Papaw
Peach
Prune
Rowan
Whort

6 letters:
Almond
Ananas
Babaco
Banana
Banian
Banyan
Carica
Casaba
Cherry

Chocho
Citron
Citrus
Damson
Durian
Durion
Emblic
Feijoa
Kiwano®
Lichee
Litchi
Longan
Loquat
Lychee
Mammee
Medlar
Narras
Nelies
Orange
Papaya
Pawpaw
Pepino
Pepper
Pomelo
Pruine
Quince
Raisin
Russet
Samara
Sapota
Sharon
Squash
Sweety

Fruits

Tomato
Wampee

7 letters:
Apricot
Avocado
Bramble
Bullace
Cedrate
Chayote
Crab-nut
Cumquat
Geebung
Genipap
Kumquat
Leechee
Litchee
Manjack
Morello
Naartje
Passion
Pimento
Pinguin
Poperin
Pumpkin
Pupunha
Ruddock
Satsuma
Soursop
Sultana
Sweetie
Tangelo
Winesap

8 letters:
Abricock
Apricock
Bergamot
Bilberry
Blimbing
Boxberry
Calabash
Dewberry
Fraughan
Goosegog
Hagberry
Hastings
Hedgehog
Kalumpit
Mandarin
May apple
Minneola

Mulberry
Physalis
Plantain
Rambutan
Sebesten
Shaddock
Sunberry
Sweetsop
Tamarind
Tayberry
Victoria

9 letters:
Algarroba
Apple-john
Asian pear
Aubergine
Bakeapple
Beach plum
Blaeberry
Blueberry
Cantaloup
Canteloup
Carambola
Chempaduk
Cherimoya
Cranberry
Greengage
Haanepoot
Hackberry
Jackfruit
Japan plum
Love apple
Mirabelle
Muskmelon
Myrobalan
Naseberry
Nectarine
Neesberry
Ogen melon
Ortanique
Persimmon
Pineapple
Plumdamas
Poppering
Raspberry
Rockmelon
Sapodilla
Saskatoon
Shadberry
Snowberry

Sour gourd
Star-apple
Tamarillo
Tangerine
Tomatillo
Victorine
Whimberry

10 letters:
Blackberry
Breadfruit
Calamondin
Canteloupe
Cherimoyer
Clementine
Cloudberry
Elderberry
Galia melon
Gooseberry
Granadilla
Grapefruit
Grenadilla
Jargonelle
Loganberry
Mangosteen
Pick-cheese
Redcurrant
Scaldberry
Sour cherry
Strawberry
Tree tomato
Watermelon
Youngberry

11 letters:
Anchovy pear
Avocado pear
Black cherry
Blood orange
Boysenberry
Chokecherry
Heart cherry
Hesperidium
Huckleberry
Jaffa orange
Marionberry
Navel orange
Pampelmoose
Pampelmouse
Pomegranate
Pompelmoose
Pompelmouse

Prickly pear
Salmonberry
Sweet cherry
Winter melon

12 letters:
Bartlett pear
Bergamot pear
Blackcurrant
Cassaba melon
Concord grape
Custard apple
Serviceberry
Victoria plum
White currant

Whortleberry
Williams pear

13 letters:
Alligator pear
Honeydew melon
Morello cherry
Sapodilla plum
Seville orange

14 letters:
Cape gooseberry
Conference pear
Queensland blue
Worcesterberry

15 letters:
Beurre Hardy pear
Bigarreau cherry
Bon Chretien pear
Cantaloupe melon
Charentais melon

16 letters:
Blackheart cherry
Strawberry tomato

17 letters:
Chinese
  gooseberry

Fungi

3 letters:
Cup

4 letters:
Bunt
Rust
Smut

5 letters:
Black
Ergot
Favus
Honey
Jelly
Morel
Mould
Mucor
Spunk
Yeast

6 letters:
Agaric
Amadou
Dry rot
Elf-cup
Empusa
Ink-cap
Mildew
Miller
Peziza
Torula
Wax cap
Wet rot

7 letters:
Amanita
Blewits
Boletus
Bracket
Candida
Jew's ear
Milk cap
Monilia
Phallus
Pythium
Russula
Tarspot
Truffle

8 letters:
Ambrosia
Bootlace
Clubroot
Death cap
Death-cup
Fuss-ball
Fuzz-ball
Merulius
Mushroom
Noble rot
Puccinia
Puckfist
Puffball
Rhizopus
Rhytisma
Sariodes
Sickener

Tremella
Tuckahoe
Ustilago

9 letters:
Beefsteak
Blackknot
Cramp ball
Earthstar
Eumycetes
Funnel cap
Horsehair
Mucorales
Shaggy cap
Stinkhorn
Toadstool

10 letters:
Gibberella
Liberty cap
Oak-leather
Orange-peel
Rust fungus
Shoestring
Sooty mould
Yellow rust

11 letters:
Anthracnose
Aspergillus
Chantarelle
Chanterelle
Cladosporum
Craterellus

Furies

Ithyphallus
Jelly fungus
Penicillium
Phycomycete
Saprolegnia
Sulphur tuft
Velvet shank

12 letters:
Cryptococcus

Discomycetes
Horn of plenty
Hypersarcoma
Trichophyton
Wood hedgehog

13 letters:
Bracket fungus
Magic mushroom
Saccharomyces

Witches' butter

14 letters:
Wood woollyfoot

15 letters:
Bird's-nest fungus
Dermatophytosis
Destroying angel

Furies

6 letters:
Alecto

7 letters:
Megaera

9 letters:
Tisiphone

Furniture

TYPES OF FURNITURE

6 letters:
Canopy
Litter
Screen
Tester

7 letters:
Bedpost
Epergne
Lectern
Trolley

8 letters:
Bedstead

Hatstand
Vanitory

9 letters:
Coatstand
Footstool
Girandola
Girandole
Hallstand
Headboard
Washstand

10 letters:
Dumbwaiter

Vanity unit

11 letters:
Cheval glass

13 letters:
Longcase clock
Umbrella stand

16 letters:
Grandfather clock
Grandmother clock

FURNITURE STYLES

5 letters:
Saxon
Tudor

6 letters:
Empire
Gothic
Norman
Shaker

7 letters:
Art Deco
Bauhaus

Puritan
Regency

8 letters:
Georgian
Jacobean
Medieval

9 letters:
Cape Dutch
Edwardian
Queen Anne
Victorian

10 letters:
Louis Seize

11 letters:
Elizabethan
Louis Quinze
Louis Treize
New Georgian
Restoration

12 letters:
Greek Revival
Second Empire

13 letters:
Louis Quatorze

14 letters:
William and Mary

FURNITURE DESIGNERS

4 letters:
Adam, *Robert*
Heal, *Ambrose*
Kent, *William*

5 letters:
Aalto, *Alvar*
Bevan, *Charles*
Jones, *Inigo*
Jones, *William*
Klint, *Kaara*
Marot, *Daniel*
Phyfe, *Duncan*
Pugin, *Augustus*
Smith, *George*

6 letters:
Breuer, *Marcel Lajos*

Burges, *William*
Morris, *William*
Voysey, *Charles*

8 letters:
Sheraton, *Thomas*

9 letters:
Pergolesi, *Michael Angelo*

10 letters:
Mackintosh, *Charles Rennie*

11 letters:
Chippendale, *Thomas*
Hepplewhite, *George*

G

4 letters:
Arp's

5 letters:
Bode's
Draco
Dwarf
Giant
Helix
Radio
Virgo

6 letters:
Baade's
Carafe
Carina
Cygnus
Fornax
Maffei
Quasar
Spiral
Zwicky

7 letters:
Barbon's
Cluster
Garland
Pancake

Regular
Seyfert
Spindle

8 letters:
Aquarius
Barnard's
Bear's Paw
Black Eye
Circinus
Holmberg
Lacertid
Milky Way
Papillon
Pinwheel
Reinmuth
Sculptor
Seashell
Sombrero

9 letters:
Andromeda
Blue fuzzy
Capricorn
Cartwheel
Centaurus
Great Wall

Irregular

10 letters:
Elliptical
Horologium
Local Group

12 letters:
Supercluster

13 letters:
Burbidge Chain

15 letters:
Exclamation Mark

17 letters:
Ambartsumian's
  Knot

19 letters:
Mini Magellanic
  Cloud

20 letters:
Large Magellanic
  Cloud
Small Magellanic
  Cloud

Games

2 letters:
Eo
Go
RU

3 letters:
Cat
Hob
Loo

Maw
Nap
Nim
Pit
Put
Swy
Tag
Tig
War

4 letters:
Base
Brag
Bull
Crap
Dibs
Fa-fi
Faro
Goff

Golf
Grab
I-spy
Keno
Kino
Loto
Ludo
Main
Mora
Polo
Pool
Putt
Ruff
Scat
Skat
Snap
Solo
Taws
Vint

5 letters:
Bingo
Bocce
Bowls
Catch
Chess
Cinch
Craps
Darts
Fives
Goose
Halma
House
Jacks
Keeno
Lotto
Lurch
Merel
Meril
Monte
Morra
Noddy
Novum
Omber
Ombre
Poker
Quino
Rebus
Roque
Rummy
Shogi

Spoof
Tarok
Tarot
Trugo
Two-up
Whisk
Whist

6 letters:
Animal
Basset
Beetle
Boston
Boules
Casino
Chemmy
Clumps
Crambo
Ecarté
Euchre
Fantan
Footer
Gammon
Gobang
Gomoku
Hockey
Hoopla
Hurley
Kitcat
Merell
Pelota
Piquet
Quinze
Quoits
Raffle
Shinny
Shinty
Soccer
Socker
Squash
Tipcat
Uckers
Vigoro

7 letters:
Anagram
Ba'spiel
Bezique
Braemar
Camogie
Canasta
Cassino

Charade
Codille
Conkers
Coon-can
Croquet
Curling
Diabolo
Hangman
Hurling
In-and-In
Jai Alai
Jukskei
Kabaddi
Lottery
Mahjong
Mancala
Marbles
Matador
Muggins
Netball
Old Maid
Pachisi
Pallone
Peekabo
Pharaoh
Pinball
Plafond
Primero
Rackets
Reversi
Ring taw
Seven-up
Snooker
Squails
Statues
Tangram
Vingt-un
War game

8 letters:
Acrostic
All-fours
Baccarat
Bumpball
Canfield
Charades
Chouette
Cottabus
Cribbage
Dominoes
Fivepins

Games

Football
Forfeits
Handball
Klondike
Klondyke
Korfball
Leapfrog
Mah-jongg
Monopoly®
Ninepins
Nintendo®
Octopush
Pachinko
Pall-mall
Pastance
Patience
Peekaboo
Pegboard
Penneech
Penneeck
Penuchle
Petanque
Ping-pong
Pinochle
Pintable
Pope Joan
Reversis
Rolypoly
Roulette
Rounders
Sack race
Scrabble®
Skipping
Skittles
Slapjack
Softball
Sphairee
Subbuteo®
Teetotum
Tray-trip
Tredille
Trictrac
Verquere
Verquire
Wall game

9 letters:
Badminton
Bagatelle
Billiards
Black-cock

Black-jack
Broomball
Crossword
Duplicate
Fillipeen
Hopscotch
Jingo-ring
Lanterloo
Level-coil
Logograph
Matrimony
Mistigris
Mumchance
Newmarket
Or mineral
Paintball
Parcheesi®
Pelmanism
Punchball
Quadrille
Quidditch®
Simon says
Solitaire
Spoilfive
Stoolball
Tip-and-run
Tredrille
Twenty-one
Vegetable
Vingt-et-un

10 letters:
Angel-beast
Basketball
Bouillotte
Candlepins
Cat's cradle
Deck tennis
Dumb Crambo
Five-stones
Handy-dandy
Horseshoes
Jackstones
Jackstraws
Knurr-spell
Lansquenet
Paddleball
Phillipina
Phillipine
Philopoena
Spillikins

Tablanette
Tchoukball
Thimblerig
Tricktrack
Troll-madam
Trou-madame
Volley-ball

11 letters:
Barley-brake
Battleships
Bumble-puppy
Catch-the-ten
Hide-and-seek
Racquetball
Rouge et noir
Sancho-pedro
Shovelboard
Speculation
Tick-tack-toe
Tiddlywinks
Troll-my-dame

12 letters:
Bar billiards
Caber tossing
Commonwealth
Consequences
Housey-housey
Jigsaw puzzle
Knur and spell
One-and-thirty
Pitch-and-toss
Shuffleboard
Span-farthing
Troll-my-dames

13 letters:
Blind man's buff
French cricket
Musical chairs
Postman's knock
Prisoner's base
Scavenger hunt

14 letters:
British bulldog
Crown and anchor
Ducks and drakes
Follow-my-leader
Shove-halfpenny
Snip-snap-snorum

Three-card monte

15 letters:
Chinese whispers
Crossword puzzle
King of the castle

Russian roulette
The Minister's Cat
Twenty questions

16 letters:
Trente-et-quarante

17 letters:
Noughts and crosses

See also:
➤ **Board games** ➤ **Chess pieces** ➤ **Computer games**

Gases

1 letter:
H
O

2 letters:
BZ
CN
CS
He
Kr
Ne
RN
VX

3 letters:
Air
CNG
LNG
LPG
Nox
SNG

4 letters:
Coal
Damp
Flue
Mace®
Neon
Tail
Tear
Town

5 letters:
Argon
Calor®
Ether
Marsh
Nerve
Ozone
Radon

Sarin
Soman
Tabun
Water
Xenon

6 letters:
Arsine
Biogas
Bottle
Butane
Butene
Ethane
Ethene
Ethine
Helium
Ketene
Oilgas
Olefin
Oxygen
Plasma
Sewage
Silane
Thoron
V-agent

7 letters:
Ammonia
Argonon
Blister
Bottled
Coal-oil
Crypton
Fluorin
Krypton
Methane
Mofette
Mustard
Natural

Olefine
Propane
Propene
Stibine

8 letters:
Chlorine
Cyanogen
Diborane
Etherion
Ethylene
Firedamp
Fluorine
Hydrogen
Laughing
Lewisite
Nitrogen
Phosgene
Producer

9 letters:
Acetylene
Afterdamp
Butadiene
Chokedamp
Phosphine
Propylene
Protostar
Solfatara
Synthesis
Whitedamp

10 letters:
Diphosgene
Greenhouse

11 letters:
Methylamine
Nitric oxide

12 letters:
Carbonic-acid
Diazomethane
Electrolytic
Formaldehyde
Nitrous oxide
Oxyacetylene

13 letters:
Carbon dioxide
Methyl bromide
Vinyl chloride

14 letters:
Carbon monoxide
Hydrogen iodide
Methyl chloride
Sulphur dioxide

15 letters:
Hydrogen bromide

Nitrogen dioxide
Nitrogen mustard

16 letters:
Hydrogen chloride
Hydrogen fluoride
Hydrogen sulphide
Synthetic natural

17 letters:
Compressed natural
Tetrafluoroethene

18 letters:
Liquefied petroleum

19 letters:
Tetrafluoroethylene

23 letters:
Dichlorodifluoromethane

Gemstones

2 letters:
ID

3 letters:
Jet

4 letters:
Jade
Onyx
Opal
Ruby
Sard

5 letters:
Agate
Balas
Beryl
Idaho
Pearl
Prase
Topaz

6 letters:
Garnet
Iolite
Jargon
Jasper
Jaspis
Morion

Plasma
Pyrope
Quartz
Sphene
Spinel
Zircon

7 letters:
Cat's-eye
Citrine
Diamond
Emerald
Girasol
Girosol
Helidor
Jacinth
Jadeite
Jargoon
Kunzite
Peridot
Sardine
Smaragd

8 letters:
Adularia
Amethyst
Corundum
Diopside

Fire opal
Girasole
Hawk's-eye
Heliodor
Hyacinth
Melanite
Menilite
Peridote
Sapphire
Sardonyx
Sunstone
Titanite

9 letters:
Almandine
Amazonite
Andradite
Aventurin
Black opal
Cairngorm
Carnelian
Cornelian
Cymophane
Demantoid
Hessonite
Hiddenite
Liver opal

Generals

Moonstone
Morganite
Moss agate
Rhodolite
Rubellite
Spodumene
Starstone
Tiger's eye
Turquoise
Uvarovite

10 letters:
Andalusite
Aquamarine
Avanturine
Aventurine
Bloodstone
Chalcedony
Chrysolite
Heliotrope

Indicolite
Indigolite
Odontolite
Rhinestone
Rose quartz
Staurolite
Topazolite
Tourmaline

11 letters:
Alexandrite
Chrysoberyl
Chrysoprase
Lapis lazuli
Smoky quartz
Spessartite
Verd antique
Vesuvianite

12 letters:
Colorado ruby

Dumortierite
Grossularite
Spanish topaz

13 letters:
Bone turquoise
Colorado topaz
Water sapphire
White sapphire

15 letters:
Oriental emerald

17 letters:
Oriental almandine

20 letters:
Madagascar
 aquamarine
New Zealand
 greenstone

Generals

3 letters:
Ike *(Dwight David Eisenhower)*
Lee, *Robert E(dward)*

5 letters:
Booth, *William*
Condé, *Louis de Bourbon,
 Prince de*
De Wet, *Christian*
Grant, *Ulysses Simpson*
Smuts, *Jan*
Wolfe, *James*

6 letters:
Custer, *George Armstrong*
Franco, *Francisco*
Gordon, *Charles George*
Joshua
Leslie, *David*
Napier, *Lord Robert*
Patton, *George*
Pompey
Raglan, *Fitzroy James Henry
 Somerset*
Rommel, *Erwin*
Scipio, *Publius Cornelius*

7 letters:
Agrippa, *Marcus Vipsanius*
Allenby, *Viscount Edmund*
Crassus, *Marcus Licinius*
Gamelin, *Maurice Gustave*
Hadrian
Sherman, *William Tecumseh*
Turenne

8 letters:
Agricola, *Gnaeus Julius*
De Gaulle, *Charles (André Joseph
 Marie)*
Hannibal
Marshall, *George Catlett*
Montcalm, *Louis Joseph de*
Napoleon *(Bonaparte)*
Pershing, *Johh Joseph*
Shrapnel, *Henry*
Stilwell, *Joseph Warren*
Stratton, *Charles Sherwood*
Tom Thumb *(Charles Sherwood
 Stratton)*

9 letters:
Agamemnon
Antigonus

Geography

Antipater
Boulanger, *George Ernest Jean Marie*
Kitchener, *Earl Herbert*
Lafayette, *Marie Joseph, Marquis de*
Macarthur, *Douglas*

10 letters:
Alcibiades
Cornwallis, *Charles, Marquis*
Eisenhower, *Dwight D(avid) (Ike)*
Holofernes

Geography

BRANCHES OF GEOGRAPHY

5 letters:
Human

7 letters:
Geology
Orology

8 letters:
Pedology
Physical

9 letters:
Chorology

Hydrology
Orography
Political

10 letters:
Demography
Glaciology
Oceanology
Seismology
Topography

11 letters:
Cartography

Chorography
Climatology
Geopolitics
Meteorology
Vulcanology

12 letters:
Biogeography
Oceanography

13 letters:
Geomorphology

GEOGRAPHY TERMS AND FEATURES

3 letters:
Bay
Col
Cwm
Map
Tor

4 letters:
Core
Crag
Dyke
Fell
Glen
Loch
Reef
Rill
Spit
Spur
Tarn
Veld
Wadi

5 letters:
Arête

Atlas
Atoll
Basin
Beach
Cliff
Crust
Delta
Fault
Fjord
Glade
Levée
Ocean
Ridge
Scree
Stack
Veldt

6 letters:
Canyon
Cirque
Coombe
Corrie
Crater
Desert

Ice cap
Isobar
Jungle
Lagoon
Mantle
Sierra
Spring
Steppe
Suburb
Tundra

7 letters:
Climate
Contour
Culvert
Equator
Erosion
Estuary
Glacier
Isobath
Isohyet
Isthmus
Meander
Moraine

New town
Rivulet
Sand bar
Savanna
Subsoil
Topsoil
Tropics
Tsunami
Volcano
Wetland

8 letters:
Crevasse
Eastings
Headland
Isotherm
Latitude
Oriental
Salt flat
Salt lake
Sandbank
Sand dune
Savannah
Snow line

9 letters:
Antipodes
Continent
Coral reef
Dormitory
Epicentre
Green belt
Longitude
Northings
North Pole

Pollution
Relief map
South Pole
Temperate
Waterfall
Watershed
Whirlpool

10 letters:
Atmosphere
Earthquake
Escarpment
Flood plain
Glaciation
Irrigation
Occidental
Ozone layer
Permafrost
Rainforest
Rain shadow
Rift valley
River basin
Third World
Water cycle
Water table
Weathering

11 letters:
Conurbation
Environment
Watercourse

12 letters:
Conservation
Urbanization

13 letters:
Afforestation
Deforestation
Global warming
Grid reference
Hanging valley
Precipitation

14 letters:
Infrastructure
Longshore drift
Ordnance Survey
Plate tectonics

15 letters:
Desertification

16 letters:
Continental drift
Continental shelf
Greenhouse effect

18 letters:
Mercator
 projection
Northern
 hemisphere
Southern
 hemisphere

21 letters:
International Date
 Line

GEOGRAPHERS

6 letters:
Kremer, *Gerhard*
Strabo

7 letters:
Hakluyt, *Richard*
Ptolemy

8 letters:
Mercator, *Gerardus*

9 letters:
Mackinder, *Sir
 Halford John*
Pausanias

10 letters:
Somerville, *Mary*

See also:
➤ **Canals** ➤ **Capes** ➤ **Capitals** ➤ **Channels** ➤ **Cities**
➤ **Continents** ➤ **Countries** ➤ **Deserts** ➤ **Earth's crust**
➤ **Hills** ➤ **Islands and island groups** ➤ **Lakes, lochs and
loughs** ➤ **Peninsulas** ➤ **Ports** ➤ **Rivers** ➤ **Seas and oceans**
➤ **Sounds** ➤ **Straits** ➤ **Towns** ➤ **Volcanoes** ➤ **Waterfalls**

Geology

Geology

GEOLOGICAL ERAS

8 letters:
Cenozoic
Mesozoic

10 letters:
Palaeozoic

11 letters:
Precambrian

GEOLOGICAL PERIODS

7 letters:
Permian

8 letters:
Cambrian
Devonian
Jurassic

Silurian
Tertiary
Triassic

10 letters:
Cretaceous
Ordovician

Quaternary

13 letters:
Carboniferous

EPOCHS OF THE CENOZOIC ERA

6 letters:
Eocene

7 letters:
Miocene

8 letters:
Holocene
Pliocene

9 letters:
Oligocene

10 letters:
Palaeocene

11 letters:
Pleistocene

See also:
➤ **Earth's crust** ➤ **Minerals** ➤ **Rocks**
➤ **Stones**

Giants and giantesses

2 letters:
Og

3 letters:
Gog

4 letters:
Anak
Bran
Otus
Ymir

5 letters:
Argus
Balan
Balor
Cacus
Hymir
Idris

Magog
Mimir
Talos
Talus
Thrym

6 letters:
Coltys
Cottus
Gefion
Krasir
Pallas
Tityus
Triton
Typhon
Urizen

7 letters:
Antaeus

Cyclops
Despair
Gabbara
Geirred
Goliath
Harapha
Skrymir

8 letters:
Ascapart
Bellerus
Briareus
Colbrand
Cormoran
Cyclopes
Ferragus
Hrungnir
Slaygood

9 letters:
Alcyoneus
Archiloro
Colbronde
Enceladus
Ephialtes
Gargantua
Lestrigon

Leviathan
Rounceval
Tregeagle
Tryphoeus

10 letters:
Pantagruel
Patagonian

Polyphemus

11 letters:
Alifanfaron
Blunderbore
Galligantus

Glands

3 letters:
Oil

4 letters:
Silk

5 letters:
Green
Liver
Lymph
Mucus
Ovary
Scent
Sweat

6 letters:
Ink-sac
Pineal
Tarsel
Testis
Thymus
Tonsil

7 letters:
Adenoid
Adrenal
Cowper's
Eccrine

Mammary
Musk-sac
Nectary
Parotid
Parotis
Thyroid

8 letters:
Apocrine
Conarium
Exocrine
Lacrimal
Pancreas
Pope's eye
Prostate
Salivary
Testicle

9 letters:
Digestive
Endocrine
Epiphysis
Holocrine
Lachrymal
Meibomian
Pituitary
Sebaceous

Uropygial

10 letters:
Bartholin's
Hypophysis
Osmeterium
Suprarenal

11 letters:
Colleterial
Paranephros
Parathyroid
Prothoracic

12 letters:
Hypothalamus

13 letters:
Bulbourethral

18 letters:
Islets of
  Langerhans

19 letters:
Islands of
  Langerhans

Glass, types of

3 letters:
Cut

4 letters:
Eden
Jena
Lead
Milk
Opal

Spun
Vita
Wire

5 letters:
Crown
Flint
Float
Paste

Plate
Pyrex®
Silex
Smalt

6 letters:
Bottle
Cullet
Quartz

Gods and Goddesses

Smalto
Strass

7 letters:
Baccara
Crookes
Crystal
Favrile
Lalique
Murrine
Opaline
Perlite
Schmelz
Stained
Tektite

Tiffany
Triplex®
Vitrail

8 letters:
Baccarat
Murrhine
Obsidian
Pearlite
Venetian
Volcanic

9 letters:
Fulgurite
Lanthanum
Tachilite

Tachylite
Tachylyte
Waterford

10 letters:
Avanturine
Aventurine
Calcedonio
Latticinio
Millefiori
Mousseline
Pitchstone

12 letters:
Vitro-di-trina

Gods and Goddesses

AZTEC

3 letters:
Atl

4 letters:
Tena

5 letters:
Innan
Itzli
Teteo

6 letters:
Atlaua
Paynal
Tlaloc
Xolotl

7 letters:
Amimitl
Ehecatl
Omacatl
Xilonen

8 letters:
Camaxtli
Centeotl
Chantico
Mayahuel
Mixcoatl
Patecatl
Techlotl

Tonatiuh
Tzapotla
Xippilli

9 letters:
Coatlicue
Cochimetl
Ixtlilton
Techalotl
Tzintetol
Tzontemoc
Xipe Totec
Xiuhcoatl

10 letters:
Acolmiztli
Chiconahui
Cihuacoatl
Nanauatzin
Omecihuatl
Xochipilli

11 letters:
Huehueteotl
Itzpapalotl
Ometecuhtli
Tepeyollotl
Tlazolteotl
Uixtociuatl
Xiuhteuctli

12 letters:
Chicomecoatl
Coyolxauhqui
Malinalxochi
Quetzalcoatl
Tecciztecatl
Tezcatlipoca
Tlaltecuhtli
Xochiquetzal
Yacatecuhtli

13 letters:
Acolnahuacatl
Huixtocihuatl
Ilamatecuhtli
Macuilxochitl

14 letters:
Chicomexochtli
Itzlacoliuhque
Mictlantecutli
Tonacatecuhtli

15 letters:
Centzonuitznaua
Chalchiuhtlicue
Chalchiutotolin
Chalmecacihuilt
Huitzilopochtli

16 letters:
Mictlantecihuatl

21 letters:
Tlahuixcalpantecuhtli

17 letters:
Chalchiuhtlatonal

CELTIC

3 letters:
Anu
Dôn
Lir

4 letters:
Áine
Badb
Bíle
Bodb
Dana
Danu
Donn
Ériu
Esus
Fand
Llyr
Lugh
Medb
Ogma

5 letters:
Artio

Balor
Banba
Bóand
Dagda
Epona
Mabon
Macha
Midir
Núadu

6 letters:
Bécuma
Brigid
Nemain
Sirona

7 letters:
Belenus
Nechtan
Sequana
Taranis

8 letters:
Ceridwen

Manannán
Morrígan
Nemetona
Rhiannon
Rosmerta
Sucellus
Teutates

9 letters:
Arianhrod
Blodeuedd
Cernunnos
Manawydan

11 letters:
Nantosuelta
Óengus Mac Óc

14 letters:
Lleu Llaw Gyffes
Vagdavercustis

EGYPTIAN

2 letters:
Ra
Re

3 letters:
Set

4 letters:
Isis

Maat
Ptah

5 letters:
Horus
Thoth

6 letters:
Amen-Ra

Anubis
Hathor
Osiris

7 letters:
Serapis

GREEK

God or goddess
Aeolus
Aphrodite
Apollo
Ares
Artemis
Asclepius
Athene *or* Pallas Athene
Bacchus

Area or place ruled
Winds
Love and beauty
Light, youth, and music
War
Hunting and the moon
Healing
Wisdom
Wine

Gods and Goddesses

God or goddess	Area or place ruled
Boreas	North wind
Cronos	Fertility of the earth
Demeter	Agriculture
Dionysus	Wine
Eos	Dawn
Eros	Love
Fates	Destiny
Gaea *or* Gaia	The earth
Graces	Charm and beauty
Hades	Underworld
Hebe	Youth and spring
Hecate	Underworld
Helios	Sun
Hephaestus	Fire and metalworking
Hera	Queen of the gods
Hermes	Messenger of the gods
Horae *or* the Hours	Seasons
Hymen	Marriage
Hyperion	Sun
Hypnos	Sleep
Iris	Rainbow
Momus	Blame and mockery
Morpheus	Sleep and dreams
Nemesis	Vengeance
Nike	Victory
Pan	Woods and shepherds
Poseidon	Sea and earthquakes
Rhea	Fertility
Selene	Moon
Uranus	Sky
Zephyrus	West wind
Zeus	King of the gods

HINDU

4 letters:
Agni
Devi
Kali
Kama
Maya
Rama
Siva

5 letters:
Durga
Indra
Shiva
Ushas

6 letters:
Brahma
Ganesa

Varuna
Vishnu

7 letters:
Hanuman
Krishna
Lakshmi

INCAN

3 letters:
Apo

4 letters:
Inti

5 letters:
Huaca
Supay

6 letters:
Chasca

Ekkeko
Illapa

7 letters:
Paricia
Punchau

Vichama

8 letters:
Catequil
Cocomama
Coniraya
Copacati
Zaramama

9 letters:
Apu Illapu

MAYAN

2 letters:
Ix

3 letters:
Kan
K'in

4 letters:
Acan
Acat
Alom
Chac
Naum
Zotz

5 letters:
Ah Kin
Ah Mun
Ajbit
Balam
Bitol
Cauac
Cizin
Ixtab
Mulac
Tohil
Votan
Yaluk

6 letters:
Ah Peku
Ah Puch
Chamer
Coyopa
Cum Hau

NORSE

3 letters:
Hel
Tyr

Cavillaca
Mama Allpa
Mama Cocha
Mama Oello
Mama Pacha
Pariacaca
Urcaguary
Viracocha

10 letters:
Apu Punchau

Ghanan
Ixchel
Kianto
Tzakol

7 letters:
Ac Yanto
Ahau-Kin
Ah Ciliz
Ahmakiq
Ah Tabai
Ahulane
Cakulha
Ekchuah
Hunab Ku
Hun Came
Hurakan
Itzamna
Xaman Ek
Yum Caax

8 letters:
Ah Cancum
Ah Cun Can
Ah Cuxtal
Ah Hulneb
Cabaguil
Camaxtli
Camazotz
Caprakan
Colel Cab
Gucumatz
Ixzaluoh
Kukulcan

4 letters:
Frey
Hela

Mama Quilla
Manco Capac
Pachacamac

11 letters:
Apocatequil

13 letters:
Chasca Coyllur
Ka-Ata-Killa Kon

9 letters:
Ah Chuy Kak
Akhushtal
Chibirias
Hacha'kyum
Kan-xib-yui
Tlacolotl

10 letters:
Ah Chun Caan
Ah Muzencab
Ah Uuc Ticab
Hun Hunahpu
Kinich Ahau

11 letters:
Alaghom Naom
Cit Bolon Tum
Itzananohk'u
Ix Chebel Yax
Kan-u-Uayeyab
Nohochacyum

12 letters:
Backlum Chaam
Buluc Chabtan
Chac Uayab Xoc

13 letters:
Ah Bolom Tzacab
Colop U Uichkin

14 letters:
Ah Uincir Dz'acab

Idun
Loki
Odin

Gods and Goddesses

Thor
Tyrr

5 letters:
Aegir
Aesir
Bragi
Freya
Freyr
Frigg

Njord
Norns
Othin
Vanir

6 letters:
Balder
Freyja
Frigga
Ithunn

Njorth

7 letters:
Heimdal

8 letters:
Heimdall

9 letters:
Heimdallr

ROMAN

God or goddess	Area or place ruled
Aesculapius	Medicine
Apollo	Light, youth, and music
Aurora	Dawn
Bacchus	Wine
Bellona	War
Bona Dea	Fertility
Ceres	Agriculture
Cupid	Love
Cybele	Nature
Diana	Hunting and the moon
Faunus	Forests
Flora	Flowers
Janus	Doors and beginnings
Juno	Queen of the gods
Jupiter *or* Jove	King of the gods
Lares	Household
Luna	Moon
Mars	War
Mercury	Messenger of the gods
Minerva	Wisdom
Neptune	Sea
Penates	Storeroom
Phoebus	Sun
Pluto	Underworld
Quirinus	War
Saturn	Agriculture and vegetation
Sol	Sun
Somnus	Sleep
Trivia	Crossroads
Venus	Love
Victoria	Victory
Vulcan	Fire and metalworking

Golfers

3 letters:
Els, *Ernie*

4 letters:
Lyle, *Sandy*

5 letters:
Braid, *James*
Faldo, *Nick*
Furyk, *Jim*
Hagen, *Walter*
Hogan, *Ben*
Jones, *Bobby*
Lopez, *Nancy*
Snead, *Sam*
Woods, *Tiger*

6 letters:
Carner, *JoAnne*

Foster, *Mark*
Garcia, *Sergio*
Gibson, *Althea*
Lawrie, *Paul*
Nelson, *Byron*
Norman, *Greg*
Palmer, *Arnold*
Player, *Gary*
Vardon, *Harry*
Watson, *Tom*

7 letters:
Bradley, *Pat*
Jacklin, *Tony*
Sarazen, *Gene*
Stewart, *Payne*
Trevino, *Lee*
Woosnam, *Ian*

8 letters:
Crenshaw, *Ben*
Nicklaus, *Jack*
Olazabal,
  José-Maria
Torrance, *Sam*
Zaharias, *Babe*

9 letters:
Whitworth, *Kathy*

11 letters:
Ballesteros,
  Severiano
Montgomerie,
  Colin

Golf terms

3 letters:
Ace
Bag
Cup
Cut
Lag
Lie
Par
Pin
Run
Tee
Top

4 letters:
Ball
Chip
Club
Draw
Duff
Fade
Fore
Grip
Half
Heel
Hole
Hook

Iron
Loft
Pull
Putt
Thin
Trap
Wood
Yips

5 letters:
Apron
Blade
Bogey
Carry
Divot
Drive
Eagle
Fluff
Gimme
Green
Hosel
Links
Rough
Round
Score
Shaft

Shank
Slice
Spoon
Swing
Tiger
Wedge

6 letters:
Bandit
Birdie
Borrow
Bunker
Caddie
Course
Dormie
Driver
Foozle
Hazard
Honour
Marker
Putter
Rabbit
Sclaff
Single
Stance
Stroke

Gorgons

Stymie
Waggle

7 letters:
Air shot
Fairway
Midiron
Scratch
Trolley

8 letters:
Approach
Back nine
Four-ball
Foursome
Green fee
Half shot
Handicap
Long iron
Medal tee
Plus twos
Recovery
Sand trap
Slow play
Take-away

9 letters:
Albatross
Backswing
Caddie car
Clubhouse
Downswing
Front nine
Greensome
Hole in one
Ladies' tee
Match play
Medal play
Pitch shot
Plus fours
Sand wedge
Score card
Short iron
Sweetspot
Threesome

10 letters:
Better-ball
Local rules
Stroke play

11 letters:
Casual water
Green keeper
Pitch and run
Play through

12 letters:
Driving range
Fresh air shot
Putting green

13 letters:
Pitching wedge
Practice swing
Rub of the green

14 letters:
Nine-hole course
Nineteenth hole

15 letters:
Royal and Ancient

16 letters:
Stableford system

Gorgons

6 letters:

Medusa

Stheno

7 letters:

Euryale

Governments

Name	Meaning
Absolutism	By an absolute ruler
Anarchy	Absence of government
Aristocracy	By nobility
Autarchy or autocracy	By an unrestricted individual
Bureaucracy	By officials
Communalism	By self-governing communities
Constitutionalism	According to a constitution
Corporatism	By corporate groups
Democracy	By the people
Despotism	By a despot or absolute ruler
Diarchy or dyarchy	By two rulers
Dictatorship	By dictator
Ergatocracy	By the workers
Gerontocracy	By old people
Gynaecocracy or gynarchy	By women
Hagiocracy or hagiarchy	By holy men

Name	Meaning
Heptarchy	By seven rulers
Hexarchy	By six rulers
Hierocracy *or* hierarchy	By priests
Imperialism	By an emperor or empire
Isocracy	By equals
Meritocracy	By rulers chosen according to ability
Mobocracy	By the mob
Monarchy	By monarch
Monocracy	By one ruler
Nomocracy	By rule of law
Ochlocracy	By mob
Octarchy	By eight rulers
Oligarchy	By the few
Pantisocracy	By all equally
Pentarchy	By five rulers
Plutocracy	By the rich
Pornocracy	By whores
Ptochocracy	By the poor
Quangocracy	By quangos
Slavocracy	By slaveholders
Squirearchy *or* squirarchy	By squires
Stratocracy	By the army
Technocracy	By experts
Tetrarchy	By four rulers
Theocracy *or* thearchy	By a deity
Triarchy	By three rulers
Tyranny	By a tyrant

Graces

6 letters:
Aglaia
Thalia

10 letters:
Euphrosyne

Grammatical cases

6 letters:
Dative

7 letters:
Elative
Oblique

8 letters:
Ablative

Agentive
Ergative
Genitive
Illative
Locative
Vocative

9 letters:
Objective

10 letters:
Accusative
Nominative
Possessive
Subjective

12 letters:
Instrumental

Grand Prix circuits

Grand Prix circuits

5 letters:
Monza

6 letters:
Monaco
Sepang
Suzuka

7 letters:
Bahrain

8 letters:
Shanghai

9 letters:
Catalunya

10 letters:
Albert Park

11 letters:
Hungaroring
Nurburgring
Silverstone

12 letters:
Indianapolis

13 letters:
Francorchamps

14 letters:
Hockenheimring
Jose Carlos Pace

16 letters:
Enzo e Dino Ferrari
Gilles Villeneuve
Nevers-Magny
  Cours

Grapes

3 letters:
Fox

5 letters:
Gamay
Pinot
Steen
Syrah
Tokay
Viura

6 letters:
Malbec
Merlot
Muscat
Shiraz
Spanna

7 letters:
Aligoté
Barbera
Catawba
Concord
Furmint
Hamburg
Malmsey
Sercial

8 letters:
Cabernet
Cinsault
Delaware
Dolcetto
Garnacha

Grenache
Hamburgh
Hanepoot
Honeypot
Malvasia
Malvesie
Marsanne
Moscatel
Muscadel
Muscatel
Nebbiolo
Pinotage
Riesling
Ruländer
Sémillon
Silvaner
Sylvaner
Verdelho
Viognier

9 letters:
Colombard
Haanepoot
Lambrusco
Malvoisie
Mourvèdre
Muscadine
Pinot gris
Pinot noir
Sauvignon
Scheurebe
Trebbiano
Ugni blanc

Véronique
Zinfandel

10 letters:
Chardonnay
Hárslevelü
Kékfrankos
Muscadelle
Negroamoro
Pinot blanc
Sangiovese
Sweet-water
Verdicchio

11 letters:
Chenin blanc
Pinot grigio
Scuppernong
Seyval blanc
Tempranillo

12 letters:
Laski rizling
Olasz rizling

13 letters:
Cabernet franc
Montepulciano
Müller-thurgau
Rhine riesling
Spätburgunder

14 letters:
Gewürztraminer
Sauvignon blanc

Tokay-Pinot Gris
Welschriesling

15 letters:
Grüner veltliner

17 letters:
Cabernet sauvignon

Grasses

3 letters:
Eel
Lop
Oat
Poa
Rye
Saw
Seg
Tef

4 letters:
Alfa
Bent
Cane
Cord
Crab
Culm
Dari
Diss
Doob
Dura
Hair
Kans
Knot
Lyme
Milo
Rami
Reed
Rice
Rips
Rusa
Salt
Snow
Stag
Star
Tape
Teff
Tell
Wire
Worm

5 letters:
Alang
Avena
Bahia

Blady
Canna
Chess
Cogon
Couch
Cutty
Dhura
Doura
Durra
Emmer
Flote
Goose
Grama
Halfa
Heath
Jawar
Jowar
Kunai
Lemon
Maize
Manna
Melic
Oryza
Pamir
Panic
Peach
Plume
Quack
Quick
Ramee
Ramie
Roosa
Sedge
Sisal
Spear
Spelt
Starr
Stipa
Storm
Sword
Wheat
Witch

6 letters:
Bamboo

Barley
Bennet
Bladey
Bromus
Buffel
Canary
Carpet
Clover
Cotton
Cuscus
Darnel
Dhurra
Eddish
Fescue
Fiorin
Jawari
Jowari
Kikuyu
Lalang
Lolium
Lucern
Marram
Marrum
Melick
Millet
Pampas
Phleum
Puszta
Quitch
Redtop
Ribbon
Scurvy
Scutch
Sesame
Toetoe
Toitoi
Twitch
Zoysia

7 letters:
Alfalfa
Bermuda
Bristle
Buffalo
Cannach

Greeks

Clivers
Esparto
Feather
Foxtail
Heather
Johnson
Locusta
Lucerne
Matweed
Quaking
Sacaton
Sea-reed
Sorghum
Squitch
Timothy
Vetiver
Wallaby
Whangee
Whitlow
Wild oat
Wild rye
Zizania
Zostera

8 letters:
Barnyard
Cat's tail
Cleavers
Dactylis
Dogstail
Eelwrack
Elephant
Flinders
Kangaroo
Khuskhus
Materass
Paspalum
Rye-grass
Scorpion
Spinifex
Teosinte

9 letters:
Bluegrass
Cocksfoot
Corkscrew
Danthonia

Deergrass
Gama-grass
Harestail
Job's tears
Porcupine
Snowgrass
Sour-gourd
Sugar cane
Triticale

10 letters:
Brome-grass
Citronella
Cochlearia
Cortaderia
Miscanthus
Pennisetum
Persicaria

12 letters:
Kentucky blue
Squirrel-tail
Yorkshire fog

Greeks

4 letters:
Ajax
Nike

5 letters:
Homer
Momus
Timon
Zorba

6 letters:
Epirus
Euclid
Nestor
Nostos

Strabo

7 letters:
Orestes
Paestum
Pelopid
Perseus
Theseus

8 letters:
Achilles
Diomedes
Leonidas
Xenophon

9 letters:
Agamemnon
Aristides
Isocrates
Patroclus
Spartacus
Thersites

10 letters:
Archimedes
Pythagoras

11 letters:
Epaminondas

Green, shades of

3 letters:
Pea
Sea

4 letters:
Aqua

Cyan
Jade
Lime
Nile
Pine
Teal

5 letters:
Apple
Olive

6 letters:
Almond

Citron

Lincoln

Turquoise

7 letters:
Avocado
Celadon
Emerald

8 letters:
Eau de nil

9 letters:
Pistachio

10 letters:
Aquamarine
Chartreuse

Guns

2 letters:
HA

3 letters:
BAR
Dag
Gat
Ray
Tea
Uzi®
Zip

4 letters:
Bren
Burp
Colt
Owen
Pump
Riot
Sten
Stun
Tier

5 letters:
Flame
Fusil
Lewis
Luger®
Maxim
Radar
Rifle
Saker
Siege
Spear
Spray
Taser®
Tommy

6 letters:
Ack-ack
Archie
Barker

Bofors
Breech
Falcon
Fowler
Garand
Gingal
Jezail
Jingal
Magnum®
Mauser
Minnie
Minute
Mortar
Musket
Pistol
Pom-pom
Quaker
Roscoe
Squirt
Staple
Swivel
Tupelo

7 letters:
Bazooka
Bulldog
Bundook
Caliver
Carbine
Coehorn
Gatling
Gingall
Hackbut
Long Tom
Machine
Noonday
Pedrero
Pelican
Perrier
Shotgun

8 letters:
Amusette
Armalite®
Arquebus
Biscayan
Browning
Culverin
Deringer
Electron
Elephant
Falconet
Firelock
Howitzer
Oerlikon
Paderero
Paterero
Pederero
Petronel
Pistolet
Repeater
Revolver
Starting
Sterling
Thompson

9 letters:
Archibald
Automatic
Big Bertha
Brown Bess
Carronade
Chassepot
Chokebore
Derringer
Escopette
Flintlock
Forty-five
Harquebus
Matchlock
Morris Meg

Gymnastic events

Musketoon
Sarbacane
Snaphance
Sterculia

10 letters:
Scatter-gun
Self-cocker
Six-shooter
Smoothbore
Snaphaunce

11 letters:
Blunderbuss

Garand rifle
Kalashnikov
Stern-cannon
Stern-chaser
Thirty eight

12 letters:
Anti-aircraft
Breech-loader
Enfield rifle
Fowlingpiece
Martini-Henry®
Mitrailleuse

Muzzle-loader
Trench mortar

13 letters:
Sub-machine-gun

15 letters:
Winchester rifle

16 letters:
Springfield rifle

21 letters:
Thompson sub-
machine gun®

Gymnastic events

4 letters:
Beam

5 letters:
Rings

7 letters:
High bar

10 letters:
Horse vault

11 letters:
Pommel horse

12 letters:
Parallel bars

13 letters:
Horizontal bar

14 letters:
Asymmetric bars

Floor exercises
Side horse vault

18 letters:
Rhythmic
gymnastics

Hairstyles

2 letters:
DA

3 letters:
Bob
Bun

4 letters:
Afro
Crop
Perm
Pouf

5 letters:
Plait
Wedge

6 letters:
Marcel
Mullet

7 letters:
Beehive
Bunches
Buzz cut
Chignon
Corn row
Crew cut
Flat top
Mohican
Pageboy
Pigtail
Shingle

8 letters:
Bouffant
Eton crop
Ponytail
Razor-cut

Skinhead

9 letters:
Duck's arse
Pompadour

10 letters:
Dreadlocks
Feather-cut
French roll
Marcel wave

11 letters:
French pleat

13 letters:
Permanent wave

Harpies

5 letters:
Aello

7 letters:
Celaeno

Ocypete

Hats

3 letters:
Cap
Fez
Lum
Mob
Nab
Red
Taj
Tam
Tin
Tit

Top

4 letters:
Coif
Hard
Hood
Kepi
Poke
Silk
Sola
Tile
Topi

Ugly
Veil

5 letters:
Akuba
Ascot
Beany
Beret
Boxer
Busby
Crown
Curch

Hats

Derby
Envoy
Gibus
Mitre
Mutch
Opera
Pagri
Paper
Pilos
Salet
Shako
Snood
Solah
Straw
Tammy
Terai
Tiara
Topee
Toque
Tuque
Visor
Vizor

6 letters:
Akubra®
Anadem
Barret
Basher
Beanie
Beaver
Boater
Bonnet
Bowler
Breton
Calash
Calpac
Castor
Cloche
Cocked
Coolie
Cornet
Cowboy
Diadem
Fedora
Gaucho
Heaume
Helmet
Hennin
Kalpak
Lum-hat
Mobcap

Morion
Panama
Pilion
Pinner
Safari
Sailor
Salade
Sallet
Shacko
Shovel
Slouch
Sunhat
Titfer
Toorie
Topper
Tourie
Trilby
Turban
Wimple

7 letters:
Bandana
Bandeau
Basinet
Biretta
Bluecap
Caleche
Calotte
Calpack
Capouch
Capuche
Chaplet
Circlet
Commode
Coronet
Cossack
Crusher
Curchef
Earmuff
Flat cap
Frontal
Hattock
Homburg
Kufiyah
Laurels
Leghorn
Matador
Montero
Petasus
Picture
Pillbox

Pilleus
Plateau
Pork-pie
Profile
Puritan
Skimmer
Songkok
Stetson
Sundown
Tarbush
Tricorn

8 letters:
Babushka
Balmoral
Bandanna
Bascinet
Bearskin
Berretta
Blackcap
Capotain
Cloth cap
Coonskin
Dunce cap
Fool's cap
Frontlet
Havelock
Headband
Kaffiyeh
Keffiyeh
Mountie's
Mushroom
Nightcap
Planter's
Puggaree
Ramilies
Runcible
Skullcap
Snap-brim
Sola-topi
Sombrero
Tarboosh
Tarboush
Trencher
Tricorne
Tyrolean
Watch cap
Yarmulke

9 letters:
Astrakhan
Balaclava

Billycock
Bollinger
Broadbrim
Cartwheel
Cockle-hat
Dunstable
Forage cap
Gandhi cap
Glengarry
Headdress
Juliet cap
Nor'wester
Peaked cap
Ramillies
Shower cap
Sou'wester
Stovepipe
Sugarloaf

Sunbonnet
Tarbouche
Tarpaulin
Ten-gallon
Wide-awake

10 letters:
Balibuntal
Bluebonnet
Chimneypot
Fascinator
Liberty cap
Pith helmet
Poke bonnet
Sola-helmet

11 letters:
Baseball cap
Crash helmet

Deerstalker
Dolly Varden
Kamelaukion
Mortarboard
Phrygian cap
Stocking cap
Tam-o'-shanter
Trencher cap

12 letters:
Cheese cutter
Fore-and-after
Steeple-crown

15 letters:
Balaclava helmet

Hawks

4 letters:
Eyas
Kite
Nyas
Soar
Sore

5 letters:
Eagle
Hobby
Marsh
Soare

6 letters:
Auceps
Elanet
Falcon
Keelie
Lanner
Merlin
Musket

Osprey
Sorage
Tarsal
Tarsel
Tassel
Tercel

7 letters:
Buzzard
Cooper's
Goshawk
Haggard
Harrier
Kestrel
Sparrow
Staniel
Tarsell
Tiersel

8 letters:
Caracara

Lanneret
Ringtail
Tercelet

9 letters:
Gerfalcon
Gier-eagle
Ossifraga
Ossifrage
Peregrine
Sore-eagle
Wind-hover

10 letters:
Hen harrier

11 letters:
Accipitrine
Lammergeier

12 letters:
Marsh harrier

Heart, parts of

5 letters:
Aorta

6 letters:
Atrium

Septum

7 letters:
Auricle

8 letters:
Vena cava

9 letters:
Ventricle

Heraldry terms

13 letters:
Bicuspid valve
Pulmonary vein

14 letters:
Semilunar valve
Tricuspid valve

15 letters:
Pulmonary artery

Heraldry terms

2 letters:
Or

3 letters:
Bar
Fur
Vol

4 letters:
Bars
Base
Bend
Coue
Fess
File
Fret
Golp
Lion
Lyon
Orle
Pale
Pall
Paly
Pean
Pile
Semé
Urdé
Vair
Vert
Yale

5 letters:
Azure
Baton
Chief
Crest
Cross
Crown
Eagle
Fesse
Field
Flory
Fusil
Giron
Golpe

Gules
Gyron
Label
Party
Rebus
Sable
Scarp
Semée
Torse
Trick
Urdée

6 letters:
Argent
Armory
Bezant
Blazon
Byzant
Canton
Charge
Checky
Coupee
Coward
Dexter
Empale
Erased
Ermine
Falcon
Fecial
Fetial
Fillet
Fleury
Herald
Impale
Lionel
Lodged
Mascle
Moline
Mullet
Naiant
Norroy
Pallet
Parted
Potent

Proper
Sejant
Shield
Verdoy
Voided
Volant
Vorant
Wreath
Wyvern

7 letters:
Annulet
Armiger
Bandeau
Bearing
Bezzant
Bordure
Cadency
Chaplet
Chevron
Compone
Company
Coronet
Dormant
Endorse
Gardant
Garland
Gironny
Griffon
Gyronny
Issuant
Leopard
Lozenge
Lozengy
Martlet
Nascent
Nombril
Passant
Purpure
Quarter
Rampant
Red Hand
Roundel
Roundle

Salient
Saltire
Sea lion
Sejeant
Statant
Trangle
Trundle
Urinant

8 letters:
Bendwise
Blazonry
Caboched
Cicerone
Couchant
Crescent
Crosslet
Emblazon
Guardant
Hauriant
Heraldic
Mantling
Naissant
Octofoil
Opinicus
Ordinary
Segreant
Sinister

Tressure
Trippant
Umbrated

9 letters:
Abatement
Dimidiate
Displayed
Embattled
Hatchment
Quartered
Quarterly
Regardant
Scutcheon
Supporter

10 letters:
Bloody Hand
Bluemantle
Cinquefoil
Clarenceux
Coat armour
Coat of arms
Cockatrice
Cognisance
Cognizance
Difference
Escutcheon
Fleur-de-lis

Fleur-de-lys
King-of-arms
Lambrequin
Portcullis
Pursuivant
Quartering

11 letters:
Achievement
Canting arms
Clarencieux
Spread eagle
Subordinary

12 letters:
Bend sinister
Inescutcheon

13 letters:
College of arms
Matriculation
Officer of arms
Voided lozenge

14 letters:
Armes parlantes
Counter-passant
Lyon King of Arms
Sun in splendour

Herbs, spices and seasonings

3 letters:
Bay
Oca
Pia
Rue

4 letters:
Dill
Forb
Mace
Mint
Miso
Moly
Sage
Salt
Wort

5 letters:
Anise

Avens
Basil
Chive
Clove
Cress
Cumin
Eruca
Inula
Maror
Medic
Orval
Senna
Shoyu
Tacca
Tansy
Thyme
Typha
Yerba

6 letters:
Bennet
Borage
Capers
Chilli
Cummin
Exacum
Fennel
Ferula
Garlic
Ginger
Hyssop
Lovage
Madder
Nam pla
Nutmeg
Origan
Purpie

Hercules, labours of

Savory
Sesame
Sorrel
Tamari
Wasabi
Willow
Yarrow

7 letters:
Aconite
Aniseed
Arugula
Bayleaf
Canella
Chervil
Cilanto
Coconut
Comfrey
Dittany
Felicia
Gentian
Gunnera
Madwort
Mustard
Oregano
Origane
Paprika
Parsley
Saffron
Salsify
Vervain

8 letters:
Allspice
Angelica
Bergamot
Cardamom
Centaury
Cinnamon
Costmary
Feverfew
Fireweed

Fluellin
Galangal
Knapweed
Mandrake
Marjoram
Origanum
Plantain
Purslane
Rosemary
Soapwort
Soy sauce
Staragen
Szechuan
Szechwan
Tarragon
Turmeric
Valerian
Wormwood

9 letters:
Asafetida
Calendula
Chamomile
Coriander
Echinacea
Eyebright
Fenugreek
Fish sauce
Galingale
Germander
Haworthia
Kalanchoe
Lamb's ears
Laserwort
Poppy seed
Pussytoes
Red pepper
Rhizocarp
Rocambole
Rodgersia
Soya sauce

Spearmint
Star anise
Tormentil

10 letters:
Asafoetida
Cassia bark
Lemon grass
Peppercorn
Pipsissewa
Rest-harrow
Sesame seed

11 letters:
Black pepper
Caraway seed
Coconut milk
Curry powder
Fines herbes
Garam masala
Laserpicium
Sweet cicely
White pepper

12 letters:
Aristolochia
Ornithogalum
Southernwood

13 letters:
Cayenne pepper
Good-King-Henry
Sunflower seed

14 letters:
Kaffir lime leaf

15 letters:
Alligator pepper
Five spice powder

18 letters:
Sichuan
 peppercorns

Hercules, labours of

Number	Labour
First	The slaying of the Nemean lion
Second	The slaying of the Lernaean hydra
Third	The capture of the hind of Ceryneia
Fourth	The capture of the wild boar of Erymanthus
Fifth	The cleansing of the Augean stables

Number	Labour
Sixth	The shooting of the Stymphalian birds
Seventh	The capture of the Cretan bull
Eighth	The capture of the horses of Diomedes
Ninth	The taking of the girdle of Hippolyte
Tenth	The capture of the cattle of Geryon
Eleventh	The recovery of the golden apples of Hesperides
Twelfth	The taking of Cerberus

Heroes

3 letters:
Cid

4 letters:
Aitu
Ajax
Eric
Finn
Kami
Lion
Tell

5 letters:
Faust
Jason

6 letters:
Amadis
Cyrano
Fingal
Hector
Kaleva
Nestor
Oliver
Onegin
Roland
Rustem
Rustum
Sigurd

7 letters:
Alcides
Beowulf
Couplet
Lothair
Marmion
Paladin
Perseus
Rinaldo
Saladin
Tancred
Theseus
Tristam
Tristan
Ulysses
Volsung

8 letters:
Achilles
Crockett
Heracles
Hercules
Hiawatha
Leonidas
Meleager
Owlglass
Parsifal
Pericles

Roderego
Roderick
Superman
Tristram

9 letters:
Agamemnon
Cuchulain
Garibaldi
Lochinvar
Owleglass
Owspiegle
Siegfried

10 letters:
Cuchullain
Howleglass
Owlspiegle

11 letters:
Bellerophon
Finn MacCool
Tam o'Shanter
Triptolemus
White knight

13 letters:
Vercingetorix

Hills

3 letters:
How
Kip
Kop
Law
Man
Nab

Tel

4 letters:
Bent
Chin
Cone
Kipp
Knot

Loma
Mesa
Pike
Pnyx
Sion
Tara
Tell

Hindu denominations and sects

Zion

5 letters:
Bluff
Cleve
Gebel
Horst
Jebel
Kopje
Morro
Pingo
Wolds

6 letters:
Arafar
Broken
Calvan
Coteau
Djebel
Mendip
Wrekin

7 letters:
Beverly
Caelian

Capitol
Drumlin
Hammock
Ludgate
Mamelon
Merrick
Nanatak
Silbury
Viminal

8 letters:
Aventine
Cheviots
Chiltern
Golgotha
Highgate
Lavender
Palatine
Pennines
Quirinal

9 letters:
Areopagus
Esquiline

Grampians
Helvellyn
Janiculum
Monadnock
Monticule
Quantocks

10 letters:
Capitoline
Lammermuir
North Downs
Saddleback
Tweedsmuir

11 letters:
Crag-and-tail
Otway Ranges

12 letters:
Golan Heights

16 letters:
Mount Lofty
  Ranges

Hindu denominations and sects

6 letters:
Saktas

8 letters:
Saivaism

11 letters:
Hare Krishna
Vaishnavism

Historians

4 letters:
Bede, *the Venerable*
Livy
Oman, *Sir Charles William
  Chadwick*

5 letters:
Acton, *John Emerich Edward
  Dalberg*
Green, *John Richard*
Pliny *(the Elder)*
Renan, *(Joseph) Ernest*
Wells, *H(erbert) G(eorge)*

6 letters:
Arrian

Bryant, *Sir Arthur (Wynne
  Morgan)*
Buckle, *Henry Thomas*
Camden, *William*
Froude, *James Anthony*
Gibbon, *Edward*
Gildas
Taylor, *A(lan) J(ohn) P(ercivale)*
Thiers, *(Louis) Adolphe*

7 letters:
Asellio, *Sempronius*
Carlyle, *Thomas*
Sallust
Starkey, *David*
Tacitus

Toynbee, *Arnold Joseph*

8 letters:
Macaulay, *Thomas Babbington*
Plutarch
Ponsonby, *Lord Arthur*
Strachey, *(Giles) Lytton*
Xenophon

9 letters:
Herodotus

Suetonius
Trevelyan, *G(eorge) M(acaulay)*

10 letters:
Thucydides

11 letters:
Trevor-Roper, *Hugh*

13 letters:
Knickerbocker, *Diedrick*

History

HISTORICAL CHARACTERS

3 letters:
Lee, *Robert E(dward)*

4 letters:
Cody, *William Frederick*
Cook, *Captain James*
Dong, *Mao Ze*
Khan, *Genghis*
King, *Martin Luther*
Polo, *Marco*

5 letters:
Drake, *Francis*
El Cid
James, *Jesse*
Jesus
Lenin, *Vladimir Ilyich*
Oates, *Lawrence Edward Grace*
Scott, *Robert Falcon*

6 letters:
Borgia, *Lucrezia*
Brutus
Buddha
Caesar, *Julius*
Cortés, *Hernando*
Custer, *George Armstrong*
Fawkes, *Guy*
Gandhi, *Mahatma*
Hickok, *James Butler*
Hickok, *Wild Bill*
Hitler, *Adolf*
Luther, *Martin*
Nelson, *Horatio*
Pompey
Stalin, *Joseph*

Stuart, *Charles Edward*
Wright, *Orville and Wilbur*
Zapata, *Emiliano*

7 letters:
À Becket, *Thomas*
Gagarin, *Yuri*
Guevara, *Che*
Lincoln, *Abraham*
Raleigh, *Walter*
Saladin
Trotsky, *Leon*
Tse-tung, *Mao*
Wallace, *William*

8 letters:
Augustus
Boadicea
Boudicca
Columbus, *Christopher*
Crockett, *Davy*
Cromwell, *Oliver*
Geronimo
Hannibal
Hiawatha
Mohammed
Muhammad
Pericles
Rasputin, *Grigori Efimovich*
Selassie, *Haile*
Socrates

9 letters:
Bonaparte, *Napoleon*
Churchill, *Winston*
Cleopatra

History

Garibaldi, *Giuseppe*
Joan of Arc
Montezuma
Mussolini, *Benito*

10 letters:
Antoinette, *Marie*
Crazy Horse
Mark Antony
Washington, *George*

11 letters:
Billy the Kid
Buffalo Bill
Charlemagne
Nightingale, *Florence*
Sitting Bull

12 letters:
Attila the Hun
Captain Oates
Clive *of India*
De Torquemada, *Tomás*

HISTORICAL EVENTS

4 letters:
D-day

5 letters:
Alamo

7 letters:
Boer War
Cold War

8 letters:
Civil War
Crusades
Waterloo

9 letters:
Agincourt
Armistice
Great Trek
Hiroshima
Holocaust
Korean War
Long March
Trafalgar
Watergate

10 letters:
Black Death
Crimean War

14 letters:
Alfred the Great
Robert the Bruce
The Black Prince

15 letters:
Hereward the Wake
Ivan the Terrible

16 letters:
Duke *of Wellington*
Gordon *of Khartoum*
Lawrence *of Arabia*

17 letters:
Alexander the Great
Catherine the Great
Mary, *Queen of Scots*

19 letters:
Bonnie Prince Charlie
Richard the Lionheart
Warwick the Kingmaker
William the Conqueror

Depression
Magna Carta
Suez Crisis
Vietnam War

11 letters:
Diet of Worms
Gordon Riots
Great Schism
Pearl Harbor
Reformation
Renaissance
Restoration

12 letters:
Bloody Sunday
Crystal Night
Easter Rising
Indian Mutiny
Potato Famine
Risorgimento

13 letters:
General Strike
Gunpowder Plot
Kristallnacht
Reign of Terror
Spanish Armada

14 letters:
Boston Tea Party
Boxer Rebellion
Napoleonic Wars
Norman Conquest
Peasants' Revolt
South Sea Bubble
Thirty Years' War
Wars of the Roses

15 letters:
Hundred Years War
Munich Agreement
Spanish Civil War
Wall Street Crash

16 letters:
American Civil War
Battle of Hastings
French Revolution
Peterloo Massacre

17 letters:
Gettysburg Address
Great Fire of London

Hungarian Uprising
Jacobite Rebellion
Russian Revolution

18 letters:
Cultural Revolution
Glorious Revolution
Spanish Inquisition
Treaty of Versailles

20 letters:
Industrial Revolution
Night of the Long Knives

22 letters:
The War between the States

23 letters:
Charge of the Light Brigade
Tiananmen Square Massacre

25 letters:
Declaration of Independence

26 letters:
Saint Valentine's Day Massacre

Homes

2 letters:
Ho

3 letters:
Cot
Hut
Inn
Mas

4 letters:
Bush
Casa
Chez
Cote
Crib
Dail
Digs
Drum
Flat
Gite
Hall
Home
Iglu
Keys

Mews
Pent
Rath
Safe
Semi
Slum
Tent
Tied
Town
York

5 letters:
Adobe
Booth
Cabin
Croft
Dacha
Dower
Frame
Hogan
Hotel
House
Hovel
Igloo

Lodge
Lords
Manor
Manse
Motel
Opera
Ranch
Shack
Tepee
Tower
Tudor
Tupek
Tupik
Usher
Villa
Wendy
Whare

6 letters:
Bhavan
Bhawan
Biggin
Bunker
Castle

Homes

Chalet
Custom
Des res
Duplex
Flotel
Garret
Grange
Hostel
Insula
Maison
Mobile
Mud hut
Orange
Palace
Prefab
Priory
Shanty
Stuart
Tavern
Wigwam

7 letters:
Althing
Barrack
Bastide
Caboose
Caravan
Chamber
Chapter
Charnel
Château
Commons
Convent
Cottage
Council
Crannog
Customs
Deanery
Embassy
Fashion
Flatlet
Habitat
Halfway
Hanover
Harbour

Knesset
Mansion
Meeting
Osborne
Rectory
Schloss
Starter
Stately
Terrace
Theatre
Trailer
Trinity
Windsor

8 letters:
Boarding
Bungalow
Burghley
Camboose
Clearing
Dwelling
Hacienda
Lagthing
Log cabin
Longleat
Montagne
Rest-home
Somerset
Tenement
Vicarage

9 letters:
Admiralty
Apartment
Bedsitter
Bundestag
But and ben
Clapboard
Consulate
Doss house
Farmhouse
Flophouse
Houseboat
Lancaster
Long house
Mattamore

Odelsting
Parsonage
Penthouse
Roadhouse
Show house
Single-end
Town house
Tree house

10 letters:
Back-to-back
Black house
Brownstone
Chatsworth
Commercial
Guest house
Heartbreak
Maisonette
Odelsthing
Parliament
Pied-à-terre
Studio flat

11 letters:
Cottage flat
Plantagenet
Shooting box

12 letters:
Broadcasting
Chattel house
Lake dwelling
Motor caravan
Weatherboard

13 letters:
Boarding house

14 letters:
Cape Cod cottage

15 letters:
Board-and-shingle
Duplex apartment

17 letters:
Bachelor
  apartment

Homophones

2 letters:
Be / Bee
By / Buy
Hi / High
Ho / Hoe
In / Inn
Lo / Low
Mo / Mow
No / Know
Oh / Owe
Pa / Pah
Pi / Pie
So / Sew
To / Two
We / Wee

3 letters:
Ail / Ale
Air / Heir
Ale / Ail
All / Awl
Arc / Ark
Ark / Arc
Awe / Ore
Awl / All
Aye / Eye
Baa / Bah
Bad / Bade
Bah / Baa
Bay / Bey
Bee / Be
Bey / Bay
Bow / Bough
Boy / Buoy
Bur / Burr
But / Butt
Buy / By
Can / Cannes
Coo / Coup
Cox / Cocks
Dam / Damn
Daw / Door
Dew / Due
Die / Dye
Doe / Dough
Due / Dew
Dug / Doug
Dun / Done

Dye / Die
Ewe / Yew
Eye / Aye
Few / Phew
Fin / Finn
Fir / Fur
For / Four
Fur / Fir
Gym / Jim
Haw / Whore
Hay / Hey
Hew / Hue
Hey / Hay
Him / Hymn
Hoe / Ho
Hue / Hew
Inn / In
Ion / Iron
Jam / Jamb
Jim / Gym
Key / Quay
Lax / Lacks
Lay / Ley
Lea / Leigh
Led / Lead
Lee / Lea
Ley / Lay
Lie / Lye
Loo / Lieu
Low / Lo
Lye / Lie
Mat / Matt
Mow / Mo
Nap / Knap
Nay / Neigh
Née / Nay
Net / Nett
New / Knew
Nix / Nicks
Nob / Knob
Not / Knot
Nun / None
Oar / Ore
Ode / Owed
One / Won
Ore / Oar
Our / Hour
Owe / Oh

Pah / Pa
Par / Parr
Pax / Packs
Pea / Pee
Pee / Pea
Per / Purr
Pie / Pi
Rap / Wrap
Red / Read
Rex / Wrecks
Roe / Row
Row / Roe
Rye / Wry
Sac / Sack
Set / Sett
Sew / So
Sic / Sick
Son / Sun
Spa / Spar
Sty / Stye
Sue / Sioux
Sum / Some
Sun / Son
Tax / Tacks
Tic / Tick
Toe / Tow
Ton / Tun
Too / To
Tor / Tore
Tow / Toe
Tun / Ton
Two / To
Urn / Earn
Use / Ewes
War / Wore
Wax / Whacks
Way / Whey
We'd / Weed
Wee / We
Wen / When
Wet / Whet
Wig / Whig
Win / Whin
Wit / Whit
Woe / Whoa
Won / One
Wry / Rye
Yew / Ewe

Homophones

4 letters:

Airy / Eyrie
Alms / Arms
Ante / Anti
Anti / Ante
Aran / Arran
Arms / Alms
Away / Aweigh
Bade / Bad
Bail / Bale
Bait / Bate
Bald / Balled
Bale / Bail
Ball / Bawl
Balm / Barm
Bang / Bhang
Bare / Bear
Bark / Barque
Barm / Balm
Base / Bass
Bass / Base
Bate / Bait
Bawd / Board
Bawl / Ball
Bays / Baize
Bean / Been
Bear / Bare
Beat / Beet
Beau / Bow
Been / Bean
Beer / Bier
Beet / Beat
Bell / Belle
Berg / Burg
Bier / Beer
Bite / Bight
Blew / Blue
Blue / Blew
Boar / Bore
Bode / Bowed
Bold / Bowled
Bole / Bowl
Boos / Booze
Bore / Boar
Born / Borne
Bosh / Boche
Bowl / Bole
Brae / Bray
Bray / Brae
Bred / Bread
Buoy / Boy

Burg / Berg
Burr / Bur
Bury / Berry
Butt / But
Call / Caul
Cash / Cache
Cast / Caste
Caul / Call
Cede / Seed
Cell / Sell
Cent / Scent
Choc / Chock
Cite / Sight
Coal / Kohl
Coat / Cote
Coax / Cokes
Coin / Coign
Cops / Copse
Copt / Copped
Copy / Kopje
Cord / Chord
Core / Corps
Cork / Caulk
Cote / Coat
Coup / Coo
Cows / Cowes
Crew / Crewe
Curb / Kerb
Damn / Dam
Dane / Deign
Days / Daze
Daze / Days
Dear / Deer
Deer / Dear
Dire / Dyer
Done / Dun
Door / Daw
Dost / Dust
Doug / Dug
Dual / Duel
Duct / Ducked
Duel / Dual
Dust / Dost
Dyer / Dire
Earn / Urn
Eddy / Eddie
Eves / Eaves
Ewes / Use
Fain / Feign
Fair / Fare
Fare / Fair

Fate / Fête
Faun / Fawn
Fawn / Faun
Feat / Feet
Feet / Feat
Fête / Fate
Find / Fined
Finn / Fin
Firs / Furze
Flaw / Floor
Flea / Flee
Flee / Flea
Flew / Flue
Flex / Flecks
Floe / Flow
Flow / Floe
Flue / Flew
Fold / Foaled
Foul / Fowl
Four / For
Fowl / Foul
Gael / Gale
Gaff / Gaffe
Gage / Gauge
Gait / Gate
Gale / Gael
Gall / Gaul
Gate / Gait
Gaul / Gall
Gays / Gaze
Gaze / Gays
Gibe / Jibe
Gild / Guild
Gill / Jill
Gilt / Guilt
Guys / Guise
Hail / Hale
Hair / Hare
Hale / Hail
Hall / Haul
Hare / Hair
Hart / Heart
Haul / Hall
Heal / Heel
Hear / Here
Heel / Heal
Heir / Air
Herd / Heard
Here / Hear
Hide / Hied
Hied / Hide

High / Hi
Hire / Higher
Hoar / Whore
Hoes / Hose
Hold / Holed
Hole / Whole
Hose / Hoes
Hour / Our
Hymn / Him
Idle / Idol
Idol / Idle
Iron / Ion
Isle / Aisle
Jamb / Jam
Jibe / Gibe
Jill / Gill
Kail / Kale
Kale / Kail
Kerb / Curb
Knap / Nap
Knew / New
Knob / Nob
Knot / Not
Know / No
Kohl / Coal
Lade / Laid
Laid / Lade
Lain / Lane
Lama / Llama
Lane / Lain
Laps / Lapse
Laud / Lord
Lava / Larva
Lawn / Lorn
Lays / Laze
Laze / Leys
Lead / Led
Leaf / Lief
Leak / Leek
Leek / Leak
Lent / Leant
Levy / Levee
Leys / Laze
Liar / Lyre
Lief / Leaf
Lieu / Loo
Limb / Limn
Limn / Limb
Load / Lode
Loan / Lone
Lode / Lowed

Lone / Loan
Loos / Lose
Loot / Lute
Lord / Laud
Lorn / Lawn
Lose / Loos
Lute / Loot
Lynx / Links
Lyre / Liar
Made / Maid
Maid / Made
Mail / Male
Main / Mane
Male / Mail
Mane / Main
Mare / Mayor
Mark / Marque
Mask / Masque
Matt / Mat
Maze / Maize
Mead / Meed
Mean / Mien
Meat / Meet
Meed / Mead
Meet / Mete
Mete / Meet
Mews / Muse
Mien / Mean
Mind / Mined
Minx / Minks
Mist / Missed
Mite / Might
Moan / Mown
Moat / Mote
Mode / Mowed
Moor / More
More / Moor
Morn / Mourn
Mote / Moat
Mown / Moan
Muse / Mews
Must / Mussed
Nave / Knave
Need / Knead
Neil / Kneel
Nell / Knell
Nett / Net
None / Nun
Nose / Knows
Oral / Aural
Ours / Hours

Owed / Ode
Pact / Packed
Pail / Pale
Pain / Pane
Pair / Pear
Pale / Pail
Pall / Paul
Pane / Pain
Pare / Pair
Parr / Par
Past / Passed
Paul / Pall
Pawl / Pall
Pawn / Porn
Paws / Pause
Peak / Peek
Peal / Peel
Pear / Pair
Peat / Pete
Peek / Peak
Peel / Peal
Peer / Pier
Pete / Peat
Phew / Few
Pier / Peer
Plum / Plumb
Pole / Poll
Poll / Pole
Poof / Pouffe
Pore / Pour
Porn / Pawn
Pour / Pore
Pray / Prey
Prey / Pray
Pros / Prose
Purl / Pearl
Purr / Per
Quay / Key
Rack / Wrack
Rain / Rein
Rapt / Wrapped
Raze / Raise
Read / Red
Reed / Read
Rein / Rain
Rest / Wrest
Ring / Wring
Rite / Right
Road / Rode
Roam / Rome
Rode / Road

Homophones

Role / Roll
Roll / Role
Rome / Roam
Rood / Rude
Room / Rheum
Root / Route
Rose / Rows
Rota / Rotor
Rote / Wrote
Rows / Rouse
Rude / Rood
Rues / Ruse
Ruff / Rough
Rung / Wrung
Ruse / Rues
Sack / Sac
Sail / Sale
Sale / Sail
Sane / Seine
Seam / Seem
Sear / Seer
Seed / Cede
Seek / Sikh
Seem / Seam
Seen / Scene
Seer / Sear
Sell / Cell
Serf / Surf
Sett / Set
Shoe / Shoo
Shoo / Shoe
Sick / Sic
Side / Sighed
Sign / Sine
Sikh / Seek
Sine / Sign
Size / Sighs
Slay / Sleigh
Sloe / Slow
Slow / Sloe
Soar / Sore
Sold / Soled
Sole / Soul
Some / Sum
Sore / Soar
Sort / Sought
Soul / Sole
Spar / Spa
Spec / Speck
Step / Steppe
Stye / Sty

Styx / Sticks
Surf / Serf
Swat / Swot
Swot / Swat
Tact / Tacked
Tail / Tale
Tale / Tail
Talk / Torque
Tare / Tear
Taut / Taught
Team / Teem
Tear / Tier
Teem / Team
Tern / Turn
Tick / Tic
Tide / Tied
Tied / Tide
Tier / Tear
Time / Thyme
Tire / Tyre
Toad / Towed
Told / Tolled
Tore / Tor
Tuba / Tuber
Tuna / Tuner
Turn / Tern
Tyre / Tire
Vain / Vein
Vale / Veil
Vane / Vain
Veil / Vale
Vein / Vain
Vial / Viol
Viol / Vial
Wade / Weighed
Wail / Whale
Wain / Wane
Wait / Weight
Wale / Whale
Wane / Wain
Ward / Warred
Ware / Where
Warn / Worn
Watt / What
Wave / Waive
Weak / Week
Wear / Ware
Weed / We'd
Week / Weak
Weld / Welled
Were / Whirr

What / Watt
When / Wen
Whet / Wet
Whey / Way
Whig / Wig
Whin / Win
Whit / Wit
Whoa / Woe
Who's / Whose
Wile / While
Wine / Whine
Won't / Wont
Wood / Would
Wore / War
Worn / Warn
Wrap / Rap
Yaws / Yours
Yoke / Yolk
Yolk / Yoke
Yore / You're
Your / Yore
Yule / You'll

5 letters:
Aisle / Isle
Aloud / Allowed
Altar / Alter
Alter / Altar
Arran / Aran
Auger / Augur
Aught / Ought
Augur / Auger
Aural / Oral
Baize / Bays
Balmy / Barmy
Barmy / Balmy
Baron / Barren
Based / Baste
Baste / Based
Beach / Beech
Beech / Beach
Belle / Bell
Berry / Bury
Berth / Birth
Betel / Beetle
Bhang / Bang
Bight / Bite
Birth / Berth
Board / Bored
Boche / Bosh
Booze / Boos

Bored / Board
Borne / Born
Bough / Bow
Bowed / Bode
Brake / Break
Bread / Bred
Break / Brake
Brews / Bruise
Brood / Brewed
Brows / Browse
Bruit / Brute
Brute / Bruit
Build / Billed
Cache / Cash
Calve / Carve
Canon / Cannon
Carat / Carrot
Carve / Calve
Caste / Cast
Caulk / Cork
Cause / Cores
Chard / Charred
Cheap / Cheep
Check / Czech
Cheep / Cheap
Chews / Choose
Chock / Choc
Choir / Quire
Chord / Cord
Chute / Shoot
Claws / Clause
Climb / Clime
Clime / Climb
Cocks / Cox
Coign / Coin
Cokes / Coax
Copse / Cops
Cores / Cause
Corps / Core
Court / Caught
Cowes / Cows
Cozen / Cousin
Creak / Creek
Creek / Creak
Crewe / Crew
Crews / Cruise
Crude / Crewed
Czech / Check
Deign / Dane
Derek / Derrick
Dough / Doe

Douse / Dowse
Dowse / Douse
Draft / Draught
Draws / Drawers
Droop / Drupe
Drupe / Droop
Eaves / Eves
Eddie / Eddy
Eerie / Eyrie
Eyrie / Eerie
Faint / Feint
Feign / Fain
Feint / Faint
Fined / Find
Flair / Flare
Flare / Flair
Floor / Flaw
Flour / Flower
Franc / Frank
Frank / Franc
Frays / Phrase
Friar / Frier
Frier / Friar
Furze / Firs
Gaffe / Gaff
Gauge / Gage
Gauze / Gores
Gores / Gauze
Grate / Great
Great / Grate
Groan / Grown
Groin / Groyne
Grown / Groan
Guest / Guessed
Guide / Guyed
Guild / Gild
Guilt / Gilt
Guise / Guys
Guyed / Guide
Heard / Herd
Heart / Hart
Hertz / Hurts
Hoard / Horde
Holed / Hold
Horde / Hoard
Horse / Hoarse
Hours / Ours
Hurts / Hertz
Islet / Eyelet
Knave / Nave
Knead / Need

Kneel / Neil
Knell / Nell
Knows / Nose
Kooky / Cookie
Kopje / Copy
Lacks / Lax
Lager / Laager
Lapse / Laps
Larva / Lava
Leach / Leech
Leads / Leeds
Leant / Lent
Least / Leased
Leech / Leach
Leeds / Leads
Leigh / Lea
Levee / Levy
Lewes / Lewis
Lewis / Lewes
Liken / Lichen
Links / Lynx
Llama / Lama
Lowed / Lode
Maize / Maze
Manor / Manner
Mayor / Mare
Medal / Meddle
Metal / Mettle
Meter / Metre
Metre / Meter
Might / Mite
Mined / Mind
Miner / Minor
Minks / Minx
Minor / Mynah
Moose / Mousse
Mourn / Morn
Mowed / Mode
Mucus / Mucous
Mynah / Minor
Naval / Navel
Navel / Naval
Neigh / Nay
Nicks / Nix
Night / Knight
Ought / Aught
Paced / Paste
Packs / Pax
Paste / Paced
Pause / Paws
Pawed / Pored

Homophones

Peace / Piece
Pearl / Purl
Pedal / Peddle
Phlox / Flocks
Piece / Peace
Place / Plaice
Plain / Plane
Plane / Plain
Pleas / Please
Plumb / Plum
Pored / Pawed
Prays / Praise
Prise / Prize
Prize / Prise
Prose / Pros
Putty / Puttee
Quire / Choir
Raise / Raze
Reams / Rheims
Reign / Rain
Retch / Wretch
Revue / Review
Rheum / Room
Right / Write
Roads / Rhodes
Rotor / Rota
Rough / Ruff
Rouse / Rows
Route / Root
Sauce / Source
Saver / Savour
Scene / Seen
Scent / Cent
Scull / Skull
Seine / Sane
Semen / Seaman
Sewer / Sower
Shake / Sheik
Shear / Sheer
Sheer / Shear
Sheik / Shake
Shire / Shyer
Shoot / Chute
Shyer / Shire
Sighs / Size
Sight / Cite
Sioux / Sue
Skull / Scull
Soled / Sold
Sonny / Sunny
Sower / Sewer

Spade / Spayed
Speck / Spec
Staid / Stayed
Stair / Stare
Stake / Steak
Stalk / Stork
Stare / Stair
Steak / Stake
Steal / Steel
Steel / Steal
Sties / Styes
Stile / Style
Stoop / Stoup
Stork / Stalk
Story / Storey
Stoup / Stoop
Styes / Sties
Style / Stile
Suite / Sweet
Sunny / Sonny
Sweet / Suite
Sword / Soared
Tacks / Tax
Taper / Tapir
Tapir / Taper
Tenor / Tenner
Their / They're
There / Their
Threw / Through
Throe / Throw
Throw / Throe
Thyme / Time
Titan / Tighten
Towed / Toad
Troop / Troupe
Trust / Trussed
Tuber / Tuba
Tuner / Tuna
Venus / Venous
Waist / Waste
Waive / Wave
Waste / Waist
Waver / Waiver
Weald / Wield
Weigh / Way
Whale / Wale
Where / Ware
Which / Witch
While / Wile
Whine / Wine
Whirl / Whorl

Whirr / Were
White / Wight
Whole / Hole
Whore / Hoar
Whorl / Whirl
Whose / Who's
Wield / Weald
Wight / White
Witch / Which
World / Whirled
Would / Wood
Wrack / Rack
Wrest / Rest
Wring / Ring
Write / Right
Wrote / Rote
Wrung / Rung
You'll / Yule
You're / Yore
Yours / Yaws

6 letters:

Ascent / Assent
Assent / Ascent
Aweigh / Away
Balled / Bald
Baring / Bearing
Barque / Bark
Barren / Baron
Beetle / Betel
Billed / Build
Bolder / Boulder
Border / Boarder
Bowled / Bold
Breach / Breech
Breech / Breach
Brewed / Brood
Bridal / Bridle
Bridle / Bridal
Briton / Britain
Broach / Brooch
Brooch / Broach
Browse / Brows
Bruise / Brews
Callus / Callous
Cannes / Can
Cannon / Canon
Canvas / Canvass
Carrot / Carat
Caster / Castor
Castor / Caster

Caught / Court
Cellar / Seller
Censer / Censor
Censor / Censer
Cereal / Serial
Chased / Chaste
Chaste / Chased
Chilli / Chilly
Chilly / Chilli
Choler / Collar
Choose / Chews
Citrus / Citrous
Claude / Clawed
Clause / Claws
Clawed / Claude
Coarse / Course
Collar / Choler
Conker / Conquer
Cookie / Kooky
Copped / Copt
Corral / Chorale
Course / Coarse
Cousin / Cozen
Coward / Cowered
Crewed / Crude
Cruise / Crews
Cygnet / Signet
Cymbal / Symbol
Cyprus / Cypress
Denary / Deanery
Desert / Dessert
Dollar / Dolour
Dolour / Dollar
Ducked / Duct
Elicit / Illicit
Ensure / Insure
Ernest / Earnest
Eyelet / Islet
Father / Farther
Fillip / Philip
Fisher / Fissure
Flecks / Flex
Flocks / Phlox
Floury / Flowery
Flower / Flour
Foaled / Fold
Freeze / Frieze
Frieze / Freeze
Gallop / Gallup
Gallup / Gallop
Gamble / Gambol

Gambol / Gamble
Geezer / Geyser
Geyser / Geezer
Gilder / Guilder
Grater / Greater
Groyne / Groin
Hangar / Hanger
Hanger / Hangar
Hansom /
Handsome
Heroin / Heroine
Higher / Hire
Hoarse / Horse
Hookah / Hooker
Hooker / Hookah
Insure / Ensure
Invade / Inveighed
Kernel / Colonel
Knight / Night
Laager / Lager
Leader / Lieder
Leased / Least
Lessen / Lesson
Lesson / Lessen
Lichen / Liken
Lieder / Leader
Lumbar / Lumber
Lumber / Lumbar
Manner / Manor
Marque / Mark
Marten / Martin
Martin / Marten
Masque / Mask
Meddle / Medal
Medlar / Meddler
Mettle / Metal
Missed / Mist
Mousse / Moose
Mucous / Mucus
Muscle / Mussel
Mussed / Must
Mussel / Muscle
Oriole / Aureole
Packed / Pact
Pallet / Palette
Passed / Past
Patten / Pattern
Peddle / Pedal
Pedlar / Peddler
Petrel / Petrol
Petrol / Petrel

Philip / Fillip
Phrase / Frays
Pistil / Pistol
Pistol / Pistil
Plaice / Place
Please / Pleas
Pouffe / Poof
Praise / Prays
Profit / Prophet
Puttee / Putty
Quarts / Quartz
Quartz / Quarts
Racket / Racquet
Ranker / Rancour
Revere / Revers
Revers / Revere
Review / Revue
Rheims / Reams
Rhodes / Roads
Rigger / Rigour
Rigour / Rigger
Ringer / Wringer
Roomer / Rumour
Rumour / Roomer
Savour / Saver
Schema / Schemer
Seaman / Semen
Seller / Cellar
Serial / Cereal
Sighed / Side
Signet / Cygnet
Sleigh / Slay
Slight / Sleight
Soared / Sword
Sought / Sort
Source / Sauce
Spayed / Spade
Stayed / Staid
Steppe / Step
Sticks / Styx
Storey / Story
Strait / Straight
Sucker / Succour
Sundae / Sunday
Sunday / Sundae
Symbol / Cymbal
Tacked / Tact
Taught / Taut
Tenner / Tenor
They're / Their
Throne / Thrown

Homophones

Thrown / Throne
Tolled / Told
Torque / Talk
Troupe / Troop
Venous / Venus
Waists / Wastes
Waiver / Waver
Warred / Ward
Wastes / Waists
Weight / Wait
Welled / Weld
Wether / Whether
Whacks / Wax
Wither / Whither
Wrecks / Rex
Wretch / Retch
Wright / Right

7 letters:

Allowed / Aloud
Aureole / Oriole
Bearing / Baring
Boarder / Border
Boulder / Bolder
Britain / Briton
Callous / Callus
Canvass / Canvas
Ceiling / Sealing
Cession / Session
Charred / Chard
Chorale / Corral
Citrous / Citrus
Clanger / Clangour
Coarser / Courser
Colonel / Kernel
Conquer / Conker
Council / Counsel
Counsel / Council
Courser / Coarser
Cowered / Coward
Cubical / Cubicle
Cubicle / Cubical
Currant / Current
Current / Currant
Cypress / Cyprus
Deanery / Denary
Derrick / Derek
Descent / Dissent
Dessert / Desert
Dissent / Descent
Draught / Draft

Drawers / Draws
Earnest / Ernest
Elusive / Illusive
Farther / Father
Fissure / Fisher
Flowery / Floury
Gorilla / Guerrilla
Greater / Grater
Greaves / Grieves
Grieves / Greaves
Guessed / Guest
Guilder / Gilder
Heroine / Heroin
Humerus /
  Humorous
Illicit / Elicit
Literal / Littoral
Manikin /
  Mannequin
Marshal / Martial
Martial / Marshal
Meddler / Medlar
Morning /
  Mourning
Mustard /
  Mustered
Nightly / Knightly
Palette / Pallet
Pattern / Patten
Peddler / Pedlar
Pervade / Purveyed
Prophet / Profit
Racquet / Racket
Radical / Radicle
Radicle / Radical
Rancour / Ranker
Reining / Reigning
Schemer / Schema
Sealing / Ceiling
Session / Cession
Slaying / Sleighing
Sleight / Slight
Storied / Storeyed
Succour / Sucker
Summary /
  Summery
Summery /
  Summary
Through / Threw
Tighten / Titan
Trooper / Trouper

Trouper / Trooper
Trussed / Trust
Weather / Wether
Weighed / Wade
Whether / Wether
Whirled / World
Whither / Wither
Wrapped / Rapt
Wringer / Ringer

8 letters:

Brighten / Brighton
Brighton / Brighten
Clangour / Clanger
Discreet / Discrete
Discrete / Discreet
Formally /
  Formerly
Formerly /
  Formally
Handsome /
  Hansom
Humorous /
  Humerus
Illusive / Elusive
Knightly / Nightly
Lineally / Linearly
Linearly / Lineally
Littoral / Literal
Mourning /
  Morning
Mustered /
  Mustard
Overseas /
  Oversees
Oversees /
  Overseas
Populace /
  Populous
Populous /
  Populace
Purveyed / Pervade
Reigning / Reining
Sterling / Stirling
Stirling / Sterling
Storeyed / Storied
Straight / Strait
Windlass /
  Windless
Windless /
  Windlass

9 letters:
Guerrilla / Gorilla
Inveighed / Invade
Lightning / Lightening
Mannequin / Manikin
Principal / Principle
Principle / Principal
Sleighing / Slaying
Veracious / Voracious
Voracious / Veracious

Councillor / Counsellor
Counsellor / Councillor
Indiscreet / Indiscrete
Indiscrete / Indiscreet
Lightening / Lightning
Stationary / Stationery
Stationery / Stationary

10 letters:
Complement / Compliment
Compliment / Complement

13 letters:
Complementary /
  Complimentary
Complimentary /
  Complementary

Hoods

4 letters:
Coif
Cope
Cowl

5 letters:
Amaut
Amice
Amowt
Pixie
Snood

6 letters:
Almuce
Apache
Biggin
Calash
Mantle

7 letters:
Bashlik
Calèche
Capuche
Jacobin

8 letters:
Calyptra
Capeline
Capuccio
Chaperon
Trot-cozy

9 letters:
Balaclava
Chaperone
Trot-cosey

Hormones

3 letters:
Sex

5 letters:
Auxin
Kinin

6 letters:
Growth

7 letters:
Gastrin
Inhibin
Insulin
Relaxin
Steroid
Thyroid

8 letters:
Androgen

Autacoid
Bursicon
Ecdysone
Estrogen
Florigen
Glucagon
Juvenile
Oestriol
Oestrone
Oxytocin
Secretin
Thymosin

9 letters:
Adrenalin®
Corticoid
Cortisone
Cytokinin

Endocrine
Melatonin
Oestrogen
Prolactin
Secretion
Serotonin
Thyroxine

10 letters:
Adrenaline
Calcitonin
Intermedin
Lactogenic
Lipotropin
Oestradiol

11 letters:
Aldosterone
Angiotensin

Horses

Epinephrine
Gibberellin
Luteinizing
Parathyroid
Progestogen
Somatomedin
Thyrotropin
Vasopressin

12 letters:
Androsterone
Antidiuretic
Biosynthesis
Corpus luteum
Gonadotropin
Luteotrophin
Noradrenalin
Pancreozymin
Progesterone
Secretagogue
Somatostatin
Somatotropin
Stilboestrol
Testosterone
Thyrotrophin

13 letters:
Gonadotrophic
Gonadotrophin
Noradrenaline
Prostaglandin
Somatotrophin

14 letters:
Corticosteroid
Corticosterone
Enterogastrone
Erythropoietin
Hydrocortisone

15 letters:
Cholecystokinin
Gibberellic acid

16 letters:
Triiodothyronine

18 letters:
Thyroid-stimulating

19 letters:
Deoxycorticosterone
Follicle-stimulating

20 letters:
Adrenocorticotrophic

22 letters:
Chorionic gonadotrophin

26 letters:
Trichlorophenoxyacetic acid

27 letters:
Interstitial-cell-stimulating
Luteinizing hormone-releasing

Horses

TYPES/BREEDS OF HORSE

2 letters:
Kt

3 letters:
Ass
Bay
Cob
Don
Dun
Nag
Pad
Pot
Rip
Tit

4 letters:
Arab
Aver
Barb
Colt
Dale
Deli
Fell
Foal
Hack
Jade
Mare
Plug
Pole

Pony
Post
Prad
Roan
Shan
Snow
Stud
Taki
Turk
Weed
Wild
Yale
Yaud

5 letters:
Airer
Arion
Arkle
Batak
Bevis
Bidet
Borer
Caple
Capul
Crock
Favel
Filly
Genet
Huçul
Iomud
Konik
Lokai
Morel
Neddy
Night
Pacer
Pinto
Poler
Punch
Rogue
Screw
Seian
Shire
Spiti
Steed
Tacky
Takhi
Waler
Wheel
White
Zebra

6 letters:
Ambler
Basuto
Bayard
Breton
Bronco
Brumby
Calico
Canuck
Cayuse
Chaser
Cooser
Crollo

Curtal
Cusser
Danish
Exmoor
Favell
Garran
Garron
Gennet
Gidran
Hogget
Hunter
Jennet
Kanuck
Keffel
Lampos
Morgan
Mudder
Nonius
Novice
Pad-nag
Plater
Poster
Quagga
Randem
Remuda
Roarer
Rouncy
Runner
Sabino
Saddle
Shagya
Sorrel
Stayer
String
Summer
Tandem
Tarpan
Tracer
Vanner
Viatka

7 letters:
Beetewk
Bobtail
Burmese
Cavalry
Charger
Clipper
Courser
Cow pony
Criollo

Cuisser
Dappled
Eclipse
Eventer
Finnish
Flemish
Gelding
Hackney
Hobbler
Jutland
Kabarda
Klepper
Liberty
Manipur
Marengo
Marocco
Marwari
Morocco
Mustang
Palfrey
Piebald
Quarter
Rhenish
Saddler
Sheltie
Shirazi
Smudish
Spanker
Starter
Strelet
Suffolk
Sumpter
Swallow
Swinger
Trigger
Trooper
Walking
Wheeler
Yamoote
Zeeland
Zmudzin

8 letters:
Aquiline
Ardennes
Balearic
Bangtail
Bathorse
Boerperd
Camargue
Clay-bank

Horses

Cocktail
Dartmoor
Destrier
Eohippus
Fell pony
Friesian
Galloway
Gulf Arab
Highland
Holstein
Hyperion
Karabair
Karabakh
Karadagh
Kochlani
Limousin
Lusitano
Palomino
Polo pony
Schimmel
Shetland
Skewbald
Sleipnir
Springer
Stalking
Stallion
Stibbler
Turkoman
Warhorse
Warragal
Warragle
Warragul
Warregal
Warrigal
Welsh Cob
Whistler
Yarraman
Yearling

9 letters:
Akhal-Teke
Anglo-Arab
Appaloosa
Black Bess
Brabançon
Caballine
Carthorse
Clavileno
Coldblood

Connemara
Dales pony
Drayhorse
Esthonian
Fjord pony
Gringolet
Groningen
Houyhnhnm
Icelandic
Kladruber
Knabstrup
Miohippus
Mongolian
Oldenburg
Packhorse
Percheron
Pinzgauer
Racehorse
Rosinante
Rozinante
Schleswig
Tarbenian
Timor pony
Trakehner
Warmblood
Welsh pony
Workhorse

10 letters:
Andalusian
Bloodstock
Bucephalus
Buckjumper
Buttermilk
Clydesdale
Copenhagen
Gelderland
Hafflinger
Hanoverian
Kathiawari
Lipizzaner
Lippizaner
Pliohippus
Polish Arab
Przewalski
Show jumper
Stockhorse
Svadilfari
Zemaitukas

11 letters:
Anglo-Norman
High-stepper
Iceland pony
Mecklenburg
Merychippus
Persian Arab
Przewalski's
Running mate

12 letters:
Cleveland Bay
Dartmoor pony
Dutch Draught
Gudbrandsdal
Hambletonian
Highland pony
North Swedish
Orlov Trotter
Shetland pony
Standard Bred
Suffolk Punch
Thoroughbred

13 letters:
Hyracotherium
Kurdistan pony
New Forest pony
Russian saddle
Spanish Jennet
Stalking-horse

14 letters:
American Saddle
Polish Half-bred
Yorkshire Coach

15 letters:
American Quarter
Orlov Rostopchin
Swedish Ardennes

16 letters:
Tennessee Walking

17 letters:
Welsh Mountain
pony

18 letters:
Polish
Thoroughbred

LEGENDARY/FICTIONAL/HISTORICAL HORSES

5 letters:
Boxer

6 letters:
Bayard
Flicka
Silver

7 letters:
Pegasus
Trigger

8 letters:
Champion
Hercules
Mister Ed
Sleipnir
Traveler

9 letters:
Black Bess
El Fideldo

Incitatus
Rosinante

10 letters:
Bucephalus

11 letters:
Black Beauty

HORSE COLOURS

3 letters:
Bay
Dun

4 letters:
Grey
Roan

5 letters:
Black
Cream
Mealy

Pinto

6 letters:
Albino
Dapple
Sorrel

7 letters:
Piebald

8 letters:
Blue roan
Chestnut

Claybank
Palomino
Skewbald

10 letters:
Dapplegrey
Fleabitten

14 letters:
Strawberry roan

HORSE MARKINGS

4 letters:
Snip
Sock
Star

5 letters:
Blaze

6 letters:
Stripe

7 letters:
Coronet

8 letters:
Stocking

9 letters:
White face

HORSE GAITS

4 letters:
Lope
Pace
Rack
Trot
Walk

5 letters:
Amble

6 letters:
Canter
Gallop
Prance

7 letters:
Jog trot

10 letters:
Rising trot

Single-foot

11 letters:
Sitting trot

12 letters:
Extended trot

Horses

HORSE PARTS

3 letters:
Bar
Haw
Toe

4 letters:
Back
Dock
Frog
Heel
Hock
Hoof
Mane
Neck
Poll
Sole
Tail
Tusk
Wall

5 letters:
Croup
Ergot
Flank
Loins

Shank

6 letters:
Barrel
Croupe
Gaskin
Haunch
Muzzle
Saddle
Sheath

7 letters:
Brisket
Counter
Forearm
Foreleg
Gambrel
Off-fore
Off-hind
Pastern
Quarter
Shannon
Withers

8 letters:
Buttress

Chestnut
Coupling
Diagonal
Forehand
Forelock
Near-fore
Near-hind

9 letters:
Hamstring
White line

10 letters:
Cannon bone
Chin groove
Coffin bone
Splint bone

11 letters:
Coronet band
Second thigh
Stifle joint

12 letters:
Fetlock joint
Forequarters

PEOPLE ASSOCIATED WITH HORSES

3 letters:
Lad

5 letters:
Coper
Groom
Rider

6 letters:
Buster
Cowboy
Hussar
Jockey
Knight
Ostler

7 letters:
Cavalry

Currier
Equerry
Equites
Farrier
Knacker
Picador
Rustler
Saddler
Trainer

8 letters:
Cavalier
Coachman
Horseman
Wrangler

9 letters:
Caballero

Chevalier
Postilion
Postrider
Stable lad

10 letters:
Equestrian
Horsewoman
Jockey Club
Roughrider

12 letters:
Broncobuster
Equestrienne

14 letters:
Horse whisperer

TACK AND EQUIPMENT AND THEIR PARTS

3 letters:
Bar
Bit

4 letters:
Bard
Boot
Curb
Flap
Rein
Spur
Tack
Wisp

5 letters:
Barde
Cinch
Girth
Plate
Skirt
Trace

6 letters:
Bridle
Cantle
Day rug
Gag-bit
Halter
Numnah
Pelham
Pommel
Roller
Saddle
Twitch

7 letters:
Bridoon
Crupper
Curb bit
Gambado
Harness
Kneecap
Nosebag
Snaffle
Stirrup

Trammel

8 letters:
Blinkers
Browband
Cavesson
Chamfron
Hockboot
Hoof pick
Lip strap
Mane comb
Night rug
Noseband
Saddlery
Sliphead
Tail comb

9 letters:
Body brush
Breeching
Check rein
Curb chain
Curb reins
Curry comb
Front arch
Headpiece
Horseshoe
Nosepiece
Overcheck
Pad saddle
Saddlebag
Surcingle
Tailguard
Trappings

10 letters:
Cheek-piece
Crownpiece
Dandy brush
Girth strap
Kimblewick
Martingale
Sidesaddle
Snaffle bit
Stirrup bar

Throatlash
Water brush

11 letters:
Bearing rein
Breastplate
Saddlecloth
Stirrup iron
Summer sheet
Swingletree
Tail bandage
Throatlatch
Whiffletree
Whippletree

12 letters:
Anti-sweat rug
Double bridle
Plain snaffle
Stable rubber
Sweat scraper
Underblanket

13 letters:
Fulmer snaffle
New Zealand rug

14 letters:
Hackamore plate
Stirrup leather
Twisted snaffle

15 letters:
Weymouth curb
 bit

16 letters:
Split-eared bridle

20 letters:
Double-jointed
 snaffle

21 letters:
Jointed egg-butt
 snaffle

Household items

HORSES, RHINOS AND OTHER PERISSODACTYLS

3 letters:
Ass

4 letters:
Mule

5 letters:
Horse
Kiang
Kulan
Tapir

See also:
➤ **Races**

Zebra

6 letters:
Donkey
Onager

7 letters:
Keitloa

8 letters:
Chigetai

Elephant

9 letters:
Dziggetai

10 letters:
Rhinoceros

13 letters:
White elephant

Household items

3 letters:
Bib
Box
Cup
Fan
Gas
Hob
Jar
Key
Log
Mop
Mug
Pan
Peg
Pot
Rug
Tap
Tin

4 letters:
Beam
Bell
Bowl
Bulb
Case
Coal
Dish
Door
Ewer
Flue
Fork
Fuel

Gong
Hi-fi
Hose
Iron
Jamb
Lamp
Lift
Lock
Oven
Pail
Pipe
Plug
Safe
Sash
Seat
Sink
Soap
Soda
Sofa
Spit
Tank
Tidy
Tile
Tray
Vase
Zarf

5 letters:
Apron
Ashet
Basin
Bench

Besom
Bidet
Blind
Board
Broil
Brush
Caddy
Chore
Cigar
Clock
Cloth
Cover
Crock
Cruet
Cruse
Diota
Doily
Duvet
Flask
Frame
Glass
Grate
Hinge
Juice
Knife
Ladle
Latch
Linen
Mixer
Mural
Paint

Household items

Panel
Poker
Quilt
Radio
Sheet
Shelf
Sieve
Spoon
Stove
Straw
Timer
Tongs
Torch
Towel
Trunk
Whisk

6 letters:
Aerial
Ash-bin
Ash-can
Awning
Basket
Beaker
Biggin
Bleach
Bluing
Boiler
Bucket
Bunker
Burner
Candle
Caster
Coffer
Colmar
Cooker
Cradle
Damper
Dishes
Dolium
Drawer
Duster
Egg-cup
Fender
Fiasco
Fingan
Flacon
Flagon
Fridge
Frieze
Gas-jet

Gas tap
Geyser
Grater
Hamper
Handle
Hearth
Heater
Ice-box
Jumble
Kaross
Kettle
Ladder
Lagena
Lintel
Locker
Log bin
Louvre
Mangle
Menage
Mincer
Mobile
Napkin
Patina
Pelmet
Pillow
Plaque
Polish
Pouffe
Pulley
Rhyton
Salver
Saucer
Scales
Sconce
Shovel
Shower
Skewer
Sponge
Starch
String
Switch
Teapot
Teaset
Tea-urn
Toy box
Trivet
Tureen
Vessel
Washer
Window
Wiring

7 letters:
Adaptor
Amphora
Ashtray
Bath tub
Bedding
Blanket
Bolster
Bouquet
Cake tin
Canteen
Ceiling
Chalice
Chamois
Chimney
Chopper
Cistern
Cleaver
Coaster
Coconut
Crystal
Cushion
Cutlery
Deed box
Dish mop
Doorway
Dustbin
Dust-pan
Faience
Fitting
Fixture
Furbish
Furnace
Fuse box
Gas-ring
Griddle
Hammock
Heating
Hickory
High tea
Hip bath
Holdall
Keyhole
Lacquer
Lagging
Lantern
Lattice
Matches
Oil lamp
Overall
Padella

Household items

Parquet
Pass-key
Pie-dish
Pitcher
Platter
Play pen
Pottery
Ramekin
Roaster
Samovar
Sanctum
Service
Serving
Shelves
Skillet
Spatula
Spy-hole
Stamnos
Steamer
Stewpot
Sundial
Sweeper
Tankard
Tea-cosy
Tea tray
Thermos
Thimble
Ticking
Toaster
Toby jug
Tool kit
Transom
Trellis
Trolley
Tumbler
Utensil
Valance
Varnish
Washday
Washtub
Worktop
Wringer

8 letters:
Atomiser
Ballcock
Barbecue
Bassinet
Bath cube
Bath soap
Bed cover

Bed linen
Bell pull
Billy can
Bird bath
Bookends
Cache-pot
Canister
Casement
Cauldron
Cigar box
Colander
Coverlet
Cream jug
Crockery
Cupboard
Cuspidor
Cut glass
Decanter
Doorbell
Doorknob
Doorpost
Doorstep
Doorstop
Driptray
Eggslice
Eggspoon
Eggtimer
Eggwhisk
Emulsion
Fanlight
Filament
Fireside
Firewood
Fixtures
Flat iron
Flour bin
Fly paper
Food-mill
Fuse-wire
Gallipot
Gas-meter
Handbell
Handrail
Hangings
Hip flask
Hollands
Homespun
Hot-plate
Immerser
Jelly bag
Jewel box

Kickshaw
Kindling
Linoleum
Matchbox
Mattress
Meatsafe
Monogram
Moth ball
Moulding
New broom
Ornament
Ovenware
Painting
Pannakin
Paraffin
Patty pan
Pendulum
Pipe rack
Polisher
Portrait
Pot plant
Radiator
Rosebowl
Saucepan
Scissors
Scrubber
Shoehorn
Shredder
Shutters
Side-door
Sink unit
Sitz bath
Skylight
Slop bowl
Slop pail
Snuff box
Soap dish
Soapsuds
Soft soap
Solarium
Spice jar
Spittoon
Squeezer
Strainer
Sunblind
Surround
Tablemat
Tapestry
Tea chest
Tea cloth
Teaspoon

Trapdoor
Underlay
Wainscot
Water jug
Water tap
Wig-block
Wireless
Yale lock

9 letters:
Ansaphone
Auto-timer
Baking tin
Barometer
Bath salts
Bath towel
Bay window
Bedspread
Beer glass
Blank door
Cakestand
Cantharus
Casserole
Chandlier
Chinaware
Cigarette
Clepsydra
Coffee cup
Container
Corkscrew
Crossbeam
Cullender
Demitasse
Desk light
Detergent
Directory
Dishcloth
Dish towel
Distemper
Dog basket
Doorplate
Drainpipe
Dust-sheet
Dutch oven
Dutch wife
Egg beater
Egg slicer
Eiderdown
Facecloth
Face towel
Fire alarm

Fireguard
Fire irons
Firelight
Fireplace
Fish knife
Fish slice
Flower pot
Foodmixer
Front door
Fruit bowl
Fruit dish
Frying pan
Gas burner
Gas cooker
Girandole
Glass door
Gold plate
Gravy boat
Hand towel
Hourglass
Housewife
Housework
Japanning
Jewel case
Joss-stick
Lamplight
Lampshade
Lampstand
Letterbox
Light bulb
Log basket
Loving cup
Master key
Mousetrap
Objet d'art
Panelling
Partition
Patchwork
Phone book
Pie-funnel
Place-card
Porcelain
Porringer
Punchbowl
Radiogram
Safety pin
Salad bowl
Sauceboat
Serviette
Shakedown
Shoeblack

Shower cap
Side light
Silver-wax
Slop basin
Soup plate
Soup spoon
Spin-drier
Sponge-bag
Staircase
Statuette
Steam iron
Steel wool
Storm door
Stovepipe
Sugar bowl
Swing door
Table lamp
Tableware
Tea kettle
Tea-waggon
Telephone
Threshold
Timepiece
Tinder-box
Tin opener
Toast-rack
Toilet bag
Underfelt
Wall clock
Wall light
Wallpaper
Washbasin
Washboard
Water butt
Water cock
Water pipe
Water tank
Wax polish
Whitewash
Window box
Wine glass

10 letters:
Abstergent
Alarm clock
Anthracite
Apple-cover
Baking bowl
Baking tray
Bedclothes
Bedsprings

Household items

Bellarmine
Boot polish
Bread board
Breadknife
Butter dish
Candelabra
Cassolette
Chafing pan
Chopsticks
Clothes peg
Coal-bucket
Coal-bunker
Coat-hanger
Coffee mill
Curtain rod
Deep-freeze
Dinner gong
Dishwasher
Doorhandle
Drawing pin
Dutch clock
Featherbed
Finger bowl
Fire-basket
Fire-escape
Firescreen
Fish kettle
Floor-cloth
Forcing bag
Fruit-knife
Glass-cloth
Gramophone
Grand piano
Hollow ware
Knickknack
Lamp socket
Letter-rack
Loose cover
Matchstick
Milk bottle
Mixing bowl
Musical box
Mustard pot
Napkin ring
Night-light
Nutcracker
Oven gloves
Paint-brush
Paper knife
Pepper mill
Percolator

Persian rug
Persiennes
Photograph
Pillowcase
Pillow slip
Pilot light
Pin cushion
Plate glass
Plate piece
Pot scourer
Pot scraper
Power point
Rain barrel
Ration book
Rolling pin
Rose-window
Salt cellar
Sealing wax
Silverware
Soap flakes
Soap powder
Spirit lamp
Step ladder
Storage jar
Strip-light
Tablecloth
Table-knife
Table-linen
Tablespoon
Tea service
Television
Thermostat
Time-switch
Tobacco jar
Toilet roll
Toilet soap
Toothbrush
Toothpaste
Transistor
Trinket box
Vanity lamp
Ventilator
Waffle-iron
Wall-socket
Warming pan
Washbasket
Wassai bowl
Watchglass
Water clock
Whisk broom
Window-pane

Window-sash
Window-seat
Window-sill
Wine basket
Wine bottle
Wine cooler
Wooden ware
Work basket
Worry beads

11 letters:
Airtight jar
Baking sheet
Broom handle
Butter-knife
Candelabrum
Candlestick
Centrepiece
Chafing dish
Cheese board
China figure
Chinoiserie
Clothes line
Clothes pole
Coal scuttle
Cookery book
Cooling tray
Counterpane
Cuckoo clock
Curtain hook
Curtain rail
Curtain ring
Dessert fork
Door-knocker
Earthenware
Eating irons
Elbowgrease
Family album
Firelighter
First-aid box
Floor polish
French chalk
Garden party
Garden swing
Hearth brush
Kitchen sink
Kitchen unit
Laundry room
Light switch
Linen basket
Loving spoon

Mantelpiece
Meat chopper
Meat cleaver
Metal polish
Non-stick pan
Oil painting
Oriental rug
Paperweight
Picture rail
Plant-holder
Pocket flask
Primus stove
Pudding bowl
Pumice stone
Record album
Roasting tin
Rotary whisk
Sauce bottle
Scouring pad
Serving dish
Shopping bag
Shower-cloth
Silver plate
Silver spoon
Skeleton key
Sliding door
Spring clean
Storm window
Table napkin
Tape measure
Tea-strainer
Thermometer
Vacuum flask
Vinaigrette
Washing line
Washing soap
Washing soda
Water closet
Water heater
Window blind
Window frame
Window-light
Wintergreen
Wooden spoon
Work-surface
Wrought iron

12 letters:
Adhesive tape
Antimacassar
Apron-strings

Ball of string
Bedside light
Bottle-opener
Bottom drawer
Bread curtain
Candleholder
Candle-sconce
Carpet beater
Carriage lamp
Carving-knife
Cheese-grater
Chiming clock
Chimney piece
Chimney-stack
Cigarette box
Clothes-brush
Clothes-drier
Clothes-horse
Companion set
Convex mirror
Cooking range
Dessert spoon
Disinfectant
Double boiler
Electric fire
Electric iron
Electric lamp
Extractor fan
Firelighters
Fireside seat
Flower holder
French polish
Hot water tank
Ironing board
Kettle-holder
Labour-saving
Light fitting
Looking-glass
Lunch counter
Magazine rack
Mulligatawny
Paraffin lamp
Passe-partout
Perambulator
Picnic basket
Picnic hamper
Picture frame
Place-setting
Pudding basin
Radiant plate
Record-player

Reel of cotton
Reel of thread
Refrigerator
Serving hatch
Serving spoon
Stain remover
Standard lamp
Swizzle stick
Table lighter
Table service
Talcum powder
Tape-recorder
Thermos flask
Toasting fork
Turkish towel
User-friendly
Visiting card
Washing board
Washing cloth

13 letters:
Backscratcher
Blanket stitch
Blotting paper
Candle snuffer
Carpet sweeper
Carriage clock
Chopping-block
Chopping-board
Clothes basket
Cocktail stick
Darning-needle
Dinner service
Draught screen
Electric mixer
Electric razor
Emulsion paint
Feather duster
Fire-resistant
Food processor
Household gods
Hurricane lamp
Lawn sprinkler
Microwave oven
Mowing-machine
Petrol lighter
Pinking-shears
Preserving-pan
Saratoga trunk
Sewing-machine
Smoothing iron

Humours of the body

Soldering iron
Storage heater
Vacuum-cleaner
Venetian blind
Washing powder
Water softener

14 letters:
Cartridge-paper
Casement-window
Central heating
Chinese lantern
Cocktail shaker
Coconut-matting
Corrugated iron
Cut-throat razor

Electric cooker
Electric kettle
Electric shaver
Hot-water bottle
Hot-water system
Household goods
Household linen
Insulating tape
Kitchen utensil
Knitting-needle
Knives and forks
Luncheon basket
Pair of scissors
Patchwork quilt
Pressure-cooker

Scrubbing-brush
Spring cleaning
Spring mattress
Washing-machine

15 letters:
Cigarette holder
Combination lock
Corrugated paper
Electric blanket
Electric toaster
Immersion heater
Knitting-machine
Pencil sharpener
Photograph album
Weighing machine

Humours of the body

5 letters:
Blood

6 letters:
Phlegm

9 letters:
Black bile

10 letters:
Yellow bile

Huts

4 letters:
Shed
Skeo
Skio
Tilt

5 letters:
Banda
Booth
Bothy
Cabin
Hogan
Humpy
Igloo
Shack
Sheal
Shiel
Wilja

6 letters:
Bothie
Bustee
Chalet
Gunyah
Mia-mia
Nissen
Pondok
Rancho
Shanty
Succah
Sukkah
Tolsel
Tolsey
Tolzey
Wigwam
Wikiup

Wiltja
Wurley

7 letters:
Choltry
Quonset®
Shebang
Wanigan
Wickiup

8 letters:
Rondavel
Shealing
Shieling
Wannigan

9 letters:
Pondokkie
Rancheria

Hydrocarbons

3 letters:
Wax

5 letters:
Alkyl
Arene
Diene
Gutta
Halon
Hexyl
Phene
Xylol

6 letters:
Aldrin
Alkane
Alkene
Alkyne
Butane
Butene
Cetane
Cubane
Decane
Dioxin
Ethane
Hexane
Hexene
Indene

Nonane
Octane
Pinene
Pyrene
Retene
Xylene

7 letters:
Amylene
Benzene
Heptane
Ligroin
Naphtha
Olefine
Pentane
Pentene
Polyene
Propane
Styrene
Terpene
Toluene

8 letters:
Camphane
Camphene
Carotene
Diphenyl
Hexylene

Isoprene
Limonene
Paraffin
Squalene
Stilbene
Triptane

9 letters:
Acetylene
Butadiene
Isobutane
Isooctane
Pentylene

10 letters:
Asphaltite
Mesitylene

11 letters:
Cycloalkane
Cyclohexane
Hatchettite
Naphthalene

12 letters:
Cyclopropane
Phenanthrene

15 letters:
Cyclopentadiene

Inflammations

3 letters:
Sty

4 letters:
Acne
Noma
Stye

5 letters:
Croup
Felon

6 letters:
Ancome
Angina
Bunion
Eczema
Garget
Iritis
Otitis
Quinsy
Thrush
Ulitis

7 letters:
Colitis
Ecthyma
Founder
Ignatis
Onychia
Pinkeye
Prurigo
Sunburn
Sycosis
Tylosis
Whitlow

8 letters:
Adenitis
Aortisis
Bursitis
Carditis

Cystisis
Fibrosis
Hyalitis
Mastitis
Metritis
Mycetoma
Myelitis
Myositis
Neuritis
Orchitis
Osteitis
Ovaritis
Phlegmon
Pleurisy
Pyelitis
Rachitis
Rhinitis
Uvulitis
Windburn

9 letters:
Arteritis
Arthritis
Balanitis
Cheilitis
Enteritis
Gastritis
Glossitis
Keratitis
Laminitis
Nephritis
Parotitis
Phlebitis
Phrenitis
Pneumonia
Proctitis
Pyorrhoea
Retinitis
Scleritis
Sinusitis

Splenitis
Strumitis
Synovitis
Typhlitis
Vaginitis

10 letters:
Asbestosis
Bronchitis
Cellulitis
Cervicitis
Dermatitis
Erysipelas
Fibrositis
Gingivitis
Hepatitis A
Hepatitis B
Intertrigo
Laryngitis
Meningitis
Oophoritis
Ophthalmia
Paronychia
Phlegmasia
Stomatitis
Tendinitis
Thrombosis
Tracheitis
Urethritis
Valvulitis
Vasculitis

11 letters:
Blepharitis
Farmer's lung
Mastoiditis
Myocarditis
Peritonitis
Pharyngitis
Prostatitis
Salpingitis

Shin splints
Spondylitis
Thoroughpin
Thyroiditis
Tonsillitis

12 letters:
Appendicitis
Encephalitis
Endocarditis
Folliculitis
Mesenteritis
Osteoporosis
Pancreatitis
Pericarditis

Polyneuritis
Swimmer's itch

13 letters:
Enterocolitis
Labyrinthitis
Osteomyelitis
Perihepatitis
Perinephritis
Periodontisis
Perityphlitis
Tenosynovitis

14 letters:
Conjunctivitis

Diverticulitis
Osteoarthritis
Vincent's angina

15 letters:
Gastroenteritis

16 letters:
Bronchopneumonia

17 letters:
Encephalomyelitis
Meningocephalitis

Inhabitants

Place	Inhabitant
Aberdeen	Aberdonian
Afghanistan	Afghan
Alabama	Alabaman *or* Alabamian
Alaska	Alaskan
Albania	Albanian
Alberta	Albertan
Algeria	Algerian
Alsace	Alsatian
American continent	American
American Samoa	American Samoan
Amsterdam	Amsterdammer
Anatolia	Anatolian
Andorra	Andorran
Angola	Angolan
Anjou	Angevin
Antigua	Antiguan
Argentina	Argentine *or* Argentinian
Arizona	Arizonan
Arkansas	Arkansan *or (informal)* Arkie
Armenia	Armenian
Asia	Asian
Assam	Assamese
Assyria	Assyrian
Australia	Australian *or (informal)* Aussie
Austria	Austrian
Azerbaijan	Azerbaijani *or* Azeri
Babylon	Babylonian
Bahamas	Bahamian
Bahrain	Bahraini
Bali	Balinese
Bangladesh	Bangladeshi

Inhabitants

Place	Inhabitant
Barbados	Barbadian, Bajan *(informal), or* Bim *(informal)*
Barbuda	Barbudan *or* Barbudian
Bavaria	Bavarian
Belarus *or* Byelorussia	Belarussian *or* Byelorussian
Belau	Belauan
Belgium	Belgian
Benin	Beninese *or* Beninois
Berlin	Berliner
Bhutan	Bhutanese
Birmingham	Brummie
Bohemia	Bohemian
Bolivia	Bolivian
Bordeaux	Bordelais
The Borders	Borderer
Bosnia	Bosnian
Boston	Bostonian *or (U.S. slang)* Bean-eater
Botswana	Botswanan
Brazil	Brazilian
Bristol	Bristolian
British Columbia	British Columbian
Brittany	Breton
Bulgaria	Bulgarian
Burgundy	Burgundian
Burkina-Faso	Burkinabe
Burma	Burmese
Burundi	Burundian
Byzantium	Byzantine
California	Californian
Cambodia	Cambodian
Cambridge	Cantabrigian
Cameroon	Cameroonian
Canada	Canadian *or (informal)* Canuck
Canada, Maritime Provinces	Downeaster
Cape Verde	Cape Verdean
Castile	Castilian
Catalonia	Catalan
The Caucasus	Caucasian
Cayman Islands	Cayman Islander
Chad	Chadian *or* Chadean
Chicago	Chicagoan
Chile	Chilean
China	Chinese
Circassia	Circassian
Colombia	Colombian
Colorado	Coloradan
Comoros Islands	Comorian
Connecticut	Nutmegger
Congo Republic	Congolese

Place	Inhabitant
Cork	Corkonian
Cornwall	Cornishman, Cornishwoman
Corsica	Corsican
Costa Rica	Costa Rican
Côte d'Ivoire	Ivorian *or* Ivorean
Croatia	Croat *or* Croatian
Cuba	Cuban
Cumbria	Cumbrian
Cyprus	Cypriot
Czechoslovakia	Czechoslovak *or* Czechoslovakian
Czech Republic	Czech
Delaware	Delawarean
Delphi	Pythian
Denmark	Dane
Devon	Devonian
Djibouti	Djiboutian *or* Djiboutien
Dominica	Dominican
Dominican Republic	Dominican
Dublin	Dubliner
Dundee	Dundonian
East Timor	East Timorese
Ecuador	Ecuadorean *or* Ecuadoran
Edinburgh	Edinburgher
Egypt	Egyptian
El Salvador	Salvadoran, Salvadorean, *or* Salvadorian
England	Englishman, Englishwoman
Ephesus	Ephesian
Equatorial Guinea	Equatorian
Eritrea	Eritrean
Estonia	Estonian
Ethiopia	Ethiopian
Europe	European
Euzkadi	Basque
Faeroe Islands	Faeroese
Falkland Islands	Falkland Islanders *or* Falklander
Fife	Fifer
Fiji	Fijian
Finland	Finn
Flanders	Fleming
Florence	Florentine
Florida	Floridian
France	Frenchman, Frenchwoman
French Guiana	Guianese
Friesland	Frisian
Friuili	Friulian
Gabon	Gabonese
Galicia	Galician
Galilee	Galilean
Galloway	Gallovidian

Inhabitants

Place	Inhabitant
Galway	Galwegian
Gambia	Gambian
Gascony	Gascon
Genoa	Genoese
Georgia (country)	Georgian
Georgia (U.S. state)	Georgian
Germany	German
Ghana	Ghanaian *or* Ghanian
Glasgow	Glaswegian
Greece	Greek
Greenland	Greenlander
Grenada	Grenadian
Guam	Guamanian
Guatemala	Guatemalan
Guinea	Guinean
Guyana	Guyanese *or* Guyanan
Haiti	Haitian
Havana	Habanero
Hawaii	Hawaiian
Hesse	Hessian
Honduras	Honduran
Hungary	Hungarian *or* Magyar
Hyderabad state	Mulki
Ibiza	Ibizan
Iceland	Icelander
Idaho	Idahoan
Illinois	Illinoian *or* Illinoisian
India	Indian
Indiana	Indianan, Indianian, *or* *(informal)* Hoosier
Indonesia	Indonesian
Iowa	Iowan
Iran	Iranian
Iraq	Iraqi
Ireland	Irishman, Irishwoman
Isle of Man	Manxman, Manxwoman
Israel	Israeli
Italy	Italian
Jamaica	Jamaican
Japan	Japanese
Java	Javanese
Jordan	Jordanian
Kansas	Kansan
Karelia	Karelian
Kazakhstan	Kazakh
Kent (East)	Man, Woman of Kent
Kent (West)	Kentish Man, Woman
Kentucky	Kentuckian
Kenya	Kenyan
Kirghizia	Kirghiz

Place	Inhabitant
Korea	Korean
Kuwait	Kuwaiti
Lancashire	Lancastrian
Lancaster	Lancastrian
Laos	Laotian
Latvia	Latvian *or* Lett
Lebanon	Lebanese
Liberia	Liberian
Libya	Libyan
Liechtenstein	Liechtensteiner
Lincolnshire	Yellow belly *(dialect)*
Lithuania	Lithuanian
Liverpool	Liverpudlian *or (informal)* Scouse *or* Scouser
Lombardy	Lombard
London	Londoner *or* Cockney
Los Angeles	Angeleno
Louisiana	Louisianan *or* Louisianian
Luxembourg	Luxembourger
Lyon	Lyonnais
Macao	Macaonese
Macedonia	Macedonian
Madagascar	Madagascan *or* Malagasy
Madrid	Madrileño, Madrileña
Maine	Mainer *or* Downeaster
Majorca	Majorcan
Malawi	Malawian
Malaya	Malayan
Malaysia	Malaysian
Maldive Islands	Maldivian
Malta	Maltese
Manchester	Mancunian
Manitoba	Manitoban
Marquesas Islands	Marquesan
Mars	Martian
Marseilles	Marsellais
Marshall Islands	Marshall Islander
Martinique	Martiniquean
Maryland	Marylander
Massachusetts	Bay Stater
Mauritania	Mauritanian
Mauritius	Mauritian
Melanesia	Melanesian
Melbourne	Melburnian
Mexico	Mexican
Michigan	Michigander, Michiganite, *or* Michiganian
Micronesia	Micronesian
Milan	Milanese
Minnesota	Minnesotan

Inhabitants

Place	Inhabitant
Mississippi	Mississippian
Missouri	Missourian
Moldavia	Moldavian
Monaco	Monegasque
Mongolia	Mongolian
Montana	Montanan
Montenegro	Montenegrin
Montserrat	Montserratian
Moravia	Moravian
Morocco	Moroccan
Moscow	Muscovite
Mozambique	Mozambican
Namibia	Namibian
Naples	Neapolitan
Nauru	Nauruan
Nebraska	Nebraskan
The Netherlands	Dutchman, Dutchwoman
New Brunswick	New Brunswicker
Newcastle upon Tyne	Geordie
New England	New Englander *or (informal)* Yankee *or* Downeaster
Newfoundland	Newfoundlander *or (informal)* Newfie
Newfoundland fishing village	Outporter
New Hampshire	New Hampshirite
New Jersey	New Jerseyan *or* New Jerseyite
New Mexico	New Mexican
New South Wales	New South Welshman, New South Welshwoman
New York	New Yorker *or* Knickerbocker
New Zealand	New Zealander *or (informal)* Kiwi *or* Enzedder
Nicaragua	Nicaraguan
Niger	Nigerien
Nigeria	Nigerian
Normandy	Norman
North Carolina	North Carolinian *or* Tarheel
North Dakota	North Dakotan
Northern Ireland	Northern Irishman, Northern Irishwoman
Northern Territory	Territorian
Northern Territory, northern part of	Top Ender
North Korea	North Korean
Northumbria	Northumbrian
Norway	Norwegian
Nova Scotia	Nova Scotian *or (informal)* Bluenose
Ohio	Ohioan
Okinawa	Okinawan

Place	Inhabitant
Oklahoma	Oklahoman *or (slang)* Okie
Oman	Omani
Ontario	Ontarian *or* Ontarioan
Oregon	Oregonian
Orkney	Orcadian
Oxford	Oxonian
Pakistan	Pakistani
Palestine	Palestinian
Panama	Panamanian
Papua New Guinea	Papua
Paraguay	Paraguayan
Paris	Parisian *or* Parisienne
Pennsylvania	Pennsylvanian
Persia	Persian
Perth	Perthite
Peru	Peruvian
The Philippines	Filipino
Poland	Pole
Pomerania	Pomeranian
Portugal	Portuguese
Prince Edward Island	Prince Edward Islander
Provence	Provençal
Prussia	Prussian
Puerto Rico	Puerto Rican
Qatar	Qatari
Quebec	Quebecer, Quebecker, *or* Quebecois
Queensland	Queenslander
Rhode Island	Rhode Islander
Rhodes	Rhodian
Rhodesia	Rhodesian
Rio de Janeiro	Cariocan
Romania	Romanian
Rome	Roman
Russian Federation	Russian
Ruthenia	Ruthenian
Rwanda	Rwandan
Samaria	Samaritan
San Marino	San Marinese *or* Sammarinese
Sardinia	Sardinian
Saskatchewan	Saskatchewanian
Saudi Arabia	Saudi *or* Saudi Arabian
Savoy	Savoyard
Saxony	Saxon
Scandinavia	Scandinavian
Scotland	Scot, Scotsman, Scotswoman, *or* Caledonian
Scottish Highlands	Highlander *or (old-fashioned)* Hielanman
Senegal	Senegalese

Inhabitants

Place	Inhabitant
Serbia	Serb *or* Serbian
Seychelles	Seychellois
Shetland	Shetlander
Sierra Leone	Sierra Leonean
Sind	Sindhi
Singapore	Singaporean
Slovakia	Slovak
Slovenia	Slovene *or* Slovenian
Solomon Islands	Solomon Islander
South Africa	South African
South Australia	South Australian *or (informal)* Croweater
South Carolina	South Carolinian
South Dakota	South Dakota
South Korea	South Korean
Spain	Spaniard
Sri Lanka	Sri Lankan
Sudan	Sudanese
Suriname	Surinamese
Swaziland	Swazi
Sweden	Swede
Switzerland	Swiss
Sydney	Sydneysider
Sydney, Western suburbs of	Westie
Syria	Syrian
Taiwan	Taiwanese
Tajikistan	Tajik
Tanzania	Tanzanian
Tasmania	Tasmanian *or (informal)* Tassie *or* Apple Islander
Tennessee	Tennessean
Texas	Texan
Thailand	Thai
Thessalonika	Thessalonian
Tibet	Tibetan
Togo	Togolese
Tonga	Tongan
Tobago	Tobagan *or* Tobagonian
Trinidad	Trinidadian
Troy	Trojan
Tunisia	Tunisian
Turkey	Turk
Turkmenistan	Turkmen
Tuscany	Tuscan
Tuvalu	Tuvaluan
Tyneside	Geordie
Tyre	Tyrian
Uganda	Ugandan
Ukraine	Ukrainian
Ulster	Ulsterman, Ulsterwoman

Place	Inhabitant
Umbria	Umbrian
United Kingdom	Briton, Brit *(informal)*, *or* Britisher
United States of America	American *or (informal)* Yank *or* Yankee
Uruguay	Uruguayan
Utah	Utahan *or* Utahn
Uzbekistan	Uzbek
Venezuela	Venezuelan
Venice	Venetian
Vermont	Vermonter
Victoria	Victorian
Vienna	Viennese
Vietnam	Vietnamese
Virginia	Virginian
Wales	Welshman, Welshwoman
Washington	Washingtonian
Wearside	Mackem
Wessex	West Saxon
Western Australia	Western Australian, Westralian, *or (informal)* Sandgroper
Western Sahara	Sahwari
West Virginia	West Virginian
Winnipeg	Winnipegger
Wisconsin	Wisconsinite
Wyoming	Wyomingite
Yemen	Yemeni
Yorkshire	Yorkshireman, Yorkshirewoman
The Yukon	Yukoner
Zaire	Zairean
Zambia	Zambian
Zanzibar	Zanzibari
Zimbabwe	Zimbabwean

Insects

TYPES OF INSECT

3 letters:
Ant
Bee
Bot
Fly
Lac
Nit
Wax

4 letters:
Crab
Flea
Gnat
Grig
Kutu
Lice
Mite
Moth
Pium
Tick
Wasp
Weta
Zimb

5 letters:
Aphis
Cimex
Emmet
Louse
Midge
Ox-bot
Scale
Stick

Insects

Zebub

6 letters:
Acarid
Breeze
Capsid
Chigoe
Cicada
Cicala
Cootie
Day-fly
Earwig
Gadfly
Hopper
Hornet
Locust
Looper
Mantid
Mantis
Mayfly
Psocid
Psylla
Punkie
Redbug
Sawfly
Scarab
Slater
Spider
Tettix
Thrips
Walker
Weevil

7 letters:
Antlion
Buzzard
Chalcid
Chigger
Cornfly
Cricket
Daphnid
Ergates
Firefly
Gallfly
Grayfly
Hive-bee
Humbuzz
Katydid
Ladybug
Odonata
Oestrus
Oniscus

Phasmid
Pill-bug
Pyralis
Sandfly
Spectre
Stylops
Termite

8 letters:
Alderfly
Bollworm
Bookworm
Caseworm
Circutio
Coccidae
Crane-fly
Dipteras
Firebrat
Gall-wasp
Glossina
Horntail
Horsefly
Inchworm
Itchmite
Lacewing
Ladybird
Lygus bug
Mealybug
Metabola
Milliped
Mosquito
Myriapod
Puss-moth
Reduviid
Ruby-tail
Scarabee
Sheep ked
Silkworm
Snowflea
Stinkbug
Stonefly
Waterbug
Wheel bug
Whitefly
Wireworm
Woodworm

9 letters:
Ametabola
Body louse
Booklouse
Caddis-fly

Centipede
Clipshear
Cochineal
Cockroach
Compodeid
Crab louse
Croton bug
Damselfly
Dobsonfly
Dragonfly
Ephemerid
Hemiptera
Homoptera
Mecoptera
Millepede
Millipede
Rearhorse
Sheep tick
Tabanidae
Tiger-moth
Woodlouse

10 letters:
Apterygota
Bark mantis
Bluebottle
Caddis worm
Cankerworm
Casebearer
Chironomid
Clipshears
Cockchafer
Coleoptera
Collembola
Fan-cricket
Fen-cricket
Froghopper
Harvestman
Leaf-cutter
Leafhopper
Mallophaga
Orthoptera
Phylloxera
Plant-louse
Pond-skater
Psocoptera
Rhipiptera
Silverfish
Springtail
Thysanuran
Treehopper

Web spinner

11 letters:
Apple maggot
Bristletail
Cabbageworm
Dermopteran
Grasshopper
Greenbottle
Hymenoptera
Mole cricket
Neuropteran
Tiger-beetle
Trichoptera

12 letters:
Bishop's mitre
Dictyopteran
Heteropteran
Rhipidoptera
Strepsiptera
Sucking louse
Thousand-legs
Thysanoptera
Walking stick

13 letters:
Cotton stainer
Daddy-long-legs
Jenny-longlegs

Leatherjacket
Measuring worm
Praying mantis
Staphylinidae

15 letters:
German cockroach
Tent caterpillar

16 letters:
Periodical cicada

19 letters:
Seventeen-year
  locust

PARTS OF INSECTS

3 letters:
Jaw

4 letters:
Coxa

5 letters:
Femur
Ileum
Notum
Scape
Snout
Thigh
Tibia

6 letters:
Air sac
Arista
Cercus
Cirrus
Corium
Glossa
Labium
Labrum
Ligula
Proleg
Scutum

Stigma
Tarsus
Tegmen
Thorax

7 letters:
Antenna
Clasper
Clypeus
Elytron
Gonopod
Hamulus
Maxilla
Ocellus
Pedicel
Trachea

8 letters:
Forewing
Mandible
Pronotum
Spiracle

9 letters:
Flagellum
Proboscis
Prothorax

Pulvillus
Scutellum
Spinneret
Underwing

10 letters:
Acetabulum
Epicuticle
Exocuticle
Haustellum
Hemelytron
Mesothorax
Metathorax
Ovipositor
Prosternum
Trochanter

11 letters:
Compound eye
Endocuticle
Ventriculus

14 letters:
Proventriculus

16 letters:
Malpighian tubule

See also:
➤ **Ants, bees and wasps** ➤ **Beetles** ➤ **Bugs** ➤ **Butterflies and moths** ➤ **Flies**

Instruments

3 letters:
Fan

4 letters:
Celt
Clam
Fork
Mike
Prog
Rasp
Rote
Tram

5 letters:
Brake
Fleam
Float
Gadge
Groma
Meter
Miser
Probe
Sonde
Wecht

6 letters:
Bougie
Broach
Etalon
Scythe
Strobe
Trocar

7 letters:
Alidade
Cadrans
Caltrop
Curette
Forceps
Pelican
Pointel
Probang
Scriber
Sextant
Spatula
Strigil
Swazzle
Swingle
Swozzle
Syringe

Trammel

8 letters:
Ablative
Barnacle
Diagraph
Dividers
Ecraseur
Odometer
Otoscope
Oximeter
Quadrant
Scissors
Strickle
Trephine
Waywiser

9 letters:
Alphonsin
Astrolabe
Atmometer
Auxometer
Barometer
Baryscope
Bolometer
Coelostat
Crows-bill
Cymograph
Dermatome
Dip-circle
Dropsonde
Eriometer
Haemostat
Heliostat
Hodometer
Konimeter
Machmeter
Manometer
Marigraph
Megascope
Metronome
Nocturnal
Potometer
Raspatory
Retractor
Rheometer
Tasimeter
Telemeter
Telescope

Tellurian
Tellurion
Tenaculum
Tonometer
Tripmeter
Voltmeter
Wavemeter

10 letters:
Almacantar
Almucantar
Altazimuth
Anemometer
Ceilometer
Clinometer
Colposcope
Cryophorus
Cystoscope
Fibrescope
Hydrometer
Hydroscope
Hygrometer
Hypsometer
Micrometer
Microphone
Pilliwinks
Protractor
Radiosonde
Spirograph
Spirometer
Tachigraph
Tachometer
Tensometer
Theodolite
Tribometer

11 letters:
Auxanometer
Chronograph
Chronometer
Chronoscope
Helicograph
Jacob's staff
Laparoscope
Pinnywinkle
Polarimeter
Rocketsonde
Seismograph
Solarimeter

Insults and terms of abuse

Stauroscope
Stethoscope
Stroboscope
Synthesizer
Tacheometer
Tensiometer
Thermometer
Voltammeter

12 letters:
Aethrioscope
Bronchoscope

Cephalometer
Keraunograph
Myringoscope
Penetrometer
Pinniewinkle
Respirometer
Scarificator
Sensitometer
Spectroscope
Synchroscope
Turbidimeter

Zenith-sector

13 letters:
Tachistoscope

14 letters:
Interferometer
Ophthalmoscope

16 letters:
Sphygmomanometer

Insults and terms of abuse

2 letters:
'ho

3 letters:
Cow
Git
Mug
Nit
Oaf

4 letters:
Berk
Bozo
Clod
Clot
Coot
Dope
Dork
Drip
Fool
Geek
Jerk
Loon
Mong
Nerd
Nurd
Ogre
Prat
Scab
Slag
Tart
Twit
Wimp
Wuss

5 letters:
Bitch
Chump
Clown
Devil
Divvy
Dumbo
Dummy
Dunce
Dweeb
Eejit
Galah
Goose
Idiot
Moron
Ninny
Plank
Rogue
Twerp
Twirp
Wally
Whore

6 letters:
Cretin
Dimwit
Donkey
Doofus
Heifer
Mincer
Minger
Muppet
Nitwit
Numpty

Rascal
Thicko
Wretch

7 letters:
Airhead
Article
Bushpig
Cabbage
Charlie
Chicken
Chuckie
Dumb-ass
Fathead
Halfwit
Pillock
Plonker
Scutter
Slapper

8 letters:
Bonehead
Dipstick
Doughnut
Imbecile
Numskull
Pea-brain
Scrubber

9 letters:
Bird-brain
Blockhead
Lamebrain
Numbskull
Scoundrel

Internet domain names

| Simpleton | **10 letters:** | **12 letters:** |
| Thickhead | Nincompoop | Cheeky monkey |

Internet domain names

GENERAL DOMAIN NAMES

Abbreviation	Top-level domain
.aero	Air-transport industry
.arpa	Internet infrastructure
.biz	Business
.co	Commercial company (used with country)
.com	Commercial company
.coop	Cooperative
.edu	Educational establishment
.eu	European Union
.gov	Government organization
.info	General use
.int	International organization
.mil	US military
.museum	Museum
.name	Individual user
.net	Company *or* organization
.org	Organization, usually nonprofit
.pro	Professionals (accountants, lawyers, etc.)

COUNTRY DOMAIN NAMES

Abbreviation	Country
.ac	Ascension Island
.ad	Andorra
.ae	United Arab Emirates
.af	Afghanistan
.ag	Antigua and Barbuda
.ai	Anguilla
.al	Albania
.am	Armenia
.an	Netherlands Antilles
.ao	Angola
.aq	Antarctica
.ar	Argentina
.as	American Samoa
.at	Austria
.au	Australia
.aw	Aruba
.az	Azerbaijan
.ba	Bosnia and Herzegovina
.bb	Barbados
.bd	Bangladesh
.be	Belgium

Internet domain names

Abbreviation	Country
.bf	Burkina Faso
.bg	Bulgaria
.bh	Bahrain
.bi	Burundi
.bj	Benin
.bm	Bermuda
.bn	Brunei Darussalam
.bo	Bolivia
.br	Brazil
.bs	Bahamas
.bt	Bhutan
.bv	Bouvet Island
.bw	Botswana
.by	Belarus
.bz	Belize
.ca	Canada
.cc	Cocos (Keeling) Islands
.cd	Congo, Democratic Republic of the
.cf	Central African Republic
.cg	Congo, Republic of
.ch	Switzerland
.ci	Côte d'Ivoire
.ck	Cook Islands
.cl	Chile
.cm	Cameroon
.cn	China
.co	Colombia
.cr	Costa Rica
.cu	Cuba
.cv	Cap Verde
.cx	Christmas Island
.cy	Cyprus
.cz	Czech Republic
.de	Germany
.dj	Dijibouti
.dk	Denmark
.dm	Dominica
.do	Dominican Republic
.dz	Algeria
.ec	Ecuador
.ee	Estonia
.eg	Egypt
.eh	Western Sahara
.er	Eritrea
.es	Spain
.et	Ethiopia
.fi	Finland
.fj	Fiji
.fk	Falkland Islands (Malvina)
.fm	Micronesia, Federal State of

Internet domain names

Abbreviation	Country
.fo	Faroe Islands
.fr	France
.ga	Gabon
.gd	Grenada
.ge	Georgia
.gf	French Guiana
.gg	Guernsey
.gh	Ghana
.gi	Gibraltar
.gl	Greenland
.gm	Gambia
.gn	Guinea
.gp	Equatorial Guinea
.gr	Greece
.gs	South Georgia and the South Sandwich Islands
.gt	Guatemala
.gu	Guam
.gw	Guinea-Bissau
.gy	Guyana
.hk	Hong Kong
.hm	Heard and McDonald Islands
.hn	Honduras
.hr	Croatia/Hrvatska
.ht	Haiti
.hu	Hungary
.id	Indonesia
.ie	Ireland
.il	Israel
.im	Isle of Man
.in	India
.io	British Indian Ocean Territory
.iq	Iraq
.ir	Iran (Islamic Republic of)
.is	Iceland
.it	Italy
.je	Jersey
.jm	Jamaica
.jo	Jordan
.jp	Japan
.ke	Kenya
.kg	Kyrgyzstan
.kh	Cambodia
.ki	Kiribati
.km	Comoros
.kn	Saint Kitts and Nevis
.kp	Korea, Democratic People's Republic
.kr	Korea, Republic of
.kw	Kuwait
.ky	Cayman Islands
.kz	Kazakhstan

Abbreviation	Country
.la	Lao People's Democratic Republic
.lb	Lebanon
.lc	Saint Lucia
.li	Liechtenstein
.lk	Sri Lanka
.lr	Liberia
.ls	Lesotho
.lt	Lithuania
.lu	Luxembourg
.lv	Latvia
.ly	Libyan Arab Jamahiriya
.ma	Morocco
.mc	Monaco
.md	Moldova, Republic of
.mg	Madagascar
.mh	Marshall Islands
.mk	Macedonia, Former Yugoslav Republic
.ml	Mali
.mm	Myanmar
.mn	Mongolia
.mo	Macau
.mp	Northern Mariana Islands
.mq	Martinique
.mr	Mauritania
.ms	Montserrat
.mt	Malta
.mu	Mauritius
.mv	Maldives
.mw	Malawi
.mx	Mexico
.my	Malaysia
.mz	Mozambique
.na	Namibia
.nc	New Caledonia
.ne	Niger
.nf	Norfolk Island
.ng	Nigeria
.ni	Nicaragua
.nl	Netherlands
.no	Norway
.np	Nepal
.nr	Nauru
.nu	Niue
.nz	New Zealand
.om	Oman
.pa	Panama
.pe	Peru
.pf	French Polynesia
.pg	Papua New Guinea
.ph	Philippines

Internet domain names

Abbreviation	Country
.pk	Pakistan
.pl	Poland
.pm	St. Pierre and Miquelon
.pn	Pitcairn Island
.pr	Puerto Rico
.ps	Palestinian Territories
.pt	Portugal
.pw	Palau
.py	Paraguay
.qa	Qatar
.re	Reunion Island
.ro	Romania
.ru	Russian Federation
.rw	Rwanda
.sa	Saudi Arabia
.sb	Soloman Islands
.sc	Seychelles
.sd	Sudan
.se	Sweden
.sg	St. Helena
.si	Slovenia
.sj	Svalbard and Jan Mayen Islands
.sk	Slovak Republic
.sl	Sierra Leone
.sm	San Marino
.sn	Senegal
.so	Somalia
.sr	Suriname
.st	Sao Tome and Principe
.sv	El Salvador
.sy	Syrian Arab Republic
.sz	Swaziland
.tc	Turks and Caicos Islands
.td	Chad
.tf	French Southern Territories
.tg	Togo
.th	Thailand
.tj	Tajikistan
.tk	Tokelau
.tm	Turkmenistan
.tn	Tunisia
.to	Tongo
.tp	East Timor
.tr	Turkey
.tt	Trinidad and Tobago
.tv	Tuvalu
.tw	Taiwan
.tz	Tanzania
.ua	Ukraine
.ug	Uganda

Abbreviation	Country
.uk	United Kingdom
.um	US Minor Outlying Islands
.us	United States
.uy	Uruguay
.uz	Uzbekistan
.va	Holy See (City Vatican State)
.vc	Saint Vincent and the Grenadines
.ve	Venezuela
.vg	Virgin Islands (British)
.vi	Virgin Islands (USA)
.vn	Vietnam
.vu	Vanuatu
.wf	Wallis and Futuna Islands
.ws	Western Samoa
.ye	Yemen
.yt	Mayotte
.yu	Yugoslavia
.za	South Africa
.zm	Zambia
.zw	Zimbabwe

Invertebrates

3 letters:
Lug

4 letters:
Clam
Cone
Kina
Pipi
Worm

5 letters:
Ameba
Bardi
Bardy
Coral
Cunje
Gaper
Leech
Polyp
Squid
Ugari

6 letters:
Amoeba
Bardie
Chiton
Cockle

Cuttle
Mussel
Oyster
Quahog
Sea mat
Sea pen
Sponge
Tellin
Teredo

7 letters:
Bivalve
Blubber
Catworm
Crinoid
Daphnia
Decapod
Eelworm
Lobworm
Lugworm
Mollusc
Octopus
Piddock
Ragworm
Rotifer
Scallop

Sea lily
Sea wasp
Sunstar
Trepang
Tubifex

8 letters:
Ammonite
Annelida
Argonaut
Bryozoan
Clamworm
Cunjevoi
Echinoid
Gapeworm
Lancelet
Lungworm
Milleped
Nautilus
Parazoan
Pauropod
Pumpworm
Red coral
Sandworm
Sea mouse
Shipworm

Invertebrates

Starfish
Tapeworm
Tube worm
Whipworm
White cat
Zoophyte

9 letters:
Amphioxus
Anthozoan
Arrowworm
Arthropod
Belemnite
Brandling
Centipede
Clabby-doo
Clappy-doo
Comb jelly
Cone shell
Devilfish
Earthworm
Gastropod
Hard-shell
Hydrozoan
Jellyfish
Lamp shell
Millepede
Millipede
Peritrich
Poriferan
Razor clam
Round clam
Roundworm
Sea slater
Sea squirt
Sea urchin
Soft-shell
Trilobite
Tusk shell
Water bear

Wheatworm
White worm
Woodborer

10 letters:
Animalcule
Balmain bug
Bêche-de-mer
Bluebottle
Brachiopod
Ctenophore
Cuttlefish
Echinoderm
Euripterid
Eurypterid
Gasteropod
Graptolite
Guinea worm
Horseleech
Liver fluke
Otter shell
Paddle worm
Protostome
Razor-shell
Scyphozoan
Sea anemone
Seed oyster
Stony coral
Tardigrade
Tooth shell
Venus shell
Vinegar eel
Water louse

11 letters:
Animalculum
Bladder worm
Bluff oyster
Feather star
Globigerina
Sea cucumber

Stomach worm
Vinegar worm
Water slater

12 letters:
Box jellyfish
Chicken louse
Gastropodart
Onychophoran
Trochelminth
Venus's-girdle

13 letters:
Crown-of-thorns
Hard-shell clam
Paper nautilus
Precious coral
Soft-shell clam
Water measurer

14 letters:
Pearly nautilus

15 letters:
Coat-of-mail shell

16 letters:
Water stick insect

17 letters:
Blue-ringed
  octopus
Chambered
  nautilus

18 letters:
Portuguese
  man-of-war
Venus's flower
  basket

21 letters:
Crown-of-thorns
  starfish

See also:
➤ **Insects** ➤ **Shellfish** ➤ **Snails, slugs and other gastropods**
➤ **Spiders and other arachnids** ➤ **Worms**

Islands and island groups

2 letters:
TT

3 letters:
Aru
Cos
Diu
Fyn
Hoy
Kos
Man
May
Rat
Rum
Sea
Yap

4 letters:
Amoy
Aran
Arru
Attu
Bali
Biak
Bute
Calf
Cebú
Coll
Cook
Cuba
Dogs
Eigg
Elba
Erin
Fair
Fiji
Guam
Heat
Herm
Holy
Hova
Idse
Iona
Java
Jolo
Jura
Keos
King
Line

Long
Mahé
Malé
Maui
Mazu
Mona
Motu
Muck
Mull
Niue
Oahu
Rhum
Rona
Ross
Saba
Sark
Seil
Skye
Truk
Uist
Ulva
Unst
Wake
Yell

5 letters:
Aland
Apple
Arran
Aruba
Banka
Banks
Barra
Batan
Belau
Belle
Bioko
Bohol
Bonin
Caldy
Canna
Capri
Ceram
Cheju
Chios
Clare
Cocos
Coney

Coral
Corfu
Crete
Delos
Disko
Ellis
Faial
Farne
Faroe
Fayal
Foula
Funen
Gigha
Haiti
Handa
Ibiza
Islay
Isola
Jerba
Kauai
Kiska
Kuril
Lanai
Lewis
Leyte
Longa
Luing
Lundy
Luzon
Maewo
Malta
Matsu
Melos
Nauru
Naxos
Nevis
North
Oland
Ormuz
Panay
Páros
Pemba
Qeshm
Qishm
Reil's
Rhode
Samar
Samoa

Islands and island groups

Samos
Saria
Seram
South
Spice
Sumba
Sunda
Thera
Thule
Timor
Tiree
Tombo
Tonga
Turks
Upolu
Whale
White
Wight
Youth
Zante

6 letters:
Achill
Aegean
Aegina
Amager
Andros
Avalon
Azores
Baffin
Banaba
Bangka
Barrow
Bikini
Borneo
Bounty
Butung
Caicos
Canary
Canvey
Cayman
Ceylon
Chiloé
Cyprus
Devil's
Diomed
Djerba
Easter
Ellice
Euboea
Flores

Fraser
Hainan
Harris
Hawaii
Hobart
Honshu
Hormuz
Icaria
Imbros
Indies
Insula
Ionian
Ischia
Ithaca
Jersey
Kiushu
Kodiak
Kosrae
Kurile
Kyushu
Labuan
Laputa
Lemnos
Lesbos
Leucas
Leukas
Levkás
Lipari
Lizard
Lombok
Madura
Majuro
Marajó
Mercer
Mersea
Midway
Negros
Ogygia
Orkney
Paphos
Patmos
Penang
Pharos
Philae
Pladdy
Ponape
Quemoy
Raasay
Ramsey
Rhodes
Rialto

Rjukyu
Robben
Ryukyu
Safety
Saipan
Saltee
Savaii
Scilly
Scyros
Sicily
Skerry
Skomer
Skyros
Snares
Soemba
Soenda
Staffa
Staten
St. John
Stroma
Summer
Tahiti
Taiwan
Thanet
Thásos
Tobago
Tresco
Tubuai
Tuvalu
Unimak
Ushant
Veneti
Virgin
Walney

7 letters:
Aeolian
Aldabra
Amboina
Andaman
Antigua
Austral
Bahamas
Baranof
Barbuda
Bardsey
Basilan
Battery
Bedloe's
Bermuda
Bonaire

British
Cartier
Celebes
Channel
Chatham
Cipango
Corsica
Crannog
Curaçao
Cythera
Diomede
Emerald
Eriskay
Faeroes
Falster
Flannan
Frisian
Fur Seal
Gambier
Gilbert
Gotland
Grenada
Hawaiki
Hayling
Heimaey
Howland
Iceland
Ireland
Iwo Jima
Jamaica
Kerrera
Laaland
La Palma
Leeward
Liberty
Lismore
Lofoten
Lolland
Madeira
Majorca
Masbate
Mayotte
Mindoro
Minorca
Molokai
Moreton
Mykonos
Nicobar
Norfolk
Oceania
Okinawa

Orcades
Orkneys
Palawan
Palmyra
Phoenix
Rathlin
Réunion
Roanoke
Rockall
Salamis
San Juan
Sao Tomé
Scalpay
Sheppey
Shikoku
Skikoku
Society
Socotra
Solomon
St. Croix
Stewart
St. Kilda
St. Kitts
St. Lucia
Sumatra
Sumbawa
Surtsey
Tenedos
Tokelau
Tortola
Tortuga
Tuamotu
Tutuila
Vanuatu
Visayan
Volcano
Waihake
Western
Wrangel
Zealand
Zetland

8 letters:
Alcatraz
Alderney
Aleutian
Anglesey
Anguilla
Antilles
Atlantis
Auckland

Balearic
Barbados
Bathurst
Billiton
Blefuscu
Bora Bora
Bornholm
Canaries
Caroline
Catalina
Choiseul
Colonsay
Cyclades
Dominica
Falkland
Farquhar
Flinders
Foulness
Friendly
Gothland
Gottland
Guernsey
Hamilton
Hebrides
Hokkaido
Hong Kong
Jan Mayen
Kangaroo
Kermadec
Krakatau
Krakatoa
Ladrones
Lavongai
Lilliput
Lord Howe
Luggnagg
Mackinac
Mainland
Maldives
Mallorca
Marianas
Marquesa
Marshall
Melville
Mindanao
Miquelon
Moluccas
Mustique
Pelagian
Pitcairn
Portland

Islands and island groups

Pribilof
Principe
Sakhalin
Sardinia
Schouten
Shetland
Sjælland
Skokholm
Soembawa
Somerset
Sporades
Sri Lanka
St. Helena
St. Martin
Sulawesi
Sverdrup
Tasmania
Tenerife
Terceira
Thousand
Thursday
Trinidad
Tsushima
Unalaska
Venetian
Victoria
Viti Levu
Windward
Zanzibar

9 letters:
Admiralty
Alexander
Andreanof
Anticosti
Antipodes
Ascension
Barataria
Benbecula
Calf of Man
Chichagof
Christmas
Elephanta
Ellesmere
Falklands
Fortunate
Galápagos
Governors
Greenland
Hainan Tao

Halmahera
Innisfree
Jamestown
Kerguelen
Lampedusa
Lanzarote
Macquarie
Manhattan
Margarita
Marquesas
Mascarene
Mauritius
Melanesia
Nantucket
New Guinea
North Uist
Polynesia
Rangitoto
Rarotonga
Runnymede
Sao Miguel
Shetlands
Singapore
Sjaelland
South Uist
Stromboli
St. Tudwal's
St. Vincent
Teneriffe
Trobriand
Vancouver
Vanua Levu
Walcheren

10 letters:
Basse-Terre
Bermoothes
Campobello
Cape Breton
Cephalonia
Corregidor
Dodecanese
Formentera
Grand Manan
Grand Terre
Grenadines
Heligoland
Hispaniola
Isle Royale
Kiritimati

Langerhans
Madagascar
Manitoulin
Marinduque
Martinique
Micronesia
Montserrat
New Britain
New Georgia
New Ireland
Pescadores
Poor Knight
Samothrace
Seychelles
Three Kings
West Indies
Whitsunday

11 letters:
Dry Tortugas
Florida Keys
Glubdubdrib
Grand Bahama
Grand Canary
Grande-Terre
Guadalcanal
Lakshadweep
Lindisfarne
Mount Desert
New Siberian
Pantelleria
Philippines
San Salvador
Southampton
South Orkney
Spitsbergen

12 letters:
Bougainville
Cassiterides
Glubbdubdrib
Greater Sunda
Marie Galante
New Caledonia
Newfoundland
Nusa Tenggara
Prince Edward
San Cristóbal
Santa Barbara
South Georgia
Torres Strait

Ivy League universities

13 letters:
Espíritu Santo
Forneaux Group
Fuerteventura
Juan Fernández
New Providence
Prince of Wales
Santa Catalina
South Shetland
St. Christopher

14 letters:
D'Entrecasteaux
Franz Josef Land
Lesser Antilles

Lewis and Harris
Queen Charlotte
Queen Elizabeth
Tristan da Cunha
Turks and Caicos
Vestmannaeyjar

15 letters:
Greater Antilles
Lewis with Harris
Wallis and Futuna

16 letters:
French West Indies
Heard and
  McDonald

17 letters:
Andaman and
  Nicobar
Fernando de
  Noronha

19 letters:
Netherlands
Antilles

Ivy League universities

4 letters:
Yale

5 letters:
Brown

7 letters:
Cornell
Harvard

8 letters:
Columbia

9 letters:
Princeton

16 letters:
Dartmouth College

24 letters:
University of
  Pennsylvania

J

3 letters:
Bed
Cag
Mao
Pea
Tux

4 letters:
Baju
Boxy
Bush
Coat
Eton
Flak
Life
Mess
Sack

5 letters:
Acton
Bania
Biker
Cymar
Denim
Duvet
Gilet
Grego
Jupon
Nehru
Parka
Pilot
Polka
Shell
Shrug
Simar
Tunic
Wamus
Water

6 letters:
Amauti

Anorak
Báinín
Banian
Banyan
Basque
Battle
Blazer
Bolero
Bomber
Cagoul
Combat
Dinner
Dolman
Donkey
Jerkin
Kagool
Lumber
Monkey
Reefer
Sacque
Safari
Sports
Strait
Tabard
Tuxedo
Wammus
Wampus
Zouave

7 letters:
Amautik
Barbour®
Blouson
Cagoule
Doublet
Fustian
Hacking
Leather
Mae West
Matinée

Norfolk
Reefing
Simarre
Smoking
Spencer
Vareuse

8 letters:
Camisole
Cardigan
Gambeson
Gendarme
Haqueton
Mackinaw
Mandarin
Tailcoat
Toreador

9 letters:
Habergeon
Hacqueton
Newmarket
Pourpoint
Shortgown
Waistcoat

10 letters:
Body warmer
Bumfreezer
Carmagnole
Fearnought
Hug-me-tight
Windjammer

11 letters:
Afghanistan
Windbreaker®
Windcheater

12 letters:
Lumberjacket
Mackinaw coat

Jazz forms

3 letters:
Bop

4 letters:
Free
Scat
Trad

5 letters:
Swing

6 letters:
Modern

7 letters:
Hard bop
Ragtime

8 letters:
Highlife

9 letters:
Afro-Cuban
Dixieland
Gutbucket
West Coast

10 letters:
Mainstream
New Orleans

11 letters:
Barrelhouse
Thirdstream
Traditional

12 letters:
Boogie-woogie
Western swing

Jazz musicians

3 letters:
Bix

4 letters:
Getz, *Stanley 'Stan'*
Pine, *Courtney*
Shaw, *Artie*

5 letters:
Basie, *William*
Davis, *Miles (Dewey)*
Haden, *Charles (Edward)*
Tatum, *Art (Arthur Tatum)*

6 letters:
Bechet, *Leon Bismarcke*
Bechet, *Sidney*
Blakey, *Art(hur)*
Garner, *Erroll*
Gordon, *Dexter*
Mingus, *Charles 'Charlie'*
Oliver, *Joseph*
Waller, *Fats (Thomas Waller)*

7 letters:
Brubeck, *Dave*
Coleman, *Ornette*
Hampton, *Lionel*
Hawkins, *Coleman*
Jarrett, *Keith*
Vaughan, *Sarah (Lois)*

8 letters:
Coltrane, *John (William)*
Marsalis, *Wynton*
Peterson, *Oscar (Emmanuel)*

9 letters:
Carpenter, *John Alden*
Christian, *Charlie*
Dankworth, *John (Philip William)*
Grappelli, *Stéphane*
Lyttelton, *Humphrey*

10 letters:
Count Basie
Fitzgerald, *Ella*
King Oliver

Jazz terms

3 letters:
Gig

4 letters:
Band

Cool
Jazz
Jive
Riff
Skin

5 letters:
Combo
Jazzy
Major
Minor

Sound
Stomp
Swing
Vocal

6 letters:
Hepcat
Jazz up
Number
Vibist

7 letters:
Bassist
Big band

Hipster
Jug band
Sideman
Stomper

8 letters:
Slap bass
Vocalist

9 letters:
Augmented
Jitterbug
Mouldy fig
Ring-shout

Saxophone

10 letters:
Added sixth
Diminished
Jam session
Ninth chord
Vibraphone

13 letters:
Eleventh chord

15 letters:
Thirteenth chord

Jewish denominations and sects

7 letters:
Zionism

8 letters:
Hasidism

9 letters:
Chasidism
Hassidism

10 letters:
Chassidism

13 letters:
Reform Judaism

14 letters:
Liberal Judaism

15 letters:
Orthodox Judaism

19 letters:
Conservative
  Judaism

Judges

3 letters:
Ito, *Lance A(llan)*

4 letters:
Coke, *Sir Edward*
More, *Sir Thomas*

5 letters:
Draco
Solon
Woolf, *Lord Henry*

6 letters:
Gideon
Holmes, *Oliver Wendell*
Hutton, *Lord (James) Brian (Edward)*
Irvine, *Lord Alexander*
Mackay, *Lord James*

7 letters:
Deborah
De Burgh, *Hubert*

Denning, *Lord Alfred*
Jephtha
Pickles
Roy Bean
Solomon

8 letters:
Falconer, *Lord Charles*
Hailsham, *Viscount Quintin McGarel Hogg*
Jeffreys, *Lord George*
Marshall, *Thurgood*

9 letters:
Judge Judy

10 letters:
Elwyn-Jones, *Lord Frederick*

13 letters:
Judge 'Joe' Dredd
Pontius Pilate

K

Kings

2 letters:
ER
Og

3 letters:
Asa
Ine
Lir
Log
Lud
Roi
Zog

4 letters:
Agag
Agis
Ahab
Brut
Ceyx
Cnut
Cole
Edwy
Fahd
Jehu
Lear
Nudd
Numa
Offa
Olaf
Saul

5 letters:
Balak
Brute
Creon
Cyrus
David
Edgar
Edwin
Gyges
Herod

Hiram
Idris
Ixion
James
Lludd
Louis
Midas
Minos
Mpret
Ninus
Penda
Priam
Rufus
Uther

6 letters:
Aegeus
Alfred
Alonso
Amasis
Arthur
Attila
Baliol
Brutus
Canute
Cheops
Clovis
Darius
Duncan
Edmund
Egbert
Farouk
Fergus
Harold
Hyksos
Lucomo
Ludwig
Memnon
Nestor
Oberon

Ogyges
Paphos
Philip
Ramses
Rhesus
Xerxes

7 letters:
Acestes
Baldwin
Balliol
Beowulf
Busiris
Caradoc
Cecrops
Croesus
Elidure
Evander
Kenneth
Macbeth
Malcolm
Oedipus
Ptolemy
Pyrrhus
Rameses
Servius
Solomon
Stephen
Tarquin
Umberto

8 letters:
Cambyses
Cophetua
Endymion
Ethelred
Hezekiah
Jereboam
Jonathan
Leonidas
Menander

Kitchen equipment

Menelaus
Milesius
Odysseus
Rehoboam
Tantalus
Thyestes
Tigranes
Zedekiah

9 letters:
Agamemnon
Ahasuerus
Alexander
Athelstan
Bretwalda
Brian Boru

Conchobar
Cunobelin
Cymbeline
Ethelbert
Florestan
Frederick
Gargantua
Pygmalion
Ras Tafari
Tarquinus
Vortigern
Wenceslas

10 letters:
Belshazzar
Cadwaladar

Caractacus
Ozymandias
Wenceslaus

11 letters:
Charlemagne
Hardicanute
Jehoshaphat
Sennacherib

12 letters:
Wayland Smith

14 letters:
Nebuchadnezzar
Uther Pendragon

Kitchen equipment

3 letters:
Aga®
Pot
Wok

4 letters:
Fork
Olla
Oven

5 letters:
Grill
Knife
Ladle
Mould
Ricer
Sieve
Spoon
Whisk

6 letters:
Barbie
Cooker
Girdle
Grater
Juicer
Kettle
Masher
Peeler
Scales
Tagine
Teapot

7 letters:
Blender
Cake tin
Chip pan
Flan tin
Griddle
Loaf tin
Poacher
Ramekin
Skillet
Spatula
Spurtle
Steamer
Tandoor
Timbale
Toaster

8 letters:
Barbecue
Colander
Egg whisk
Icing bag
Jelly bag
Pot-au-feu
Saucepan
Strainer
Teaspoon

9 letters:
Bain-marie
Cafetiere
Casserole

Coffeepot
Corkscrew
Egg beater
Fish slice
Frying pan
Gravy boat
Mandoline
Mezzaluna
Microwave
Sauce boat
Tin-opener

10 letters:
Baking tray
Bread knife
Chopsticks
Liquidizer
Mixing bowl
Nutcracker
Pepper mill
Percolator
Rolling pin
Rotisserie
Tablespoon
Tenderizer

11 letters:
Cooling rack
Wooden spoon

12 letters:
Bottle opener

Carving knife
Deep fat fryer
Dessertspoon
Double boiler
Measuring jug
Pastry cutter
Toasting fork

13 letters:
Chopping board

Coffee grinder
Food processor
Ice-cream maker
Lemon squeezer
Microwave oven

14 letters:
Double saucepan
Juice extractor

15 letters:
Fan-assisted oven
Mortar and pestle

17 letters:
Batterie de cuisine

Knights

3 letters:
Kay

4 letters:
Bors

5 letters:
Guyon
Pinel

6 letters:
Bliant
Cambel
Gareth
Gawain
Lionel
Melius
Modred
Ritter

7 letters:
Accolon
Artegal
Caradoc
Galahad
Launfal
Orlando
Paladin
Tristan

8 letters:
Alphagus
Banneret
Bedivere
Calidore
Lancelot
Maecenas
Palmerin
Parsifal

Perceval
Percival
Tristram
Vavasour

9 letters:
Aguecheek
Britomart
Caballero
Launcelot
Lochinvar
Lohengrin
Pharamond
Valvassor

10 letters:
Tannhauser

11 letters:
Perceforest

Knitting stitches

3 letters:
Box
Rib

4 letters:
Moss
Seed
Slip

5 letters:
Cable

6 letters:
Garter

7 letters:
Layette

8 letters:
Pavilion
Stocking

9 letters:
Garter rib

10 letters:
Double moss
Double seed
Mistake rib

Moss panels

11 letters:
Diagonal rib
Roman stripe

13 letters:
Fisherman's rib

Knots

3 letters:
Bow
Tie

4 letters:
Bend
Flat
Loop
Love
Mesh
Reef
Slip
Wale
Wall

5 letters:
Hitch
Mouse
Picot
Quipu
Thumb
Water

6 letters:
Clinch
French
Granny
Lover's
Prusik
Shroud

Square

7 letters:
Barrell
Bowknot
Bowline
Cat's paw
Crochet
Diamond
Gordian
Rosette
Running
Sailor's
Windsor

8 letters:
Hangman's
Overhand
Slipknot
Surgeon's
Truelove

9 letters:
Bowstring
Half-hitch
Sheet bend
Swab hitch
Turk's-head

10 letters:
Becket bend

Clove hitch
Fisherman's
Girth hitch
Hawser bend
Monkey fist
Sheepshank
Stevedore's
Truelover's

11 letters:
Carrick bend
Englishman's
Magnus hitch
Timber hitch

12 letters:
Harness hitch
Rolling hitch
Weaver's hitch

13 letters:
Figure of eight
Matthew Walker
Slippery hitch

14 letters:
Blackwall hitch
Englishman's tie
Fisherman's bend
Running bowline

L

Lakes, lochs and loughs

2 letters:
No

3 letters:
Ard
Awe
Ewe
Tay
Van
Zug

4 letters:
Bala
Biel
Bled
Chad
Como
Earn
Erie
Erne
Eyre
Fyne
Kivu
Mead
Ness
Nyos
Taal
Tana
Thun
Tien

5 letters:
Allen
Atlin
Cowan
Frome
Garda
Gatún
Huron
Ilmen
Léman

Leven
Lochy
Lower
Malar
Meech
Morar
Mungo
Mweru
Myall
Nam Co
Neagh
Nyasa
Onega
Patos
Playa
Poopó
Pskov
Sevan
Sween
Tahoe
Taupo
Tsana
Urmia
Volta

6 letters:
Albert
Annecy
Argyle
Averno
Baikal
Barlee
Bitter
Broads
Cayuga
Corrib
Edward
Geneva
Kariba
Ladoga

Laggan
Linnhe
Lomond
Lugano
Malawi
Miveru
Mobutu
Nakuru
Nam Tso
Nasser
Oneida
Peipus
P'o-yang
Rudolf
Saimaa
Te Anau
Tekapo
Tummel
Vanern
Zürich

7 letters:
Amadeus
Aral Sea
Avernus
Axolotl
Balaton
Belfast
Dead Sea
Iliamna
Katrine
Koko Nor
Kuku Nor
Lucerne
Managua
Nipigon
Ontario
Rannoch
Rotorua
Toronto

Languages

Torrens
Turkana

8 letters:
Balkhash
Bodensee
Carnegie
Dongting
Gairdner
Grasmere
Issyk-Kul
Kootenay
Lake Aral
Maggiore
Manitoba
Menindee
Menteith
Michigan
Naumachy
Okanagan
Onondaga
Regillus
Reindeer
Superior
Titicaca
Tonle Sap
Torridon
Veronica
Victoria
Wakatipu
Wanawaka
Winnipeg

9 letters:
Athabasca

Athabaska
Bangweulu
Champlain
Constance
Ennerdale
Everglade
Great Bear
Great Salt
Innisfree
Killarney
Macquarie
Manapouri
Maracaibo
Naumachia
Neuchâtel
Nicaragua
Nipissing
Saint John
Serbonian
Thirlmere
Trasimene
Trasimono
Ullswater
Wairarapa
Wast Water
Winnebago
Ysselmeer

10 letters:
Buttermere
Caspian Sea
Clearwater
Great Lakes
Great Slave

Hawes Water
Ijsselmeer
Miraflores
Mistassini
Okeechobee
Okefenokee
Saint Clair
Serpentine
Tanganyika
Washington
Windermere

11 letters:
Great Bitter
Lesser Slave
Stanley Pool

12 letters:
Derwentwater
Little Bitter
Memphremagog
Sea of Galilee
Waikaremoana

13 letters:
Bassenthwaite
Coniston Water
Crummock Water
Pontchartrain

14 letters:
Disappointment
Ennerdale Water
Lake of the Woods

Languages

AFRICAN LANGUAGES

2 letters:
Ga
Gã

3 letters:
Edo
Ewe
Ibo
Luo
Tiv
Twi

4 letters:
Akan
Beni
Bini
Efik
Fang
Fula
Hutu
Igbo
Krio
Lozi

Luba
Nama
Nuba
Nupe
Pedi
Susu
Zulu

5 letters:
Bemba
Chewa

Duala
Dyula
Fanti
Fulah
Galla
Ganda
Hausa
Kongo
Masai
Moore
Mossi
Nyoro
Pondo
Sango
Shona
Sotho
Swazi
Temne
Tigré
Tonga
Venda
Wolof
Xhosa

6 letters:
Berber

Coptic
Damara
Fulani
Grikwa
Griqua
Herero
Ibibio
Kabyle
Kikuyu
Nyanja
Ovambo
Rwanda
Somali
Tsonga
Tswana
Tuareg
Yoruba

7 letters:
Adamawa
Amharic
Ashanti
Bambara
Barotse
Bashkir
Kirundi

Luganda
Malinke
Maninke
Namaqua
Ndebele
Sesotho
Songhai
Swahili

8 letters:
Chichewa
Fanagalo
Fanakalo
Kingwana
Malagasy
Matabele
Tigrinya
Tshiluba

9 letters:
Afrikaans
Hottentot

13 letters:
Northern Sotho

ASIAN LANGUAGES

3 letters:
Lao
Mon

4 letters:
Ainu
Cham
Moro
Naga
Nuri
Shan
Thai
Urdu

5 letters:
Dinka
Farsi
Gondi
Hindi
Karen
Kazak
Khmer
Malay
Oriya

Tamil
Tatar
Uigur
Uzbek
Yakut

6 letters:
Abkhaz
Adygei
Adyghe
Afghan
Arabic
Bihari
Brahui
Buriat
Buryat
Divehi
Evenki
Hebrew
Kafiri
Kalmyk
Kazakh
Korean

Lahnda
Lepcha
Manchu
Mishmi
Mongol
Nepali
Ostyak
Pashto
Pushto
Pushtu
Sindhi
Telegu
Telugu
Tungus
Uighur

7 letters:
Abkhazi
Aramaic
Balochi
Baluchi
Bengali
Burmese

Languages

Chinese
Chukchi
Chuvash
Dzongka
Iranian
Kalmuck
Kannada
Khalkha
Kirghiz
Kurdish
Marathi
Ossetic
Punjabi
Sogdian
Tadzhik
Tagalog
Tibetan
Turkman
Turkmen

8 letters:
Armenian

Assamese
Balinese
Canarese
Chukchee
Filipino
Gujarati
Gujerati
Gurkhali
Japanese
Javanese
Kanarese
Kashmiri
Mahratti
Mandarin
Ossetian
Tadzhiki
Turkoman

9 letters:
Abkhazian
Cantonese
Kabardian

Malayalam
Mongolian
Sinhalese

10 letters:
Circassian
Hindostani
Hindustani
Kara-Kalpak
Kazan Tatar
Malayalaam
Vietnamese

11 letters:
Azerbaijani
Hindoostani

15 letters:
Bahasa Indonesia

AUSTRALASIAN LANGUAGES

4 letters:
Krio
Motu

5 letters:
Dinka
Māori

6 letters:
Aranda
Fijian
Papuan
Samoan

Tongan

7 letters:
Moriori
Nauruan
Pintubi

8 letters:
Gurindji
Hawaiian
Hiri Motu
Tuvaluan
Warlpiri

9 letters:
Kamilaroi

10 letters:
Beach-la-Mar
Police Motu

13 letters:
Neo-Melanesian

20 letters:
Solomon Islands
  Pidgin

EUROPEAN LANGUAGES

4 letters:
Erse
Komi
Lapp
Manx

5 letters:
Czech
Dutch
Greek
Ladin
Vogul
Welsh

6 letters:
Basque
Bokmål
Breton
Cymric
Danish
French
Gaelic
German
Kymric
Ladino
Lallan

Magyar
Polish
Romany
Shelta
Slovak
Udmurt
Votyak
Zyrian

7 letters:
Catalan
Cornish
English

Finnish
Flemish
Frisian
Gagauzi
Italian
Lallans
Latvian
Lettish
Maltese
Mingrel
Mordvin
Nynorsk
Romanes
Romansh
Russian
Samoyed
Slovene
Sorbian
Spanish
Swedish

Turkish
Yiddish

8 letters:
Albanian
Bohemian
Cheremis
Croatian
Estonian
Faeroese
Friulian
Galician
Georgian
Karelian
Landsmål
Lusatian
Romanian
Romansch

9 letters:
Alemannic

Bulgarian
Castilian
Cheremiss
Hungarian
Icelandic
Norwegian
Provençal
Sardinian
Ukrainian

10 letters:
Lithuanian
Macedonian
Mingrelian
Portuguese
Serbo-Croat

12 letters:
Byelorussian

13 letters:
Serbo-Croatian

NORTH AMERICAN LANGUAGES

3 letters:
Fox
Ute

4 letters:
Crow
Erie
Hopi
Zuñi

5 letters:
Aleut
Creek
Haida
Huron
Osage
Piute
Sioux
Taino

6 letters:
Abnaki
Apache
Cayuga
Eskimo
Micmac
Mixtec
Mohave
Mohawk

Mojave
Navaho
Navajo
Nootka
Ojibwa
Oneida
Paiute
Pawnee
Pequot
Seneca

7 letters:
Arapaho
Caddoan
Catawba
Chinook
Choctaw
Mahican
Mohican
Shawnee
Tahltan
Tlingit

8 letters:
Aleutian
Algonkin
Cherokee
Cheyenne
Comanche

Delaware
Iroquois
Kwakiutl
Menomini
Nez Percé
Okanagan
Okanogan
Okinagan
Onondaga
Sahaptan
Sahaptin
Seminole
Shoshone
Shoshoni

9 letters:
Algonquin
Blackfoot
Chickasaw
Inuktitut
Sahaptian
Tuscarora
Winnebago

11 letters:
Assiniboine
Massachuset
Narraganset

Languages

12 letters:
Narragansett

13 letters:
Massachusetts

SOUTH AMERICAN LANGUAGES

4 letters:
Tupi

6 letters:
Aymara
Galibi
Kechua

7 letters:
Guarani
Nahuatl
Quechua
Quichua
Zapotec

8 letters:
Chibchan

10 letters:
Araucanian

ANCIENT LANGUAGES

4 letters:
Avar
Ge'ez
Inca
Maya
Norn
Pali

5 letters:
Aztec
Ionic
Koine
Latin
Mayan
Oscan
Punic
Vedic

6 letters:
Gothic
Hebrew
Libyan
Lycian
Lydian
Sabean
Syriac

7 letters:
Avestan
Avestic
Chaldee
Edomite

Elamite
Hittite
Pahlavi
Pehlevi
Pictish
Sabaean
Umbrian
Venetic
Wendish

8 letters:
Akkadian
Assyrian
Egyptian
Ethiopic
Etruscan
Faliscan
Frankish
Illyrian
Messapïc
Old Norse
Phrygian
Sanskrit
Scythian
Sumerian
Thracian
Ugaritic
Volscian

9 letters:
Canaanite

Langue d'oc
Messapian
Sabellian
Tocharian
Tokharian

10 letters:
Anglo-Saxon
Babylonian
Gallo-Roman
Himyaritic
Langue d'oïl
Phoenician

11 letters:
Celtiberian
Langobardic
Old Prussian
Osso-Umbrian

12 letters:
Ancient Greek
Gallo-Romance

13 letters:
Old High German

14 letters:
Thraco-Phrygian

17 letters:
Old Church
  Slavonic

ARTIFICIAL LANGUAGES

3 letters:
Ido

7 letters:
Volapuk

Volapük

9 letters:
Esperanto

11 letters:
Interlingua

LANGUAGE GROUPS

3 letters:
Gur
Kwa
San

5 letters:
Bantu
Carib
Indic
Mande
Mayan
Munda
Nguni
Norse
Ugric
Yuman

6 letters:
Altaic
Baltic
Celtic
Chadic
Cymric
Dardic
Eskimo
Finnic
Italic
Na-Déné
Pahari
Salish
Siouan
Turkic
Uralic

7 letters:
Caddoan
Hamitic
Iranian
Khoisan
Nilotic
Oceanic
Romance
Saharan

Semitic
Sinitic
Sudanic
Voltaic

8 letters:
Albanian
Arawakan
Armenian
Cushitic
Germanic
Hellenic
Mongolic
Mon-Khmer
Penutian
Rhaetian
Salishan
Slavonic
Tungusic
Wakashan

9 letters:
Algonkian
Anatolian
Brythonic
Caucasian
Chari-Nile
Dravidian
Indo-Aryan
Iroquoian
Muskogean
Semi-Bantu

10 letters:
Algonquian
Athabascan
Athabaskan
Athapascan
Athapaskan
Australian
Benue-Congo
Canaanitic
Hindustani

Melanesian
Muskhogean
Niger-Congo
Polynesian
Sanskritic
Shoshonean
Uto-Aztecan

11 letters:
Afro-Asiatic
East Iranian
Indo-Iranian
Indo-Pacific
Kordofanian
Micronesian
Nilo-Saharan
Pama-Nyungan
Sino-Tibetan
Tupi-Guarani
West Iranian

12 letters:
Austronesian
East Germanic
Indo-European
Tibeto-Burman
West Atlantic
West Germanic
West Slavonic

13 letters:
Austro-Asiatic
Hamito-Semitic
North Germanic
Semito-Hamitic

16 letters:
Malayo-Polynesian

20 letters:
Trans-New Guinea
  phylum

Law

LAW TERMS

2 letters:
On

3 letters:
Ban
Bar
CAV
Doe
Dot
Jus
Run
Sue
Try
Use

4 letters:
Abet
Able
Aver
Avow
Bail
Bond
Case
Cite
Deed
Eyre
Fact
Feme
File
Find
Flaw
Free
Gist
Hear
Heir
Jury
Land
Lien
Mise
Mute
Nisi
Nude
Oath
Open
Oyer
Plea
Real

Rest
Riot
Rout
Rule
Sign
Sine
Soke
Sole
Suit
Term
Tort
Udal
Upon
User
View
Waif
Ward
Will
Writ

5 letters:
Abate
Adopt
Adult
Agist
Alibi
Array
Avoid
Award
Baron
Bench
Brief
Bring
Cause
Cheat
Chose
Close
Costs
Count
Court
Covin
Culpa
Demur
Devil
Donee
Donor
Dower

Droit
Enter
Estop
Evict
Folio
Grant
Grith
Heres
In fee
In rem
Issue
Joint
Judge
Jural
Jurat
Juror
Lapse
Libel
Limit
Manus
Mesne
Moral
Naked
Novel
Offer
Overt
Panel
Parol
Party
Petit
Petty
Plead
Posse
Privy
Proof
Prove
Pupil
Remit
Reply
Retry
Salvo
Sound
Squat
Stale
Swear
Tales

Tenor
Thing
Title
Trial
Venue
Waive
Waste
Wrong

6 letters:
Abator
Accrue
Accuse
Acquit
Action
Affirm
Affray
Allege
Amerce
Answer
Appeal
Assets
Assign
Attach
Attorn
Bailee
Bailor
Bigamy
Capias
Caveat
Cessor
Charge
Come on
Common
Custom
Cy pres
Decree
Defeat
De jure
Delict
Demand
Depose
Devise
Digest
Disbar
Docket
Domain
Duress
Enjoin
Equity
Escrow

Estray
Extend
Extent
Factor
Fiscal
Forest
Guilty
Haeres
Holder
In banc
Infant
Infirm
Injury
Intent
Junior
Jurist
Laches
Lawyer
Legist
Maihem
Malice
Matter
Mayhem
Merger
Merits
Motion
Nonage
Owelty
Pardon
Plaint
Prayer
Prefer
Queen's
Recoup
Rejoin
Relief
Remand
Remise
Report
Rescue
Retain
Return
Review
Ruling
Saving
Script
Socage
Suitor
Surety
Tender
Termer

Termor
Trover
Vacant
Vacate
Vendee
Vendor
Verify
Versus
Viewer
Waiver

7 letters:
Accused
Ad litem
Affiant
Alienee
Alienor
Alimony
Amnesty
Ancient
Approve
Arraign
Assault
Attaint
Bailiff
Bencher
Bequest
Capital
Caption
Case law
Caution
Circuit
Codicil
Commute
Condemn
Condone
Connive
Convene
Convert
Coroner
Counsel
Cruelty
Culprit
Custody
Damages
Damnify
Default
Defence
Deodand
Deraign
Detinue

Devolve
Dies non
Dismiss
Dissent
Dowable
Earnest
Empanel
Engross
Escheat
Estreat
Examine
Execute
Exhibit
Ex parte
Fiction
Filiate
Finding
Foreign
Foreman
Forfeit
Garnish
Grantee
Grantor
Hearing
Hearsay
Heiress
Heritor
Impanel
Implead
Ingoing
In posse
Inquest
Joinder
Juryman
Jus soli
Justice
Justify
Larceny
Lawsuit
Law term
Lex loci
Manager
Mandate
Mens rea
Misuser
Movable
Nol. pros.
Non pros.
Nonsuit
Obscene
Onerous

Opening
Portion
Precept
Presume
Privity
Probate
Proceed
Process
Purview
Recital
Recover
Relator
Release
Replevy
Residue
Reverse
Scandal
Session
Settlor
Several
Slander
Sound in
Stand by
Succeed
Summary
Summons
Suo jure
Suo loco
Swear in
Tenancy
Testate
Testify
Triable
Verdict
Vesture
Vitiate
Voucher
Warrant
Witness

8 letters:
Abeyance
Absolute
Act of God
Advocate
Alienate
Alluvion
Appellee
Assessor
Assignee
Assignor

Attorney
Avulsion
Bailable
Bailment
Bailsman
Bankrupt
Barratry
Barretry
Bequeath
Bondsman
Caveator
Chambers
Chancery
Citation
Complete
Compound
Contempt
Contract
Copyhold
Covenant
Darraign
Dead hand
Decedent
Deed poll
Demurrer
Deponent
Detainer
Disannul
Disclaim
Distrain
Distress
Dividend
Dotation
Estoppel
Estovers
Evidence
Executor
Felo de se
Feme sole
Fiducial
Forensic
Forjudge
Fungible
Gravamen
Guardian
Hand down
Handling
Heirship
Heritage
Hung jury
Hypothec

In camera
In escrow
Innuendo
Insanity
In specie
Instruct
In venter
Ipso jure
Issuable
Jeopardy
Jointure
Judgment
Judicial
Juratory
Juristic
Law Lords
Litigant
Mandamus
Material
Mistrial
Mittimus
Monopoly
Mortmain
Moveable
Novation
Nuisance
Oblivion
Occupant
Ordinary
Parcener
Peculium
Personal
Petition
Pleading
Post-obit
Premises
Presents
Promisee
Promisor
Propound
Pursuant
Question
Rebutter
Recorder
Recovery
Relation
Replevin
Reporter
Reprieve
Schedule
Scienter

Sentence
Sergeant
Serjeant
Solatium
Solution
Spinster
Stranger
Stultify
Subpoena
Sui juris
Swear out
Tenantry
Tipstaff
Tortious
Transfer
Traverse
Trespass
Tribunal
Variance
Voidable
Voir dire
Warranty

9 letters:
Abandonee
Accessary
Accessory
Accretion
Adjective
Adminicle
Affidavit
Affiliate
Alienable
Annulment
Appellant
Appellate
Appendant
Arbitrary
Assumpsit
Attainder
Authentic
Authority
Avoidance
Bailiwick
Barrister
Blasphemy
Bona fides
Briefless
Cartulary
Cassation
Challenge

Champerty
Collusion
Committal
Commonage
Common law
Competent
Complaint
Condition
Contumacy
Coparceny
Counselor
Coverture
Criminate
Custodian
Customary
Debatable
Declarant
Defalcate
Defendant
Demandant
Desertion
Determine
Devisable
Diligence
Disaffirm
Discharge
Discommon
Discovert
Discovery
Disforest
Distraint
Effectual
Equitable
Evocation
Exception
Execution
Executory
Executrix
Exemplify
Extradite
Fiduciary
Filiation
Foreclose
Forejudge
Garnishee
Gavelkind
Grand jury
Guarantee
Heritable
Immovable
Imperfect

Law

Indemnity
Indenture
Instanter
Intention
Interdict
Intervene
Intestate
Jointress
Judge-made
Judgement
Judicable
Judiciary
Juridical
Jurywoman
Law French
Leasehold
Litigable
Mortgagee
Muniments
Nisi prius
Nolle pros.
Non liquet
Not guilty
Obreption
Occupancy
Onomastic
Pecuniary
Petit jury
Petty jury
Plaintiff
Pleadings
Precedent
Prescribe
Principal
Privilege
Proponent
Prosecute
Public law
Pupillage
Quitclaim
Recaption
Re-examine
Reference
Refresher
Rejoinder
Remission
Res gestae
Residuary
Sequester
Servitude
Severable

Severance
Signatory
Sine prole
Solemnity
Solicitor
Specialty
Stand down
Statement
Stipulate
Subrogate
Summation
Summing-up
Surcharge
Surrender
Testament
Testimony
Under oath
Venireman
Vexatious
Vindicate
Voluntary
Volunteer

10 letters:

Absente reo
Acceptance
Accusation
Actionable
Admissible
Advocation
Alienation
Ambulatory
Appearance
Assignment
Attachment
Automatism
Beneficial
Bill of sale
Case stated
Certiorari
Cessionary
Chargeable
Chartulary
Civil death
Coexecutor
Cognisable
Cognisance
Cognizable
Cognizance
Commitment
Commutable

Competence
Competency
Conclusion
Confiscate
Connivance
Consensual
Consortium
Constitute
Contraband
Contractor
Conversion
Conveyance
Convincing
Coparcener
Copyholder
Counsellor
Crown court
Cur. adv. vult
Dead letter
Decree nisi
Defamation
Defeasible
Deposition
Disinherit
Disorderly
Distrainee
Distringas
Emblements
Expectancy
Extinguish
Feme covert
Gratuitous
Ground rent
Hereditary
Homologate
Impartible
Impediment
In articles
Incapacity
In chancery
Inducement
Injunction
In personam
Institutes
Instrument
Intendment
Interplead
Inter vivos
Invalidate
Judicative
Judicatory

Judicature
Jus gentium
Left-handed
Lex scripta
Limitation
Lis pendens
Litigation
Magistrate
Memorandum
Misjoinder
Moratorium
Morganatic
Negligence
Next friend
Nonjoinder
Obligation
Perception
Peremptory
Personalty
Petitioner
Possessory
Predispose
Pre-emption
Preference
Prima facie
Private law
Privileged
Prize court
Proceeding
Propositus
Prosecutor
Recognisee
Recognisor
Recognizee
Recognizor
Repetition
Resolutive
Respondent
Returnable
Secularise
Secularize
Separation
Settlement
Smart money
Spoliation
Stated case
Statute law
Stillicide
Submission
Subreption
Surplusage

Suspension
Third party
Tort-feasor
Trial court
Ultra vires
Unilateral
Vindictive
Wager of law

11 letters:
Affiliation
Affirmation
Arbitration
Beneficiary
Commutation
Complainant
Composition
Constituent
Contentious
Continuance
Coparcenary
Corpus juris
Counterpart
Countersign
County court
Declaration
Declaratory
Dereliction
Descendable
Descendible
Disafforest
Discontinue
Distributee
Disturbance
Encumbrance
Enfranchise
Engrossment
Examination
Expropriate
Fieri facias
Forbearance
Fornication
Garnishment
Hypothecate
Incompetent
Incorporeal
Incriminate
Inheritance
Inquisition
Judges' rules
Jury process

Jus naturale
Justiciable
Law merchant
Leaseholder
Lex talionis
Locus standi
Maintenance
Malfeasance
Mare clausum
Mare liberum
Ministerial
Misfeasance
Mispleading
Necessaries
Nonfeasance
Nudum pactum
Port of entry
Presentment
Presumption
Preterition
Procuration
Procuratory
Prohibition
Prosecution
Protonotary
Provocation
Quo warranto
Replication
Reservation
Res judicata
Restitution
Scire facias
Self-defence
Sequestrate
Special case
Subrogation
Substantive
Surrebuttal
Surrebutter
Unalienable
Unavoidable
Ward of court
Year and a day

12 letters:
Accusatorial
Amicus curiae
Bona vacantia
Chance-medley
Chief justice
Codification

Law

Compurgation
Constructive
Contributory
Conventional
Co-respondent
Coroner's jury
Counterclaim
Cross-examine
Denunciation
Determinable
Distribution
Earnest money
Encumbrancer
Extraditable
Force majeure
Grand larceny
Habeas corpus
Incapacitate
Indefeasible
Instructions
Interpleader
Jail delivery
Jurisconsult
Jurisprudent
Jus sanguinis
Justice court
Manslaughter
Misadventure
Notary public
Obiter dictum
Onus probandi
Pendente lite
Petit larceny
Petty larceny
Prescription
Prothonotary
Real property
Receivership
Recognisance
Recognizance
Surrejoinder
Testamentary
Traffic court
Unappealable
Uncovenanted
Unwritten law
Venire facias
Verification

13 letters:

A mensa et thoro

Articled clerk
Attorney-at-law
Body corporate
Breach of trust
Burden of proof
Certification
Change of venue
Civil marriage
Consideration
Consolidation
Corpus delicti
Countercharge
Determination
Documentation
Eminent domain
Extrajudicial
First offender
Inferior court
Inquisitorial
Interlocutory
Irrepleviable
Jurisprudence
Juvenile court
King's evidence
Legal medicine
Lex non scripta
Nolle prosequi
Paraphernalia
Paterfamilias
Paternity suit
Petty sessions
Premeditation
Primogeniture
Probable cause
Process-server
Question of law
Recrimination
Res adjudicata
Right of common
Self-executing
Sequestration
Sergeant at law
Serjeant at law
Treasure-trove

14 letters:

Arrest judgment
Barrister-at-law
Chamber counsel
Counselor-at-law
Decree absolute

Direct evidence
Examine-in-chief
Family Division
Fideicommissum
Irreplevisable
Justices in eyre
Mental disorder
Napoleonic Code
Nolo contendere
Non prosequitur
Plea bargaining
Posse comitatus
Property centre
Public defender
Public nuisance
Question of fact
Representation
State's evidence
Summary offence
Time immemorial
Ultimogeniture
Unincorporated
Utter barrister

15 letters:

Attorney general
Bill of attainder
Breach of promise
Carnal knowledge
Coroner's inquest
Disorderly house
Due process of law
Fideicommissary
Imprescriptable
Interrogatories
Non compos
  mentis
Official Referee
Oyer and terminer
Private nuisance
Quarter sessions
Res ipsa loquitur
Special pleading
Writ of execution

16 letters:

Affiliation order
Anton Piller order
Bill of indictment
Blasphemous libel
Breach of the peace
Conscience clause

Deferred sentence
Demisit sine prole
Dies non juridicus
Exemplary
  damages
Flagrante delicto
Forensic medicine
Goods and chattels
Magistrates' court
Mental impairment
Personal property
Public prosecutor
Restraining order
Statement of claim
Territorial court
Transitory action
Unlawful assembly
Without prejudice

17 letters:
Arrest of judgement
Compliance officer
Curia advisari vult
Disorderly conduct
False
  imprisonment
Insurable interest
Judgment by
  default
Justice of the peace
Persistent cruelty

18 letters:
Clerk to the justices

Corpus Juris Civilis
Cumulative
  evidence
In flagrante delicto
Judicial separation
Particulars of Claim
Pecuniary
  advantage
Place of safety
  order

19 letters:
Administration
  order
Challenge to the
  array
Challenge to the
  polls
Prosecuting
  attorney
Restrictive
  covenant
Specific
  performance
Summary
  jurisdiction

20 letters:
Court of first
  instance
Criminal
  conversation
Medical
  jurisprudence

Obtaining by
  deception
Psychopathic
  disorder
Statutory
  declaration
Voluntary
  arrangement

21 letters:
Indeterminate
  sentence
Unreasonable
  behaviour

22 letters:
Affiliation
  proceedings
Contributory
  negligence
Divorce from bed
  and board

23 letters:
Letters of
  administration

24 letters:
Diminished
  responsibility

26 letters:
Certificate of
  incorporation

CRIMINAL LAW TERMS

5 letters:
Arson
Entry
Felon
Force
Theft
Thief
Utter

6 letters:
Felony
Suborn

7 letters:
Battery

Embrace
Forgery
Impeach
Perjure
Perjury
Riot Act
Robbery

8 letters:
Bailment
Burglary
Embracer
Infamous
True bill

9 letters:
Acquittal
Deception
Embraceor
Embracery
Felonious
Personate

10 letters:
Hard labour
Indictable
Indictment

12 letters:
Misdemeanant

Law

Misdemeanour

13 letters:
Housebreaking

14 letters:
False pretences

Penal servitude

16 letters:
Actual bodily harm

18 letters:
Grievous bodily

harm
Malice
  aforethought

PROPERTY LAW TERMS

3 letters:
Fee

4 letters:
Oust
Tail

5 letters:
Entry

6 letters:
Assure
Convey
Demise
Divest
Entail
Estate
Ouster
Result
Revert
Seisin
Seizin
Tenure
Vested

7 letters:
Abutter
Adverse
Appoint
Chattel
Deforce
Demesne
Descent
Devisee
Devisor
Enfeoff
Fee tail
Fixture
Heirdom

8 letters:
Abuttals

Amortise
Amortize
Disseise
Dominion
Dominium
Easement
Freehold
Heirloom
Hotchpot
Messuage
Remitter
Riparian
Survivor
Warranty

9 letters:
Abatement
Accession
Ademption
Appointee
Appointor
Disentail
Ejectment
Fee simple
Heir-at-law
Intrusion
Mortgager
Mortgagor
Partition
Party wall
Reconvert
Remainder
Reversion
Severalty

10 letters:
Betterment
Freeholder
Particular
Perpetuity
Transferee

Transferor

11 letters:
Advancement
Appointment
Chattel real
Reversioner
Transferrer

12 letters:
Appurtenance
Dilapidation
Heir apparent
Heriditament
Remainderman

13 letters:
Administrator

14 letters:
Administration
Vested interest

15 letters:
Abstract of title
Chattel personal
Unity of interest

16 letters:
Dominant
  tenement
Servient tenement

18 letters:
Equity of
  redemption
Power of
  appointment

SCOTS LAW TERMS

3 letters:
Feu

5 letters:
Agent
Poind
Pupil
Tutor

6 letters:
Assize
Decern
Delict
Depone
Desert
Fiscal
Notour
Repone
Sasine
Wadset

7 letters:
Aliment
Curator
Decreet
Feu duty
Mandate

8 letters:
Advocate
Continue
Defender
Hypothec
Law agent
Location
Lockfast
Poinding
Thirlage

9 letters:
Approbate
Avizandum
Interdict
Not proven
Tradition

10 letters:
Alimentary
Arrestment
Crown agent
Declarator
Repetition

11 letters:
Assignation
Fire raising

Sequestrate
Warrant sale

12 letters:
Interlocutor
Precognition

13 letters:
District court

14 letters:
Advocate Depute
Condescendence
Notour bankrupt
Sheriff officer

16 letters:
Culpable homicide
Multiplepoinding
Procurator fiscal

21 letters:
Approbate and
  reprobate

22 letters:
Justice of the peace
  court

Law sittings

6 letters:
Easter
Hilary

7 letters:
Trinity

10 letters:
Michaelmas

Leather

3 letters:
Kid
Kip

4 letters:
Buff
Calf
Cuir
Hide
Napa
Roan
Yuft

5 letters:
Mocha
Nappa
Suede

6 letters:
Corium
Deacon
Levant
Nubuck®
Oxhide
Patent

Rexine®
Russia
Shammy

7 letters:
Box-calf
Chamois
Cowhide
Dogskin
Hog-skin
Kip-skin
Morocco

Pigskin
Rawhide
Saffian

8 letters:
Buckskin
Cabretta
Capeskin
Cheverel
Cordovan

Cordwain
Deerskin
Marocain
Maroquin
Rough-out
Shagreen

9 letters:
Chevrette
Horsehide

Sharkskin
Sheepskin

10 letters:
Checklaton
Shecklaton

11 letters:
Cuir-bouilli
Whitleather

Lilies

3 letters:
Day

4 letters:
Aloe
Arum
Corn
Lent
Lote
Sego

5 letters:
Calla
Camas
Lotus
Padma
Regal
Tiger
Water
Yucca

6 letters:
Camash
Camass
Canada
Crinum
Easter

Jacob's
Nerine
Nuphar
Smilax
Zephyr

7 letters:
African
Candock
Madonna
Nelumbo
Quamash

8 letters:
Asphodel
Galtonia
Martagon
Nenuphar
Phormium
Plantain
Trillium
Turk's cap
Victoria

9 letters:
Amaryllis
Colchicum

Colocasia
Herb-paris
Kniphofia

10 letters:
Agapanthus
Aspidistra
Belladonna
Fleur de lys
Haemanthus

11 letters:
Convallaria

12 letters:
Annunciation
Hemerocallis
Skunk cabbage
Solomon's seal

14 letters:
Chincherinchee

15 letters:
Star of Bethlehem

Literature

LITERATURE TERMS

2 letters:
SF

4 letters:
Coda
Epic

Myth
Plot
Saga

5 letters:
Beats

Cento
Drama
Essay
Fable
Gloss

Maxim
Motif
Novel
Roman
Story
Theme
Trope
Verse

6 letters:
Bathos
Comedy
Gothic
Legend
Parody
Pathos
Satire
Simile
Sketch
Theory
Thesis

7 letters:
Bombast
Byronic
Chiller
Conceit
Epistle
Epitaph
Erasure
Faction
Fantasy
Homeric
Imagery
Janeite
Joycean
Kenning
Lampoon
Novella
Polemic
Realism
Subplot
Subtext
Tragedy

8 letters:
Allegory
Allusion
Anti-hero
Aphorism
Archaism
Augustan

Causerie
Dialogue
Epilogue
Exegesis
Fabulist
Foreword
Futurism
Horatian
Jacobean
Kailyard
Kiddy lit
Metaphor
Narrator
Oxymoron
Pastiche
Pastoral
Samizdat
Swiftian
Vignette

9 letters:
Amphigory
Antinovel
Anti-roman
Brechtian
Bricolage
Cyberpunk
Decadence
Derridian
Dialectic
Discourse
Gongorism
Hellenism
Invective
Melodrama
Modernism
Narrative
Novelette
Pot-boiler

10 letters:
Amphigouri
Bakhtinian
Belletrist
Ciceronian
Classicism
Denouement
Dickensian
Johnsonian
Journalese
Juvenalian
Kafkaesque

Laurentian
Lawrentian
Mock-heroic
Mythopoeia
Naturalism
Nom de plume
Palindrome
Paraphrase
Picaresque
Plagiarism
Post-theory
Roman à clef
Short story
Spoonerism
Surrealism

11 letters:
Black comedy
Campus novel
Courtly love
Fantastique
Festschrift
Fin de siècle
Foucauldian
Hagiography
Historicism
Littérateur
Metafiction
Narratology
Pornography
Queer theory
Romanticism
Tragicomedy

12 letters:
Alliteration
Bibliography
Bodice-ripper
Hermeneutics
Magic realism
Metalanguage
New criticism
Nouveau roman
Onomatopoeia
Splatterpunk

13 letters:
Angry Young Men
Belles-lettres
Bildungsroman
Carnivalesque
Celtic Revival

Literature

Colloquialism
Expressionism
Marxist theory
Postmodernism
Structuralism
Sturm und Drang

14 letters:
Beat Generation
Bowdlerization
Cut-up technique
Deconstruction
Double entendre
Feminist theory
Figure of speech
Locus classicus
Lost Generation
Magical realism

New historicism
Science fiction

15 letters:
Bloomsbury group
Comedy of
  manners
Epistolary novel
Historical novel
Intertextuality
Post-colonialism

16 letters:
Commedia
  dell'arte
Death of the
  author
Hudibrastic verse
Sentimental novel

Socialist realism

17 letters:
Interior monologue
Literary criticism
Post-structuralism
Restoration
  comedy

19 letters:
Cultural
  materialism

21 letters:
Signifier and
  signified
Stream of
  consciousness

LITERARY CHARACTERS

Character	Book	Author
Captain Ahab	Moby Dick	Herman Melville
Aladdin	The Arabian Nights' Entertainments	Traditional
Alice	Alice's Adventures in Wonderland, Through the Looking-Glass	Lewis Carroll
Bridget Allworthy	Tom Jones	Henry Fielding
Squire Allworthy	Tom Jones	Henry Fielding
Blanch Amory	Pendennis	William Makepeace Thackeray
Harry Angstrom	Rabbit, Run et al.	John Updike
Artful Dodger	Oliver Twist	Charles Dickens
Jack Aubrey	Master and Commander et al.	Patrick O'Brian
Aunt Polly	Tom Sawyer	Mark Twain
Joe Bagstock	Dombey and Son	Charles Dickens
David Balfour	Kidnapped, Catriona	Robert Louis Stevenson
Mrs. Bardell	The Pickwick Papers	Charles Dickens
Barkis	David Copperfield	Charles Dickens
Jake Barnes	The Sun Also Rises	Ernest Hemingway
Adam Bede	Adam Bede	George Eliot
Seth Bede	Adam Bede	George Eliot
Laura Bell	Pendennis	William Makepeace Thackeray
Elizabeth Bennet	Pride and Prejudice	Jane Austen
Jane Bennet	Pride and Prejudice	Jane Austen
Kitty Bennet	Pride and Prejudice	Jane Austen
Lydia Bennet	Pride and Prejudice	Jane Austen

Character	Book	Author
Mary Bennet	Pride and Prejudice	Jane Austen
Mr. Bennet	Pride and Prejudice	Jane Austen
Mrs. Bennet	Pride and Prejudice	Jane Austen
Edmund Bertram	Mansfield Park	Jane Austen
Julia Bertram	Mansfield Park	Jane Austen
Lady Bertram	Mansfield Park	Jane Austen
Maria Bertram	Mansfield Park	Jane Austen
Sir Thomas Bertram	Mansfield Park	Jane Austen
Tom Bertram	Mansfield Park	Jane Austen
Biddy	Great Expectations	Charles Dickens
Charles Bingley	Pride and Prejudice	Jane Austen
Stephen Blackpool	Hard Times	Charles Dickens
Anthony Blanche	Brideshead Revisited	Evelyn Waugh
Leopold Bloom	Ulysses	James Joyce
Molly Bloom	Ulysses	James Joyce
Mr. Boffin	Our Mutual Friend	Charles Dickens
Mrs. Boffin	Our Mutual Friend	Charles Dickens
Farmer Boldwood	Far from the Madding Crowd	Thomas Hardy
Josiah Bounderby	Hard Times	Charles Dickens
Madeline Bray	Nicholas Nickleby	Charles Dickens
Alan Breck	Kidnapped, Catriona	Robert Louis Stevenson
Sue Bridehead	Jude the Obscure	Thomas Hardy
Miss Briggs	Vanity Fair	William Makepeace Thackeray
Dorothea Brooke	Middlemarch	George Eliot
Mr. Brooke	Middlemarch	George Eliot
Mr. Brownlow	Oliver Twist	Charles Dickens
Daisy Buchanan	The Great Gatsby	F. Scott Fitzgerald
Rosa Bud	Edwin Drood	Charles Dickens
Billy Budd	Billy Budd, Foretopman	Herman Melville
Mr. Bulstrode	Middlemarch	George Eliot
Bumble	Oliver Twist	Charles Dickens
Mrs. Cadwallader	Middlemarch	George Eliot
Carker	Dombey and Son	Charles Dickens
Richard Carstone	Bleak House	Charles Dickens
Sydney Carton	A Tale of Two Cities	Charles Dickens
Mr. Casaubon	Middlemarch	George Eliot
Casby	Little Dorrit	Charles Dickens
Flora Casby	Little Dorrit	Charles Dickens
Dunstan Cass	Silas Marner	George Eliot
Godfrey Cass	Silas Marner	George Eliot
Lady Castlewood	Henry Esmond	William Makepeace Thackeray
Lord Castlewood	Henry Esmond	William Makepeace Thackeray
Holden Caulfield	The Catcher in the Rye	J. D. Salinger
Chadband	Bleak House	Charles Dickens

Literature

Character	Book	Author
Constance Chatterley	Lady Chatterley's Lover	D. H. Lawrence
The Cheeryble Brothers	Nicholas Nickleby	Charles Dickens
Edward Chester	Barnaby Rudge	Charles Dickens
Sir James Chettam	Middlemarch	George Eliot
Chuffey	Martin Chuzzlewit	Charles Dickens
Frank Churchill	Emma	Jane Austen
Jonas Chuzzlewit	Martin Chuzzlewit	Charles Dickens
Martin Chuzzlewit	Martin Chuzzlewit	Charles Dickens
Ada Clare	Bleak House	Charles Dickens
Angel Clare	Tess of the D'Urbervilles	Thomas Hardy
Arthur Clennam	Little Dorrit	Charles Dickens
Humphry Clinker	Humphry Clinker	Tobias Smollett
William Collins	Pride and Prejudice	Jane Austen
Benjy Compson	The Sound and the Fury	William Faulkner
David Copperfield	David Copperfield	Charles Dickens
Emily Costigan	Pendennis	William Makepeace Thackeray
Bob Cratchit	A Christmas Carol	Charles Dickens
Henry Crawford	Mansfield Park	Jane Austen
Mary Crawford	Mansfield Park	Jane Austen
Bute Crawley	Vanity Fair	William Makepeace Thackeray
Miss Crawley	Vanity Fair	William Makepeace Thackeray
Mrs. Bute Crawley	Vanity Fair	William Makepeace Thackeray
Pitt Crawley	Vanity Fair	William Makepeace Thackeray
Rawdon Crawley	Vanity Fair	William Makepeace Thackeray
Sir Pitt Crawley	Vanity Fair	William Makepeace Thackeray
Septimus Crisparkle	Edwin Drood	Charles Dickens
Vincent Crummles	Nicholas Nickleby	Charles Dickens
Jerry Cruncher	A Tale of Two Cities	Charles Dickens
Robinson Crusoe	Robinson Crusoe	Daniel Defoe
Captain Cuttle	Dombey and Son	Charles Dickens
Sebastian Dangerfield	The Ginger Man	J. P. Donleavy
Fitzwilliam Darcy	Pride and Prejudice	Jane Austen
Charles Darnay	A Tale of Two Cities	Charles Dickens
Elinor Dashwood	Sense and Sensibility	Jane Austen
John Dashwood	Sense and Sensibility	Jane Austen
Margaret Dashwood	Sense and Sensibility	Jane Austen
Marianne Dashwood	Sense and Sensibility	Jane Austen
Mrs. Henry Dashwood	Sense and Sensibility	Jane Austen
Dick Datchery	Edwin Drood	Charles Dickens

Character	Book	Author
Fancy Day	Under The Greenwood Tree	Thomas Hardy
Lady Catherine de Bourgh	Pride and Prejudice	Jane Austen
Stephen Dedalus	A Portrait of the Artist as a Young Man, Ulysses	James Joyce
Sir Leicester Dedlock	Bleak House	Charles Dickens
Lady Dedlock	Bleak House	Charles Dickens
Madame Defarge	A Tale of Two Cities	Charles Dickens
Dick Dewy	Under The Greenwood Tree	Thomas Hardy
Mr. Dick	David Copperfield	Charles Dickens
Jim Dixon	Lucky Jim	Kingsley Amis
William Dobbin	Vanity Fair	William Makepeace Thackeray
Mr. Dombey	Dombey and Son	Charles Dickens
Florence Dombey	Dombey and Son	Charles Dickens
Don Quixote	Don Quixote de la Mancha	Miguel de Cervantes
Arabella Donn	Jude the Obscure	Thomas Hardy
Lorna Doone	Lorna Doone	R. D. Blackmore
Amy Dorrit or Little Dorrit	Little Dorrit	Charles Dickens
Fanny Dorrit	Little Dorrit	Charles Dickens
Tip Dorrit	Little Dorrit	Charles Dickens
William Dorrit	Little Dorrit	Charles Dickens
Edwin Drood	Edwin Drood	Charles Dickens
Bentley Drummle	Great Expectations	Charles Dickens
Catriona Drummond	Catriona	Robert Louis Stevenson
Alec D'Urberville	Tess of the D'Urbervilles	Thomas Hardy
Tess Durbeyfield	Tess of the D'Urbervilles	Thomas Hardy
Catherine Earnshaw	Wuthering Heights	Emily Brontë
Hareton Earnshaw	Wuthering Heights	Emily Brontë
Hindley Earnshaw	Wuthering Heights	Emily Brontë
Anne Elliot	Persuasion	Jane Austen
Elizabeth Elliot	Persuasion	Jane Austen
Sir Walter Elliot	Persuasion	Jane Austen
Em'ly	David Copperfield	Charles Dickens
Eppie	Silas Marner	George Eliot
Esmeralda	Notre Dame de Paris	Victor Hugo
Beatrix Esmond	Henry Esmond	William Makepeace Thackeray
Henry Esmond	Henry Esmond	William Makepeace Thackeray
Estella	Great Expectations	Charles Dickens
Bathsheba Everdene	Far from the Madding Crowd	Thomas Hardy
Jane Eyre	Jane Eyre	Charlotte Brontë
Fagin	Oliver Twist	Charles Dickens

Literature

Character	Book	Author
Andrew Fairservice	Rob Roy	Sir Walter Scott
Donald Farfrae	The Mayor of Casterbridge	Thomas Hardy
Jude Fawley	Jude the Obscure	Thomas Hardy
Edward Ferrars	Sense and Sensibility	Jane Austen
Huck *or* Huckleberry Finn	Tom Sawyer, Huckleberry Finn	Mark Twain
Miss Flite	Bleak House	Charles Dickens
Julia Flyte	Brideshead Revisited	Evelyn Waugh
Sebastian Flyte	Brideshead Revisited	Evelyn Waugh
Phileas Fogg	Around the World in Eighty Days	Jules Verne
Man Friday	Robinson Crusoe	Daniel Defoe
Sarah Gamp	Martin Chuzzlewit	Charles Dickens
Joe Gargery	Great Expectations	Charles Dickens
Jay Gatsby	The Great Gatsby	F. Scott Fitzgerald
Walter Gay	Dombey and Son	Charles Dickens
Solomon Gills	Dombey and Son	Charles Dickens
Louisa Gradgrind	Hard Times	Charles Dickens
Thomas Gradgrind	Hard Times	Charles Dickens
Tom Gradgrind	Hard Times	Charles Dickens
Mary Graham	Martin Chuzzlewit	Charles Dickens
Edith Granger	Dombey and Son	Charles Dickens
Dorian Gray	The Picture of Dorian Gray	Oscar Wilde
Mr. Grewgious	Edwin Drood	Charles Dickens
Mrs. Grundy	Speed the Plough	T. Morton
Ben Gunn	Treasure Island	Robert Louis Stevenson
Chris Guthrie	Sunset Song et al.	Lewis Grassic Gibbon
Ham	David Copperfield	Charles Dickens
Richard Hannay	The Thirty-nine Steps et al.	John Buchan
Emma Haredale	Barnaby Rudge	Charles Dickens
John Harmon	Our Mutual Friend	Charles Dickens
James Harthouse	Hard Times	Charles Dickens
Miss Havisham	Great Expectations	Charles Dickens
Sir Mulberry Hawk	Nicholas Nickleby	Charles Dickens
Jim Hawkins	Treasure Island	Robert Louis Stevenson
Bradley Headstone	Our Mutual Friend	Charles Dickens
Heathcliff	Wuthering Heights	Emily Brontë
Uriah Heep	David Copperfield	Charles Dickens
Michael Henchard	The Mayor of Casterbridge	Thomas Hardy
Lizzy Hexam	Our Mutual Friend	Charles Dickens
Betty Higden	Our Mutual Friend	Charles Dickens
Sherlock Holmes	The Adventures of Sherlock Holmes et al.	Sir Arthur Conan Doyle
Humbert Humbert	Lolita	Vladimir Nabokov
Mr. Hyde	The Strange Case of Dr. Jekyll and Mr. Hyde	Robert Louis Stevenson

Character	Book	Author
Injun Joe	Tom Sawyer	Mark Twain
Ishmael	Moby Dick	Herman Melville
Jaggers	Great Expectations	Charles Dickens
John Jarndyce	Bleak House	Charles Dickens
Bailie Nicol Jarvie	Rob Roy	Sir Walter Scott
John Jasper	Edwin Drood	Charles Dickens
Jeeves	My Man Jeeves et al.	P. G. Wodehouse
Dr. Jekyll	The Strange Case of Dr. Jekyll and Mr. Hyde	Robert Louis Stevenson
Mrs. Jellyby	Bleak House	Charles Dickens
Mrs. Jennings	Sense and Sensibility	Jane Austen
Jim	Huckleberry Finn	Mark Twain
Lord Jim	Lord Jim	Joseph Conrad
Jingle	The Pickwick Papers	Charles Dickens
Jo	Bleak House	Charles Dickens
Cissy Jupe	Hard Times	Charles Dickens
Joseph K.	The Trial	Franz Kafka
George Knightley	Emma	Jane Austen
Krook	Bleak House	Charles Dickens
Kurtz	Heart of Darkness	Joseph Conrad
Will Ladislaw	Middlemarch	George Eliot
Helena Landless	Edwin Drood	Charles Dickens
Neville Landless	Edwin Drood	Charles Dickens
Edgar Linton	Wuthering Heights	Emily Brontë
Isabella Linton	Wuthering Heights	Emily Brontë
Dr. Livesey	Treasure Island	Robert Louis Stevenson
Tertius Lydgate	Middlemarch	George Eliot
Rob Roy Macgregor	Rob Roy	Sir Walter Scott
Randle P. McMurphy	One Flew Over the Cuckoo's Nest	Ken Kesey
Abel Magwitch	Great Expectations	Charles Dickens
Dr. Manette	A Tale of Two Cities	Charles Dickens
Lucie Manette	A Tale of Two Cities	Charles Dickens
Madame Mantalini	Nicholas Nickleby	Charles Dickens
The Marchioness	The Old Curiosity Shop	Charles Dickens
Jacob Marley	A Christmas Carol	Charles Dickens
Philip Marlowe	The Big Sleep et al.	Raymond Chandler
Silas Marner	Silas Marner	George Eliot
Stephen Maturin	Master and Commander et al.	Patrick O'Brian
Oliver Mellors	Lady Chatterley's Lover	D. H. Lawrence
Merdle	Little Dorrit	Charles Dickens
Mrs. Merdle	Little Dorrit	Charles Dickens
Wilkins Micawber	David Copperfield	Charles Dickens
Walter Mitty	The Secret Life of Walter Mitty	James Thurber
Lord Mohun	Henry Esmond	William Makepeace Thackeray
Monks	Oliver Twist	Charles Dickens

Literature

Character	Book	Author
Dean Moriarty	On the Road	Jack Kerouac
Professor Moriarty	The Adventures of Sherlock Holmes et al.	Sir Arthur Conan Doyle
Dinah Morris	Adam Bede	George Eliot
Murdstone	David Copperfield	Charles Dickens
Mrs. Grundy	Hard Times	Charles Dickens
Baron Münchhausen	Münchhausen, Baron, Narrative of His Marvellous Travels	R. E. Raspe
Nancy	Oliver Twist	Charles Dickens
Little Nell	The Old Curiosity Shop	Charles Dickens
Captain Nemo	Twenty Thousand Leagues under the Sea	Jules Verne
Kate Nickleby	Nicholas Nickleby	Charles Dickens
Nicholas Nickleby	Nicholas Nickleby	Charles Dickens
Ralph Nickleby	Nicholas Nickleby	Charles Dickens
Newman Noggs	Nicholas Nickleby	Charles Dickens
Susan Nipper	Dombey and Son	Charles Dickens
Kit Nubbles	The Old Curiosity Shop	Charles Dickens
Gabriel Oak	Far from the Madding Crowd	Thomas Hardy
Glorvina O'Dowd	Vanity Fair	William Makepeace Thackeray
Major O'Dowd	Vanity Fair	William Makepeace Thackeray
Mrs. O'Dowd	Vanity Fair	William Makepeace Thackeray
Francis Osbaldistone	Rob Roy	Sir Walter Scott
Rashleigh Osbaldistone	Rob Roy	Sir Walter Scott
George Osborne	Vanity Fair	William Makepeace Thackeray
Pancks	Little Dorrit	Charles Dickens
Sancho Panza	Don Quixote de la Mancha	Miguel de Cervantes
Sal Paradise	On the Road	Jack Kerouac
Passepartout	Around the World in Eighty Days	Jules Verne
Pecksniff	Martin Chuzzlewit	Charles Dickens
Charity Pecksniff	Martin Chuzzlewit	Charles Dickens
Mercy Pecksniff	Martin Chuzzlewit	Charles Dickens
Peggoty	David Copperfield	Charles Dickens
Arthur Pendennis	Pendennis	William Makepeace Thackeray
Helen Pendennis	Pendennis	William Makepeace Thackeray
Pew	Treasure Island	Robert Louis Stevenson
Samuel Pickwick	The Pickwick Papers	Charles Dickens
Ruth Pinch	Martin Chuzzlewit	Charles Dickens
Tom Pinch	Martin Chuzzlewit	Charles Dickens

Character	Book	Author
Pip *or* Philip Pirrip	Great Expectations	Charles Dickens
Herbert Pocket	Great Expectations	Charles Dickens
Charles Pooter	The Diary of a Nobody	G. and W. Grossmith
Martin Poyser	Adam Bede	George Eliot
Mrs. Poyser	Adam Bede	George Eliot
Fanny Price	Mansfield Park	Jane Austen
J. Alfred Prufrock	Prufrock and Other Observations	T. S. Eliot
Pumblechook	Great Expectations	Charles Dickens
Quasimodo	Notre Dame de Paris	Victor Hugo
Queequeg	Moby Dick	Herman Melville
Daniel Quilp	The Old Curiosity Shop	Charles Dickens
Roderick Random	Roderick Random	Tobias Smollett
Riah	Our Mutual Friend	Charles Dickens
Rogue Riderhood	Our Mutual Friend	Charles Dickens
Fanny Robin	Far from the Madding Crowd	Thomas Hardy
Mr. Rochester	Jane Eyre	Charlotte Brontë
Barnaby Rudge	Barnaby Rudge	Charles Dickens
Lady Russell	Persuasion	Jane Austen
Charles Ryder	Brideshead Revisited	Evelyn Waugh
Tom Sawyer	Tom Sawyer	Mark Twain
Scrooge	A Christmas Carol	Charles Dickens
Amelia Sedley	Vanity Fair	William Makepeace Thackeray
Jos Sedley	Vanity Fair	William Makepeace Thackeray
Tristram Shandy	The Life and Opinions of Tristram Shandy	Laurence Sterne
Becky *or* Rebecca Sharp	Vanity Fair	William Makepeace Thackeray
Bill Sikes	Oliver Twist	Charles Dickens
Long John Silver	Treasure Island	Robert Louis Stevenson
Harold Skimpole	Bleak House	Charles Dickens
Sleary	Hard Times	Charles Dickens
Smike	Nicholas Nickleby	Charles Dickens
Harriet Smith	Emma	Jane Austen
Winston Smith	1984	George Orwell
Augustus Snodgrass	The Pickwick Papers	Charles Dickens
Hetty Sorrel	Adam Bede	George Eliot
Lady Southdown	Vanity Fair	William Makepeace Thackeray
Mrs. Sparsit	Hard Times	Charles Dickens
Dora Spenlow	David Copperfield	Charles Dickens
Wackford Squeers	Nicholas Nickleby	Charles Dickens
Starbuck	Moby Dick	Herman Melville
Lucy Steele	Sense and Sensibility	Jane Austen
James Steerforth	David Copperfield	Charles Dickens

Literature

Character	Book	Author
Lord Steyne	Vanity Fair	William Makepeace Thackeray
Esther Summerson	Bleak House	Charles Dickens
Dick Swiveller	The Old Curiosity Shop	Charles Dickens
Mark Tapley	Martin Chuzzlewit	Charles Dickens
Tartuffe	Tartuffe	Molière
Mr. Tartar	Edwin Drood	Charles Dickens
Tarzan	Tarzan of the Apes	Edgar Rice Burroughs
Becky Thatcher	Tom Sawyer	Mark Twain
Montague Tigg	Martin Chuzzlewit	Charles Dickens
Tiny Tim	A Christmas Carol	Charles Dickens
Mrs. Todgers	Martin Chuzzlewit	Charles Dickens
Toots	Dombey and Son	Charles Dickens
Traddles	David Copperfield	Charles Dickens
Squire Trelawney	Treasure Island	Robert Louis Stevenson
Fred Trent	The Old Curiosity Shop	Charles Dickens
Job Trotter	The Pickwick Papers	Charles Dickens
Betsey Trotwood	David Copperfield	Charles Dickens
Sergeant Troy	Far from the Madding Crowd	Thomas Hardy
Tulkinghorn	Bleak House	Charles Dickens
Tracy Tupman	The Pickwick Papers	Charles Dickens
Thomas Tusher	Henry Esmond	William Makepeace Thackeray
Oliver Twist	Oliver Twist	Charles Dickens
Gabriel Varden	Barnaby Rudge	Charles Dickens
Dolly Varden	Barnaby Rudge	Charles Dickens
Mr. Veneering	Our Mutual Friend	Charles Dickens
Mrs. Veneering	Our Mutual Friend	Charles Dickens
Diggory Venn	Return of the Native	Thomas Hardy
Diana Vernon	Rob Roy	Sir Walter Scott
Rosamond Vincy	Middlemarch	George Eliot
Johann Voss	Voss	Patrick White
Eustacia Vye	Return of the Native	Thomas Hardy
George Warrington	Pendennis	William Makepeace Thackeray
Dr. Watson	The Adventures of Sherlock Holmes et al.	Sir Arthur Conan Doyle
Silas Wegg	Our Mutual Friend	Charles Dickens
Sam Weller	The Pickwick Papers	Charles Dickens
Wemmick	Great Expectations	Charles Dickens
Frank Wentworth	Persuasion	Jane Austen
Agnes Wickfield	David Copperfield	Charles Dickens
George Wickham	Pride and Prejudice	Jane Austen
Damon Wildeve	Return of the Native	Thomas Hardy
Bella Wilfer	Our Mutual Friend	Charles Dickens
John Willoughby	Sense and Sensibility	Jane Austen
Nathaniel Winkle	The Pickwick Papers	Charles Dickens

Character	Book	Author
Dolly Winthrop	Silas Marner	George Eliot
Allan Woodcourt	Bleak House	Charles Dickens
Emma Woodhouse	Emma	Jane Austen
Mr. Woodhouse	Emma	Jane Austen
Bertie Wooster	My Man Jeeves et al.	P. G. Wodehouse
Eugene Wrayburn	Our Mutual Friend	Charles Dickens
Jenny Wren	Our Mutual Friend	Charles Dickens
Clym Yeobright	Return of the Native	Thomas Hardy
Thomasin Yeobright	Return of the Native	Thomas Hardy
Yossarian	Catch-22	Joseph Heller
Yuri Zhivago	Doctor Zhivago	Boris Pasternak
Zorba or Alexis Zorbas	Zorba the Greek	Nikos Kazantzakis

See also:
➤ **Diarists** ➤ **Dramatists** ➤ **Musketeers** ➤ **Novelists**
➤ **Poetry** ➤ **Shakespeare** ➤ **Works of literature and music**
➤ **Writers**

Lizards

3 letters:
Eft
Jew

4 letters:
Abas
Gila
Newt
Sand
Tegu
Wall
Worm

5 letters:
Agama
Anole
Draco
Gecko
Guana
Skink
Snake
Tokay
Varan

6 letters:
Anguis
Goanna

Horned
Iguana
Komodo
Leguan
Moloch
Worral
Worrel

7 letters:
Bearded
Frilled
Geckone
Lacerta
Leguaan
Monitor
Perenty
Stellio
Tuatara
Tuatera
Zandoli

8 letters:
Basilisk
Dinosaur
Hatteria
Menopome
Mosasaur

Perentie
Stellion
Sungazer
Teguexin
Whiptail

9 letters:
Blindworm
Chameleon
Galliwasp
Mastigure

10 letters:
Chuckwalla
Glass snake
Hellbender
Kabaragoya
Mosasaurus

11 letters:
Amphisboena
Blue-tongued
Brontosurus

12 letters:
Komodo dragon

Locomotives

Locomotives

7 letters:
Mallard

9 letters:
Blue Peter
Britannia
City Class
Hall Class
King Class

10 letters:
Black Class

The General

11 letters:
Golden Arrow
West Country

12 letters:
General Stamp
Merchant Navy
Schools Class

14 letters:
Flying Scotsman

15 letters:
Coronation Class
Midland
  Compound

16 letters:
Duke of Gloucester

19 letters:
Thomas the Tank
  Engine

London, boroughs of

5 letters:
Brent

6 letters:
Barnet
Bexley
Camden
Ealing
Harrow
Merton
Newham
Sutton

7 letters:
Bromley
Croydon
Enfield
Hackney

Lambeth

8 letters:
Haringey
Havering
Hounslow
Kingston
Lewisham
Richmond

9 letters:
Greenwich
Islington
Redbridge
Southwark

10 letters:
Hillingdon
Wandsworth

11 letters:
Westminster

12 letters:
Tower Hamlets

13 letters:
Waltham Forest

18 letters:
Barking and
  Dagenham

20 letters:
Hammersmith and
  Fulham
Kensington and
  Chelsea

Lovers

Antony and Cleopatra
Bonnie (Parker) and Clyde
  (Barrow)
Richard Burton and Elizabeth
  Taylor
Julius Caesar and Cleopatra
Casanova
Cathy and Heathcliffe
Dante and Beatrice
Darby and Joan
Dido and Aeneas

Don Juan
Edward VIII and Wallis
  Simpson
Eloise and Abelard
Harlequin and Columbine
Hero and Leander
Jane Eyre and Edward
  Rochester
Lancelot and Guinevere
Lochinvar and Ellen
Napoleon and Josephine

Scarlett O'Hara and Rhett Butler
Orpheus and Eurydice
Paris and Helen of Troy
Pelleas and Melisande
Petrarch and Laura
Porgy and Bess
Pyramus and Thisbe

Robin Hood and Maid Marian
Romeo and Juliet
Rosalind and Orlando
Samson and Delilah
Tosca and Cavaradossi
Tristan and Isolde
Troilus and Cressida
Zeus and Hera

M

Mammals, extinct

6 letters:
Apeman
Quagga
Tarpan

7 letters:
Aurochs
Mammoth

8 letters:
Creodont
Eohippus
Irish elk
Mastodon

9 letters:
Dinoceras
Dinothere
Megathere

10 letters:
Glyptodont
Uintathere

11 letters:
Nototherium
Titanothere

12 letters:
Chalicothere

13 letters:
Dryopithecine

14 letters:
Baluchitherium
Labyrinthodont

15 letters:
Sabre-toothed cat

17 letters:
Australopithecine
Sabre-toothed
 tiger

See also:
➤ **Anteaters and other edentates** ➤ **Antelopes** ➤ **Bats**
➤ **Carnivores** ➤ **Cats** ➤ **Cattle, breeds of** ➤ **Cows** ➤ **Dogs**
➤ **Horses** ➤ **Marsupials** ➤ **Monkeys, apes and other**
primates ➤ **Pigs** ➤ **Rabbits and hares** ➤ **Rodents** ➤ **Seals**
➤ **Sea mammals** ➤ **Sheep** ➤ **Shrews and other insectivores**
➤ **Whales and dolphins**

Mania

Mania	**Object**
Ablutomania	Washing
Agoramania	Open spaces
Ailuromania	Cats
Andromania	Men
Anglomania	England
Anthomania	Flowers
Apimania	Bees
Arithmomania	Counting
Automania	Solitude
Autophonomania	Suicide
Balletomania	Ballet
Ballistomania	Bullets
Bibliomania	Books

Mania	Object
Chionomania	Snow
Choreomania	Dancing
Chrematomania	Money
Cremnomania	Cliffs
Cynomania	Dogs
Dipsomania	Alcohol
Doramania	Fur
Dromomania	Travelling
Egomania	Your self
Eleuthromania	Freedom
Entheomania	Religion
Entomomania	Insects
Ergasiomania	Work
Eroticomania	Erotica
Erotomania	Sex
Florimania	Plants
Gamomania	Marriage
Graphomania	Writing
Gymnomania	Nakedness
Gynomania	Women
Hamartiomania	Sin
Hedonomania	Pleasure
Heliomania	Sun
Hippomania	Horses
Homicidomania	Murder
Hydromania	Water
Hylomania	Woods
Hypnomania	Sleep
Ichthyomania	Fish
Iconomania	Icons
Kinesomania	Movement
Kleptomania	Stealing
Logomania	Talking
Macromania	Becoming larger
Megalomania	Your own importance
Melomania	Music
Mentulomania	Penises
Micromania	Becoming smaller
Monomania	One thing
Musicomania	Music
Musomania	Mice
Mythomania	Lies
Necromania	Death
Noctimania	Night
Nudomania	Nudity
Nymphomania	Sex
Ochlomania	Crowds
Oikomania	Home
Oinomania	Wine
Ophidiomania	Reptiles

Marsupials

Mania	Object
Orchidomania	Testicles
Ornithomania	Birds
Phagomania	Eating
Pharmacomania	Medicines
Phonomania	Noise
Photomania	Light
Plutomania	Great wealth
Potomania	Drinking
Pyromania	Fire
Scribomania	Writing
Siderodromomania	Railway travel
Sitomania	Food
Sophomania	Your own wisdom
Thalassomania	The sea
Thanatomania	Death
Theatromania	Theatre
Timbromania	Stamps
Trichomania	Hair
Verbomania	Words
Xenomania	Foreigners
Zoomania	Animals

Marsupials

3 letters:
Roo

4 letters:
Dama
Marl
Tait
Tuan
Uroo

5 letters:
Bilby
Damar
Koala
Mardo
Marlu
Pongo
Quoll
Tungo
Yapok

6 letters:
Badger
Bobuck
Boodie
Cuscus

Glider
Jerboa
Kowari
Merrin
Mongan
Numbat
Possum
Quenda
Quokka
Tammar
Toolah
Tungoo
Warabi
Wogoit
Wombat
Woylie
Yapock

7 letters:
Bettong
Biggada
Dalgite
Dalgyte
Dasyure
Dibbler

Dunnart
Kultarr
Mulgara
Munning
Ningaui
Opossum
Potoroo
Wallaby
Wild cat
Wurrung
Yallara

8 letters:
Boongary
Burramys
Dasyurid
Duckbill
Forester
Kangaroo
Karrabul
Macropod
Platypus
Ringtail
Squeaker
Tiger cat

Toolache
Wallaroo
Wintarro
Wuhl-wuhl

9 letters:
Bandicoot
Boodie rat
Didelphia
Koala bear
Larapinta
Native cat
Pademelon
Petaurist
Phalanger
Thylacine
Wambenger

10 letters:
Antechinus
Diprotodon
Honey mouse
Native bear
Noolbenger
Notoryctes
Paddymelon
Phascogale
Red wallaby
Rock possum
Satanellus

11 letters:
Diprotodont
Fairy possum
Flying mouse
Hare-wallaby
Honey possum
Nototherium
Pygmy glider
Pygmy possum
Rat kangaroo
Red kangaroo
Rock wallaby
Sugar glider
Tcharibeena

12 letters:
Agile wallaby
Black wallaby
Fluffy glider
Grey forester
Marsupial cat

Parma wallaby
Pitchi-pitchi
River wallaby
Sandy wallaby
Scrub wallaby
Swamp wallaby
Tree kangaroo

13 letters:
Brush kangaroo
Feather glider
Marsupial mole
Rufous wallaby
Sooty kangaroo
Striped possum
Tasmanian wolf
Ursine dasyure

14 letters:
Banded anteater
Brown bandicoot
Flying squirrel
Forest kangaroo
Gunn's bandicoot
Jerboa kangaroo
Jungle kangaroo
Mallee kangaroo
Marsupial mouse
Mountain possum
Plains kangaroo
Ringtail possum
Squirrel glider
Tasmanian devil
Tasmanian tiger

15 letters:
Barred bandicoot
Bennett's wallaby
Brush-tail possum
Desert bandicoot
Flying phalanger
Golden bandicoot
Naked-nose wombat
Rabbit bandicoot
Whiptail wallaby

16 letters:
Antelope kangaroo
Hairy-nosed wombat
Musky rat- kangaroo
Red-necked wallaby
Ringtailed possum

Spotted native cat

17 letters:
Antilopine wallaby
Brindled bandicoot
Brush-tailed possum
Cannings' little dog
Desert-rat kangaroo
Great grey kangaroo
Grey's brush wallaby
Leadbeater's possum
Northern native cat
Pretty-face wallaby
Rufous rat-kangaroo

18 letters:
Black-faced kangaroo
Black-tailed wallaby
Brush-tailed bettong
Brush-tailed wallaby
Duck-billed platypus
Jerboa pouched mouse
Long-eared bandicoot
Long-nosed bandicoot
Pig-footed bandicoot

19 letters:
Darling Downs dunnart
Eastern brush wallaby
Eastern grey kangaroo
Green ringtail possum
Lesueur's rat-kangaroo
Mountain pygmy possum
Short-eared bandicoot

Short-nosed bandicoot
Western grey kangaroo
Yellow-bellied glider

20 letters:
Bennett's tree kangaroo
Burrowing rat-kangaroo
Rabbit-eared bandicoot

21 letters:
Lumholtz's tree kangaroo
Ring-tailed rock wallaby
Short-nosed rat kangaroo

22 letters:
Bridled nail-tail wallaby
Lemuroid ringtail possum
Northern brown bandicoot
Southern brown bandicoot
Yellow-footed antechinus

23 letters:
Crescent nail-tail wallaby
Mountain brushtail possum
Northern nail-tail wallaby
Yellow-footed rock wallaby

24 letters:
Tasmanian barred bandicoot

25 letters:
Crest-tailed marsupial mouse

26 letters:
Herbert River ringtail possum

Martial arts

MARTIAL ARTS

4 letters:
Judo
Sumo

5 letters:
Iai-do
Kendo
Kyudo

6 letters:
Aikido
Karate
Kung fu

Tukido®

7 letters:
Hapkido
Ju jitsu
Ju-jutsu

8 letters:
Capoeira
Iai-jutsu
Jiu jitsu
Karate-do
Muay Thai

Ninjitsu
Ninjutsu
Wing Chun

9 letters:
Tae kwon-do
Yari-jutsu

10 letters:
Jeet Kune Do
Kick boxing
Naginata-do
Thai boxing

11 letters:
Tai chi chuan

12 letters:
Tai chi qi gong
Tomiki aikido

13 letters:
Goju Kai karate
Goju Ryu karate
Hung Gar kung fu
Sumo wrestling
Wado Ryu karate

14 letters:
Ishin Ryu karate
Sankukai karate
Shito Ryu karate

Shotokai karate
Shotokan karate
Shukokai karate
Wing Tsun kung fu

16 letters:
Crane style kung fu
Ta Sheng Men kung fu
Tiger style kung fu

17 letters:
Monkey style kung fu

18 letters:
Kyokushinkai karate

24 letters:
Praying Mantis style kung fu

MARTIAL ARTS TERMS

Term	**Meaning**
Basho	Sumo turnament
Bo	Staff
Bogu	Kendo armour
Bokuto	Kendo wooden sword
Budo *or* bushido	Warrior's way
Dan	Black belt grade
Do	Kendo breastplate
-do	The way
Dohyo	Sumo ring
Dojo	Practice room or mat
Gi	Suit
Hachimaki *or* tenugui	Kendo headcloth
Hakama	Divided skirt
Ippon	One competition point
Jiu-kumite	Freestyle karate competition
-jutsu	Fighting art
-ka	Student
Kama	Hand sickle
Kata	Sequence of techniques
Katana	Kendo sword
Katsu	Resuscitation techniques
Keikogi	Kendo jacket
Kesho-mawashi	Embroidered sumo apron
Ki, chi, *or* qi	Inner power
Kiai	Yell accompanying movement
Kihon	Repetition of techniques
Kote	Kendo gauntlets
Kyu	Student grade
Makiwara	Practice block
Mawashi	Sumo fighting belt
Men	Kendo mask

Materials

Term	Meaning
Nage-waza *or* tachi-waza	Ju jitsu competition
Naginata	Curved-blade spear
Ne-waza	Ju jitsu competition
Ninin-dori	Aikido competition
Ninja	Japanese trained assassin
Nunchaku	Hinged flails
Obi	Coloured belt
Ozeki	Sumo champion
Qi gong	Breath control
Randori kyoghi	Aikido competition
Rikishi	Sumo wrestler
Rokushakubo	Six-foot staff
Ryu	Martial arts school
Sai	Short trident
Samurai	Japanese warrior caste
Sensei	Teacher
Shinai	Kendo bamboo sword
Sifu	Teacher
Suneate	Naginata shin guards
Tanto randori	Aikido competition
Tare	Kendo apron
Te	Hand fighting
Ton-fa *or* tui-fa	Hardwood weapon
Tsuna	Sumo grand champion's belt
Waza-ari	Half competition point
Yari	Spear
Yokozuna	Sumo grand champion
Zanshin	Total awareness

Materials

3 letters:
Say

4 letters:
Lamé
Lawn
Tape
Wool

5 letters:
Crash
Toile
Twill

6 letters:
Canvas
Cermet
Coburg
Dimity

Russel
Soneri
Tusser

7 letters:
Batiste
Cambric
Ceramic
Chiffon
Galatea
Genappe
Hessian
Oilskin
Sagathy

8 letters:
Cretonne
Gossamer
Homespun

Illusion
Jeanette
Marocain
Moquette
Prunella
Toilinet

9 letters:
Calamanco
Cellulose
Charmeuse®
Fibrefill
Gaberdine
Macintosh
Pina-cloth
Polyester
Sackcloth
Stockinet

Swansdown
Tarpaulin
Towelling
Worcester

10 letters:
Fibreglass
Toilinette
Winceyette

11 letters:
Stockinette

Mathematics

BRANCHES OF MATHEMATICS

4 letters:
Pure

6 letters:
Conics

7 letters:
Algebra
Applied

8 letters:
Analysis
Calculus
Geometry
Topology

9 letters:
Set theory

10 letters:
Arithmetic
Game theory
Nomography
Statistics

11 letters:
Group theory

12 letters:
Number theory
Trigonometry

13 letters:
Chaos geometry

14 letters:
Boolean algebra

16 letters:
Integral calculus

17 letters:
Euclidean geometry
Numerical analysis
Probability theory

18 letters:
Analytical geometry
Coordinate geometry

20 letters:
Differential calculus
Non-Euclidean geometry

MATHEMATICAL TERMS

2 letters:
Pi

3 letters:
Arc
Log
Odd
Set
Sum

4 letters:
Area
Axis
Base
Cone

Cube
Cusp
Even
Mean
Mode
Node
Plus
Root
Sine
Surd
Zero

5 letters:
Angle
Chord

Curve
Digit
Graph
Helix
Index
Locus
Minus
Power
Prism
Proof
Ratio
Solid
Torus
Union

Mathematics

Value
X-axis
Y-axis
Z-axis

6 letters:
Binary
Circle
Cosine
Cuboid
Denary
Equals
Factor
Matrix
Median
Number
Oblong
Origin
Radian
Radius
Scalar
Secant
Sector
Sphere
Square
Subset
Vector
Volume

7 letters:
Average
Decagon
Decimal
Ellipse
Formula
Hexagon
Integer
Nonagon
Octagon
Open set
Polygon
Product
Rhombus
Scalene
Tangent

8 letters:
Addition
Algorism
Binomial
Constant
Cosecant

Cube root
Cylinder
Diagonal
Diameter
Division
Equation
Fraction
Function
Heptagon
Infinity
Integral
Operator
Parabola
Parallel
Pentagon
Quadrant
Quotient
Triangle
Variable

9 letters:
Algorithm
Closed set
Cotangent
Factorial
Frequency
Hyperbola
Isosceles
Logarithm
Numerator
Operation
Rectangle
Remainder
Slide rule
Trapezium

10 letters:
Acute angle
Concentric
Co-ordinate
Hemisphere
Hypotenuse
Octahedron
Percentage
Polyhedron
Polynomial
Real number
Reciprocal
Right angle
Semicircle
Square root

11 letters:
Coefficient
Denominator
Equilateral
Exponential
Icosahedron
Obtuse angle
Prime number
Probability
Reflex angle
Subtraction
Tetrahedron
Venn diagram

12 letters:
Common factor
Dodecahedron
Intersection
Universal set

13 letters:
Circumference
Complex number
Mandelbrot set
Natural number
Ordinal number
Parallelogram
Perfect number
Quadrilateral

14 letters:
Cardinal number
Multiplication
Proper fraction
Rational number
Vulgar fraction

15 letters:
Imaginary number

16 letters:
Improper fraction
Irrational number
Natural logarithm
Recurring decimal
Strange attractor

17 letters:
Common
   denominator
Pythagoras'
   theorem
Quadratic equation

18 letters:
Significant figures

19 letters:
Right-angled triangle

20 letters:
Cartesian coordinates

MATHEMATICIANS

3 letters:
Dee, *John*
Lie, *Marius Sophus*

4 letters:
Hero
Kahn, *Herman*
Weyl, *Hermann*
Zeno *(of Elea)*

5 letters:
Aiken, *Howard Hathaway*
Bondi, *Hermann*
Boole, *George*
Comte, *Isidore Auguste*
Euler, *Leonhard*
Gauss, *Karl Friedrich*
Gibbs, *Josiah Willard*
Gödel, *Kurt*

6 letters:
Agnesi, *Maria Gaetana*
Ampère, *André Marie*
Balmer, *Johann Jakob*
Bessel, *Friedrich Wilhelm*
Briggs, *Henry*
Cantor, *Georg*
Cauchy, *Augustin Louis*
Cayley, *Arthur*
Cocker, *Edward*
Darwin, *George Howard*
Euclid
Fermat, *Pierre De*
Gunter, *Edmund*
Halley, *Edmund*
Jacobi, *Karl Gustav Jacob*
Napier, *John*
Newton, *Isaac*
Pappus *of Alexandria*
Pascal, *Blaise*
Peirce, *Charles Sanders*
Penney, *William George*
Taylor, *Brook*

Lowest common multiple

21 letters:
Simultaneous equations

23 letters:
Lowest common denominator

Thales
Turing, *Alan Mathison*
Wiener, *Norbert*

7 letters:
Babbage, *Charles*
D'Oresme, *Nicole*
Eudoxus *of Cnidus*
Fourier, *Jean Baptiste Joseph*
Galileo
Hawking, *Stephen William*
Hilbert, *David*
Khayyám, *Omar*
Laplace, *Pierre Simon*
Leibniz
Pearson, *Karl*
Penrose, *Roger*
Poisson, *Siméon Denis*
Ptolemy
Pytheas
Riemann, *Georg Friedrich Bernhard*
Russell, *Bertrand*
Shannon, *Claude*

8 letters:
Archytas
Clausius, *Rudolf Julius*
Dedekind, *Julius Wilhelm Richard*
De Fermat, *Pierre*
Einstein, *Albert*
Goldbach, *Christian*
Hamilton, *William Rowan*
Lagrange, *Joseph Louis*
Legendre, *Adrien Marie*
Lovelace, *Ada*
Mercator, *Gerardus*
Playfair, *John*
Poincaré, *Jules Henri*

9 letters:
Bernoulli, *Daniel*
Bernoulli, *Jacques*

Meals

Bernoulli, *Jean*
Descartes, *René*
Dirichlet, *Peter Gustav Lejeune*
Dunstable, *John*
Fibonacci, *Leonardo*
Minkowski, *Hermann*
Whitehead, *Alfred North*

10 letters:
Apollonius *of Perga*
Archimedes
Diophantos
Kolmogorov, *Andrei Nikolaevich*
Pythagoras
Torricelli, *Evangelista*

Von Neumann, *John*

11 letters:
Anaximander
Lobachevsky, *Nikolai Ivanovich*
Von Leibnitz, *Gottfried Wilhelm*

12 letters:
De Maupertuis, *Pierre Louis Moreau*
Eratosthenes

13 letters:
Regiomontanus, *Johann Müller*

14 letters:
Le Rond Alembert, *Jean*

Meals

3 letters:
Tea

5 letters:
Feast
Lunch
Snack
Tapas

6 letters:
Barbie
Brunch
Buffet

Dinner
Picnic
Supper
Tiffin

7 letters:
Banquet
Fish fry
High tea

8 letters:
Barbecue
Cream tea

Luncheon

9 letters:
Beanfeast
Breakfast
Elevenses

11 letters:
Smorgasbord

12 letters:
Afternoon tea

Meats

3 letters:
Ham
Leg
Rib

4 letters:
Beef
Chop
Duck
Game
Hock
Hogg
Lamb
Loin
Pork
Rack

Rump
Spam®
Veal

5 letters:
Bacon
Chuck
Chump
Devon
Gigot
Goose
Hough
Liver
Mince
Offal
Round

Scrag
Shank
Skirt
Steak
T-bone
Tripe

6 letters:
Breast
Collar
Cutlet
Fillet
Gammon
Haslet
Hogget
Kidney

Lights
Mutton
Oxtail
Pigeon
Polony
Saddle
Salami
Tongue
Turkey

7 letters:
Beef-ham
Brisket
Charqui
Chicken
Chorizo
Gristle
Numbles
Sausage
Saveloy
Sirloin
Topside
Venison

8 letters:
Bath chap
Cervelat
Chitlins
Cold cuts
Escalope
Forehock

Lamb's fry
Noisette
Oxtongue
Parma ham
Pastrami
Pemmican
Pheasant
Pope's eye
Salt pork
Shoulder
Sparerib
Undercut

9 letters:
Bockwurst
Boerewors
Bratwurst
Chipolata
Chitlings
Entrecôte
Foreshank
Pepperoni
Tournedos

10 letters:
Chuck steak
Corned beef
Crown roast
Knackwurst
Knockwurst
Liverwurst

Médaillons
Mortadella
Prosciutto
Rolled lamb
Silverside
Sweetbread
Tenderloin

11 letters:
Baron of beef
Minute steak
Parson's nose
Square slice

12 letters:
Black pudding
Chitterlings
Liver sausage
Lorne sausage
Luncheon meat
Stewing steak

13 letters:
Chateaubriand
Colonial goose
Square sausage

16 letters:
Porterhouse steak

17 letters:
Cumberland
  sausage

Medals

9 letters:
Iron Cross

10 letters:
Bronze Star
Silver Star

11 letters:
George Cross
Purple Heart

13 letters:
Croix de Guerre
Legion of Merit

Royal Red Cross
Victoria Cross

14 letters:
Légion d'Honneur

20 letters:
Militaire Willemsorde

25 letters:
Congressional Medal of Honor
Distinguished Service Cross
Distinguished Service Order

Medicine

BRANCHES OF MEDICINE

5 letters:
Legal
Space

6 letters:
Sports

7 letters:
Anatomy
Myology
Nuclear
Otology
Surgery
Urology

8 letters:
Aviation
Etiology
Forensic
Internal
Nosology
Oncology
Physical
Posology
Serology
Tocology
Tokology
Virology

9 letters:
Aetiology
Anaplasty
Andrology
Angiology
Audiology
Chiropody
Dentistry
Midwifery
Neurology
Nostology
Nutrition
Optometry
Orthotics
Osteology
Pathology
Radiology
Rhinology

10 letters:
Balneology

Cardiology
Embryology
Exodontics
Geratology
Geriatrics
Gynecology
Hematology
Immunology
Industrial
Nephrology
Obstetrics
Odontology
Orthoptics
Pediatrics
Preventive
Proctology
Psychiatry
Psychology
Toxicology
Trichology
Veterinary

11 letters:
Biomedicine
Dermatology
Diagnostics
Eccrinology
Endodontics
Gerontology
Gynaecology
Haematology
Laryngology
Neonatology
Oral hygiene
Orthodontia
Orthopedics
Osteoplasty
Paediatrics
Physiatrics
Stomatology
Syphilology
Venereology

12 letters:
Anaesthetics
Bacteriology
Epidemiology
Neuroanatomy
Neurosurgery

Orthodontics
Orthopaedics
Periodontics
Pharyngology
Rheumatology
Therapeutics

13 letters:
Dental hygiene
Dental surgery
Endocrinology
Genitourinary
Materia medica
Morbid anatomy
Ophthalmology
Physiotherapy
Speech therapy

14 letters:
Neuropathology
Otolaryngology
Plastic surgery
Psychoanalysis
Symptomatology

15 letters:
Bioastronautics
Encephalography
Immunochemistry
Neurophysiology
Neuropsychiatry

16 letters:
Gastroenterology
Spare-part surgery

17 letters:
Electrophysiology
Hydrotherapeutics
Veterinary science

18 letters:
Neuroendocrinology

19 letters:
Electrotherapeutics

MEDICAL PRACTITIONERS AND SPECIALISTS

2 letters:
GP

3 letters:
Vet

5 letters:
Nurse

6 letters:
Doctor
Extern
Intern
Matron
Physio

7 letters:
Dentist
Externe
Interne
Midwife
Orderly
Surgeon

8 letters:
Houseman
Optician
Resident

9 letters:
Anatomist
Dietitian
Internist
Myologist
Orthotist
Otologist
Paramedic
Registrar
Therapist
Urologist

10 letters:
Consultant
Etiologist
Exodontist
Geriatrist
Nosologist
Oncologist
Orthoptist
Serologist
Virologist

11 letters:
Aetiologist
Andrologist
Audiologist
Chiropodist
Endodontist
Neurologist
Optometrist
Orthopedist
Osteologist
Pathologist
Radiologist
Rhinologist

12 letters:
Anaesthetist
Balneologist
Cardiologist
Embryologist
Geriatrician
Gynecologist
Hematologist
Immunologist
Junior doctor
Nephrologist
Neurosurgeon
Nutritionist
Obstetrician
Odontologist
Orthodontist
Orthopaedist
Pediatrician
Proctologist
Psychiatrist
Psychologist
Radiographer
Toxicologist
Trichologist
Veterinarian

13 letters:
Dental surgeon
Dermatologist
Diagnostician
District nurse
Gerontologist
Gynaecologist
Haematologist
Health visitor

Laryngologist
Neonatologist
Oral hygienist
Paediatrician
Psychoanalyst
Syphilologist
Venereologist

14 letters:
Bacteriologist
Barefoot doctor
Epidemiologist
House physician
Hydrotherapist
Neuroanatomist
Nursing officer
Pharyngologist
Plastic surgeon
Rheumatologist

15 letters:
Dental hygienist
Endocrinologist
Ophthalmologist
Physiotherapist
Speech therapist

16 letters:
Neuropathologist
Otolaryngologist

17 letters:
Forensic scientist
Neurophysiologist
Neuropsychiatrist
Veterinary surgeon

18 letters:
Gastroenterologist

19 letters:
Electrophysiologist
General
  practitioner

20 letters:
Laboratory
  technician

21 letters:
Occupational
  therapist

Medicine

MEDICAL AND SURGICAL INSTRUMENTS AND EQUIPMENT

4 letters:
Swab

5 letters:
Clamp
Curet
Drain
Lance
Probe
Sling
Sound
Stupe

6 letters:
Bedpan
Canula
Lancet
Needle
Splint
Stylet
Suture
Trepan
Trocar

7 letters:
Bandage
Cannula
Catling
Curette
Forceps
Packing
Scalpel
Scanner
Syringe
Wet pack

8 letters:
Bistoury
Catheter
Heat lamp
Hemostat
Iron lung
Otoscope
Pulmotor®
Speculum
Trephine

9 letters:
Aspirator
CT scanner
Cymograph

Depressor
Endoscope
Fetoscope
Haemostat
Inhalator
Kymograph
Nebulizer
Pacemaker
Perimeter
Raspatory
Retractor
Rheometer
Skiascope
Stretcher

10 letters:
CAT scanner
Colposcope
Compressor
Cystoscope
Fiberscope
Fibrescope
Gonioscope
Hypodermic
Inspirator
Microscope
Orthoscope
Oxygen mask
Oxygen tent
Respirator
Rhinoscope
Spirograph
Spirometer
Tourniquet
Urinometer
Ventilator

11 letters:
Arthroscope
Cardiograph
Colonoscope
Fluoroscope
Gamma camera
Gastroscope
Laparoscope
Nephroscope
Plaster cast
Pneumograph
Proctoscope

Retinoscope
Stethoscope
Stomach pump
X-ray machine

12 letters:
Bronchoscope
Laryngoscope
Resuscitator
Sphygmograph
Thoracoscope
Urethroscope

13 letters:
Defibrillator
Encephalogram
Esophagoscope
Kidney machine
Pharyngoscope
Pneumatometer
Röntgenoscope
Styptic pencil

14 letters:
Oesophagoscope
Ophthalmoscope
Roentgenoscope
Specimen bottle

15 letters:
Artificial heart
Dialysis machine
Electromyograph

16 letters:
Artificial kidney
Heart-lung
  machine
Hypodermic
  needle
Sphygmomanometer

17 letters:
Hypodermic
  syringe
Ultrasound scanner

18 letters:
Electrocardiograph
Life-support
  machine

Medicine

19 letters:
Clinical thermometer

21 letters:
Electroencephalograph

BRANCHES OF ALTERNATIVE MEDICINE

7 letters:
Massage
Shiatsu

8 letters:
Hypnosis

9 letters:
Herbalism
Iridology
Radionics

10 letters:
Homeopathy

11 letters:
Acupressure
Acupuncture
Biofeedback
Homoeopathy
Kinesiology
Moxibustion
Naturopathy
Reflexology

12 letters:
Aromatherapy

Osteopathy
Chiropractic
Hydrotherapy
Hypnotherapy

16 letters:
Bach flower remedy

17 letters:
Autogenic training

18 letters:
Alexander
technique

PEOPLE IN MEDICINE

4 letters:
Bell, *Sir Charles*
Drew, *Charles*
Jung, *Carl*
Koch, *Robert*
Lind, *James*
Mayo, *Charles*
Reed, *Walter*
Ross, *Sir Ronald*
Salk, *Jonas E(dward)*

5 letters:
Broca, *Paul*
Bruce, *Sir David*
Cajal, *Santiago Ramon y*
Crick, *Francis*
Curie, *Marie*
Freud, *Sigmund*
Galen
Henle, *Friedrich*
Kenny, *Elizabeth*
Krebs, *Sir Edwin*
Leach, *Penelope*
Lower, *Richard*
Osler, *Sir William*
Paget, *Sir James*
Remak, *Robert*
Sharp, *Phillip*
Spock, *Benjamin*
Steno, *Nicolaus*

6 letters:
Barton, *Clara*
Bichat, *Marie*
Bishop, *Michael*
Bright, *Richard*
Carrel, *Alexis*
Cavell, *Edith Louisa*
Cooper, *Sir Astley*
Cuvier, *Georges*
Fernel, *Jean*
Finsen, *Niels*
Garrod, *Sir Archibald*
Harvey, *William*
Hunter, *John*
Inglis, *Elsie*
Jenner, *Edward*
Lister, *Joseph*
Manson, *Sir Patrick*
Mesmer, *Franz Anton*
Mullis, *Kary*
Pavlov, *Ivan*
Sanger, *Margaret*
Treves, *Sir Frederick*
Varmus, *Harold*
Watson, *James*
Watson, *John*
Willis, *Thomas*

7 letters:
Addison, *Thomas*
Axelrod, *Julius*

Membranes

Banting, *Sir Frederick*
Barnard, *Christiaan*
Bethune, *Henry Norman*
Burkitt, *Denis*
Cushing, *Harvey*
Ehrlich, *Paul*
Eijkman, *Christian*
Fleming, *Sir Alexander*
Gilbert, *William*
Hodgkin, *Dorothy*
Hodgkin, *Thomas*
Laennec, *Rene*
Laveran, *Charles*
Linacre, *Thomas*
MacEwen, *Sir William*
McIndoe, *Sir Archibald*
Medawar, *Sir Peter*
Nicolle, *Charles*
Pasteur, *Louis*
Röntgen, *Wilhelm Conrad*
Seacole, *Mary Jane*
Simpson, *Sir James Young*
Warburg, *Otto*
Winston, *Lord Robert*

8 letters:
Anderson, *Elizabeth Garrett*
Avicenna
Beaumont, *William*
Billroth, *Theodor*
Charnley, *Sir John*
Delbruck, *Max*
Duchenne, *Guillaume*
Dulbecco, *Renato*
Geronimo

Jex-Blake, *Sophia*
Leishman, *Sir William*
Magendie, *Francois*
Malpighi, *Marcello*
Morgagni, *Giovanni*
Pattison, *Dorothy*
Stoppard, *Miriam*
Sydenham, *Thomas*
Tournier, *Paul*
Vesalius

9 letters:
Alzheimer, *Alois*
Bartholin, *Erasmus*
Blackwell, *Elizabeth*
Boerhaave, *Hermann*
Dupuytren, *Guillaume*
Dutrochet, *Henri*
Hahnemann, *Samuel*
Mackenzie, *Sir James*
Parkinson, *James*

10 letters:
Fracastoro, *Girolamo*
Greenfield, *Susan*
Langerhans, *Paul*
Paracelsus
Stephenson, *Elsie*

11 letters:
Hippocrates
Livingstone, *David*
Nightingale, *Florence*
Szent-Gyorgi, *Albert*

12 letters:
Erasistratus

Membranes

3 letters:
Haw

4 letters:
Dura

5 letters:
Exine
Mater

6 letters:
Amnion
Cornea

Extine
Intima
Intine
Meninx
Mucosa
Mucous
Pleura
Sclera
Serosa
Serous
Tympan

7 letters:
Chorion
Choroid
Decidua
Hyaloid
Periost
Putamen

8 letters:
Axilemma
Ependyma
Frenulum

Indusium
Patagium
Pericarp
Pia mater
Synovial
Tympanic
Vacuolar

9 letters:
Arachnoid
Dura mater
Endostium
Involucre
Mesentery
Tonoplast

Vitelline

10 letters:
Periosteum
Peritoneum
Sarcolemma

11 letters:
Chromoplast
Conjunctiva
Dissepiment
Endocardium
Endometrium
Mediastinum
Nictitating

Pericardium
Pericranium
Peritonaeum
Third eyelid
Trophoblast

12 letters:
Schneiderian

13 letters:
Choroid plexus
Perichondrium

15 letters:
Chorioallantois

Metals

Metal	Symbol
Actinium	Ac
Aluminium	Al
Americium	Am
Antimony	Sb
Barium	Ba
Berkelium	Bk
Beryllium	Be
Bismuth	Bi
Cadmium	Cd
Caesium *or* cesium	Cs
Calcium	Ca
Californium	Cf
Cerium	Ce
Chromium	Cr
Cobalt	Co
Copper	Cu
Curium	Cm
Dysprosium	Dy
Einsteinium	Es
Erbium	Er
Europium	Eu
Fermium	Fm
Francium	Fr
Gadolinium	Gd
Gallium	Ga
Germanium	Ge
Gold	Au
Hafnium	Hf
Holmium	Ho
Indium	In
Iridium	Ir

Metals

Metal	Symbol
Iron	Fe
Lanthanum	La
Lawrencium	Lr
Lead	Pb
Lithium	Li
Lutetium	Lu
Magnesium	Mg
Manganese	Mn
Mendelevium	Md
Mercury	Hg
Molybdenum	Mo
Neodymium	Nd
Neptunium	Np
Nickel	Ni
Niobium	Nb
Nobelium	No
Osmium	Os
Palladium	Pd
Platinum	Pt
Plutonium	Pu
Polonium	Po
Potassium	K
Praseodymium	Pr
Promethium	Pm
Protactinium	Pa
Radium	Ra
Rhenium	Re
Rhodium	Rh
Rubidium	Rb
Ruthenium	Ru
Samarium	Sm
Scandium	Sc
Silver	Ag
Sodium	Na
Strontium	Sr
Tantalum	Ta
Technetium	Tc
Terbium	Tb
Thallium	Tl
Thorium	Th
Thulium	Tm
Tin	Sn
Titanium	Ti
Tungsten *or* wolfram	W
Uranium	U
Vanadium	V
Ytterbium	Yb
Yttrium	Y
Zinc	Zn
Zirconium	Zr

Meteor showers

6 letters:
Boötes
Cetids
Lyrids
Ursids
Velids

7 letters:
Corvids
Cygnids
Hydrids
Leonids
Librids
Mensids
Normids
Piscids
Puppids
Scutids
Taurids

8 letters:
Aquilids
Arietids
Aurigids
Cancrids
Geminids
Orionids
Pavonids
Pegasids
Perseids

9 letters:
Aquariids
Craterids
Draconids
Eridanids
Herculids
Scorpiids
Virginids

10 letters:
Centaurids
Phoenicids
Sextantids

11 letters:
Andromedids
Quadrantids
Triangulids

12 letters:
Capricornids
Monocerotids
Sagittariids
Ursa Majorids

13 letters:
Canis Minorids

14 letters:
Coma Berenicids

Military ranks

2 letters:
AB
AC
AM
BO
CO
FM
FO
Lt
MO
OS
PO
QM
RA
SM
VA
WO

3 letters:
ACM
Adm
AVM
Cdr

Col
COS
Cpl
CPO
CSM
Gen
LAC
Maj
NCO
Pte
RSM
Sgt
SMO
Tpr

4 letters:
Brig
Capt
Cdre
C-in-C
Corp
Genl
L-Cpl

MRAF
Sub L

5 letters:
Flt Lt
G Capt
Lt-Col
Lt-Gen
Major
Sergt

6 letters:
Col Sgt
Flt Sgt
Lt-Comm
Maj-Gen
Marine
Sqn-Ldr

7 letters:
Admiral
Captain
Colonel
General

Military ranks

Marshal
Private

8 letters:
Corporal
Sergeant

9 letters:
Brigadier
Commander
Commodore
Drum major
Subaltern

10 letters:
Able rating
Able seaman
Air marshal
Air officer
Lieutenant
Midshipman

11 letters:
Aircraftmen
Rear admiral
Vice admiral

12 letters:
Air commodore
Chief of staff
Field marshal
Field officer
Fleet admiral
Group captain
Major general
Petty officer
Pilot officer

13 letters:
Branch officer
Flying officer
Lance corporal
Leading rating
Master aircrew
Quartermaster
Sergeant major
Staff sergeant
Sublieutenant
Wing commander

14 letters:
Air vice-marshal

Colour sergeant
Flight engineer
Flight mechanic
Flight sergeant
Medical officer
Ordinary rating
Ordinary seaman
Squadron leader
Warrant officer

15 letters:
Air chief marshal
Chief technician

16 letters:
Able-bodied seaman
Commander in chief
Flight lieutenant
Junior technician
Second lieutenant

17 letters:
Admiral of the fleet
Chief petty officer
Commanding officer
Lieutenant colonel
Lieutenant general
Senior aircraftman

18 letters:
Leading aircraftman

19 letters:
Acting sublieutenant
Commissioned officer
Lieutenant commander

20 letters:
Company sergeant major
Senior medical officer

22 letters:
Fleet chief petty officer
Noncommissioned officer

23 letters:
Regimental sergeant major

25 letters:
Marshal of the Royal Air Force

Minerals

4 letters:
Gang
Mica
Opal
Sard
Spar
Talc
Trap
Urao

5 letters:
Agate
Balas
Beryl
Borax
Chert
Emery
Flint
Fluor
Mafic
Nitre
Prase
Topaz
Trona
Umber

6 letters:
Acmite
Albite
Augite
Blende
Galena
Gangue
Garnet
Glance
Gypsum
Halite
Hauyne
Illite
Jargon
Jasper
Lithia
Norite
Nosean
Pinite
Pyrite
Quartz
Rutile
Schorl

Silica
Sphene
Spinel
Tincal
Zircon

7 letters:
Alunite
Amalgam
Anatase
Apatite
Axinite
Azurite
Barytes
Bauxite
Biotite
Bornite
Brucite
Calcite
Calomel
Catseye
Cuprite
Cyanite
Diamond
Dysodil
Epidote
Euclase
Eucrite
Fahlore
Felspar
Gahnite
Göthite
Gummite
Hessite
Ice spar
Jadeite
Jargoon
Kainite
Kernite
Kunzite
Kyanite
Leucite
Mellite
Mullite
Nacrite
Olivine
Pennine
Peridot

Pyrites
Realgar
Rosaker
Sylvine
Sylvite
Thorite
Thulite
Tripoli
Turgite
Ulexite
Uralite
Uranite
Uranium
Zeolite
Zincite
Zoisite
Zorgite

8 letters:
Adularia
Allanite
Analcime
Analcite
Andesine
Ankerite
Antimony
Aphanite
Asbestos
Autunite
Blue john
Boehmite
Boracite
Braunite
Brookite
Calamine
Cerusite
Chlorite
Chromite
Cinnabar
Cleveite
Corundum
Crocoite
Cryolite
Datolite
Dendrite
Diallage
Diaspore
Diopside

Minerals

Dioptase
Disthene
Dolomite
Dysodile
Dysodyle
Epsomite
Erionite
Euxenite
Fayalite
Feldspar
Flinkite
Fluorite
Galenite
Gibbsite
Goethite
Graphite
Gyrolite
Hematite
Hyacinth
Idocrase
Ilmenite
Iodyrite
Jarosite
Lazulite
Lazurite
Lewisite
Limonite
Massicot
Melilite
Metamict
Mimetite
Monazite
Nephrite
Noselite
Orpiment
Petuntse
Petuntze
Prehnite
Pyroxene
Resalgar
Rock-salt
Sanidine
Saponite
Siderite
Smaltite
Smectite
Sodalite
Stannite
Stibnite
Stilbite
Taconite

Tenorite
Titanite
Troilite
Xenotime
Zaratite

9 letters:
Alabaster
Allophane
Amazonite
Amphibole
Anglesite
Anhydrite
Anorthite
Aragonite
Argentite
Atacamite
Blackjack
Blacklead
Carnelian
Carnotite
Celestine
Celestite
Cerussite
Chabazite
Cheralite
Chondrule
Cobaltine
Cobaltite
Coccolite
Columbate
Columbite
Covellite
Elaeolite
Enhydrite
Enstatite
Erythrite
Fibrolite®
Fluorspar
Gehlenite
Germanite
Geyserite
Gmelinite
Goslarite
Haematite
Harmotome
Hercynite
Hiddenite
Kaolinite
Kermesite
Kieserite

Magnesite
Magnetite
Malachite
Manganite
Marcasite
Margarite
Marialite
Microlite
Microlith
Millerite
Mispickel
Mizzonite
Monzonite
Moonstone
Muscovite
Natrolite
Nepheline
Nephelite
Niccolite
Nitratine
Olivenite
Ottrelite
Ozocerite
Ozokerite
Pargasite
Pectolite
Periclase
Pericline
Phenacite
Phenakite
Pleonaste
Polianite
Pollucite
Powellite
Proustite
Rhodonite
Rubellite
Scapolite
Scheelite
Scolecite
Spodumene
Sylvanite
Tantalite
Tremolite
Troostite
Tungstite
Turquoise
Uraninite
Uvarovite
Variscite
Vulpinite

Wavellite
Wernerite
Willemite
Witherite
Wulfenite
Zinkenite

10 letters:
Actinolite
Alabandine
Alabandite
Andalusite
Bastnasite
Calaverite
Carnallite
Chalcocite
Chessylite
Chrysolite
Chrysotile
Colemanite
Cordierite
Crocoisite
Dyscrasite
Forsterite
Gadolinite
Garnierite
Glauconite
Halloysite
Heulandite
Honey-stone
Hornblende
Indicolite
Indigolite
Jamesonite
Laurdalite
Meerschaum
Microcline
Oligoclase
Orthoclase
Perovskite
Phosgenite
Polybasite
Polyhalite
Pyrolusite

Pyroxenite
Pyrrhotine
Pyrrhotite
Redruthite
Riebeckite
Ripidolite
Samarskite
Sapphirine
Serpentine
Smaragdite
Sperrylite
Sphalerite
Staurolite
Tennantite
Thaumasite
Thenardite
Thorianite
Tiemannite
Torbernite
Tourmaline
Triphylite
Vanadinite
Wolframite
Zinckenite

11 letters:
Alexandrite
Amblygonite
Annabergite
Apophyllite
Baddeleyite
Bastnaesite
Cassiterite
Cerargyrite
Chiastolite
Chrysoberyl
Clay mineral
Clinochlore
Crocidolite
Dendrachate
Franklinite
Greenockite
Hypersthene
Josephinite

Labradorite
Lapis lazuli
Molybdenite
Pentlandite
Phosphorite
Piedmontite
Pitchblende
Psilomelane
Pyrargyrite
Sillimanite
Smithsonite
Tetradymite
Vermiculite
Vesuvianite
Ythro-cerite

12 letters:
Arfvedsonite
Arsenopyrite
Babingtonite
Bismuthinite
Chalcanthite
Chalcopyrite
Cristobalite
Dumortierite
Feldspathoid
Fluorapatite
Hemimorphite
Pyromorphite
Pyrophyllite
Senarmontite
Skutterudite
Strontianite
Synadelphite
Tetrahedrite
Wollastonite

13 letters:
Bismuth glance
Clinopyroxene
Cummingtonite
Rhodochrosite

15 letters:
Montmorillonite

Missiles

3 letters:
SAM
SSM

UAM

4 letters:
Ammo

Ball
Bolt
Bomb

Molecules

Dart
ICBM
MIRV
Scud
Shot
SLBM
SLCM
Styx
Thor

5 letters:
Arrow
Atlas
Bolas
Kiley
Kyley
Kylie
Onion
Shell
Spear
Titan

6 letters:
Bullet
Cruise
Dum-dum
Exocet
Guided
Pellet
Rocket
Tracer

7 letters:
Dingbat
Grenade
Harpoon
Patriot
Polaris
Quarrel
Torpedo
Trident
Warhead

8 letters:
Air-to-air
Buzz bomb
Maverick
Pershing
Poseidon
Snowball
Standoff

9 letters:
Ballistic
Boomerang
Doodlebug
Fléchette
Minuteman
Smart bomb

10 letters:
Blue streak
Flying bomb

Side-winder

11 letters:
Interceptor

12 letters:
Surface to air

13 letters:
Anti-ballistic

16 letters:
Surface to surface

17 letters:
Sea-launched cruise

25 letters:
Intercontinental ballistic

26 letters:
Submarine-launched ballistic

43 letters:
Multiple independently targeted re-entry vehicle

Molecules

3 letters:
DNA

5 letters:
Codon
Dimer
Kinin

6 letters:
Chiral
Hapten
Isomer
Ligand
Trimer

7 letters:
Carbene
Monomer

Peptide
Polymer
Uridine

8 letters:
Acceptor
Cavitand
Coenzyme
Cofactor
Replicon

9 letters:
Buckyball
Cobalamin
Fullerene
Long-chain
Metameric

Semantide

10 letters:
Metabolite

11 letters:
Chromophore
Closed chain
Footballene

12 letters:
Enantiomorph
Stereoisomer

14 letters:
Polysaccharide

Monastic orders

6 letters:
Sangha

7 letters:
Cluniac
Saivite
Shaolin

8 letters:
Basilian
Trappist
Vaisnava

9 letters:
Capuchins
Carmelite
Celestine

Dominican
Mathurins
Red Friars

10 letters:
Bendictine
Carthusian
Cistercian
Feuillants
Franciscan

11 letters:
Augustinian
Bridgettine
Camaldolese
Gilbertines
Tironensian

White Canons

12 letters:
Redemptorist
Trinitarians

14 letters:
Knights Templar
Premonstratian

17 letters:
Christian Brothers
Premonstratensian
Visitation Sisters

20 letters:
Mendicant
  Augustinian

Monkeys, apes and other primates

3 letters:
Pug
Sai

4 letters:
Douc
Leaf
Mico
Mona
Nala
Saki
Tana
Titi
Zati

5 letters:
Cebus
Chimp
Diana
Drill
Green
Indri
Jocko
Lemur
Loris
Magot
Midas
Orang
Sajou

Silen
Toque

6 letters:
Aye-aye
Baboon
Bandar
Bonnet
Bonobo
Chacma
Coaita
Colugo
Galago
Gelada
Gibbon
Grison
Grivet
Guenon
Howler
Indris
Jackey
Langur
Macaco
Malmag
Monkey
Rhesus
Sagoin
Saguin

Sifaka
Simpai
Spider
Tee-tee
Uakari
Vervet
Wou-wou
Wow-wow

7 letters:
Cebidae
Colobus
Gorilla
Guereza
Hanuman
Hoolock
Jacchus
Macaque
Meerkat
Mycetes
Nasalis
Ouakari
Sagouin
Saimiri
Sapajou
Siamang
Silenus
Tamarin

Monks

Tarsier
Wistiti

8 letters:
Bushbaby
Capuchin
Durukuli
Entellus
Mandrill
Mangabey
Marmoset
Ouistiti
Squirrel
Talapoin
Wanderoo

9 letters:
Hylobates
Orang-utan
Phalanger
Proboscis

10 letters:
Barbary ape
Chimpanzee
Cynomolgus
Jackanapes
Silverback

11 letters:
Douroucouli
Flying lemur

Green monkey
Orang-outang
Platyrrhine

12 letters:
Bonnet monkey
Howler monkey
Rhesus monkey
Slender loris
Spider monkey

14 letters:
Squirrel monkey

15 letters:
Proboscis monkey

Monks

3 letters:
Dan
Dom

4 letters:
Bede
Lama

5 letters:
Abbot
Arhat
Black
Bonze
Bruno
Friar
Prior

6 letters:
Austin
Bhikhu
Culdee
Jerome
Mendel
Oblate
Sangha

7 letters:
Beghard

Brother
Caedmon
Caloyer
Cluniac
Félibre
Hegumen
Jacobin
Maurist

8 letters:
Acoemeti
Basilian
Cenobite
Jacobite
Olivetan
Pelagian
Rasputin
Salesian
Talapoin
Theatine
Trappist

9 letters:
Celestine
Coenobite
Dominican
Gyrovague

Hesychast
Thelemite

10 letters:
Bernardine
Carthusian
Cistercian
Hildebrand
Norbertine
Savonarola
Thelonious

11 letters:
Abbey-lubber
Augustinian
Benedictine
Bonaventura
Ignorantine
Mekhitarist
Tironensian

12 letters:
Bethlehemite
Mechitharist

13 letters:
Archimandrite
Thomas à Kempis

Monsters

3 letters:
Orc

4 letters:
Eten
Ogre

5 letters:
Ettin
Giant
Harpy
Hydra
Lamia
Snark
Teras
Troll
Yowie

6 letters:
Alecto
Bunyip
Dragon
Erebus
Geryon
Gorgon
Kraken
Medusa
Moloch

Nessie
Scylla
Simorg
Simurg
Sphinx
Typhon
Wyvern

7 letters:
Caliban
Chimera
Cyclops
Grendel
Simurgh
Taniwha
Vampire
Wendego
Wendigo
Werwolf
Ziffius

8 letters:
Asmodeus
Behemoth
Cerberus
Chimaera
Mastodon

Minotaur
Opinicus
Stegodon
Typhoeus
Werewolf

9 letters:
Dinoceras
Fire-drake
Leviathan
Stegosaur
Wasserman

10 letters:
Cockatrice
Hippogriff
Jabberwock
Sarsquatch

11 letters:
Chichevache
Hippocampus
Triceratops

12 letters:
Bandersnatch
Frankenstein

Mosses

3 letters:
Fog
Hag

4 letters:
Club
Hagg
Peat
Rose

5 letters:
Agate
Irish
Marsh
Usnea

6 letters:
Ceylon
Hypnum
Lichen
Litmus

7 letters:
Acrogen
Iceland
Lycopod
Muscoid
Parella
Spanish

8 letters:
Reindeer

Sphagnum
Staghorn

9 letters:
Carrageen
Lecanoram
Wolf's claw

10 letters:
Carragheen
Fontinalis

11 letters:
Polytrichum
Selaginella

Motor sports

Motor sports

7 letters:
Karting

8 letters:
Rallying
Speedway

9 letters:
Autocross

Motocross

10 letters:
Drag racing
Rallycross
Scrambling

11 letters:
Motor racing

13 letters:
Motor rallying

14 letters:
Stock car racing

16 letters:
Motor-cycle racing

Mountaineers

5 letters:
Munro, *Sir HT*

6 letters:
Conway, *Sir Martin*
Harrer, *Heinrich*
Norgay, *Tenzing*
Willss, *Sir Alfred*

7 letters:
Corbett, *JR*
Hillary, *Sir Edmund*
Mallory, *George*

Messner, *Reinhold*
Shipman, *Eric*
Simpson, *Joe*
Whymper, *Edward*
Workman, *Fannie Bullock*

8 letters:
Petzoldt, *Paul*

9 letters:
Bonington, *Chris*

10 letters:
Freshfield, *DW*

Mountains

2 letters:
K2

3 letters:
Apo
Ida
Kaf
Ore

4 letters:
Alai
Blue
Bona
Cook
Etna
Fuji
Harz
Hoss

Isto
Jaya
Jura
Meru
Nebo
Oeta
Ossa
Rigi
Rosa
Viso
Zeil

5 letters:
Abora
Adams
Aldan
Altai
Amara

Andes
Aneto
Arber
Athos
Atlas
Badon
Black
Blanc
Coast
Corno
Djaja
Eiger
Ellis
Ghats
Green
Guyot
Hekla

Horeb
Idris
Kamet
Kenya
Leone
Logan
Marcy
Munro
Ozark
Rocky
Rydal
Sinai
Siple
Snowy
Table
Tabor
Tatra
Teide
Tyree
Urals
Welsh

6 letters:

Amhara
Anadyr
Arafat
Ararat
Averno
Balkan
Bogong
Carmel
Cho Oyu
Dragon
Egmont
Elbert
Elberz
Elbrus
Erebus
Gilead
Hermon
Hoggar
Hoosac
Kunlun
Lhotse
Makalu
Mourne
Musala
Negoiu
Ortles
Pamirs

Pelion
Pisgah
Pocono
Robson
Scopus
Sorata
Steele
Tasman
Taunus
Taurus
Vernon
Vosges
Zagros

7 letters:

Aorangi
Aragats
Arcadia
Belukha
Bernina
Brocken
Buffalo
Calvary
Cariboo
Cascade
Chianti
Corbett
Dapsang
Everest
Helicon
Kennedy
Khingan
Kuenlun
Lebanon
Lucania
Manaslu
Markham
Nan Shan
Olympus
Palomar
Perdido
Pilatus
Rainier
Rhodope
Scafell
Selkirk
Skiddaw
Snowdon
Sperrin
Stanley

Sudeten
Toubkal
Travers
Troglav
Whitney
Wicklow
Zard Kuh

8 letters:

Anai Mudi
Ben Nevis
Cambrian
Cevennes
Demavend
Estrella
Grampian
Hymettus
Illimani
Jungfrau
Kinabalu
King Peak
Klínovec
Leibnitz
McKinley
Mitchell
Mulhacén
Pennines
Pyrenees
Rushmore
Skalitsy
Smólikas
St Helen's
Taraniki
Tien Shan
Vesuvius
Victoria
Waun Fach
Wrangell

9 letters:

Aconcagua
Allegheny
Annapurna
Apennines
Argentera
Ben Lomond
Blackburn
Blue Ridge
Cairngorm
Catskills

Mountains

Caucasian
Connemara
Corcovado
Demavrand
Dolomites
El Capitan
Emi Koussi
Grampians
Guadalupe
Helvellyn
Highlands
Himalayas
Hindu Kush
Inselberg
Jebel Musa
Karakoram
Kings Peak
Kosciusko
Lenin Peak
Longs Peak
Mansfield
Marmolada
Mont Blanc
Nanda Devi
Narodnaya
Parnassus
Pikes Peak
Puy de Dôme
Rock Creek
Sugarloaf
Tirich Mir
Vancouver
Venusberg
Weisshorn
Woodroffe
Zugspitze

10 letters:
Arakan Yoma
Ben Macdhui
Blanca Peak
Cantabrian
Carpathian
Delectable
Dhaulagiri
Erymanthus
Erzgebirge
Gannet Peak
Grand Teton
Great Gable

Harney Peak
Horselberg
Kongur Shan
Laurentian
Masharbrum
Matterhorn
Monte Corno
Montserrat
Pentelikon
Piz Bernina
Pobeda Peak
Puncak Jaya
Puy de Sancy
St Michael's
Tengri Khan
Timpanogos
Waddington
Washington
Wellington

11 letters:
Adirondacks
Alaska Range
Appalachian
Aran Fawddwy
Bartle Frere
Bimberi Peak
Brooks Range
Drakensberg
Fairweather
Gerlachovka
Kilimanjaro
Kolyma Range
Munku-Sardyk
Nanga Parbat
Salmon River
Scafell Pike
Schneekoppe
Sierra Madre
Sir Sandford

12 letters:
Albert Edward
Cascade Range
Citlaltépetl
Godwin Austen
Gran Paradiso
Kanchenjunga
Ruahine Range
Sierra Nevada

Slieve Donard
Tararua Range
Ulugh Muztagh
Victoria Peak
Vinson Massif
Western Ghats

13 letters:
Carmarthen Van
Carrantuohill
Clingman's Dome
Croagh Patrick
Flinders Range
Grossglockner
Humphreys Peak
Kangchenjunga
Massif Central
Mount of Olives
Petermann Peak
San Bernardino
Slide Mountain
Table Mountain
White Mountain

14 letters:
Bohemian Forest
Carnarvon Range
Finsteraarhorn
Hamersley Range
Kaikoura Ranges
Kommunizma
  Peak
Liverpool Range
Musgrove Ranges
Ruwenzori Range
Stirling Ranges

15 letters:
Cerro de Mulhacén
Uncompahgre
  Peak

16 letters:
Blue Mountain
  Peak
Macdonnell Ranges
Thabana Ntlenyana

17 letters:
Continental Divide
Sir Wilfrid Laurier

Sugar Loaf
  Mountain
Transylvanian Alps

19 letters:
Macgillicuddy's Reeks

20 letters:
Salmon River Mountains

Murderers

Murderers

4 letters:
Cain
Gacy, *John*
Gein, *Ed*
Ruby, *Jack*
West, *Fred*
West, *Rosemary*

5 letters:
Booth, *John Wilkes*
Brady, *Ian*
Ellis, *Ruth*

6 letters:
Bonney, *William*
Borden, *Lizzie*
Corday, *Charlotte*
Graham, *Barbara*
Manson, *Charles*
Oswald, *Lee Harvey*
Pearce, *Charlie*
Sirhan, *Sirhan*

7 letters:
Chapman, *Mark*

Crippen, *Hawley*
Gilmore, *Gary*
Hindley, *Myra*
Huntley, *Ian*
Macbeth
Panzram, *Carl*
Shipman, *Harold*
Wuornos, *Aileen*

8 letters:
Chessman, *Caryl*
Christie, *John*

9 letters:
Bible John
Hauptmann, *Bruno*
Sutcliffe, *Peter*

11 letters:
Billy the Kid

13 letters:
Jack the Ripper

14 letters:
Leopold and Loeb

17 letters:
The Moors
  Murderers

18 letters:
The Boston
  Strangler
The Yorkshire
  Ripper

Muscles

3 letters:
Abs
Lat
Pec

4 letters:
Pecs
Quad

5 letters:
Psoas
Teres
Tonus

6 letters:
Biceps
Flexor
Pathos
Rectus
Smooth
Soleus
Tensor
Thenar

7 letters:
Agonist
Ciliary

Deltoid
Dilator
Erecter
Erector
Evertor
Gluteus
Iliacus
Laxator
Levator
Pylorus
Rotator
Sarcous
Scalene

Sthenic
Triceps

8 letters:
Abductor
Adductor
Effector
Elevator
Extensor
Glutaeus
Kreatine
Masseter
Occlusor
Omohyoid
Opponent
Pectoral
Peroneus
Platysma
Pronator
Risorius
Scalenus
Serratus
Splenial

Striated

9 letters:
Arytenoid
Attollens
Cremaster
Depressor
Diaphragm
Digastric
Hamstring
Perforans
Quadratus
Retractor
Sartorius
Sphincter
Supinator
Suspensor
Tenaculum
Trapezius
Voluntary

10 letters:
Antagonist
Buccinator

Compressor
Contractor
Corrugator
Perforatus
Protractor
Quadriceps
Sarcolemma
Suspensory

11 letters:
Accelerator
Accessorius
Constrictor
Lumbricalis
Rhomboideus

13 letters:
Gastrocnemius

14 letters:
Gluteus maximus
Peroneal muscle

15 letters:
Latissimus dorsi

Muses

Name	Muse of
Calliope	Epic poetry
Clio	History
Erato	Love poetry
Euterpe	Lyric poetry and music
Melpomene	Tragedy
Polyhymnia	Singing, mime, and sacred dance
Terpsichore	Dance and choral song
Thalia	Comedy and pastoral poetry
Urania	Astronomy

Mushrooms and other edible fungi

3 letters:
Cep

5 letters:
Enoki
Horse
Hypha
Magic
Morel

6 letters:
Agaric
Blewit
Button
Hyphal
Ink-cap
Meadow
Oyster
Waxcap

7 letters:
Blewits
Parasol
Porcini
Porcino
Truffle

8 letters:
Penny-bun
Puffball

Shiitake

9 letters:
Fly agaric
Gyromitra

10 letters:
Champignon
Lawyer's wig
Liberty cap
Shaggymane

11 letters:
Chanterelle

Velvet shank

12 letters:
Black truffle
Horn of plenty
Scotch bonnet
Shaggy ink cap
White truffle

13 letters:
Straw mushroom

14 letters:
Button mushroom

Meadow
  mushroom
Oyster mushroom

15 letters:
Wood ear
  mushroom

16 letters:
Shiitake
  mushroom

Music

CLASSICAL MUSIC GENRES

5 letters:
Early
Salon

6 letters:
Galant
Gothic
Rococo
Serial

7 letters:
Ars nova
Baroque

8 letters:
Romantic

9 letters:
Classical

10 letters:
Ars antiqua
Minimalist
Twelve-tone

11 letters:
Nationalist

Renaissance

12 letters:
Dodecaphonic
Neoclassical
Post-romantic

13 letters:
Expressionist
Impressionist
Music concrète

TYPES OF COMPOSITION

3 letters:
Air
Duo

4 letters:
Aria
Duet
Lied
Mass
Raga
Reel
Song
Trio

5 letters:
Canon
Dirge
Dumka

Elegy
Étude
Fugue
Galop
Gigue
March
Motet
Nonet
Octet
Opera
Polka
Psalm
Suite
Waltz

6 letters:
Anthem
Ballet

Bolero
Chorus
Lament
Medley
Minuet
Pavane
Septet
Sextet
Sonata

7 letters:
Ballade
Bourrée
Cantata
Canzona
Canzone
Chorale
Czardas

Music

Fantasy
Gavotte
Ländler
Mazurka
Partita
Passion
Pibroch
Prelude
Quartet
Quintet
Requiem
Romance
Scherzo
Toccata

8 letters:
Barceuse
Canticle
Cavatina
Chaconne
Concerto
Fantasia
Galliard
Hornpipe
Madrigal
Nocturne
Notturno
Operetta
Oratorio
Overture

Part song
Pastiche
Phantasy
Rhapsody
Ricercar
Rigadoon
Rigadoun
Serenade
Sonatina
Symphony
Tone poem

9 letters:
Allemande
Bagatelle
Barcarole
Capriccio
Ecossaise
Farandole
Impromptu
Interlude
Passepied
Pastorale
Polonaise
Quadrille
Ricercare
Singspiel
Song cycle

10 letters:
Albumblatt

Canzonetta
Concertino
Grand opera
Humoresque
Opera buffa
Opera seria
Strathspey
Trio sonata

11 letters:
Concertante
Contradance
Contredanse
Passacaglia
Schottische
Sinfonietta

12 letters:
Concertstück
Divertimento

13 letters:
Symphonic poem

14 letters:
Concerto grosso
Divertissement

19 letters:
Sinfonia
  concertante

POPULAR MUSIC TYPES

3 letters:
AOR
Bop
Dub
Pop
Rag
Rai
Rap
Ska

4 letters:
Folk
Funk
Go-go
Goth
Jazz
Loco
Punk
Rave

Rock
Romo
Soca
Soul
Trad
Zouk

5 letters:
Bebop
Blues
Cajun
Cu-bop
Disco
Dream
Early
House
Indie
Kwela
Muzak®

Neume
P-funk
Piped
Ragga
Salon
Salsa
Sokah
Swing

6 letters:
Bebung
Doo-wop
Fusion
Gagaku
Garage
Gospel
Gothic
Grunge
Hip-hop

Jungle	Flamenco	Industrial
Khayal	Folk rock	Merseybeat
Marabi	Free jazz	Modern jazz
Motown®	Glam rock	New Country
New Age	Hardcore	Rockabilly
Reggae	Hard rock	Rocksteady
Techno	High life	Urban blues
Thrash	Jazz-funk	World music
Trance	Jazz-rock	
Zydeco	Karnatak	**11 letters:**
	Lollipop	Country rock
7 letters:	Mariachi	Harmolodics
Ambient	Mbaqanga	Motor rhythm
Bhangra	Punk rock	New romantic
Britpop	Trad jazz	Psychobilly
Calypso		Raggamuffin
Ceilidh	**9 letters:**	Rock and roll
Chamber	Acid house	Stadium rock
Country	Bluegrass	Third stream
Gangsta	Bubblegum	Thrash metal
Hardbag	Dixieland	
Hardbop	Folk music	**12 letters:**
Klezmer	Hillbilly	Boogie-woogie
New Wave	Honky-tonk	Country blues
Pibroch	Rock'n'roll	
Qawwali	Spiritual	**13 letters:**
Ragtime	Surf music	Detroit techno
Skiffle	Swingbeat	
Soukous	Technopop	**14 letters:**
Trip hop	Warehouse	Mainstream jazz
Ziganka		New Orleans jazz
	10 letters:	Rhythm and blues
8 letters:	Chopsticks	
Acid jazz	Death metal	**15 letters:**
Acid rock	Gangsta rap	Musique concrete
Bluebeat	Gothic rock	Progressive rock
Concrete	Heavy metal	
Cool jazz	Hindustani	**17 letters:**
		Country and
		western

MUSICAL EXPRESSIONS AND TEMPO INSTRUCTIONS

Instruction	**Meaning**
Accelerando	With increasing speed
Adagio	Slowly
Agitato	In an agitated manner
Allegretto	Fairly quickly or briskly
Allegro	Quickly, in a brisk, lively manner
Amoroso	Lovingly
Andante	At a moderately slow tempo
Andantino	Slightly faster than andante
Animato	In a lively manner
Appassionato	Impassioned

Music

Instruction	Meaning
Assai	(in combination) very
Calando	With gradually decreasing tone and speed
Cantabile	In a singing style
Con	(in combination) with
Con affeto	With tender emotion
Con amore	Lovingly
Con anima	With spirit
Con brio	Vigorously
Con fuoco	With fire
Con moto	Quickly
Crescendo	Gradual increase in loudness
Diminuendo	Gradual decrease in loudness
Dolce	Gently and sweetly
Doloroso	In a sorrowful manner
Energico	Energetically
Espressivo	Expressively
Forte	Loud or loudly
Fortissimo	Very loud
Furioso	In a frantically rushing manner
Giocoso	Merry
Grave	Solemn and slow
Grazioso	Graceful
Lacrimoso	Sad and mournful
Largo	Slowly and broadly
Larghetto	Slowly and broadly, but less so than largo
Legato	Smoothly and connectedly
Leggiero	Light
Lento	Slowly
Maestoso	Majestically
Marziale	Martial
Mezzo	(in combination) moderately
Moderato	At a moderate tempo
Molto	(in combination) very
Non troppo *or* non tanto	(in combination) not too much
Pianissimo	Very quietly
Piano	Softly
Più	(in combination) more
Pizzicato	(in music for stringed instruments) to be plucked with the finger
Poco *or* un poco	(in combination) a little
Pomposo	In a pompous manner
Presto	Very fast
Prestissimo	Faster than presto
Quasi	(in combination) almost, as if
Rallentando	Becoming slower
Rubato	With a flexible tempo
Scherzando	In jocular style
Sciolto	Free and easy
Semplice	Simple and unforced
Sforzando	With strong initial attack

Instruction	Meaning
Smorzando	Dying away
Sospirando	'sighing', plaintive
Sostenuto	In a smooth and sustained manner
Sotto voce	Extremely quiet
Staccato	(of notes) short, clipped, and separate
Strascinando	Stretched out
Strepitoso	Noisy
Stringendo	With increasing speed
Tanto	(in combination) too much
Tardo	Slow
Troppo	(in combination) too much
Vivace	In a brisk lively manner
Volante	'flying', fast and light

MUSICAL MODES

Mode	Final note
I Dorian	D
II Hypodorian	A
III Phrygian	E
IV Hypophrygian	B
V Lydian	F
VI Hypolydian	C
VII Mixolydian	G
VIII Hypomixolydian	D
IX Aeolian	A
X Hypoaeolian	E
XI Ionian	C
XII Hypoionian	G

MUSICAL INSTRUMENTS

2 letters:
Ax
Gu

3 letters:
Axe
Gue
Kit
Lur
Oud
Saz
Uke
Zel

4 letters:
Bell
Crwd
Drum
Fife
Gong

Harp
Horn
Kora
Koto
Lure
Lute
Lyre
Moog®
Oboe
Pipa
Pipe
Rate
Reed
Rote
Sang
Tuba
Vina
Viol
Whip

Zeze

5 letters:
Aulos
Banjo
Bongo
Bugle
Cello
Chime
Clave
Cobza
Conga
Corno
Crowd
Crwth
Dobro®
Flute
Guiro
Gusla
Gusle

Music

Gusli
Kazoo
Mbira
Naker
Nebel
Ngoma
Organ
Piano
Quena
Rebec
Regal
Sanko
Sansa
Sarod
Shalm
Shawm
Sitar
Tabla
Tabor
Tibia
Veena
Viola
Zanze
Zinke

6 letters:
Antara
Cither
Citole
Cornet
Cymbal
Euphon
Fiddle
Flugel
Guitar
Kanoon
Maraca
Poogye
Racket
Rebeck
Ribibe
Sancho
Santir
Santur
Shalme
Sittar
Spinet
Syrinx
Tabour
Tam-tam
Timbal

Tom-tom
Trigon
Tymbal
Vielle
Violin
Zither
Zufolo

7 letters:
Alphorn
Althorn
Bagpipe
Bandore
Bandura
Baryton
Bassoon
Bazooka
Bodhrán
Celesta
Celeste
Cembalo
Chikara
Cithara
Cithern
Cittern
Clarion
Clavier
Console
Cornett
Cowbell
Cymbalo
Dichord
Dulcian
Fagotto
Flutina
Gamelan
Gittern
Hautboy
Helicon
High-hat
Kalimba
Kantela
Kantele
Kithara
Klavier
Lyricon
Mandola
Marimba
Musette
Ocarina
Pandora

Pandore
Pandura
Pianola®
Piccolo
Poogyee
Posaune
Rackett
Sackbut
Sambuca
Samisen
Santour
Sarangi
Saxhorn
Saxtuba
Serpent
Sistrum
Tambour
Tambura
Theorbo
Timbrel
Timpani
Trumpet
Tympani
Tympany
Ukelele
Ukulele
Vihuela
Violone
Vocoder
Whistle
Zuffolo

8 letters:
Angklung
Archlute
Autoharp®
Bagpipes
Barytone
Bass drum
Bass viol
Bouzouki
Calliope
Canorous
Carillon
Charango
Cimbalom
Cimbalon
Clarinet
Clarsach
Clavecin
Cornetto

Cornpipe
Cromorna
Cromorne
Crumhorn
Cymbalon
Dulcimer
Gemshorn
Guarneri
Guimbard
Handbell
Hautbois
Hornpipe
Humstrum
Jew's-harp
Keyboard
Key-bugle
Langspel
Lyra viol
Mandolin
Manzello
Martenot
Melodeon
Melodica
Melodion
Mirliton
Ottavino
Panpipes
Phorminx
Polyphon
Psaltery
Recorder
Reco-reco
Reed pipe
Side drum
Slughorn
Spinette
Sticcado
Sticcato
Surbahar
Tamboura
Tamburin
Tenoroon
Theremin®
Triangle
Trombone
Virginal
Vocalion
Zambomba
Zampogna

9 letters:
Accordion

Alpenhorn
Baby grand
Balalaika
Bandoneon
Baryulele
Böhm flute
Bombardon
Castanets
Chalumeau
Cornemuse
Decachord
Euphonium
Flageolet
Flexatone
Gittarone
Gran cassa
Gutbucket
Harmonica
Harmonium
Idiophone
Kent-bugle
Krummhorn
Langspiel
Mandoline
Monochord
Mouth-harp
Nose flute
Octachord
Orpharion
Pantaleon
Pastorale
Polyphone
Reed organ
Saxophone
Seraphine
Slughorne
Snare drum
Sopranino
Stockhorn
Trompette
Washboard
Welsh harp
Wood block
Wurlitzer®
Xylophone
Xylorimba

10 letters:
Basset horn
Bass guitar
Bullroarer
Chitarrone

Clavichord
Concertina
Contrabass
Cor anglais
Didgeridoo
Double bass
Flugelhorn
French horn
Gramophone
Grand piano
Hurdy-gurdy
Kettledrum
Mellophone
Mouth organ
Oboe d'amore
Ophicleide
Orpheoreon
Pantachord
Shakuhachi
Sousaphone
Squeeze-box
Steam organ
Stylophone
Symphonium
Tambourine
Thumb piano
Vibraphone

11 letters:
Aeolian harp
Bach trumpet
Barrel organ
Chordophone
Clairschach
Contrabasso
Drum machine
English horn
Harmoniphon
Harpsichord
Heckelphone
Hunting horn
Nickelodeon
Orchestrina
Orchestrion
Phonofiddle
Player piano
Slide guitar
Square piano
Steel guitar
Straduarius
Synthesizer
Trump-marine

Viola d'amore
Violoncello

12 letters:
Boudoir grand
Chamber organ
Chapman stick®
Chinese block
Clavicembalo
Concert grand
Cottage piano
Glockenspiel
Hammond organ®
Harmoniphone
Metallophone
Oboe da caccia

Penny whistle
Sarrusophone
Stock and horn
Stradivarius
Tromba-marina
Tubular bells
Uillean pipes
Upright piano
Viola da gamba

13 letters:
Contrabassoon
Contrafagotto
Double bassoon
Ondes Martenot
Panharmonicon

Physharmonica
Spanish guitar

14 letters:
Electric guitar
Glass harmonica
Hawaiian guitar
Portative organ
Viola da braccio

15 letters:
Electronic organ

16 letters:
Pedal steel guitar

See also:
➤ **Composers** ➤ **Orchestral instruments** ➤ **Jazz forms**
➤ **Jazz terms** ➤ **Jazz musicians** ➤ **Notes and rests** ➤ **Works**
of literature and music

Musketeers

5 letters:
Athos

6 letters:
Aramis

7 letters:
Porthos

9 letters:
D'Artagnan

Muslim denominations and sects

4 letters:
Shia

5 letters:
Druse
Druze
Imami
Shiah
Sunni

Zaidi

6 letters:
Nizari
Senusi
Shiite
Sufism

7 letters:
Isma'ili

Senussi

8 letters:
Alawites
Wahabism

9 letters:
Alaouites
Wahhabism

Mythology

CHARACTERS IN CLASSICAL MYTHOLOGY

2 letters:
Io

4 letters:
Ajax

Dido
Echo
Leda

5 letters:
Atlas

Circe
Helen
Ixion
Jason
Medea

Midas
Minos
Muses
Niobe
Orion
Paris
Priam
Remus
Sibyl

6 letters:
Adonis
Aeneas
Castor
Charon
Europa
Hector
Hecuba
Icarus
Medusa
Pollux
Psyche
Semele
Thisbe

7 letters:
Actaeon
Amazons
Arachne

Ariadne
Calypso
Electra
Galatea
Jocasta
Oedipus
Orestes
Orpheus
Pandora
Perseus
Pyramus
Romulus
Silenus
Theseus
Ulysses

8 letters:
Achilles
Antigone
Atalanta
Callisto
Daedalus
Eurydice
Ganymede
Heracles
Hercules
Menelaus
Odysseus

Penelope
Pleiades
Sisyphus
Tantalus
Tiresias

9 letters:
Agamemnon
Andromeda
Argonauts
Cassandra
Narcissus
Pygmalion

10 letters:
Andromache
Cassiopeia
Hippolytus
Hyacinthus
Persephone
Polydeuces
Polyphemus
Prometheus
Proserpina

12 letters:
Clytemnestra

14 letters:
Hermaphroditus

PLACES IN CLASSICAL MYTHOLOGY

4 letters:
Styx
Troy

5 letters:
Hades
Lethe

6 letters:
Erebus
Thebes

7 letters:
Acheron
Colchis
Elysium
Helicon
Olympus

8 letters:
Tartarus

9 letters:
Parnassus

10 letters:
Phlegethon

19 letters:
Islands of the
    Blessed

MYTHOLOGICAL CREATURES

3 letters:
Elf
Fay
Nix
Orc
Roc

4 letters:
Faun

Fury
Peri

5 letters:
Afrit
Dryad
Dwarf
Fairy
Genie

Giant
Harpy
Hydra
Jinni
Kylin
Lamia
Naiad
Nixie

Mythology

Nymph
Oread
Pixie
Satyr
Siren
Sylph
Troll

6 letters:
Afreet
Bunyip
Djinni
Djinny
Dragon
Geryon
Goblin
Gorgon
Hobbit
Jinnee
Kelpie
Kraken
Merman
Nereid

Scylla
Sphinx

7 letters:
Banshee
Centaur
Chimera
Cyclops
Echidna
Erlking
Gremlin
Grendel
Griffin
Griffon
Gryphon
Mermaid
Oceanid
Phoenix
Tricorn
Unicorn

8 letters:
Basilisk
Behemoth

Cerberus
Chimaera
Minotaur

9 letters:
Charybdis
Hamadryad
Hobgoblin
Impundulu
Leviathan
Tokoloshe
Wood nymph

10 letters:
Cockatrice
Hippogriff
Hippogryph
Leprechaun
Salamander
Water nymph

11 letters:
Androsphinx
Hippocampus

CHARACTERS IN NORSE MYTHOLOGY

3 letters:
Ask
Lif

4 letters:
Atli

5 letters:
Mimir
Regin

6 letters:
Fafnir
Gudrun
Gunnar
Sigurd

7 letters:
Andvari
Sigmund
Wayland

8 letters:
Brynhild
Gutthorn
Hreidmar

10 letters:
Lifthrasir

PLACES IN NORSE MYTHOLOGY

3 letters:
Hel

4 letters:
Hela

6 letters:
Asgard
Utgard

7 letters:
Asgarth
Bifrost
Midgard

8 letters:
Midgarth
Niflheim

Valhalla

9 letters:
Jotunheim

10 letters:
Jotunnheim

See also:
➤ **Actaeon's hounds** ➤ **Ancient cities** ➤ **Arthurian legend**
➤ **Fates** ➤ **Giants and giantesses** ➤ **Gods and Goddesses**
➤ **Gorgons** ➤ **Graces** ➤ **Greeks** ➤ **Harpies** ➤ **Hercules**
➤ **Monsters** ➤ **Muses** ➤ **Rivers of Hell** ➤ **Seven against
Thebes** ➤ **Wonders of the ancient world**

N

Nerves

4 letters:
Axon

5 letters:
Cyton
Nidus
Optic
Ulnar
Vagus

6 letters:
Bouton
Facial
Myelon
Radial

7 letters:
Cranial
Excitor
Sciatic
Synapse

8 letters:
Acoustic
Ganglion

9 letters:
Depressor
Epicritic
Trochlear

10 letters:
Commissure
Perikaryon
Trigeminal

11 letters:
Octulomotor
Solar plexus

12 letters:
Baroreceptor
Electrotonus

13 letters:
Proprioceptor

Newspapers and magazines

2 letters:
GQ
OK

3 letters:
FHM
Red
She
Viz
Zoo

4 letters:
Best
Chat
Chic
Elle
Mind
Mojo
More
Nuts
Time
Word

5 letters:
Bella
Blick
Bliss
Hello
Metro
Prima
Punch
Ta Nea
Uncut
Vogue
Which
Wired
Woman

6 letters:
El Pais
Forbes
Granta
Loaded
Nature
Pepper

Record
The Sun
War Cry

7 letters:
Company
Die Welt
Die Zeit
Esquire
Fortune
Hustler
Le Monde
Mayfair
Newsday
Options
Playboy
The Face
The Lady
The Star
Time Out
Tribune

Newspapers and magazines

8 letters:
Big Issue
Campaign
Gay Times
Il Giorno
La Stampa
Le Figaro
Navy News
Newsweek
New Woman
Observer
The Oldie
The Onion
The Times
USA Today

9 letters:
Classic FM
Dagbladet
Daily Mail
Daily Star
Expressen
Ideal Home
L'Humanité
New Yorker
Smash Hits
The Lancet
The Tablet
The Tatler
Total Film
Woman's Own

10 letters:
Asian Times
Daily Sport
Denver Post
Film Review
France-Soir
Il Giornale
Irish Times
La Lanterne
Libération
Private Eye
Racing Post
Radio Times
Sunday Mail
Sunday Post
Vanity Fair

11 letters:
Bild Zeitung
Boston Globe
Daily Mirror
De Telegraaf
El Periodico
Marie Claire
Melody Maker
Miami Herald
Morning Star
New York Post
Ouest France
Sunday Sport
Sunday World
The European
The Guardian
The Scotsman
The Universe
Woman's Realm

12 letters:
Angling Times
Boston Herald
Cosmopolitan
Daily Express
Family Circle
Fortean Times
History Today
Il Messaggero
La Repubblica
La Voix du Nord
New Scientist
New Statesman
New York Times
Nursing Times
Poetry Review
Seattle Times
Sunday Herald
Sunday Mirror
Sunday People
The Economist
The Spectator
Woman and Home
Woman's Weekly

13 letters:
Evening Herald
Horse and Hound

Just Seventeen
Mother and Baby
Reader's Digest
The Bookseller
The Watchtower
Wales on Sunday
Woman's Journal

14 letters:
Chicago Tribune
Daily Telegraph
Financial Times
France-Dimanche
House and Garden
Kansas City Star
Literary Review
News of the World
Publishing News
The Independent
The Sunday Times
Washington Post

15 letters:
Algemeen Dagblad
Berliner Zeitung
Chicago Sun-
  Times
Evening Standard
Exchange and Mart
Express on Sunday
Harpers and
  Queen
Homes and
  Gardens
Los Angeles Times
The Mail on
  Sunday

16 letters:
Dazed and
  Confused
Detroit Free Press
Diario de Noticias
Houston Chronicle
Irish Independent
National Enquirer
New York Daily
  News
Scotland on Sunday

The People's Friend
The Scots Magazine

17 letters:
Corriere della Sera
Dallas Morning News
New Musical Express
Sunday Independent
Wall Street Journal

18 letters:
National Geographic
The Sunday Telegraph

20 letters:
Orange County Register

Philadelphia Enquirer

21 letters:
British Medical Journal
San Francisco Chronicle

22 letters:
The Independent on Sunday

26 letters:
International Herald Tribune
The Times Literary Supplement

28 letters:
Frankfurter Allgemeine Zeitung

Nobility

RANKS OF BRITISH NOBILITY (IN ORDER OF PRECEDENCE)

Royal duke
Royal duchess
Duke
Duchess
Marquess

Marquis
Marchioness
Earl
Countess
Viscount

Viscountess
Baron
Baroness
Baronet

RANKS OF FOREIGN NOBILITY

5 letters:
Boyar
Count

6 letters:
Prince

7 letters:
Grandee
Marquis
Vicomte

8 letters:
Archduke

Burgrave
Countess
Marchesa
Marchese
Margrave
Marquise
Princess

9 letters:
Grand duke
Landgrave

10 letters:
Margravine

Vicomtesse

11 letters:
Archduchess
Landgravine

12 letters:
Grand duchess

Notes and rests

British name	American name
Breve	Double-whole note
Semibreve	Whole note
Minim	Half note
Crotchet	Quarter note

Novelists

British name	American name
Quaver	Eighth note
Semiquaver	Sixteenth note
Demisemiquaver	Thirty-second note
Hemidemisemiquaver	Sixty-fourth note

Novelists

2 letters:
Mo, *Timothy*
Oë, *Kenzaburo*

3 letters:
Eco, *Umberto*
Lee, *Harper*
Lee, *Laurie*
Nye, *Robert*
Rao, *Raja*

4 letters:
Amis, *Kingsley*
Amis, *Martin (Louis)*
Behn, *Aphra*
Bely, *Andrei*
Böll, *Heinrich*
Boyd, *William*
Buck, *Pearl*
Cela, *Camilo José*
Dunn, *Nell*
Fast, *Howard*
Ford, *Ford Madox*
Ford, *Richard*
Gide, *André (Paul Guillaume)*
Gold, *Herbert*
Gray, *Alasdair*
Hill, *Susan*
Hogg, *James*
Hope (Hawkins), *Sir Anthony*
Hugo, *Victor (Marie)*
Jong, *Erica*
King, *Francis*
King, *Stephen (Edwin)*
Levi, *Primo*
Mann, *Thomas*
Okri, *Ben*
Puzo, *Mario*
Read, *Piers Paul*
Rhys, *Jean*
Roth, *Henry*
Saki
Sand, *George*

Snow, *C(harles) P(ercy)*
Uris, *Leon*
Wain, *John*
West, *Morris*
West, *Rebecca*
Wouk, *Herman*
Zola, *Émile*

5 letters:
Adams, *Douglas*
Adams, *Richard*
Anand, *Mulk Raj*
Banks, *Iain*
Banks, *Lynne Reid*
Barth, *John*
Bates, *H(erbert) E(rnest)*
Bowen, *Elizabeth*
Bragg, *Melvin*
Brink, *André*
Brown, *George Douglas*
Brown, *George Mackay*
Byatt, *A(ntonia) S(usan)*
Camus, *Albert*
Carey, *Peter*
Crane, *Stephen*
Defoe, *Daniel*
Desai, *Anita*
Doyle, *Arthur Conan*
Doyle, *Roddy*
Duffy, *Maureen*
Dumas, *Alexandre*
Eliot, *George*
Elkin, *Stanley*
Ellis, *Alice Thomas*
Elton, *Ben*
Figes, *Eva*
Frame, *Janet Paterson*
Frayn, *Michael*
Gogol, *Nikolai Vasilievich*
Gorky, *Maxim*
Gosse, *Sir Edmund (William)*
Grass, *Günter (Wilhelm)*

Hardy, *Thomas*
Hesse, *Hermann*
Heyer, *Georgette*
Hines, *Barry*
Hoban, *Russell*
Hulme, *Keri*
Innes, *(Ralph) Hammond*
James, *Henry*
James, *P(hyllis) D(orothy)*
Joyce, *James (Augustine Aloysius)*
Kafka, *Franz*
Keane, *Molly*
Kesey, *Ken*
Lewis, *(Harry) Sinclair*
Llosa, *Mario Vargos*
Lodge, *David (John)*
Lowry, *(Clarence) Malcolm*
Lurie, *Alison*
Marsh, *Ngaio*
Moore, *Brian*
Newby, *P(ercy) H(oward)*
Oates, *Joyce Carol*
O'Hara, *John*
Orczy, *Baroness Emmuska*
Ouida
Ozick, *Cynthia*
Paton, *Alan (Stewart)*
Peake, *Mervyn*
Powys, *John Cowper*
Queen, *Ellery*
Rolfe, *Frederick William*
Scott, *Sir Walter*
Selby, *Hubert Jr*
Shute, *Nevil*
Simon, *Claude*
Smith, *Iain Crichton*
Smith, *Zadie*
Spark, *Dame Muriel (Sarah)*
Stead, *C K*
Stein, *Gertrude*
Stone, *Robert*
Stowe, *Harriet Elizabeth Beecher*
Swift, *Graham*
Swift, *Jonathan*
Toole, *John Kennedy*
Tuohy, *Frank*
Twain, *Mark (Samuel L Clemens)*
Tyler, *Anne*
Verne, *Jules*
Vidal, *Gore*
Waugh, *Evelyn (Arthur St John)*

Wells, *H(erbert) G(eorge)*
Welsh, *Irvine*
Welty, *Eudora*
White, *Antonia*
White, *Patrick*
White, *T(erence) H(anbury)*
Wilde, *Oscar (Fingal O'Flahertie Wills)*
Wolfe, *Thomas Clayton*
Wolfe, *Tom*
Wolff, *Tobias*
Woolf, *(Adeline) Virginia*
Yerby, *Frank*

6 letters:

Achebe, *Chinua*
Aldiss, *Brian*
Ambler, *Eric*
Archer, *Jeffrey*
Asimov, *Isaac*
Atwood, *Margaret*
Austen, *Jane*
Barker, *Elspeth*
Barker, *Pat*
Barnes, *Julian*
Bawden, *Nina*
Bellow, *Saul*
Berger, *John*
Berger, *Thomas*
Binchy, *Maeve*
Bowles, *Paul*
Braine, *John (Gerard)*
Brontë, *Anne*
Brontë, *Charlotte*
Brontë, *Emily (Jane)*
Brophy, *Brigid*
Buchan, *John*
Bunyan, *John*
Burney, *Fanny*
Butler, *Samuel*
Capote, *Truman*
Carter, *Angela*
Cather, *Willa*
Clarke, *Arthur C(harles)*
Cleary, *Jon*
Condon, *Richard*
Conrad, *Joseph*
Cooper, *James Fenimore*
Cooper, *Jilly*
Cooper, *William*
Davies, *(William) Robertson*

Novelists

De Sade, *Marquis*
Didion, *Joan*
Farmer, *Philip José*
Fowles, *John (Robert)*
Fraser, *Antonia*
French, *Marilyn*
Fuller, *Roy*
Gaddis, *William*
Garner, *Helen*
Gibbon, *Lewis Grassic*
Godden, *(Margaret) Rumer*
Godwin, *William*
Goethe, *Johann Wolfgang von*
Graham, *Winston*
Graves, *Robert (Ranke)*
Greene, *(Henry) Graham*
Hailey, *Arthur*
Heller, *Joseph*
Hilton, *James*
Holtby, *Winifred*
Horgan, *Paul*
Howard, *Elizabeth Jane*
Hughes, *Thomas*
Hunter, *Evan*
Huxley, *Aldous (Leonard)*
Irving, *John*
Kaplan, *Johanna*
Kelman, *James*
Le Fanu, *(Joseph) Sheridan*
Le Guin, *Ursula*
Lively, *Penelope*
London, *Jack*
Mailer, *Norman (Kingsley)*
Malouf, *David*
Massie, *Allan*
McEwan, *Ian*
Miller, *Henry (Valentine)*
Mosley, *Nicholas*
O'Brien, *Edna*
O'Brien, *Flann*
Orwell, *George*
Passos, *John Roderigo Dos*
Porter, *Harold*
Porter, *Katherine Anne*
Powell, *Anthony*
Proulx, *E Annie*
Proust, *Marcel*
Rankin, *Ian*
Sartre, *Jean-Paul*
Sayers, *Dorothy L(eigh)*
Sharpe, *Tom*

Singer, *Isaac Bashevis*
Spring, *Howard*
Sterne, *Laurence*
Stoker, *Bram*
Storey, *David (Malcolm)*
Styron, *William*
Symons, *Julian*
Trevor, *William*
Updike, *John (Hoyer)*
Upward, *Edward (Falaise)*
Walker, *Alice*
Warner, *Marina*
Warren, *Robert Penn*
Weldon, *Fay*
Wesley, *Mary*
Wilder, *Thornton*
Wilson, *A(ndrew) N(orman)*
Wright, *Richard Nathaniel*

7 letters:

Ackroyd, *Peter*
Alvarez, *Al*
Angelou, *Maya*
Ballard, *J(ames) G(raham)*
Barstow, *Stanley*
Bedford, *Sybille*
Bennett, *(Enoch) Arnold*
Burgess, *Anthony*
Burrows, *Edgar Rice*
Calvino, *Italo*
Canetti, *Elias*
Clavell, *James*
Coetzee, *J(ohn) M(ichael)*
Colette, *(Sidonie-Gabrielle)*
Collins, *Wilkie (William)*
Connell, *Evan*
Cookson, *Catherine*
DeLillo, *Don*
De Vries, *Peter*
Dickens, *Charles (John Huffam)*
Dickens, *Monica*
Dinesen, *Isak*
Drabble, *Margaret*
Durrell, *Gerald (Malcolm)*
Durrell, *Laurence*
Fleming, *Ian*
Forster, *E(dward) M(organ)*
Forsyth, *Frederick*
Francis, *Dick*
Gaskell, *Elizabeth*
Gibbons, *Stella*

Gilliat, *Penelope*
Gissing, *George (Robert)*
Glasgow, *Ellen*
Golding, *Sir William (Gerald)*
Goldman, *William*
Grisham, *John*
Haggard, *Sir H(enry) Rider*
Hartley, *L(eslie) P(oles)*
Hazzard, *Shirley*
Hurston, *Zora Neale*
Kennedy, *Margaret*
Kerouac, *Jack*
Kipling, *(Joseph) Rudyard*
Kundera, *Milan*
Lamming, *George*
Le Carré, *John*
Lehmann, *Rosamond*
Lessing, *Doris*
MacLean, *Alistair*
Mahfouz, *Naguib*
Malamud, *Bernard*
Manning, *Olivia*
Márquez, *Gabriel García*
Marryat, *(Captain) Frederick*
Maugham, *W(illiam) Somerset*
Mauriac, *François*
Mishima, *Yukio*
Mitford, *Nancy*
Murdoch, *Dame (Jean) Iris*
Nabokov, *Vladimir (Vladimirovich)*
Naipaul, *Sir V(idiadhar) S(urajprasad)*
Peacock, *Thomas Love*
Pynchon, *Thomas*
Raphael, *Frederic*
Renault, *Mary*
Rendell, *Ruth*
Richler, *Mordecai*
Robbins, *Harold*
Rushdie, *(Ahmed) Salman*
Saroyan, *William*
Shelley, *Mary (Wollstonecraft)*
Shields, *Carol*
Simenon, *Georges (Joseph Christian)*
Stewart, *J(ohn) I(nnes) M(ackintosh)*
Stewart, *Mary*
Süskind, *Patrick*
Tennant, *Emma*
Theroux, *Paul*

Tolkien, *J(ohn) R(onald) R(euel)*
Tolstoy, *Count Leo (Nikolayevich)*
Tranter, *Nigel*
Tremain, *Rose*
Tutuola, *Amos*
Walpole, *Horace*
Wharton, *Edith (Newbold)*
Wilding, *Michael*

8 letters:
Abrahams, *Peter*
Aldridge, *James*
Apuleius, *Lucius*
Beerbohm, *Max*
Bradbury, *Malcolm*
Bradford, *Barbara Taylor*
Brittain, *Vera*
Brookner, *Anita*
Bulgakov, *Mikhail Afanaseyev*
Cartland, *Barbara*
Chandler, *Raymond*
Christie, *Dame Agatha (Mary Clarissa)*
Correlli, *Maria*
Davidson, *Lionel*
De Balzac, *Honoré*
Deighton, *Len*
De Laclos, *Pierre Choderlos*
De Quincy, *Thomas*
Disraeli, *Benjamin*
Donleavy, *J(ames) P(atrick)*
Faulkner, *William*
Fielding, *Helen*
Fielding, *Henry*
Flaubert, *Gustave*
Forester, *C(ecil) S(cott)*
Freeling, *Nicholas*
Galloway, *Janice*
Gordimer, *Nadine*
Guterson, *David*
Heinlein, *Robert A(nson)*
Ishiguro, *Kazuo*
Jhabvala, *Ruth Prawer*
Keneally, *Thomas*
Kingsley, *Charles*
Lawrence, *D(avid) H(erbert)*
Macauley, *Rose*
MacInnes, *Colin*
Melville, *Herman*
Meredith, *George*
Michener, *James A(lbert)*

Novelists

Mitchell, *Julian*
Mitchell, *Margaret*
Moorcock, *Michael*
Morrison, *Toni*
Mortimer, *John*
Mortimer, *Penelope*
Oliphant, *Margaret*
Ondaatje, *Michael*
Remarque, *Erich Maria*
Salinger, *J(erome) D(avid)*
Sillitoe, *Alan*
Smollett, *Tobias George*
Stendhal
Trollope, *Anthony*
Trollope, *Joanna*
Turgenev, *Ivan Sergeyevich*
Voltaire
Vonnegut, *Kurt*
Zamyatin, *Evgeny Ivanovich*

9 letters:
Blackmore, *R(ichard)*
  D(oddridge)
Bleasdale, *Alan*
Bromfield, *Louis*
Burroughs, *William*
Delafield, *E M*
Du Maurier, *Dame Daphne*
Edgeworth, *Maria*
Feinstein, *Elaine*
Gerhardie, *William Alexander*
Goldsmith, *Oliver*
Goncharov, *Ivan Aleksandrovich*
Grossmith, *George*
Grossmith, *Weedon*
Hawthorne, *Nathaniel*
Hemingway, *Ernest (Millar)*
Highsmith, *Patricia*
Isherwood, *Christopher (William*
  Bradshaw)
Lermontov, *Mikhail Yurievich*
MacDonald, *George*
Mackenzie, *Sir (Edward*
  Montague) Compton
MacKenzie, *Henry*
Mankowitz, *(Cyril) Wolf*
McCullers, *Carson*
McLaverty, *Bernard*
Mitchison, *Naomi*

Monsarrat, *Nicholas*
O'Flaherty, *Liam*
Pasternak, *Boris Leonidovich*
Pratchett, *Terry*
Priestley, *J(ohn) B(oynton)*
Pritchett, *V(ictor) S(awdon)*
Radcliffe, *Ann*
Schreiner, *Olive*
Sholokhov, *Mikhail*
  Aleksandrovich
Steinbeck, *John (Ernest)*
Stevenson, *Robert Louis (Balfour)*
Thackeray, *William Makepeace*
Wa Thiong'o, *Ngugi*
Winterson, *Jeanette*
Wodehouse, *Sir P(elham)*
  G(renville)
Yourcenar, *Marguerite*

10 letters:
Bainbridge, *Beryl*
Ballantyne, *R(obert) M(ichael)*
Benedictus, *David*
Brooke-Rose, *Christina*
Chesterton, *G(ilbert) K(eith)*
De Beauvoir, *Simone*
Dostoevsky, *Fyodor Mikhailovich*
Fairbairns, *Zöe*
Fitzgerald, *F(rancis) Scott (Key)*
Fitzgerald, *Penelope*
Galsworthy, *John*
Markandaya, *Kamala*
McIlvanney, *William*
Richardson, *Dorothy*
Richardson, *Samuel*
Van der Post, *Laurens*
Vansittart, *Peter*
Waterhouse, *Keith*

11 letters:
Auchincloss, *Louis*
De Cervantes, *Miguel*
Di Lampedusa, *Guiseppe Tomasi*

12 letters:
De Maupassant, *(Henri René*
  Albert) Guy
Kazantazakis, *Nikos*
Solzhenitsyn, *Alexander*
  Isayevich

13 letters:
Alain-Fournier
Sackville-West, *Vita (Victoria Mary)*

14 letters:
Compton-Burnett, *Ivy*
De Saint-Exupéry, *Antoine*

Nuts

3 letters:
Cob

4 letters:
Cola
Kola
Mast
Pine
Rhus

5 letters:
Acorn
Areca
Arnut
Beech
Betel
Hazel
Lichi
Pecan

6 letters:
Acajou
Almond
Bauple
Brazil
Cashew

Cobnut
Illipe
Lichee
Litchi
Lychee
Marron
Monkey
Peanut
Pignut
Supari
Walnut

7 letters:
Arachis
Babassu
Coquina
Filberd
Filbert
Hickory
Praline
Prawlin

8 letters:
Chestnut
Earthnut
Hazelnut

Quandong
Sapucaia

9 letters:
Amygdalus
Barcelona
Beech-mast
Butternut
Chincapin
Chinkapin
Coco de mer
Groundnut
Macadamia
Mockernut
Pistachio
Sassafras

10 letters:
Chinquapin
Pine kernel
Queensland

12 letters:
Bertholletia

13 letters:
Dwarf chestnut

O

Occupations

2 letters:
AB
BA
CA
DD
GP
MA
MC
MD
MO
MP
Mr
PA
PM

3 letters:
BSc
CID
Deb
Doc
Don
Dux
Fan
Guy
Job
Kid
Lad
Man
Mrs
Nun
Pay
Rep
Sir
Spy

4 letters:
Aide
Babe
Baby
Bard
Beak

Bear
Beau
Boss
Bull
Chap
Char
Chef
Cook
Crew
Cure
Dean
Demy
Dick
Diva
Doxy
Dyer
Feed
Firm
Girl
G-man
Hack
Hand
Head
Hero
Hobo
Host
Lass
Lead
Magi
Maid
Miss
Monk
Page
Peer
Peon
Poet
Pope
Sage
Salt
Seer

Serf
Silk
Star
Tyro
Wage
Ward
Whip

5 letters:
Abbot
Actor
Ad-man
Adult
Agent
Baker
Belle
Boots
Bosun
Boxer
Buyer
Caddy
Cadet
Canon
Chief
Chips
Clerk
Coach
Crier
Crone
Crony
Crook
Decoy
Demon
Devil
Diver
Donor
Doyen
Dummy
Dutch
Elder

Envoy
Extra
Fakir
Felon
Fence
Fifer
Friar
Galen
Garbo
Ghost
Gipsy
Grass
Guard
Guest
Guide
Hewer
Issue
Judge
Juror
Laird
Limey
Local
Locum
Loser
Lover
Luter
Madam
Major
Maker
Maori
Mason
Mayor
Medic
Miner
Minor
Model
Nanny
Navvy
Nurse
Odist
Owner
Padre
Party
Pilot
Pin-up
Piper
Posse
Prior
Proxy
Pupil
Quack

Quill
Rabbi
Racer
Rider
Rishi
Rival
Rover
Saver
Sawer
Scout
Sewer
Slave
Smith
Sower
Staff
Tenor
Thief
Tiler
Tommy
Tramp
Tuner
Tutor
Uhlan
Usher
Valet
Vicar
Viner
Wench
Witch
Woman
Yokel
Youth

6 letters:
Abbess
Ad-mass
Air ace
Airman
Albino
Alumna
Archer
Artist
Au pair
Aurist
Author
Backer
Bandit
Banker
Barber
Bargee
Barker

Barman
Batman
Batter
Beadle
Bearer
Beater
Beggar
Beldam
Berber
Bishop
Boffin
Bookie
Bowman
Broker
Bugler
Bursar
Busker
Butler
Cabbie
Caddie
Caller
Camper
Cantor
Captor
Career
Carter
Carver
Casual
Censor
Cleric
Client
Codist
Co-heir
Consul
Coolie
Cooper
Copier
Copper
Co-star
Coster
Couper
Cowboy
Creole
Critic
Curate
Cutler
Cutter
Damsel
Dancer
Deacon
Dealer

Occupations

Debtor
Deputy
Divine
Docker
Doctor
Double
Dowser
Draper
Drawer
Driver
Drudge
Duenna
Editor
Ensign
Escort
Eskimo
Etcher
Expert
Fabler
Factor
Feeder
Fellow
Fitter
Flunky
Flyman
Forger
Friend
Fuller
Gaffer
Gagman
Ganger
Gaoler
Garcon
Gaucho
German
Gigolo
Gillie
Glazer
Glover
Golfer
Graver
Grocer
Grower
Gunman
Gunner
Hatter
Hawker
Healer
Helper
Herald
Hermit

Het-man
High-up
Hippie
Hosier
Hunter
Hussar
Hymner
Ice-man
Inmate
Intern
Jailer
Jester
Jet set
Jobber
Jockey
Joiner
Jumper
Junior
Junker
Keener
Keeper
Killer
Lackey
Lancer
Lascar
Lawyer
Leader
Lector
Legate
Lender
Lessee
Levite
Limner
Living
Lodger
Lutist
Lyrist
Mahout
Maiden
Marine
Marker
Master
Matron
Medico
Medium
Member
Menial
Mentor
Mercer
Mikado
Miller

Minion
Mister
Moiler
Monger
Moppet
Mortal
Mummer
Munshi
Musico
Mystic
Nannie
Native
Norman
Notary
Novice
Nudist
Nuncio
Oboist
Odd job
Office
Oilman
Optime
Oracle
Orator
Ostler
Outlaw
Packer
Parson
Pastor
Patron
Pedlar
Penman
Pen-pal
Picket
Pieman
Pirate
Pitman
Plater
Player
Pommie
Porter
Potter
Prater
Priest
Punter
Purser
Ragman
Ranger
Rating
Reader
Reaper

Rector
Regius
Rhymer
Rigger
Ringer
Rioter
Robber
Rookie
Runner
Sailor
Sapper
Sartor
Savage
Savant
Sawyer
Scorer
Scouse
Scribe
Sea-dog
Sealer
Seaman
Second
Seller
Senior
Sentry
Server
Sexton
Shadow
Sheila
Shower
Shrink
Singer
Sister
Skater
Skivvy
Skyman
Slater
Slavey
Slayer
Sleuth
Smoker
Sniper
Soutar
Souter
Sowter
Sparks
Squire
Status
Stoker
Suitor
Sutler

Tailor
Talent
Tanner
Tartar
Tarvet
Taster
Tatter
Teller
Tenant
Teuton
Tiller
Tinker
Tinner
Toiler
Trader
Truant
Turner
Tycoon
Typist
Tyrant
Umpire
Urchin
Usurer
Valuer
Vanman
Vendor
Verger
Victor
Viking
Waiter
Walk-on
Warden
Warder
Weaver
Welder
Whaler
Winner
Wizard
Worker
Wright
Writer
Yeoman

7 letters:
Abetter
Abigail
Acolyte
Acrobat
Actress
Actuary
Admiral

Adviser
Almoner
Alumnus
Amateur
Analyst
Apostle
Arbiter
Artisan
Artiste
Assayer
Athlete
Attache
Auditor
Aviator
Bailiff
Ballboy
Bandman
Barmaid
Baronet
Bassist
Bedouin
Beldame
Bellboy
Bellhop
Big name
Big shot
Bit-part
Blender
Boarder
Boatman
Bookman
Bouncer
Breeder
Brigand
Builder
Burglar
Bushman
Butcher
Buttons
Callboy
Calling
Cambist
Captain
Captive
Carrier
Cashier
Caulker
Caveman
Cellist
Chemist
Chindit

Occupations

Chorist
Citizen
Cleaner
Climber
Clippie
Coalman
Cobbler
Cockney
Colleen
Collier
Colonel
Commere
Company
Compere
Comrade
Convert
Convict
Co-pilot
Copyist
Copyman
Coroner
Corsair
Cossack
Counsel
Courier
Cowherd
Cowpoke
Creator
Crofter
Crooner
Cropper
Curator
Custode
Cyclist
Danseur
Daysman
Debater
Denizen
Dentist
Diviner
Dominie
Doorman
Dragoon
Drayman
Dresser
Driller
Drummer
Dustman
Elogist
Embassy
Entrant

Equerry
Escapee
Escaper
Esquire
Farceur
Farcist
Farrier
Fiddler
Fighter
Fireman
Flagman
Flapper
Flesher
Florist
Footboy
Footman
Footpad
Foreman
Founder
Frogman
Furrier
Gambler
Gate-man
General
Ghillie
Glazier
Gleaner
Grown up
Gun moll
Gymnast
Handler
Hangman
Harpist
Haulier
Head boy
Headman
Heckler
Heiress
Heroine
Hipster
Histrio
Hostess
Hymnist
Imagist
Invalid
Jack-tar
Janitor
Jemedar
Juggler
Junkman
Justice

Knacker
Knitter
Learner
Lineman
Linkboy
Linkman
Lockman
Look-out
Lorimer
Maestro
Magnate
Mailman
Manager
Mariner
Marshal
Masseur
Matador
Matelot
Meatman
Midwife
Milkman
Mobsman
Mobster
Modiste
Monitor
Moulder
Mourner
Mudlark
Navarch
Newsboy
Newsman
Oarsman
Oculist
Officer
Old salt
Omnibus
Oratrix
Orderly
Page-boy
Painter
Partner
Passman
Patient
Patroon
Pearler
Peasant
Pianist
Picador
Pierrot
Pilgrim
Pioneer

Planner
Planter
Plumber
Poacher
Poetess
Pollman
Poloist
Pontiff
Poor man
Pop idol
Pop star
Post-boy
Postman
Prefect
Prelate
Premier
Presser
Primate
Printer
Privado
Private
Proctor
Proofer
Prophet
Protégé
Provost
Prowler
Puddler
Punster
Pursuer
Railman
Rancher
Rat race
Realtor
Redskin
Referee
Refugee
Regular
Remover
Rentier
Rescuer
Reserve
Retinue
Rich man
Routine
Rustler
Saddler
Sagaman
Samurai
Sandman
Scalper

Scenist
Scholar
Scraper
Sea-cook
Sea-king
Sea-lord
Sea-wolf
Seminar
Senator
Servant
Service
Settler
Sevitor
Sharper
Shearer
Sheriff
Shopman
Shopper
Showman
Skinner
Skipper
Soldier
Soloist
Soprano
Spartan
Speaker
Spinner
Sponsor
Spotter
Stand-by
Starlet
Starman
Starter
Station
Steward
Stipend
Student
Supremo
Surgeon
Swagman
Tapster
Teacher
Tipster
Tourist
Trainee
Trainer
Trapper
Trawler
Tripper
Trooper
Trouper

Tumbler
Turfman
Veteran
Viceroy
Vintner
Visitor
Warrior
Webster
Whipper
Wiseman
Witness
Wolf cub
Woodman
Woolman
Workman

8 letters:

Abductor
Adherent
Adjutant
Advocate
Aeronaut
Alderman
Alienist
Allopath
Ambivert
Anchoret
Armorist
Armourer
Arranger
Assassin
Assessor
Attacker
Attorney
Axemaker
Bagmaker
Banjoist
Bankrupt
Banksman
Bargeman
Baritone
Beadsman
Bedesman
Bedmaker
Beginner
Bigamist
Blackleg
Blind man
Boardman
Bohemian
Bondsman

Occupations

Boniface	Delegate	Fugitive
Borrower	Deserter	Fusilier
Botanist	Designer	Gangsman
Bowmaker	Detainee	Gangster
Boxmaker	Dictator	Gaolbird
Boy scout	Diet cook	Gardener
Brakeman	Diocesan	Garroter
Brunette	Diplomat	Gendarme
Bummaree	Director	Goatherd
Cabin boy	Disciple	Governor
Call-girl	Dogsbody	Gownsman
Canoness	Domestic	Graduate
Cardinal	Dragoman	Guardian
Castaway	Druggist	Gunsmith
Ceramist	Duettist	Ham actor
Chairman	Educator	Handmaid
Chambers	Elegiast	Handyman
Champion	Embalmer	Hatmaker
Chandler	Emeritus	Hawkshaw
Chaperon	Emigrant	Haymaker
Chaplain	Emissary	Head cook
Choirboy	Employee	Head girl
Cicerone	Engineer	Headship
Cicisbeo	Engraver	Hebraist
Civilian	Epic poet	Helmsman
Claimant	Essayist	Henchman
Clansman	Eulogist	Herdsman
Classman	Examinee	Hijacker
Clerkess	Executor	Hired gun
Clothier	Explorer	Hired man
Co-author	Exponent	Hireling
Comedian	Fabulist	Home help
Commando	Factotum	Horseman
Commoner	Falconer	Hotelier
Compiler	Fanfaron	Houseboy
Composer	Fanmaker	Hula girl
Conjurer	Farm hand	Huntsman
Convener	Ferryman	Idyllist
Corporal	Figurant	Importer
Coryphee	Film idol	Inceptor
Cottager	Filmstar	Informer
Courtier	Finalist	Initiate
Coxswain	Finisher	Inkmaker
Creditor	Fishwife	Inventor
Croupier	Flatfoot	Islander
Cupmaker	Flautist	Jailbird
Cutpurse	Floorman	Jet pilot
Dairyman	Forester	Jeweller
Danseuse	Forgeman	Jongleur
Dead-head	Freshman	Juvenile
Deck-hand	Front-man	Knife-boy

Labourer
Land-girl
Landlady
Landlord
Landsman
Lapidary
Law agent
Lawgiver
Lawmaker
Laywoman
Lecturer
Licensee
Life-peer
Linesman
Linguist
Listener
Logician
Loiterer
Looker-on
Lumberer
Luminary
Lyricist
Magician
Mandarin
Mapmaker
Marauder
Marksman
Masseuse
Mechanic
Mediator
Melodist
Mercator
Merchant
Milkmaid
Millgirl
Millhand
Milliner
Minister
Ministry
Minstrel
Mistress
Modeller
Moralist
Motorist
Muleteer
Muralist
Murderer
Musician
Narrator
Naturist
Neophyte

Netmaker
Newcomer
News-hawk
Nightman
Norseman
Novelist
Objector
Occupant
Official
Onlooker
Op artist
Operator
Opponent
Optician
Oratress
Ordinand
Organist
Overlord
Overseer
Pardoner
Parodist
Party man
Passer-by
Patentee
Penmaker
Perfumer
Perjurer
Picaroon
Pilferer
Pillager
Plagiary
Poetling
Poisoner
Polisher
Pontifex
Position
Potmaker
Practice
Preacher
Pressman
Prioress
Prisoner
Prizeman
Producer
Promoter
Prompter
Psychist
Publican
Pugilist
Purveyor
Quarrier

Radar man
Rag trade
Ragwoman
Receiver
Recorder
Reformer
Reporter
Resident
Retailer
Retainer
Reveller
Revenant
Reviewer
Rewriter
Ridleman
Rivetter
Road-gang
Rotarian
Rugmaker
Saboteur
Salesman
Salvager
Satirist
Sawbones
Sawsmith
Sciolost
Scullion
Sculptor
Seafarer
Seedsman
Selector
Sentinel
Sergeant
Shepherd
Shipmate
Shopgirl
Showgirl
Side-kick
Sidesman
Silk gown
Sketcher
Sky-scout
Small fry
Smuggler
Solitary
Songster
Sorcerer
Spaceman
Spearman
Speed cop
Sprinter

Occupations

Stageman
Star turn
Stockman
Storeman
Stowaway
Stranger
Stripper
Stroller
Stunt man
Superior
Superman
Supplier
Surveyor
Survivor
Swagsman
Tallyman
Taxpayer
Teddy boy
Teenager
Thatcher
Thespian
Thurifer
Tin miner
Tinsmith
Tom Thumb
Tone post
Top brass
Toreador
Torturer
Townsman
Trainman
Trappist
Tripeman
Tunester
Unionist
Union man
Vagabond
Valuator
Vanguard
Vigilate
Virtuoso
Vocalist
Vocation
Waitress
Ward maid
Wardress
Watchman
Waterman
Wayfarer
Wet nurse
Wheelman

Whiphand
Whipjack
Whittler
Wig maker
Woodsman
Workfolk
Workgirl
Workhand
Wrangler
Wrestler
Yodeller

9 letters:
Aborigine
Absconder
Aerialist
Alchemist
Anatomist
Anchoress
Anchorite
Annotator
Announcer
Annuitant
Antiquary
Apologist
Applicant
Appraiser
Arch-enemy
Architect
Archivist
Art critic
Art dealer
Artificer
Assistant
Associate
Astronaut
Attendant
Authoress
Authority
Automaton
Axlesmith
Balladist
Ballerina
Bargainer
Barrister
Barrow-boy
Beefeater
Bee keeper
Beermaker
Beggarman
Bellmaker

Biologist
Bit player
Boatswain
Bodyguard
Bodymaker
Boilerman
Boltsmith
Bookmaker
Bootblack
Bootmaker
Bradmaker
Brass hats
Brigadier
Buccaneer
Bunny girl
Bus driver
Bush pilot
Byrewoman
Bystander
Cab driver
Cabin crew
Café owner
Cakemaker
Cameraman
Candidate
Canvasser
Cardsharp
Caretaker
Carpenter
Casemaker
Celebrity
Cellarman
Centurion
Chain gang
Charterer
Charwoman
Chauffeur
Choralist
Chorus boy
Clergyman
Clinician
Clogmaker
Coadjutor
Coal miner
Coenobite
Colleague
Collector
Columnist
Combatant
Commander
Commodore

Companion
Concierge
Concubine
Conductor
Confessor
Confidant
Conqueror
Conscript
Constable
Contender
Contralto
Cornerboy
Cosmonaut
Cost clerk
Costumier
Court fool
Couturier
Covergirl
Crackshot
Cracksman
Crayonist
Cricketer
Cupbearer
Custodian
Cutthroat
Cymbalist
Daily help
Day-labour
Deaconess
Dean of men
Debutante
Decorator
Defendant
Dependent
Designate
Desk clerk
Detective
Dialogist
Dietician
Dispenser
Dog walker
Dollmaker
Dramatist
Drum major
Drysalter
Ecologist
Economist
Embezzler
Emolument
Enamelist

Enchanter
Engrosser
Entourage
Errand boy
Espionage
Estimator
Exchanger
Exchequer
Exciseman
Executive
Eye doctor
Fieldwork
Figurante
Film actor
Film extra
Film maker
Financier
Fire guard
First mate
Fisherman
Foreigner
Foundling
Free lance
Freemason
Fruiterer
Furnisher
Garreteer
Garrotter
Gas fitter
Gazetteer
Gem cutter
Geologist
Girl guide
Gladiator
Gluemaker
Go-between
Goldsmith
Gondolier
Governess
Grapevine
Grenadier
Guarantor
Guardsman
Guerrilla
Guest star
Guitarist
Gunrunner
Handsewer
Harbinger
Harbourer

Harlequin
Harmonist
Harpooner
Harvester
Head clerk
Herbalist
Hillbilly
Hired hand
Hired help
Historian
Home maker
Homeopath
Hottentot
House dick
Housemaid
Husbandry
Hypnotist
Immigrant
Innkeeper
Inscriber
In service
Inside man
Inspector
Interview
Ironminer
Ironsmith
Jay walker
Jitterbug
Jobholder
Key worker
Kidnapper
Lacemaker
Lady's maid
Lampmaker
Lampooner
Land agent
Land force
Landowner
Landreeve
Land shark
Larcenist
Launderer
Laundress
Lawmonger
Lay figure
Lay reader
Lay sister
Legionary
Lensmaker
Librarian

Occupations

Lifeguard
Linotyper
Liontamer
Lip-reader
Liveryman
Loan agent
Lockmaker
Locksmith
Log-roller
Lord mayor
Lowlander
Lumberman
Machinist
Major domo
Major poet
Make-up man
Male model
Male nurse
Man-at-arms
Man Friday
Medallist
Mendicant
Mercenary
Mesmerist
Messenger
Middleman
Minor poet
Model girl
Monitress
Moonraker
Mortician
Muscleman
Musketeer
Mythmaker
Navigator
Neighbour
Newsagent
Newshound
Nursemaid
Occultist
Odd job man
Office boy
Old master
Old stager
Ombudsman
Operative
Osteopath
Otologist
Outfitter
Panellist
Pantomime

Paparazzo
Part-owner
Passenger
Patrolman
Patroness
Paymaster
Paysagist
Pedagogue
Pen friend
Pen pusher
Pensioner
Performer
Personnel
Phone girl
Physician
Physicist
Picksmith
Pierrette
Pistoleer
Pitwright
Plaintiff
Plasterer
Ploughboy
Ploughman
Plunderer
Poetaster
Policeman
Pop artist
Pop singer
Portrayer
Portreeve
Possessor
Postulant
Postwoman
Poulterer
Precentor
Precursor
Prelector
Presbyter
President
Priestess
Principal
Privateer
Professor
Profiteer
Prud'homme
Publicist
Publisher
Puppeteer
Raconteur
Rainmaker

Ransacker
Ranzelman
Ratefixer
Ratepayer
Recordist
Reference
Registrar
Residency
Rhymester
Ringsider
Roadmaker
Rocketeer
Rocket man
Ropemaker
Roundsman
Rum runner
Rural dean
Sackmaker
Sacristan
Safemaker
Sailmaker
Sales girl
Sales team
Sassenach
Scarecrow
Scavenger
Scenarist
Schoolma'm
Scrapegut
Scribbler
Scrivener
Sea-lawyer
Secretary
Seneschal
Sentryman
Seraskier
Serenader
Sermonist
Servitude
Shoemaker
Signaller
Signalman
Situation
Skin diver
Solicitor
Songsmith
Sonneteer
Sophister
Sophomore
Sorceress
Soubrette

Space crew
Speedster
Spider man
Spokesman
Sportsman
Stagehand
Stage idol
Star gazer
Statesman
Stationer
Steersman
Stevedore
Strike pay
Subaltern
Sub-editor
Subsitute
Suffragan
Swineherd
Tablemaid
Tailoress
Tap dancer
Tax evader
Tentmaker
Test pilot
Therapist
Timberman
Toolsmith
Town clerk
Towncrier
Tradesman
Traveller
Tribesman
Trumpeter
Tympanist
Undergrad
Usherette
Violinist
Volunteer
Wassailer
Waxworker
Weekender
Wheelsman
Winemaker
Woodreeve
Workwoman
Yachtsman
Youngster
Zitherist
Zoologist

10 letters:
Able seaman
Accomplice
Accountant
Advertiser
Aeronomist
Agrologist
Agronomist
Aide-de-camp
Air hostess
Air steward
Amanuensis
Ambassador
Anglo-Saxon
Anvilsmith
Apothecary
Apprentice
Arbitrator
Archbishop
Archdeacon
Archpriest
Aristocrat
Astrologer
Astronomer
Auctioneer
Audit clerk
Au pair girl
Babe in arms
Baby sitter
Ballet girl
Ballplayer
Bandmaster
Bank robber
Baseballer
Bassoonist
Bear leader
Beautician
Bellringer
Benefactor
Billbroker
Billposter
Biochemist
Biographer
Blacksmith
Bladesmith
Blockmaker
Bludgeoner
Bluebottle
Bluejacket
Boatwright

Bogtrotter
Bombardier
Bonesetter
Bonus clerk
Bookbinder
Book dealer
Bookfolder
Bookholder
Bookkeeper
Bookseller
Bookwright
Bootlegger
Brain drain
Brakemaker
Brass smith
Bricklayer
Brickmaker
Broom maker
Brushmaker
Bulb grower
Bumbailiff
Bureaucrat
Burlesquer
Camera team
Campaigner
Cartoonist
Cat breeder
Cat burglar
Catechumen
Cavalryman
Ceramicist
Chainmaker
Chairmaker
Chancellor
Changeling
Chargehand
Charity boy
Chauffeuse
Chorus girl
Chronicler
Cider maker
Cigar maker
Claim agent
Clapper boy
Cloakmaker
Clockmaker
Clocksmith
Clog dancer
Cloisterer
Cloistress

Occupations

Clothmaker	Dry cleaner	Handshaker
Clubmaster	Duty roster	Hatchetman
Coachmaker	Early riser	Headhunter
Coastguard	Empiricist	Headmaster
Co-director	Equestrian	Head porter
Collar-work	Evangelist	Head waiter
Coloratura	Eye witness	Hedgesmith
Colporteur	Fabricator	Henchwoman
Comedienne	Faith curer	Highlander
Commandant	Farmer's boy	High priest
Commission	Fellmonger	Highwayman
Competitor	Fictionist	Hitchhiker
Compositor	Film editor	Holy orders
Concertist	Firemaster	Honorarium
Consultant	Fire raiser	Horn player
Contestant	Fishmonger	Horologist
Contractor	Flag bearer	House agent
Controller	Flight crew	Husbandman
Copyreader	Flower girl	Impresario
Copywriter	Folk singer	Incendiary
Corn doctor	Footballer	Inhabitant
Cornettist	Foot doctor	Inquisitor
Coryphaeus	Forecaster	Instructor
Councillor	Forerunner	Iol painter
Counsellor	Forty-niner	Ironmaster
Country boy	Frame maker	Ironmonger
Countryman	Freebooter	Ironworker
Couturiere	Fund raiser	Jewel thief
Cover agent	Gamekeeper	Job printer
Crackbrain	Game warden	Journalist
Cultivator	Garage hand	Junk dealer
Customs man	Gatekeeper	Kennelmaid
Cytologist	Gatewright	Kitchenboy
Day tripper	Geisha girl	Kitchenman
Demoiselle	Geneticist	Knifesmith
Dilettante	Geochemist	Land holder
Dirty nurse	Geographer	Land jobber
Disc jockey	Glassmaker	Landlubber
Discounter	Glossarist	Land pirate
Discoverer	Goalkeeper	Land waiter
Dishwasher	Gold beater	Lapidarist
Dispatcher	Gold digger	Laundryman
Dog breeder	Goldworker	Law officer
Donkey work	Grammarian	Lay brother
Doorkeeper	Grand prior	Leading man
Dramatizer	Groceryman	Legislator
Dramaturge	Gubernator	Liberty man
Dressmaker	Gunslinger	Librettist
Drug pusher	Hall porter	Licentiate
Drummer boy	Handmaiden	Lieutenant

Lighterman
Lime burner
Linotypist
Lobsterman
Lock keeper
Loggerhead
Loomworker
Lumberjack
Machineman
Magistrate
Mail robber
Management
Manageress
Manicurist
Manservant
Medical man
Medicaster
Message boy
Midshipman
Militiaman
Millwright
Mind-curist
Mind healer
Mindreader
Ministress
Missionary
Model maker
Monopolist
Moonshiner
Motley fool
Mouthpiece
Naturalist
Nautch girl
Naval cadet
Negotiator
Neutralist
Newscaster
News editor
Newsvendor
Newswriter
Night float
Night nurse
Notability
Nurseryman
Obituarist
Occupation
Pallbearer
Pantomimic
Pantry maid
Papermaker
Park keeper

Park ranger
Pastrycook
Pathfinder
Pawnbroker
Peacemaker
Pearl diver
Pearly king
Pedestrian
Pediatrist
Pedicurist
Penologist
Perruquier
Personnage
Petitioner
Pharmacist
Piano tuner
Piccoloist
Pickpocket
Piermaster
Plagiarist
Platelayer
Playbroker
Playwright
Playwriter
Poet-artist
Poet-farmer
Poet-priest
Politician
Postmaster
Prebendary
Priesthood
Prima donna
Private eye
Procurator
Programmer
Prolocutor
Proprietor
Prospector
Proveditor
Questioner
Quizmaster
Railwayman
Raw recruit
Recitalist
Researcher
Retirement
Revenue man
Revivalist
Rhapsodist
Ringmaster
Roadmender

Ropedancer
Ropewalker
Safeblower
Sales clerk
Sales force
Saleswoman
Saltworker
Sand-dancer
Scientists
Scrutineer
Sculptress
Sea-captain
Seamstress
Second mate
Sematicist
Seminarian
Sempstress
Serologist
Serviceman
Session man
Shanghaier
Shipwright
Shopfitter
Shopkeeper
Signwriter
Songstress
Sound mixer
Spacewoman
Specialist
Speculator
Spy catcher
Staff nurse
Starmonger
Steelmaker
Steepljack
Step dancer
Stewardess
Stick-up man
Stockrider
Stocktaker
Stonemason
Storesmith
Strategist
Submariner
Subscriber
Supercargo
Supervisor
Supplicant
Swordsmith
Symphonist
Syncopator

Occupations

Tally clerk
Tallywoman
Taskmaster
Taxi driver
Technician
Technocrat
Televiewer
Tenderfoot
Third party
Tilewright
Timekeeper
Trafficker
Translator
Tripehound
Tripewoman
Trombonist
Troubadour
Tweedledee
Tweedledum
Typesetter
Typing pool
Underagent
Understudy
Undertaker
Vegetarian
Versemaker
Versesmith
Veterinary
Vice-consul
Vice-master
Victualler
Vine grower
Wage earner
Wage worker
Wainwright
Watchmaker
Water guard
Wharfinger
Wholesaler
Winebibber
Winewaiter
Wireworker
Woodcarver
Woodcutter
Woodworker
Wool carder
Wool comber
Wool sorter
Wool winder
Workfellow
Working man

Workmaster
Workpeople
Worshipper

11 letters:
Abecedarian
Academician
Accompanist
Actor's agent
Antiquarian
Appointment
Army officer
Astrologist
Astronomist
Audio typist
Backroom boy
Bag snatcher
Bank cashier
Bank manager
Bargemaster
Basketmaker
Beauty queen
Bell founder
Beneficiary
Billsticker
Bingo caller
Bird fancier
Bird watcher
Board member
Body builder
Body servant
Boilermaker
Boilersmith
Breadwinner
Bridgemaker
Broadcaster
Bronzesmith
Bullfighter
Bushfighter
Businessman
Candlemaker
Car salesman
Chamberlain
Chambermaid
Charcoalist
Cheerleader
Cheesemaker
Chiropactor
Chiropodist
Choirmaster
Clairvoyant

Clergywoman
Coachwright
Co-authoress
Coffinmaker
Cognoscenti
Commentator
Congressman
Conspirator
Contributor
Conveyancer
Co-ordinator
Coppersmith
Court jester
Crane driver
Crimewriter
Crown lawyer
Cub reporter
Cypher clerk
Day labourer
Dean of women
Delivery man
Demographer
Distributor
Double agent
Draughtsman
Drill master
Drug peddler
Duty officer
Electrician
Embroiderer
Enlisted man
Entertainer
Estate agent
Etymologist
Executioner
Extortioner
Factory hand
Faith healer
Field worker
Fifth column
Fighting man
Filing clerk
Fingersmith
Fire brigade
Fire watcher
Flag captain
Flag officer
Flat dweller
Flying squad
Foot soldier
Fruit picker

Funambulist
Functionary
Galley slave
Gamesmaster
Gentlewoman
Ghostwriter
Ginger group
Glass blower
Glass cutter
Grave digger
Greengrocer
Gunman's moll
Haberdasher
Hairdresser
Hair stylist
Hammersmith
Handservant
Hardwareman
Head teacher
Hedgepriest
High sheriff
High society
Home crofter
Horse doctor
Horse trader
Housemaster
Housemother
Housewright
Ice-cream man
Illuminator
Illusionist
Illustrator
Infantryman
Interpreter
Interviewer
Iron founder
Kitchenmaid
Lamplighter
Landscapist
Land steward
Laundrymaid
Leading lady
Leaseholder
Ledger clerk
Leter writer
Lifeboatman
Locum tenens
Lollipop man
Lord Provost
Lorry driver
Madrigalist

Maidservant
Mandolinist
Manipulator
Masquerader
Master baker
Matinee idol
Mechanician
Medicine man
Merchantman
Metalworker
Method actor
Military man
Millionaire
Mimographer
Miniaturist
Momorialist
Money lender
Moonlighter
Mother's help
Mountaineer
Music critic
Naval rating
Needlewoman
Neurologist
Night hunter
Night porter
Night sister
Night worker
Novelettist
Numismatist
Office party
Onion Johnny
Optometrist
Ornamentist
Orthopedist
Palaestrian
Pamphleteer
Panelbeater
Panel doctor
Papal nuncio
Paperhanger
Paragrapher
Parish clerk
Parlourmaid
Pathologist
Pearlfisher
Pearly queen
Penny-a-liner
Petrologist
Philatelist
Philologist

Philosopher
Phonologist
Piece worker
Police cadet
Policewoman
Portraitist
Predecessor
Prizewinner
Probationer
Proof reader
Protagonist
Purseholder
Questionist
Quill driver
Radiologist
Rag merchant
Rank and file
Rear admiral
Relic monger
Research man
Rhetorician
River keeper
Roadsweeper
Rocket pilot
Rugby player
Safebreaker
Safecracker
Sandwichman
Saxophonist
School nurse
Scorekeeper
Scoutmaster
Scrap dealer
Scythesmith
Search party
Secret agent
Semaphorist
Semi-skilled
Senior clerk
Sharebroker
Sheep farmer
Shepherdess
Shipbuilder
Ship's cooper
Ship's tailor
Ship's writer
Shop steward
Silversmith
Sinologoist
Sister tutor
Slaughterer

Occupations

Slave trader
Smallholder
Sociologist
Space doctor
Spacewriter
Speechmaker
Stage player
Stagewright
Stallholder
Stenotypist
Stereotyper
Stipendiary
Stockbroker
Stockfarmer
Stockjobber
Stonecutter
Storekeeper
Storyteller
Straight man
Stripteaser
Subordinate
Surrebutter
Swordmaster
Talent scout
Taxidermist
Telegrapher
Telepathist
Telephonist
Terpsichore
Testimonial
Ticket agent
Toastmaster
Tobacconist
Tommy Atkins
Tooth doctor
Tooth drawer
Town planner
Toxophilite
Train bearer
Train robber
Transcriber
Travel agent
Tree surgeon
Truck farmer
Typographer
Upholsterer
Van salesman
Versemonger
Vine dresser
Viola player
War reporter

Washerwoman
Water doctor
Water finder
Welfare work
Whalefisher
Wheelwright
White-collar
White hunter
Witch doctor
Woodshopper
Wool stapler
Working girl
Xylophonist
Youth leader

12 letters:
Actor-manager
Advance party
Air commodore
Aircraftsman
Air-sea rescue
Ambulance man
Anaesthetist
Armour bearer
Artilleryman
Balladmonger
Ballad singer
Ballet dancer
Bibliologist
Bibliopegist
Body snatcher
Booking clerk
Bookstitcher
Border sentry
Bottlewasher
Boulevardier
Bridgemaster
Brigade major
Cabinet maker
Calligrapher
Camp follower
Candlewright
Caricaturist
Carpet bagger
Carpet fetter
Cartographer
Casual labour
Cattle lifter
Cerographist
Check-weigher
Chicken thief

Chief cashier
Chief justice
Chief mourner
Chief of staff
Chimney sweep
Chirographer
Churchwarden
Circuit rider
Civil servant
Civil service
Clarinettist
Clerk of works
Coachbuilder
Coatguardman
Collaborator
Commissioner
Confectioner
Conquistador
Contemporary
Corn chandler
Costermonger
Customs clerk
Deep-sea diver
Demonstrator
Desk sergeant
Doctor's round
Dramaturgist
Ecclesiastic
Electrotyper
Elocutionist
Entomologist
Entrepreneur
Escapologist
Exhibitioner
Experimenter
Ex-serviceman
Exterminator
Family doctor
Father figure
Field-marshal
Figure dancer
Filed officer
Filibusterer
Film director
Film producer
First officer
First reserve
Flying column
Flying doctor
Footplateman
Garret master

General agent
Geriatrician
Globetrotter
Grandstander
Group captain
Guest speaker
Gynecologist
Headmistress
Headshrinker
Heir apparent
High official
Hockey player
Holidaymaker
Hotel manager
Housebreaker
Houseekeeper
Housepainter
Hydropathist
Immunologist
Impersonator
Improvisator
Instructress
Intermediary
Jazz musician
Junior rating
Juvenile lead
King's counsel
Kitchen staff
Knifegrinder
Knifethrower
Lady superior
Landed gentry
Land surveyor
Law stationer
Lay-out artist
Leader writer
Leathernecks
Legal adviser
Lexicologist
Line sergeant
Literary hack
Literary lion
Lithographer
Longshoreman
Loss adjuster
Maid of honour
Maitre d'hotel
Major-general
Make-up artist
Man of letters
Man of science

Manual worker
Manufacturer
Mass-producer
Master-at-arms
Mastersinger
Metallurgist
Metropolitan
Mezzo soprano
Mineralogist
Money-changer
Monographist
Motorcyclist
Musicologist
Naval officer
Newspaperman
Notary public
Nutritionist
Obstetrician
Office bearer
Office junior
Pastoral poet
Patent office
Pediatrician
Penitentiary
Petty officer
Photographer
Physiologist
Plant manager
Ploughwright
Plumber's mate
Poet laureate
Post graduate
Postmistress
Practitioner
Press officer
Principal boy
Prison warder
Prison worker
Quarrymaster
Racing driver
Radiodontist
Radiographer
Receptionist
Restaurateur
Retaining fee
Sales manager
Scene-painter
Scene-shifter
Schoolmaster
Screenwriter
Scriptwriter

Scullery maid
Sister german
Site engineer
Snake-charmer
Social worker
Soil mechanic
Sole occupant
Special agent
Speechwriter
Spiritualist
Sportscaster
Sports master
Sportswriter
Staff officer
Stage manager
Statistician
Steel erector
Stenographer
Stereotypist
Stonedresser
Stormtrooper
Street-trader
Tax-collector
Technologist
Telegraph boy
Telephone man
Tennis player
Test engineer
Theatre nurse
Ticket holder
Ticket writer
Top executive
Trained nurse
Trichologist
Trick-cyclist
Troutbreeder
Undermanager
Vaudevillist
Vice-director
Vice-governor
Vicie-admiral
Warehouseman
Water-diviner
Wind musician
Wine merchant
Wood-engraver
Worker priest
Working party
Workmistress
Works manager

Occupations

Officials

2 letters:
MC
SL

3 letters:
Aga
GOC

4 letters:
Agha
Cigs
Dean
Exon
Imam
Prog
Suit

5 letters:
Amban
Chair
Ephor
Imaum
Jurat
Mayor
Mirza
Sewer
Usher

6 letters:
Ataman
Beadle
Bursar
Censor
Consul
Datary
Deacon
Hetman
Keeper
Lictor
Master
Notary
Purser
Sexton
Syndic
Verger
Warden
Yeoman

7 letters:
Agistor
Attaché
Bailiff
Coroner
Darogha
Equerry
Filacer
Filazer
Hayward
Jamadar
Jemadar
Jemidar
Marshal
Mueddin
Pooh-Bah
Proctor
Provost
Sheriff
Speaker
Steward
Tribune

8 letters:
Bimbashi
Black rod
Chairman
Claviger
Cursitor
Decurion
Delegate
Mandarin
Palatine
Tipstaff
Verderer
Whiffler

9 letters:
Apparitor
Catchpole
Catchpoll
Commissar
Constable
Ealdorman
Escheator
Exciseman
Gauleiter

Intendant
Jobsworth
Landdrost
Moderator
Ombudsman
Polemarch
Precentor
President
Principal
Tahsildar
Treasurer
Waldgrave

10 letters:
Ambassador
Bumbailiff
Bureaucrat
Chairwoman
Chancellor
Magistrate
Postmaster
Procurator
Proveditor
Pursuivant
Silentiary
Subchanter
Supercargo
Tidewaiter
Timekeeper

11 letters:
Chairperson
Chamberlain
Functionary
Infirmarian
Shop steward

12 letters:
Commissioner
Jack-in-office
Remembrancer

13 letters:
Quartermaster

14 letters:
Provost-marshal

Oils

Oils

13 letters:
Pentyl acetate
Sunflower seed

14 letters:
Glutaraldehyde

15 letters:
Evening primrose

Orange, shades of

4 letters:
Gold

5 letters:
Amber
Ochre

Peach

9 letters:
Grenadine
Tangerine

10 letters:
Terracotta

11 letters:
Burnt sienna

Orchestral instruments

4 letters:
Gong
Harp
Oboe
Tuba

5 letters:
Cello
Flute
Piano
Viola

6 letters:
Violin

7 letters:
Bassoon
Celesta
Piccolo
Timpani
Trumpet

8 letters:
Bass-drum
Clarinet
Trombone

9 letters:
Snare drum
Xylophone

10 letters:
Cor anglais
Double bass
French horn

11 letters:
Violoncello

12 letters:
Tubular bells

13 letters:
Contra-bassoon

Ores

3 letters:
Tin
Wad

4 letters:
Alga
Wadd

6 letters:
Copper
Glance

7 letters:
Bauxite
Bornite
Niobite
Oligist
Peacock

Realgar

8 letters:
Calamine
Cerusite
Crocoite
Galenite
Ilmenite
Limonite
Smaltite
Tenorite

9 letters:
Coffinite
Haematite
Hedyphane
Ironstone

Phacolite
Proustite
Stream-tin

10 letters:
Calaverite
Chalcocite
Horseflesh
Iridosmine
Melaconite
Sphalerite
Stephanite

11 letters:
Pitchblende
Psilomelane
Pyrargyrite

Organizations and treaties

12 letters:
Babingtonite
Chalcopyrite

Pyromorphite
Tetrahedrite

15 letters:
Stilpnosiderite

Organizations and treaties

2 letters:
EU

3 letters:
CAP
CBI
ECO
EEA
EMS
EMU
IFC
ILO
IMF
TUC
WTO

4 letters:
ACAS
CACM
ECSC
EFTA
GATT
NEDC
OECD
OPEC

5 letters:
LAFTA
NAFTA
UNIDO

6 letters:
ECOSOC
ECOWAS
UNCTAD

7 letters:
CARICOM
CARIFTA
COMECON

8 letters:
Advisory

9 letters:
World Bank

12 letters:
Conciliation
Treaty of Rome

13 letters:
European Union

14 letters:
Lomé agreements

16 letters:
Maastricht Treaty

18 letters:
Bretton Woods System

19 letters:
Office of Fair Trading
Trades Union Congress

20 letters:
European Economic Area

21 letters:
And Arbitration Service
European Monetary Union

22 letters:
Caribbean Free Trade Area
European Investment Bank
European Monetary System
World Trade Organization

23 letters:
Single European Market Act

24 letters:
Common Agricultural Policy
Economic and Social Council
European Coal Organization

25 letters:
International Monetary Fund

27 letters:
Central American Common
    Market

28 letters:
European Free Trade association

29 letters:
European Coal and Steel Community

30 letters:
Confederation of British Industry
Monopolies and Mergers Commission

31 letters:
European Monetary Cooperation Fund
European Regional Development Fund
International Finance Corporation
International Labour Organization
North American Free Trade Agreement

33 letters:
Caribbean Community and Common Market
General Agreement on Tariffs and Trade
Latin American Free Trade Association

34 letters:
Council for Mutual Economic Assistance
National Economic Development Council

36 letters:
Economic Community Of West African States

40 letters:
New Zealand and Australia Free Trade Agreement

41 letters:
Organization of Petroleum Exporting Countries

43 letters:
European Bank for Reconstruction and Development

44 letters:
United Nations Conference on Trade and Development

46 letters:
United Nations Industrial Development Organization

48 letters:
International Bank for Reconstruction and Development
Organization for Economic Cooperation and Development

Organs

Organs

3 letters:
Ear
Fin

4 letters:
Gill

5 letters:
Corti
Ctene
Gonad
Liver
Serra

6 letters:
Carpel
Feeler
Fundus
Kidney
Radula
Spleen
Stamen
Syrinx

Thymus
Tongue
Tonsil
Uterus
Viscus
Vitals

7 letters:
Isomere
Medulla
Nectary
Oogonia
Saprobe
Viscera

8 letters:
Hapteron
Pancreas
Placenta
Pulmones
Receptor
Tentacle

Tympanum

9 letters:
Sensillum
Spinneret

10 letters:
Nephridium
Ovipositor
Parapodium
Photophore
Sporangium
Sporophore

11 letters:
Archegonium

12 letters:
Exteroceptor

13 letters:
Chemoreceptor
Photoreceptor

Oxbridge colleges

3 letters:
New

5 letters:
Clare
Green
Jesus
Keble
King's
Oriel

6 letters:
Darwin
Exeter
Girton
Merton
Queen's
Selwyn
Wadham

7 letters:
Balliol

Christ's
Downing
Kellogg
Linacre
Lincoln
New Hall
Newnham
St Anne's
St Cross
St Hugh's
St John's
Trinity
Wolfson

8 letters:
All Souls
Emmanuel
Homerton
Magdalen
Nuffield
Pembroke

Robinson
St Hilda's
St Peter's

9 letters:
Brasenose
Churchill
Clare Hall
Magdalene
Mansfield
St Antony's
St Edmund's
Templeton
Worcester

10 letters:
Greyfriars
Hughes Hall
Peterhouse
Somerville
St Stephen's
University

Oxbridge colleges

11 letters:
Blackfriars
Campion Hall
Fitzwilliam
Regent's Park
Trinity Hall

12 letters:
Christ Church

Sidney Sussex
St Benet's Hall
St Catharine's
St Catherine's
St Edmund Hall
Wycliffe Hall

13 letters:
Corpus Christi

Lucy Cavendish

16 letters:
Gonville and Caius
Harris Manchester
Lady Margaret Hall

P

Palms

3 letters:
Ita

4 letters:
Atap
Coco
Date
Doum
Nipa

5 letters:
Areca
Assai
Betel
Bussu
Macaw
Nikau
Ratan
Sabal

6 letters:
Buriti
Corozo

Elaeis
Gomuti
Gomuto
Gru-gru
Jupati
Kentia
Macoya
Raffia
Raphia
Rattan
Trooly

7 letters:
Babassu
Calamus
Coquito
Corypha
Euterpe
Jipyapa
Moriche
Palmyra
Paxiuba

Pupunha
Talipat
Talipot
Troelie
Troolie

8 letters:
Carnauba
Date tree
Groo-groo
Jipi-Japa
Macahuba

9 letters:
Burrawang
Carnahuba

10 letters:
Chamaerops
Jippi-Jappa

12 letters:
Chiqui-chiqui
Washingtonia

Papers

3 letters:
Art
Rag
Wax

4 letters:
Bond
Chad
Demy
Exam
File
Laid
Note
Rice

Test
Wove

5 letters:
Bible
Brown
Crepe
Crown
Emery
Flock
Glass
Graph
Green
India

Kraft
Linen
Sheet
Sugar
Touch
Waste
Waxed
White

6 letters:
Ballot
Baryta
Carbon
Filter

Garnet
Litmus
Manila
Retree
Tissue
Toilet
Vellum

7 letters:
Bromide
Manilla
Papyrus
Torchon
Tracing

Whatman®
Writing

8 letters:
Document
Foolscap
Glassine
Turmeric
Wrapping

9 letters:
Cartridge
Chiyogami
Cigarette

Cream-laid
Cream-wove
Hieratica
Onion-skin
Papillote
Parchment
Willesden

10 letters:
Cellophane®

11 letters:
Greaseproof

Parasites

3 letters:
Bot
Ked
Nit

4 letters:
Conk
Flea
Kade
Tick
Tryp

5 letters:
Leech
Louse
Worms

6 letters:
Coccus
Dodder
Isopod
Viscum

7 letters:
Ascarid
Bonamia
Candida
Copepod
Epizoon
Giardia
Hair-eel
Lamprey

Pinworm
Stylops

8 letters:
Entozoon
Epiphyte
Filarium
Hook-worm
Lungworm
Nematode
Puccinia
Sporozoa
Tapeworm
Trichina

9 letters:
Bilharzia
Ectophyte
Endamoeba
Endophyte
Entophyte
Heartworm
Ichneumon
Inquiline
Macdonald
Mistletoe
Orobanche
Rafflesia
Roundworm
Sporozoan
Strongyle

Trematode

10 letters:
Autoecious
Babesiasis
Liverfluke
Monogenean
Plasmodium
Rickettsia
Smut-fungus
Toxoplasma

11 letters:
Bladder-worm
Cryptozoite
Gregarinida
Haematozoon
Schistosoma
Strongyloid
Trypanosoma

12 letters:
Heteroecious
Licktrencher
Mallophagous
Rhipidoptera
Strepsiptera

15 letters:
Cryptosporidium

Parliaments

4 letters:
Dail
Diet
Rump
Sejm

5 letters:
Lords
Thing

6 letters:
Cortes
Majlis
Seanad

7 letters:
Althing
Commons
Knesset

Lagting
Riksdag
Tynwald

8 letters:
Congress
Lagthing
Lok Sabha
Stannary
Stormont
Storting

9 letters:
Barebones
Bundestag
Eduskunta
Folketing
Landsting

Odelsting
Reichstag
Sanhedrin
Stirthing
Storthing

10 letters:
Landsthing
Odelsthing
Rajya Sabha
St Stephens

11 letters:
Volkskammer
Westminster

13 letters:
Seanad Eireann

Pasta

4 letters:
Pipe
Zita
Ziti

5 letters:
Penne
Ruote

6 letters:
Ditali

7 letters:
Bavette
Fusilli
Gnocchi
Lasagne
Lumache
Noodles
Ravioli

Spätzle

8 letters:
Bucatini
Farfalle
Linguine
Macaroni
Rigatoni
Spaetzle
Taglioni

9 letters:
Agnolotti
Fettucine
Fettucini
Spaghetti

10 letters:
Bombolotti
Cannelloni

Cellentani
Conchiglie
Fettuccine
Gnocchetti
Lasagnette
Tortellini
Tortelloni
Vermicelli

11 letters:
Cappelletti
Maultaschen
Orecchiette
Pappardelle
Tagliatelle
Tortiglioni

12 letters:
Paglia e fieno

Pastry

4 letters:
Filo
Puff
Suet

5 letters:
Choux

Flaky

8 letters:
Hot water

9 letters:
Rough puff

10 letters:
Pâte brisée
Pâte sucrée
Shortcrust

14 letters:
Pâte feuilletée

Peninsulas

4 letters:
Ards
Cape
Eyre
Kola

5 letters:
Gaspé
Gower
Lleyn
Malay
Sinai
Yorke

6 letters:
Alaska
Avalon
Balkan
Bataan
Crimea
Deccan
Iberia
Istria

Palmer
Tasman
Wirral

7 letters:
Arabian
Boothia
Cape Cod
Chukchi
Florida
Iberian
Jutland
Kintyre
Kowloon
Leizhou

8 letters:
Delmarva
East Cape
Labrador
Melville

9 letters:
Antarctic

Cape Verde
Gallipoli
Indo-China
Kamchatka
Kathiawar
The Lizard

10 letters:
Chalcidice
Chersonese
Nova Scotia

11 letters:
Peloponnese

12 letters:
Scandinavian

14 letters:
Baja California

17 letters:
Wilson's
  Promontory

Peoples

AFRICAN PEOPLES

3 letters:
Edo
Ewe
Ibo
Luo
Rif
San
Tiv
Twi

4 letters:
Akan
Boer
Efik
Fang
Fula
Hutu
Igbo
Lozi

Luba
Moor
Munt
Mzee
Nama
Nuba
Nuer
Nupe
Pedi

Peoples

Riff
Rifi
Susu
Tshi
Xosa
Zulu

5 letters:
Bantu
Bemba
Bintu
Chewa
Dinka
Duala
Dyula
Fanti
Fingo
Fulah
Galla
Ganda
Hausa
Ibibi
Kongo
Lango
Mande
Masai
Mende
Mossi
Muntu
Negro
Nguni
Nilot
Nyoro
Oromo
Pigmy
Pondo
Pygmy
Shluh
Shona
Sotho
Swazi
Temne
Tonga
Tutsi
Venda
Wolof
Xhosa

6 letters:
Basuto
Beento
Berber
Damara
Grikwa
Griqua
Hamite
Herero
Ibibio
Kabyle
Kenyan
Kikuyu
Libyan
Malawi
Malian
Nilote
Nubian
Nyanja
Ovambo
Somali
Tsonga
Tswana
Tuareg
Watusi
Yoruba

7 letters:
Angolan
Ashanti
Baganda
Bambara
Barbary
Barotse
Basotho
Biafran
Bushman
Cairene
Flytaal
Gambian
Ghanian
Gullash
Lesotho
Lowveld
Maghreb
Maghrib
Malinke

Maninke
Mashona
Mosotho
Namaqua
Ndebele
Shilluk
Songhai
Swahili
Voltaic
Watutsi
Yoruban
Zairean

8 letters:
Botswana
Cushitic
Eritrean
Gabonese
Ghanaian
Khoikhoi
Liberian
Mandingo
Matabele
Moroccan
Namibian
Negrillo
Shangaan
Sudanese
Transkei
Tunisian

9 letters:
Congolese
Ethiopian
Gazankulu
Hottentot
Rhodesian
Transvaal

10 letters:
Abyssinian
Mozambican

11 letters:
Rastafarian
Strandloper

12 letters:
Carthaginian

ASIAN PEOPLES

3 letters:
Hui
Hun
Jat
Lao
Mon

4 letters:
Ainu
Arab
Cham
Chin
Dani
Dard
Dyak
Gond
Jain
Kurd
Mede
Moro
Motu
Naga
Nair
Nuri
Shan
Sikh
Sind
Thai
Turk

5 letters:
Dayak
Hindu
Kafir
Karen
Kazak
Khmer
Kisan
Malay
Mogul
Munda
Nayar
Nogay
Oriya
Parsi
Sindh
Tajik
Tamil
Tatar

Uigur
Uzbek
Vedda
Yakut

6 letters:
Beduin
Bihari
Buryat
Cumans
Essene
Evenki
Fulani
Gurkha
Harsha
Igorot
Jewish
Kalmyk
Kazakh
Khalsa
Lepcha
Lycian
Lydian
Mazhbi
Mishmi
Mongol
Parsee
Pashto
Pathan
Pushto
Pushtu
Sabean
Semite
Sherpa
Sindhi
Tadjik
Tartar
Telegu
Tongan
Tungus
Uighur
Veddah

7 letters:
Adivasi
Adivisi
Amorite
Balochi
Baluchi

Bashkir
Bedouin
Bengali
Bisayan
Burmese
Chinese
Chukchi
Chuvash
Cossack
Elamite
Harijan
Hittite
Hurrian
Israeli
Kalmuck
Kassite
Maratha
Maratta
Negrito
Panjabi
Punjabi
Sabaean
Samoyed
Saracen
Sogdian
Tadzhik
Tagalog
Talaing
Turkmen
Visayan

8 letters:
Accadian
Akkadian
Canarese
Chaldean
Chukchee
Ephesian
Gujarati
Gujerati
Igorrote
Kanarese
Kashmiri
Mahratta
Sumerian
Turanian

9 letters:
Amalekite

Peoples

Bakhtyari
Chaldaean
Dravidian
Kabardian
Sinhalese
Tocharian

Tokharian

10 letters:
Andamanese
Babylonian
Ephraimite
Kara-Kalpak

Kshatriyas
Montagnard
Phoenician

11 letters:
Palestinian

AUSTRALASIAN PEOPLES

5 letters:
Dayak
Māori

6 letters:
Aranda

7 letters:
Tagalog

8 letters:
Gurindji

9 letters:
Aborigine

10 letters:
Melanesian
Polynesian

CENTRAL AND SOUTH AMERICAN INDIAN PEOPLES

2 letters:
Ge

4 letters:
Inca
Maya
Tupi

5 letters:
Aztec
Carib
Chimú

6 letters:
Aymara
Chibca
Kechua
Makuna
Mixtec
Toltec

7 letters:
Guarani
Nahuatl

Quechua
Quichua
Zapotec

8 letters:
Arawakan

10 letters:
Araucanian
Cashinahua

INUIT PEOPLES

5 letters:
Aleut
Inuit
Yupik

6 letters:
Innuit

8 letters:
Aleutian

13 letters:
Caribou Eskimo

EUROPEAN PEOPLES

4 letters:
Celt
Dane
Finn
Gaul
Goth
Jute
Komi
Lapp
Manx
Pict
Pole
Scot

Slav
Sorb
Turk
Wend

5 letters:
Angle
Aryan
Azeri
Croat
Cymry
Czech
Dutch

Frank
Gipsy
Greek
Gypsy
Iceni
Irish
Kymry
Latin
Norse
Saxon
Swede
Swiss
Vlach

Welsh

6 letters:
Basque
Belgae
Breton
Briton
Bulgar
Cimbri
Dorian
Eolian
French
Gaelic
Gascon
German
Goidel
Ingush
Ionian
Magyar
Norman
Ostyak
Sabine
Salain
Slovak
Teuton
Ugrian
Vandal
Viking
Volsci
Votyak
Walach

7 letters:
Achaean
Achaian
Aeolian
Azorean
Brython
Catalan
Chechen
Cornish
English

Fleming
Frisian
Iberian
Latvian
Lombard
Maltese
Mordvin
Russian
Samnite
Samoyed
Serbian
Silures
Slovene
Swabian
Walloon

8 letters:
Albanian
Alemanni
Armenian
Austrian
Bavarian
Cheremis
Corsican
Croatian
Ephesian
Estonian
Etrurian
Etruscan
Faeroese
Galician
Georgian
Hellenic
Illyrian
Karelian
Lusatian
Prussian
Romanian
Scythian
Sephardi
Sicilian

Thracian
Tyrolese
Visigoth

9 letters:
Aragonese
Ashkenazi
Bulgarian
Castilian
Celtiberi
Cheremiss
Esthonian
Icelandic
Langobard
Norwegian
Ostrogoth
Provençal
Sabellian
Sardinian
Ukrainian

10 letters:
Andalusian
Anglo-Saxon
Burgundian
Carinthian
Lithuanian
Macedonian
Portuguese

11 letters:
Anglo-Norman
Azerbaijani
Belorussian
Celtiberian
Montenegrin

12 letters:
Indo-European
Luxembourger

13 letters:
Bosnian Muslim

NATIVE AMERICAN TRIBES

3 letters:
Fox
Ute

4 letters:
Cree
Crow
Dene

Hopi
Hupa
Inca
Iowa
Maya
Moki
Pima

Pomo
Sauk
Tewa
Tico
Tiwa
Tupi
Yuma

Peoples

Zuni

5 letters:
Aztec
Blood
Caddo
Cajun
Campa
Carib
Creek
Haida
Huron
Kansa
Kiowa
Lipan
Miami
Moqui
Olmec
Omaha
Osage
Ponca
Sioux
Teton
Wappo
Yaqui
Yuchi
Yuman
Yunca

6 letters:
Abnaki
Apache
Aymara
Biloxi
Cayuga
Cocopa
Dakota
Dogrib
Kechua
Kichai
Lakota
Mandan
Micmac
Mistec
Mixtec
Mohave
Mohawk
Mojave
Navaho
Navajo
Nootka
Oglala

Ojibwa
Oneida
Ostiak
Ottawa
Paiute
Papago
Pawnee
Pequot
Pericu
Piegan
Plains
Pueblo
Quakaw
Quapaw
Salish
Santee
Sarcee
Seneca
Siwash
Toltec
Warrau
Yanqui

7 letters:
Abenaki
Arapaho
Araucan
Arikara
Caddoan
Catawba
Chibcha
Chilcal
Chinook
Choctaw
Hidatsa
Kutenai
Mahican
Mapuche
Mohegan
Mohican
Nahuatl
Natchez
Ojibway
Orejone
Palouse
Pontiac
Quechua
Quichua
Senecan
Serrano
Shawnee

Stonies
Tlingit
Tonkawa
Wichita
Wyandot
Yalkama

8 letters:
Aguaruna
Algonkin
Cherokee
Cheyenne
Chippewa
Comanche
Delaware
Flathead
Illinois
Iroquois
Kickapoo
Kootenai
Kootenay
Kwakiutl
Malecite
Menomini
Mikasuki
Mogollon
Muskogee
Nez Percé
Okanagon
Onondaga
Powhatan
Seminole
Shoshone
Shoshoni
Shushwap

9 letters:
Algonkian
Algonquan
Algonquin
Apalachee
Ashochimi
Blackfoot
Chickasaw
Chipewyan
Chippeway
Karankawa
Manhattan
Melungeon
Menominee
Mescalero
Muskogean

Penobscot
Potawatom
Suquamash
Tsimshian
Tuscarora
Wampanoag
Winnebago
Wyandotte

10 letters:
Algonquian
Athabascan
Bella Coola
Leni-Lenapé
Miniconjou

Minnetaree
Montagnais
Montagnard
Muskhogean
Root-digger
Tarahumara

11 letters:
Assiniboine
Kiowa Apache
Massachuset
Minneconjou
Narraganset
Susquehanna

12 letters:
Mound Builder
Pasamaquoddy

13 letters:
Massachusetts
Northern Piute
Southern Piute
Susquehannock

14 letters:
Northern Paiute
Southern Paiute

Philosophy

PHILOSOPHICAL SCHOOLS AND DOCTRINES

5 letters:
Deism

6 letters:
Monism
Taoism
Theism

7 letters:
Animism
Atomism
Dualism
Fideism
Marxism
Realism
Thomism

8 letters:
Cynicism
Fatalism
Hedonism
Humanism
Idealism
Nihilism
Stoicism

9 letters:
Platonism
Pluralism

10 letters:
Eleaticism
Empiricism
Kantianism
Nominalism
Positivism
Pragmatism
Pyrrhonism
Scepticism
Utopianism

11 letters:
Determinism
Hegelianism
Materialism
Rationalism

12 letters:
Behaviourism
Cartesianism
Confucianism
Epicureanism
Essentialism
Neo-Platonism

13 letters:
Conceptualism
Immaterialism

Phenomenalism
Scholasticism
Structuralism

14 letters:
Existentialism
Logical atomism
Pythagoreanism
Sensationalism
Utilitarianism

15 letters:
Aristotelianism
Conventionalism
Critical realism

16 letters:
Consequentialism

17 letters:
Logical positivism

Philosophy

PHILOSOPHERS

2 letters:
Xi, *Chu*
Zi, *Lao*
Zi, *Xun*
Zu, *Han Fei*

4 letters:
Ayer, *A(lfred) J(ules)*
Cato, *Marcus Porcius*
Hume, *David*
Kant, *Immanuel*
Mach, *Ernst*
Marx, *Karl*
Mill, *James*
Mill, *John Stuart*
More, *Henry*
Mo-Zi
Reid, *Thomas*
Ryle, *Gilbert*
Vico, *Giovanni Battista*
Weil, *Simone*
Wolf, *Friedrich August*

5 letters:
Amiel, *Henri Frédéric*
Bacon, *Francis*
Bacon, *Roger*
Bayle, *Pierre*
Benda, *Julien*
Bruno, *Giordano*
Buber, *Martin*
Burke, *Edmund*
Comte, *Auguste*
Croce, *Benedetto*
Dewey, *John*
Frege, *Gottlob*
Fromm, *Erich*
Godel, *Kurt*
Green, *T(homas) H(ill)*
Hegel, *Georg Wilhelm Friedrich*
Iqbal, *Muhammad*
James, *William*
Locke, *John*
Lully, *Ramón*
Moore, *G(eorge) E(dward)*
Paine, *Thomas*
Paley, *William*
Plato
Rawls, *John*

Renan, *(Joseph) Ernest*
Royce, *Josiah*
Smith, *Adam*
Sorel, *Georges*
Taine, *Hippolyte Adophe*

6 letters:
Adorno, *Theodor Wiesengrund*
Agnesi, *Maria Gaetana*
Arendt, *Hannah*
Austin, *J(ohn) L(angshaw)*
Berlin, *Isaiah*
Carnap, *Rudolf*
Cicero, *Marcus Tallius*
Cousin, *Victor*
Engels, *Friedrich*
Eucken, *Rudolph Christoph*
Fichte, *Johann Gottlieb*
Ficino, *Marsilio*
Gasset, *José Ortega y*
Godwin, *William*
Herder, *Johann Gottfried*
Herzen, *Aleksandr Ivanovich*
Hobbes, *Thomas*
Langer, *Suzanne*
Lukács, *Georg*
Magnus, *Albertus*
Marcel, *Gabriel*
Newton, *Isaac*
Ortega (y Gasset), *José*
Pascal, *Blaise*
Peirce, *Charles Sanders*
Popper, *Karl*
Pyrrho
Sartre, *Jean-Paul*
Scotus, *John Duns*
Seneca, *Lucius Annaeus*
Tagore, *Rabindranath*
Tarski, *Alfred*
Thales

7 letters:
Abelard, *Peter*
Aquinas, *Thomas*
Bentham, *Jeremy*
Bergson, *Henri Louis*
Bradley, *F(rancis) H(erbert)*
Buridan, *Jean*
Derrida, *Jacques*

Diderot, *Denis*
Emerson, *Ralph Waldo*
Erasmus, *Desiderius*
Erigena, *John Scotus*
Fechner, *Gustav Theodor*
Gentile, *Giovanni*
Gorgias
Haeckel, *Ernst Heinrich*
Hah-Levi, *Judah*
Hartley, *David*
Herbart, *Johann Friedrich*
Herbert, *Edward*
Husserl, *Edmund*
Hypatia
Jaspers, *Karl*
Judaeus, *Philo*
Leibniz, *Gottfried Wilhelm*
Malthus, *Thomas Robert*
Marcuse, *Herbert*
Masaryk, *Tomáš Garrigue*
Mencius
Meng-tse
Murdoch, *Dame (Jean) Iris*
Proclus
Ricoeur, *Paul*
Russell, *Bertrand*
Sankara
Sankhya
Schlick, *Moritz*
Spencer, *Herbert*
Spinoza, *Baruch*
Steiner, *Rudolf*
Tillich, *Paul Johannes*
Tolstoy, *Count Leo (Nikolayevich)*

8 letters:

Al-Farabi, *Mohammed ibn Tarkhan*
Averroës
Avicenna
Berkeley, *George*
Boethius, *Anicius Manlius Severinus*
Cassirer, *Ernst*
Cudworth, *Ralph*
Davidson, *Donald*
De Suárez, *Francisco*
Diogenes
Eberhard, *Johann August*
Epicurus
Foucault, *Michel*

Gassendi, *Pierre*
Hamilton, *William*
Harrison, *Frederic*
Leopardi, *Giacomo*
Maritain, *Jacques*
Menippus
Plotinus
Plutarch
Poincaré, *Jules Henri*
Porphyry
Ramanuja
Rousseau, *Jean Jacques*
Shankara
Socrates
Spengler, *Oswald*
Strawson, *Peter*
Voltaire, *François-Marie Arouet de*
Von Hayek, *Friedrich August*
Williams, *Bernard*
Xenophon
Zhuangzi

9 letters:

Althusser, *Louis*
Aristotle
Berdyayev, *Nikolai Aleksandrovich*
Bosanquet, *Bernard*
Chuang-tzu
Cleanthes
Confucius
Copleston, *Frederick (Charles)*
De Chardin, *Pierre Teilhard*
Descartes, *René*
De Unamuno, *Miguel*
Epictetus
Euhemerus
Feuerbach, *Ludwig Andreas*
Heidegger, *Martin*
Helvétius, *Claude Adrien*
Hutcheson, *Francis*
Leucippus
Lévy-Bruhl, *Lucien*
Lucretius
Nietzsche, *Friedrich Wilhelm*
Santayana, *George*
Schelling, *Friedrich Wilhelm Joseph Von*
Von Herder, *Johann Gottfried*
Whitehead, *A(lfred) N(orth)*

10 letters:

Anacharsis

Phobias

Anaxagoras
Anaximenes
Apemanthus
Apollonius
Aristippus
Baumgarten, *Alexander Gottlieb*
Campanella, *Tommaso*
Chrysippus
Chrysostom, *Dio*
Churchland, *Paul*
Cumberland, *Richard*
De Beauvoir, *Simone*
Democritus
Empedocles
Heraclitus
Ibn-Gabirol, *Solomon*
Ibn-Khaldun
Maimonides
Parmenides
Protagoras
Pythagoras
Schweitzer, *Albert*
Swedenborg, *Emanuel*
Xenocrates
Xenophanes
Zeno *of Elea*

11 letters:
Anaximander
Antisthenes
Bonaventura
De Condillac, *Étienne Bonnot*
Heracleides
Kierkegaard, *Søren Aabye*
Machiavelli, *Niccolò*
Malebranche, *Nicolas*
Montesquieu, *Charles de Secondat (Baron de la Brède et de)*
Reichenbach, *Hans*

Von Leibnitz, *Gottfried Wilhelm*
Von Schlegel, *Friedrich*

12 letters:
Callisthenes
De Fontenelle, *Bernard le Bovier*
De Saint-Simon, *Comte*
Merleau-Ponty, *Maurice*
Schopenhauer, *Arthur*
Theophrastus
Von Pufendorf, *Samuel*
Von Schelling, *Friedrich Wilhelm Joseph*
Wittgenstein, *Ludwig Josef Johann*
Zeno *of Citium*

13 letters:
De Montesquieu, *Baron de la Brède et*
Van Orman Quine, *Willard*

14 letters:
Della Mirandola, *Giovanni Pico*
Nicholas *of Cusa*
Rosmini-Serbati, *Antonio*
Schleiermacher, *Friedrich Ernst Daniel*
Shankaracharya

15 letters:
Le Rond d'Alembert, *Jean*
William *of Ockham*

16 letters:
Marsilius *of Padua*

18 letters:
De Caritat Condorcet, *Marie Jean Antoine Nicholas*
St Augustine *of Hippo*

Phobias

Phobia	Object
Acerophobia	Sourness
Achluophobia	Darkness
Acrophobia	Heights
Aerophobia	Air
Agoraphobia	Open spaces
Aichurophobia	Points

Phobia	Object
Ailurophobia	Cats
Akousticophobia	Sound
Algophobia	Pain
Amakaphobia	Carriages
Amathophobia	Dust
Androphobia	Men
Anemophobia	Wind
Anginophobia	Narrowness
Anthropophobia	Man
Antlophobia	Flood
Apeirophobia	Infinity
Aquaphobia	Water
Arachnophobia	Spiders
Asthenophobia	Weakness
Astraphobia	Lightning
Atephobia	Ruin
Aulophobia	Flute
Bacilliphobia	Microbes
Barophobia	Gravity
Basophobia	Walking
Batrachophobia	Reptiles
Belonephobia	Needles
Bibliophobia	Books
Brontophobia	Thunder
Cancerophobia	Cancer
Cheimaphobia	Cold
Chionophobia	Snow
Chrematophobia	Money
Chronophobia	Duration
Chrystallophobia	Crystals
Claustrophobia	Closed spaces
Cnidophobia	Stings
Cometophobia	Comets
Cromophobia	Colour
Cyberphobia	Computers
Cynophobia	Dogs
Demonophobia	Demons
Demophobia	Crowds
Dermatophobia	Skin
Dikephobia	Justice
Doraphobia	Fur
Eisoptrophobia	Mirrors
Electrophobia	Electricity
Enetephobia	Pins
Entomophobia	Insects
Eosophobia	Dawn
Eremophobia	Solitude
Ereuthophobia	Blushing
Ergasiophobia	Work
Genophobia	Sex

Phobias

Phobia	Object
Geumaphobia	Taste
Graphophobia	Writing
Gymnophobia	Nudity
Gynophobia	Women
Hadephobia	Hell
Haematophobia	Blood
Hamartiophobia	Sin
Haptophobia	Touch
Harpaxophobia	Robbers
Hedonophobia	Pleasure
Helminthophobia	Worms
Hodophobia	Travel
Homichlophobia	Fog
Homophobia	Homosexuals
Hormephobia	Shock
Hydrophobia	Water
Hypegiaphobia	Responsibility
Hypnophobia	Sleep
Ideophobia	Ideas
Kakorraphiaphobia	Failure
Katagelophobia	Ridicule
Kenophobia	Void
Kinesophobia	Motion
Kleptophobia	Stealing
Kopophobia	Fatigue
Kristallophobia	Ice
Laliophobia	Stuttering
Linonophobia	String
Logophobia	Words
Lyssophobia	Insanity
Maniaphobia	Insanity
Mastigophobia	Flogging
Mechanophobia	Machinery
Metallophobia	Metals
Meteorophobia	Meteors
Misophobia	Contamination
Monophobia	One thing
Musicophobia	Music
Musophobia	Mice
Necrophobia	Corpses
Nelophobia	Glass
Neophobia	Newness
Nephophobia	Clouds
Nosophobia	Disease
Nyctophobia	Night
Ochlophobia	Crowds
Ochophobia	Vehicles
Odontophobia	Teeth
Oikophobia	Home
Olfactophobia	Smell

Phobia	Object
Ommatophobia	Eyes
Oneirophobia	Dreams
Ophidiophobia	Snakes
Ornithophobia	Birds
Ouranophobia	Heaven
Panphobia	Everything
Pantophobia	Everything
Parthenophobia	Girls
Pathophobia	Disease
Peniaphobia	Poverty
Phasmophobia	Ghosts
Phobophobia	Fears
Photophobia	Light
Pnigerophobia	Smothering
Poinephobia	Punishment
Polyphobia	Many things
Potophobia	Drink
Pteronophobia	Feathers
Pyrophobia	Fire
Russophobia	Russia
Rypophobia	Soiling
Satanophobia	Satan
Selaphobia	Flesh
Siderophobia	Stars
Sitophobia	Food
Spermaphobia	Germs
Spermatophobia	Germs
Stasiphobia	Standing
Stygiophobia	Hell
Taphephobia	Being buried alive
Technophobia	Technology
Teratophobia	Giving birth to a monster
Thaasophobia	Sitting
Thalassophobia	Sea
Thanatophobia	Death
Theophobia	God
Thermophobia	Heat
Tonitrophobia	Thunder
Toxiphobia	Poison
Tremophobia	Trembling
Triskaidekaphobia	Thirteen
Xenophobia	Strangers *or* foreigners
Zelophobia	Jealousy
Zoophobia	Animals

Photography terms

Photography terms

3 letters:
Cam
Pan
TTL

4 letters:
Cock
Film
Gate
Gobo
Grip
Load
Shot
Stop

5 letters:
Blimp
Crane
Dolly
F-stop
Set up
Track
T-stop

6 letters:
Mosaic
Screen
Target
Tripod
Unipod

7 letters:
Hot shoe
Key grip

Release
Saticon
Shutter
T-number
Vidicon

8 letters:
Cassette
Film pack
Lens hood
Long shot
Orthicon
Snapshot
Stop down
Zoom lens

9 letters:
Amplifier
Cameraman
Cartridge
Cokuloris
Ferrotype
Film speed
Macro lens
Objective
Paparazzo
Plumbicon

10 letters:
Autowinder
Camera tube
Focal plane
Iconoscope

Viewfinder
Vignetting

11 letters:
Caméra stylo
Focus puller
Large-format

12 letters:
Cable release
Depth of focus
Synchroflash
Tracking shot

13 letters:
Accessory shoe
Cinematograph
Delayed action
Extension ring
Image orthicon
Telephoto lens
Wide-angle lens

14 letters:
Automatic focus
Kinetheodolite
Pan and tilt head
Shooting script

18 letters:
Hyperfocal distance

19 letters:
Photoreconnaissance

Physics

BRANCHES OF PHYSICS

5 letters:
Solar

6 letters:
Atomic
Optics
Sonics

7 letters:
Applied
Nuclear

Quantum
Statics

8 letters:
Dynamics
Kinetics
Particle
Rheology

9 letters:
Acoustics

Cosmology
Harmonics
Magnetics
Magnetism
Mechanics

10 letters:
Biophysics
Cryogenics
Geophysics

High-energy
Nucleonics
Photometry
Pneumatics
Solid-state

11 letters:
Aerostatics
Electronics
Mesoscopics
Theoretical
Thermometry
Ultrasonics

12 letters:
Aerodynamics

PHYSICS TERMS

3 letters:
Ohm

4 letters:
Atom
Fuse
Lens
Mass
Muon
Volt
Watt
Wave
X-ray

5 letters:
Anion
Diode
Earth
Farad
Field
Force
Hertz
Joule
Laser
Meson

6 letters:
Ampere
Baryon
Cacion
Charge
Energy
Fusion
Kelvin

Astrophysics
Macrophysics
Microphysics
Spectroscopy

13 letters:
Thermostatics

14 letters:
Electrostatics
Low-temperature
Magnetostatics
Thermodynamics

15 letters:
Condensed-matter

Lepton
Matter
Moment
Newton
Pascal
Proton
Vacuum

7 letters:
Calorie
Coulomb
Current
Decibel
Density
Fission
Gravity
Hyperon
Impetus
Inertia
Neutron
Nucleon
Nucleus
Ohm's law
Quantum
Tension

8 letters:
Angstrom
Electron
Friction
Gamma ray
Half-life
Infrared
Momentum

16 letters:
Electromagnetism
Quantum
  mechanics

17 letters:
Superaerodynamics

20 letters:
Statistical
  mechanics

Neutrino
Particle
Red shift
Spectrum
Velocity

9 letters:
Amplifier
Becquerel
Boyle's law
Conductor
Cosmic ray
Cyclotron
Diffusion
Frequency
Generator
Microwave
Radiation
Radio wave
Viscosity

10 letters:
Antimatter
Cathode ray
Charles' law
Convection
Inductance
Reflection
Refraction
Relativity
Resistance
Rutherford
Thermostat
Transistor

Physics

Wavelength

11 letters:
Capacitance
Diffraction
Electricity
Tau particle
Transformer
Ultraviolet

12 letters:
Acceleration
Fluorescence
Luminescence

13 letters:
Direct current
Doppler effect

Kinetic energy
Radioactivity
Semiconductor
Superfluidity

14 letters:
Brownian motion
Planck constant
Surface tension

15 letters:
Centre of gravity
Planck's constant
Potential energy

16 letters:
Centrifugal force
Centripetal force

Terminal velocity

17 letters:
Static electricity
Subatomic particle
Superconductivity

18 letters:
Alternating current
Electromotive force

19 letters:
Potential
   difference

20 letters:
Simple harmonic
   motion

PHYSICISTS

3 letters:
Lee, *Tsung-Dao*
Ohm, *Georg Simon*

4 letters:
Abbe, *Ernst*
Bohr, *Aage Niels*
Bohr, *Niels (Henrik David)*
Born, *Max*
Bose, *Jagadis Chandra*
Bose, *Satyendra Nath*
Hahn, *Otto*
Hess, *Victor Francis*
Kerr, *John*
Lamb, *Willis Eugene*
Lawe, *William C*
Mach, *Ernst*
Néel, *Louis*
Rabi, *Isidor Isaac*
Snow, *C(harles) P(ercy)*
Swan, *Joseph Wilson*
Ting, *Samuel Chao Chung*
Wien, *Wilhelm*
Yang, *Chen Ning*

5 letters:
Aston, *Francis William*
Auger, *Pierre*
Basov, *Nikolai*
Bethe, *Hans Albrecht*
Bloch, *Felix*
Bothe, *Walter*

Boyle, *Robert*
Bragg, *Sir William Henry*
Braun, *Karl Ferdinand*
Curie, *Marie*
Curie, *Pierre*
Debye, *Peter Joseph Wilhelm*
Dewar, *James*
Dirac, *Paul Adrien Maurice*
Fabry, *Charles*
Fermi, *Enrico*
Fuchs, *Klaus*
Gauss, *Carl Friedrich*
Gibbs, *Josiah Willard*
Henry, *Joseph*
Hertz, *Gustav*
Hertz, *Heinrich Rudolph*
Hooke, *Robert*
Jeans, *James Hopwood*
Joule, *James Prescott*
Lodge, *Oliver*
Pauli, *Wolfgang*
Popov, *Alexander Stepanovich*
Sègre, *Emilio*
Stark, *Johannes*
Volta, *Alessandro*
Weber, *Wilhelm Eduard*
Young, *Thomas*

6 letters:
Alfren
Alfvén, *Hannes Olaf Gösta*
Ampère, *André Marie*

Physics

Barkla, *Charles Glover*
Binnig, *Gerd*
Carnot, *Nicolas Leonard Sadi*
Cooper, *Leon*
Cronin, *James Watson*
Dalton, *John*
Franck, *James*
Frisch, *Otto*
Geiger, *Hans*
Giorgi, *Filippo*
Glaser, *Donald Arthur*
Graham, *Thomas*
Kelvin, *William Thomson*
Landau, *Lev Davidovich*
Newton, *Isaac*
Pascal, *Blaise*
Perrin, *Jean Baptiste*
Picard, *Jean*
Planck, *Max (Karl Ernst Ludwig)*
Powell, *Celic*
Talbot, *William Henry Fox*
Teller, *Edward*
Townes, *Charles Hard*
Walton, *Ernest Thomas Sinton*
Wigner, *Eugene Paul*
Wilson, *Charles Thomson Rees*
Yukawa, *Hideki*
Zwicky, *Fritz*

7 letters:
Alvarez, *Luis Walter*
Babinet, *Jacques*
Bardeen, *John*
Bravais, *Auguste*
Broglie, *Maurice*
Charles, *Jacques*
Compton, *Arthur Holly*
Coulomb, *Charles Augustin De*
Crookes, *William*
Doppler, *C(hristian) J(ohann)*
Faraday, *Michael*
Fechner, *Gustav*
Feynman, *Richard*
Fresnel, *Augustin*
Galilei, *Galileo*
Galileo
Gell-Man, *Murray*
Gilbert, *William*
Goddard, *Robert Hutchings*
Hawking, *Stephen William*
Heitler, *Walter*

Huygens, *Christiaan*
Kapitza, *Piotr Leonidovich*
Langley, *Samuel Pierpont*
Laplace, *Pierre Simon*
Lippman, *Gabriel*
Lorentz, *Hendrik Antoon*
Marconi, *Guglielmo*
Maxwell, *James Clerk*
Meitner, *Lise*
Milikin, *Robert*
Moseley, *Henry Gwyn-Jeffreys*
Oersted, *Hans Christian*
Penrose, *Roger*
Piccard, *Auguste*
Prandtl, *Ludwig*
Purcell, *Edward Mill*
Réaumur, *René Antoine Ferchault De*
Richter, *Burton*
Röntgen, *Wilhelm Konrad Von*
Seaborg, *Glenn*
Szilard, *Leo*
Thomson, *Benjamin*
Thomson, *George Paget*
Thomson, *Joseph John*
Tyndall, *John*
Von Laue, *Max Theodor Felix*
Wheeler, *John Archibald*

8 letters:
Anderson, *Carl David*
Anderson, *Elizabeth Garrett*
Anderson, *Philip Warren*
Ångström, *Anders Jonas*
Appleton, *Edward*
Avogadro, *Amedeo*
Blackett, *Patrick Maynard Stuart*
Brattain, *Walter Houser*
Brewster, *David*
Bridgman, *Percy*
Chadwick, *James*
Cherwell, *Frederick Alexander Lindemann*
Clausius, *Rudolf*
Davisson, *Clinton Joseph*
Einstein, *Albert*
Foucault, *Jean Bernard Léon*
Gassendi, *Pierre*
Ipatieff, *Vladimir Nikolaievich*
Lawrence, *Ernest Orlando*
McMillan, *Edwin*

Pigments

Mullikin, *Robert Sanderson*
Oliphant, *Mark Laurence Elwin*
Poincaré, *Jules Henri*
Rayleigh, *John William Strutt*
Roentgen, *Wilhelm Konrad*
Sakharov, *Andrei*
Shockley, *William Bradfield*
Siegbahn, *Kai*
Van Allen, *James*
Von Mayer, *Julius Robert*
Weinberg, *Steven*
Zworykin, *Vladimir Kosma*

9 letters:
Arrhenius, *Svante August*
Becquerel, *Antoine Henri*
Bernoulli, *Daniel*
Boltzmann, *Ludwig*
Cavendish, *Henry*
Cherenkov, *Pavel Alekseyevich*
Cockcroft, *John Douglas*
De Coulomb, *Charles Augustin*
Eddington, *Arthur Stanley*
Gay-Lussac, *Joseph Louis*
Heaviside, *Oliver*
Josephson, *Brian David*
Kirchhoff, *Gustav*
Lindemann, *Frederick*
Michelson, *Albert*
Von Békésy, *Georg*

Von Eötvös, *Roland*

10 letters:
Archimedes
Barkhausen, *Heinrich Georg*
Fahrenheit, *Gabriel Daniel*
Heisenburg, *Werner Karl*
Richardson, *Owen Willans*
Rutherford, *Ernest*
Torricelli, *Evangelista*
Watson-Watt, *Robert Alexander*

11 letters:
Chamberlain, *Owen*
Joliot-Curie, *Irène*
Oppenheimer, *J(ulius) Robert*
Schrödinger, *Erwin*
Van de Graaff, *R(obert) J(emison)*
Van der Waals, *Johannes Diderik*
Von Guericke, *Otto*

12 letters:
Von Helmholtz, *Hermann Ludwig Ferdinand*

13 letters:
Von Fraunhofer, *Joseph*

14 letters:
Le Rond Alembert, *Jean*

15 letters:
Kamerlingh-Onnes, *Heike*

See also:
➤ **Molecules** ➤ **Subatomic particles**

Pigments

3 letters:
Hem

4 letters:
Haem
Heme

5 letters:
Ochre
Opsin
Sepia
Smalt
Umber

6 letters:
Bister
Bistre
Chrome
Cobalt
Flavin
Lutein
Madder
Naevus
Pterin
Sienna

7 letters:
Argyria
Carmine
Carotin
Etiolin
Flavine
Gamboge
Melanin
Sinopia
Tapetum
Tempera

8 letters:
Carotene
Gossypol
Iodopsin
Luteolin
Orpiment
Retinene
Verditer
Viridian

9 letters:
Anthocyan
Bilirubin
Chromogen
Colcothar
Lamp-black
Lithopone
Liverspot
Nigrosine

Porphyrin
Quercetin
Rhodopsin
Urochrome

10 letters:
Anthoclore
Betacyanin
Biliverdin
Carotenoid
Carotinoid
Hemocyanin
Hemoglobin
Paris-green
Riboflavin
Terre-verte

11 letters:
Anthocyanin

Chlorophyll
Fucoxanthin
Haemocyanin
Haemoglobin
Phytochrome
Xanthophyll

12 letters:
Cappagh-brown
Phycoxanthin
Xanthopterin

13 letters:
Phycoerythrin
Xanthopterine

14 letters:
Phthalocyanine

Pigs

5 letters:
Duroc
Welsh

8 letters:
Cheshire
Landrace
Pietrain
Tamworth

9 letters:
Berkshire

Hampshire

10 letters:
Large Black
Large White
Saddleback
Small White

11 letters:
Middle White

12 letters:
Chester White

17 letters:
Gloucester Old Spot

20 letters:
Vietnamese
  pot-bellied

Pirates

4 letters:
Smee

7 letters:
Ben Gunn

8 letters:
Black Dog
Blind Pew
Mary Read
Redbeard

9 letters:
Anne Bonny
Thomas Tew

10 letters:
Barbarossa
Blackbeard
Calico Jack

11 letters:
Captain Hook
Edward Teach
Sir Henry Morgan
Jean Laffite
John Rackham

12 letters:
Sir Francis Drake

13 letters:
Basil Ringrose

14 letters:
Captain Pugwash
Long John Silver
William Dampier

18 letters:
Bartholomew
  Roberts
William (Captain)
  Kidd

Places and their nicknames

Places and their nicknames

Place	Nickname
Aberdeen	The Granite City
Adelaide	The City of Churches
Amsterdam	The Venice of the North
Birmingham	Brum *or* the Venice of the North
Boston	Bean Town
Bruges	The Venice of the North
California	The Golden State
Chicago	The Windy City
Dallas	The Big D
Detroit	The Motor City
Dresden	Florence on the Elbe
Dublin	The Fair City
Dumfries	Queen of the South
Edinburgh	Auld Reekie *or* the Athens of the North
Florida	The Sunshine State
Fraserburgh	The Broch
Fremantle	Freo
Glasgow	The Dear Green Place
Hamburg	The Venice of the North
Indiana	The Hoosier State
Iowa	The Hawkeye State
Ireland	The Emerald Isle
Jamaica	J.A. *or* the Yard
Jerusalem	The Holy City
Kentucky	The Bluegrass State
Kuala Lumpur	K.L.
London	The Big Smoke *or* the Great Wen
Los Angeles	L.A.
New Jersey	The Garden State
New Orleans	The Crescent City *or* the Big Easy
New South Wales	Ma State
New York (City)	The Big Apple
New York (State)	The Empire State
New Zealand	Pig Island
North Carolina	The Tarheel State
Nottingham	Queen of the Midlands
Oklahoma	The Sooner State
Pennsylvania	The Keystone State
Philadelphia	Philly
Portsmouth	Pompey
Prince Edward Island	Spud Island
Queensland	Bananaland *or* the Deep North (*both derogatory*)
Rome	The Eternal City
San Francisco	Frisco
Southeastern U.S.A.	Dixie, Dixieland, *or* the Deep South
Tasmania	Tassie *or* the Apple Isle

Place	Nickname
Texas	The Lone Star State
Utah	The Beehive State
Venice	La Serenissima

Planets

4 letters:
Mars

5 letters:
Earth
Pluto (dwarf
  planet)

6 letters:
Saturn
Uranus

7 letters:
Jupiter

Venus

Mercury
Neptune

Plants

VARIETIES OF PLANT

3 letters:
Dal
Kex
Meu
Pia
Rue
Set
Til
Udo
Urd
Yam

4 letters:
Alga
Aloe
Anil
Deme
Fern
Forb
Herb
Ixia
Kali
Loco
More
Nard
Ombu
Rhus
Sego
Sola
Sunn

Taro
Thea
Vine
Yarr

5 letters:
Ajwan
Anise
Aroid
Benni
Blite
Boree
Buchu
Bucku
Bugle
Calla
Canna
Clary
Clote
Cress
Fouat
Fouet
Gemma
Glaux
Gorse
Guaco
Hosta
Inula
Jalap
Kenaf

Kudzu
Lathe
Lotus
Lurgi
Medic
Morel
Murva
Musci
Orpin
Orris
Oshac
Panax
Sedge
Sedum
Spink
Tetra
Timbo
Urena

6 letters:
Acacia
Acorus
Ajowan
Alisma
Alpine
Arnica
Bablah
Betony
Burnet
Cactus

Plants

Cassia
Catnep
Cnicus
Cosmea
Cosmos
Croton
Datura
Derris
Dodder
Exogen
Gnetum
Hyssop
Iberis
Knawel
Madder
Mallow
Medick
Mimosa
Moorva
Nerium
Nettle
Nuphar
Orchis
Orpine
Pachak
Phloem
Protea
Rattle
Reseda
Retama
Rubber
Sesame
Silene
Smilax
Spider
Spurge
Spurry
Squill
Styrax
Teasel
Thrift
Tulipa
Tutsan
Yarrow

7 letters:
Alkanet
All-good
Allseed
Alyssum
Brinjal

Burdock
Caltrop
Cardoon
Carduus
Carline
Cat's ear
Chervil
Dasheen
Dioecia
Dittany
Ephedra
Filaree
Fly-trap
Freesia
Frogbit
Gentian
Gerbera
Haemony
Henbane
Ipomoea
Isoetes
Lantana
Lucerne
Lychnis
Mahonia
Melilot
Mercury
Mullein
Nemesia
Nigella
Nonsuch
Opuntia
Palmiet
Pareira
Petunia
Ragwort
Rhodora
Ruellia
Saffron
Salfern
Salsola
Sampire
Sanicle
Scandix
Setwall
Skirret
Spignel
Spiraea
Spurrey
Stapela
Syringa

Tagetes
Thallus
Triffid
Tritoma
Vanilla
Vervain
Zedoary

8 letters:
Acanthus
Agrimony
Angelica
Arenaria
Asphodel
Bindi-eye
Buckbean
Buplever
Camomile
Canaigre
Centaury
Costmary
Diandria
Dielytra
Dumbcane
Fluellin
Fumitory
Geophyte
Gesneria
Gnetales
Gromwell
Hag-taper
Henequen
Hepatica
Hibiscus
Larkspur
Lavender
Mandrake
Monstera
Oleander
Opopanax
Plumbago
Psilotum
Putchock
Ratsbane
Roly-poly
Samphire
Scammony
Self-heal
Silphium
Sparaxis
Spergula

Plants

Stapelia
Staragen
Starwort
Tamarisk
Tritonia
Tuberose
Tuckahoe
Wait-a-bit

9 letters:
Adderwort
Andromeda
Arrowroot
Artemisia
Aubrietia
Bald-money
Brooklime
Broom-rape
Butterbur
Colocasia
Coltsfoot
Cordaites
Coreopsis
Coriander
Dittander
Erythrina
Euphorbia
Eyebright
Fenugreek
Germander
Groundsel
Herb-paris
Horse-tail
Liver-wort
Lousewort
Mare's-tail
Moneywort

Moschatel
Patchouli
Pimpernel
Portulaca
Rocambole
Screwpine
Spearmint
Spearwort
Spikenard
Stone-crop
Sweet-gale
Tomatillo
Tormentil
Wake-robin
Wincopipe
Wolf's bane

10 letters:
Alexanders
Angiosperm
Aspidistra
Astralagus
Dyer's-broom
Earth-smoke
Five-finger
Fraxinella
Fritillary
Goat-sallow
Goats-thorn
Goat-willow
Goldilocks
Icosandria
Maidenhair
Mignonette
Parkleaves
Rest-harrow
Salicornia

Touch-me-not
Tropophyte
Yellowroot

11 letters:
Acidanthera
Bears-breech
Bristle-fern
Callitriche
Convolvulus
Dusty-miller
Hurtleberry
Loosestrife
Meadowsweet
Nancy-pretty
Schizophyte
Sempervivum
Thallophyte

12 letters:
Adam's flannel
Epacridaceae
Midsummermen
Morning glory
Parsley-piert
Pasqueflower
Phytobenthos
Southernwood
Water-soldier

13 letters:
Townhall clock

14 letters:
Chincherinchee
Lords and ladies
Shepherd's purse

PARTS OF PLANTS

3 letters:
Bud
Lip
Pod

4 letters:
Cyme
Head
Leaf
Root
Seed
Spur
Stem

5 letters:
Bract
Calyx
Costa
Fruit
Glume
Joint
Lemma
Ovary
Ovule
Palea
Petal

Sepal
Spike
Stoma
Style
Tepal
Torus
Umbel
Xylem

6 letters:
Anther
Bulbil
Carpel

Poetry

Catkin
Caulis
Corymb
Floret
Phloem
Pistil
Pollen
Raceme
Rachis
Sheath
Spadix
Spathe
Stamen
Stigma
Tassel

7 letters:
Blossom
Corolla
Foliage
Nectary
Panicle
Pedicel
Root cap

Seed pod
Taproot

8 letters:
Cyathium
Filament
Nucellus
Offshoot
Peduncle
Perianth
Placenta
Root hair
Spikelet
Thalamus

9 letters:
Capitulum
Dichasium
Epidermis
Guard cell
Gynoecium
Internode
Involucel
Involucre
Micropyle

Pollinium
Secundine

10 letters:
Androecium
Anthophore
Carpophore
Commissure
Hypanthium
Receptacle

11 letters:
Clinandrium
Gametophore
Monochasium
Pollen grain

12 letters:
Hibernaculum

13 letters:
Inflorescence

14 letters:
Floral envelope
Vascular bundle

See also:
➤ **Algae** ➤ **Botany** ➤ **Ferns** ➤ **Flowers** ➤ **Fungi**
➤ **Grasses** ➤ **Lilies** ➤ **Mosses** ➤ **Palms** ➤ **Seaweeds**
➤ **Shrubs** ➤ **Trees**

Poetry

POETRY AND PROSODY TERMS

3 letters:
Bob

4 letters:
Foot
Iamb

5 letters:
Arsis
Canto
Envoi
Envoy
Epode
Ictus
Ionic
Metre

Octet
Paeon
Rhyme
Wheel

6 letters:
Adonic
Alcaic
Cesura
Cretic
Dactyl
Dipody
Iambic
Iambus
Octave
Rhythm

Septet
Sestet
Stanza
Tercet

7 letters:
Anapest
Cadence
Cadency
Caesura
Couplet
Distich
Elision
Paeonic
Pyhrric
Quintet

Refrain
Sapphic
Sestina
Sextain
Spondee
Stichic
Strophe
Triplet
Trochee

8 letters:
Amoebean
Anapaest
Bacchius
Choriamb
Dactylic
Dieresis
Eye rhyme
Pindaric
Quatrain
Quintain
Scansion
Spondaic
Trochaic

9 letters:
Amoebaean
Anacrusis
Anapestic
Assonance
Diaeresis
Free verse
Full rhyme
Half-rhyme
Hemistich
Hexameter
Long metre

Macaronic
Octameter
Pararhyme
Rime riche
Terza rima
Tetrapody
Unstopped
Vers libre

10 letters:
Amphibrach
Amphimacer
Anapaestic
Blank verse
Catalectic
Choriambus
Consonance
Consonancy
End-stopped
Heptameter
Heptastich
Hypermeter
Ottava rima
Pentameter
Pentastich
Rhyme royal
Short metre
Tetrabrach
Tetrameter
Tetrastich

11 letters:
Alexandrine
Antistrophe
Common metre
Enjambement
Jabberwocky

Rhyme scheme

12 letters:
Alliteration
Ballad stanza
Leonine rhyme
Onomatopoeia
Perfect rhyme
Sprung rhythm

13 letters:
Closed couplet
Common measure
Feminine rhyme
Heroic couplet
Internal rhyme
Syllabic metre

14 letters:
Accentual metre
Feminine ending
Masculine rhyme
Verse paragraph

15 letters:
Masculine ending

16 letters:
Spenserian stanza

17 letters:
Quantitative metre

19 letters:
Stress-syllabic
metre

22 letters:
Accentual-syllabic
metre

POETRY MOVEMENTS AND GROUPINGS

8 letters:
Imagists

9 letters:
Decadents
Lake Poets
Romantics

10 letters:
Symbolists

11 letters:
Petrarchans
The Movement

12 letters:
Alexandrians

13 letters:
Georgian Poets

14 letters:
Liverpool Poets

17 letters:
Metaphysical Poets

19 letters:
Scottish
Chaucerians

Poetry

Brooks, *Gwendolyn*
Butler, *Samuel*
Carver, *Raymond*
Clough, *Arthur Hugh*
Cowper, *William*
Crabbe, *George*
Dowson, *Ernest Christopher*
Dryden, *John*
Dunbar, *William*
Dutton, *Geoffrey*
Elliot, *Ebenezer*
Éluard, *Paul*
Empson, *William*
Ennius, *Quintus*
George, *Stefan*
Glycon
Goethe, *Johann Wolfgang von*
Graves, *Robert (Ranke)*
Heaney, *Seamus*
Hesiod
Horace
Hughes, *Ted*
Jonson, *Ben(jamin)*
Landor, *Walter Savage*
Larkin, *Philip*
Lawman
Lowell, *Amy*
Lowell, *Robert*
Millay, *Edna St Vincent*
Milton, *John*
Morgan, *Edwin (George)*
Morris, *Sir Lewis*
Motion, *Andrew*
Neruda, *Pablo*
Ossian
Patten, *Brian*
Pindar
Porter, *Peter*
Racine, *Jean (Baptiste)*
Rhymer, *Corn Law*
Riding, *Laura*
Sappho
Seaman, *Sir Owen*
Shanks, *Edward*
Sidney, *Sir Philip*
Tagore, *Sir Rabindranath*
Thomas, *Dylan (Marlais)*
Thomas, *Edward*
Thomas, *R(onald) S(tuart)*
Trench, *Frederick Herbert*

Villon, *François*
Virgil
Waller, *Edmund*
Wright, *Judith*

7 letters:
Addison, *Joseph*
Alcaeus
Angelou, *Maya*
Aretino, *Pietro*
Ariosto, *Ludovico*
Beddoes, *Thomas*
Belleau, *Rémy*
Blunden, *Edmund*
Bridges, *Robert Seymour*
Brodsky, *Joseph*
Caedmon
Campion, *Thomas*
Causley, *Charles*
Chapman, *George*
Chaucer, *Geoffrey*
Collins, *Wilkie (William)*
Corinna
Cynwulf
De Vigny, *Alfred Victor*
Emerson, *Ralph Waldo*
Flaccus, *Horace (Quintus Horatius)*
Flecker, *James Elroy*
Herbert, *George*
Heredia, *José María*
Herrick, *Robert*
Hodgson, *Ralph*
Hopkins, *Gerard Manley*
Housman, *A(lfred) E(dward)*
Johnson, *Samuel*
Juvenal
Khayyam, *Omar*
Kipling, *(Joseph) Rudyard*
Layamon
Leonard, *Tom*
MacCaig, *Norman*
MacLean, *Sorley*
Martial
Marvell, *Andrew*
McGough, *Roger*
Mistral, *Frédéric*
Newbolt, *Sir Henry John*
Orpheus
Pushkin, *Aleksander Sergeyevich*
Rimbaud, *Arthur*

Poetry

Roethke, *Theodore Huebner*
Ronsard, *Pierre de*
Russell, *George William*
Sassoon, *Siegfried (Louvain)*
Schwarz, *Delmore*
Seifert, *Jaroslav*
Service, *Robert William*
Shelley, *Percy Bysshe*
Sitwell, *Edith*
Skelton, *John*
Southey, *Robert*
Spender, *Stephen*
Spenser, *Edmund*
Statius, *Publius Papinius*
Stevens, *Wallace*
Terence *(Publius Terentius Afer)*
Thomson, *James*
Vaughan, *Henry*
Vaughan, *William*
Walcott, *Derek*
Whitman, *Walt(er)*

8 letters:
Anacreon
Berryman, *John*
Betjeman, *John*
Browning, *Elizabeth Barrett*
Browning, *Robert*
Campbell, *Thomas*
Catullus, *Gaius Valerius*
Clampitt, *Amy*
Cummings, *E(dward) E(stlin)*
Cynewulf
Davenant, *Sir William*
de la Mare, *Walter (John)*
Ginsberg, *Allen*
Hamilton, *William*
Henryson, *Robert*
Jennings, *Elizabeth*
Kavanagh, *Patrick*
Kynewulf
Langland, *William*
Leopardi, *Giacomo*
Lovelace, *Richard*
Macauley, *Thomas*
MacNeice, *Louis*
Mallarmé, *Stéphane*
Menander
Petrarch
Rossetti, *Christina Georgina*
Rossetti, *Dante Gabriel*

Schiller, *(Johann Cristoph) Friedrich von*
Shadwell, *Thomas*
Stephens, *James*
Suckling, *John*
Taliesin
Tennyson, *Lord Alfred*
Thompson, *Francis*
Traherne, *Thomas*
Tyrtaeus
Verlaine, *Paul*
Whittier, *John Greenleaf*

9 letters:
Aeschylus
Akhmatova, *Anna*
Bunthorne, *Reginald*
Coleridge, *Samuel Taylor*
De Camoëns, *Luis Vaz*
Dickinson, *Emily*
Doolittle, *Hilda (H D)*
Euripides
Goldsmith, *Oliver*
Lamartine, *Alphone Marie Loius De*
Lucretius
Marinetti, *Emilio Filippo Tommaso*
Masefield, *John*
Quasimodo, *Salvatore*
Rochester, *(John Wilmot)*
Rosenberg, *Isaac*
Shenstone, *William*
Simonides *(of Ceos)*
Sophocles
Stevenson, *Robert Louis (Balfour)*
Swinburne, *Algernon Charles*

10 letters:
Baudelaire, *Charles Pierre*
Chatterton, *Thomas*
Cumberland, *Richard*
Drinkwater, *John*
Fitzgerald, *Edward*
Fitzgerald, *Robert*
Longfellow, *Henry Wadsworth*
MacDiarmid, *Hugh*
Propertius, *Sextus*
Szymborska, *Wislawa*
Tannhauser
Theocritus
Wordsworth, *William*

Apollinaire, *Guillaume*
Archilochus
Asclepiades
Callimachus
De Lamartine, *Alphonse Marie*
   Louis de Prat
Maeterlinck, *Count Maurice*

Shakespeare, *William*

12 letters:
Aristophanes
De La Fontaine, *Jean*

15 letters:
Ettrick Shepherd

Poisons

POISONOUS SUBSTANCES AND GASES

4 letters:
Bane
Lead
Tutu
Upas

5 letters:
Aspic
Conin
Ergot
Sarin
Sassy
Soman
Timbo
Urali

6 letters:
Aldrin
Antiar
Arsine
Cicuta
Conine
Curare
Curari
Datura
Dioxin
Emetin
Hebona
Ourali
Ourari
Phenol
Wabain

7 letters:
Aconite
Amanita
Aniline
Arsenic

Atropin
Benzene
Brucine
Cacodyl
Coniine
Cowbane
Cyanide
Emetine
Hebenon
Hemlock
Henbane
Lindane
Neurine
Ouabain
Phallin
Red lead
Safrole
Solpuga
Stibine
Stibium
Surinam
Tanghin
Tropine
Woorali
Woorara
Wourali

8 letters:
Acrolein
Adamsite
Apocynum
Atropine
Barbasco
Botulism
Cyanogen
Cyanuret
Daturine

Death cap
Dumbcane
Foxglove
Gossypol
Laburnum
Lewisite
Lobeline
Locoweed
Methanol
Mezereon
Nerve gas
Oleander
Paraquat
Phosgene
Pokeroot
Pokeweed
Ratsbane
Samnitis
Santonin
Sasswood
Solanine
Thallium
Thebaine
Urushiol
Veratrin
Warfarin

9 letters:
Aflatoxin
Afterdamp
Baneberry
Benzidine
Coyotillo
Digitalin
Echidnine
Fly agaric
Gelsemine

Poisons

Monkshood
Muscarine
Nux vomica
Poison gas
Poison ivy
Poison oak
Pokeberry
Sassy wood
Saxitoxin
Stonefish
Tanghinin
Toxaphene
Veratrine
Whitedamp
Wolf's-bane
Yohimbine

10 letters:
Aqua-tofana
Belladonna
Cadaverine
Colchicine
Cyanic acid
Death angel
Hydrastine
Liberty cap
Limberneck
Manchineel
Mandragora
Mustard gas
Oxalic acid
Paris green
Phalloidin
Picrotoxin
Stavesacre
Strychnine
Tetrotoxin

Thorn apple

11 letters:
Agent Orange
Black bryony
Calabar-bean
Death camass
Dog's mercury
Gelseminine
Hyoscyamine
Pilocarpine
Poison elder
Prussic acid
Staggerbush
Sugar of lead
Veratridine

12 letters:
Allyl alcohol
Formaldehyde
Lead monoxide
Noogoora burr
Poison sumach
Strophanthus
Tetrodotoxin
Water hemlock
Zinc chloride

13 letters:
Dieffenbachia
Mercuric oxide
Methyl bromide
Poison dogwood
Silver nitrate
Sodium cyanide

14 letters:
Carbon monoxide

Castor-oil plant
Hydrogen iodide
Mountain laurel

15 letters:
Arsenic trioxide
Barium hydroxide
Black nightshade
Destroying angel
Hydrogen cyanide
Indian liquorice
Nitrogen dioxide
Osmium tetroxide
Woody nightshade

16 letters:
Carbon disulphide
Deadly nightshade
Hydrogen fluoride
Hydrogen sulphide
Mercuric chloride
Potassium cyanide

19 letters:
Sodium
 fluoroacetate
Tetramethyldiarsine

21 letters:
Potassium
 permanganate

25 letters:
Antimony
potassium
 tartrate

TYPES OF POISONING

4 letters:
Lead

6 letters:
Iodism

7 letters:
Bromism

8 letters:
Botulism

Ergotism
Plumbism
Ptomaine

9 letters:
Fluorosis
Saturnism

10 letters:
Digitalism
Salmonella

11 letters:
Hydrargyria
Listeriosis
Phosphorism

12 letters:
Mercurialism
Strychninism

Political parties

AUSTRALIA

20 letters:
Australian Labor Party

23 letters:
Liberal Party of Australia

24 letters:
National Party of Australia

AUSTRIA

3 letters:
FPÖ
ÖVP
SPÖ

12 letters:
Freedom Party
People's Party

14 letters:
Socialist Party

BELGIUM

2 letters:
PS
SP
VB

3 letters:
CVP
PRL
PSC
PVV

5 letters:
Ecolo

6 letters:
Agalev

11 letters:
Flemish Bloc

16 letters:
French Green Party

17 letters:
Flemish Green Party

19 letters:
Flemish Liberal Party

20 letters:
French Socialist Party

21 letters:
Flemish Socialist Party

24 letters:
French Liberal Reform Party

26 letters:
French Social Christian Party

27 letters:
Flemish Social Christian Party

CANADA

11 letters:
Reform Party

12 letters:
Liberal Party

13 letters:
Bloc Quebecois

17 letters:
Social Credit Party

18 letters:
New Democratic Party

23 letters:
Progressive Conservative

Political parties

DENMARK

1 letter:
V

2 letters:
CD
FP
KF
RV
SD
SF

3 letters:
KrF

8 letters:
Liberals

FINLAND

2 letters:
KP
SD

3 letters:
KOK
SFP
SMP

4 letters:
SKDL

10 letters:
Green Party

11 letters:
Centre Party

FRANCE

2 letters:
PC
PR
PS

3 letters:
RDR
UDF

13 letters:
National Front

13 letters:
Progress Party

14 letters:
Left Socialists

15 letters:
Centre Democrats
Radical Liberals
Social Democrats

21 letters:
Christian People's Party
Socialist People's Party

24 letters:
Conservative People's Party

17 letters:
Finnish Rural Party

19 letters:
Swedish People's Party

21 letters:
Democratic Alternative
Social Democratic Party

22 letters:
National Coalition Party

30 letters:
Finnish People's Democratic League

14 letters:
Communist Party
Socialist Party

15 letters:
Republican Party

19 letters:
Rally for the Republic

23 letters:
Union for French Democracy

GERMANY

3 letters:
CDU
CSU
FDP
PDS
SPD

10 letters:
Green Party

19 letters:
Free Democratic Party

20 letters:
Christian-Social Union

21 letters:
Social Democratic Party

24 letters:
Christian-Democratic Union

26 letters:
Party of Democratic Socialism

GREECE

2 letters:
ND

5 letters:
PASOK

12 letters:
New Democracy

14 letters:
Politiki Aniksi

15 letters:
Political Spring

19 letters:
Greek Communist Party

28 letters:
Pan-Hellenic Socialist
  Movement

INDIA

1 letter:
I

3 letters:
BJP

8 letters:
Congress

9 letters:
Janata Dal

20 letters:
Bharitiya Janata Party

IRISH REPUBLIC

8 letters:
Fine Gael

10 letters:
Fianna Fáil

11 letters:
Labour Party

14 letters:
Democratic Left

20 letters:
Progressive Democrats

ISRAEL

5 letters:
Likud

11 letters:
Labour Party

Political parties

ITALY

3 letters:
PDS

11 letters:
Centre Union
Forza Italia

14 letters:
Northern League

JAPAN

7 letters:
Komeito

21 letters:
Social Democratic Party

LUXEMBOURG

2 letters:
PD

3 letters:
PCS

4 letters:
POSL

14 letters:
Communist Party

MALTA

16 letters:
Malta Labour Party
Nationalist Party

MEXICO

3 letters:
PAN
PRD
PRI

19 letters:
National Action Party

25 letters:
Revolutionary Workers' Party

16 letters:
National Alliance

22 letters:
Christian Democrat Party

24 letters:
Democratic Party of the Left

22 letters:
Liberal Democratic Party

24 letters:
Democratic Socialist Party

15 letters:
Democratic Party

20 letters:
Christian Social Party

31 letters:
Luxembourg Socialist Workers'
Party

30 letters:
Party of the Democratic
Revolution

31 letters:
Institutional Revolutionary Party

THE NETHERLANDS

3 letters:
CDA
VVD

4 letters:
PvdA

11 letters:
Labour Party

25 letters:
Christian Democratic Appeal

34 letters:
People's Party for Freedom and Democracy

NEW ZEALAND

11 letters:
Labour Party

13 letters:
National Party

NORTHERN IRELAND

4 letters:
SDLP

8 letters:
Sinn Féin

23 letters:
Democratic Unionist Party

27 letters:
Official Ulster Unionist Party

30 letters:
Social Democratic and Labour
  Party

PORTUGAL

2 letters:
PS

3 letters:
CDS
PRD
PSD

14 letters:
Socialist Party

21 letters:
Social Democratic Party

22 letters:
Democratic Renewal Party

27 letters:
Democratic Social Centre Party

SOUTH AFRICA

3 letters:
ANC
PAC

13 letters:
National Party

19 letters:
Inkatha Freedom Party

21 letters:
Pan-Africanist Congress

23 letters:
African National Congress

Political parties

SPAIN

2 letters:
HB
IU
PP

3 letters:
CiU
PNV

4 letters:
PSOE

10 letters:
United Left

12 letters:
People's Party

13 letters:
Herri Batasuna

16 letters:
Convergencia i Uni

21 letters:
Socialist Workers' Party

22 letters:
Basque Nationalist Party

SWEDEN

3 letters:
SAP

9 letters:
Left Party

10 letters:
Green Party

11 letters:
Centre Party

12 letters:
Liberal Party

13 letters:
Moderate Party

24 letters:
Christian Democratic Party

27 letters:
Social Democratic Labour Party

TURKEY

3 letters:
PKK

4 letters:
ANAP

13 letters:
True Path Party

15 letters:
Motherland Party

19 letters:
Kurdish Workers' Party

29 letters:
Social Democratic Populist Party

UNITED KINGDOM (MAINLAND)

10 letters:
Plaid Cymru

11 letters:
Labour Party

16 letters:
Liberal Democrats

21 letters:
Scottish National Party

28 letters:
Conservative and Unionist Party

UNITED STATES OF AMERICA

15 letters:
Democratic Party
Republican Party

Politicians

4 letters:
Eden, *Sir (Robert) Anthony*

5 letters:
Laski, *Harold Joseph*

6 letters:
Bright, *John*

7 letters:
Parnell, *Charles Stewart*

Trotsky, *Leon*

8 letters:
Disraeli, *Benjamin*

11 letters:
Wilberforce, *William*

12 letters:
Chesterfield, *Philip Dormer Stanhope*

See also:
➤ **Presidents of the U.S.** ➤ **Prime Ministers**

Popes

Pope	Pontificate	Pope	Pontificate
Peter	Until c.64	Dionysius	259–68
Linus	c.64–c.76	Felix I	269–74
Anacletus	c.76–c.90	Eutychianus	275–83
Clement I	c.90–c.99	Caius	283–96
Evaristus	c.99–c.105	Marcellinus	296–304
Alexander I	c.105–c.117	Marcellus I	308–09
Sixtus I	c.117–c.127	Eusebius	310
Telesphorus	c.127–c.137	Miltiades	311–14
Hyginus	c.137–c.140	Sylvester I	314–35
Pius I	c.140–c.154	Mark	336
Anicetus	c.154–c.166	Julius I	337–52
Soter	c.166–c.175	Liberius	352–66
Eleutherius	175–89	Damasus I	366–84
Victor I	189–98	Siricius	384–99
Zephyrinus	198–217	Anastasius I	399–401
Callistus I	217–22	Innocent I	402–17
Urban I	222–30	Zosimus	417–18
Pontian	230–35	Boniface I	418–22
Anterus	235–36	Celestine I	422–32
Fabian	236–50	Sixtus III	432–40
Cornelius	251–53	Leo I	440–61
Lucius I	253–54	Hilarus	461–68
Stephen I	254–57	Simplicius	468–83
Sixtus II	257–58	Felix III (II)	483–92

Popes

Pope	Pontificate	Pope	Pontificate
Gelasius I	492–96	Hadrian I	772–95
Anastasius II	496–98	Leo III	795–816
Symmachus	498–514	Stephen IV (V)	816–17
Hormisdas	514–23	Paschal I	817–24
John I	523–26	Eugenius II	824–27
Felix IV (III)	526–30	Valentine	827
Boniface II	530–32	Gregory IV	827–44
John II	533–35	Sergius II	844–47
Agapetus I	535–36	Leo IV	847–55
Silverius	536–37	Benedict III	855–58
Vigilius	537–55	Nicholas I	858–67
Pelagius I	556–61	Hadrian II	867–72
John III	561–74	John VIII	872–82
Benedict I	575–79	Marinus I	882–84
Pelagius II	579–90	Hadrian III	884–85
Gregory I	590–604	Stephen V (VI)	885–91
Sabinianus	604–06	Formosus	891–96
Boniface III	607	Boniface VI	896
Boniface IV	608–15	Stephen VI (VII)	896–97
Deusdedit *or* Adeodatus I	615–18	Romanus	897
		Theodore II	897
Boniface V	619–25	John IX	898–900
Honorious I	625–38	Benedict IV	900–03
Severinus	640	Leo V	903
John IV	640–42	Sergius III	904–11
Theodore I	642–49	Anastasius III	911–13
Martin I	649–54	Lando	913–14
Eugenius I	654–57	John X	914–28
Vitalian	657–72	Leo VI	928
Adeotatus II	672–6	Stephen VII (VIII)	928–31
Donus	676–78	John XI	931–35
Agatho	678–81	Leo VII	936–39
Leo II	682–83	Stephen IX	939–42
Benedict II	684–85	Marinus II	942–46
John V	685–86	Agapetus II	946–55
Cono	686–87	John XII	955–64
Sergius I	687–701	Leo VIII	963–65
John VI	701–05	Benedict V	964–66
John VII	705–07	John XIII	965–72
Sisinnius	708	Benedict VI	973–74
Constantine	708–15	Benedict VII	974–83
Gregory II	715–31	John XIV	983–84
Gregory III	731–41	John XV	985–96
Zacharias	741–52	Gregory V	996–99
Stephen II (not consecrated)	752	Sylvester II	999–1003
		John XVII	1003
Stephen II (III)	752–7	John XVIII	1004–09
Paul I	757–67	Sergius IV	1009–12
Stephen III (IV)	768–72	Benedict VIII	1012–24

Pope	Pontificate	Pope	Pontificate
John XIX	1024–32	Nicholas IV	1288–92
Benedict IX (first reign)	1032–44	Celestine V	1294
		Boniface VIII	1294–1303
Sylvester III	1045	Benedict XI	1303–04
Benedict IX (second reign)	1045	Clement V	1305–14
		John XXII	1316–34
Gregory VI	1045–46	Benedict XII	1334–42
Clement II	1046–47	Clement VI	1342–52
Benedict IX (third reign)	1047–48	Innocent VI	1352–62
		Urban V	1362–70
Damasus II	1048	Gregory XI	1370–78
Leo IX	1048–54	Urban VI	1378–89
Victor II	1055–57	Boniface IX	1389–1404
Stephen IX (X)	1057–58	Innocent VII	1404–06
Nicholas II	1059–61	Gregory XII	1406–15
Alexander II	1061–73	Martin V	1417–41
Gregory VII	1073–85	Eugenius IV	1431–47
Victor III	1086–87	Nicholas V	1447–55
Urban II	1088–99	Callistus III	1455–58
Paschal II	1099–1118	Pius II	1458–64
Gelasius II	1118–19	Paul II	1464–71
Callistus II	1119–24	Sixtus IV	1471–84
Honorious II	1124–30	Innocent VIII	1484–92
Innocent II	1130–43	Alexander VI	1492–1503
Celestine II	1143–44	Pius III	1503
Lucius II	1144–45	Julius II	1503–13
Eugenius III	1145–53	Leo X	1513–21
Anastasius IV	1153–54	Hadrian VI	1522–23
Hadrian IV	1154–59	Clement VII	1523–34
Alexander III	1159–81	Paul III	1534–49
Lucius III	1181–85	Julius III	1550–55
Urban III	1185–87	Marcellus II	1555
Gregory VIII	1187	Paul IV	1555–59
Clement III	1187–91	Pius IV	1559–65
Celestine III	1191–98	Pius V	1566–72
Innocent III	1198–1216	Gregory XIII	1572–85
Honorious III	1216–27	Sixtus V	1585–90
Gregory IX	1227–41	Urban VII	1590
Celestine IV	1241	Gregory XIV	1590–91
Innocent IV	1243–54	Innocent IX	1591
Alexander IV	1254–61	Clement VIII	1592–1605
Urban IV	1261–64	Leo XI	1605
Clement IV	1265–68	Paul V	1605–21
Gregory X	1271–76	Gregory XV	1621–23
Innocent V	1276	Urban VIII	1623–44
Hadrian V	1276	Innocent X	1644–55
John XXI	1276–77	Alexander VII	1655–67
Nicholas III	1277–80	Clement IX	1667–69
Martin IV	1281–85	Clement X	1670–76
Honorious IV	1285–87	Innocent XI	1676–89

Ports

Pope	Pontificate	Pope	Pontificate
Alexander VIII	1689–91	Gregory XVI	1831–46
Innocent XII	1691–1700	Pius IX	1846–78
Clement XI	1700–21	Leo XIII	1878–1903
Innocent XIII	1721–24	Pius X	1903–14
Benedict XIII	1724–30	Benedict XV	1914–22
Clement XII	1730–40	Pius XI	1922–39
Benedict XIV	1740–58	Pius XII	1939–58
Clement XIII	1758–69	John XXIII	1958–63
Clement XIV	1769–74	Paul VI	1963–78
Pius VI	1775–99	John Paul I	1978
Pius VII	1800–23	John Paul II	1978–2005
Leo XII	1823–29	Benedictus XVI	2005–
Pius VIII	1829–30		

Ports

3 letters:
Abo
Ayr
Gao
Hué
Rio
Rye

4 letters:
Acre
Aden
Akko
Amoy
Apia
Baku
Bari
Cebu
Cóbh
Cork
Deal
Dill
Elat
Hilo
Hull
Icel
Kiel
Kobe
Lima
Lomé
Oban
Omsk
Oran
Oslo
Perm
Pula
Puri
Riga
Said
Suez
Suva
Tyre
Vigo
Wick

5 letters:
Accra
Aqaba
Arhus
Arica
Aulis
Barry
Basra
Batum
Beira
Belem
Brest
Cádiz
Cairo
Colón
Dakar
Derry
Dilli
Dover
Dubai
Eilat
Emden
Galle
Genoa
Gijón
Haifa
Izmir
Jaffa
Jedda
Jidda
Kerch
Kochi
Lagos
Larne
Leith
Lulea
Macao
Malmo
Mocha
Newry
Osaka
Ostia
Poole
Pusan
Rabat
Salto
Sidon
Sligo
Split
Surat
Tampa
Tokyo
Tunis
Turku
Visby

Yalta

6 letters:
Aarhus
Abadan
Agadir
Albany
Ancona
Ashdod
Bastia
Batumi
Beirut
Belize
Bergen
Bilbao
Bissau
Bombay
Bootle
Boston
Bremen
Burgas
Calais
Callao
Cannes
Canton
Cochin
Danzig
Darwin
Dieppe
Duluth
Dundee
Durban
Elblag
Galata
Galway
Gdańsk
Gdynia
Harbin
Havana
Hobart
Iloilo
Inchon
Juneau
Kisumu
Kuwait
Lisbon
Lobito
London
Luanda
Lübeck
Madras

Malaga
Manama
Manaus
Manila
Maputo
Mobile
Muscat
Nantes
Naples
Narvik
Nassau
Nelson
Odense
Odessa
Oporto
Ostend
Padang
Quincy
Ragusa
Recife
Rimini
Rostov
Santos
Smyrna
St Malo
Sydney
Tacoma
Tallin
Venice
Whitby
Yangon

7 letters:
Abidjan
Ajaccio
Algiers
Antibes
Antwerp
Augusta
Bangkok
Belfast
Bristol
Buffalo
Cardiff
Catania
Chicago
Cologne
Colombo
Conakry
Corinth
Dunedin

Dunkirk
Ephesus
Esbjerg
Foochow
Funchal
Geelong
Glasgow
Grimsby
Halifax
Hamburg
Harwich
Incheon
Iquique
Iquitos
Karachi
Kinsale
Kowloon
Latakia
Legaspi
Le Havre
Lerwick
Livorno
Lorient
Marsala
Messina
Milazzo
Mombasa
Munster
Newport
New York
Oakland
Okayama
Palermo
Piraeus
Rangoon
Rapallo
Rosario
Rostock
Runcorn
Salerno
San Juan
Seattle
Seville
Stettin
Swansea
Tallinn
Tampico
Tangier
Taranto
Trieste
Tripoli

Ports

Ushuaia
Wexford
Wicklow

8 letters:
Aberdeen
Acapulco
Alicante
Arbroath
Auckland
Batangas
Bathurst
Benghazi
Bordeaux
Boulogne
Brindisi
Brisbane
Cagliari
Calcutta
Cape Town
Djibouti
Flushing
Freetown
Geropiga
Göteborg
Greenock
Hamilton
Harfleur
Helsinki
Holyhead
Honolulu
Istanbul
Kanazawa
Kawasaki
Keflavik
Kingston
La Coruña
La Guaira
Limassol
Limerick
Monrovia
Montreal
Murmansk
Nagasaki
Newhaven
Penzance
Pevensey
Plymouth
Portland
Port Said
Ramsgate

Rosslare
Salvador
San Diego
Sandwich
Savannah
Schiedam
Shanghai
Syracuse
Szczecin
Takoradi
Valencia
Veracruz
Weymouth
Yokohama

9 letters:
Amsterdam
Anchorage
Angostura
Annapolis
Archangel
Baltimore
Barcelona
Cartagena
Cherbourg
Dartmouth
Dubrovnik
Dunkerque
Ellesmere
Esperance
Europoort
Famagusta
Fishguard
Fleetwood
Fremantle
Gallipoli
Gateshead
Gravesend
Guayaquil
Immingham
Inhambane
Kao-hsiung
Kirkcaldy
Las Palmas
Liverpool
Lowestoft
Marseille
Melbourne
Mogadishu
Morecambe
Newcastle

Phnom Penh
Port Louis
Port Sudan
Reykjavik
Rotterdam
Santander
Schleswig
Sheerness
Singapore
Stavanger
Stockholm
Stornoway
Stranraer
Tarragona
Trondheim
Tynemouth
Vancouver
Volgograd
Walvis Bay
Waterford
Zeebrugge

10 letters:
Alexandria
Birkenhead
Bratislava
Bridgetown
Caernarfon
Cap-Haitien
Casablanca
Charleston
Chittagong
Copenhagen
East London
Folkestone
Fray Bentos
Georgetown
Gothenburg
Hammerfest
Launceston
Los Angeles
Mogadiscio
Montego Bay
Montevideo
New Orleans
Paramaribo
Portsmouth
Port Talbot
Queenstown
Sevastopol
Sunderland

Townsville
Valparaíso
Wellington

11 letters:
Buenos Aires
Dar es Salaam
Grangemouth
Londonderry
Mar del Plata
Port Moresby
Punta Arenas
Scarborough
Southampton
Trincomalee
Vladivostok

12 letters:
Barranquilla
Buenaventura
Dún Laoghaire
Jacksonville
Milford Haven
Port Adelaide
Port au Prince
Rio de Janeiro
San Francisco
San Sebastian
Santo Domingo
South Shields

13 letters:
Ellesmere Port

Great Yarmouth
Ho Chi Minh City
Hook of Holland
Port Elizabeth
Tandjungpriok

14 letters:
Vishakhapatnam

15 letters:
Saint Petersburg

17 letters:
Newcastle upon
 Tyne

Potatoes

4 letters:
Cara

5 letters:
Wilja

6 letters:
Estima
Romano

7 letters:
Desiree
Marfona
Roseval

8 letters:
Catriona

9 letters:
Charlotte
Kerr's Pink
Maris Bard

10 letters:
Arran Comet
Arran Pilot
King Edward
Maris Piper

11 letters:
Jersey Royal

12 letters:
Arran Victory

Golden Wonder
Pentland Dell
Pink Fir Apple

13 letters:
Pentland Crown
Ulster Sceptre

14 letters:
Pentland Squire
Sharpe's Express

15 letters:
Belle de Fontenay
Pentland Javelin

Pottery

4 letters:
Delf
Ming
Raku
Sung
Ware

5 letters:
China
Delft
Spode

6 letters:
Bisque
Wemyss

7 letters:
Celadon
Ceramic
Etruria
Faience
Satsuma

8 letters:
Flatback
Gombroon
Majolica
Slipware
Wedgwood®
Whieldon

9 letters:
Agatewear
Creamware

Presidents of the U.S.

Stoneware	Spongeware
10 letters:	**11 letters:**
Crouch-ware	Granitewear
Hollowware	

Presidents of the U.S.

President	Party	Term of office
1. George Washington	Federalist	1789–97
2. John Adams	Federalist	1797–1801
3. Thomas Jefferson	Democratic Republican	1801–1809
4. James Madison	Democratic Republican	1809–1817
5. James Monroe	Democratic Republican	1817–25
6. John Quincy Adams	Democratic Republican	1825–29
7. Andrew Jackson	Democrat	1829–37
8. Martin Van Buren	Democrat	1837–41
9. William Henry Harrison	Whig	1841
10. John Tyler	Whig	1841–45
11. James K. Polk	Democrat	1845–49
12. Zachary Taylor	Whig	1849–50
13. Millard Fillmore	Whig	1850–53
14. Franklin Pierce	Democrat	1853–57
15. James Buchanan	Democrat	1857–61
16. Abraham Lincoln	Republican	1861–65
17. Andrew Johnson	Republican	1865–69
18. Ulysses S. Grant	Republican	1869–77
19. Rutherford B. Hayes	Republican	1877–81
20. James A. Garfield	Republican	1881
21. Chester A. Arthur	Republican	1881–85
22. Grover Cleveland	Democrat	1885–89
23. Benjamin Harrison	Republican	1889–93
24. Grover Cleveland	Democrat	1893–97
25. William McKinley	Republican	1897–1901
26. Theodore Roosevelt	Republican	1901–1909
27. William Howard Taft	Republican	1909–13
28. Woodrow Wilson	Democrat	1913–21
29. Warren G. Harding	Republican	1921–23
30. Calvin Coolidge	Republican	1923–29
31. Herbert C. Hoover	Republican	1929–33
32. Franklin D. Roosevelt	Democrat	1933–45
33. Harry S. Truman	Democrat	1945–53
34. Dwight D. Eisenhower	Republican	1953–61
35. John F. Kennedy	Democrat	1961–63
36. Lyndon B. Johnson	Democrat	1963–69
37. Richard M. Nixon	Republican	1969–74
38. Gerald R. Ford	Republican	1974–77
39. James E. Carter, Jr	Democrat	1977–81
40. Ronald W. Reagan	Republican	1981–89
41. George H. W. Bush	Republican	1989–93

President	Party	Term of office
42. William J. Clinton	Democrat	1993–2001
43. George W. Bush	Republican	2001–

Prey, birds of

3 letters:
Ern
Owl

4 letters:
Erne
Gled
Hawk
Kite
Ruru

5 letters:
Eagle
Glede
Hobby
Saker

6 letters:
Condor
Falcon
Lanner
Merlin
Mopoke
Osprey

7 letters:
Barn owl
Boobook
Buzzard
Goshawk
Harrier
Hawk owl
Hoot owl
Kestrel

Red kite
Vulture

8 letters:
Brown owl
Bush-hawk
Caracara
Duck hawk
Falconet
Karearea
Sea eagle
Snowy owl
Tawny owl

9 letters:
Accipiter
Bald eagle
Eagle-hawk
Fish eagle
Gerfalcon
Gier-eagle
Gyrfalcon
Horned owl
Little owl
Ossifraga
Ossifrage
Wind-hover

10 letters:
Hen harrier
Screech owl

11 letters:
Chicken hawk

Cooper's hawk
Golden eagle
Lammergeier
Lammergeyer
Sparrowhawk

12 letters:
Honey buzzard
Long-eared owl
Marsh harrier

13 letters:
Bateleur eagle
Secretary bird
Turkey buzzard

14 letters:
Bearded vulture

15 letters:
Montagu's harrier
Peregrine falcon

16 letters:
Wedge-tailed eagle

17 letters:
Australian goshawk

18 letters:
Rough-legged
 buzzard

Prime Ministers

BRITISH PRIME MINISTERS

Prime Minister	Party	Term of office
Robert Walpole	Whig	1721–42
Earl of Wilmington	Whig	1742–43
Henry Pelham	Whig	1743–54
Duke of Newcastle	Whig	1754–56
Duke of Devonshire	Whig	1756–57

Prime Ministers

Prime Minister	Party	Term of office
Duke of Newcastle	Whig	1757–62
Earl of Bute	Tory	1762–63
George Grenville	Whig	1763–65
Marquess of Rockingham	Whig	1765–66
Duke of Grafton	Whig	1766–70
Lord North	Tory	1770–82
Marquess of Rockingham	Whig	1782
Earl of Shelburne	Whig	1782–83
Duke of Portland	Coalition	1783
William Pitt	Tory	1783–1801
Henry Addington	Tory	1801–04
William Pitt	Tory	1804–06
Lord Grenville	Whig	1806–7
Duke of Portland	Tory	1807–09
Spencer Perceval	Tory	1809–12
Earl of Liverpool	Tory	1812–27
George Canning	Tory	1827
Viscount Goderich	Tory	1827–28
Duke of Wellington	Tory	1828–30
Earl Grey	Whig	1830–34
Viscount Melbourne	Whig	1834
Robert Peel	Conservative	1834–35
Viscount Melbourne	Whig	1835–41
Robert Peel	Conservative	1841–46
Lord John Russell	Liberal	1846–52
Earl of Derby	Conservative	1852
Lord Aberdeen	Peelite	1852–55
Viscount Palmerston	Liberal	1855–58
Earl of Derby	Conservative	1858–59
Viscount Palmerston	Liberal	1859–65
Lord John Russell	Liberal	1865–66
Earl of Derby	Conservative	1866–68
Benjamin Disraeli	Conservative	1868
William Gladstone	Liberal	1868–74
Benjamin Disraeli	Conservative	1874–80
William Gladstone	Liberal	1880–85
Marquess of Salisbury	Conservative	1885–86
William Gladstone	Liberal	1886
Marquess of Salisbury	Conservative	1886–92
William Gladstone	Liberal	1892–94
Earl of Rosebery	Liberal	1894–95
Marquess of Salisbury	Conservative	1895–1902
Arthur James Balfour	Conservative	1902–05
Henry Campbell–Bannerman	Liberal	1905–08
Herbert Henry Asquith	Liberal	1908–15
Herbert Henry Asquith	Coalition	1915–16
David Lloyd George	Coalition	1916–22
Andrew Bonar Law	Conservative	1922–23
Stanley Baldwin	Conservative	1923–24
James Ramsay MacDonald	Labour	1924

Prime Minister	Party	Term of office
Stanley Baldwin	Conservative	1924–29
James Ramsay MacDonald	Labour	1929–31
James Ramsay MacDonald	Nationalist	1931–35
Stanley Baldwin	Nationalist	1935–37
Arthur Neville Chamberlain	Nationalist	1937–40
Winston Churchill	Coalition	1940–45
Clement Attlee	Labour	1945–51
Winston Churchill	Conservative	1951–55
Anthony Eden	Conservative	1955–57
Harold Macmillan	Conservative	1957–63
Alec Douglas–Home	Conservative	1963–64
Harold Wilson	Labour	1964–70
Edward Heath	Conservative	1970–74
Harold Wilson	Labour	1974–76
James Callaghan	Labour	1976–79
Margaret Thatcher	Conservative	1979–90
John Major	Conservative	1990–97
Tony Blair	Labour	1997–2007
Gordon Brown	Labour	2007–

AUSTRALIAN PRIME MINISTERS

Prime Minister	Party	Term of office
Edmund Barton	Protectionist	1901–03
Alfred Deakin	Protectionist	1903–04
John Christian Watson	Labor	1904
George Houston Reid	Free Trade	1904–05
Alfred Deakin	Protectionist	1905–08
Andrew Fisher	Labor	1908–09
Alfred Deakin	Fusion	1909–10
Andrew Fisher	Labor	1910–13
Joseph Cook	Liberal	1913–14
Andrew Fisher	Labor	1914–15
William Morris Hughes	National Labor	1915–17
William Morris Hughes	Nationalist	1917–23
Stanley Melbourne Bruce	Nationalist	1923–29
James Henry Scullin	Labor	1929–31
Joseph Aloysius Lyons	United	1931–39
Earle Christmas Page	Country	1939
Robert Gordon Menzies	United	1939–41
Arthur William Fadden	Country	1941
John Joseph Curtin	Labor	1941–45
Joseph Benedict Chifley	Labor	1945–49
Robert Gordon Menzies	Liberal	1949–66
Harold Edward Holt	Liberal	1966–67
John McEwen	Country	1967–68
John Grey Gorton	Liberal	1968–71
William McMahon	Liberal	1971–72
Edward Gough Whitlam	Labor	1972–75
John Malcolm Fraser	Liberal	1975–83

Prime Ministers

Prime Minister	Party	Term of office
Robert James Lee Hawke	Labor	1983–91
Paul Keating	Labor	1991–96
John Howard	Liberal	1996–2007
Kevin Rudd	Labor	2007–

CANADIAN PRIME MINISTERS

Prime Minister	Party	Term of office
John A. MacDonald	Conservative	1867–73
Alexander Mackenzie	Liberal	1873–78
John A. MacDonald	Conservative	1878–91
John J.C. Abbot	Conservative	1891–92
John S.D. Thompson	Conservative	1892–94
Mackenzie Bowell	Conservative	1894–96
Charles Tupper	Conservative	1896
Wilfrid Laurier	Liberal	1896–1911
Robert Borden	Conservative	1911–20
Arthur Meighen	Conservative	1920–21
William Lyon Mackenzie King	Liberal	1921–26
Arthur Meighen	Conservative	1926
William Lyon Mackenzie King	Liberal	1926–30
Richard Bedford Bennet	Conservative	1930–35
William Lyon Mackenzie King	Liberal	1935–48
Louis St. Laurent	Liberal	1948–57
John George Diefenbaker	Conservative	1957–63
Lester Bowles Pearson	Liberal	1963–68
Pierre Elliott Trudeau	Liberal	1968–79
Joseph Clark	Conservative	1979–80
Pierre Elliott Trudeau	Liberal	1980–84
John Turner	Liberal	1984
Brian Mulroney	Conservative	1984–93
Kim Campbell	Conservative	1993
Joseph Jacques Jean Chrétien	Liberal	1993–2003
Paul Martin	Liberal	2003–6
Stephen Joseph Harper	Conservative	2006–

NEW ZEALAND PRIME MINISTERS

Prime Minister	Party	Term of office
Henry Sewell	—	1856
William Fox	—	1856
Edward William Stafford	—	1856–61
William Fox	—	1861–62
Alfred Domett	—	1862–63
Frederick Whitaker	—	1863–64
Frederick Aloysius Weld	—	1864–65
Edward William Stafford	—	1865–69
William Fox	—	1869–72
Edward William Stafford	—	1872
William Fox	—	1873
Julius Vogel	—	1873–75

Prime Minister	Party	Term of office
Daniel Pollen	—	1875–76
Julius Vogel	—	1876
Harry Albert Atkinson	—	1876–77
George Grey	—	1877–79
John Hall	—	1879–82
Frederick Whitaker	—	1882–83
Harry Albert Atkinson	—	1883–84
Robert Stout	—	1884
Harry Albert Atkinson	—	1884
Robert Stout	—	1884–87
Harry Albert Atkinson	—	1887–91
John Ballance	—	1891–93
Richard John Seddon	Liberal	1893–1906
William Hall-Jones	Liberal	1906
Joseph George Ward	Liberal/National	1906–12
Thomas Mackenzie	National	1912
William Ferguson Massey	Reform	1912–25
Francis Henry Dillon Bell	Reform	1925
Joseph Gordon Coates	Reform	1925–28
Joseph George Ward	Liberal/National	1928–30
George William Forbes	United	1930–35
Michael Joseph Savage	Labour	1935–40
Peter Fraser	Labour	1940–49
Sidney George Holland	National	1949–57
Keith Jacka Holyoake	National	1957
Walter Nash	Labour	1957–60
Keith Jacka Holyoake	National	1960–72
John Ross Marshall	National	1972
Norman Eric Kirk	Labour	1972–74
Wallace Edward Rowling	Labour	1974–75
Robert David Muldoon	National	1975–84
David Russell Lange	Labour	1984–89
Geoffrey Palmer	Labour	1989–90
Mike Moore	Labour	1990
Jim Bolger	National	1990–97
Jenny Shipley	National	1997–99
Helen Clark	Labour	1999–

Programming languages

1 letter:
C

3 letters:
Ada
RPG
SQL

4 letters:
Java

LISP
LOGO
Perl

5 letters:
Algol
BASIC
Basic
COBOL

CORAL
FORTH
OCCAM

6 letters:
Pascal
PROLOG
Simula
SNOBOL

7 letters:	9 letters:	10 letters:
FORTRAN	Smalltalk	Postscript
Haskell		

Proteins

4 letters:
Zein

5 letters:
Abrin
Actin
Opsin
Prion
Renin
Ricin

6 letters:
Avidin
Capsid
Enzyme
Fibrin
Globin
Gluten
Lectin
Leptin
Myosin
Ossein

7 letters:
Adipsin
Albumen
Albumin
Aleuron
Amyloid
Elastin
Fibroin
Gliadin
Hordein
Keratin

Legumin
Opsonin
Sericin
Spongin
Tubulin

8 letters:
Aleurone
Amandine
Collagen
Cytokine
Ferritin
Gliadine
Globulin
Prolamin
Spectrin
Troponin
Vitellin

9 letters:
Capsomere
Flagellin
Myoglobin
Ovalbumin
Phaseolin
Prolamine
Properdin
Protamine
Repressor
Sclerotin

10 letters:
Actomyosin
Apoprotein

Bradykinin
Calmodulin
Caseinogen
Conchiolin
Dystrophin
Factor VIII
Fibrinogen
Interferon
Lymphokine
Thrombogen
Toxalbumin

11 letters:
Angiotensin
Haploglobin
Interleukin
Lactalbumin
Transferrin
Tropomyosin

12 letters:
Lactoprotein
Serum albumin

13 letters:
Ceruloplasmin
Serum globulin

14 letters:
Immunoglobulin

16 letters:
Alpha-fetoprotein

Provinces of Canada

Province	Abbreviation
Alberta	AB
British Columbia	BC
Manitoba	MB
New Brunswick	NB
Newfoundland	NF
Northwest Territories	NWT
Nova Scotia	NS

Province	Abbreviation
Nunavut	NU
Ontario	ON
Prince Edward Island	PE
Quebec	PQ
Saskatchewan	SK
Yukon Territory	YT

Provinces of South Africa

Province	Capital
Eastern Cape	Bisho
Free State	Bloemfontein
Gauteng	Johannesburg
KwaZulu-Natal	Pietermaritzburg
Limpopo	Pietersburg
Mpumalanga	Nelspruit
North-West	Mafikeng
Northern Cape	Kimberley
Western Cape	Cape Town

Psychology

BRANCHES OF PSYCHOLOGY

5 letters:
Child

6 letters:
Social

8 letters:
Analytic
Clinical
Hedonics

10 letters:
Industrial

Psychiatry

11 letters:
Comparative
Educational

12 letters:
Experimental

13 letters:
Developmental
Psychometrics
Psychophysics

14 letters:
Organizational
Parapsychology

15 letters:
Neuropsychology

16 letters:
Psychophysiology

17 letters:
Psycholinguistics

PSYCHOLOGY TERMS

2 letters:
Id

3 letters:
Ego

4 letters:
Anal
Mind
Self

5 letters:
Angst
Mania

6 letters:
Phobia
Psyche
Stress
Trauma

7 letters:
Anxiety
Complex
Persona

8 letters:
Alter ego
Analysis
Delusion

Purple, shades of

Dementia
Fixation
Hypnosis
Hysteria
Neurosis
Paranoia
Superego
Syndrome

9 letters:
Death wish
Extrovert
Introvert
Obsession
Psychosis

10 letters:
Compulsion
Depression

Regression
Repression

11 letters:
Inkblot test
Personality
Sublimation
Unconscious

12 letters:
Conditioning
Freudian slip
Group therapy
Hypochondria
Subconscious

13 letters:
Consciousness
Primal therapy
Psychosomatic

Rorschach test
Schizophrenia

14 letters:
Electra complex
Gestalt therapy
Oedipus complex
Psychoanalysis

18 letters:
Inferiority complex
Persecution
  complex

19 letters:
Personality
  disorder
Primal scream
  therapy

PSYCHOLOGISTS

4 letters:
Coué, *Émile*
Jung, *Carl Gustav*

5 letters:
Adler, *Alfred*
Freud, *Sigmund*
Fromm, *Erich*
James, *William*
Janet, *Pierre Marie Félix*
Luria, *Alexander Romanovich*
Reich, *Wilhelm*
Wundt, *Wilhelm Max*

6 letters:
Hering, *Ewald*
Horney, *Karen*
Köhler, *Wolfgang*

Müller, *Johannes Peter*
Pavlov, *Ivan Petrovich*
Piaget, *Jean*
Watson, *John*

7 letters:
Eysenck, *Hans Jürgen*
Fechner, *Gustav Theodor*
Skinner, *B(urrhus) F(rederic)*

9 letters:
Thorndike, *Edward Lee*

10 letters:
Ebbinghaus, *Hermann*

11 letters:
Münsterberg, *Hugo*

Purple, shades of

4 letters:
Plum
Puce
Wine

5 letters:
Lilac
Mauve
Pansy

Royal

6 letters:
Claret
Indigo
Tyrian
Violet

7 letters:
Carmine

Gentian
Heather
Magenta

8 letters:
Amethyst
Burgundy
Dubonnet
Lavender

Purple, shades of

Mulberry

Peach-blow

Periwinkle

9 letters:
Aubergine

10 letters:
Heliotrope

11 letters:
Gentian blue

Q

Queens

3 letters:
Mab
May

4 letters:
Anna
Anne
Bess
Dido
Juno
Leda
Mary

5 letters:
Helen
Maeve
Sheba

6 letters:
Atossa
Balkis
Esther
Hecuba

Isabel
Ishtar
Isolde

7 letters:
Camilla
Candace
Eleanor
Jocasta
Matilda
Omphale
Titania

8 letters:
Adelaide
Alcestis
Boadicea
Boudicca
Brunhild
Caroline
Eleanora
Gertrude
Hermione

Penelope
Phaedram
Victoria

9 letters:
Alexandra
Artemesia
Brunhilde
Cleopatra
Elizabeth
Guinevere
Hippolyta
Nefertiti
Semiramis

10 letters:
Hatshepset
Hatshepsut
Persephone
Proserpina

15 letters:
Marie Antoinette

R

Rabbits and hares

4 letters:
Cony
Hare
Pika

5 letters:
Coney

6 letters:
Rabbit

10 letters:
Arctic hare
Cottontail
Jack rabbit

11 letters:
Belgian hare

12 letters:
Angora rabbit

Snowshoe hare

14 letters:
Snowshoe rabbit

Races

2 letters:
TT

4 letters:
Boat
Milk
Oaks

5 letters:
Derby
Palio

6 letters:
Le Mans

7 letters:
St Leger

8 letters:
Olympics
RAC Rally

10 letters:
Epsom Derby
Royal Ascot

11 letters:
Admiral's Cup
America's Cup

12 letters:
Melbourne Cup
National Hunt
Tour de France

13 letters:
Dubai World Cup
Grand National
Kentucky Derby
Manx Grand Prix

15 letters:
Monte Carlo Rally

17 letters:
Cheltenham Gold
 Cup

Red, shades of

3 letters:
Bay

4 letters:
Foxy
Pink
Plum
Puce

Rose
Rosy
Ruby
Rust
Wine

5 letters:
Coral

Flame
Flesh
Gules
Henna
Liver
Peach
Poppy

Regimental nicknames

Sandy

6 letters:
Auburn
Cerise
Cherry
Claret
Copper
Damask
Ginger
Maroon
Russet
Titian
Turkey

7 letters:
Carmine
Carroty
Coppery

Crimson
Fuchsia
Magenta
Old rose
Oxblood
Roseate
Scarlet
Tea rose
Vermeil

8 letters:
Baby pink
Burgundy
Cardinal
Chestnut
Cinnabar
Cyclamen
Dubonnet

Mulberry

9 letters:
Carnation
Grenadine
Peach-blow
Raspberry
Shell pink
Vermilion

10 letters:
Oyster pink
Salmon pink
Strawberry
Terracotta

11 letters:
Burnt sienna

Regimental nicknames

Regiment	Nickname
Army Service Corps	Ally Sloper's Cavalry
21st SAS	Artist's Rifles
13th Hussars	Baker's Dozen
2nd Dragoon Guards	The Bays
Royal Leicestershire Regiment	Bengal Tigers
17th Lancers	Bingham's Dandies
Royal Dragoons	Birdcatchers
7th Dragoon Guards	Black Horse
North Staffordshire Regiment	Black Knots
50th Foot Regiment	Blind *or* Dirty Half Hundred
Manchester Regiment	Bloodsuckers
11th Foot	Bloody Eleventh
4th/7th Royal Dragoon Guards	Blue Horse
Royal Horse Guards	Blues
Royal Scots Greys	Bubbly Jocks
3rd Foot	Buffs, Nutcrackers *or* Resurrectionists
4th (Royal Irish) Dragoon Guards	Buttermilks
26th & 90th Foot	Cameronians *or* Scottish Rifles
3rd Prince of Wales Dragoon Guards	Carabineers, Carbs *or* Tichborne's Own
55th Foot	Castle Reeves
Royal Army Medical Corps	Castor Oil Dragoons
11th Hussars (Prince Albert's Own)	Cherry Pickers *or* Cherubims
Coldstream Guards	Coldies
8th (King's Royal Irish) Hussars	Cross Belts
17th/21st Lancers	Death *or* Glory Boys

Regiment	Nickname
9th (Queen's Royal) Lancers	Delhi Spearmen
7th Armoured Division	Desert Rats
Inns of Court Regiment	Devil's Own
46th Foot (Duke of Cornwall's Light Infantry)	Docs *or* Red Feathers
18th (Queen Mary's Own) Hussars	Drogheda Light Horse
33rd Foot (Duke of Wellington's)	Duke's
Royal Scots Fusiliers	Earl of Mar's Grey Breeks
15th (The King's) Hussars	Eliott's Tailors
Territorial Army Emergency Reserve	Ever Readies
40th (XL) Foot	Excellers
68th Foot (Durham Light Infantry)	Faithful Durhams
Royal Berkshire Regiment	Farmers' Boys
87th Foot (Royal Irish Fusiliers)	Faugh-a-ballagh Boys *or* Old Fogs
15th (King's) Hussars	Fighting Fifteenth
5th Foot (Royal Northumberland Fusiliers)	Fighting Fifth
9th Foot (Royal Norfolk Regiment)	Fighting Ninth, Holy Boys *or* Norfolk Howards
Worcestershire Regiment	Firms
Welsh Regiment	First Invalids
Queen's Royal Regiment (West Surrey)	First Tangerines
Royal Ulster Rifles	Fitch and Grenadiers
54th Foot (Dorset Regiment)	Flamers
Gloucestershire Regiment	Fore and Aft
42nd Foot (Black Watch)	Forty-Twas
Royal Scots (1st Foot)	First and Wurst
Royal Highland Fusiliers	Fusil Jocks
Royal Horse Artillery	Galloping Gunners
3rd (King's Own) Hussars	Galloping Third
Gordon Highlanders	Gay Gordons
70th Foot (East Surrey)	Glasgow Greys
Highland Light Infantry	Glesca Keelies
5th (Princess Charlotte of Wales) Dragoon Guards	Green Horse
Alexandra Princess of Wales Own Yorkshire Regiment	Green Howards
King's Royal Rifle Corps	Green Jackets
21st (Empress of Indian's) Lancers	Grey Lancers
Royal Scots Greys	Greys
Royal Hampshire Regiment	Hampshire Tigers
33rd Foot (Duke of Wellington's Regiment)	Havercake Lads
Royal Army Veterinary Corps	Horse Doctors
17th (Duke of Cambridge's Own) Lancers	Horse Marines
South Wales Borderers	Howard's Greens
Royal Army Pay Corps	Ink Slingers
King's Royal Rifle Corps	Jaegers

Regimental nicknames

Regiment	Nickname
Royal Marines	Jollies
Scots Guards	Kiddies
King's Own Scottish Borderers	Kokky-Olly Birds *or* Kosbies
King's Own Yorkshire Light Infantry	Kolis *or* Koylies
32nd Foot (Duke of Cornwall's Light Infantry)	Lacedaemonians
47th Foot	Lancashire Lads *or* The Loyal Regiment
8th Foot (King's Regiment)	Leather Hats
Oxfordshire & Buckinghamshire Light Infantry	Light Bobs
13th Hussars	Lily Whites
Irish Guards	Micks
Lancashire Fusiliers	Minden Boys
Royal Army Service Corps	Moke Train
Wiltshire Regiment	Moonrakers
4th (Royal Irish) Dragoon Guards	Mounted Micks
Royal Engineers	Mudlarks
Royal Marines	Neptune's Bodyguard
Welsh Regiment	Old Agamemnons
Gloucestershire Regiment	Old Braggs
53rd Foot (King's Shropshire Light Infantry)	Old Brickdusts *or* Old Five and Threepennies
3rd (Prince of Wales's) Dragoon Guards	Old Canaries
12th Foot (Suffolk Regiment)	Old Dozen
Grenadier Guards	Old Eyes
87th Foot (Royal Irish Fusiliers)	Old Fogs
7th (Queen's Own) Hussars	Old Saucy Seventh
Sherwood Foresters	Old Stubborns
35th Foot	Orange Lilies
4th (Queen's Own) Hussars	Paget's Irregular Horse
Bedfordshire & Hertfordshire Regiment	Peacemakers
90th Foot (Cameronians)	Perthshire Grey Breeks
Royal Lincolnshire Regiment	Poachers
56th Foot	Pompadours
77th Foot	Pot-Hooks
South Staffordshire Regiment	Pump and Tortoise
Royal Army Pay Corps	Quill Drivers
5th (Royal Irish) Lancers	Red Breasts
Royal Horse Artillery	Right of the Line
91st Foot (Argyll & Sutherland Highlanders)	Rorys
(1st) The Royal Dragoons	Royals
65th Foot (York & Lancaster Regiment)	Royal Tigers
2nd Dragoon Guards (Queen's Bays)	Rusty Buckles
Grenadier Guards	Sand Bags
39th Foot (Dorsetshire Regiment)	Sankey's Horse
Royal Engineers	Sappers

Regiment	Nickname
6th Foot (Royal Warwickshire Fusiliers)	Saucy Sixth
16th (Queen's Royal) Lancers	Scarlet Lancers
6th (Inniskilling) Dragoons	Skiffingers
5th Royal Inniskilling Dragoon Guards	Skins
17th (Duke of Cambridge's Own) Lancers	Skull and Crossbones
Gloucestershire Regiment	Slashers
15th Foot (East Yorkshire Regiment)	Snappers
Wiltshire Regiment	Springers
1st Northamptonshire Regiment	Steel Backs
7th (Princess of Wales's Royal) Lancers	Strawboots
12th (Prince of Wales's Royal) Lancers	Supple Twelfth
Rifle Brigade	Sweeps
Welsh Guards	Taffys
93rd Foot (2nd Battalion Argyll & Sutherland Highlanders)	Thin Red Line
30th Foot (East Lancashire Regiment)	Three Tens
Life Guards	Tin Bellies or The Tins
Yorkshire & Lancashire Regiment	Twin Roses
55th Foot (Border Regiment)	Two Fives
44th Foot (Essex Regiment)	Two Fours
20th Foot (Lancashire Fusiliers)	Two Tens
69th Foot	Ups and Downs
Royal Warwickshire Fusiliers	Warwickshire Lads
20th Hussars	The X's
31st Foot (East Surrey Regiment)	Young Buffs
7th (Queen's Own) Hussars	Young Eyes

Regions, administrative

FRENCH REGIONS

6 letters:
Alsace
Centre

7 letters:
Corsica

8 letters:
Auvergne
Brittany
Burgundy
Limousin
Lorraine
Picardie

9 letters:
Aquitaine

10 letters:
Rhône-Alpes

11 letters:
Île-de-France
Pays de Loire

12 letters:
Franche-Comté
Midi-Pyrénées

14 letters:
Basse-Normandie
Haute-Normandie

15 letters:
Nord-Pas-de-Calais

Poitou-Charentes

16 letters:
Champagne-
  Ardenne

19 letters:
Languedoc-
  Roussillon

22 letters:
Provence-Alpes-
  Côte d'Azur

Regions, administrative

FRENCH DÉPARTEMENTS

3 letters:
Ain
Lot
Var

4 letters:
Aube
Aude
Cher
Eure
Gard
Gers
Jura
Nord
Oise
Orne
Tarn

5 letters:
Aisne
Corse
Doubs
Drôme
Indre
Isère
Loire
Marne
Meuse
Paris
Rhône
Saône
Somme
Yonne

6 letters:
Allier
Ariège
Cantal
Creuse
Essone
Gayane
Landes
Loiret
Lozère
Manche

Sarthe
Savoie
Vendée
Vienne
Vosges

7 letters:
Ardèche
Aveyron
Bas Rhin
Corrèze
Cote d'Or
Gironde
Hérault
Mayenne
Moselle
Niveres
Réunion

8 letters:
Ardennes
Calvados
Charente
Dordogne
Haut Rhin
Morbihan
Val d'Oise
Vaucluse
Yvelines

9 letters:
Finistère
Puy de Dôme

10 letters:
Deux Sèvres
Eure et Loir
Guadeloupe
Haute Loire
Haute Marne
Loir et Cher
Martinique
Val de Marne

11 letters:
Côtes du Nord

Hautes Alpes
Haute Savoie
Haute Vienne
Pas de Calais

12 letters:
Haute Garonne
Hauts de Seine
Indre et Loire
Lot et Garonne
Maine et Loire
Saône et Loire
Seine et Marne

13 letters:
Ille et Vilaine
Seine Maritime
Tarn et Garonne

14 letters:
Alpes Maritimes
Bouches du Rhône
Hautes Pyrénées

15 letters:
Loire Atlantique
Seine Saint Denis

16 letters:
Charente Maritime
Meurthe et Moselle

18 letters:
Pyrénées Orientales

19 letters:
Pyrénées
  Atlantiques
Territoire de
  Belfort

20 letters:
Alpes de Haute
  Provence

GERMAN STATES

6 letters:
Berlin
Bremen
Hessen
Saxony

7 letters:
Bavaria
Hamburg

8 letters:
Saarland

9 letters:
Thuringia

11 letters:
Brandenburg

Lower Saxony

12 letters:
Saxony-Anhalt

16 letters:
Baden-Württemberg

17 letters:
Schleswig-Holstein

19 letters:
Rhineland-Palatinate

20 letters:
North Rhine-Westphalia

24 letters:
Mecklenburg-West Pomerania

ITALIAN REGIONS

5 letters:
Lazio

6 letters:
Marche
Molise
Puglia
Sicily
Umbria
Veneto

7 letters:
Abruzzo
Liguria

Tuscany

8 letters:
Calabria
Campania
Lombardy
Piedmont
Sardinia

10 letters:
Basilicata

11 letters:
Valle d'Aosta

13 letters:
Emilia-Romagna

17 letters:
Trentino-Alto
  Adige

19 letters:
Friuli-Venezia
  Giulia

ITALIAN PROVINCES

4 letters:
Asti
Bari
Como
Enna
Lodi
Pisa
Roma

5 letters:
Aosta
Cuneo
Forlì
Lecce
Lecco

Lucca
Nuoro
Parma
Pavia
Prato
Rieti
Siena
Terni
Udine

6 letters:
Ancona
Arezzo
Chieti
Foggia

Genova
Latina
Matera
Milano
Modena
Napoli
Novara
Padova
Pesaro
Ragusa
Rimini
Rovigo
Savona
Teramo
Torino

Regions, administrative

Trento
Varese
Verona

7 letters:
Belluno
Bergamo
Bologna
Bolzano
Brescia
Caserta
Catania
Cosenza
Cremona
Crotone
Ferrara
Firenze
Gorizia
Imperia
Isernia
L'Aquila
Livorno
Mantova
Messina
Palermo
Perugia
Pescara
Pistoia

Potenza
Ravenna
Salerno
Sassari
Sondrio
Taranto
Trapani
Treviso
Trieste
Venezia
Vicenza
Viterbo

8 letters:
Avellino
Brindisi
Cagliari
Grosseto
La Spezia
Macerata
Oristano
Piacenza
Siracusa
Verbania
Vercelli

9 letters:
Agrigento

Benevento
Catanzaro
Frosinone
Pordenone

10 letters:
Campobasso

11 letters:
Alessandria

12 letters:
Ascoli Piceno
Massa Carrara
Reggio Emilia
Vibo Valentia

13 letters:
Caltanissetta

16 letters:
Reggio di Calabria

21 letters:
Repubblica di San
  Marino

SPANISH REGIONS

5 letters:
Ceuta

6 letters:
Aragón
Madrid
Murcia

7 letters:
Galicia
La Rioja
Melilla
Navarra

8 letters:
Asturias

9 letters:
Andalucía
Cantabria
Catalonia

11 letters:
Extremadura

12 letters:
Castilla-León

13 letters:
Basque Country
Canary Islands

15 letters:
Balearic Islands

16 letters:
Castilla-La Mancha

18 letters:
Valencian
  Community

SPANISH PROVINCES

4 letters:
Jaén
León
Lugo

5 letters:
Álava

Ávila
Cádiz
Ceuta
Soria

6 letters:
Burgos

Cuenca
Girona
Huelva
Huesca
Lleida
Madrid
Málaga

Murcia
Orense
Teruel
Toledo
Zamora

7 letters:
Almerìa
Badajoz
Cácares
Cordoba
Granada
La Rioja
Melilla
Navarra
Segovia
Sevilla

Vizcaya

8 letters:
Albacete
Alicante
Asturias
La Coruna
Palencia
Valencia
Zaragoza

9 letters:
Alhucemas
Balearics
Barcelona
Cantabria
Castellón
Guipúzcoa

Las Palmas
Salamanca
Tarragona

10 letters:
Chafarinas
Ciudad Real
Pontevedra
Valladolid

11 letters:
Gualalajara

15 letters:
Vélez de la Gomera

19 letters:
Santa Cruz de
  Tenerife

See also:
➤ **Provinces of Canada** ➤ **Countries** ➤ **Provinces of South Africa** ➤ **States and territories** ➤ **Swiss cantons** ➤ **Territories of New Zealand**

Religion

RELIGIONS

4 letters:
Babi
Druz
Jain

5 letters:
Baha'i
Druse
Druze
Hasid
Islam
Jaina
Jewry
Sunna

6 letters:
Babism
Culdee
Gueber
Guebre
Hadith
Hassid
Jesuit

Loyola
Sabian
Shaker
Shango
Shembe
Shinto
Taoism
Voodoo
Zabian

7 letters:
Animism
Baha'ism
Bogomil
Ismaili
Jainism
Judaism
Lamaism
Macumba
Mahatma
Orphism
Parsism
Piarist

Sikhism
Tsabian
Yezidis

8 letters:
Buddhism
Druidism
Hinduism
Lutheran
Manichee
Mazdaism
Mazdeism
Paganism
Santeria
Satanism
Theatine

9 letters:
Celestine
Coenobite
Hindooism
Jansenism
Mithraism
Mormonism

Religion

Pantheist
Shamanism
Shintoism
Utraquist
Voodooism
Zoroaster

10 letters:
Carthusian
Cistercian
Gilbertine
Heliolatry
Hospitaler
Manicheism

Zend-avesta

11 letters:
Camaldolite
Hare Krishna
Hospitaller
Ignorantine
Manichaeism
Mithraicism
Ryobu Shinto
Scientology®
Zoroastrism

12 letters:
Christianity

Confucianism
Zarathustric

13 letters:
Sons of Freedom
Tractarianism

14 letters:
Rastafarianism
Zoroastrianism

15 letters:
Christadelphian
Jehovah's Witness

RELIGIOUS BOOKS

2 letters:
Lu

4 letters:
Veda

5 letters:
Bible
Koran
Li Chi
Quran
Torah

6 letters:
Granth
I Ching

Talmud

7 letters:
Rigveda
Su Ching

8 letters:
Ayurveda
Ramayana
Samaveda
Shi Ching
Tipitaka

9 letters:
Adi Granth
Apocrypha

Atharveda
Siddhanta
Tripitaka
Yajurveda

11 letters:
Mahabharata

12 letters:
Bhagavad-Gita
Book of Mormon
New Testament
Old Testament

15 letters:
Guru Granth Sahib

RELIGIOUS BUILDINGS

5 letters:
Abbey
Kaaba
Marae

6 letters:
Bethel
Chapel

Church
Mosque
Temple

7 letters:
Convent

8 letters:
Gurdwara

9 letters:
Cathedral
Monastery
Synagogue

10 letters:
Tabernacle

RELIGIOUS CLOTHING

3 letters:
Alb

4 letters:
Coif
Cope

Cowl

5 letters:
Amice
Cotta
Habit

Mitre

6 letters:
Almuce
Chimar
Chimer

Cornet
Guimpe
Peplos
Peplus
Rochet
Tippet
Wimple

7 letters:
Biretta
Calotte
Capuche
Cassock
Chimere
Gremial
Infulae

Maniple
Mozetta
Pallium
Soutane
Tunicle

8 letters:
Berretta
Capouche
Chasuble
Dalmatic
Mozzetta
Scapular
Surplice

9 letters:
Clericals

Dog collar
Shovel hat
Surcingle
Zucchetto

10 letters:
Canonicals

11 letters:
Mantelletta
Pontificals

12 letters:
Superhumeral

14 letters:
Clerical collar

RELIGIOUS FESTIVALS

4 letters:
Holi
Lent

5 letters:
Hirja
Purim
Wesak

6 letters:
Advent
Diwali
Easter
Pesach

7 letters:
Ramadan
Shavuot
Succoth
Sukkoth
Trinity
Whitsun
Yuan Tan

8 letters:
Al Hijrah
Baisakhi
Bodhi Day
Chanukah
Dussehra
Epiphany

Hanukkah
Id-ul-Adha
Id-ul-Fitr
Passover
Rogation

9 letters:
Candlemas
Ching Ming
Christmas
Eid ul-Adha
Eid ul-Fitr
Pentecost
Rama Naumi
Yom Kippur

10 letters:
Good Friday
Michaelmas
Palm Sunday
Sexagesima

11 letters:
Dhammacakka
Hola Mohalla

12 letters:
Ascension Day
Ash Wednesday
Janamashtami
Lailat ul-Qadr

Moon Festival
Quadragesima
Rosh Hashanah
Septuagesima

13 letters:
Corpus Christi
Lailat ul-Barah
Passion Sunday
Quinquagesima
Raksha Bandhan
Shrove Tuesday

14 letters:
Day of Atonement
Mahashivaratri
Maundy Thursday
Winter Festival

18 letters:
Dragon Boat
 Festival
Feast of
 Tabernacles
Guru Nanak's
 Birthday

20 letters:
Lailat ul-Isra Wal
 Mi'raj

Religious movements

Religious movements

Adidam (The Way of the Heart)
African Methodist Episcopalian Church
Alcoholics Anonymous
AME Church
Amish
Ananda Church of Self Realization
Ananda Marga Yoga Society
Anglo-Israelism
Assemblies of God
Association for Research and Enlightenment
Atheism
Atherius Society
Aum Shinrikyo
Baha'i Faith
Baptists, Primitive
Baptists, Southern
Bogomils
Boston Church of Christ
Branch Davidians
Branhamism
British-Israelism
Brownsville Revival
Bruderhof
Buddhism
Call to Renewal (Christians for a New Political Vision)
Calvary Chapel
Campus Crusade for Christ
Candomble
Cao Daism
Channeling
Charismatic Movement

Chen Tao (The Right Way)
Children of God
Christadelphians
Christian and Missionary Alliance
Christian Coalition
Christian Identity Movement
Christian Reconstructionism
Christian Reformed Church in America
Christian Science
Christianity in Japan
Church in Island Pond
Church of God International
Church of Satan
Church of Set
Church of the Nazarene
Church of the New Jerusalem
Church Universal and Triumphant
Concerned Christians
Course in Miracles
Deepak Chopra
Discordianism
Divine Light Mission
Druids
Druse
Druze
Eckankar
Elan Vital
Est
Falun Gong (Religious Freedom in China)
Father Divine
Feng Shui

First Church of Christ, Scientist
Foundation of Human
Understanding
Foursquare Gospel Church
Freemasonry
Fundamentalism
Ghebers
Gnosticism
Guebres
Hare Krishnas
Hasidism
Healthy, Happy, Holy
Organization
Heaven's Gate
Hinduism
Holy Order of MANS
Holy Spirit Association for the
Unification of World
Christianity
Huguenots
Hussites
Hutterian Brethren of New York,
Inc.
I Am
Institute of Noetic Sciences
Integral Yoga
International Church of
Scientology
International Church of the
Foursquare Gospel
International Churches Of Christ
International Peace Mission
Movement
International Raelian Religion
International Society for Krishna
Consciousness
ISKCON
Islam
Israeli School of Universal
Practical Knowledge (The
Twelve Tribes)
Jainism
Jehovah's Witnesses
Jesus Army
Jesus Fellowship Church
Jesus People USA
Jonestown
Kabbalah
Karaites
Knights of Columbus
Konkokyo

Lamaism
Landmark Education
Latter Day Saints
Latter Rain Movement
Lifespring
Local Church
Macumba Maitreya
Manichaeism
Masada
Masons
Mazdaism
Mazdeism
Meher Baba Groups
Mennonites
Messianic Jewish Alliance of
America
Methodist Church
Millennium Prophecies
Mithraism
Moody Bible Institute
Moody Church
Moonies
Moral Rearmament
Moravian Church
Mormonism (LDS)
MOVE
Movement for the Restoration of
the Ten Commandments of
God
Movement of Spiritual Inner
Awareness
MSIA
Nation of Islam
Nation of Yahweh
National Baptist Convention
Native American Religions
Nazarene
Neo-Paganism
Neturei Karta (Guardians of the
City)
New Age
New Creation Christian
Community
New Thought
Nichiren Shoshu
Northeast Kingdom Community
Church
Nubian Islamic Hebrews
Old Catholicism
Oneida Movement
Opus Dei

Religious movements

Order of the Solar Temple
Osho
Oxford
Paramahansa Yogananda
Parseeism
Parsiism
Pentacostalism
Peoples Temple
Philadelphia Church of God
Primitive Baptists
Process Church of the Final
    Judgment
Promise Keepers
Puseyism
Quakers
Raelians
Rajnesshism
Ramakrishna Order of the
    Vendanta Society
Ramtha's School of
    Enlightenment
Rastafarianism
Rebirthing
Religious Science (United
    Church of)
Reorganized Church Of Jesus
    Christ of Latter Day Saints
Restoration Movement
Restoration of the Ten
    Commandments of God
Roman Catholicism
Rosicrucian Order (AMORC)
Sabbatarian
Sabians
Sacramentarians
Sahaja Yoga
Salem Witch Trials
Salvation Army
Santeria
Satanism
Scientific Pantheism
Scientology
Secular Humanism
Seicho No Ie
Self-Realization Fellowship
Seventh-Day Adventists
Shakers
Shamanism
Shambhala International
Shinreikyo
Shinto

Shirdi Sai Baba
Sikh Dharma
Sikhs
Silva Mind Control *or* Silva
    Method
Snake Handlers
Society of Friends
Soka Gakkai
Solar Temple
Southern Baptists
Southern Christian Leadership
    Conference (SCLC)
Spiritual Discovery (Suma Ching
    Hai)
Spiritualism
Sri Chinmoy
Sukyo Mahikari
Suma Ching Hai
Swedenborgianism
Synanon
Synchronicity Contemporary
    Meditation
Taoism
Tenrikyo
The Brethren
The Church of God (Seventh
    Day)
The Church of Jesus Christ of
    Latter Day Saints
The Family
The Forum
The Process
The Temple of Set
The Way International (the way)
The Zarathushtrian Assembly
Theosophy
Toronto Blessing
Tractarianism
Transcendental Meditation
Twelve Tribes
Two X Twos
Unarius Academy of Science
Unification Church
Unitarian Universalist
United Church of Religious
    Science
United Methodist Church
United Pentacostal Church
    International
United Society of Believers
Unity School of Christianity

Universal Life Church
Universal Negro Improvement
  Association
Universal Peace Mission
  Movement
Urantia Brotherhood
Vendanta Society
Vineyard Churches
Voodooism
Watchtower and Bible Tract
  Society

Wicca
Willow Creek Community
  Church
Woman's Christian Temperance
  Union
Worldwide Church of God
Zen Buddhism
Zionism
Zoroastrianism

Religious orders

Assumptionist (A.A.)
Augustinian (O.S.A.)
Barnabite Fathers
Benedictine (O.S.B)
Bridgitine (C.S.B)
Brothers of St Gabriel
Brothers of St John of God
Brothers of the Christian
  Schools (F.S.C.)
Camaldolese Benedictines
Canossian Daughters of Charity
Carmelite (O.C., O.C.D.,
  O.C.D.S.)
Carthusian (O. Cart.)
Celestine
Cenacle Sisters
Christian Brothers
Cistercian (O. Cist.)
Claretian Missionaries
Congregation Marians
Congregation of the Holy Cross
  (C.S.C.)
Cordeliers
Daughters of St Francis of Assisi
Daughters of St Mary of
  Providence
Daughters of St Paul
Dervish
Divine Word Missionaries
  (D.V.M.)
Dominican (O.P.)
Felician Sisters
Franciscan (O.F.M.)

Handmaids of the Precious
  Blood
Hare Krishna (International
  Society for Krishna
  Consciousness or I.S.K.C.O.N.)
Institute of Charity (Rosminians)
  (I.C.)
Jesuits (S.J.)
Lasallian Brothers
Little Brothers of the Good
  Shepherd
Little Sisters of the Poor
Loretto nuns
Marianists
Marist Fathers and Brothers
Maryknoll
Missionaries of Charity (M.C.)
Missionaries of the Sacred Heart
  (M.S.C.)
Norbertines (C.R.P.)
Oblates (O.M.I.)
Observants
Passionists (C.P.)
Piarists
Poor Clares
Poor Sisters of Nazareth
Redemptorists (C.S.S.R.)
Resurrectionists (C.R.)
Salesians
Salesians of Don Bosco (S.D.B.)
Salvatorians
Servites
Sisters of Charity

Reptiles

Reptiles

2 letters:
Go

3 letters:
Asp
Boa

4 letters:
Habu

5 letters:
Adder
Agama
Anole
Cobra
Gecko
Krait
Mamba
Racer
Skink
Snake
Swift
Tokay
Viper

6 letters:
Agamid
Caiman
Cayman
Dugite
Dukite
Elapid
Freshy
Garial
Gavial
Goanna
Iguana
Leguan
Lizard
Moloch
Python
Saltie
Taipan
Turtle

7 letters:
Camoodi
Frillie
Gharial
Monitor
Ngarara
Perenty
Rattler
Tuatara

8 letters:
Anaconda
Bungarra
Cerastes
Hawkbill
Moccasin
Perentie
Pit viper
Rat snake
Ringhals
Sea snake
Slowworm
Terrapin
Tortoise

9 letters:
Alligator
Blindworm
Blue racer
Boomslang
Box turtle
Bull snake
Chameleon
Crocodile
Deaf adder
Galliwasp
Hamadryad
Hawksbill
Hoop snake
Jew lizard
King cobra
King snake
Milk snake
Mud turtle

Puff adder
Rock snake
Sand viper
Sphenodon
Tree snake
Whip snake

10 letters:
Bandy-bandy
Black snake
Blind snake
Blue tongue
Brown snake
Bushmaster
Chuckwalla
Copperhead
Coral snake
Death adder
Fer-de-lance
Glass snake
Grass snake
Horned toad
Kabaragoya
Loggerhead
Massasauga
Rock python
Sand lizard
Sidewinder
Tiger snake
Wall lizard
Water snake
Worm lizard

11 letters:
Amphisbaena
Carpet snake
Constrictor
Cottonmouth
Diamondback
Gaboon viper
Garter snake
Gila monster
Gopher snake
Green turtle

Horned viper
Indigo snake
Leatherback
Mallee snake
Rattlesnake
Smooth snake
Thorn lizard
Thorny devil

12 letters:
Diamond snake
Flying dragon
Flying lizard
Hognose snake
Komodo dragon
Komodo lizard

13 letters:
Bearded dragon
Bearded lizard
Bicycle lizard

Cycling lizard
Diamond python
Frilled lizard
Giant tortoise
Mountain devil
Water moccasin

14 letters:
Boa constrictor
Cobra de capello
Harlequin snake
Leathery turtle
Malayan monitor
Snapping turtle

15 letters:
Hawksbill turtle
Schneider python

16 letters:
Loggerhead turtle

17 letters:
Amethystine
  python
Diamondback
  turtle
Frill-necked lizard
Soft-shelled turtle

18 letters:
Saltwater crocodile

19 letters:
Diamondback
  terrapin
Freshwater
  crocodile

20 letters:
Red-bellied black
  snake

See also:
➤ **Dinosaurs** ➤ **Lizards** ➤ **Snakes**

Republics

3 letters:
UAR

4 letters:
Chad
Cuba
Eire
Fiji
Iran
Komi
Laos
Mali
Peru
Togo

5 letters:
Belau
Benin
Chile
Czech
Egypt
Gabon
Ghana
Haiti

Italy
Khmer
Malta
Nauru
Niger
Palau
Sudan
Syria
Yemen
Zaire

6 letters:
Angola
Bukavu
Gambia
Guinea
Guyana
Ingush
Israel
Kalmyk
Latvia
Malawi
Mexico
Myanma

Panama
Rwanda
Serbia
Turkey
Weimar
Zambia

7 letters:
Albania
Algeria
Andorra
Bashkir
Belarus
Bolivia
Burundi
Chechen
Comoros
Croatia
Ecuador
Estonia
Finland
Hungary
Iceland
Kalmuck

Resins

Khakass
Lebanon
Liberia
Moldova
Myanmar
Namibia
Nigeria
Romania
Senegal
Somalia
Surinam
Tunisia
Ukraine
Uruguay
Vanuatu
Vietnam

8 letters:
Botswana
Bulgaria
Cambodia
Cameroon
Chechnya
Colombia
Dagestan
Djibouti
Dominica
Esthonia
Honduras
Karelian

Kiribati
Malagasy
Maldives
Mongolia
Paraguay
Sinn Fein
Slovakia
Slovenia
Sri Lanka
Tanzania
Udmurtia
Zimbabwe

9 letters:
Argentina
Cape Verde
Costa Rica
Dominican
Guatemala
Indonesia
Kazakstan
Lithuania
Macedonia
Mauritius
Nicaragua
San Marino
Venezuela

10 letters:
Azerbaijan

Bangladesh
Belarussia
El Salvador
Kazakhstan
Kyrgyzstan
Madagascar
Mauritania
Montenegro
Mordvinian
Mozambique
Tajikistan
Ubang-Shari
Yugoslavia

11 letters:
Afghanistan
Byelorussia
Philippines
Sierra Leone
Switzerland

12 letters:
Guinea-Bissau
Turkmenistan

13 letters:
Bashkortostan

17 letters:
Bosnia-
  Herzegovina

Resins

3 letters:
Gum
Lac

4 letters:
Arar
Hing
Kino
Urea

5 letters:
Amber
Amino
Copai
Copal
Damar
Elemi
Epoxy

Myrrh
Roset
Rosin
Rosit
Rozet
Rozit
Saran®

6 letters:
Balsam
Charas
Conima
Copalm
Dammar
Dammer
Gambir
Mastic
Storax

Styrax

7 letters:
Acaroid
Benzoin
Caranna
Carauna
Churrus
Copaiba
Copaiva
Galipot
Gambier
Gamboge
Glyptal
Hashish
Jalapin
Ladanum
Polymer

Rice and other cereals

Shellac
Xylenol

8 letters:
Bakelite®
Benjamin
Cannabin
Galbanum
Guaiacum
Hasheesh
Melamine
Olibanum

Opopanax
Phenolic
Propolis
Retinite
Sandarac
Scammony
Takamaka

9 letters:
Asafetida
Courbaril
Polyester

Sagapenum
Sandarach

10 letters:
Asafoetida

11 letters:
Podophyllin

12 letters:
Dragon's blood
Frankincense

Rice and other cereals

4 letters:
Bran
Corn
Oats
Ragi
Sago

5 letters:
Maize
Wheat

6 letters:
Millet

7 letters:
Oatmeal
Tapioca

8 letters:
Couscous
Wild rice

9 letters:
Brown rice
Patna rice

10 letters:
Indian rice

11 letters:
Arborio rice
Basmati rice
Bulgur wheat

13 letters:
Long grain rice

14 letters:
Short grain rice

Rivers

2 letters:
Ob
Po
Si
Xi

3 letters:
Aar
Ain
Aln
Axe
Ayr
Bug
Cam
Dee
Don
Ems
Esk

Exe
Fal
Fly
Han
Hsi
Inn
Lee
Lot
Nar
Ord
Red
San
Tay
Tet
Ure
Usk
Var
Wye

4 letters:
Abus
Abzu
Acis
Adur
Aire
Alma
Alph
Amur
Aran
Aras
Arno
Aube
Aude
Avon
Back
Beni
Bomu

Rivers

Cher
Dart
Deva
Doon
Dove
Drin
Earn
Ebbw
Ebro
Eden
Eder
Elbe
Erne
Esla
Eure
Gila
Göta
Huon
Idle
Isar
Iser
Isis
Juba
Kama
Kill
Kura
Kwai
Lahn
Lech
Lena
Liao
Lune
Maas
Main
Meta
Milk
Miño
Mole
Nene
Neva
Nile
Nith
Oder
Ohio
Oise
Ouse
Oxus
Prut
Ruhr
Saar
Sava

Save
Soar
Spey
Styx
Swan
Swat
Taff
Tana
Tarn
Tees
Teme
Test
Tyne
Uele
Ural
Vaal
Waal
Wear
Xero
Yalu
Yare
Yate
Yser
Yüan
Yüen

5 letters:
Abana
Acton
Adige
Afton
Agate
Aisne
Aldan
Apure
Argun
Avoca
Benue
Boyne
Cauca
Chari
Clyde
Congo
Cross
Dasht
Desna
Doubs
Douro
Drava
Drave
Duero

Dvina
Eblis
Firth
Fleet
Forth
Gogra
Green
Havel
Indre
Indus
Isère
James
Jumna
Juruá
Kabul
Kasai
Kenga
Kuban
Lethe
Liard
Lippe
Loire
Marne
Meuse
Minho
Mosel
Mulla
Namoi
Negro
Neman
Niger
Ogowe
Onega
Oreti
Peace
Pearl
Pecos
Pelly
Piave
Pison
Plate
Purús
Rance
Rhein
Rhine
Rhône
Rogue
Saône
Seine
Shari
Shiré

Siang
Siret
Skien
Slave
Snake
Snowy
Somme
Spree
Staff
Stour
Swale
Tagus
Tamar
Tapti
Tarim
Teign
Terek
Tiber
Tisza
Tobol
Trent
Tweed
Volga
Volta
Warta
Weser
Xiang
Xingú
Yaqui
Yarra
Yonne
Yssel
Yukon

6 letters:
Albany
Allier
Amazon
Anadyr
Angara
Arzina
Atbara
Barcoo
Barrow
Bío-Bío
Calder
Canton
Chenab
Clutha
Crouch
Cuiaba

Cydnus
Danube
Dawson
Donets
Duddon
Durack
Finlay
Fraser
Gambia
Ganges
Glomma
Granta
Hodder
Hsiang
Hudson
Humber
Iguaçú
IJssel
Irtish
Irwell
Itchen
Japurá
Javari
Javary
Jhelum
Jordan
Kagera
Kaveri
Kennet
Kolyma
Komati
Liffey
Mamoré
Medway
Mekong
Mersey
Mohawk
Molopo
Morava
Moskva
Murray
Neckar
Neisse
Nelson
Nyeman
Ogooué
Orange
Orwell
Ottawa
Pahang
Paraná

Pripet
Rakaia
Ribble
Riffle
Rother
Sabine
Salado
Salado
Sambre
Santee
Severn
Struma
Sutlej
Sutley
Swanee
Tanana
Tarsus
Teviot
Thames
Ticino
Tigris
Tugela
Tyburn
Ubangi
Ussuri
Vardar
Vienne
Vltava
Wabash
Wairau
Wensum
Wharfe
Yarrow
Yellow

7 letters:
Acheron
Alabama
Aruwimi
Bermejo
Caquetá
Cauvery
Chagres
Cocytus
Damodar
Darling
Derwent
Detroit
Dnieper
Dubglas
Durance

Rivers

Ettrick
Fitzroy
Garonne
Genesee
Gironde
Guaporé
Helmand
Hooghly
Huang He
Hwangho
Iguassú
Irawadi
Kanawha
Krishna
Lachlan
Limpopo
Lualaba
Madeira
Manning
Marañón
Maritsa
Mataura
Meander
Moselle
Narmada
Niagara
Orinoco
Orontes
Paraíba
Pechora
Pharpar
Potomac
Rubicon
Sabrina
Salinas
Salween
Salzach
Sanders
Scheldt
Senegal
Shannon
Songhua
Swannee
Tapajós
Thomson
Ucayali
Uruguay
Vistula
Waikato
Washita
Welland

Yangtse
Yangtze
Yenisei
Yenisey
Zambese
Zambezi

8 letters:
Amu Darya
Anderson
Apurimac
Araguaia
Arkansas
Berezina
Blue Nile
Canadian
Charente
Cherwell
Chindwin
Clarence
Colorado
Columbia
Daintree
Delaware
Demerara
Dneister
Dniester
Dordogne
Flinders
Franklin
Gascoyne
Godavari
Guadiana
Illinois
Kentucky
Klondike
Kootenai
Kootenay
Maeander
Mahanadi
Menderes
Missouri
Mitchell
Okanagan
Okavango
Ouachita
Pactolus
Paraguay
Parnaíba
Putumayo
Rio Negro

Safid Rud
Saguenay
Savannah
Suwannee
Syr Darya
Torridge
Toulouse
Tunguska
Victoria
Volturno
Wanganui
Windrush
Zhu Jiang

9 letters:
Ashburton
Athabaska
Billabong
Churchill
Crocodile
Des Moines
Essequibo
Euphrates
Irrawaddy
Kuskokwim
Mackenzie
Macquarie
Magdalena
Minnesota
Murchison
Parnahiba
Pilcomayo
Porcupine
Qu'Appelle
Rangitata
Richelieu
Rio Branco
Rio Grande
Saint John
Salambria
Santa Cruz
Tennessee
Tocantins
White Nile
Wisconsin

10 letters:
Black Volta
Blackwater
Chao Phraya
Courantyne
Housatonic

Kizil Irmak
Phlegethon
Rangitaiki
Rangitikei
Sacramento
Saint Croix
St Lawrence
White Volta

11 letters:
Assiniboine
Brahmaputra

Connecticut
Cooper Creek
Lesser Slave
Madre de Dios
Mississippi
Monongahela
Shatt-al-Arab
Susquehanna
Yellowstone

12 letters:
Cooper's Creek

Guadalquivir
Murrumbidgee
Saskatchewan

13 letters:
Little Bighorn
Saint Lawrence

Rivers of Hell

4 letters:
Styx (River of Oath)

5 letters:
Lethe (River of Forgetfulness)

7 letters:
Acheron (River of Woe)

Cocytus (River of Lament)

10 letters:
Phlegethon (River of Fire)

Rocks

2 letters:
Aa

3 letters:
Gem
Gib
Jow
Tor

4 letters:
Bell
Clay
Coal
Crag
Gang
Glam
Grit
Jura
Lava
Lias
Noup
Reef
Sill
Sima
Trap

Tufa
Tuff
Zoic

5 letters:
Ayers
Brash
Calpe
Chair
Chalk
Chert
Cliff
Craig
Elvan
Flint
Geode
Glass
Krans
Loess
Magma
Nappe
Scalp
Scree
Shale
Skarn

Slate
Solid
Stone
Trass
Uluru
Wacke

6 letters:
Aplite
Arkose
Banket
Basalt
Dacite
Diapir
Dunite
Flaser
Flysch
Fossil
Gabbro
Gangue
Gibber
Gneiss
Gossan
Gozzan
Gravel

Rocks

Inlier
Kingle
Marble
Masada
Norite
Oolite
Pelite
Pluton
Pumice
Rognon
Sarsen
Schist
Sinter
Skerry
Sklate
S. Peter
Stonen
Synroc
Tephra

7 letters:
Aquifer
Boulder
Breccia
Clastic
Cuprite
Cyanean
Diamond
Diorite
Eucrite
Fastnet
Felsite
Granite
Greisen
Lignite
Lorelei
Marlite
Minette
Molasse
Moraine
Needles
Nunatak
Olivine
Ophites
Outcrop
Outlier
Peridot
Picrite
Remanie
Rhaetic
Sinking

Spilite
Syenite
Thulite
Tripoli
Wenlock

8 letters:
Adularia
Aegirine
Andesite
Aphanite
Basanite
Brockram
Burstone
Calcrete
Calc-tufa
Calc-tuff
Ciminite
Diabasic
Dolerite
Dolomite
Eclogite
Eklogite
Elvanite
Eutaxite
Fahlband
Felstone
Ganister
Hepatite
Hornfels
Idocrase
Inchcape
Laterite
Lopolith
Mesolite
Mudstone
Mylonite
Obsidian
Peperino
Perknite
Petuntse
Phyllite
Pisolite
Plutonic
Plymouth
Porphyry
Psammite
Psephite
Ragstone
Regolith
Rhyolite

Rocaille
Roe-stone
Saxatile
Saxonite
Scorpion
Sunstone
Taconite
Tarpeian
Tephrite
The Olgas
Tonalite
Trachyte
Trappean
Xenolith

9 letters:
Anticline
Argillite
Batholite
Bentonite
Bluestone
Buhrstone
Claystone
Cockhorse
Colluvium
Cornstone
Dalradian
Eddystone
Edinburgh
Evaporite
Firestone
Flowstone
Gannister
Gibraltar
Goslarite
Granulite
Graywacke
Greensand
Greystone
Greywacke
Hornstone
Impactite
Intrusion
Ironstone
Laccolite
Laccolith
Limestone
Meteorite
Migmatite
Monadnock
Monocline

Monzonite
Mortstone
Mugearite
Natrolite
Neocomian
Nunatakkr
Ophiolite
Ottrelite
Pegmatite
Petrology
Phonolite
Phosphate
Pleonaste
Protogine
Quartzite
Reservoir
Sandstone
Saprolite
Scablands
Schistose
Siltstone
Soapstone
Tachylyte
Theralite
Tinguaite
Toadstone
Travertin
Variolite
Vulcanite
Whinstone
Whunstane
Zechstein

10 letters:
Ailsa Craig

Amygdaloid
Anthracite
Camptonite
Epidiorite
Foundation
Granophyre
Greenstone
Hypabyssal
Ignimbrite
Kersantite
Kimberlite
Lherzolite
Limburgite
Novaculite
Palagonite
Peridotite
Permafrost
Phenocryst
Pitchstone
Pyroxenite
Rupestrian
Schalstein
Serpentine
Sparagmite
Stinkstone
Stonebrash
Stonehenge
Syntagmata
Teschenite
Touchstone
Travertine
Troctolite

11 letters:
Agglomerate

Amphibolite
Annabergite
Anorthosite
Carbonatite
Geanticline
Halleflinta
Lamprophyre
Monchiquite
Napoleonite
Nephelinite
Phillipsite
Pyroclastic
Sedimentary
Symplegades

12 letters:
Babingtonite
Conglomerate
Granodiorite
Grossularite
Hornblendite
Slickenslide
Stromatolite
Syntagmatite
Thunderstone

13 letters:
Hypersthenite

14 letters:
Roche moutonnée

See also:
➤ **Minerals** ➤ **Ores** ➤ **Stones**

Rodents

3 letters:
Mus
Rat

4 letters:
Cavy
Jird
Mara

Paca
Vole

5 letters:
Aguti
Bobac
Bobak
Civet

Coypu
Hutia
Hyrax
Kiore
Mouse
Murid
Ratel
Shrew

Roman numerals

Taira

6 letters:
Agouti
Beaver
Boomer
Dassie
Gerbil
Glires
Gopher
Hog-rat
Jerbil
Jerboa
Marmot
Nutria
Ratton
Suslik
Taguan

7 letters:
Acouchi
Acouchy
Cane rat
Chincha
Glutton
Hamster
Lemming
Mole rat
Muskrat
Ondatra
Pack rat
Potoroo
Souslik

8 letters:
Banxring

Biscacha
Bizcacha
Black rat
Brown rat
Capybara
Chipmunk
Cricetus
Dormouse
Gerbille
Hampster
Hedgehog
Māori rat
Musquash
Ochotona
Sciurine
Sewellel
Squirrel
Tucotuco
Tucu-tuco
Viscacha
Vizcacha
Water rat
White rat

9 letters:
Bandicoot
Bangsring
Chickaree
Deer mouse
Delundung
Desert rat
Groundhog
Guinea pig
Jerboa rat
Norway rat

Porcupine
Water vole
Woodchuck

10 letters:
Chinchilla
Dargawarra
Fieldmouse
House mouse
Springhaas
Springhase

11 letters:
Fox squirrel
Kangaroo rat
Pocket mouse
Red squirrel
Spermophile

12 letters:
Grey squirrel
Harvest mouse
Hopping mouse
Jumping mouse
Pocket gopher

14 letters:
Flying squirrel
Ground squirrel

16 letters:
White-footed
mouse

20 letters:
Spinifex hopping
mouse

Roman numerals	
Numeral	**Equivalent**
A	50
B	300
C	100
D	500
E	250
F	40
G	400
H	200
I	1
K	250
L	50

Numeral	Equivalent
M	1000
N	90
O	11
P	400
Q	500
R	80
S	7 or 70
T	160
V	5
X	10
Y	150
Z	2000

Rome, the seven hills of

7 letters:
Caelian
Viminal

8 letters:
Aventine

Palatine
Quirinal

9 letters:
Esquiline

10 letters:
Capitoline

Roofing

3 letters:
Hip

4 letters:
Bell
Dome

5 letters:
Gable
Skirt

6 letters:
French

Hipped
Pop-top
Saddle
Thatch
Thetch

7 letters:
Belfast
Gambrel
Hardtop
Mansard
Shingle

8 letters:
Imperial
Pavilion

9 letters:
Monopitch

10 letters:
Jerkin-head

12 letters:
Porte-cochère

Ropes

3 letters:
Guy
Tow

4 letters:
Balk
Cord
Fall

Jeff
Line
Stay
Vang

5 letters:
Baulk
Brail

Cable
Guide
Lasso
Longe
Lunge
Riata
Sheet
Sugan

Rugby terms

Trace
Wanty
Widdy

6 letters:
Cablet
Cordon
Earing
Halser
Halter
Hawser
Inhaul
Marlin
Prusik
Roband
Robbin
Runner
Shroud
String
Tackle

7 letters:
Bobstay

Cringle
Halyard
Lanyard
Marline
Mooring
Outhaul
Painter
Pastern
Rawhide
Stirrup
Swifter
Towline
Triatic

8 letters:
Backstay
Boltrope
Bunt-line
Downhaul
Forestay
Gantline
Halliard

Headfast
Jack-stay
Prolonge
Selvagee
Spun-yarn

9 letters:
Breeching
Foresheet
Mainbrace
Mainsheet
Reef point
Sternfast
Timenoguy

10 letters:
Hawser-laid
Kernmantel

11 letters:
Triatic stay

13 letters:
Futtock-shroud

Rugby terms

3 letters:
Try

4 letters:
Back
Ball
Mark
Maul
Pack
Pass
Punt
Ruck

5 letters:
Scrum

6 letters:
Centre
Hooker
Tackle
Winger

7 letters:
Back row

Flanker
Fly half
Forward
Knock on
Line-out
Penalty
Referee

8 letters:
Crossbar
Drop goal
Front row
Full back
Goalpost
Half back

9 letters:
Garryowen
Loose head
Scrum half
Scrummage
Second row
Tight head

10 letters:
Conversion
Five-eighth
Touch judge
Up and under

11 letters:
Lock forward
Outside half
Prop forward
Wing forward

12 letters:
Loose forward
Stand-off half
Three-quarter

18 letters:
Number eight
 forward

Rulers

TITLES OF RULERS

3 letters:
Ban
Bey
Dey
Mir
Oba
Raj
Rex

4 letters:
Amir
Cham
Czar
Doge
Duce
Duke
Emir
Imam
Inca
Khan
King
Pope
Raja
Rana
Rani
Shah
Tsar
Vali
Wali

5 letters:
Ameer
Ardri
Calif
Chief
Dewan
Diwan
Imaum
Kalif
Mogul
Mpret
Mudir
Nabob
Nawab
Negus
Nizam
Pacha

Pasha
Queen
Rajah
Ranee
Shaka
Sheik
Sophi
Sophy
Tenno

6 letters:
Atabeg
Atabek
Caesar
Caliph
Chagan
Dergue
Despot
Dynast
Exarch
Führer
Kabaka
Kaiser
Khalif
Manchu
Mikado
Prince
Regent
Sachem
Satrap
Sharif
Sheikh
Sherif
Shogun
Sirdar
Squier
Squire
Sultan
Tycoon
Tyrant

7 letters:
Abbasid
Ardrigh
Bajayet
Bajazet
Catapan

Chogyal
Elector
Emperor
Empress
Gaekwar
Gaikwar
Jamshid
Jamshyd
Khedive
Lesbian
Monarch
Pharaoh
Podesta
Shereef
Souldan
Toparch
Viceroy

8 letters:
Archduke
Autocrat
Burgrave
Caudillo
Dictator
Ethnarch
Heptarch
Hierarch
Hospodar
Maharaja
Maharani
Mameluke
Mistress
Oligarch
Padishah
Sagamore
Sassanid
Suzerain
Tetrarch

9 letters:
Bretwalda
Cosmocrat
Dalai Lama
Maharajah
Maharanee
Ochlocrat
Pendragon

Rulers

Plutocrat
Potentate
Sovereign
Vicereine

FAMOUS RULERS

4 letters:
Nero

5 letters:
Herod
Lenin
Louis

6 letters:
Castro
Cheops
Franco
Hitler
Nasser
Stalin

7 letters:
Idi Amin
Saladin

8 letters:
Augustus
Bismarck
Boadicea
Boudicca
Caligula
Cromwell
De Gaulle
Hirohito

10 letters:
Aristocrat
Great Mogul
Plantocrat
Rajpramukh

Nicholas
Pericles
Victoria

9 letters:
Churchill
Cleopatra
Elizabeth
Mao Ze Dong
Montezuma
Mussolini
Tamerlane

10 letters:
Caractacus
Kublai Khan
Mao Tse-tung

11 letters:
Charlemagne
Genghis Khan
Prester John
Tamburlaine
Tutankhamen
Tutankhamun

12 letters:
Chandragupta
Julius Caesar

Stadholder
Stratocrat

11 letters:
Stadtholder

13 letters:
Haile Selassie
Peter the Great

14 letters:
Alfred the Great

15 letters:
Ivan the Terrible

17 letters:
Alexander the
  Great
Catherine the Great
Napoleon
  Bonaparte

18 letters:
Edward the
  Confessor

19 letters:
Richard the
  Lionheart
William the
  Conqueror

22 letters:
Suleiman the
  Magnificent

ENGLISH RULERS (IN CHRONOLOGICAL ORDER)

Saxons
Egbert
Ethelwulf
Ethelbald
Ethelbert
Ethel(d)red I
Alfred the Great
Edward the Elder
Athelstan
Edmund (I)
Edred
Edwy
Edgar

Edward the Martyr
Ethel(d)red II (the Unready)
Edmund II (Ironside)
Danes
Canute
Harold I
Hardecanute
Saxons
Edward the Confessor
Harold II
Normans
William (I) the Conqueror
William II Rufus

Henry I
Stephen
Plantagenets
Henry II
Richard I The Lionheart
John
Henry III
Edward I
Edward II
Edward III
Richard II
Lancasters
Henry IV
Henry V
Henry VI
Yorks
Edward IV
Edward V
Richard III
Tudors
Henry VII
Henry VIII
Edward VI
Lady Jane Grey
Mary (I)
Elizabeth (I)

Stuarts
James I (VI of Scotland)
Charles I (Stuart)
Commonwealth Protectors
Oliver Cromwell
Richard Cromwell
Stuarts
Charles II
James II (Interregnum)
William III and Mary II
Anne
Hanovers
George I
George II
George III
George IV
William IV
Victoria
Edward VII (Saxe-Coburg-Gotha)
Windsors
George V
Edward VIII (abdicated)
George VI
Elizabeth II

SCOTTISH RULERS (IN CHRONOLOGICAL ORDER)

Kenneth (I) M(a)cAlpin
Donald
Constantine I
Aedh
Eocha
Donald
Constantine II
Malcolm I
Indulph
Dubh
Cuilean
Kenneth II
Constantine III
Malcolm II
Duncan I
Macbeth
Lulach
Malcolm III
Donald Bane

Duncan II
Donald Bane
Edmund
Edgar
Alexander I
David I
John Baliol
Robert (the) Bruce
David II
Robert II
Robert III
James I
James II
James III
James IV
James V
Mary (Queen of Scots)
James VI

Russian federal republics

VOLGA DISTRICT

6 letters:
Mari El

7 letters:
Mariy El

8 letters:
Mordovia

Udmurtia

9 letters:
Chuvashia
Mordvinia

10 letters:
Tartarstan

13 letters:
Bashkortostan

NORTHERN CAUCASUS

7 letters:
Adygeya

8 letters:
Chechnia
Chechnya
Dagestan
Kalmykia

10 letters:
Ingushetia

15 letters:
Northern Ossetia

17 letters:
Kabardino-Balkaria

18 letters:
Karachay-Cherkessia
North Ossetia-Alania

NORTHWESTERN RUSSIA

4 letters:
Komi

7 letters:
Karelia

SIBERIA

4 letters:
Tuva

5 letters:
Altay

8 letters:
Buryatia

9 letters:
Khakassia

RUSSIAN FAR EAST

5 letters:
Sakha

S

Saint	Feast day
Agatha	5 February
Agnes	31 January
Aidan	31 August
Alban	22 June
Albertus Magnus	15 November
Aloysius (patron saint of youth)	21 June
Ambrose	7 December
Andrew (Scotland)	30 November
Anne	26 July
Anselm	21 April
Anthony *or* Antony	17 January
Anthony *or* Antony of Padua	13 June
Athanasius	2 May
Augustine of Hippo	28 August
Barnabas	11 June
Bartholomew	24 August
Basil	2 January
Bede	25 May
Benedict	11 July
Bernadette of Lourdes	16 April
Bernard of Clairvaux	20 August
Bernard of Menthon	28 May
Bonaventura *or* Bonaventure	15 July
Boniface	5 June
Brendan	16 May
Bridget, Bride *or* Brigid (Ireland)	1 February
Bridget *or* Birgitta (Sweden)	23 July
Catherine of Alexandria	25 November
Catherine of Siena (the Dominican Order)	29 April
Cecilia (music)	22 November
Charles Borromeo	4 November
Christopher (travellers)	25 July
Clare of Assisi	11 August
Clement I	23 November
Clement of Alexandria	5 December
Columba *or* Colmcille	9 June
Crispin (shoemakers)	25 October
Crispinian (shoemakers)	25 October
Cuthbert	20 March

Saints

Saint	Feast day
Cyprian	16 September
Cyril	14 February
Cyril of Alexandria	27 June
David (Wales)	1 March
Denis (France)	9 October
Dominic	7 August
Dorothy	6 February
Dunstan	19 May
Edmund	20 November
Edward the Confessor	13 October
Edward the Martyr	18 March
Elizabeth	5 November
Elizabeth of Hungary	17 November
Elmo	2 June
Ethelbert *or* Æthelbert	25 February
Francis of Assisi	4 October
Francis of Sales	24 January
Francis Xavier	3 December
Geneviève (Paris)	3 January
George (England)	23 April
Gertrude	16 November
Gilbert of Sempringham	4 February
Giles (cripples, beggars, and lepers)	1 September
Gregory I (the Great)	3 September
Gregory VII *or* Hildebrand	25 May
Gregory of Nazianzus	2 January
Gregory of Nyssa	9 March
Gregory of Tours	17 November
Hilary of Poitiers	13 January
Hildegard of Bingen	17 September
Helen *or* Helena	18 August
Helier	16 July
Ignatius	17 October
Ignatius of Loyola	31 July
Isidore of Seville	4 April
James	23 October
James the Less	3 May
Jane Frances de Chantal	12 December
Jerome	30 September
Joachim	26 July
Joan of Arc	30 May
John	27 December
John Bosco	31 January
John Chrysostom	13 September
John Ogilvie	10 March
John of Damascus	4 December
John of the Cross	14 December
John the Baptist	24 June
Joseph	19 March
Joseph of Arimathaea	17 March

Saint	Feast day
Joseph of Copertino	18 September
Jude	28 October
Justin	1 June
Kentigern *or* Mungo	14 January
Kevin	3 June
Lawrence	10 August
Lawrence O'Toole	14 November
Leger	2 October
Leo I (the Great)	10 November
Leo II	3 July
Leo III	12 June
Leo IV	17 July
Leonard	6 November
Lucy	13 December
Luke	18 October
Malachy	3 November
Margaret	20 July
Margaret of Scotland	10 June, 16 November (in Scotland)
Maria Goretti	6 July
Mark	25 April
Martha	29 July
Martin de Porres	3 November
Martin of Tours (France)	11 November
Mary	15 August
Mary Magdalene	22 July
Matthew *or* Levi	21 September
Matthias	14 May
Methodius	14 February
Michael	29 September
Neot	31 July
Nicholas (Russia, children, sailors, merchants, and pawnbrokers)	6 December
Nicholas I (the Great)	13 November
Ninian	16 September
Olaf *or* Olav (Norway)	29 July
Oliver Plunket *or* Plunkett	1 July
Oswald	28 February
Pachomius	14 May
Patrick (Ireland)	17 March
Paul	29 June
Paulinus	10 October
Paulinus of Nola	22 June
Peter *or* Simon Peter	29 June
Philip	3 May
Philip Neri	26 May
Pius V	30 April
Pius X	21 August
Polycarp	26 January *or* 23 February

Salts

Saint	Feast day
Rose of Lima	23 August
Sebastian	20 January
Silas	13 July
Simon Zelotes	28 October
Stanislaw *or* Stanislaus (Poland)	11 April
Stanislaus Kostka	13 November
Stephen	26 *or* 27 December
Stephen of Hungary	16 *or* 20 August
Swithin *or* Swithun	15 July
Teresa *or* Theresa of Avila	15 October
Thérèse de Lisieux	1 October
Thomas	3 July
Thomas à Becket	29 December
Thomas Aquinas	28 January
Thomas More	22 June
Timothy	26 January
Titus	26 January
Ursula	21 October
Valentine	14 February
Veronica	12 July
Vincent de Paul	27 September
Vitus	15 June
Vladimir	15 July
Wenceslaus *or* Wenceslas	28 September
Wilfrid	12 October

Salts

2 letters:
AB

4 letters:
Corn
NaCl
Rock
Soap
Urao

5 letters:
Azide
Borax
Urate

6 letters:
Aurate
Borate
Halite
Iodide
Malate
Mucate
Oleate
Osmate
Sebate
Sodium
Uranin

7 letters:
Bromate
Bromide
Caprate
Citrate
Cyanate
Formate
Glauber
Ioduret
Lactate
Lithate
Muriate
Nitrate
Nitrite
Osmiate

Oxalate
Picrate
Sulfite
Tannate

8 letters:
Alginate
Caproate
Cerusite
Chlorate
Chlorite
Chromate
Datolite
Malonate
Plumbite
Pyruvate
Resinate
Rochelle
Selenate
Stannate
Stearate

Suberate
Sulphate
Sulphite
Tartrate
Titanate
Vanadate
Xanthate

9 letters:
Aluminate
Aspartite
Caprylate
Carbamate
Carbonate
Cyclamate
Glutamate
Magnesium

Manganate
Palmitate
Periodate
Phosphate
Phthalate
Potassium
Succinate
Tellurate
Tungstate

10 letters:
Andalusite
Bichromate
Dithionate
Isocyanide
Pandermite
Propionate

Sulphonate

11 letters:
Bicarbonate
Carboxylate
Microcosmic
Monohydrate
Perchlorate
Sal ammoniac
Sal volatile
Thiocyanate

12 letters:
Ferricyanide
Thiosulphate

13 letters:
Hydrochloride

Satellites

EARTH

4 letters:
Moon

5 letters:
Astra (artificial)

Tiros (artificial)

JUPITER

2 letters:
Io

4 letters:
Leda
Teba

5 letters:
Carme
Elara
Karme
Metis

Thebe

6 letters:
Ananke
Europa
Metida
Pacife
Sinope

7 letters:
Amaltea
Gimalia

Himalia
Lisitea

8 letters:
Adrastea
Amalthea
Callisto
Galilean
Ganymede
Lysithia
Pasiphaë

SATURN

3 letters:
Pan

4 letters:
Rhea

5 letters:
Atlas
Dione
Janus
Mimas

Titan

6 letters:
Helene
Phoebe
Tethys

7 letters:
Calypso
Iapetus
Pandora

Telesto

8 letters:
Hyperion

9 letters:
Enceladus

10 letters:
Epimetheus
Prometheus

Sauces

URANUS

4 letters:
Puck

5 letters:
Ariel

6 letters:
Bianca
Juliet
Oberon

Portia

7 letters:
Belinda
Caliban
Miranda
Ophelia
Sycorax
Titania

Umbriel

8 letters:
Cordelia
Cressida
Rosalind

9 letters:
Desdemona

NEPTUNE

5 letters:
Naian

6 letters:
Nereid

Triton

7 letters:
Despina
Galatea

Larissa
Proteus

8 letters:
Thalassa

MARS

6 letters:
Deimos
Phobos

PLUTO

6 letters:
Charon

Sauces

2 letters:
HP®

3 letters:
Soy

4 letters:
Fish
Hard
Mint
Mole
Soja
Soya
Wine

5 letters:
Apple
Bread
Brown
Caper

Cream
Curry
Fudge
Garum
Gravy
Melba
Pesto
Salsa
Satay
Shoyu
White

6 letters:
Cheese
Chilli
Coulis
Creole
Fondue
Fu yong

Fu yung
Hoisin
Mornay
Nam pia
Orange
Oxymal
Oyster
Panada
Pistou
Relish
Sambal
Tamari
Tartar
Tomato

7 letters:
À la king
Alfredo
Custard

Ketchup
Newburg
Nuoc mam
Parsley
Passata
Rouille
Sabayon
Soubise
Suprême
Tabasco®
Tartare
Velouté

8 letters:
Barbecue
Béchamel
Chasseur
Chow-chow
Fenberry
Marinara
Matelote
Meunière
Mirepoix
Piri-piri

Ravigote
Red pesto
Salpicon
Verjuice

9 letters:
Allemanse
Béarnaise
Black bean
Bolognese
Carbonara
Chocolate
Cranberry
Enchilada
Espagnole
Rémoulade
Worcester

10 letters:
Bolognaise
Bordelaise
Chaudfroid
Cumberland
Mayonnaise

Mousseline
Piccalilli
Salad cream
Salsa verde
Stroganoff

11 letters:
Hollandaise
Horseradish
Vinaigrette

12 letters:
Brandy butter
Sweet-and-sour

13 letters:
Bourguignonne
Salad dressing

14 letters:
French dressing
Worcestershire

15 letters:
Russian dressing

Sausages

3 letters:
Sav

4 letters:
Lola

5 letters:
Black
Blood
Devon
Kiska
Kiske
Liver
Lorne
Lyons
Metts
Sujuk
Wurst

6 letters:
Banger
Garlic
Haggis
Hot dog

Kishka
Kishke
Lolita
Mirkas
Polony
Salami
Summer
Tuscan
Vienna
Wiener
Wienie

7 letters:
Abruzzo
Bologna
Cheerio
Chorizo
Frizzes
Kolbasa
Merguez
Saveloy
Soujouk
Yershig

Zampone

8 letters:
Cervelat
Chaurice
Chourico
Drisheen
Kielbasa
Lap chong
Lap chung
Linguica
Linguisa
Lop chong
Morcilla
Peperoni
Rohwurst
Teewurst
Toulouse

9 letters:
Andouille
Blutwurst
Bockwurst
Boerewors

Scarves

Bratwurst
Chipolata
Cotechino
Knoblauch
Landjager
Lap cheong
Longanisa
Longaniza
Loukanika
Mettwurst
Pepperoni
Red boudin
Saucisson
Sulzwurst

10 letters:
Bauerwurst
Boerewurst
Bruehwurst
Cumberland

Knackwurst
Knockwurst
Landjaeger
Liverwurst
Mettwaurst
Mortadella
Potato korv
Weisswurst

11 letters:
Bauernwurst
Boudin blanc
Boudin rouge
Frankfurter
Genoa salami
Grutzewurst
Knublewurst
Kochwuerste
Pinkelwurst
Weisswurste

White boudin
Wienerwurst
Zungenwurst

12 letters:
Andouillette
Bierschinken
Black pudding
Fleischwurst
White pudding

13 letters:
Schinkenwurst

14 letters:
Braunschweiger
Lebanon bologna
Medisterpoelse

15 letters:
Katenrauchwurst

Scarves

4 letters:
Doek
Haik
Hyke

5 letters:
Curch
Fichu
Haick
Pagri
Stole

6 letters:
Cravat
Haique

Madras
Rebozo
Tippet

7 letters:
Belcher
Dupatta
Muffler
Orarium
Tallith

8 letters:
Babushka
Cataract
Mantilla

Neckatee
Palatine
Trot-cosy
Trot-cozy
Vexillum

9 letters:
Comforter
Muffettee

10 letters:
Lambrequin

11 letters:
Nightingale

Schools

NAMES OF SCHOOLS

3 letters:
RAM

4 letters:
Dada
Eton
RADA

5 letters:
Perse
Slade
Stowe

6 letters:
Fettes
Harrow

Oundle
Repton

7 letters:
Bauhaus
Flemish
Lancing
Loretto

Roedean
Rossall

8 letters:
Barbizon
Benenden
Downside
Mannheim

9 letters:
Chartreux
Frankfurt

Tonbridge

10 letters:
Ampleforth
Manchester
Stonyhurst
Wellington
Winchester

11 letters:
Giggleswick
Gordonstoun

Marlborough

12 letters:
Charterhouse

TYPES OF SCHOOL

3 letters:
CAT
CTC
GPS
LSE
Uni

4 letters:
Co-ed
Poly
Prep
Tech

5 letters:
Kindy
Lycée

6 letters:
Hostel
Kindie

7 letters:
Academe
Academy
College
Convent
Crammer
Nursery
Varsity
Yeshiva

8 letters:
Seminary

9 letters:
Alma mater
Day school
Gymnasien
Gymnasium

Institute
Ivy League
Madrassah
Palaestra

10 letters:
Chautauqua
Dame school
High school
Pensionnat
Prep school
University

11 letters:
Charm school
Choir school
Drama school
First school
Grade school
Hedge-school
List D school
Lower school
Mixed school
Night school
Open College
Polytechnic
Reformatory
State school
Trade school
Upper school

12 letters:
Church school
Conservatory
Infant school
Junior school
Kindergarten
Magnet school

Middle school
Multiversity
Normal school
Progymnasium
Public school
Ragged school
Reform school
Summer school
Sunday school

13 letters:
Community home
Comprehensive
Conservatoire
Convent school
Council school
Grammar school
Junior college
Nursery school
Primary school
Private school
Sabbath school
Special school

14 letters:
Approved school
Bluecoat school
Boarding school
Hospital school
National School
Open University
Schola cantorum
Separate school
Village college

15 letters:
Civic university
Community school

Sea birds

Composite school
Finishing school
Parochial school
Secondary school
Single-sex school
Tertiary college

16 letters:
Classical college
Community college
Elementary school
Grant-aided school
Integrated school
Maintained school
Sixth-form college
Technical college

17 letters:
Direct-grant school
Independent school
Preparatory school
Residential school

Technology college

18 letters:
College of education
District high school
Great Public Schools
Intermediate school

19 letters:
Collegiate institute
Comprehensive school
Land grant university

20 letters:
Correspondence school

21 letters:
City technology college
Grant-maintained school
Secondary modern school

27 letters:
College of advanced technology

See also:
➤ **Degrees** ➤ **Colleges** ➤ **Education terms** ➤ **Ivy League universities** ➤ **Oxbridge colleges**

Sea birds

3 letters:
Auk
Cob
Ern
Mew

4 letters:
Cobb
Coot
Erne
Gull
Shag
Skua
Tara
Titi

5 letters:
Booby
Kawau
Prion

6 letters:
Auklet
Fulmar
Gannet
Korora
Petrel
Scoter
Sea-cob
Sea-mew
Seapie
Takapu

7 letters:
Oldwife
Sea duck
Seagull
Taranui

8 letters:
Black cap
Blue shag

Fish hawk
Murrelet
Old squaw
Skua-gull
Surf duck

9 letters:
Albatross
Black shag
Cormorant
Guillemot
Ivory gull
Kittiwake
Razorbill

10 letters:
Gooney bird
Mutton bird
Sea swallow
Shearwater
Surf scoter

11 letters:
Blue penguin
Caspian tern
Frigate bird
Herring gull
Kahawai bird
Storm petrel

12 letters:
Fairy penguin
Glaucous gull
Man-of-war bird
Stormy petrel
Velvet scoter

13 letters:
Little penguin
Oystercatcher

Wilson's petrel

14 letters:
Black guillemot
Razor-billed auk

15 letters:
Black-backed gull

16 letters:
White-fronted tern

17 letters:
Little blue penguin

18 letters:
Wandering
  albatross

19 letters:
Mother Carey's
  chicken
Tasmanian mutton
  bird

21 letters:
Short-tailed
  shearwater

Seafood

3 letters:
Cod
Dab
Eel

4 letters:
Bass
Carp
Clam
Crab
Hake
Huss
Ling
Pike
Pipi
Pout
Shad
Sild
Sole
Tuna

5 letters:
Bream
Brill
Koura
Perch
Prawn
Roach
Shark

Skate
Snoek
Snook
Sprat
Squid
Trout
Tunny
Wahoo
Whelk
Witch
Yabby

6 letters:
Bonito
Callop
Cockle
Dorado
Kipper
Marron
Megrim
Mullet
Mussel
Oyster
Pillie
Plaice
Saithe
Salmon
Shrimp
Turbot

Winkle
Yabbie
Zander

7 letters:
Abalone
Anchovy
Bloater
Blue cod
Catfish
Codling
Crawbob
Craybob
Craydab
Dogfish
Gemfish
Haddock
Halibut
Herring
Jewfish
Kahawai
Lobster
Morwong
Mud crab
Octopus
Pollack
Pomfret
Queenie
Redfish

Seals

Sardine
Scallop
Scollop
Snapper
Sockeye
Whiting

8 letters:
Clawchie
Coalfish
Crawfish
Crayfish
Flounder
Grayling
John Dory
Kingfish
Lumpfish
Mackerel
Monkfish
Mulloway
Nannygai
Pilchard
Rockfish
Sand crab
Tarakihi
Teraglin

Terakihi
Tilefish
Trevally
Wolffish

9 letters:
Blackfish
Blue manna
Clabby-doo
Clappy-doo
Dover sole
King prawn
Lemon sole
Red salmon
Swordfish
Whitebait

10 letters:
Balmain bug
Barramundi
Butterfish
Parrotfish
Red snapper
Tiger prawn

11 letters:
Banana prawn

Blue swimmer
Langoustine
School prawn
Sea cucumber
Yellow belly

12 letters:
Queen scallop
Rainbow trout
Skipjack tuna

13 letters:
Moreton Bay bug
Norway lobster

14 letters:
Dublin Bay prawn

16 letters:
Australian salmon
Greenland halibut

18 letters:
Shovel-nosed
  lobster

Seals

4 letters:
Harp
Monk

5 letters:
Eared
Great
Otary
Phoca
Silky

6 letters:
Hooded
Hudson

Ringed
Sealch
Sealgh
Selkie
Silkie

7 letters:
Earless
Harbour
Sea-bear
Weddell

8 letters:
Elephant

Seecatch
Zalophus

9 letters:
Crab-eater
Greenland
Pintadera

10 letters:
Pinnipedia
Seecatchie

11 letters:
Bladdernose

Sea mammals

4 letters:
Seal

6 letters:
Dugong
Sea cow
Walrus

7 letters:
Manatee

Sea lion

8 letters:
Harp seal
Sea horse

9 letters:
Eared seal

10 letters:
Hooded seal

11 letters:
Earless seal

12 letters:
Elephant seal

Seas and oceans

3 letters:
Ler
Med
Red

4 letters:
Aral
Azov
Dead
Java
Kara
Ross
Sulu

5 letters:
Banda
Black
Ceram
China
Coral
Hadal
Irish
Japan
North
South
Timor
White

6 letters:
Abssal
Aegean
Arctic
Baltic
Bering
Biscay
Celtic
Euxine
Flores

Indian
Inland
Ionian
Laptev
Scotia
Tasman
Tethys
Yellow

7 letters:
Andaman
Arabian
Arafura
Barents
Caspian
Celebes
Channel
Chukchi
Euripus
Galilee
Icarian
Lincoln
Marmara
Marmora
Okhotsk
Pacific
Pelagic
Polynya
Solomon
Weddell

8 letters:
Adriatic
Amundsen
Atlantic
Beaufort
Bismarck

Bosporus
Hwang Hai
Labrador
Ligurian
Sargasso
Southern
Tiberias

9 letters:
Antarctic
Bosphorus
Caribbean
East China
Greenland
Hudson Bay
Melanesia
Norwegian
Polynesia
Skagerrak
Thalassic

10 letters:
Philippine
South China
Tyrrhenian

11 letters:
Herring-pond
Spanish main

12 letters:
East Siberian
Nordenskjöld

13 letters:
Mediterranean

14 letters:
Bellingshausen

Seasons

Season	Related adjective
Spring	Vernal
Summer	Aestival *or* estival
Autumn	Autumnal
Winter	Hibernal *or* hiemal

Seats

3 letters:
Box
Pew
Pit

4 letters:
Banc
Love
Sofa
Sunk

5 letters:
Bench
Chair
Couch
Dicky
Divan
Perch
Sedes
Siege
Squab
Stool

6 letters:
Bucket
Canapé
Dickey
Houdah
Howdah
Humpty
Pouffe
Rumble
Saddle
Settee
Settle
Sunkie
Throne

7 letters:
Ejector
Ottoman
Palfrey
Pillion
Tonneau

8 letters:
Sedilium
Woolsack

9 letters:
Banquette
Bleachers
Davenport
Deckchair
Faldstool
Palanquin

10 letters:
Faldistory
Knifeboard
Strapontin
Subsellium
Sunlounger
Synthronus

12 letters:
Chaise longue
Rumble-tumble

Seaweeds

3 letters:
Ore

4 letters:
Agar
Alga
Kelp
Kilp
Nori
Tang
Ulva
Ware

5 letters:
Algae

Arame
Dulse
Fucus
Kombu
Laver
Varec
Vraic
Wrack

6 letters:
Desmid
Diatom
Sea-mat
Varech

Wakame
Wakane

7 letters:
Oarweed
Redware
Sea-lace
Sea-moss
Seaware

8 letters:
Chondrus
Conferva
Gulfweed
Porphyra

Rockweed
Sargasso
Sea-wrack

9 letters:
Carrageen
Coralline
Cystocarp
Laminaria
Nullipore

Seabottle
Sea-tangle

10 letters:
Badderlock
Carragheen
Ceylon moss
Sea-lettuce
Sea-whistle

11 letters:
Bladderwort
Sea-furbelow

12 letters:
Bladderwrack
Enteromorpha
Heterocontae
Peacock's tail

Seven against Thebes

6 letters:
Tydeus

8 letters:
Adrasyus
Capaneus

9 letters:
Polynices

10 letters:
Amphiaraüs
Hippomedon

13 letters:
Parthenopaeus

Seven deadly sins

4 letters:
Envy
Lust

5 letters:
Anger

Pride
Sloth

7 letters:
Avarice

8 letters:
Gluttony

12 letters:
Covetousness

Shakespeare

CHARACTERS IN SHAKESPEARE

Character	Play
Sir Andrew Aguecheek	Twelfth Night
Antonio	The Merchant of Venice
Antony	Antony and Cleopatra, Julius Caesar
Ariel	The Tempest
Aufidius	Coriolanus
Autolycus	The Winter's Tale
Banquo	Macbeth
Bassanio	The Merchant of Venice
Beatrice	Much Ado About Nothing
Sir Toby Belch	Twelfth Night
Benedick	Much Ado About Nothing
Bolingbroke	Richard II
Bottom	A Midsummer Night's Dream
Brutus	Julius Caesar
Caliban	The Tempest
Casca	Julius Caesar

Shakespeare

Character	Play
Cassio	Othello
Cassius	Julius Caesar
Claudio	Much Ado About Nothing, Measure for Measure
Claudius	Hamlet
Cleopatra	Antony and Cleopatra
Cordelia	King Lear
Coriolanus	Coriolanus
Cressida	Troilus and Cressida
Demetrius	A Midsummer Night's Dream
Desdemona	Othello
Dogberry	Much Ado About Nothing
Edmund	King Lear
Enobarbus	Antony and Cleopatra
Falstaff	Henry IV Parts I and II, The Merry Wives of Windsor
Ferdinand	The Tempest
Feste	Twelfth Night
Fluellen	Henry V
Fool	King Lear
Gertrude	Hamlet
Gloucester	King Lear
Goneril	King Lear
Guildenstern	Hamlet
Hamlet	Hamlet
Helena	All's Well that Ends Well, A Midsummer Night's Dream
Hermia	A Midsummer Night's Dream
Hero	Much Ado About Nothing
Hotspur	Henry IV Part I
Iago	Othello
Jaques	As You Like It
John of Gaunt	Richard II
Juliet	Romeo and Juliet
Julius Caesar	Julius Caesar
Katharina or Kate	The Taming of the Shrew
Kent	King Lear
Laertes	Hamlet
Lear	King Lear
Lysander	A Midsummer Night's Dream
Macbeth	Macbeth
Lady Macbeth	Macbeth
Macduff	Macbeth
Malcolm	Macbeth
Malvolio	Twelfth Night
Mercutio	Romeo and Juliet
Miranda	The Tempest
Oberon	A Midsummer Night's Dream
Octavius	Antony and Cleopatra
Olivia	Twelfth Night

Character	Play
Ophelia	Hamlet
Orlando	As You Like It
Orsino	Twelfth Night
Othello	Othello
Pandarus	Troilus and Cressida
Perdita	The Winter's Tale
Petruchio	The Taming of the Shrew
Pistol	Henry IV Part II, Henry V, The Merry Wives of Windsor
Polonius	Hamlet
Portia	The Merchant of Venice
Prospero	The Tempest
Puck	A Midsummer Night's Dream
Mistress Quickly	The Merry Wives of Windsor
Regan	King Lear
Romeo	Romeo and Juliet
Rosalind	As You Like It
Rosencrantz	Hamlet
Sebastian	The Tempest, Twelfth Night
Shylock	The Merchant of Venice
Thersites	Troilus and Cressida
Timon	Timon of Athens
Titania	A Midsummer Night's Dream
Touchstone	As You Like It
Troilus	Troilus and Cressida
Tybalt	Romeo and Juliet
Viola	Twelfth Night

PLAYS OF SHAKESPEARE

6 letters:
Hamlet
Henry V

7 letters:
Macbeth
Othello

8 letters:
King John
King Lear

9 letters:
Cymbeline
Henry VIII
Richard II

10 letters:
Coriolanus
Richard III
The Tempest

11 letters:
As You Like It

12 letters:
Henry IV Part I
Henry VI Part I
Julius Caesar
Twelfth Night

13 letters:
Henry IV Part II
Henry VI Part II
Timon of Athens

14 letters:
Henry VI Part III
Romeo and Juliet
The Winter's Tale

15 letters:
Titus Andronicus

Sharks

Sharks

3 letters:
Cow
Dog

4 letters:
Blue
Huss
Mako
Noah
Rigg
Tope

5 letters:
Angel
Gummy
Nurse
Tiger
Whale

6 letters:
Beagle
Carpet
School
Sea-ape

Whaler

7 letters:
Basking
Dogfish
Requiem
Reremai
Soupfin
Zygaena

8 letters:
Mackerel
Monkfish
Penny-dog
Rhinodon
Sailfish
Thrasher
Thresher

9 letters:
Angelfish
Grey nurse
Houndfish
Lemonfish

Porbeagle
Rhineodon
Seven-gill
Six-gilled
Wobbegong

10 letters:
Blue whaler
Bonnethead
Cestracion
Demoiselle
Hammerhead
Nursehound
Shovelhead

11 letters:
Blue pointer
Plagiostomi
Smoothhound

12 letters:
Bronze whaler

Sheep

4 letters:
Down
Kent
Lonk
Mule
Soay
Udad

5 letters:
Ammon
Ancon
Jacob
Lleyn
Texel
Urial

6 letters:
Aoudad
Argali
Bharal
Bident
Burhel
Burrel
Exmoor
Masham
Merino
Muflon
Musmon
Oorial
Orkney
Oxford

7 letters:
Ancones
Bighorn
Boreray
Burrell
Caracul
Cheviot
Colbred
Dinmont
Karakul
Lincoln
Loghtan
Loghtyn
Mouflon
Musimon
Ryeland
St. Kilda

Suffolk

8 letters:
Cheviots
Cotswold
Dartmoor
Drysdale
Herdwick
Loaghtan
Moufflon
Mountain
Polwarth
Portland
Shetland

9 letters:
Blackface
Blue-faced
Broadtail
Cambridge
Coopworth
Dalesbred
Fat-tailed
Hampshire
Hebridian
Kerry Hill
Leicester
Llanwenog
Marco Polo
Perendale
Romeldale
Rough Fell
Shorthorn
Southdown
Swaledale
Teeswater
Welsh Mule

10 letters:
Clun Forest
Corriedale
Dorset Down
Dorset Horn
Exmoor Horn
Hill Radnor
Shropshire

11 letters:
Île de France
Manx Loghtan

Norfolk Horn
Rambouillet
Romney Marsh
Wensleydale

12 letters:
British Texel

13 letters:
East Friesland
Hampshire Down
Mountain sheep
Rouge de l'Ouest
Welsh Halfbred
Welsh Mountain
Wiltshire Horn

14 letters:
British Vendéen
Devon Closewool
North Ronaldsay

15 letters:
Border Leicester
English Halfbred
Hexham Leicester
Lincoln Longwool
Oxfordshire Down

16 letters:
British Friesland
British Milksheep
British Oldenburg
Scottish Halfbred

17 letters:
British Charollais
Leicester Longwool
Scottish Blackface
Welsh Hill
  Speckled
White Face
  Dartmoor

18 letters:
Beulah Speckled-
face
Black Welsh
  Mountain
British Bleu du
  Maine

Shellfish

South Wales Mountain
Whitefaced Woodland

Shellfish

19 letters:
Derbyshire Gritstone
North Country Cheviot
Wensleydale Longwool

20 letters:
Brecknock Hill Cheviot

24 letters:
Devon and Cornwall Longwool
Welsh Mountain Badger Faced

3 letters:
Mya
Top

4 letters:
Arca
Boat
Clam
Clio
Crab
Lamp
Paua
Pawa
Pipi
Tusk
Unio

5 letters:
Bulla
Capiz
Chank
Cohog
Conch
Cowry
Doris
Drill
Gaper
Helix
Koura
Murex
Olive
Ormer
Pinna
Polyp
Prawn
Razor
Sepia
Solen
Spoot
Squid

Turbo
Venus
Whelk
Yabby
Zimbi

6 letters:
Buckie
Chiton
Cockle
Cowrie
Cuttle
Limpet
Marron
Mussel
Ostrea
Oyster
Pecten
Pereia
Pholas
Poulpe
Purple
Quahog
Sea-ear
Sea-pen
Stromb
Tellen
Tellin
Teredo
Triton
Wakiki
Winkle
Yabbie

7 letters:
Abalone
Balanus
Bivalve
Crawbob
Craybob

Craydab
Isopoda
Lobster
Mud crab
Octopod
Octopus
Piddock
Quahaug
Scallop
Scollop
Sea-hare
Sea-slug
Toheroa
Torpedo
Trochus
Vitrina

8 letters:
Ammonite
Argonaut
Ark-shell
Chelonia
Clawchie
Copepoda
Crawfish
Crayfish
Deerhorn
Escallop
Haliotis
Nautilus
Ostracod
Pteropod
Sand crab
Saxicava
Sea-lemon
Shipworm
Strombus
Trivalve
Univalve
Xenophya

9 letters:
Balamnite
Belemnite
Blue manna
Clabby-doo
Clappy-doo
Cone-shell
Crustacea
Dentalium
Gastropod
King prawn
Langouste
Monocoque
Neopilina
Scalarium
Thermidor
Tusk-shell
Wing-shell

10 letters:
Acorn-shell

Amphineura
Cuttlefish
Gasteropod
Periwinkle
Razorshell
Scaphopoda
Stomatopod
Swan-mussel
Turritella
Wentletrap

11 letters:
Banana prawn
Blue swimmer
Foraminifer
Globigerina
Langoustine
Paper-sailor
School prawn
Soldier crab
Tectibranch
Trochophore

12 letters:
Malacostraca
Pelican's-foot

13 letters:
Lamellibranch
Moreton Bay bug
Norway lobster
Opisthobranch
Paper nautilus

14 letters:
Dublin Bay prawn
Pearly nautilus

16 letters:
Freshwater shrimp

18 letters:
Shovel-nosed
  lobster

Ships, parts of

3 letters:
Bow
Gyn
Jib
Rig

4 letters:
Amas
Beam
Bung
Bunk
Deck
Foil
Foot
Gaff
Hank
Head
Helm
Hull
Keel
Line
Loof
Luff
Mast
Peak

Prow
Rode
Rope
Sail
Skin
Slot
Spar
Yard

5 letters:
Berth
Bilge
Bitts
Blade
Block
Cabin
Chine
Chock
Cleat
Flare
Genoa
Hatch
Hoist
Kedge
Leech

Lines
Loofe
Oakum
Screw
Sheet
Slide
Staff
Stern
Wheel
Winch

6 letters:
Anchor
Bridge
Burgee
Colors
Davite
Dinghy
Dorade
Drogue
Fender
Fiddle
Fo'c'sle
Frames
Galley

Ships, parts of

Gunnel
Jigger
Rudder
Sheave
Shroud

7 letters:
Ballast
Bearers
Bobstay
Boomkin
Buoyage
Capstan
Channel
Coaming
Cordage
Dunnage
Fardage
Fin keel
Gallows
Gudgeon
Gunwale
Halyard
Iron-jib
Jibboom
Jib stay
Nippers
Outhaul
Quarter
Raffees
Rigging
Sea cock
Snubber
Toe rail
Topmast
Trysail
Yard arm

8 letters:
Backstay
Boom-vang
Bowsprit
Bulkhead
Bulwarks
Ditty box
Fife rail
Foredeck
Foremast
Forepeak
Foresail

Forestay
Full keel
Headsail
Headstay
Jib sheet
Leeboard
Life boat
Lifeline
Life raft
Mainmast
Mainsail
Masthead
Moonsail
Poop deck
Porthole
Scuppers
Shear pin
Staysail
Storm jib
Telltale
Trip line

9 letters:
Bilge keel
Bilge pump
Bitter end
Cabin sole
Crow's nest
Deck plate
Gang plank
Hard chine
Hawse hole
King spoke
Lazarette
Lazyjacks
Lazysheet
Main sheet
Moonraker
Outrigger
Preventer
Royal mast
Sea-anchor
Sheathing
Spinnaker
Stanchion
Traveller

10 letters:
Anchor ball
Canoe stern

Figurehead
Fore castle
Jib netting
Jib topsail
Jigger-mast
Martingale
Mizzen mast
Mizzen sail
Riding sail
Rudder post
Sailing-rig
Sidelights
Turnbuckle

11 letters:
Anchor chain
Anchor light
Bosun's chair
Carline wood
Chafing gear
Foretopmast
Heaving line
Holding tank
Main topsail
Mooring line
Planing-hull
Sampson post
Spring lines
Towing light

12 letters:
Anchor locker
Bosun's locker
Charley noble
Companionway
Forestaysail
Hatch coaming
Kicking-strap
Reefing lines

13 letters:
Flame arrester
Iron-spinnaker
Running lights
Spinnaker boom
Spinnaker lift
Spinnaker pole
Stability sail

14 letters:
Anchor windlass

Courtesy ensign
Mizzen staysail
Running rigging

15 letters:
Running backstay

16 letters:
Painted waterline

17 letters:
Spinnaker pole lift

Shirts

3 letters:
Tee

4 letters:
Bush
Hair
Polo
Sark

5 letters:
Dress
Kurta

6 letters:
Banyan
Blouse

Boiled
Camise
Guimpe
Khurta
Skivvy
Sports
T-shirt

7 letters:
Chemise
Dashiki
Grandad
Kerbaya

8 letters:
Lava-lava

Swanndri®

9 letters:
Garibaldi
Jacky Howe

10 letters:
Overblouse

11 letters:
Middy blouse

13 letters:
Cover-shoulder

Shoes and boots

3 letters:
Dap
Tie

4 letters:
Boot
Clog
Flat
Geta
Muil
Mule
Pump
Sock
Soft
Spat
Vamp
Vibs
Zori

5 letters:
Court

Gatty
Plate
Sabot
Scuff
Spike
Stoga
Stogy
Suede
Track
Wader
Wedge
Welly

6 letters:
Arctic
Ballet
Bootee
Brogan
Brogue
Buskin

Chopin
Flatty
Gaiter
Galosh
Golosh
Jandal®
Lace-up
Loafer
Mukluk
Oxford
Panton
Patten
Racket
Rivlin
Saddle
Safety
Sandal
Sannie
Slip-on
Vamper

Shrews and other insectivores

Vibram®
Wedgie

7 letters:
Blucher
Bottine
Casuals
Chopine
Cothurn
Creeper
Flattie
Galoche
Ghillie
Gumboot
Gumshoe
Gym shoe
High-low
Open-toe
Oxonian
Peeptoe
Racquet
Rubbers
Rullion
Sabaton
Slipper
Sneaker
Top boot
Trainer

8 letters:
Athletic
Balmoral
Crowboot
Deck shoe
Flip-flop

Golf shoe
Half boot
High heel
Jackboot
Larrigan
Mocassin
Moccasin
Moonboot
Overshoe
Pantofle
Platform
Plimsole
Plimsoll
Poulaine
Rock boot
Sandshoe
Snowshoe
Solleret
Stiletto
Velskoen

9 letters:
Ankle boot
Biker boot
Cothurnus
Court shoe
Doc Marten®
Field boot
Mary-Janes®
Pantoffle
Pantoufle
Rope-soled
Scarpetto
Slingback

Thigh boot
Track shoe
Veldskoen
Wedge heel

10 letters:
Bovver boot
Chukka boot
Cowboy boot
Espadrille
Kitten heel
Kurdaitcha
Tennis shoe
Veld-schoen

11 letters:
Hessian boot
Hobnail boot
Hush-puppies®
Running shoe

12 letters:
Co-respondent
Football boot

Kletterschue
Surgical boot
Training shoe
Winkle-picker

14 letters:
Brothel creeper
Wellington boot

15 letters:
Brothel creepers

Shrews and other insectivores

4 letters:
Mole

5 letters:
Shrew

6 letters:
Desman
Tenrec

7 letters:
Moon rat

9 letters:
Shrew mole
Solenodon
Tree shrew

10 letters:
Shrewmouse

Water shrew

12 letters:
Star-nose mole

13 letters:
Elephant shrew
Star-nosed mole

Shrubs

3 letters:
Box
Kat
Qat
Rue
Tea
Wax

4 letters:
Coca
Cola
Hebe
Nabk
Olea
Rhus
Rose
Ruta
Titi
Tutu

5 letters:
Aalii
Brere
Briar
Brier
Broom
Brush
Buaze
Buazi
Caper
Gorse
Hakea
Heath
Henna
Lilac
Maqui
Monte
Pyxie
Salal
Savin
Senna
Thyme
Toyon
Wahoo
Yacca
Yacka
Yapon

Yupon
Zamia

6 letters:
Acacia
Alhagi
Aucuba
Azalea
Bauera
Correa
Cotton
Crowea
Daphne
Fatsia
Feijoa
Frutex
Fynbos
Garrya
Jojoba
Laurel
Lignum
Manoao
Maquis
Matico
Mimosa
Myrica
Myrtle
Pituri
Privet
Protea
Savine
Sumach
Tawine
Tutsan
Yaupon

7 letters:
Arboret
Arbutus
Banksia
Boronia
Bramble
Bullace
Cascara
Cytisus
Dogwood
Emu bush

Epacris
Fuchsia
Geebong
Geebung
Heather
Hop-tree
Jasmine
Jibbong
Juniper
Lantana
Mesquit
Oleacea
Olearia
Rhatany
Romneya
Shallon
Skimmia
Tarwine
Tauhinu
Tea-tree
Waratah

8 letters:
Acanthus
Barberry
Bilberry
Black boy
Bluebush
Buddleia
Camellia
Clematis
Coprosma
Gardenia
Hardhack
Hawthorn
Hibiscus
Inkberry
Jetbread
Laburnum
Lavender
Magnolia
Ninebark
Ocotillo
Oleander
Rock rose
Rosemary
Saltbush

Silicas and silicates

Shadbush
Spekboom
Sweetsop
Tamarisk

9 letters:
Andromeda
Blueberry
Buckthorn
Clianthus
Coyotillo
Cranberry
Daisy bush
Firethorn
Forsythia
Grevillea
Hydrangea
Jaborandi
Jessamine
Kerrawang
Liquorice
Melaleuca
Mistletoe

Patchouli
Poison ivy
Poison oak
Raspberry
Spicebush
Waxflower
Yacca bush

10 letters:
Blackthorn
Cottonbush
Cottonwood
Crossandra
Eriostemon
Frangipani
Gooseberry
Horizontal
Joshua tree
Laurustine
Mock orange
Parkleaves
Poinsettia
Potentilla

Pyracantha
Redcurrant
Strawberry
Supplejack

11 letters:
Beautybrush
Blanket bush
Bottlebrush
Honeysuckle
Pittosporum
Steeplebush

12 letters:
Blackcurrant
Rhododendron
Southernwood

13 letters:
Christmas bush
Crown-of-thorns

18 letters:
Geraldton
   waxflower

Silicas and silicates

4 letters:
Opal

5 letters:
Chert
Silex

6 letters:
Albite
Humite
Iolite
Pinite

7 letters:
Kyanite
Olivine
Tripoli

Zeolite

8 letters:
Analcite
Datolite
Diopside
Dioptase
Saponite

9 letters:
Chabazite
Hiddenite
Penninite
Rhodonite
Scapolite
Tridymite

10 letters:
Andalusite
Float-stone
Kieselguhr
Staurolite
Ultrabasic

11 letters:
Vermiculite

12 letters:
Cristobalite
Monticellite

15 letters:
Montmorillonite

Silks

4 letters:
Corn
Flox
Pulu
Tram

5 letters:
Atlas
Crape
Crepe
Flosh
Floss
Gazar
Ninon
Satin
Seric
Surah
Tabby
Tasar
Tulle

6 letters:
Dupion
Faille
Kincob
Pongee
Samite
Sendal

Shalli
Sleave
Tussah
Tusseh
Tusser
Velvet

7 letters:
Alamode
Brocade
Chiffon
Foulard
Marabou
Organza
Ottoman
Sarsnet
Schappe
Tabaret
Taffeta
Tiffany
Tussore

8 letters:
Barathea
Chenille
Duchesse
Florence
Lustrine

Lustring
Makimono
Marabout
Paduasoy
Prunella
Prunelle
Prunello
Sarsenet
Shantung
Sien-tsan

9 letters:
Charmeuse®
Filoselle
Georgette
Matelasse
Parachute
Sericeous
Serigraph

10 letters:
Florentine
Lutestring
Peau de soie

11 letters:
Thistledown

Skin, afflictions of

4 letters:
Boba
Buba
Rash
Yaws

5 letters:
Favus
Hives
Mange
Pinta
Tinea

6 letters:
Cowpox
Dartre
Herpes
Livedo

Morula
Sapego
Scurvy
Tetter

7 letters:
Ecthyma
Prurigo
Rosacea
Scabies
Serpigo
Verruca
Verruga

8 letters:
Chloasma
Cyanosis
Dyschroa

Exanthem
Impetigo
Miliaria
Pyoderma
Ringworm
Rose-rash
Vaccinia
Vitiligo
Xanthoma

9 letters:
Chloracne
Exanthema
Pemphigus
Psoriasis

10 letters:
Dermatitis

Skirts

Dermatosis
Erysipelas
Framboesia
Ichthyosis
Pityriasis
Seborrhoea

Strophulus

11 letters:
Mal del pinto

12 letters:
Sclerodermia

13 letters:
Leishmaniasis
Lupus vulgaris

Skirts

4 letters:
Bell
Full
Hoop
Hula
Kilt
Mini
Ra-ra
Tace
Tutu

5 letters:
A-line
Grass
Harem
Pareo
Pareu
Tasse

6 letters:
Dirndl
Hobble
Pencil
Peplum

Piu-piu
Riding
Sarong
Taslet
Tasset
Tonlet

7 letters:
Culotte
Divided
Filibeg
Lamboys

8 letters:
Bouffant
Culottes
Fillibeg
Half-slip
Lava-lava
Philibeg
Puffball
Wrapover

9 letters:
Cheongsam

Crinoline
Gabardine
Gaberdine
Maxiskirt
Midiskirt
Miniskirt
Overskirt
Petticoat
Waist-slip
Wrapround

10 letters:
Fustanella
Fustanelle
Microskirt
Underskirt
Wraparound

11 letters:
Drop-waisted

13 letters:
Button-through

Snails, slugs and other gastropods

4 letters:
Slug

5 letters:
Conch
Cowry
Murex
Ormer
Snail
Whelk

6 letters:
Cowrie

Limpet
Sea-ear
Triton
Winkle

7 letters:
Abalone
Sea hare
Sea slug

8 letters:
Ear shell
Top-shell

10 letters:
Nudibranch
Periwinkle
Roman snail
Wentletrap

13 letters:
Ramshorn snail

Snakes

3 letters:
Asp
Boa
Rat

4 letters:
Boma
Bull
Corn
Habu
Hoop
King
Milk
Naga
Naia
Naja
Pipe
Rock
Seps
Tree
Whip

5 letters:
Adder
Blind
Brown
Cobra
Congo
Coral
Cribo
Elaps
Glass
Grass
Krait
Mamba
Mulga
Racer
Tiger
Viper

Water

6 letters:
Carpet
Clotho
Daboia
Dipsas
Dugite
Ellops
Garter
Indigo
Karait
Python
Ribbon
Smooth
Taipan
Thirst
Uraeus
Vasuki

7 letters:
Camoodi
Coluber
Diamond
Hognose
Langaha
Rattler

8 letters:
Anaconda
Cerastes
Jararaca
Jararaka
Lachesis
Mocassin
Moccasin
Pit-viper
Ringhals
Ringneck
Rinkhals

Slowworm
Spitting
Sucuruju
Surucucu
Takshaka

9 letters:
Blue-racer
Boomslang
Coachwhip
Hamadryad
Horsewhip
King cobra
Kingsnake
Puff-adder
River jack
Sand viper

10 letters:
Bandy-bandy
Blacksnake
Bush-master
Copperhead
Death-adder
Dendrophis
Fer-de-lance
Homorelaps
Massasauga
Sidewinder

11 letters:
Amphisbaena
Cottonmouth
Diamond-back
Horned viper

13 letters:
Water moccasin

17 letters:
Timber rattlesnake

Snooker and billiards terms

1 letter:
D

3 letters:
Lag
Pot

Red
Top

4 letters:
Ball
Blue

Draw
Foul
Kick
Kiss
Pink

Socks and tights

Rack
Rest
Side
Spot
Stun

5 letters:
Baize
Baulk
Black
Break
Brown
Carom
Chalk
Fluke
Frame
Green
In-off
Jenny
Massé
Nurse
Plant
Screw
White

6 letters:
Bridge
Cannon
Cue tip
Double
Hazard
Miscue
Pocket
Safety
Spider
Yellow

7 letters:
Bouclée
Bricole
Cue ball
Cushion
English
Scratch
Snooker

8 letters:
Free ball
Half-butt

Headrail
Spot ball
Triangle

9 letters:
Baulkline
Clearance
Long jenny
Plain ball

10 letters:
Drop cannon
Object ball
Short jenny

11 letters:
Whitechapel

12 letters:
Cue extension
Maximum break

13 letters:
Nursery cannon

Socks and tights

4 letters:
Hose
Sock

5 letters:
Putty
Stock

6 letters:
Anklet
Argyle
Nylons
Puttee
Stay-up

Tights

7 letters:
Bed sock
Maillot
Pop sock

8 letters:
Half-hose
Stocking

9 letters:
Ankle sock
Bobby sock

Legwarmer
Pantihose
Pantyhose

10 letters:
Slouch sock

12 letters:
Knee-high sock

13 letters:
Lisle stocking

Sofas

5 letters:
Couch
Divan
Futon
Squab

6 letters:
Canapé
Chaise
Day bed
Lounge
Settee

Settle

7 letters:
Bergère
Sofa bed
Vis-à-vis

8 letters:
Love seat

9 letters:
Davenport

Tête-à-tête

11 letters:
Studio couch

12 letters:
Chaise longue
Chesterfield

Sounds

4 letters:
Jura

5 letters:
Puget
Smith

6 letters:
Achill
Nootka
Tromsø

7 letters:
Mcmurdo
Milford
Pamlico

8 letters:
Plymouth
Scoresby
The Sound

9 letters:
Lancaster

10 letters:
Kilbrennan
King George

12 letters:
Sound of Sleat

14 letters:
Queen Charlotte

Spiders and other arachnids

3 letters:
Red

4 letters:
Bird
Mite
Tick
Wolf

5 letters:
Money
Water

6 letters:
Aranea
Chigoe
Diadem
Epeira
Jigger
Katipo
Lycosa
Mygale
Redbug
Violin

7 letters:
Chigger
Hunting
Jumping

Red-back
Solpuga
Spinner

8 letters:
Arachnid
Araneida
Attercop
Cardinal
Ethercap
Ettercap
Huntsman
Itch mite
Podogona
Sand flea
Trapdoor

9 letters:
Bobbejaan
Funnel-web
Harvester
Orb-weaver
Phalangid
Ricinulei
Tarantula

10 letters:
Bird spider
Black widow

Cheese mite
Harvestman
Pycnogonid
Spider mite
Wolf spider

11 letters:
House spider
Money spider
Vinegarroon
Water spider

12 letters:
Book scorpion
Jockey spider
Whip scorpion

13 letters:
Daddy-longlegs
False scorpion
Hunting spider
Jumping spider
Red-back spider

14 letters:
Cardinal spider
Trap-door spider

Sports

2 letters:
RU

4 letters:
Golf
Polo
Pool
Sumo

5 letters:
Bandy
Bowls
Darts
Fives
Rugby
Sambo
Skeet

6 letters:
Aikido
Boules
Boxing
Hockey
Hurley
Karate
Pelota
Quoits
Savate
Shinty
Soccer
Squash
Tennis

7 letters:
Angling
Archery
Camogie
Cricket
Croquet
Curling
Cycling
Fencing
Fishing
Gliding
Hurling
Jai alai
Kabbadi
Netball
Rackets
Snooker

8 letters:
Aquatics
Baseball
Coursing
Falconry
Football
Goalball
Handball
Korfball
Lacrosse
Octopush
Pétanque
Rounders
Shooting
Skittles
Softball
Speedway
Tug-of-war

9 letters:
Autocross
Badminton
Billiards
Decathlon
Ice hockey
Potholing
Skijoring
Skydiving
Stool ball
Triathlon
Water polo
Wrestling

10 letters:
Ballooning
Basketball
Candlepins
Cyclo-cross
Drag-racing
Fly-fishing
Fox-hunting
Gymnastics
Kickboxing
Lawn tennis
Paddleball
Paraskiing
Real tennis
Rugby union
Volleyball

11 letters:
Hang gliding
Parachuting
Paragliding
Parasailing
Rugby league
Table tennis
Windsurfing

12 letters:
Bullfighting
Cockfighting
Orienteering
Parascending
Pigeon racing
Rock climbing
Roller hockey
Speed-skating
Steeplechase
Trampolining
Trapshooting
Wakeboarding

13 letters:
Roller skating
Rugby football
Squash rackets
Tenpin bowling
Weightlifting

14 letters:
Gaelic football
Mountaineering
Sambo wrestling

15 letters:
Australian Rules
Greyhound racing

16 letters:
American football
Canadian football
Modern pentathlon

17 letters:
Five-a-side
    football

18 letters:
Clay pigeon
    shooting

Rhythmic
gymnastics

19 letters:
Association
football

23 letters:
Australian Rules
football

See also:

➤ **American football teams** ➤ **Athletic events** ➤ **Ball games** ➤ **Baseball teams** ➤ **Boxing weights** ➤ **Cricketers** ➤ **Equestrianism** ➤ **Fencing terms** ➤ **Football** ➤ **Football clubs** ➤ **Footballers** ➤ **Golfers** ➤ **Golf terms** ➤ **Grand Prix circuits** ➤ **Gymnastic events** ➤ **Martial arts** ➤ **Motor sports** ➤ **Rugby terms** ➤ **Snooker and billiards terms** ➤ **Sportspeople** ➤ **Swimming strokes** ➤ **Tennis players** ➤ **Tennis terms** ➤ **Water sports** ➤ **Winter sports**

Sportspeople

3 letters:
Coe, *Sebastian*

4 letters:
Anne, *Princess*
Dean, *Christopher*
Leng, *Virginia*
Lowe, *John*
Rose, *Sir Alec*
Ruth, *Babe*
Witt, *Katarina*

5 letters:
Blyth, *Sir Chay*
Curry, *John*
Davis, *Steve*
Ebdon, *Peter*
Lewis, *Carl*
Lewis, *Denise*
Meade, *Richard*
Orser, *Brian*
Ovett, *Steve*
Owens, *Jesse*
Smith, *Harvey*
Spitz, *Mark*
Stark, *Ian*
Viren, *Lasse*
Wells, *Allan*
White, *Jimmy*

6 letters:
Broome, *David*

Davies, *Sharron*
Foster, *Brendan*
Foster, *Tim*
Gunnel, *Sally*
Hendry, *Stephen*
Holmes, *Kelly*
Joiner, *Florence
Griffith*
Jordan, *Michael*
Korbut, *Olga*
Martin, *Rhona*
Palmer, *Lucinda
Prior*
Schenk, *Christaian*
Wilson, *Jockey*

7 letters:
Bristow, *Eric*
Cousins, *Robin*
Edwards, *Eddie 'The
Eagle'*
Edwards, *Jonathan*
Fosbury, *Dick*
Francis, *Claire*
Freeman, *Cathy*
Higgins, *Alex
'Hurricane'*
Johnson, *Ben*
Pinsent, *Matthew*
Reardon, *Ray*
Simpson, *O(renthal)*

J(ames)
Torvill, *Jayne*
Zvereva, *Ellina*

8 letters:
Boardman, *Chris*
Brabants, *Tim*
Chataway,
Christopher
Christie, *Linford*
Comaneci, *Nadia*
Hamilton, *Scott*
Petrenko, *Viktor*
Redgrave, *Steve*
Thompson, *Daley*
Thorburn, *Cliff*

9 letters:
Bannister, *Roger*
Bullimore, *Tony*
Cracknell, *James*
Schumaker, *Michael*

10 letters:
Chichester, *Sir
Francis*

11 letters:
Weissmuller,
Johnny

Stars and constellations

STARS

3 letters:
Sol

4 letters:
Argo
Grus
Idol
Lyra
Mira
Pavo
Pole
Ursa
Vega
Vela

5 letters:
Acrux
Agena
Algol
Ceres
Deneb
Draco
Dubhe
Hyads
Indus
Lupus
Mensa
Merak
Mizar
Norma
North
Polar
Rigel
Rigil
Venus
Virgo
Wagon
Whale

6 letters:
Alioth
Alkaid
Altair
Aquila
Auriga

Boötes
Carina
Castor
Cygnus
Dorado
Esther
Fornax
Hyades
Megrez
Merope
Octans
Phecda
Plough
Pollux
Psyche
Puppis
Saturn
Sirius
Sothis
The Sun
Uranus
Vesper
Volans

7 letters:
Antares
Calaeno
Canopus
Capella
Cepheus
Columba
Dolphin
Lucifer
Phoenix
Polaris
Procyon
Proxima
Regulus
Serpens
Triones
Wagoner

8 letters:
Achernar

Arcturus
Barnard's
Canicula
Circinus
Denebola
Equuleus
Hesperus
Pegasean
Pleiades
Pointers
Praesepe
Scorpius
Waggoner

9 letters:
Aldebaran
Andromeda
Bellatrix
Betelgeux
Big Dipper
Centaurus
Delphinus
Fomalhaut
Ophiuchus
Wolf-Rayet

10 letters:
Betelgeuse
Betelgeuze
Cassiopeia
Mogen David
Orion's belt
The Dog Star

11 letters:
The Pointers
The Pole Star

12 letters:
Little Dipper
Solomon's seal
The North Star

14 letters:
Proxima centaur

CONSTELLATIONS

Latin name	English name
Andromeda	Andromeda
Antlia	Air Pump
Apus	Bird of Paradise
Aquarius	Water Bearer
Aquila	Eagle
Ara	Altar
Argo	Ship of the Argonauts
Aries	Ram
Auriga	Charioteer
Boötes	Herdsman
Caelum	Chisel
Camelopardalis	Giraffe
Cancer	Crab
Canes Venatici	Hunting Dogs
Canis Major	Great Dog
Canis Minor	Little Dog
Capricornus	Sea Goat
Carina	Keel
Cassiopeia	Cassiopeia
Centaurus	Centaur
Cepheus	Cepheus
Cetus	Whale
Chamaeleon	Chameleon
Circinus	Compasses
Columba	Dove
Coma Berenices	Bernice's Hair
Corona Australis	Southern Crown
Corona Borealis	Northern Crown
Corvus	Crow
Crater	Cup
Crux	Southern Cross
Cygnus	Swan
Cynosure	Dog's Tail
Delphinus	Dolphin
Dorado	Swordfish
Draco	Dragon
Equuleus	Little Horse
Eridanus	River Eridanus
Fornax	Furnace
Gemini	Twins
Grus	Crane
Hercules	Hercules
Horologium	Clock
Hydra	Sea Serpent
Hydrus	Water Snake
Indus	Indian
Lacerta	Lizard

Stars and constellations

Latin name	English name
Leo	Lion
Leo Minor	Little Lion
Lepus	Hare
Libra	Scales
Lupus	Wolf
Lynx	Lynx
Lyra	Harp
Mensa	Table
Microscopium	Microscope
Monoceros	Unicorn
Musca	Fly
Norma	Level
Octans	Octant
Ophiuchus	Serpent Bearer
Orion	Orion
Pavo	Peacock
Pegasus	Winged Horse
Perseus	Perseus
Phoenix	Phoenix
Pictor	Easel
Pisces	Fishes
Piscis Austrinus	Southern Fish
Puppis	Ship's Stern
Pyxis	Mariner's Compass
Reticulum	Net
Sagitta	Arrow
Sagittarius	Archer
Scorpius	Scorpion
Sculptor	Sculptor
Scutum	Shield
Serpens	Serpent
Sextans	Sextant
Taurus	Bull
Telescopium	Telescope
Triangulum	Triangle
Triangulum Australe	Southern Triangle
Tucana	Toucan
Ursa Major	Great Bear (contains the Plough or (U.S.) Big Dipper)
Ursa Minor	Little Bear or (U.S.) Little Dipper
Vela	Sails
Virgo	Virgin
Volans	Flying Fish
Vulpecula	Fox

States and territories

AUSTRALIAN STATES AND TERRITORIES

8 letters:
Tasmania
Victoria

10 letters:
Queensland

13 letters:
New South Wales

14 letters:
South Australia

16 letters:
Western Australia

17 letters:
Northern Territory

26 letters:
Australian Capital
Territory

INDIAN STATES

3 letters:
Goa

5 letters:
Assam
Bihar

6 letters:
Kerala
Orissa
Punjab
Sikkim

7 letters:
Gujarat
Haryana
Manipur

Mizoram
Tripura

8 letters:
Jharkand
Nagaland

9 letters:
Karnataka
Meghalaya
Rajasthan
Tamil Nadu

10 letters:
West Bengal

11 letters:
Maharashtra

Uttaranchal

12 letters:
Chhattisgarh
Uttar Pradesh

13 letters:
Andhra Pradesh
Madhya Pradesh

15 letters:
Himachal Pradesh
Jammu and
Kashmir

16 letters:
Arunachal Pradesh

INDIAN UNION TERRITORIES

5 letters:
Delhi

10 letters:
Chandigarh

11 letters:
Daman and Diu
Lakshadweep

Pondicherry

19 letters:
Dadra and Nagar
Haveli

24 letters:
Andaman and
Nicobar Islands

US STATES

State	Abbreviation	Zip code	Nickname	Capital
Alabama	Ala.	AL	Cotton	Montgomery
Alaska	Alas.	AK	Last Frontier	Juneau
Arizona	Ariz.	AZ	Apache	Phoenix
Arkansas	Ark.	AR	Wonder	Little Rock
California	Cal.	CA	Golden	Sacramento

States and territories

State	Abbreviation	Zip code	Nickname	Capital
Colorado	Colo.	CO	Centennial	Denver
Connecticut	Conn.	CT	Nutmeg	Hartford
Delaware	Del.	DE	Diamond	Dover
District of Columbia	D.C.	DC	—	—
Florida	Fla.	FL	Sunshine	Tallahassee
Georgia	Ga.	GA	Peach	Atlanta
Hawaii	Haw.	HI	Aloha	Honolulu
Idaho	Id. *or* Ida.	ID	Gem	Boise
Illinois	Ill.	IL	Prairie	Springfield
Indiana	Ind.	IN	Hoosier	Indianapolis
Iowa	Ia. *or* Io.	IA	Hawkeye	Des Moines
Kansas	Kan. *or* Kans.	KS	Sunflower	Topeka
Kentucky	Ken.	KY	Blue Grass	Frankfort
Louisiana	La.	LA	Pelican	Baton Rouge
Maine	Me.	ME	Pine Tree	Augusta
Maryland	Md.	MD	Free	Annapolis
Massachusetts	Mass.	MA	Bay	Boston
Michigan	Mich.	MI	Wolverine	Lansing
Minnesota	Minn.	MN	Gopher	St Paul
Mississippi	Miss.	MS	Magnolia	Jackson
Missouri	Mo.	MO	Show-me	Jefferson City
Montana	Mont.	MT	Treasure	Helena
Nebraska	Neb.	NE	Cornhusker	Lincoln
Nevada	Nev.	NV	Sagebrush	Carson City
New Hampshire	N.H.	NH	Granite	Concord
New Jersey	N.J.	NJ	Garden	Trenton
New Mexico	N.M. *or* N.Mex.	NM	Sunshine	Santa Fe
New York	N.Y.	NY	Empire	Albany
North Carolina	N.C.	NC	Tar Heel	Raleigh
North Dakota	N.D. *or* N.Dak.	ND	Sioux	Bismarck
Ohio	O.	OH	Buckeye	Columbus
Oklahoma	Okla.	OK	Sooner	Oklahoma City
Oregon	Oreg.	OR	Beaver	Salem
Pennsylvania	Pa., Penn., *or* Penna.	PA	Keystone	Harrisburg
Rhode Island	R.I.	RI	Little Rhody	Providence
South Carolina	S.C.	SC	Palmetto	Columbia
South Dakota	S.Dak.	SD	Coyote	Pierre
Tennessee	Tenn.	TN	Volunteer	Nashville
Texas	Tex.	TX	Lone Star	Austin
Utah	Ut.	UT	Beehive	Salt Lake City
Vermont	Vt.	VT	Green Mountain	Montpelier
Virginia	Va.	VA	Old Dominion	Richmond
Washington	Wash.	WA	Evergreen	Olympia

States and territories

State	Abbreviation	Zip code	Nickname	Capital
West Virginia	W.Va.	WV	Panhandle	Charleston
Wisconsin	Wis.	WI	Badger	Madison
Wyoming	Wyo.	WY	Equality	Cheyenne

US STATES: YEAR OF ACCESSION TO THE UNION

State	Year of Accession
Alabama	1819
Alaska	1959
Arizona	1912
Arkansas	1836
California	1850
Colorado	1876
Connecticut	1788
Delaware	1787
District of Columbia	1889
Florida	1845
Georgia	1788
Hawaii	1959
Idaho	1890
Illinois	1818
Indiana	1816
Iowa	1846
Kansas	1861
Kentucky	1792
Louisiana	1812
Maine	1820
Maryland	1788
Massachusetts	1788
Michigan	1837
Minnesota	1858
Mississippi	1817
Missouri	1821
Montana	1889
Nebraska	1867
Nevada	1864
New Hampshire	1788
New Jersey	1787
New Mexico	1912
New York	1788
North Carolina	1789
North Dakota	1889
Ohio	1803
Oklahoma	1907
Oregon	1859
Pennsylvania	1787
Rhode Island	1790
South Carolina	1788
South Dakota	1889
Tennessee	1796

Stones

State	Year of Accession
Texas	1845
Utah	1896
Vermont	1791
Virginia	1788
Washington	1889
West Virginia	1863
Wisconsin	1848
Wyoming	1890

Stones

2 letters:
St

3 letters:
Gem
Hog
Pit
Rag
Tin

4 letters:
Bath
Blue
Celt
Door
Flag
Hone
Horn
Iron
Jasp
Kerb
Lias
Lime
Lode
Onyx
Opal
Plum
Ragg
Sard
Skew
Slab
Soap
Tile

5 letters:
Agate
Amber
Balas
Beryl

Black
Chalk
Chert
Coade
Culch
Drupe
Flint
Gooly
Grape
Jewel
Kenne
Lapis
Logan
Menah
Metal
Mocha
Niobe
Paste
Prase
Pumie
Quern
Quoin
Quoit
Rubin
Rufus
Rybat
Scone
Scree
Slate
Sneck
Stela
Stele
Topaz
Wacke
Wyman

6 letters:
Amazon

Ashlar
Ashler
Baetyl
Bezoar
Brinny
Cobble
Coping
Cultch
Dolmen
Flusch
Fossil
Gibber
Gooley
Goolie
Gravel
Humite
Jargon
Jasper
Kidney
Kingle
Ligure
Lithic
Menhir
Metate
Muller
Nutlet
Oamaru
Paving
Pebble
Pot-lid
Pumice
Pyrene
Rip-rap
Sarsen
Scarab
Summer
Tanist

7 letters:
Asteria
Avebury
Blarney
Bologna
Boulder
Breccia
Callais
Chuckie
Curling
Girasol
Granite
Hyacine
Hyalite
Jargoon
Lia-fail
Lithoid
Moabite
Niobean
Olivine
Parpane
Parpend
Parpent
Peridot
Perpend
Perpent
Petrous
Pudding
Purbeck
Putamen
Rocking
Rosetta
Sardine
Sarsden
Scaglia
Schanse
Schanze
Smaragd
Tektite
Telamon
Tripoli

Urolith

8 letters:
Aerolite
Aerolith
Amethyst
Asteroid
Baguette
Cabochon
Calculus
Cinnamon
Cromlech
Ebenezer
Elf-arrow
Endocarp
Essonite
Ganister
Girasole
Lapidate
Megalith
Menamber
Monolith
Nephrite
Omphalos
Onychite
Parpoint
Petrosal
Phengite
Portland
Rollrich
Sapphire
Sardonyx
Scalpins
Schantze
Tonalite
Voussoir

9 letters:
Alabaster
Asparagus
Cairngorm

Carnelian
Cholelith
Chondrite
Cornelian
Crossette
Dichroite
Firestone
Gannister
Greensand
Hessonite
Hoarstone
Lithiasis
Paleolith
Pipestone
Rubicelle
Scagliola
Trilithon
Turquoise
Ventifact

10 letters:
Adamantine
Alectorian
Aragonites
Chalcedony
Draconites
Enhydritic
Foundation
Gastrolith
Grey-wether
Kimberlite
Lherzolite
Lithophyte
Rhinestone

11 letters:
Peristalith

12 letters:
Carton-pierre
Philosopher's

See also:
➤ **Minerals** ➤ **Ores** ➤ **Rocks**

Straits

4 letters:
Bass
Cook
Mena
Palk

5 letters:
Cabot
Davis
Dover
Kerch
Korea
Sumba

6 letters:
Bangka
Barrow
Bering
Hainan
Hecate
Hudson
Lombok
Madura
Taiwan
Tartar
Torres

7 letters:
Denmark
Dolphin
Euripus
Evripos
Florida
Formosa

Foveaux
Le Maire
Malacca
Molucca
Øresund

8 letters:
Bosporus
Makassar
Minch, The
Sound, The

9 letters:
Bosphorus
Great Belt
La Pérouse
Small Belt
Solent, The

10 letters:
Gut of Canso
Juan de Fuca
Limfjorden
Little Belt
North Minch

11 letters:
Bab-el-Mandeb
Dardanelles
Kattegat, The
Little Minch
Mona Passage

12 letters:
Skagerrak, The

13 letters:
Strait of Canso
Strait of Sunda

14 letters:
Northumberland
Strait of Hormuz
Straits of Johor

15 letters:
Strait of Georgia
Strait of Malacca
Strait of Messina
Strait of Otranto
Straits of Harris
Windward Passage

16 letters:
Strait of Magellan

17 letters:
Passage of
  Colonsay
Strait of Belle
  Isle
Strait of Bonifacio
Straits of Mackinac

18 letters:
Strait of Juan de
  Fuca
Straits of
  Gibraltar

Subatomic particles

1 letter:
J
W
Z

3 letters:
Chi
Eta
Psi
Tau

4 letters:
Kaon
Muon
Pion

5 letters:
Axion
Boson
Gluon
Meson

Omega
Quark
Sigma
Tauon

6 letters:
Baryon
Hadron
Lambda
Lepton

Parton
Photon
Proton

7 letters:
Fermion
Neutron

Tachyon
Upsilon

8 letters:
Electron
Monopole
Neutrino

9 letters:
Resonance

10 letters:
Higgs boson

Sugars

3 letters:
Goo
Gur

4 letters:
Beet
Cane
Goor
Loaf
Lump
Milk
Palm
Wood

5 letters:
Brown
Candy
Grape
Icing
Maple
Sorgo
White

6 letters:
Aldose
Barley
Caster
Fucose
Hexose
Inulin

Invert
Ribose
Sorgho
Triose
Xylose

7 letters:
Caramel
Cellose
Glucose
Jaggary
Jaggery
Lactose
Maltose
Mannose
Panocha
Pentose
Penuche
Refined
Sorbose
Sorghum
Trehala

8 letters:
Demerara
Dextrose
Fructose
Furanose
Honeydew
Jagghery

Powdered
Rhamnose

9 letters:
Amygdalin
Arabinose
Cassonade
Galactose
Laevulose
Muscovado
Raffinose
Trehalose

10 letters:
Aldohexose
Cellobiose
Glucosoric
Granulated
Saccharine
Saccharoid

11 letters:
Deoxyribose

12 letters:
Crystallized
Disaccharide

14 letters:
Monosaccharide

Suits

3 letters:
Mao
Ski
Wet

4 letters:
Jump

Pant
Zoot

5 letters:
Anti-G
Dress
G-suit

Shell
Slack
Sweat

6 letters:
Boiler
Judogi

Lounge
Romper
Safari
Sailor
Sweats

7 letters:
Catsuit
Pajamas
Penguin
Pyjamas

Sunsuit
Trouser

8 letters:
Playsuit
Swimsuit

9 letters:
Buckskins
Spacesuit
Tracksuit

10 letters:
Three-piece

12 letters:
Evening dress
Morning dress

14 letters:
Double-breasted
Single-breasted

Supernatural

PEOPLE WITH SUPERNATURAL POWERS

3 letters:
Hag
Hex

4 letters:
Mage
Seer

5 letters:
Magus
Siren
Witch

6 letters:
Dowser
Medium
Shaman
Wizard

7 letters:
Diviner

Warlock

8 letters:
Conjurer
Exorcist
Magician
Sorcerer
Spaewife

9 letters:
Archimage
Enchanter
Rainmaker
Sorceress
Superhero

10 letters:
Channeller
Water witch
White witch

11 letters:
Clairvoyant
Enchantress
Necromancer
Thaumaturge
Witch doctor
Witch master

12 letters:
Clairaudient
Water diviner

13 letters:
Clairsentient
Fortune-teller

SUPERNATURAL CREATURES

3 letters:
Elf
Fay
God
Imp

4 letters:
Ogre
Peri

5 letters:
Angel
Demon
Devil

Dwarf
Fairy
Genie
Ghost
Ghoul
Giant
Gnome
Golem
Jinni
Lamia
Pixie
Sylph
Troll

Zombi

6 letters:
Djinni
Djinny
Dybbuk
Goblin
Jinnee
Kelpie
Selkie
Silkie
Sprite
Wraith

Zombie

7 letters:
Banshee
Brownie
Goddess
Gremlin
Incubus
Kachina
Monster
Phantom
Sandman

SUPERNATURAL TERMS

3 letters:
ESP
Hex
Obi

4 letters:
Aura
Fate
Jinx
Juju
Mojo
Rune
Wand

5 letters:
Charm
Curse
Obeah
Ouija®
Sigil
Spell

6 letters:
Amulet
Apport
Fetish
Grigri
Hoodoo
Kismet
Séance
Voodoo

7 letters:
Evil eye

Spectre
Vampire

8 letters:
Familiar
Succubus
Werewolf

9 letters:
Hobgoblin

10 letters:
Leprechaun

Philtre
Portent

8 letters:
Exorcism
Greegree
Grimoire
Gris-gris
Talisman

9 letters:
Ectoplasm
Magic wand
Pentagram
Telepathy

10 letters:
Black magic
Divination
Indian sign
Levitation
Magic spell
Necromancy
Possession
Sixth sense
Telegnosis
White magic
Xenoglossy

11 letters:
Abracadabra
Incantation
Magic circle
Premonition

Little folk

11 letters:
Lycanthrope
Poltergeist

12 letters:
Little people

13 letters:
Guardian angel

14 letters:
Fairy godmother

Second sight
Telekinesis
The Black Art
Xenoglossia

12 letters:
Clairvoyance
Invultuation
Telaesthesia
Witching hour

13 letters:
Clairaudience
Psychokinesis
Reincarnation

14 letters:
Clairsentience
Cryptaesthesia
Parapsychology

17 letters:
Speaking in
  tongues

22 letters:
Extrasensory
  perception

Surgical operations

5 letters:
Graft
Taxis

6 letters:
Bypass

7 letters:
Section

8 letters:
Ablation
Avulsion
Cesarean
Colotomy
Face-lift
Liposuck
Lobotomy
Tenotomy
Vagotomy

9 letters:
Anaplasty
Autograft
Caesarean
Colectomy
Colostomy
Colpotomy
Costotomy
Curettage
Cystotomy
Ileostomy
Iridotomy
Leucotomy
Lithotomy
Lobectomy
Necrotomy
Neoplasty
Neurotomy
Osteotomy
Plication
Resection
Rhizotomy
Skin graft
Tummy tuck
Vasectomy
Zooplasty

10 letters:
Adenectomy

Amputation
Autoplasty
Biosurgery
Craniotomy
Cystectomy
Enterotomy
Episiotomy
Gastrotomy
Iridectomy
Keratotomy
Laparotomy
Lithotrity
Lumpectomy
Mastectomy
Myomectomy
Nephrotomy
Neurectomy
Ovariotomy
Phlebotomy
Pleurotomy
Rachiotomy
Sclerotomy
Strabotomy
Thymectomy
Transplant
Varicotomy

11 letters:
Anastomosis
Angioplasty
Arthrectomy
Cryosurgery
Débridement
Embolectomy
Embryectomy
Enterectomy
Enterostomy
Gastrectomy
Gastrostomy
Glossectomy
Hysterotomy
Laminectomy
Laryngotomy
Liposuction
Nephrectomy
Osteoclasis
Osteoplasty
Ovariectomy

Phlebectomy
Pneumectomy
Pylorectomy
Rhinoplasty
Splenectomy
Tenorrhaphy
Thoracotomy
Tracheotomy
Vaginectomy
Venesection

12 letters:
Arthroplasty
Circumcision
Dermabrasion
Fenestration
Heteroplasty
Hysterectomy
Keratoplasty
Microsurgery
Neurosurgery
Oophorectomy
Paracentesis
Pharyngotomy
Replantation
Tonsillotomy
Tracheostomy

13 letters:
Adenoidectomy
Dermatoplasty
Mastoidectomy
Pneumonectomy
Prostatectomy
Psychosurgery
Salpingectomy
Stomatoplasty
Sympathectomy
Thoracoplasty
Thyroidectomy
Tonsillectomy
Tubal ligation

14 letters:
Appendicectomy
Blepharoplasty
Cardiocentesis
Clitoridectomy
Coronary bypass

Electrosurgery
Keyhole surgery
Plastic surgery
Staphyloplasty
Xenotransplant

15 letters:
Cholecystectomy
Cosmetic surgery
Staphylorrhaphy

16 letters:
Caesarean section

Open-heart surgery
Radial keratotomy
Spare-part surgery

17 letters:
Commando operation
Gastroenterostomy
Haemorrhoidectomy

18 letters:
Gastroduodenostomy
Gender reassignment

Sweaters

4 letters:
Aran
Polo

5 letters:
V-neck

6 letters:
Indian
Jersey
Jumper
Siwash
Skivvy

7 letters:
V-necked

8 letters:
Cardigan
Cowichan
Crew-neck
Fairisle
Guernsey
Polo neck
Pullover
Rollneck

Slipover

9 letters:
Icelandic
Sloppy joe

10 letters:
Cowl-necked
Crew-necked
Sweatshirt
Turtleneck

Swellings

3 letters:
Wen

4 letters:
Bump
Cyst
Gout
Kibe
Lump
Stye

5 letters:
Mouse
Tuber
Whelk

6 letters:
Bunion
Epulis
Goiter
Goitre

Lampas
Oedema
Struma
Tumour
Warble

7 letters:
Blister
Chancre
Entasis
Lampers

8 letters:
Anasarca
Aneurysm
Capellet
Farcy-bud
Hematoma
Lampasse
Odontoma

Ox-warble
Pulvinus
Scirrhus
Teratoma
Tubercle
Windgall
Xanthoma

9 letters:
Adenomata
Apophysis
Chilblain
Haematoma
Hydrocele
Parotitis

10 letters:
Scleriasis

13 letters:
Elephantiasis

Swimming strokes

Swimming strokes

5 letters:
Crawl

7 letters:
Trudgen

8 letters:
Buttefly

9 letters:
Back crawl
Freestyle

10 letters:
Backstroke
Front crawl
Sidestroke

11 letters:
Doggy-paddle

12 letters:
Breaststroke

20 letters:
Inverted
  breaststroke

Swiss cantons

3 letters:
Uri
Zug

4 letters:
Bern
Jura
Vaud

5 letters:
Berne

6 letters:
Aargau
Genève
Glarus
Luzern
Schwyz
Ticino

Valais
Wallis
Zürich

7 letters:
Thurgau

8 letters:
Freiburg
Fribourg
Obwalden

9 letters:
Neuchâtel
Nidwalden
Solothurn

10 letters:
Basel-Stadt

Graubünden

11 letters:
Sankt Gallen

12 letters:
Schaffhausen

15 letters:
Basel-Landschaft

20 letters:
Appenzell-
  Innerrhoden

21 letters:
Appenzell-
  Ausserrhoden

Swords and other weapons with blades

4 letters:
Bill
Chiv
Dirk
Épée
Foil
Kris
Pike

5 letters:
Bilbo
Broad
Estoc
Jerid
Kendo

Knife
Kukri
Saber
Sabre
Skean
Spear
Sword

6 letters:
Anlace
Curtax
Dagger
Espada
Glaive
Gleave

Hanger
Jereed
Katana
Khanda
Kirpan
Parang
Rapier
Toledo
Tulwar

7 letters:
Anelace
Assagai
Assegai
Ataghan

Swords and other weapons with blades

Balmung
Bayonet
Curtana
Cutlass
Gladius
Halberd
Hatchet
Jerreed
Machete
Morglay
Poleaxe
Poniard
Semitar
Shabble
Spirtle
Spurtle
Whinger
Yatagan

8 letters:
Cemitare
Claymore
Curtal-ax

Falchion
Faulchin
Partisan
Schlager
Scimitar
Semitaur
Sgian-dhu
Skene-dhu
Spadroon
Spontoon
Stiletto
Stone axe
Tomahawk
Whiniard
Whinyard
White-arm
Yataghan

9 letters:
Arondight
Backsword
Balisarda
Battle-axe

Damascene
Excalibur
Faulchion
Jackknife
Schiavone

10 letters:
Angurvadel
Bowie knife
Broadsword
Smallsword
Swordstick

11 letters:
Sheath knife
Snickersnee
Trench knife

12 letters:
Spurtleblade
Sword bayonet

13 letters:
Andrew Ferrara

T

Tables and desks

3 letters:
Bar

4 letters:
Desk

6 letters:
Buffet
Bureau
Carrel
Lowboy
Teapoy

7 letters:
Counter

8 letters:
Lapboard
Tea table

9 letters:
Card table
Davenport
Drum table

Side table
Wool table
Workbench
Worktable

10 letters:
Escritoire
Secretaire
Tea trolley
Traymobile

11 letters:
Coffee table
Dining table
Reading desk
Roll-top desk
Writing desk

12 letters:
Bedside table
Breakfast bar
Console table
Folding table

Gate-leg table
Kitchen table
Nest of tables
Pedestal desk
Snooker table
Trestle table
Writing table

13 letters:
Billiard table
Dressing table
Drop-leaf table
Pembroke table
Piecrust table

14 letters:
Breakfast table
Refectory table

15 letters:
Gate-legged table
Occasional table

Teeth

5 letters:
Molar

6 letters:
Canine

7 letters:
Incisor

8 letters:
Premolar

9 letters:
Foretooth

11 letters:
Wisdom tooth

Tennis players

MALE

4 letters:
Ashe, *Arthur*
Borg, *Bjorn*
Cash, *Pat*

Moya, *Carlos*
Rios, *Marcelo*

5 letters:
Blake, *James*

Canas, *Guillermo*
Costa, *Albert*
Laver, *Rod*
Lendl, *Ivan*

Lloyd, *John*
Novak, *Jiri*
Perry, *Fred*
Roche, *Tony*
Safin, *Marat*
Vilas, *Guillermo*

6 letters:
Agassi, *Andre*
Becker, *Boris*
Edberg, *Stefan*
Henman, *Tim*
Hewitt, *Lleyton*
Rafter, *Pat*

7 letters:
Amitraj, *Vijay*

FEMALE

4 letters:
Graf, *Steffi*
King, *Billie-Jean*
Wade, *Virginia*

5 letters:
Bueno, *Maria*
Court, *Margaret*
Dokic, *Jelena*
Evert, *Chris*
Jones, *Ann*
Rubin, *Chanda*
Seles, *Monica*
Stove, *Betty*

6 letters:
Barker, *Sue*
Casals, *Rosie*
Cawley, *Evonne*
Farina, *Silvia*
Hingis, *Martina*

Connors, *Jimmy*
Emerson, *Roy*
Federer, *Roger*
Ferrero, *Juan
Carlos*
Gambill,
Jan-Michael
Maskell, *Dan*
McEnroe, *John*
Nastase, *Ilie*
Roddick, *Andy*
Sampras, *Pete*

8 letters:
Corretja, *Alex*
Gonzalez, *Fernando*

7 letters:
Maleeva,
Magdalena
Myskina, *Anastasia*
Novotna, *Jana*

8 letters:
Capriati, *Jennifer*
Mauresmo, *Amelie*
Sabatini, *Gabriela*
Williams, *Serena*
Williams, *Venus*

9 letters:
Clijsters, *Kim*
Davenport, *Lindsay*
Goolagong, *Evonne*
Pistolesi, *Anna*
Stevenson,
Alexandra

Grosjean, *Sebastien*
Newcombe, *John*
Rosewall, *Ken*
Rusedski, *Greg*
Schalken, *Sjeng*

10 letters:
Ivanisevic, *Goran*
Kafelnikov, *Yevgeny*
Nalbandian, *David*
Srichaphan,
Paradorn

13 letters:
Philippoussis, *Mark*

10 letters:
Hantuchova,
Daniela
Kournikova, *Anna*

11 letters:
Navratilova,
Martina

13 letters:
Henin-Hardenne,
Justine

14 letters:
Sanchez-Vicario,
Arantxa

Tennis terms

3 letters:
Ace
Let
Lob
Net
Set

4 letters:
Ball
Chip
Game
Love

5 letters:
Court
Deuce
Fault
Match
Rally

Territories of New Zealand

Slice
Smash

6 letters:
Racket
Return
Server
Umpire
Volley

7 letters:
Doubles
Net cord
Racquet
Service
Singles
Topspin

8 letters:
Backhand

Baseline
Drop shot
Forehand
Line call
Linesman
Love game
Receiver
Set point
Sideline
Tie-break
Tramline
Undercut

9 letters:
Advantage
Clay court
Foot fault
Forecourt
Hard court

10 letters:
Break point
Cannonball
Centre line
Centre mark
Grass court
Half-volley
Lawn tennis
Tiebreaker

11 letters:
Double fault
Passing shot
Service line

12 letters:
Approach shot
Break of serve
Ground stroke
Mixed doubles

Territories of New Zealand

4 letters:
Niue

7 letters:
Tokelau

11 letters:
Cook Islands

12 letters:
Union Islands

14 letters:
Ross Dependency

Theatre terms

3 letters:
Act
Cue
Ham

4 letters:
Exit
Flat
Gods
Prop
Role

5 letters:
Flies
Fluff
House
Lines

Scene
Stage
Wings

6 letters:
Chorus
Circle
Corpse
Prompt
Script
Speech
Stalls

7 letters:
Curtain
Gallery
Overact

Resting
Scenery
Unities
Upstage

8 letters:
Crush bar
Entr'acte
Entrance
Juvenile
Offstage
Prompter
Scene bay
Thespian

9 letters:
Backstage

Downstage
Greenroom
Monologue
Noises off
Orchestra
Scene dock
Soliloquy
Soubrette
Stage door
Stagehand
Stage left

10 letters:
First night
Leading man
Opera house
Stage right
Understudy

11 letters:
Catastrophe
Curtain call
Greasepaint
Leading lady
Off-Broadway
Stage fright
Stage-struck

12 letters:
Front of house
Orchestra pit
Stage manager
Stage whisper

13 letters:
Coup de théâtre
Curtain-raiser

Curtain speech

14 letters:
Off-off-Broadway
Proscenium arch
Stage direction

16 letters:
Comédie Française
Dramatis personae
First-night nerves

17 letters:
Theatre-in-the-
   round

Ties and cravats

3 letters:
Boa
Tie

5 letters:
Ascot
Dicky
Fichu
Scarf
Stock
Stole

6 letters:
Bertha

Bow tie
Cravat
Madras
Rebozo

7 letters:
Foulard
Muffler
Necktie

8 letters:
Black tie
Carcanet
Dicky bow

Kerchief
White tie

9 letters:
Comforter
Neckcloth
School tie

10 letters:
Windsor tie

11 letters:
Falling band
Neckerchief

Time

RELATED VOCABULARY

2 letters:
AD
Am
BC
Mo
Pm

3 letters:
Age
Ago

Aye
Day
Due
E'en
E'er
Eld
Eos
Era
Ere
Eve

May
Oft
Old
Sec
Ult
Yet

4 letters:
Aeon
Ages

Time

Anon
Ante
Date
Dawn
Dial
Dusk
Even
Ever
Fall
Fast
Fore
Ides
Inst
Jiff
July
June
Late
Lent
Moon
Morn
Next
Noel
Noon
Once
Over
Past
Post
Prox
Slow
Soon
Span
Term
Then
Tick
Tide
Till
Time
Unto
Week
When
Xmas
Year
Yore
Yule

5 letters:
Again
Annum
April
As yet
Brief

Clock
Cycle
Daily
Dekad
Delay
Diary
Early
Epact
Epoch
Fasti
Flash
Jiffy
Later
March
Matin
Month
Never
Night
Nonce
Nones
Often
Passe
Pause
Point
Prime
Prior
Purim
Ready
Shake
Sharp
Short
Since
So far
Space
Spell
Still
Style
Sunup
Tempo
Today
Trice
Until
Watch
While
Years
Young
Youth

6 letters:
Actual
Advent

Always
Annual
At once
August
Aurora
Autumn
Bairam
Brumal
Coeval
Coming
Crisis
Curfew
Decade
Dotage
During
Easter
Elapse
Ere now
Extant
Ferial
Friday
Future
Gnomon
Heyday
Hiemal
Hourly
Ice age
In time
Jet age
Julian
Lammas
Lapsed
Lately
Latest
Latish
Lustre
Manana
May day
Midday
Minute
Modern
Moment
Monday
Morrow
New day
O'clock
Off-day
Of late
Old age
One day
On time

Period
Presto
Pre-war
Prompt
Pronto
Pro tem
Rarely
Recent
Season
Second
Seldom
Sooner
Spring
Sudden
Summer
Sunday
Sunset
Timely
To date
Update
Vernal
Vesper
Weekly
Whilst
Winter
Yearly
Yester

7 letters:
Abiding
Ack emma
Ageless
Ages ago
All over
Almanac
Already
Ancient
Anytime
Archaic
At night
Bedtime
Belated
Betimes
Boyhood
By-and-by
Calends
Century
Chiliad
Current
Dawning
Daylong

Day-peep
Daytime
Diurnal
Dog days
Earlier
Elapsed
Endless
Epochal
Equinox
Estival
Evening
Exactly
Expired
Extinct
Fast day
Flag day
Forever
For good
For life
Harvest
High day
History
Holiday
Holy day
Infancy
Instant
Interim
Iron Age
January
Journal
Jubilee
Just now
Kalends
Lady day
Long ago
Long run
Lustrum
Manhood
Manhour
Matinal
Mid-week
Monthly
Morning
Newborn
New Year
Nightly
Noonday
October
One-time
Overdue
Pending

Pip emma
Postwar
Present
Proximo
Quarter
Quondam
Ramadan
Ripe age
Sabbath
Secular
Shortly
Sine die
Some day
Stretch
Sukkoth
Sundial
Sundown
Sunrise
Teenage
Tertian
This day
Time-lag
Time was
Tonight
Too late
Too soon
Tuesday
Twinkle
Two two's
Unready
Up to now
Usually
Weekday
Weekend
Whereon
Whitsun

8 letters:
Abruptly
A long day
Antedate
As soon as
Biannual
Biennial
Birthday
Biweekly
Blue moon
Brumaire
Calendar
Civil day
Darkling

Time

Date line
Daybreak
Daylight
Deadline
December
Derby day
Directly
Dogwatch
Doomsday
Duration
Eggtimer
Enduring
Entr'acte
Epiphany
Eternity
Eventide
Evermore
Every day
Evil hour
Fast time
Feast day
February
Fleeting
Foredawn
Forenoon
Formerly
Frequent
Gain time
Gloaming
Half hour
Half past
Hanukkah
Hereunto
Hibernal
High time
Hitherto
Hogmanay
Holy days
Holy week
Horology
Ill-timed
In a flash
In a trice
Infinity
In future
In no time
In season
Interval
Juncture
Keep time
Kill time

Lang syne
Last time
Last week
Lateness
Latterly
Leap year
Lifelong
Life-span
Lifetime
Livelong
Long time
Lord's day
Lose time
Lunation
Mark time
Mean time
Medieval
Menology
Meridian
Meteoric
Midnight
Momently
Natal day
New Style
Next week
Noontide
Noontime
Not often
November
Nowadays
Obsolete
Occasion
Ofttimes
Old times
On the dot
Our times
Passover
Pass time
Postdate
Postpone
Previous
Promptly
Punctual
Recently
Right now
Ringtime
Saturday
Seasonal
Seedtime
Semester
Solar day

Solstice
Some time
Space Age
Sporadic
Steel Age
Suddenly
Take time
Temporal
This week
Thursday
Timeless
Time-worn
Tomorrow
Too early
Twilight
Ultimate
Until now
Untimely
Up-to-date
Weeklong
Whenever
Year-book
Yearlong
Years ago
Yoretime
Yuletide

9 letters:
Adulthood
Afternoon
After that
After time
All at once
Antiquity
Atomic Age
At present
Bimonthly
Boxing Day
Bronze Age
Candlemas
Canicular
Centenary
Childhood
Christmas
Chronicle
Civil time
Civil year
Clepsydra
Continual
Crepuscle
Days of old

Dayspring
Decennary
Decennial
Decennium
Due season
Earliness
Early bird
Ember days
Empire Day
Ephemeral
Ephemeris
Epochally
Erstwhile
Ever since
Every hour
Far future
First time
Foregoing
Forthwith
Fortnight
From now on
Gnomonics
Golden Age
Great year
Gregorian
Hallowe'en
Hallowmas
Happy days
Hereafter
Honeymoon
Hourglass
Immediacy
Immediate
In a second
In due time
Instanter
Instantly
Interlude
In the past
Julian day
Lammas day
Later date
Latter day
Light year
Local time
Longevity
Long-lived
Long since
Long spell
Long while
Lunar year

Many a time
Many times
Mardi Gras
Martinmas
Mature age
Matutinal
Meanwhile
Mediaeval
Menstrual
Metronome
Midday sun
Middle age
Midsummer
Midwinter
Mistiming
Momentary
Monthlong
Nevermore
Nightfall
Nightlong
Nighttide
Night time
Nocturnal
Octennial
Oftentime
Opportune
Out of date
Overnight
Pentecost
Perennial
Permanent
Postcenal
Preceding
Precisely
Premature
Presently
Quarterly
Quarter to
Quotidian
Recurrent
Regularly
Remote age
Right time
Saint's day
Salad days
Sandglass
Semestral
September
Short term
Short time
Solar time

Solar year
Sometimes
Space time
Spare time
Spend time
Stop watch
Swiss plan
Temporary
Temporize
Therewith
Till death
Time being
Time check
Time clock
Time flies
Time limit
Time of day
Timepiece
Times past
Timetable
To this day
Transient
Triennial
Twinkling
Two shakes
Upon which
Vicennial
Waste time
Wednesday
Well-timed
Wherefore
Whereunto
Whereupon
Wrong time
Yesterday

10 letters:
Afterwards
After which
Alarm clock
Allhallows
All the time
Anno Domini
At all times
At that time
At this time
Beforehand
Before long
Beforetime
Behindhand
Behind time

Time

Better days
Break of day
Bygone days
By the clock
Centennial
Childermas
Chronogram
Chronology
Close of day
Common time
Consequent
Constantly
Continuous
Cosmic time
Crepuscule
Days gone by
Days of yore
Eastertide
Easter time
Evanescent
Eventually
Father's day
Father Time
Fiscal year
Fleetingly
Frequently
Futuristic
Generation
Good Friday
Half a jiffy
Half an hour
Half a shake
Hardly ever
Hebdomadal
Hebrew Year
Henceforth
Here and now
Heretofore
Historical
Immemorial
Incidental
In good time
Invariably
Isochronon
Julian year
Just in time
Lammastide
Last chance
Last minute
Lententide
Lunar month

Methuselah
Michaelmas
Middle-aged
Middle Ages
Midmorning
Millennium
Moratorium
Mother's day
Near future
Nick of time
Now or never
Occasional
Of the clock
Olden times
One fine day
On occasion
On the eve of
Palm Sunday
Posthumous
Prehistory
Present day
Previously
Proper time
Repeatedly
Retrospect
Ripe old age
Sabbath day
Seasonable
Semiweekly
Septennial
Sextennial
Short spell
Small hours
Soon enough
Springtide
Springtime
Subsequent
Summertide
Summertime
Thereafter
This minute
Time-keeper
Timeliness
Time signal
Time to come
Time to kill
Transitory
Tricennial
Triple time
Ultimately
Very seldom

Vespertime
Water clock
Wedding day
Whensoever
Whitmonday
Whitsunday
Wintertide
Wintertime
With the sun
Wristwatch
Years on end
Yesteryear

11 letters:
Adjournment
Adolescence
After-dinner
Against time
Ahead of time
All Fools day
All Souls day
Anachronism
Anniversary
At intervals
Bicentenary
Bygone times
Ceaselessly
Chronograph
Chronometer
Chronoscope
Coincidence
Concurrence
Continually
Crack of dawn
Crepuscular
Cuckoo clock
Day after day
Day and night
Day in day out
Dead of night
Endless time
Ever and a day
Ever and anon
Everlasting
Every moment
Fin de siècle
Flower of age
For evermore
Former times
Fortnightly
Gay Nineties

Golden hours
Good old days
Halcyon days
Half a second
Hebdomadary
Hereinafter
Ides of March
Immediately
In an instant
Incessantly
In due course
Inopportune
Intercalary
Interregnum
Judgment day
Lapse of time
Leisure time
Little while
Livelong day
Long-lasting
Long overdue
March of time
Microsecond
Middle years
Millisecond
Modern times
Momentarily
Morningtide
Morningtime
Never-ending
New Year's day
New Year's eve
Night and day
Once or twice
Opportunely
Opportunity
Out of season
Passion week
Penultimate
Perennially
Perfect year
Perpetually
Play for time
Point of time
Present time
Prime of life
Promptitude
Punctuality
Quadrennial
Quarter past
Rogation Day

Sands of time
Semi-monthly
Shining hour
Short notice
Some time ago
Split second
Straightway
Synchronism
Synchronize
Tempus fugit
Thenceforth
The other day
This morning
This very day
Time and tide
Time drags by
Time machine
Time to spare
Turret clock
Twelvemonth
Ultramodern
Waiting time
Whitsuntide
With the lark
Year of Grace

12 letters:
All of a sudden
All Saints Day
A long time ago
Ancient times
Annunciation
Antediluvian
Ante meridiem
Antemeridien
Armistice day
Ascension day
Ash Wednesday
Auld lang syne
Bide one's time
Calendar year
Christmas day
Christmas eve
Consequently
Contemporary
Course of time
Decisive hour
Decline of day
Donkey's years
Eleventh hour
Feast of Weeks

Following day
Fourth of July
From that time
Greek calends
Holy Thursday
In days of yore
Indian summer
Innocents day
In olden times
Intermission
Late in the day
Long-standing
Many a long day
Metachronism
Nychthemeron
Occasionally
Old-fashioned
Once in a while
On the instant
On the morroww
Parachronism
Periodically
Postdiluvian
Postmeridiem
Postponement
Postprandial
Quadrigesima
Quinquennial
Quinquennium
Rare occasion
Red letter day
Sempiternity
Sidereal time
Simultaneous
Stall for time
Standard time
Still of night
Stitch in time
Synodic month
Tercentenary
The dawn of day
Then and there
The year round
Time and again
Time-honoured
Timelessness
Time will tell
Turning point
Twelfth night
Twelve o'clock
Unseasonable

Time

Witching hour
Without delay

13 letters:
Again and again
All Hallow's eve
April fool's day
Ascensiontide
At short notice
Broad daylight
Calendar month
Christmas-tide
Christmas-time
Chronographer
Chronological
Days of the week
Every few hours
Every few years
Every other day
Financial year
For the present
From the outset
From the word go
Generation gap
Getting on a bit
Golden jubilee
Golden wedding
Greenwich time
Michaelmas day
Old as the hills
Once upon a time
Passion Sunday
Quincentenary
Quinquagesima
Retrospective
Right up to date
Roman calendar
Round the clock
Shrove Tuesday
Silver jubilee
Silver wedding
Some of the time
Some other time
Sooner or later
Speaking clock
St Crispin's day
St Luke's summer
St Swithin's day
Summer holiday

Synchronology
The time is ripe
Time after time
Time marches on
Time of arrival
Time out of mind
Tomorrow night
Trinity Sunday
Tropical month
Turn of the year
Up-to-the-minute
Up with the lark
Vernal equinox
Week in, week out
Year in, year out

14 letters:
Advancing years
Before and after
Behind schedule
Breathing space
Chronometrical
Day in and day out
Daylight saving
Declining years
Diamond jubilee
Diamond wedding
During the night
Easter holidays
For ever and a day
For ever and ever
For the duration
From time to time
Fullness of time
Geological time
In ancient times
In course of time
Interval of time
In the afternoon
In the beginning
In the meanwhile
Julian calendar
Keep early hours
Maundy Thursday
Midsummer night
Month of Sundays
Pancake Tuesday
Past and present
Remembrance Day

Sabbatical year
Septuagenarian
Walpurgis night
Witches' Sabbath

15 letters:
Against the clock
Ahead of schedule
Chronologically
Contemporaneity
Contemporaneous
Continental time
Continuation day
Dominical letter
Equinoctial year
Every now and then
For a year and a
   day
Fourth dimension
How goes the
   enemy
In the nick of time
Month after month
Months and
   months
Months of the year
Mothering Sunday
Night after night
Once in a blue
   moon
Once in a lifetime
Put back the clock
Put the clock back
Quatercentenary
Retrospectively
Spur of the
   moment
St Valentine's day
Thanksgiving day
The morning after
This year of grace
Tomorrow evening
Tomorrow morning
World without end

17 letters:
Gregorian calendar

GREGORIAN CALENDAR

January	May	September
February	June	October
March	July	November
April	August	December

JEWISH CALENDAR

Tishri	Shebat	Tammuz
Cheshvan	Adar	Av
Heshvan	Nisan	Ab
Kislev	Iyar	Elul
Tevet	Iyyar	
Shevat	Sivan	

MUSLIM CALENDAR

Muharram	Jumada I	Rhamadhan
Moharram	Jumada II	Ramazan
Safar	Rajab	Shawwal
Saphar	Shaban	Dhu'l-Qa'dah
Rabia I	Shaaban	Dhu'l-Hijjah
Rabia II	Ramadan	

FRENCH REVOLUTIONARY CALENDAR

Vendémiaire	Ventôse	Thermidor
Brumaire	Germinal	Fervidor
Frimaire	Floréal	Fructidor
Nivôse	Prairial	
Pluviôse	Messidor	

TIME ZONES

17 letters:
British Summer Time
Greenwich Mean Time
Yukon Daylight Time
Yukon Standard Time

19 letters:
Central Daylight Time
Central European Time
Central Standard Time
Eastern Daylight Time
Eastern Standard Time

Pacific Daylight Time
Pacific Standard Time

20 letters:
Atlantic Daylight Time
Atlantic Standard Time
Mountain Daylight Time
Mountain Standard Time

24 letters:
Newfoundland Daylight Time
Newfoundland Standard Time

Tobacco

TYPES OF TOBACCO

4 letters:
Shag

5 letters:
Snout
Snuff

6 letters:
Burley
Filler
Rappee

7 letters:
Caporal

Perique
Sumatra
Turkish

8 letters:
Canaster
Makhorka
Maryland
Virginia

9 letters:
Broadleaf
Fire-cured

Flue-cured

11 letters:
Cigar binder
Cigar filler

12 letters:
Cigar wrapper
Dark air-cured

14 letters:
Chewing tobacco
Cuban cigar leaf

TYPES OF CIGAR AND CIGARETTE

5 letters:
Breva
Claro
Stogy

6 letters:
Concha
Corona
Havana
Maduro

Manila
Roll-up
Stogey

7 letters:
Cheroot

8 letters:
Perfecto
Puritano

9 letters:
Cigarillo
Imperiale
Panatella

10 letters:
Tailor-made

11 letters:
Roll-your-own

PIPES

4 letters:
Clay

5 letters:
Briar
Peace

6 letters:
Hookah

7 letters:
Corncob

8 letters:
Calabash

10 letters:
Meerschaum

12 letters:
Churchwarden
Hubble-bubble

GENERAL SMOKING TERMS

3 letters:
Ash

4 letters:
Bowl
Butt
Pipe
Plug
Stem

5 letters:
Flint

6 letters:
Dottle
Smoker
Splint

7 letters:
Ashtray

Humidor
Lighter
Makings
Matches
Pigtail

8 letters:
Calabash
Pipe rack

Rollings
Snuffbox

Smoking room
Tobacconist

14 letters:
Cigarette paper

9 letters:
Filter tip
Smoke room

12 letters:
Tobacco pouch

15 letters:
Cigarette holder

11 letters:
Pipe cleaner

13 letters:
Cigarette case
Smoking jacket

18 letters:
Smoking
   compartment

Tools

3 letters:
Awl
Axe
Bit
Gab
Gad
Hob
Hoe
Saw
Sax

4 letters:
Bosh
Comb
File
Fork
Froe
Frow
Hack
Hone
Maul
Pick
Rake
Spud

5 letters:
Auger
Borer
Broad
Burin
Clink
Croze
Drift
Drill
Drove
Facer
Float
Gavel
Kevel
Plane

Punch
Shave
Slick
Snake
Spade
Swage

6 letters:
Beetle
Bodkin
Broach
Chaser
Chisel
Comber
Cradle
Dibble
Fillet
Flange
Former
Fraise
Fuller
Gimlet
Gouger
Graver
Gympie
Hammer
Jumper
Mallet
Padsaw
Pestle
Pliers
Rabble
Ripple
Rocker
Router
Sander
Scutch
Scythe
Shears
Sickle

Spider
Stylus
Trepan
Trowel
Wimble
Wrench

7 letters:
Bolster
Dresser
Flatter
Ice pick
Jointer
Mattock
Nibbler
Nippers
Rabbler
Rounder
Scauper
Scorper
Scriber
Slasher
Spanner
Spudder

8 letters:
Allen key
Billhook
Bitstock
Clippers
Driftpin
Edge tool
Screw tap
Scutcher
Stiletto

9 letters:
Alligator
Drawknife
Drawshave
Eyeleteer

Torture

10 letters:
Bushhammer
Claw hammer
Cold chisel
Drill press
Hack hammer
Icebreaker
Jackhammer
Piledriver
Power drill
Tack hammer
Tilt hammer
Triphammer

11 letters:
Brace and bit

Centre punch
Countersink
Drove chisel
Hammer drill
Mitre square
Ploughstaff
Pruning hook
Screwdriver
Spitsticker

12 letters:
Diamond point
Firmer chisel
Floatcut file
Monkey wrench
Pitching tool

Sledgehammer

13 letters:
Rawhide hammer
Soldering iron

14 letters:
Ball-peen hammer
Knapping hammer
Percussion tool

15 letters:
Half-round chisel
Pneumatic hammer

Torture

INSTRUMENTS OF TORTURE

4 letters:
Boot
Rack

5 letters:
Brake
Wheel

7 letters:
Scourge

10 letters:
Iron maiden
Pilliwinks
Thumbscrew

13 letters:
Cat-o'-nine-tails

14 letters:
Procrustean bed

TYPES OF TORTURE

5 letters:
Water

8 letters:
Gauntlet

9 letters:
Bastinado
Strappado
Water cure

12 letters:
Chinese water

Towns

3 letters:
Ems
Gao
Ife
Lod
Niš
Spa
Zug

4 letters:
Agen
Albi
Asti

Biel
Bury
Bute
Cheb
Cork
Deal
Edam
Eton
Genk
Györ
Hamm
Hove
Hyde

Kent
Lens
León
Lodi
Mayo
Melk
Mons
Mull
Niue
Oahu
Sale
Sfax
Skye

Thun
Toul
Trim
Tyre
Wick

5 letters:
Aarau
Aduwa
Ahwaz
Aksum
Alloa
Alost
Aosta
Arlon
Arras
Aruba
Ascot
Aswan
Aulis
Aydin
Balkh
Banff
Bohol
Capua
Cavan
Clare
Cluny
Conwy
Copán
Corby
Cowes
Crewe
Daman
Delft
Dinan
Doorn
Dubna
Egham
Elche
Elgin
Emmen
Ennis
Epsom
Esher
Faial
Flint
Gotha
Gouda
Hilla
Hotan
Ikeja

Ipsus
Irbid
Issus
Izmit
Jerez
Jinja
Kauai
Kells
Kerry
Korçë
Krems
Lahti
Laois
Leigh
Lewes
Leyte
Lorca
Louth
Luton
Luxor
Lydia
Maraş
Massa
Meath
Namur
Negev
Nikko
Niort
Noyon
Öland
Omagh
Ostia
Otago
Pavia
Pelée
Pemba
Płock
Ponce
Pydna
Qeshm
Rugby
Sedan
Sibiu
Sitka
Skien
Sligo
Stans
Ta`izz
Tomsk
Tours
Trier
Truro

Ujiji
Upolu
Vaduz
Vichy
Wigan
Youth
Ypres
Zarqa

6 letters:
Abydos
Actium
Aegina
Agadir
Almada
Al Marj
Amalfi
Anadyr
Antrim
Anyang
Armagh
Arnold
Ashdod
Assisi
Atbara
Aveiro
Ayodha
Bangor
Bastia
Batley
Battle
Bauchi
Bayeux
Bethel
Bingen
Biskra
Bodmin
Bolton
Bouaké
Brecon
Butung
Buxton
Can Tho
Carlow
Celaya
Cognac
Crosby
Cuenca
Dachau
Dawson
Denton
Deurne

Towns

Dinant
Dodona
Dudley
Dunoon
Eccles
Edessa
Edirne
Epping
Évreux
Flores
Forfar
Galway
Gibeon
Glarus
Guyana
Hameln
Harlow
Havant
Hawick
Huambo
Huesca
Hwange
Ilesha
Ilkley
Irvine
Kalisz
Kendal
Kirkby
Kiruna
Kokura
Kumasi
Labuan
Lashio
Latina
Lemnos
Lesbos
Lombok
Ludlow
Lugano
Lützen
Macapá
Maldon
Medway
Megara
Menton
Merano
Mérida
Miseno
Morley
Nablus
Nakuru
Nelson

Newark
Oakham
Offaly
Oldham
Örebro
Osijek
Ottawa
Owerri
Pernik
Phuket
Pleven
Poitou
Pudsey
Ragusa
Rashid
Rijeka
Sarnen
Schwyz
Sennar
Sestos
Seveso
Shache
Shiloh
Sintra
Slough
Sokoto
Soweto
Tarbes
Tivoli
Tralee
Tyumen
Verdun
Vienne
Warley
Welkom
Widnes
Woking
Zabrze
Zwolle

7 letters:
Airdrie
Alençon
Ålesund
Al Hufuf
Almadén
Altdorf
Amboise
Antibes
Appleby
Armenia
Arundel

Ashford
Augusta
Auxerre
Baalbek
Bacolod
Bamberg
Banbury
Bedford
Belfort
Bien Hoa
Blaydon
Bonaire
Burnley
Cabimas
Cambrai
Cannock
Carlton
Carrara
Caserta
Cassino
Chatham
Cholula
Chorley
Clacton
Clonmel
Colditz
Concord
Consett
Corinth
Cortona
Crawley
Crotone
Cwmbran
Cythera
Devizes
Dhahran
Donegal
Donetsk
Dongola
Douglas
Dundalk
Eleusis
Entebbe
Evesham
Exmouth
Falkirk
Falster
Fareham
Farnham
Fashoda
Felling
Fiesole

Görlitz
Gosport
Halifax
Harlech
Hasselt
Herisau
Heywood
Hoylake
Ipswich
Iqaluit
Karbala
Keswick
Khojent
Kildare
Kutaisi
La Línea
La Palma
Legnica
Leitrim
Lerwick
Leuctra
Lifford
Lisieux
Locarno
Lourdes
Louvain
Malvern
Margate
Matlock
Megiddo
Meissen
Melilla
Minorca
Morpeth
Moulins
Newbury
Newport
Newtown
Numidia
Okinawa
Olsztyn
Orvieto
Otranto
Paisley
Papeete
Peebles
Penrith
Pereira
Plovdiv
Punakha
Pushkin
Reading

Red Deer
Reigate
Renfrew
Runcorn
Sagunto
Saint-Lô
Segovia
Setúbal
Seville
Shakhty
Sheppey
Shkodër
Skipton
Sovetsk
Staines
Stanley
Swindon
Tampere
Tanagra
Taunton
Telford
Thapsus
Tobolsk
Torquay
Tripoli
Tutuila
Urmston
Üsküdar
Valence
Vellore
Walsall
Warwick
Watford
Wexford
Wicklow
Windsor
Wisbech
Woomera
Worksop
Wrexham
Zaandam
Zealand

8 letters:
Abeokuta
Aberdare
Abingdon
Amravati
Aquileia
Armidale
Aubusson
Aycliffe

Ballarat
Banstead
Barbados
Barnsley
Basildon
Bastogne
Beauvais
Bedworth
Benfleet
Beverley
Biarritz
Billiton
Boa Vista
Bornholm
Budapest
Buraydah
Caerleon
Calabria
Campania
Chamonix
Chartres
Chepstow
Chertsey
Cheshunt
Chigwell
Courtrai
Damietta
Dartford
Daventry
Demerara
Dewsbury
Dumfries
Ebbw Vale
El Faiyûm
Erlangen
Fribourg
Galloway
Golconda
Grantham
Guernica
Hamilton
Hastings
Hatfield
Hertford
Hinckley
Holyhead
Ilkeston
Jemappes
Junagadh
Keighley
Kerkrade
Kilkenny

Towns

Kirkwall
Le Cateau
Limerick
Llandaff
Llanelli
Longford
Lüneburg
Lyonnais
Mafikeng
Mainland
Maitland
Manassas
Maubeuge
Mézières
Mindanao
Monaghan
Monmouth
Montreux
Mufulira
Murmansk
Nanterre
Nazareth
Nijmegen
Nishapur
Normandy
Nuneaton
Omdurman
Paignton
Pembroke
Penzance
Peterlee
Piacenza
Piedmont
Portland
Redditch
Richmond
Rijswijk
Rochdale
Rothesay
Sabadell
Sarajevo
Seremban
Solihull
Spalding
Stafford
Subotica
Tamworth
Ternopol
Timbuktu
Touraine
Tübingen
Uxbridge

Viti Levu
Wallasey
Wallsend
Waterloo
Zlatoust
Zululand

9 letters:
Abbeville
Agrigento
Alcántara
Aldershot
Ambleside
Apeldoorn
Appenzell
Auschwitz
Aylesbury
Bebington
Beersheba
Bethlehem
Bethsaida
Blackpool
Bracknell
Brentwood
Brighouse
Capernaum
Castlebar
Chaeronea
Chantilly
Charleroi
Chernobyl
Chiengmai
Chinatown
Clydebank
Coleraine
Colwyn Bay
Deauville
Dodge City
Dolgellau
Doncaster
Dumbarton
Dunstable
Eastleigh
Elizabeth
Esslingen
Five Towns
Gällivare
Galwegian
Gelligaer
Godesberg
Gold Coast
Gütersloh

Halesowen
Harrogate
Inveraray
Jamestown
Kettering
Killarney
King's Lynn
Kitchener
Kitzbühel
Lambaréné
Lancaster
Le Creusot
Llandudno
Lockerbie
Long Eaton
Los Alamos
Lower Hutt
Lymington
Maidstone
Mansfield
Middleton
Mullingar
Neuchâtel
Newmarket
New Romney
Northwich
Ogbomosho
Paderborn
Palm Beach
Périgueux
Perpignan
Pharsalus
Pontypool
Portadown
Port Royal
Prestwich
Prestwick
Princeton
Roscommon
Rotherham
Saint Gall
Saint-Ouen
Salamanca
Santa Cruz
Sherborne
Solothurn
Sosnowiec
Southport
Stevenage
Stockport
Stralsund
Stranraer

Towns

Stretford
Surakarta
Tipperary
Tombstone
Tonbridge
Tourcoing
Tullamore
Vancouver
Viareggio
Wadi Halfa
Wad Medani
Waterford
Westmeath
Woodstock
Worcester
Wuppertal

10 letters:
Accrington
Altrincham
Amersfoort
Anderlecht
Austerlitz
Barnstaple
Bellinzona
Bennington
Bridgwater
Bromsgrove
Buckingham
Caerphilly
Canterbury
Carmarthen
Castleford
Chadderton
Cheltenham
Ciudad Real
Coatbridge
Colchester
Coldstream
Darjeeling
Darlington
Dorchester
Eisenstadt
Ffestiniog
Frauenfeld
Galashiels
Gettysburg
Gillingham
Glenrothes
Hammerfest
High Street
Huntingdon

Interlaken
Kalgoorlie
Kapfenberg
Kenilworth
Kilmarnock
Kragujevac
Letchworth
Leverkusen
Linlithgow
Livingston
Llangollen
Longbenton
Los Angeles
Maidenhead
Middelburg
Monte Carlo
Montego Bay
Motherwell
Neumünster
New Castile
New Ireland
Paramaribo
Pontefract
Pontypridd
Portlaoise
Regensburg
Ruda Śląska
Sacramento
Saint Croix
Saint-Denis
San Antonio
Scunthorpe
Shrewsbury
Simferopol
Tewkesbury
Trowbridge
Twickenham
Vijayawada
Warrington
Washington
Whitehorse
Winchester
Winterthur
Xochimilco

11 letters:
Aberystwyth
Aix-les-Bains
Alessandria
Armentières
Basingstoke
Cirencester

Clackmannan
Cumbernauld
Dawson Creek
Downpatrick
Enniskillen
Farnborough
Fort William
Glastonbury
Grande-Terre
Halberstadt
High Wycombe
Kanchipuram
Kigoma-Ujiji
Leatherhead
Marlborough
Mississauga
Missolonghi
Montbéliard
Montpellier
Nakhichevan
Northampton
Novosibirsk
Nyíregyháza
Prestonpans
Rambouillet
Saint-Brieuc
Saint David's
Saint Helena
Saint Helens
Saint Helier
Saint Pierre
San Fernando
Sharpeville
Sierra Leone
Stourbridge
Wanne-Eickel

12 letters:
Alice Springs
Anuradhapura
Ascoli Piceno
Beaconsfield
Bielsko-Biała
Bougainville
Cerro de Pasco
Chesterfield
Chilpancingo
Christchurch
East Kilbride
Huddersfield
Kristianstad
Loughborough

Towns

Luang Prabang
Macclesfield
Marie Galante
Matabeleland
Milton Keynes
Newtownabbey
Peterborough
Saint Austell
Saint-Étienne
Saint-Quentin
San Ildefonso
Schaffhausen
Secunderabad
Seringapatam
Skelmersdale
Valenciennes
Villahermosa
Villeurbanne
Wattenscheid
West Bromwich

13 letters:
Berchtesgaden
Blantyre-Limbe
Bury St Edmunds
Carrickfergus
Cayman Islands
Évian-les-Bains
Fontainebleau
Hertfordshire
Hradec Králové
Kidderminster
Leamington Spa
Lipari Islands
Llano Estacado
Lons-le-Saunier
Melton Mowbray
Merthyr Tydfil
Middlesbrough
New Providence
Northallerton
Ryukyu Islands
Southend-on-Sea

14 letters:
Annapolis Royal
Ashby-de-la-Zouch
Bishop Auckland
Château-Thierry
Griqualand East

Griqualand West
Hemel Hempstead
Henley-on-Thames
Mariánské Lázně
Saint Augustine
Tunbridge Wells
Wellingborough

15 letters:
Ashton-under-Lyne
Barrow-in-Furness
Burton-upon-Trent
Camborne-Redruth
Falkland Islands
Lewis with Harris
Neuilly-sur-Seine
Scottish Borders
Stratford-on-Avon
Sunbury-on-Thames
Sutton Coldfield
Weston-super-Mare

16 letters:
Alcazar de San Juan
Berwick-upon-Tweed
Eastern Townships
Houghton-le-Spring
Sutton-in-Ashfield
Welwyn Garden City

17 letters:
Talavera de la Reina

18 letters:
Aldridge-Brownhills
Newcastle-under-Lyme
Prince Edward Island
Saint-Maur-des-Fossés

19 letters:
Bismarck Archipelago
Charleville-Mézières
Dumfries and Galloway

21 letters:
Queenborough in Sheppey

28 letters:
Saint Vincent and the
  Grenadines

Trade terms

2 letters:
CA
Co
HP
Rd

3 letters:
Bag
Bar
Bid
Bob
BOT
Buy
Cap
COD
Con
Dot
Due
Dun
EEC
Fee
IOU
Job
Lot
Ltd
Net
Oof
Owe
Par
Pay
Pit
Pro
Put
Rig
Sag
SET
Sum
Tag
Tax
Tin
Tip
VAT
Wad

4 letters:
Agio
Back
Bank
Bear

Body
Bond
Boom
Buck
Bulk
Bull
Bury
Call
Cant
Cash
Cess
Char
Chip
Coin
Co-op
Corn
Cost
Crop
Curb
Deal
Dear
Debt
Desk
Dibs
Dole
Drug
Dues
Dump
Dust
Duty
Earn
EFTA
Fair
Fees
Fine
Fire
Firm
Fisc
Free
Fund
Gain
Game
Gift
Gild
Gilt
Giro
Glut
Gold

Good
Haul
Hawk
Heap
Hire
Hive
Hold
Hype
Idle
IOUs
Item
Lend
Levy
Line
List
Loan
Long
Loss
Make
Mart
Meed
Milk
Mill
Mint
Nail
Note
Paid
Pawn
PAYE
Peag
Perk
Pool
Post
Rags
Raid
Rate
Reap
Rent
Risk
Roll
Roup
Ruin
Sack
Safe
Sale
Salt
Save
Scab

Trade terms

Sell
Shop
Sink
Slug
Sold
Stag
Swap
Tare
Task
Tick
Till
Tout
Vend
Visa
Wage
Ware
Work

5 letters:
Agent
Amass
Angel
Assay
Asset
At par
Audit
Baron
Batch
Beans
Bears
Bid up
Block
Blunt
Board
Bogus
Bones
Bonus
Boost
Booth
Brand
Brass
Broke
Bucks
Bulls
Bunce
Buyer
Buy up
By-bid
Cadge
Cargo
Cheap

Check
Chink
Chips
Chore
Clear
Clerk
Costs
Craft
Crash
Cycle
Debit
Depot
Dives
Dough
Dowry
Draft
Entry
Ernie
Exact
Files
Float
Forge
Funds
Gilts
Gnome
Goods
Gross
Guild
Hoard
House
Index
Ingot
Issue
Lease
Lucre
Maker
Means
Midas
Money
Ochre
Offer
Order
Owing
Panic
Paper
Piece
Pitch
Plant
Pound
Price
Prize

Purse
Queer
Quota
Quote
Rails
Rally
Rebuy
Remit
Repay
Rhino
Rocks
Salve
Scalp
Scoop
Score
Scrip
Set up
Share
Shark
Shift
Short
Skill
Slash
Slump
Smash
Smith
Snide
Spend
Spiel
Spots
Stake
Stall
Stand
Stint
Stock
Store
Strop
Tally
Taxes
Terms
Tithe
Token
Trade
Treat
Trend
Truck
Trust
Usury
Utter
Value
Venal

Wages
Wares
Welsh
Works
Worth
Yield

6 letters:

Abacus
Accept
Accrue
Admass
Afford
Agency
Agenda
Amount
Appeal
Arrear
Assets
At cost
Avails
Backer
Banker
Barker
Barter
Bazaar
Bearer
Boodle
Borrow
Bought
Bounce
Bounty
Bourse
Branch
Broker
Budget
Bureau
Bursar
Button
Buying
Buy out
Cambio
Career
Cartel
Cash in
Change
Charge
Cheque
Client
Coffer
Consol

Copper
Corner
Costly
Coupon
Cowrie
Credit
Crisis
Custom
Dealer
Deal in
Debtee
Debtor
Defray
Demand
Dicker
Drawer
Dunner
Emptio
Enrich
Equity
Errand
Estate
Excise
Expend
Export
Figure
Fiscal
Fold up
Freeze
Future
Garage
Gazump
Godown
Go slow
Gratis
Grease
Growth
Guinea
Haggle
Hammer
Hard up
Hawker
Import
Impose
Impost
In bulk
In cash
Income
In debt
In-tray
Jobber

Job lot
Labour
Leader
Ledger
Lender
Liable
Living
Luxury
Mammon
Merger
Minute
Moneys
Monger
Monies
Notice
Nugget
Octroi
Odd job
Odd lot
Office
On call
Oncost
On tick
Option
Outbid
Outcry
Outlay
Outlet
Output
Packet
Parity
Patron
Pauper
Pay day
Pay for
Paying
Pay-off
Payola
Pay out
Peddle
Pedlar
Picket
Pirate
Pledge
Plunge
Plutus
Pocket
Policy
Profit
Public
Purvey

Trade terms

Racket
Raffle
Rating
Ration
Realty
Rebate
Recoup
Redeem
Refund
Reject
Remedy
Render
Rental
Resale
Resell
Resign
Retail
Retire
Return
Reward
Rialto
Riches
Ruined
Salary
Save up
Saving
Sell up
Settle
Shares
Shorts
Silver
Simony
Smithy
Specie
Spiral
Sponge
Spread
Stable
Staker
Stocks
Strike
Sundry
Supply
Surtax
Swings
Tariff
Taxman
Teller
Tender
Tenths
Ticker

Ticket
Towage
Trader
Treaty
Tycoon
Unload
Unpaid
Usurer
Valuta
Vendor
Vendue
Wallet
Wampum
Wealth
Worker
Wright

7 letters:
Abscond
Account
Actuary
Allonge
Annuity
Arrears
Article
Atelier
Auction
Auditor
Automat
Average
Backing
Bad debt
Balance
Ballast
Banking
Bargain
Berries
Bidding
Bonanza
Bondage
Boycott
Bullets
Bullion
Bursary
Buy back
Cabbage
Calling
Cambist
Capital
Cash box
Cashier

Ceiling
Chapman
Charity
Chinker
Clinker
Coinage
Coining
Company
Concern
Consols
Contact
Convert
Coppers
Corn pit
Cottons
Counter
Croesus
Cumshaw
Customs
Cut-rate
Damages
Daybook
Dealing
Declare
Default
Deficit
Deflate
Deposit
Deviser
Dockage
Draw out
Due bill
Dumping
Economy
Effects
Embargo
Emption
Endorse
Engross
Entrust
Expense
Exploit
Exports
Factory
Failure
Fall due
Finance
Flutter
Foot lot
Foreman
Forgery

For sale	Oddment	Room man
Fortune	On offer	Rouleau
Foundry	On terms	Royalty
Freebie	On trust	Sacking
Freight	Opening	Salable
Full lot	Opulent	Salt tax
Futures	Out-tray	Salvage
Gabelle	Package	Savings
Gift box	Parlour	Seconds
Go broke	Parvenu	Selling
Good buy	Payable	Sell out
Good sum	Pay cash	Service
Go under	Payment	Shekels
Guerdon	Pay rise	Shopman
Half-day	Payroll	Shopper
Harvest	Payslip	Skilled
Haulage	Peddlar	Smelter
Head tax	Pending	Solvent
Holding	Pension	Sponger
Imports	Pet bank	Squeeze
Inflate	Plunger	Stipend
In funds	Poll tax	Storage
Intrust	Poor man	Striker
Invoice	Portage	Subsidy
Iron men	Pre-empt	Surplus
Jingler	Premium	Swindle
Jobbers	Prepaid	Takings
Jobbing	Pricing	Taxable
Jobless	Produce	Tax-free
Journal	Profits	Terrier
Killing	Promote	The city
Land tax	Pro rata	Tidy sum
Leading	Prosper	Trade in
Lending	Provide	Trading
Lettuce	Pursuit	Traffic
Limited	Pyramid	Tranche
Lockout	Realize	Trustee
Lombard	Realtor	Utility
Long-run	Refusal	Vacancy
Lottery	Regrate	Vending
Lump sum	Reissue	Venture
Manager	Release	Voucher
Man-made	Requite	Walkout
Mintage	Reserve	War bond
Mission	Retiral	Warrant
Moneyed	Returns	Wealthy
Nest egg	Revenue	Welfare
Net gain	Rich man	Well off
Notions	Rigging	Welsher
Nummary	Rollers	Wildcat

Trade terms

Workday

8 letters:
Above par
Accredit
Affluent
After tax
Agiotage
Agronomy
Amortize
Appraise
At a price
Auditing
Automate
Badly off
Bad money
Ballyhoo
Bankbook
Bank loan
Bank note
Bank roll
Bankrupt
Base coin
Basic pay
Bear pool
Bear raid
Beat down
Below par
Blackleg
Blue chip
Board lot
Boardman
Bondager
Boom town
Borrower
Boutique
Breakage
Brochure
Bull pool
Bull raid
Business
Buying in
Campaign
Carriage
Cashbook
Cash down
Cash sale
Circular
Clientry
Close out
Cold cash

Commands
Commerce
Consumer
Contango
Contract
Converts
Counting
Creditor
Credit to
Currency
Customer
Cut-price
Day shift
Dealings
Defrayal
Director
Disburse
Discount
Disposal
Dividend
Dry goods
Earnings
Embezzle
Employee
Employer
Emporium
Entrepot
Estimate
Evaluate
Exchange
Expended
Expenses
Exporter
Face ruin
Finances
Fire sale
Flat rate
Floorman
For a song
Free gift
Free port
Function
Gasworks
Gazetted
Gazumper
Gift shop
Gilt edge
Giveaway
Gold mine
Gold rush
Good will

Gratuity
Grow rich
Hallmark
Hard cash
Hard sell
Hardware
Hoarding
Homework
Hot money
Huckster
Importer
In arrear
Increase
Indebted
Industry
In pocket
Interest
In the red
Investor
Issuance
Issue par
Jeweller
Junkshop
Keep shop
Kitemark
Knitwork
Labourer
Lame duck
Largesse
Large sum
Legation
Levanter
Lifework
Live high
Live well
Long side
Low price
Low water
Make a bid
Make good
Manifest
Man power
Mark down
Material
Maturity
Merchant
Mint drop
Monetary
Moneybag
Moneybox
Monopoly

Mortgage
Net price
Net worth
No charge
Notation
Notecase
Oddments
Off price
On credit
On demand
On strike
Operator
Opulence
Ordinary
Overhaul
Overhead
Overseer
Overtime
Par value
Passbook
Pawn shop
Pay talks
Pin money
Pipeline
Pittance
Position
Post paid
Poundage
Practice
Premises
Price cut
Price war
Proceeds
Producer
Property
Prospect
Purchase
Put price
Quit rent
Rack rent
Rag trade
Rainy day
Receipts
Reckoner
Recorder
Recovery
Refinery
Register
Regrater
Rent-free
Rent roll

Requital
Reserves
Retailer
Retainer
Richesse
Richling
Round lot
Round sum
Rush hour
Salaried
Saleroom
Salesman
Salt down
Sanction
Scalping
Scarcity
Schedule
Security
Self-made
Shipment
Shipyard
Shopping
Short-run
Showcase
Showroom
Sideline
Sinecure
Small sum
Soft cell
Solatium
Solidity
Solvency
Spending
Spot cash
Spot sale
Square up
Sterling
Sundries
Supertax
Supplies
Swapping
Takeover
Take stop
Tallyman
Taxation
Tax dodge
Taxpayer
Time bill
Tolbooth
Tool shop
Toolwork

Top price
Trade gap
Trade off
Treasure
Treasury
Turnover
Underbid
Undercut
Usufruct
Valorize
Valuable
Venality
Vendible
Vocation
Wash sale
Watchdog
Well-to-do
Wharfage
Workaday
Work late
Workroom
Workshop
Write off

9 letters:
Absconder
Ad valorem
Affiliate
Affluence
Aggregate
Allowance
Amount due
Appraisal
Arbitrage
Arrearage
Assigment
Avocation
Back shift
Bad cheque
Bank clerk
Bank stock
Barrow boy
Bartering
Bear panic
Blind pool
Board room
Bond issue
Bon marché
Bonus bond
Borrowing
Box office

Trade terms

Brand name	Excise tax	Job of work
Breadline	Executive	Joint bank
Brokerage	Expansion	Keep books
Bucketing	Expensive	Knock down
Bull panic	Exploiter	Late shift
Buy in bulk	Export tax	Legal bond
By auction	Extortion	Liability
By-bidding	Face value	Life's work
By-product	Fair price	Liquidate
Cable code	Fair trade	List price
Cable rate	Fat profit	Long purse
Call price	Fiat money	Lossmaker
Cash grain	Financial	Low-priced
Catalogue	Financier	Luxury tax
Cellarage	Firm offer	Mail order
Cheapjack	Firm price	Make a sale
Check rate	Flash note	Market day
Clearance	Flat broke	Marketing
Clientage	Flotation	Means test
Clientele	Free trade	Middleman
Co-emption	Full purse	Moneybags
Coin money	Gilt-edged	Money belt
Commodity	Going rate	Mortgagee
Costerman	Gold piece	Mortgager
Cost price	Good price	Neat price
Craftsman	Greenback	Negotiate
Death duty	Guarantee	Net income
Debenture	Guarantor	Night safe
Deduction	Half-price	Officiate
Defaulter	Handiwork	Off market
Deflation	Hard goods	On account
Depositor	Hard money	On the nail
Dime store	Head buyer	Operative
Directors	Heavy cost	Order book
Direct tax	High price	Outgoings
Dirt-cheap	High value	Out of debt
Discharge	Holy stone	Out of work
Dishonour	Hot market	Outworker
Dismissal	Hush money	Overdraft
Dollar gap	Import tax	Overdrawn
Draw wages	In arrears	Overheads
Drug store	Incentive	Overspend
Easy money	Income tax	Patronage
Easy terms	In deficit	Patronize
Economics	Indemnity	Pay dearly
Economies	Inflation	Pay in kind
Economise	Insolvent	Paymaster
Emolument	Insurance	Pecuniary
Establish	In the city	Pecunious
Exchequer	Invention	Penniless
Exciseman	Inventory	Penny wise

Petty cash
Piecework
Piggy bank
Plutocrat
Poorly off
Portfolio
Pound note
Pourboire
Practical
Priceless
Price list
Price ring
Price rise
Prime cost
Principal
Profiteer
Promotion
Purchaser
Qualified
Quittance
Quotation
Ratepayer
Ready cash
Real wages
Recession
Reckoning
Reduction
Redundant
Reference
Refinance
Reflation
Registrar
Reimburse
Repayment
Resources
Restraint
Sacrifice
Sale block
Salesgirl
Sales talk
Secretary
Sell short
Shift work
Shop floor
Short sale
Short side
Sight bill
Single tax
Situation
Soft goods
Sole agent

Soundness
Speculate
Spendings
Spot grain
Spot price
Stability
Stamp duty
Statement
Stock list
Stockpile
Stock rate
Strike pay
Strongbox
Subsidize
Substance
Sumptuary
Surcharge
Sweatshop
Sweet shop
Syndicate
Synthetic
Tax return
Technical
The actual
The market
The street
Tie-in sale
Timocracy
Tollbooth
Trade fair
Trademark
Trade name
Trade sale
Tradesman
Traffic in
Treadmill
Treasurer
Undersell
Union card
Unit trust
Unsalable
Unskilled
Up for sale
Utilities
Utterance
Valuation
Vendition
Wage claim
Wage scale
Warehouse
Wash sales

Wealth tax
Well-lined
Whitewash
Wholesale
Work force
Workhouse
Work study
World Bank

10 letters:

Acceptance
Accountant
Accounting
Accumulate
Adjustment
Advertiser
Appreciate
Apprentice
Assessment
At a bargain
At a premium
At the spear
Auctioneer
Auction off
Automation
Average out
Bank credit
Bankruptcy
Bearer bond
Bear market
Best seller
Bill broker
Bill of sale
Blood money
Bondholder
Bonus stock
Bookkeeper
Bucket shop
Bulk buying
Buy and sell
Buy futures
Calculator
Capitalism
Capitalist
Capitalize
Chain banks
Chain store
Chancellor
Chargeable
Chargehand
Cheapening

Trade terms

Cheap skate
Cheque book
Chrematist
Chrysology
Closed shop
Closing bid
Collateral
Colporteur
Commercial
Commission
Compensate
Conference
Consortium
Contraband
Cost centre
Coupon bond
Credit card
Credit slip
Curb broker
Curb market
Daily bread
Dead market
Deep in debt
Defalcator
Defrayment
Del credere
Deliquence
Demand bill
Department
Depository
Depreciate
Depression
Direct cost
Dirty money
Dividend on
Dollar bill
Dummy share
Dutch treat
Easy market
Economizer
Efficiency
Employment
Encumbered
End product
Enterprise
Estate duty
Eurodollar
Evaluation
Ex-dividend
Exorbitant
Exposition

False money
Fancy goods
Fancy price
Fancy stock
Filthy rich
First offer
Fiscal year
Fixed price
Fixed trust
Flat market
Floor price
Floor trade
Forced sale
Free gratis
Free market
Free sample
Free trader
Freightage
Full stocks
Funded debt
Give credit
Gold nugget
Go on strike
Go shopping
Government
Green pound
Grindstone
Half stocks
Handicraft
Hand market
Have in hand
Head office
Heavy purse
High-priced
Hold office
Honorarium
Import duty
Imposition
In business
Income bond
Incumbered
Incur a debt
Industrial
Insolvency
Instalment
In the black
In the money
Investment
Job-hunting
Joint bonds
Joint stock

Jumble sale
Laboratory
Lighterage
Liquidator
Livelihood
Living wage
Loan market
Long market
Long seller
Loss leader
Management
Man of means
Marked down
Marketable
Market hall
Mass market
Meal ticket
Member bank
Mercantile
Merchantry
Midas touch
Monetarism
Monetarist
Moneyed man
Money order
Monopolise
Monopolist
Moratorium
Negotiable
Never never
Nightshift
Nominal fee
Nominal par
Nonpayment
Note of hand
Numismatic
Obligation
Occupation
Off licence
Oil of palms
On the block
On the cheap
On the rocks
On the shelf
Opening bid
Open market
Out of funds
Overcharge
Paper money
Pawnbroker
Peppercorn

Percentage
Picket duty
Pig in a poke
Pilot plant
Plutocracy
Pocket book
Power plant
Pre-emption
Preference
Prepayment
Price index
Price level
Printworks
Prix unique
Production
Profession
Profitable
Prospector
Prospectus
Prosperity
Provide for
Purchasing
Pure profit
Put and call
Ration book
Ready money
Real estate
Recompense
Recoupment
Redeemable
Redundancy
Remittance
Remunerate
Repair shop
Reparation
Repository
Repurchase
Retail shop
Retirement
Rock bottom
Round trade
Run up a bill
Salability
Sales force
Saving bank
Saving game
Scrip issue
Second-hand
Securities
Serial bond
Settlement

Settle with
Share index
Shoestring
Shopkeeper
Shop window
Short bonds
Sick market
Skilled man
Slave trade
Slow market
Smart money
Soft market
Sole agency
Speciality
Speculator
Split shift
Spondulies
Statistics
Steelworks
Steep price
Stock issue
Stockpiles
Stony broke
Straitened
Stronghold
Strongroom
Sum of money
Swap horses
Take a flier
Taskmaster
Tax evasion
Technician
Technocrat
The needful
Thin margin
Third World
Ticker tape
Tour of duty
Trade board
Trade cycle
Trade guild
Trade price
Trade route
Trade union
Treaty port
Typewriter
Typing pool
Underwrite
Unemployed
Upset price
Wad of notes

Wage freeze
Wage policy
Walk of life
Wall Street
Waterworks
Wealthy man
Well afford
Well-heeled
Wholesaler
Window-shop
Working day
Work to rule
Written off

11 letters:
Accountancy
Account book
Acquittance
Advertising
Agriculture
Antique shop
Appointment
Asking price
Assemby line
Association
At face value
Auction ring
Bank account
Bank balance
Bank holiday
Bank manager
Bank of issue
Barclaycard
Bargain sale
Bear account
Bear the cost
Betting shop
Big business
Billionaire
Bill of costs
Black market
Blank cheque
Bonus scheme
Book-keeping
Bottom price
Bread winner
Brisk market
Budget price
Bull account
Businessman
Capital gain

Trade terms

Carbon paper
Cash account
Catallactic
Caught short
Central bank
Certificate
Chamberlain
Chancellery
Chemist shop
Chrysocracy
Circulation
Closing down
Come to terms
Commodities
Common stock
Company rule
Competition
Competitive
Comptometer
Consumption
Cool million
Co-operative
Copperworks
Corn in Egypt
Corporation
Cost-benefit
Counterfeit
Cover charge
Cum dividend
Custom house
Customs duty
Danger money
Defence bond
Demand curve
Demarcation
Deposit slip
Devaluation
Display case
Distributor
Dividend off
Double entry
Down payment
Drive a trade
Dutch aution
Earn a living
Economic law
Economic man
Economy size
Embarrassed
Endorsement
Established

Estate agent
Expenditure
Fabrication
Fetch a price
Filthy lucre
Fixed assets
Fixed income
Floor broker
Fluctuation
Foot the bill
Foreclosure
Free harbour
Future grain
Future price
Gingerbread
Gross income
Hard bargain
High finance
Horse market
Hypermarket
Impecunious
Indirect tax
Industrials
Inexpensive
Institution
Intercourse
Ironmongery
Joint return
Key industry
King's ransom
Lap of luxury
Legal tender
Liberty bond
Life savings
Line of goods
Liquidation
Local branch
Local office
Long account
Long service
Loose change
Machine-made
Machine shop
Made of money
Manufactory
Manufacture
Market place
Market price
Mass-produce
Merchandise
Millionaire

Minimum wage
Mint of money
Money broker
Money dealer
Money lender
Money's worth
Money to burn
Negotiation
Nest factory
Net interest
Net receipts
Nuisance tax
Numismatics
On easy terms
On good terms
On the market
Open account
Open-end bond
Out of pocket
Outstanding
Overpayment
Package deal
Paper credit
Partnership
Pay cash down
Pay on demand
Pay spot cash
Pay the piper
Piece of work
Pilot scheme
Place of work
Pocket money
Polytechnic
Possessions
Postal order
Pots of money
Poverty line
Poverty trap
Premium bond
Pretty penny
Price-fixing
Price freeze
Price spiral
Price ticket
Property tax
Proposition
Purchase tax
Put-up market
Queer Street
Quoted price
Raw material

Reserve bank
Resignation
Restriction
Retiring age
Risk capital
Rummage sale
Run into debt
Safe deposit
Sales ledger
Salesperson
Savings bank
Self-service
Sell at a loss
Sell forward
Sell futures
Sharebroker
Shareholder
Share ledger
Shopping bag
Short change
Short seller
Single entry
Sinking fund
Slot machine
Small change
Small trader
Sole emption
Speculation
Sponsorship
Stagflation
Stockbroker
Stock dealer
Stockholder
Stockjobber
Stock ledger
Stock market
Stockpiling
Stocktaking
Storekeeper
Subsistence
Supermarket
Take-home pay
Take-over bid
Tattersall's
Tax assessor
Tax gatherer
Technocracy
The have-nots
Tight budget
Tight market
Time bargain

Tired market
To the tune of
Trade school
Trading post
Transaction
Travel agent
Truck system
Undercharge
Underwriter
Vendibility
Wherewithal
Working life
Workmanlike
Workmanship
Works outing
World market

12 letters:

Active market
Ad valorem tax
Amalgamation
Amortization
Amortizement
Arithmometer
Auction stand
Balance sheet
Bank examiner
Bargain offer
Bargain price
Barter system
Be in business
Bill of lading
Board meeting
Board of Trade
Bond to bearer
Bottom dollar
Bottomry bond
Branch office
Broker's agent
Brokers board
Business deal
Business life
Businesslike
Buyer's market
Buying public
Callable bond
Capital gains
Capital goods
Capital stock
Cash and carry
Cash register

Casual labour
Catallactics
Circular note
Clearing bank
Closing price
Common market
Compensation
Consumer good
Cook the books
Costermonger
Cost of living
Counting-room
Credit rating
Critical path
Currency note
Current price
Customs union
Denomination
Depreciation
Direct labour
Disbursement
Discount rate
Distribution
Dollar crisis
Durable goods
Early closing
Earned income
Econometrics
Economy drive
Entrepreneur
Exchange rate
Exhaust price
Extend credit
Extravagance
Fair exchange
Fill an office
First refusal
Fiscal policy
Fixed capital
Floating debt
Folding money
Foreign trade
Gate receipts
General store
Get rich quick
Going concern
Gold standard
Goods for sale
Great expense
Haberdashery
Hard currency

Trade terms

High pressure
Hire purchase
Hungry market
Impulse buyer
In conference
Indebtedness
Interest rate
Internal bond
In the gazette
Joint account
Keep accounts
Labour of love
Laissez-faire
Leather goods
Line of credit
Live in clover
Lively market
Long interest
Make a bargain
Make a fortune
Make delivery
Make one's pile
Manipulation
Manufacturer
Marginal cost
Mass-produced
Mercantilism
Monetization
Money changer
Money matters
Mortgage bond
National bank
Nearest offer
Nine till five
Nominal price
Nominal value
Nouveau riche
Odd-lot dealer
Offered price
Offer for sale
Office junior
Open-end trust
Opening price
Organization
Packing house
Pay as you earn
Pay in advance
Pegged market
Peg the market
Ply one's trade
Porte-monnaie

Pressure belt
Price ceiling
Price control
Price current
Price of money
Price rigging
Productivity
Professional
Profiteering
Profit margin
Profit motive
Purse strings
Rags to riches
Rate of growth
Redeployment
Regional bank
Remuneration
Remunerative
Reserve price
Retaining fee
Retrenchment
Rigged market
Rig the market
Rising prices
Rolling stock
Rubber cheque
Sale by outcry
Sale or return
Sales gimmick
Sales manager
Salesmanship
Satisfaction
Sell on credit
Severance pay
Share company
Shareholding
Short account
Show business
Slender means
Sliding scale
State lottery
Steady market
Sterling area
Stock company
Stock dealing
Stockholding
Stock in trade
Stockjobbery
Street market
Strike action
Strike it rich

Strong market
Superannuate
Sustain a loss
Tax collector
Tax exemption
Ten-cent store
The long green
Ticker market
Trade balance
Trade mission
Trading stamp
Travel agency
Treasury bill
Treasury note
Trial balance
Trustee stock
Unemployment
Variety store
Watered stock
Welfare State
Without a bean
Working class
Working order

13 letters:
Advertisement
Asset stripper
Bank messenger
Bank of England
Bank overdraft
Bank statement
Budget account
Budget surplus
Bulls and bears
Burial society
Business hours
Cash dispenser
Cash in advance
Cash on the nail
Clearance sale
Clearing-house
Commercialism
Commercialist
Company report
Concessionary
Confetti money
Confidence man
Consumer goods
Copartnership
Cost-effective
Counting-house

Credit account
Credit balance
Credit company
Credit squeeze
Crossed cheque
Current assets
Depressed area
Discount house
Discount store
Excess profits
Eye to business
Falling prices
Filing cabinet
Financial year
Fire insurance
Free-trade area
Fringe benefit
Going for a song
Impulse buying
Incorporation
Industrialism
In Queer Street
Life assurance
Life insurance
Lombard Street
Man of business
Millionairess
Modernisation
Money no object
Multinational
Multiple store
Parkinson's Law
Payment in kind
Payment in lieu
Penalty clause
Petticoat lane
Price increase
Private income
Private sector
Profitability
Profit and loss
Profit sharing
Protectionism
Protectionist
Public company
Purchase price
Raise the money
Rate for the job
Rates and texes
Regular income
Sellers market

Service charge
Small business
Small investor
Spending spree
Stock exchange
Strike breaker
Subcontractor
Tax-deductible
Trade discount
Trade unionism
Trade unionist
Trading estate
Value added tax
White elephant
Wild-cat strike

14 letters:
Accident policy
Asset stripping
Balance of trade
Bargain counter
Bill discounter
Capitalisation
Cash on delivery
Certain annuity
Clearance house
Company meeting
Concessionaire
Consumer demand
Corporation tax
Cost accountant
Cost accounting
Cost efficiency
Current account
Deposit account
Direct-debiting
Discount broker
Distressed area
Electricty bill
Expense account
Eye for business
Family business
Finance company
Free enterprise
Free of interest
Full employment
Gnomes of Zurich
Holding company
Imprest account
Inertia selling
Letter of credit

Lighting-up time
Limited company
Lloyd's register
Market research
Mass production
Merchant banker
Monthly payment
National income
National wealth
Ordinary shares
Over production
Over the counter
Penny-in-the-slot
Peppercorn rent
Peter principle
Private company
Production line
Pyramid selling
Quality control
Rate of exchange
Rate of interest
Second-hand shop
Shopping centre
Simple interest
Superannuation
Surrender value
Tariff reformer
Three mile limit
Under the hammer
Unearned income
Vending machine
Vested interest
Visible exports
Window shopping
Working capital

15 letters:
American Express
Bargain basement
Building society
Business as usual
Business circles
Business contact
Business manager
Business studies
Business venture
Capital gains tax
Carriage forward
Cash transaction
Closing-down sale
Commission agent

Trees

Company director
Company promoter
Complete annuity
Cottage industry
Deferred annuity
Deferred payment
Department store
Development area
Distress warrant
Dividend warrant
Do a roaring trade
Endowment policy
Entrepreneurial
Exchange control
Family allowance
Floating capital
Foreign exchange

Franking machine
Friendly society
Golden handshake
Income-tax
  demand
Income-tax rebate
Income-tax relief
Income-tax return
Insurance broker
Insurance policy
Investment trust
Invisible import
Labour intensive
Lightning strike
Marine insurance
Money for old rope
National savings

No-claim discount
Non-profit-making
Preference stock
Public ownership
Purchasing power
Registration fee
Regular customer
Reserve currency
Rock-bottom price
Service industry
Settle an account
Sleeping partner
Supply and demand
Suspense account
Under the counter
Unemployment pay
World of commerce

Trees

2 letters:
Bo
Ti

3 letters:
Ash
Asp
Bay
Bel
Ben
Box
Elm
Fig
Fir
Gum
Ita
Jak
Koa
Mot
Nim
Oak
Sal
Tea
Til
Ule
Wax
Yew

4 letters:
Acer
Akee

Aloe
Amla
Arar
Atap
Bael
Bhel
Bito
Boab
Bosk
Cade
Coco
Cola
Cork
Dali
Deal
Dhak
Dika
Dita
Eugh
Gean
Hule
Ilex
Jack
Kaki
Kiri
Kola
Lime
Lind
Lote
Mako

Ming
Mott
Mowa
Nipa
Ombu
Palm
Pear
Pine
Plum
Poon
Rata
Rhus
Rimu
Shea
Silk
Sloe
Sorb
Tawa
Teak
Teil
Titi
Toon
Tung
Tutu
Upas
Yang

5 letters:
Abele
Abies

Ackee
Afara
Alamo
Alder
Alnus
Anona
Apple
Areca
Argan
Aspen
Balsa
Beech
Belah
Belar
Birch
Bodhi
Boree
Bunya
Butea
Cacao
Carap
Carob
Cedar
Ceiba
China
Cocoa
Cocus
Coral
Ebony
Elder
Fagus
Fever
Flame
Guava
Hakea
Hazel
Hevea
Holly
Iroko
Jambu
Jarul
Judas
Karri
Kauri
Khaya
Kiaat
Kokum
Larch
Lemon
Lilac
Lotus

Mahoe
Mahua
Mahwa
Mamey
Mango
Maple
Marri
Matai
Melia
Motte
Mugga
Mulga
Mvule
Myall
Ngaio
Nyssa
Olive
Opepe
Osier
Palas
Palay
Panax
Papaw
Peach
Pecan
Pinon
Pipal
Pipul
Plane
Quina
Ramin
Roble
Rowan
Sabal
Saman
Sassy
Scrog
Silva
Smoke
Sumac
Taxus
Thorn
Thuja
Thuya
Tilia
Tsuga
Tuart
Tulip
Vitex
Wahoo
Wilga

Witch
Xylem
Yacca
Yucca
Yulan
Zaman
Zamia

6 letters:
Abroma
Acacia
Alerce
Almond
Angico
Annona
Antiar
Arbute
Arolla
Balsam
Banana
Banyan
Baobab
Bilian
Billar
Bombax
Bonsai
Bo-tree
Bottle
Brazil
Buriti
Cadaga
Cadagi
Carapa
Carica
Cashew
Cassia
Cembra
Cerris
Chaste
Chenar
Cherry
Chinar
Citron
Citrus
Coffee
Cordon
Cornel
Cornus
Deodar
Diana's
Dragon

Trees

Durian
Durion
Emblic
Eumong
Eumung
Feijoa
Fustet
Fustic
Gallus
Garjan
Gidgee
Gidjee
Gingko
Ginkgo
Glinap
Gnetum
Gopher
Guango
Gurjun
Gympie
Illipe
Illipi
Jarool
Jarrah
Joshua
Jujube
Kamala
Kamela
Kanuka
Karaka
Karite
Kowhai
Laurel
Lebbek
Linden
Locust
Longan
Loquat
Lucuma
Macoya
Mallee
Manuka
Mastic
Mimosa
Mopane
Mopani
Myrtle
Nutmeg
Obeche
Orange
Padauk

Padouk
Pagoda
Papaya
Pawpaw
Peepul
Pepper
Platan
Pomelo
Poplar
Popple
Protea
Puriri
Quince
Raffia
Red-bud
Ricker
Roucou
Rubber
Sabicu
Sallow
Samaan
Sapele
Sapium
Sapota
Saxaul
She-oak
Sinder
Souari
Spruce
Stemma
Styrax
Sumach
Sunder
Sundra
Sundri
Tamanu
Tewart
Titoki
Tooart
Totara
Tupelo
Waboom
Walnut
Wandoo
Wattle
Wicken
Willow
Witgat
Yarran
Zamang

7 letters:

Ailanto
Amboina
Apricot
Arbutus
Avodire
Bebeeru
Bilimbi
Bilsted
Bubinga
Buck-eye
Bursera
Cabbage
Cajeput
Cajuput
Calamus
Camphor
Camwood
Canella
Carbean
Carbeen
Catalpa
Champac
Champak
Chayote
Coconut
Coquito
Cork oak
Corylus
Corypha
Cumquat
Cypress
Dagwood
Dogwood
Dryades
Durmast
Geebung
Genipap
Gluinap
Grey gum
Hemlock
Hickory
Holm-oak
Iron gum
Jipyapa
Juniper
Karbeen
Kumquat
Lacquer
Lagetto
Lentisk

Logwood
Lumbang
Madrono
Mahaleb
Manjack
Marasca
Margosa
Mazzard
Mesquit
Moringa
Morrell
Pereira
Pimento
Platane
Pollard
Populus
Quassia
Quicken
Quillai
Quinain
Radiata
Rampike
Redwood
Rock elm
Saksaul
Sandbox
Saouari
Sapling
Sausage
Sequoia
Seringa
Service
Shittah
Snow gum
Sourgum
Soursop
Spindle
Sundari
Tea-tree
Varnish
Wallaba
Wirilda
Witchen
Wych-elm
Xylopia
Zelkova

8 letters:
Aguacate
Algaroba
Aquillia

Bangalay
Bangalow
Banyalla
Basswood
Beefwood
Benjamin
Berrigan
Black boy
Black oak
Blimbing
Bountree
Bourtree
Breadnut
Brigalow
Bulwaddy
Calabash
Chestnut
Cinchona
Cinnamon
Cocoplum
Coolabah
Coolibah
Corkwood
Date palm
Dendroid
Dracaena
Espalier
Eucalypt
Flittern
Fraxinus
Garcinia
Ghost gum
Gnetales
Guaiacum
Hagberry
Hawthorn
Hoop pine
Hornbeam
Huon pine
Igdrasil
Ironbark
Ironwood
Jelutong
Kingwood
Laburnum
Lacebark
Lecythis
Loblolly
Magnolia
Mahogany
Makomako

Mangrove
Manna-ash
Mesquite
Mulberry
Ocotillo
Oiticica
Oleaceae
Oleaster
Palmetto
Pichurim
Pinaster
Pyinkado
Quandang
Quandong
Quantong
Quillaia
Quillaja
Quondong
Raintree
Rambutan
Rangiora
Rewa-rewa
Rivergum
Rosewood
Sago-palm
Sandarac
Santalum
Sapindus
Sapucaia
Scots fir
Sea grape
Silky oak
Simaruba
Soapbark
Sourwood
Stinging
Sweet gum
Sweetsop
Sycamine
Sycamore
Sycomore
Tamarack
Tamarind
Tamarisk
Taxodium
Umbrella
White ash
Whitegum
Witch elm
Ygdrasil

Trees

Ylang-ylang

11 letters:
Appleringie
Black wattle
Blanket-leaf
Cabbage-palm
Chaulmoogra
Chokecherry
Cryptomeria
Dipterocarp
Eriodendron
Flamboyante
Fothergilla
Leatherwood
Lignum vitae
Liquidambar
Maceranduba
Mountain ash
Pomegranate
Purpleheart
Pussy willow
Radiata pine
River red gum
Scribbly gum
Shittimwood

Silver birch
Sitka spruce
Stringy-bark

12 letters:
Bangalow palm
Golden wattle
Gympie nettle
Hercules' club
Insignis pine
Liriodendron
Mammee-sapota
Masseranduba
Monkey puzzle
Monterey pine
Washingtonia

13 letters:
Camphor laurel
Celery-top pine
Horse chestnut
Moreton Bay ash
Moreton Bay fig
Paper-mulberry
Peppermint gum
Queensland nut

Weeping willow

14 letters:
Antarctic beech
Bunya-bunya pine
Cedar of Lebanon
Illawarra flame
Stinking wattle

15 letters:
Bastard mahogany
Cabbage tree palm

16 letters:
Tasmanian blue
  gum

17 letters:
Bat's wing
  coral-tree
Norfolk Island pine

18 letters:
Moreton Bay
  chestnut

5 letters:
Cords
Jeans
Levis®
Loons
Slops
Trews

6 letters:
Breeks
Capris
Chinos
Denims
Flares
Slacks
Trouse

7 letters:
Combats
Joggers
Kachera
Pyjamas

Shalwar

8 letters:
Bloomers
Breeches
Britches
Culottes
Flannels
Hipsters
Hot pants
Jodhpurs
Knickers
Leggings
Overalls
Ski pants

9 letters:
Buckskins
Churidars
Corduroys
Dungarees
Loon pants

Plus fours
Trunk hose
Wranglers®

10 letters:
Capri pants
Cargo pants
Drainpipes
Hip-huggers
Lederhosen
Oxford bags
Pantaloons
Salopettes
Stovepipes

11 letters:
Bell-bottoms

12 letters:
Galligaskins
Gallygaskins
Palazzo pants
Pedal pushers

Smallclothes

13 letters:
Bermuda shorts
Cycling shorts
Spatterdashes
Toreador pants

14 letters:
Knickerbockers
Riding breeches

15 letters:
Jogging trousers

17 letters:
Sweat-suit trousers
Tracksuit trousers

Tumours

3 letters:
Wen
Yaw

4 letters:
Crab
Mole
Wart

5 letters:
Grape
Gumma
Myoma
Talpa
Wilm's

6 letters:
Anbury
Cancer
Epulis
Glioma
Lipoma
Myxoma
Struma

7 letters:
Adenoma
Angioma
Dermoid
Fibroid
Fibroma

Myeloma
Neuroma
Osteoma
Polypus
Sarcoma
Thymoma

8 letters:
Crab-yaws
Ganglion
Hepatoma
Lymphoma
Melanoma
Seminoma
Steatoma
Teratoma
Windgall
Xanthoma

9 letters:
Carcinoid
Carcinoma
Chondroma
Condyloma
Encanthis
Exostosis
Granuloma
Haematoma
Papilloma

10 letters:
Meningioma

11 letters:
Astrocytoma
Encephaloma
Gioblastoma
Haemangioma

12 letters:
Angiosarcoma
Endothelioma
Mesothelioma
Osteosarcoma

13 letters:
Neuroblastoma
Osteoclastoma

14 letters:
Carcinosarcoma
Retinoblastoma

15 letters:
Burkitt lymphoma
Medullablastoma

16 letters:
Burkitt's lymphoma

Typefaces

3 letters:
Gem

4 letters:
Pica
Quad
Ruby

5 letters:
Agate
Canon
Elite
Pearl
Roman
Ronde

Serif

6 letters:
Aldine
Caslon
Cicero
Gothic

Minion
Primer

7 letters:
Braille
Brevier
Elzevir
Emerald
Fraktur
Old-face
Paragon
Plantin

Quadrat

8 letters:
Bold face
Egyptian
Garamond
Old style
Sanserif
Semibold

9 letters:
Bourgeois
Brilliant

Clarendon
Columbian
Non-pareil

10 letters:
Longprimer

11 letters:
Baskerville
Black-letter
Great primer

U

Underwear

3 letters:
Bra

4 letters:
Body
Vest

5 letters:
Pants
Shift
Teddy

6 letters:
Basque
Boxers
Briefs
Bustle
Corset
Garter
Girdle
Shorts
Trunks
T-shirt

7 letters:
Drawers
G-string
Pannier
Panties

Singlet
Step-ins
Y-fronts

8 letters:
Balmoral
Bloomers
Broekies
Camisole
Corselet
Half-slip
Knickers
Lingerie
Thermals

9 letters:
Brassiere
Crinoline
Jockstrap
Long johns
Petticoat
Suspender
Undervest
Union suit
Waist-slip

10 letters:
Chemisette
Garter belt

String vest
Underpants
Undershirt
Underskirt

11 letters:
Boxer shorts
Panty girdle
Undershorts

12 letters:
Body stocking
Camiknickers
Combinations
Underdrawers

13 letters:
Liberty bodice
Suspender belt

14 letters:
French knickers

15 letters:
Athletic support

17 letters:
Foundation
 garment

Units

1 letter:
K

2 letters:
SI

3 letters:
Amp
Bar

Bit
Erg
Gal
GeV
Lux
Mho
Mil
Nit

Ohm
Rem
Rep
Tog

4 letters:
Baud
Byte

Dyne
Foot
Gram
Gray
Hour
Inch
Mile
Octa
Okta
Phot
Pint
Slug
Sone
Torr
Volt
Watt
Yard

5 letters:
Crith
Cusec
Daraf
Darcy
Debye
Farad
Fermi
Gauss
Henry
Hertz
Joule
Litre
Lumen
Metre
Neper
Nepit
Ounce
Pixel
Pound
Quart
Remen
Sabin
Stilb
Stoke
Stone

Tesla
Therm
Weber
Yrneh

6 letters:
Dalton
Degree
Denier
Dobson
Gallon
Jansky
Kelvin
Kilerg
Lexeme
Micron
Morgen
Newton
Pascal
Probit
Radian
Second
Sememe
Stokes

7 letters:
Candela
Congius
Coulomb
Dioptre
Energid
Fresnel
Gigabit
Gilbert
Lambert
Man-hour
Maxwell
Megaton
Micella
Micelle
Minute
Oersted
Phoneme
Poundal
Rontgen

Semeion
Siemens
Sievert
Syntagm
Tagmeme

8 letters:
Abampere
Angstrom
Chaldron
Electron
Glosseme
Kilowatt
Magneton
Megabyte
Megawatt
Morpheme
Roentgen
Syntagma
Terabyte
Therblig

9 letters:
Becquerel
Kilderkin
Kilometre
Megahertz
Microinch
Steradian

10 letters:
Centimetre
Centipoise
Dessiatine
Microcurie
Millilitre
Millimetre
Nanosecond
Picosecond
Ploughgate
Rutherford

11 letters:
Centimorgan
Pennyweight

V

Vegetables

3 letters:
Cos
Oca
Pea
Udo
Yam

4 letters:
Beet
Cole
Corn
Guar
Kail
Kale
Leek
Neep
Okra
Okro
Puha
Sium
Spud
Taro

5 letters:
Ackee
Beans
Chard
Chive
Choko
Chufa
Cress
Ingan
Mooli
Navew
Onion
Orach
Pease
Puwha
Savoy
Swede
Syboe

6 letters:
Adjigo
Allium
Batata
Bhindi
Calalu
Carrot
Celery
Daikon
Endive
Fennel
Frisee
Greens
Jicama
Kumara
Kumera
Lablab
Mangel
Marrow
Orache
Pepper
Potato
Pratie
Quinoa
Radish
Rapini
Sorrel
Sprout
Squash
Tomato
Turnip
Warran

7 letters:
Bok choy
Cabbage
Calaloo
Cardoon
Chayote
Chicory

Cocoyam
Collard
Gherkin
Lettuce
Mangold
Pak-choi
Parsnip
Pimento
Pumpkin
Rauriki
Romaine
Salsify
Shallot
Skirret
Spinach
Spinage
Sprouts

8 letters:
Baby corn
Beetroot
Brassica
Broccoli
Capsicum
Celeriac
Cucumber
Eggplant
Escarole
Eschalot
Hastings
Kohlrabi
Pimiento
Rutabaga
Samphire
Scallion
Zucchini

9 letters:
Artichoke
Asparagus
Aubergine

Broad bean
Calabrese
Corn salad
Courgette
Finocchio
Mangetout
Radicchio
Rocambole
Succotash
Sweet corn
Tonka-bean

10 letters:
Alexanders
Bean sprout
Beef tomato
Bell pepper
Cos lettuce
Salad onion

See also:
➤ **Potatoes**

Scorzonera
Silver beet

11 letters:
Cauliflower
Chinese leaf
Horseradish
Lady's finger
Oyster plant
Spinach-beet
Spring onion
Sweet potato

12 letters:
Cherry tomato
Corn on the cob
Lamb's lettuce
Mangel-wurzel
Marrow squash

Savoy cabbage
Spanish onion
Spring greens

13 letters:
Pe-tsai cabbage

14 letters:
Brussels sprout
Chinese cabbage
Globe artichoke
Iceberg lettuce

15 letters:
Vegetable marrow

16 letters:
Butternut pumpkin

18 letters:
Jerusalem artichoke

Vehicles

3 letters:
ATV
Bus
Cab
Car
Hog
JCB®
LEM
Ute
Van

4 letters:
Bike
Boat
Cart
Dray
Jeep®
Kago
Kart
Luge
Pram
Quad
Scow
Shay
Ship
Sled

Tank
Taxi
Tram
Trap

5 letters:
Artic
Brake
Buggy
Coach
Coupé
Crate
Cycle
Float
Hatch
Lorry
Moped
Ratha
Soyuz
Sulky
Tip-up
Tonga
Towie
Train
Truck
Turbo

Vespa
Wagon

6 letters:
Barrow
Camion
Camper
Chaise
Dennet
Fiacre
Gharri
Gharry
Go-cart
Go-kart
Hansom
Hearse
Jet ski
Jingle
Jinker
Jitney
Koneke
Launch
Limber
Litter
Pick-up
Rocket

Vehicles

Samlor
Skibob
Skidoo®
Sledge
Sleigh
Sno-Cat®
Spider
Surrey
Tandem
Tanker
Telega
Tourer
Tricar
Troika
Tuk tuk
Vahana
Waggon

7 letters:
Amtrack
Bicycle
Caravan
Chariot
Dog-cart
Gritter
Growler
Jeepney
Kibitka
Komatik
Minibus
Minicab
Minivan
Norimon
Omnibus
Pedicab
Phaeton
Postbus
Railcar
Ricksha
Scooter
Sidecar
Tempera
Tipcart
Tracked
Tractor
Trailer
Tramcar
Travois
Trishaw
Trolley
Tumbrel

Tumbril
Utility
Volante
Wildcat

8 letters:
Aircraft
Brancard
Carriage
Carry-all
Curricle
Dustcart
Motorbus
Motorcar
Panda car
Rickshaw
Runabout
Scout car
Stanhope
Steam-car
Tarantas
Toboggan
Tow truck
Tricycle
Unicycle

9 letters:
Ambulance
Autocycle
Bulldozer
Cabriolet
Camper van
Charabanc
Dormobile®
Dump truck
Dune buggy
Estate car
Gladstone
Half-track
Hansom cab
Hatchback
Jaunty car
Jinriksha
Landaulet
Land Rover
Limousine
Low-loader
Milk float
Motorbike
Police car
Racing car
Road train

Sand-yacht
Spaceship
Sports car
Streetcar
Tarantass
Trail bike
Tumble-car
Wagonette

10 letters:
Black Maria
Fire engine
Hovercraft
Jinricksha
Jinrikisha
Juggernaut
Locomotive
Motorcycle
Panel truck
Post chaise
Roadroller
Shandrydan
Snowmobile
Snow plough
Spacecraft
Space probe
Stagecoach
Tank engine
Touring car
Trolleybus
Trolley car
Tumble-cart
Two-wheeler
Velocipede
Waggonette

11 letters:
Articulated
Caterpillar®
Delivery van
Dumper-truck
Jaunting car
Jinrickshaw
Landaulette
Light engine
Steamroller
Tipper lorry
Tipper truck
Wheelbarrow

12 letters:
Autorickshaw

Breakdown van
Double-decker
Garbage truck
Motorbicycle
Motor caravan
Motor scooter
Motor vehicle
Pantechnicon
Perambulator
Single-decker
Space capsule

Space shuttle
Station wagon
Three-wheeler
Troop carrier
Utility truck

13 letters:
Fork-lift truck
Paddock-basher
Penny-farthing
People carrier

14 letters:
Conestoga wagon
Off-road vehicle
Traction engine

16 letters:
Articulated lorry
Combine harvester

See also:
➤ **Aircraft** ➤ **Bicycles** ➤ **Boats and ships** ➤ **Cars**
➤ **Carriages and carts** ➤ **Locomotives**

Veins

4 letters:
Spur

6 letters:
Portal
Radius

7 letters:
Basilic
Femoral

Jugular
Saphena

8 letters:
Terminal
Vena cava

9 letters:
Arteriole
Pulmonary

Sectorial

10 letters:
Subclavian

11 letters:
Subscapular

Verse forms

3 letters:
Lay
Ode

4 letters:
Epic
Sijo
Song

5 letters:
Ditty
Elegy
Epode
Haiku
Idyll
Lyric
Rhyme
Tanka
Verse

6 letters:
Ballad
Epopee
Ghazal
Monody
Sonnet

7 letters:
Bucolic
Couplet
Eclogue
Epigram
Georgic
Pantoum
Rondeau
Sestina
Triolet
Virelay

8 letters:
Acrostic
Cinquain
Clerihew
Jintishi
Limerick
Lipogram
Madrigal
Palinode
Pastoral
Thin poem
Verselet
Versicle

9 letters:
Free verse
Roundelay
Shape poem

10 letters:
Villanelle

12 letters:
Concrete poem
Epithalamium

Nursery rhyme
Prothalamion

Volcanoes

3 letters:
Apo
Aso
Puy

4 letters:
Etna
Fuji
Maui
Pelé
Taal

5 letters:
Askja
Elgon
Hekla
Kauai
Kenya
Mayon
Misti
Pelée
Teide
Teyde
Thira

6 letters:
Ararat
Asosan
Egmont
Erebus
Ischia
Katmai
Kazbek
Llaima
Semeru
Tolima

7 letters:
Aragats

El Misti
Hornito
Huascán
Iliamna
Iwo Jima
Kilauea
Ruapehu
Semeroe
Tambora

8 letters:
Antisana
Cameroon
Cotopaxi
Krakatau
Krakatoa
Mauna Kea
Mauna Loa
St Helens
Taraniki
Vesuvius

9 letters:
Aniakchak
Corcovado
Haleakala
Helgafell
Huascarán
Paricutín
Pozzolana
Puzzolana
Soufrière
Stromboli
Suribachi
Tangariro

10 letters:
Chimborazo
Lassen Peak

Montserrat
Nyiragongo
Pozzuolana
Santa Maria
Tungurahua

11 letters:
Erciyas Dagi
Kilimanjaro
Mount Erebus
Mount Katmai
Nyamuragira
Olympus Mons

12 letters:
Citlaltépetl
Ixtaccihuatl
Iztaccihuatl
National Park
Popocatépetl

13 letters:
Mount Demavend
Mount St. Helens

14 letters:
Nevado de Colima
Nevado de Toluca
Soufrière Hills
Tristan da Cunha

17 letters:
Warrumbungle
 Range

Warfare terms

2 letters:
AB
GI
MP
RA
RE
RN

3 letters:
Arm
Axe
Bow
Cap
Cut
Dud
Foe
Gat
Gun
Hun
NCO
POW
RAF
Ram
Rat
Rod
Row
Sap
Spy
Sub
TNT
Tyr
Van
Vet
War

4 letters:
Ally
Ammo
Ares
Arms
Army

A-war
AWOL
Ball
Band
Barb
Bard
Bill
Bird
Bola
Bolt
Bomb
Bone
Bout
Bren
Butt
Camp
Club
Cock
Coif
Colt
Cosh
Dart
D-day
Dike
Dirk
Dove
Duck
Duel
Dump
Duty
Epee
Exon
Feud
File
Fire
Fish
Flak
Foil
Fort
Fray

Guns
Hate
Hawk
Helm
Hero
Hilt
Hold
Host
H-war
ICBM
Impi
Jack
Jamb
Jeep
Jock
Keep
Kill
Kris
Levy
Load
Lock
Mail
Mars
Mere
Mine
MIRV
Moat
Mole
Navy
Odin
Peel
Peon
Pike
Post
Rack
Rank
Rath
Riot
Rock
Rout

Warfare terms

Rush
Shot
Slug
Spit
Spur
Stab
Tank
Tuck
Unit
WACS
Wage
Wall
Ward
WAVE
Wing
WRNS
Yomp
Zone
Zulu

5 letters:
AA gun
A-bomb
Aegis
Arena
Armed
Armet
Array
Arrow
At bay
At war
Baton
Beset
Blade
Blank
Blast
Blitz
Boche
Bolas
Brave
Broch
Buffs
Burst
Cadre
Chute
Clash
Corps
Cover
Ditch
Draft
Drive

Enemy
Feint
Fence
Field
Fight
Flail
Flank
Fleet
Foray
Fosse
Front
Fusee
Fusil
Grape
Guard
Harry
H-bomb
H-hour
Jerid
Jerry
Jihad
Jingo
Knife
Kukri
Lager
Lance
Leave
Luger
Melee
Mound
Muket
Onset
Orgue
Parry
Pavis
Plate
Poilu
Posse
Power
Provo
Rally
Range
Ranks
Rebel
Recce
Redan
Repel
Rifle
Rowel
Sally
Salvo

Scarp
Scene
Scout
Sepoy
Serve
Shaft
Shako
Shell
Shoot
Siege
Skean
Sling
Snake
Sowar
Spahi
Spear
Spike
Spray
Spurs
Squad
Staff
Steel
Stick
Stone
Storm
Sword
Targe
Tasse
Tommy
Train
Troop
Truce
U-boat
Uhlan
Visor
WAACS
WAAFS
Waddy
Woden
Wound
WRACS
Wrens

6 letters:
Abatis
Ack-ack
Action
Air arm
Air gun
Alpeen
Amazon

Ambush
Animus
Anzacs
Archer
Archie
Argosy
Armada
Armour
Askari
Assail
Attack
Barbel
Barrel
Batman
Battle
Beaver
Bellum
Big gun
Billet
Bomber
Breech
Bugler
Bullet
Bunker
Camail
Cannon
Casque
Castle
Casual
Charge
Cohort
Column
Combat
Convoy
Cordon
Corium
Creese
Cudgel
Cuisse
Curfew
Curtal
Dagger
Defeat
Defend
Detail
Donjon
Dry run
Duello
Dugout
Dumdum
Enlist

Ensign
Escarp
Escort
Exocet
Fewter
Flight
Foeman
Forage
Forces
Gabion
Galoot
Glacis
Glaive
Gorget
Greave
Gunner
Gun shy
Gurkha
Gusset
Hagbut
Hammer
Hanger
Hanjar
Harass
Heaume
Helmet
Hot war
Hussar
Impact
Impale
In arms
Inroad
Jereed
Jingal
Laager
Labrys
Lancer
Legion
Lorica
Mailed
Maquis
Marine
Mauser
Merlon
Minnie
Morion
Mortar
Muster
Muzzle
Oilcan
Outfit

Panzer
Parade
Parole
Patrol
Pavise
Pellet
Pepper
Petard
Picket
Pierce
Pistol
Pogrom
Pompom
Powder
Pow-pow
Quiver
Rafale
Rajput
Ramrod
Rapier
Rappel
Ray gun
Razzia
Rebuff
Reduit
Report
Revolt
Rioter
Rocket
Rookie
Salade
Sallet
Salute
Sangar
Sapper
Sconce
Scutum
Sentry
Set gun
Shield
Slogan
Sniper
Sortie
Sparth
Spying
Strafe
Strike
Swivel
Talion
Target
Tenail

Warfare terms

Thrust
To arms
Tocsin
Toledo
Tom-tom
Trench
Troops
Tulwar
Turret
Vallum
Valour
Vandal
Victor
Volley
War cry
War god
Weapon
Womera
Yeoman
Zouave

7 letters:
Abattis
Advance
Air raid
Amnesty
Archery
Armoury
Arsenal
Assault
Assegai
Atom gun
Atom war
Baldric
Barrack
Barrage
Barrier
Bar shot
Basinet
Bastion
Battery
Bayonet
Bazooka
Beat off
Bellona
Big guns
Big shot
Blowgun
Boer War
Bombard
Bombing

Booster
Bravado
Bren gun
Bricole
Brigade
Buckler
Bulldog
Bulwark
Caisson
Caitiff
Calibre
Caliver
Caltrop
Canonry
Cap-a-pie
Carbine
Carcass
Carrier
Cashier
Cavalry
Chamade
Chamber
Charger
Chicken
Citadel
Cold war
Command
Company
Conchie
Conquer
Cordite
Corslet
Cossack
Coupure
Courage
Courser
Crusade
Cudgels
Cuirass
Curtain
Curtana
Cutlass
Dastard
Defence
Disband
Distaff
Dragoon
Draught
Dry fire
Dudgeon
Dueller

Dungeon
Echelon
Enomoty
Fall-out
Fend off
Fighter
Firearm
Fortify
Fortlet
Foxhole
Gallant
Gallery
Gas bomb
Gas mask
Germ war
Gisarme
Go to war
Grapnel
Grenade
Gunboat
Gundeck
Gunfire
Gunlock
Gunnage
Gunnery
Gunning
Gun park
Gunplay
Gun port
Gunroom
Gunshot
Hackbut
Halberd
Handjar
Harness
Hatchet
Hauberk
Heroism
Hessian
Heyduck
Hold off
Holster
Holy war
Hostage
Invader
Jackman
Jambeau
Jankers
Javelin
Jollies
Jump jet

Knifing
Kremlin
Lambast
Lamboys
Longbow
Long Tom
Lookout
Lunette
Lyddite
Machete
Make war
Maniple
Mantlet
Marines
Martial
Matross
Megaton
Militia
Missile
Mission
Neutral
Offence
On guard
Open war
Outpost
Outwork
Paladin
Panoply
Parados
Parapet
Patriot
Pedrero
Petrary
Phalanx
Pikeman
Pillbox
Platoon
Poleaxe
Poniard
Private
Quarrel
Rampage
Rampart
Ravelin
Recruit
Red army
Redcoat
Redoubt
Regular
Repulse
Retreat

Riposte
Sabaoth
Sabaton
Salient
Samurai
Sandbag
Seabees
Section
Self bow
Service
Shoot at
Shooter
Shotgun
Soldier
Spartan
Sparthe
Spinner
Sten gun
Supremo
Tactics
Tear-gas
Tenable
Testudo
Theatre
The fray
Torpedo
Traitor
Trigger
Trooper
Tumbril
Uniform
Veteran
Victory
Wage war
War club
Ward off
War drum
Warfare
War game
Warhead
Warlike
Warlord
Warpath
Warring
Warrior
Warship
War song
Weapons
Wind gun
Woomera
Wounded

Yatagan
Yomping

8 letters:
Aceldama
Activate
Air force
Air rifle
Air-to-air
All-clear
Alliance
Ammo dump
Anabasis
Anti-mine
Arbalest
Armament
Armature
Armoured
Arms race
Arquebus
Art of war
Atom bomb
Attacker
Aventail
Ballista
Banderol
Barbette
Barbican
Barracks
Bartisan
Baselard
Battalia
Battling
Bear arms
Besieger
Betrayer
Blockade
Blowpipe
Bludgeon
Bomb rack
Bomb site
Brattice
Brickbat
Broadaxe
Browning
Buckshot
Buttress
Buzzbomb
Campaign
Casemate
Catapult

Warfare terms

Cavalier
Chaffron
Chamfron
Champion
Chasseur
Chivalry
Civil war
Claymore
Cold feet
Commando
Conflict
Crossbow
Cry havoc
Culverin
Cylinder
Defender
Demilune
Deserter
Destrier
Division
Doughboy
Drum call
Drumfire
Drumhead
Duellist
Dynamite
Embattle
Enfilade
Enlistee
Entrench
Envelope
Errantry
Escalade
Exercise
Falchion
Falconet
Fasthold
Fastness
Fencible
Field gun
Fighting
File fire
Fireball
Fire bomb
Firelock
Fire upon
Flotilla
Fortress
Fugleman
Furlough
Fusilier

Gambeson
Garrison
Gauntlet
Great War
Guerilla
Gunflint
Gunmetal
Gunpoint
Gunsmith
Gunstick
Gunstock
Hang fire
Heavy gun
Hedgehog
Herisson
Hill fort
Hireling
Hornwork
Howitzer
Infantry
Informer
Invading
Invasion
Ironclad
Janizary
Jazerant
Jingoism
Jump area
Killadar
Knuckles
Lancegay
Land-army
Land-mine
Langrage
Last post
Launcher
Leon mine
Lewis gun
Loophole
Magazine
Mailclad
Man-of-war
Mantelet
Marksman
Martello
Massacre
Maxim gun
Melinite
Militant
Military
Mobilize

Morrison
Muniment
Munition
Mushroom
Musketry
Nerve gas
Open fire
Ordnance
Orillion
Outguard
Overkill
Pacifist
Palisade
Palstaff
Palstave
Partisan
Password
Pauldron
Petronel
Pikehead
Poltroon
Puncheon
Quisling
Quo vadis
Recreant
Regiment
Renegade
Repulsor
Reserves
Reveille
Revolver
Ricochet
Rifleman
Risalder
Runagate
Safehold
Scabbard
Scimitar
Sentinel
Shrapnel
Side arms
Siege cap
Skean dhu
Skirmish
Soldiery
Solleret
Space gun
Spadroon
Spearman
Spontoon
Squadron

Stabbing
Stalwart
Star Wars
Stave off
Stiletto
Stockade
Strafing
Strategy
Struggle
Surprise
Surround
Take arms
Tenaille
The front
The sword
Time bomb
Tomahawk
Tommy gun
Total war
Transfix
Trenches
Turnback
Turncoat
Turntail
Up in arms
Uprising
Vambrace
Vamplate
Vanguard
Vanquish
Vendetta
War cloud
Warcraft
War dance
Warfarer
War horse
War hound
War paint
War whoop
Waterloo
Wayfarer
Weaponry
World war
Yeomanry
Zero hour

9 letters:
Accoutred
Aggressor
Air-to-ship
Ambuscade

Arch enemy
Army corps
Army issue
Army lists
Arrowhead
Artillery
Assailant
Atomic gun
Atomic war
Attacking
Attrition
Automatic
Auto-rifle
Backplate
Ballistic
Banderole
Bandolier
Bastinado
Battalion
Battleaxe
Battlecry
Beachhead
Beefeater
Beleaguer
Bellicism
Bellicose
Big Bertha
Blackjack
Bloodshed
Bomb-happy
Bombs away
Bombshell
Bombsight
Booby trap
Boomerang
Broadside
Brown Bess
Brown bill
Camouflet
Cannonade
Cannoneer
Caparison
Carronade
Carry arms
Cartouche
Cartridge
Casemated
Castellan
Cease fire
Chain mail
Chain shot

Challenge
Chamfrain
Chassepot
Cold steel
Combatant
Combative
Conqueror
Conscript
Corselect
Crackshot
Cross fire
Defensive
Derringer
Desert rat
Deterrent
Detonator
Discharge
Doodlebug
Double sap
Drop a bomb
Earthwork
Embattled
Encompass
Enemy camp
Enemy fire
Escopette
Espionage
Explosive
Face guard
Fence wall
Field army
Fieldwork
Fire a shot
Firepower
Fireworks
First line
Flintlock
Flying sap
Fortalice
Fortified
Fourth arm
Free-lance
Front line
Fulgurite
Fusillade
Gas attack
Gelignite
Gladiator
Grapeshot
Grenadier
Guardsman

Warfare terms

Gun battle
Guncotton
Gunpowder
Gun turret
Habergeon
Harguebus
Headpiece
Heavy fire
Heroic act
Home Guard
Hostility
Hydrobomb
Incursion
Incursive
In defence
Ironbound
Irregular
Irruption
Janissary
Jesserant
Katabasis
Keep guard
Keep vigil
Lance-jack
Langridge
Last ditch
Legionary
Levy war on
Lie in wait
Lionheart
Logistics
Long-range
Luftwaffe
Make war on
Man-at-arms
Manoeuvre
March past
Matchlock
Mercenary
Militancy
Minefield
Minuteman
Monomachy
Munitions
Musketeer
Musketoon
Needle gun
Nose guard
Nosepiece
Offensive
Onslaught

Open order
Operation
Other side
Overthrow
Panoplied
Parachute
Peel-house
Peel-tower
Pikestaff
Prick-spur
Projector
Pugnacity
Pyroxylin
Ram rocket
Rearguard
Rebel call
Rebellion
Rerebrace
Ressalder
Rifle ball
Rocket gun
Rocket man
Roundhead
Round shot
Rowel spur
Royal Navy
Sally port
Saltpetre
Sea battle
Seat of war
Sentry box
Shellfire
Signalman
Single sap
Ski troops
Skyrocket
Sky troops
Slaughter
Slingshot
Slungshot
Small arms
Small bore
Small-shot
Smoke bomb
Soldierly
Soldier on
Sonic mine
Son of a gun
Spearhead
Spring gun
Stand fire

Stink bomb
Strategic
Subaltern
Submarine
Super bomb
Surprisal
Surrender
Swivel gun
Sword-play
Take sides
Tank corps
Target day
Task force
Tit for tat
Torpedoed
Torpedoer
Trainband
Trench gun
Troopship
Truncheon
Under arms
Under fire
Vigilante
Volunteer
Warmonger
War Office
War rocket
Watchword
White flag
Woomerang
Zumbooruk

10 letters:

Activation
Active army
Active duty
Active list
Adventurer
Aerial bomb
Aerial mine
Aggression
Aggressive
Air Command
Air service
Ambushment
Ammunition
Antagonism
Armageddon
Armed force
Armed guard
Armed truce

Armigerous
Armipotent
Arm's length
Atomic bomb
Atomic pile
Atom-rocket
Ballistics
Barbed-wire
Battleship
Battle flag
Battle hymn
Battle line
Battlement
Blitzkrieg
Blockhouse
Bold stroke
Bombardier
Bowie knife
Box barrage
Breastwork
Bridgehead
Brigandine
Broadsword
Bugle corps
Call to arms
Camel corps
Camouflage
Campaigner
Cannon ball
Cannon shot
Cantonment
Carabineer
Carry on war
Cavalryman
Coastguard
Coat of mail
Combat area
Combat team
Commandant
Contingent
Cross-staff
Cuirassier
Declare war
Defendable
Defensible
Demobilize
Detachment
Direct fire
Dragonnade
Dragoonade
Drawbridge

Drummer boy
Embankment
Encampment
Engarrison
Eprouvette
Escalation
Expedition
Faint heart
Fieldpiece
Field train
Fiery cross
Fire trench
Firing area
Flying bomb
Flying tank
Foot Guards
Foot rifles
Gatling gun
Ground fire
Ground mine
Ground-zero
Halberdier
Heavy-armed
Impalement
Incendiary
Investment
Jingoistic
Knighthood
Knobkerrie
Kriegspiel
Lambrequin
Lay siege to
Life Guards
Light-armed
Line of fire
Loaded cane
Long knives
Lookout man
Machine gun
Martiality
Militarism
Militarize
Militiaman
Missile man
Mob tactics
Mount guard
Mural crown
Musket shot
Mustard gas
Napalm bomb
No man's land

Nuclear war
Obsidional
Occupation
Old soldier
On the march
Operations
Other ranks
Over the top
Oyster mine
Paratroops
Percussion
Petrol bomb
Picket duty
Point blank
Portcullis
Private war
Projectile
Raking fire
Rally round
Raw recruit
Resistance
Revolution
Rifle range
Rocket bomb
Rocket fire
Rules of war
Run-through
Second line
Sentry duty
Serviceman
Shellshock
Shillelagh
Short-range
Siegecraft
Siege train
Six-shooter
Slit trench
Smallsword
Smooth bore
Spill blood
Stand guard
State of war
Strategist
Stronghold
Submachine
Sure as a gun
Sword fight
Swordstick
Sworn enemy
Take to arms
Tenderfoot

Warfare terms

Ten-pounder
Test rocket
Touch paper
Trajectile
Trajectory
Under siege
Vanquisher
Volunteers
War goddess
Winchester

11 letters:

Air-to-ground
Anti-missile
Anti-tank gun
Area bombing
Armed combat
Armed forces
Armoured car
Auxiliaries
Barnstormer
Battle array
Battledress
Battlefield
Battle order
Battle plane
Battle royal
Beach master
Bersaglieri
Besiegement
Blockbuster
Bloody shirt
Blunderbuss
Bombardment
Bomber pilot
Bomb-release
Bow and arrow
Breastplate
British Army
British Navy
Buck private
Bulletproof
Buoyant mine
Bushwhacker
Camaraderie
Castellated
Castle guard
Caterpillar
Change sides
Combat train
Contentious

Countermine
Crack troops
Declaration
Demibastion
Depth charge
Dive-bombing
Emplacement
Enemy action
Engine of war
Enlisted man
Envelopment
Fighting man
Fire a volley
Fire tactics
Firing party
Firing squad
Firing table
First strike
Fission bomb
Flare rocket
Flying corps
Footed arrow
Footslogger
Foot soldier
Forced march
Force of arms
Friend or foe
Full harness
Full of fight
Gang warfare
Generalship
Germ warfare
Giant powder
Ground-to-air
Guerrillero
Guncarriage
Hair trigger
Hand grenade
Heavy armour
Heavy bomber
High dudgeon
Hill station
Horse Guards
Horse pistol
Hostilities
Infantrymen
Irish Guards
Iron rations
Land warfare
Light bomber
Lionhearted

Lochaber axe
Loggerheads
Look daggers
Magazine gun
Maginot line
Marine Corps
Might of arms
Military man
Mine thrower
Moral defeat
Mountain gun
Naval bomber
Naval forces
Nitre powder
Nitrocotton
Nuclear bomb
Open warfare
Pattern bomb
Peace treaty
Picket guard
Plate armour
Platoon fire
Postern gate
Powder grain
Provisional
Put to flight
Rallying cry
Rank and file
Rebel action
Reconnoitre
Recruitment
Regular army
Retro-rocket
Rolling fire
Safe-conduct
Safety catch
Scots Guards
Service call
Ship-to-shore
Shock troops
Shooting war
Shoot to kill
Shuttle raid
Signal Corps
Smell powder
Smoke screen
Sneak attack
Soldatesque
Soldierlike
Soldiership
Spent bullet

Stand at ease
Stand of arms
Step rockets
Stormtroops
Stray bullet
Subdivision
Swiss Guards
Sword in hand
Take by storm
Thin red line
Tommy Atkins
Torpedo boat
Trench knife
Trigger talk
True colours
Trusty sword
Under attack
Underground
Up and at them
Warlikeness
War of nerves
Warriorlike
War to end war
Water cannon
Wooden horse
Wooden walls

12 letters:

Acoustic mine
Anti-aircraft
Appeal to arms
Armour-plated
Army reserves
Artilleryman
Atomic cannon
Awkward squad
Banzai charge
Battering ram
Battleground
Beat a retreat
Belligerence
Breakthrough
Breechloader
Buccaneering
Bushfighting
Cannon fodder
Cannon's mouth
Civil defence
Council of war
Counter march
Court martial

Cut-and-thrust
Daggers drawn
Deadly weapon
Demi-culverin
Dumdum bullet
Dutch courage
Electron bomb
Encirclement
Engines of war
Entrenchment
Escaramouche
False colours
Field of blood
Flame-thrower
Floating mine
Flying column
Forward march
Fowling piece
Gladiatorial
Go over the top
Grand tactics
Ground forces
Guerrilla war
Guided weapon
Heavy dragoon
Home reserves
Homing rocket
Horse and foot
Horse marines
Hydrogen bomb
Lady from hell
Launching pad
Leathernecks
Light Brigade
Light dragoon
Line of action
Line of battle
Machicolated
Magnetic mine
March against
Marching song
Medical Corps
Medium bomber
Military zone
Mine detector
Mobilization
Moral courage
Moral support
Moral victory
Muzzle-loader
Naval militia

Naval reserve
Naval warfare
On the warpath
Parthian shot
Pearl Harbour
Picked troops
Pioneer corps
Plunging fire
Powder charge
Pyrotechnics
Quarterstaff
Reactivation
Religious war
Rifled cannon
Rifle grenade
Rocket attack
Second strike
Sharpshooter
Shock tactics
Shoulder a gun
Shoulder arms
Siege warfare
Signal rocket
Single combat
Smoker rocket
Standing army
Stormtrooper
Stouthearted
Sudden attack
Supply troops
Sword bayonet
Tactical unit
Take the field
Theatre of war
Tooth and nail
Trench mortar
Trigger happy
Under the flag
Vertical fire
Virus warfare
Warmongering
White feather
Who goes there
Yellow streak

13 letters:

Active service
Andrew Ferrara
Armaments race
Armed conflict
Arms and the man

Warfare terms

Army exercises
Articles of war
Assault course
Baptism of fire
Battle cruiser
Battle honours
Battle-scarred
Bayonet charge
Beleaguerment
Bomber command
Breechloading
British Legion
Cartridge-belt
Cavalry charge
Cheval-de-frise
Churchill tank
Cobelligerent
Combat fatigue
Comrade in arms
Counter-attack
Desert warfare
Disengagement
Dispatch-rider
Drill sergeant
Evasive action
Exocet missile
Field hospital
Field of battle
Fighter patrol
First world war
Flammenwerfer
Flying colours
Flying officer
Force de frappe
Foreign legion
Fortification
Generalissimo
Guard of honour
Guided missile
Gunnery school
High-explosive
Lance-corporal
Light infantry
Line of defence
Listening post
Machine gunner
Messerschmitt
Military Cross
Military Medal
Mine detection

Mini-submarine
Muzzle loading
Non-resistance
Nuclear weapon
Order of battle
Order of the day
Passage of arms
Peninsular War
Pitched battle
Prisoner of war
Put to the sword
Quarter-gunner
Quartermaster
Reinforcement
Royal air force
Running battle
Sabre-rattling
Scorched earth
Senior service
Sergeant-major
Siegfried line
Staff-sergeant
Striking force
Sublieutenant
Sub-machine gun
Trench warfare
Two-edged sword
Unarmed combat
Victoria Cross
War department
War to the death
Wing commander
Yeoman service

14 letters:

Action stations
Airborne forces
Airborne troops
Aircraftswoman
Air Vice-Marshal
Ammunition dump
Army cadet force
Army manoeuvres
Barrage balloon
Battle stations
Blank-cartridge
Blockade runner
Captain-general
Cavalry officer
Chevaux-de-frise

Cloak-and-dagger
Coastal battery
Coastal command
Colonel-in-chief
Colour-sergeant
Comrades in arms
Conquering hero
Demobilisation
Field ambulance
Field artillery
Fifth columnist
Fighter command
Fight to a finish
Flag-lieutenant
Freedom fighter
Guerrilla chief
Guerrilla force
Heavy artillery
Horse artillery
Incendiary bomb
Liaison officer
Light artillery
Marching orders
Militarisation
Military police
Military tattoo
Muzzle velocity
Non-operational
Nuclear warfare
Nuclear warhead
Operations room
Orderly officer
Ordinary seaman
Pincer movement
Powder magazine
Pyrrhic victory
Reconnaissance
Regimental band
Royal Artillery
Royal Engineers
Royal Fusiliers
Royal Tank Corps
Squadron-leader
Street fighting
Supreme command
Unknown soldier
Unknown warrior
Urban guerrilla
Warrant officer
Wars of the Roses

Winter quarters

15 letters:
Adjutant general
Air chief marshal
Aircraft carrier
Anderson shelter
Armed to the teeth
Armoured cruiser
Brigade of Guards
Chemical warfare
Displaced person
First lieutenant
Gentleman-at-arms
Grenadier Guards
Light machine-gun

Military mission
Military service
Molotov cocktail
Morrison shelter
Mulberry harbour
National defence
National service
Naval engagement
Naval operations
Non-commissioned
Observation post
Officer of the day
On active service
Orderly corporal
Orderly sergeant

Parachute troops
Rearguard action
Recruiting drive
Regimental march
Second-in-
  command
Spoils of victory
Sword-and-buckler
Telescopic sight
Territorial army

17 letters:
Up guards and at
  them

Waterfalls

5 letters:
Angel
Pilao
Tysse

6 letters:
Iguaçú
Kabiwa
Mardel
Ormeli
Ribbon
Tugela

7 letters:
Mtarazi
Niagara
Roraima

8 letters:
Cuquenan
Itatinga
Kaieteur
Takakkaw
Victoria
Yosemite

9 letters:
Churchill

10 letters:
Cleve-Garth
Sutherland

11 letters:
Yellowstone

13 letters:
Vestre Mardola

Water sports

6 letters:
Diving
Rowing

7 letters:
Sailing
Surfing

8 letters:
Canoeing
Swimming

Yachting

9 letters:
Canoe polo
Water polo

10 letters:
Skin diving

11 letters:
Aquabobbing
Parasailing

Water-skiing
Windsurfing

12 letters:
Powerboating

15 letters:
Powerboat racing

20 letters:
Synchronized
  swimming

Weapons

2 letters:
V1

3 letters:
Dag
Gad
Gun

4 letters:
Bill
Bolo
Bomb
Club
Cosh
Dart
Gade
Gaid
Kris
Mace®
Nuke
Spat
Sten

5 letters:
Arrow
Baton
Estoc
Flail
Maxim
Orgue
Pilum
Rifle
Sabre
Saker
Sting
Sword
Taser®
Vouge

6 letters:
Airgun
Binary
Cestus
Cohorn
Cudgel
Dagger
Gingal
Glaive
Jingal
Mauser®

Mortar
Musket
Napalm
Onager
Pistol
Sparke
Sparth
Taiaha
Tomboc
Voulge

7 letters:
Arblast
Assegai
Ataghan
Bayonet
Bazooka
Bondook
Caliver
Caltrap
Caltrop
Carbine
Coehorn
Cutlass
Dragoon
Enfield
Fougade
Gingall
Gisarme
Grenade
Halberd
Halbert
Harpoon
Javelin
Longbow
Machete
Matchet
Quarrel
Sandbag
Shotgun
Torpedo
Trident

8 letters:
Arbalest
Armalite®
Arquebus
Ballista
Blowpipe

Bludgeon
Calthrop
Catapult
Crossbow
Culverin
Death ray
Elf-arrow
Fougasse
Howitzer
Mangonel
Nunchaku
Partisan
Petronel
Revolver
Skean-dhu
Skene-dhu
Spontoon
Stiletto
Stinkpot
Whirl-bat
Whorl-bat

9 letters:
Arquebuse
Backsword
Battleaxe
Derringer
Doodlebug
Excalibur
Fléchette
Flintlock
Forty-five
Grapeshot
Greek fire
Harquebus
Poison gas
Sarbacane
Trebuchet
Trebucket
Truncheon

10 letters:
Broadsword
Mustard gas

11 letters:
Germ warfare
Morgenstern
Snickersnee

12 letters:
Flame-thrower
Quarterstaff
Rifle grenade

13 letters:
Knuckle-duster

Life-preserver
Manrikigusari

14 letters:
Nunchaku sticks

15 letters:
Chemical warfare

17 letters:
Biological warfare

22 letters:
Bacteriological
  warfare

Weather

WEATHER DESCRIPTIONS

3 letters:
Dry
Hot
Icy
Raw
Wet

4 letters:
Cold
Dull
Fine
Foul
Hazy
Mild

5 letters:
Balmy
Bland
Clear
Close
Dirty
Foggy

Fresh
Humid
Misty
Muggy
Nippy
Parky
Rainy
Snowy
Sunny
Windy

6 letters:
Arctic
Baking
Breezy
Clammy
Cloudy
Dreich
Filthy
Sticky
Stormy

Sultry
Wintry

7 letters:
Clement
Drizzly
Showery

8 letters:
Blustery
Freezing
Overcast
Thundery
Tropical

9 letters:
Inclement
Perishing
Scorching

10 letters:
Blistering

WEATHER PHENOMENA

3 letters:
Fog
Ice

4 letters:
Gale
Gust
Haar
Hail
Mist
Rain
Snow
Thaw

Wind

5 letters:
Cloud
Sleet
Smirr
Storm

6 letters:
Breeze
Freeze
Shower
Squall

Zephyr

7 letters:
Cyclone
Drizzle
Tempest
Thunder
Tornado
Tsunami
Typhoon

8 letters:
Acid rain

Weather

Cold snap
Heatwave
Pressure
Sunshine

9 letters:
Dust devil
Dust storm
Hurricane

Lightning
Peasouper
Sandstorm
Tidal wave
Whirlwind

10 letters:
Waterspout
Willy-willy

13 letters:
Ball lightning
Precipitation

14 letters:
Sheet lightning

METEOROLOGICAL TERMS

4 letters:
Scud

5 letters:
Front
Ridge
Virga

6 letters:
Isobar
Trough

7 letters:
Cyclone
Lee wave
Thermal

9 letters:
Cold front
Isallobar
Warm front

10 letters:
Depression

Heat-island

11 letters:
Anticyclone

13 letters:
Occluded front
Synoptic chart

GATHERERS OF WEATHER DATA

9 letters:
Dropsonde
Met. Office

10 letters:
Radiosonde
Weatherman

11 letters:
Weather ship

12 letters:
Meteorograph
Pilot balloon
Weatherwoman

14 letters:
Weather station

20 letters:
Meteorological
  Office

WEATHER MEASURING INSTRUMENTS

Instrument	Phenomenon measured
Anemometer	Wind velocity
Anemoscope	Wind direction
Atmometer	Rate of water evaporation into atmosphere
Barograph	Atmospheric pressure
Barometer	Atmospheric pressure
Baroscope	Atmospheric pressure
Hygrometer	Humidity
Maximum-minimum thermometer	Temperature variation
Nephoscope	Cloud velocity, altitude, and direction of movement
Psychrometer	Humidity
Rain gauge	Rainfall and snowfall
Rawinsonde	Atmospheric wind velocity
Stevenson's screen	Temperature

Instrument	Phenomenon measured
Sunshine recorder	Hours of sunshine
Thermometer	Temperature
Weathercock	Wind direction
Weather vane	Wind direction
Wet-and-dry-bulb thermometer	Humidity
Wind gauge	Wind velocity
Wind tee	Wind direction

See also:
➤ **Atmosphere, layers of** ➤ **Clouds** ➤ **Winds**

Weeds

3 letters:
Ers

4 letters:
Alga
Dock
Nard
Ragi
Sudd
Tare
Tine
Ulva
Yarr

5 letters:
Couch
Daisy
Dulse
Lemna
Reate
Runch
Tansy
Vetch

6 letters:
Blinks
Clover
Cockle
Dallop
Darnel
Dollop
Elodea
Fat hen

Fucoid
Indian
Joe-pye
Knawel
Nettle
Nostoc
Oxygen
Sorrel
Spurge
Twitch
Widow's
Winnow

7 letters:
Allseed
Burdock
Femitar
Fenitar
Helodea
Mayweed
Ragwort
Ruderal
Senecio
Spurrey
Thistle

8 letters:
Arenaria
Bedstraw
Bell-bind
Charlock
Fumitory
Knapweed

Matfelon
Pilewort
Piri-piri
Plantain
Purslane
Sargasso

9 letters:
Adderwort
Anacharis
Chickweed
Chlorella
Coltsfoot
Groundsel
Knot-grass
Mare's-tail
Pearlwort
Sun-spurge
Tormentil
Wartcress

10 letters:
Carpetweed
Corncockle
Nipplewort
Rest-harrow
Sagittaria

11 letters:
Potamogeton
Swine's-cress
Ulotrichale

Weights and measures

Weights and measures

IMPERIAL SYSTEM

Linear	**Square**	**Weight**
Mile	Square mile	Ton
Furlong	Acre	Hundredweight
Rod	Square rod	Stone
Yard	Square yard	Pound
Foot	Square foot	Ounce
Inch	Square inch	—
Mil	—	—

Land	**Volume**	**Liquid volume**
Square mile	Cubic yard	Gallon
Acre	Cubic foot	Quart
Square rod	Cubic inch	Pint
Square yard	—	Fluid ounce

METRIC SYSTEM

Linear	**Square**	**Weight**
Kilometre	Square kilometre	Tonne
Metre	Square metre	Kilogram
Centimetre	Square centimetre	Gram
Millimetre	Square millimetre	—

Land	**Volume**	**Liquid volume**
Square kilometre	Cubic metre	Litre
Hectare	Cubic decimetre	Millilitre
Are	Cubic centimetre	—
—	Cubic millimetre	—

Whales and dolphins

4 letters:
Orca

6 letters:
Beluga
Dorado

7 letters:
Bowhead
Grampus
Narwhal
Rorqual

8 letters:
Bay whale
Cachalot
Greyback
Porpoise
Sei whale

9 letters:
Blackfish
Blue whale
Grey whale

10 letters:
Black whale
Minke whale
Pilot whale
Right whale
Sperm whale
White whale

11 letters:
Baleen whale
Killer whale

12 letters:
Toothed whale

13 letters:
Humpback whale

Sulphur-bottom

14 letters:
Greenland whale
Whalebone whale

17 letters:
Bottlenose dolphin

Windows

3 letters:
Bay
Bow

4 letters:
Rose
Sash

5 letters:
Gable
Jesse
Judas
Ogive
Oriel
Ox-eye
Storm

6 letters:
Dormer
French
Garret
Lancet
Monial

Oculus
Rosace
Wicket

7 letters:
Compass
Guichet
Lattice
Lucarne
Lunette
Luthern
Mullion
Picture
Transom
Trellis
Ventana
Weather
Windock
Winnock

8 letters:
Casement

Fanlight
Fenestra
Porthole

9 letters:
Companion
Deadlight
Dream-hole
Loop-light
Mezzanine

10 letters:
Fenestella

11 letters:
Lychnoscope
Oeil-de-boeuf

12 letters:
Quarterlight

14 letters:
Catherine-wheel

Winds

4 letters:
Berg
Bise
Bora
Bura
Föhn
Gale
Gust
Puna

5 letters:
Blore
Buran
Eurus
Foehn
Gibli
Noser

Notus
Trade
Zonda

6 letters:
Aquilo
Auster
Baguio
Boreas
Ghibli
Haboob
Kamsin
Levant
Samiel
Sciroc
Simoom
Simoon

Solano
Squall
Wester
Zephyr

7 letters:
Aeolian
Aquilon
Bluster
Chinook
Cyclone
Draught
Etesian
Gregale
Kamseen
Khamsin
Meltemi

Mistral
Monsoon
Nor'east
Norther
Pampero
Shimaal
Sirocco
Snifter
Snorter
Souther
Sumatra
Tornado
Twister
Typhoon

8 letters:
Argestes

Easterly
Favonian
Favonius
Levanter
Libeccio
Scirocco
Williwaw
Zephyrus

9 letters:
Anti-trade
Dust devil
Euraquilo
Harmattan
Hurricane
Hurricano
Libecchio

Nor'wester
Volturnus

10 letters:
Cape doctor
Euroclydon
Rip-snorter
Tourbillon
Tramontana
Tramontane
Whirlblast
Willy-willy

11 letters:
White squall

13 letters:
Northwesterly

Wines

WINE-PRODUCING AREAS

Area	Country
Ahr	Germany
Alsace	France
Alto Adige *or* Südtirol	Italy
Anjou	France
Argentina	—
Austria	—
Baden	Germany
Barossa Valley	Australia
Bordeaux	France
Bulgaria	—
Burgundy	France
California	U.S.A.
Chablis	France
Champagne	France
Chianti	Italy
Chile	—
Clare Valley	Australia
Coonawarra	Australia
Côte d'Or	France
Finger Lakes	U.S.A.
Franken	Germany
Friuli	Italy
Gisborne	New Zealand
Goulburn Valley	Australia
Greece	—
Hawkes Bay	New Zealand

Area	Country
Hessiches Bergstrasse	Germany
Hungary	—
Hunter Valley	Australia
Languedoc	France
Loire	France
Margaret River	Australia
Marlborough	New Zealand
Martinborough	New Zealand
McLaren Vale	Australia
Mendocino	U.S.A.
Mittelrhein	Germany
Moldavia	—
Mornington Peninsula	Australia
Mosel-Saar-Ruwer	Germany
Nahe	Germany
Napa Valley	U.S.A.
Navarra	Spain
New York State	U.S.A.
Oregon	U.S.A.
Padthaway	Australia
Penedès	Spain
Piedmont	Italy
Portugal	—
Provence	France
Rheingau	Germany
Rheinhessen	Germany
Rheinpfalz	Germany
Rhône	France
Ribera del Duro	Spain
Rioja	Spain
Romania	—
Sicily	Italy
Sonoma	U.S.A.
South Africa	—
Switzerland	—
Touraine	France
Tuscany	Italy
Umbria	Italy
Valdepeñas	Spain
Veneto	Italy
Washington State	U.S.A.
Württemberg	Germany
Yarra Valley	Australia

Wines

2 letters:
AC
NV

3 letters:
AOC
DOC
Dry
LBV
QbA
QmP
Sec
TBA

4 letters:
Aszú
Brix
Brut
DOCG
Fino
Flor
Rosé
Sekt
VDQS

5 letters:
Baumé
Cream
Cuvée
Dolce
Plonk
Secco
Sweet
Tinto

6 letters:
Medium
Solera
Sur lie
Tannin

7 letters:
Amabile
Auslese
Crianza
Demi-sec
Eiswein
Malmsey
Oechsle
Oloroso
Organic

Passito
Recioto
Récolte
Reserva
Riserva
Terroir
Trocken
Vin gris
Vintage
Weingut

8 letters:
Ausbruch
Botrytis
Grand cru
Kabinett
Moelleux
Mousseux
Noble rot
Prädikat
Ruby Port
Spätlese
Spumante
Varietal
Vigneron
Vignoble

9 letters:
Abbocatto
Cru classé
Grosslage
Medium-dry
Pale cream
Pétillant
Puttonyos
Table wine
Tafelwein
Tawny Port
Vin de pays

10 letters:
Botrytized
Einzellage
Garrafeira
Manzanilla
Non-vintage
Premier cru
Second wine
Sin crianza
Vin de table

11 letters:
Amontillado
Dessert wine
Gran reserva
Halbtrocken
Late harvest
Medium-sweet
Weissherbst

12 letters:
Cru bourgeois
Vino da tavola

13 letters:
Beerenauslese
Estate bottled
Fortified wine
Qualitätswein
Sparkling wine

14 letters:
Vendage tardive
Vieilles vignes
Vin doux naturel

15 letters:
Pourriture noble
Sigle Quinta Port

17 letters:
Erzeugerabfüllung

18 letters:
Late-Bottled Vintage

See also:
➤ **Drinks**

Méthode champenoise

20 letters:
Appellation contrôlée
Trockenbeerenauslese
Winzergenossenschaft

22 letters:
Late-Bottled Vintage Port
Malolactic fermentation

24 letters:
Qualitätswein mit Prädikat

28 letters:
Appellation d'origine contrôlée

30 letters:
Vin Délimité de Qualité
  Supérieure

33 letters:
Denominazione di origine
  controllata

34 letters:
Qualitätswein bestimmter
  Anbaugebiet

43 letters:
Denominazione di origine
  controllata e garantita

Winter sports

4 letters:
Luge

6 letters:
Skiing
Slalom
Super-G

7 letters:
Curling
Skating

8 letters:
Biathlon

9 letters:
Bobsleigh
Ice hockey
Skijoring

10 letters:
Ice dancing
Ice skating
Skibobbing
Ski jumping

11 letters:
Tobogganing

12 letters:
Alpine skiing
Nordic skiing
Snowboarding
Speed skating

13 letters:
Figure skating

14 letters:
Downhill racing

Wonders of the ancient world

Wonders of the ancient world

Colossus of Rhodes
Hanging Gardens of Babylon
Mausoleum of Halicarnassus
Pharos of Alexandria
Phidias' statue of Zeus at
 Olympia
Pyramids of Egypt
Temple of Artemis at Ephesus

Wood, types of

3 letters:
Ash
Box
Elm
Fir
Koa
Oak
Red
Yew

4 letters:
Beef
Cade
Eugh
Iron
Lana
Lime
Pear
Pine
Poon
Rata
Teak
Toon
Yang

5 letters:
Agila
Algum
Almug
Apple
Balsa
Beech
Birch
Cedar
Ebony
Hazel
Heben
Iroko
Jarul
Kauri
Kiaat

Kokra
Larch
Maple
Myall
Olive
Opepe
Plane
Ramin
Rowan
Sapan
Sassy
Stink
Sumac
Thorn
Tulip
Zante

6 letters:
Alerce
Bamboo
Bog oak
Brasil
Brazil
Canary
Carapa
Cherry
Citron
Fustet
Fustic
Fustoc
Gaboon
Gopher
Jarool
Jarrah
Lignum
Locust
Obeche
Orache
Orange
Padauk

Padouk
Poplar
Red fir
Red gum
Red oak
Sabele
Sabicu
Sandal
Sapele
Sappan
Sissoo
Sponge
Spruce
Sumach
Tupelo
Waboom
Walnut
Willow

7 letters:
Amboina
Amboyna
Assagai
Assegai
Barwood
Boxwood
Camwood
Cypress
Durmast
Gumtree
Gumwood
Hemlock
Hickory
Meranti
Nutwood
Palmyra
Pimento
Quassia
Sanders
Sapwood

Shawnee
Shittim
Wallaba

8 letters:
Agalloch
Alburnum
Basswood
Beefwood
Chestnut
Corkwood
Crabwood
Guaiacum
Guaiocum
Hardwood
Harewood
Hornbeam
Ironwood
Jelutong
Kingwood
Laburnum
Mahogany
Pulpwood
Pyengadu
Pyinkado
Red cedar
Rosewood
Sandarac
Sapucaia
Sasswood
Shagbark
Softwood

Southern
Sycamore
Tamarack
Tamarind

9 letters:
Briarwood
Butternut
Caliature
Campeachy
Coachwood
Eaglewood
Hackberry
Jacaranda
Lancewood
Partridge
Persimmon
Pitch pine
Quebracho
Satinwood
Scots pine
Shellbark
Stinkwood
Torchwood
Tulipwood
White pine
Whitewood
Zebrawood

10 letters:
Afrormosia
Bulletwood

Calamander
Candlewood
Coromandel
Durmast oak
Fiddlewood
Greenheart
Hackmatack
Marblewood
Nettle-tree
Orangewood
Palisander
Paraná pine
Ribbonwood
Sandalwood
Sappanwood
Sneezewood
Spotted gum
Summerwood
White cedar
Yellowwood

11 letters:
Black walnut
Lignum-vitae
Sanderswood
Slippery elm

13 letters:
Partridge-wood

15 letters:
African mahogany
Western red cedar

Works of literature and music

3 letters:
Job
Kim
She

4 letters:
Aida
Emma
Lulu
Maud

5 letters:
Brand
Comus
Faust
Fetes

Kipps
La Mer
Manon
Medea
Norma
Scoop
Tosca

6 letters:
Alcina
Amelia
Becket
Ben Hur
Carmen
En Saga

Ghosts
Hassan
Helena
Iberia
Jenufa
Lolita
Martha
Mignon
Nuages
Oberon
Otello
Rienzi
Rob Roy
Rokeby
Salome

Works of literature and music

Semele
Sylvia
Trilby
Utopia
Walden

7 letters:
Adonais
Aladdin
Amadeus
Babbitt
Beowulf
Camilla
Candida
Don Juan
Dracula
Electra
Erewhon
Euphues
Fidelio
Giselle
Ivanhoe
Lord Jim
Lycidas
Macbeth
Manfred
Marmion
Ma Vlast
Mazeppa
Messiah
Nabucco
Othello
Rebecca
Ring, The
Shirley
Sirenes
Ulysses
Volpone
Werther
Wozzeck

8 letters:
Adam Bede
Adam Zero
Alcestis
Anabasis
Antigone
Arabella
Bells, The
Born Free
Carnaval
Carnival

Catriona
Cenci, The
Coppelia
Cranford
Endymion
Everyman
Falstaff
Gloriana
Hay Fever
Hiawatha
Hudibras
Hyperion
Idiot, The
Idomeneo
Iliad, The
In the Wet
Iolanthe
Jane Eyre
King Lear
LA Boheme
L'Allegro
Lavengro
Les Noces
Lucky Jim
Moby Dick
Parsifal
Patience
Peer Gynt
Pericles
Rasselas
Sea Drift
Swan Lake
Tom Jones
Turandot
Villette
Waves, The

9 letters:
Aeneid, The
Agamemnon
Beau Geste
Billy Budd
Brigg Fair
Capriccio
Cavalcade
Checkmate
Choephori
Coningsby
Cox and Box
Critic, The
Cymbeline

Dandy Dick
Don Carlos
Dr Zhivago
Dubliners
East Lynne
Egoist, The
Eumenides
Euryanthe
Hard Times
Hobbit, The
I, Claudius
I Puritani
Kidnapped
Kubla Khan
Les Biches
Lohengrin
Mein Kampf
Men at Arms
Mikado, The
No Highway
On Liberty
Papillons
Prince, The
Pygmalion
Rigoletto
Rivals, The
Ruddigore
Saint Joan
Siegfried
Tom Sawyer
Venusberg
Vice Versa
Warden, The

10 letters:
All for Love
Animal Farm
Appalachia
Bleak House
Borough, The
Cannery Row
Casablanca
Cinderella
Citadel, The
Coriolanus
Das Kapital
Die Walkure
Don Quixote
Dunciad, The
Dynasts, The
Howards End

Works of literature and music

Il Seraglio
Inferno, The
In Memoriam
Intermezzo
I Pagliacci
Jamaica Inn
John Gilpin
Kenilworth
Kingdom, The
La Gioconda
La Traviata
Les Troyens
Lorna Doone
Lysistrata
My Fair Lady
My Son, My Son
Nelson Mass
Odyssey, The
Oedipus Rex
Only Way, The
On the Beach
Our Village
Pantagruel
Persuasion
Petroushka
Planets, The
Prelude, The
Prince Igor
Relapse, The
Rural Rides
Seagull, The
Seasons, The
Semiramide
Tannhauser
Tempest, The
Tono-Bungay
Trojans, The
Uncle Remus
Uncle Vanya
Vanity Fair
Vile Bodies
War Requiem
Water Music
Westward Ho

11 letters:
American, The
Apostles, The
As You Like It
Big Sleep, The
Black Beauty

Blue Bird, The
Boule de Suif
Cakes and Ale
Child Harold
Creation, The
Cruel Sea, The
Doll's House, A
Don Giovanni
Don Pasquale
Firebird, The
Georgics, The
Greenmantle
Harp Quartet
Hedda Gabler
High Windows
HMS Pinafore
Hymn of Jesus
I Like It Here
Il Penseroso
Il Trovatore
Jack and Jill
Journey's End
Judith Paris
Little Eyolf
Little Women
Loved One, The
Love for Love
Luisa Miller
Mary Poppins
Middlemarch
Minute Waltz
Mrs Dalloway
Mr Standfast
Newcomes, The
Now We Are Six
Noye's Fludde
Ode to Autumn
Oliver Twist
Peter Grimes
Peter Simple
Pippa Passes
Princess Ida
Princess, The
Puss in Boots
Redgauntlet
Rosmersholm
Salut d'Amour
Sea Symphony
Silas Marner
Sorcerer, The
South Riding

Stalky and Co
Stenka Razin
Tale of a Tub, A
Talisman, The
Tam o'Shanter
Trial by Jury
What Katy Did
Wild Duck, The
William Tell
Women in Love
Wrong Box, The

12 letters:
Alchemist, The
Anna Karenina
Antiquary, The
Apple Cart, The
Archduke Trio
Areopagitica
Ash Wednesday
Barnaby Rudge
Blithe Spirit
Brighton Rock
Buddenbrooks
Caretaker, The
Charley's Aunt
Cosi fan Tutte
Danse Macabre
Decameron, The
Dogs of War, The
Dombey and Son
Epithalamion
Eugene Onegin
Excursion, The
Four Quartets
Frankenstein
Golden Ass, The
Grand Duke, The
Guy Mannering
Handley Cross
Julius Caesar
Karelia Suite
Khovanschina
Kinderscenen
Kreisleriana
La Sonnambula
Le Pere Goriot
Les Huguenots
Les Sylphides
Linz Symphony
Little Dorrit

Works of literature and music

Locksley Hall
Lost Chord, The
Madame Bovary
Major Barbara
Manon Lescaut
Moll Flanders
Moonstone, The
Old Mortality
Owen Wingrave
Paradise Lost
Piers Plowman
Porgy and Bess
Precious Bane
Private Lives
Prothalamion
Rheingold, Das
Rip Van Winkle
Rogue Herries
Romany Rye, The
Sardanapalus
Spring Sonata
Trout Quintet
Twelfth Night
Valkyries, The
Whisky Galore

13 letters:

Albert Herring
Almayer's Folly
Andrea Chenier
Angel Pavement
Arms and the Man
Art of Fugue, The
Bab Ballads, The
Black Arrow, The
Black Mischief
Blue Danube, The
Boris Godounov
Brave New World
Cancer Ward, The
Carmina Burana
Chanson de Nuit
Clock Symphony
Crown Imperial
Death in Venice
Der Freischutz
Dido and Aeneas
Doctor Faustus
Doctor Zhivago
Fame is the Spur
Finnegan's Wake

Ghost Train, The
Gondoliers, The
Harold in Italy
Hatter's Castle
Jungle Book, The
Just So Stories
La Cenerentola
L'Elisir d'Amore
Mabinogion, The
Magic Flute, The
Magistrate, The
Mansfield Park
Metamorphosen
Nutcracker, The
Odessa File, The
Orb and Sceptre
Path to Rome, The
Peg Woffington
Private Angelo
Religio Medici
Schindler's Ark
Sketches by Boz
Songs of Travel
Sons and Lovers
Stamboul Train
Tarka the Otter
Timon of Athens
Under Milk Wood
Utopia Limited
Virginians, The
White Devil, The
Winnie-the-Pooh
Winslow Boy, The
Zuleika Dobson

14 letters:

Ambassadors, The
Andrea del Sarto
Battle Symphony
Bee's Wedding, The
Book of Snobs, The
Brief Encounter
Chanson de Matin
Choral Symphony
Cider with Rosie
Claudius the God
Coral Island, The
Country Wife, The
Crotchet Castle
Darkness at Noon
Decline and Fall

Works of literature and music

Deep Blue Sea, The
Die Zauberflote
Ein Heldenleben
Emperor Quartet
Entertainer, The
Eroica Symphony
Forsyte Saga, The
Four Just Men, The
Gay Lord Quex, The
Golden Bough, The
Goodbye Mr Chips
Goodby to Berlin
Great Gatsby, The
Handful of Dust, A
Horse's Mouth, The
Jude the Obscure
Kreutzer Sonata
Le Morte d'Arthur
London Symphony
Loom of Youth, The
Lord of the Flies
Lord of the Rings
Lost Horizon, The
Lyrical Ballads
Madam Butterfly
Man and Superman
Masterman Ready
National Velvet
Nightmare Abbey
Nine Tailors, The
Of Human Bondage
Our Man in Havana
Passage to India
Pickwick Papers
Plain Dealer, The
Prague Symphony
Quentin Durward
Rhapsody in Blue
Rights of Man, The
Robinson Crusoe
Roderick Random
Romeo and Juliet
Separate Tables
Shropshire Lad, A
Siegfried Idyll
Sinister Street
Sins of my Old Age
Slavonic Dances
Spring Symphony
Stones of Venice
Time Machine, The

Town Like Alice, A
Tragic Symphony
Treasure Island
Tristram Shandy
Uncle Tom's Cabin
Venus and Adonis
Vicar of Bray, The
Voices of Spring
Water Babies, The
Widowers Houses
Winter's Tale, The
Woodlanders, The

15 letters:
African Queen, The
Allan Quatermain
Ariadne auf Naxos
Bartholomew Fair
Beggar's Opera, The
Child of our Time, A
Christmas Carol, A
Clarissa Harlowe
Dangerous Corner
Daphnis and Chloe
Divine Comedy, The
Emperor Concerto
Emperor Waltz, The
Essays of Elia, The
Faerie Queene, The
Fanny by Gaslight
Farewell to Arms, A
Frenchman's Creek
From the New World
Golden Legend, The
Gone with the Wind
Gotterdammerung
Haffner Symphony
Hansel and Gretel
Heartbreak House
Huckleberry Finn
Iceman Cometh, The
Invisible Man, The
Italian Symphony
Jupiter Symphony
Le Nozze di Figaro
Letters of Junius
Life for the Tsar, A
Look Back in Anger
Moonlight Sonata
Northanger Abbey
Old Wives Tale, The

Worms

3 letters:
Bob
Dew
Fan
Lob

4 letters:
Tube

5 letters:
Acorn
Arrow
Fluke
Leech
Lytta
Piper

6 letters:
Caddis
Guinea
Nereid
Paddle
Palmer
Palolo
Ribbon
Scolex
Taenia
Teredo
Tongue

7 letters:
Ascarid
Bladder
Bristle
Catworm
Cestode
Cestoid

Filaria
Gordius
Hair-eel
Ragworm
Sabella
Serpula
Stomach
Tag-tail
Tenioid
Triclad
Tubifex
Vinegar

8 letters:
Bootlace
Capeworm
Caseworm
Clamworm
Filander
Gilt-tail
Hairworm
Hookworm
Inchworm
Nematoda
Nematode
Nemertea
Paste-eel
Seamouse
Strongyl
Toxocara
Trichina
Wheat-eel
Whipworm

9 letters:
Bilharzia

Brandling
Diplozoon
Heartworm
Horsehair
Lumbricus
Peripatus
Planarian
Strawworm
Strongyle
Tiger tail
Trematode
Wheatworm

10 letters:
Anguillula
Liver-fluke
Polychaete
Threadworm

11 letters:
Oligochaete
Schistosome
Scoleciform
Trichinella
Trichinosed
Turbellaria

12 letters:
Enteropneust
Hemichordata
Night-crawler
Sipunculacea

13 letters:
Platyhelminth
Sipunculoidea

3 letters:
Eco, *Umberto*
Lee, *Sophia*
Paz, *Octavio*
Poe, *Edgar Allan*
RLS

4 letters:
Amis, *Martin (Louis)*
Asch, *Sholem*
Aymé, *Marcel*
Bede, *the Venerable*
Bolt, *Robert (Oxton)*
Cary, *(Arthur) Joyce Lunel*
Cole, *Babette*
Dahl, *Roald*
Fine, *Ann*
Gide, *André (Paul Guillaume)*
Hope (Hawkins), *Sir Anthony*
Hugo, *Victor (Marie)*
Hunt, *E(verette) Howard*
King, *Stephen (Edwin)*
Lamb, *Charles*
Loos, *Anita*
Loti, *Pierre*
Lyly, *John*
Mann, *Thomas*
More, *Henry*
Nash, *(Frederic) Ogden*
Opie, *Iona*
Ovid
Pope, *Alexander*
Saki *(Hector Hugh Munro)*
Sand, *George*
Shaw, *George Bernard*
Snow, *C(harles) P(ercy)*
Ward, *Mary Augusta*
West, *Nathanael*
Zola, *Émile*

5 letters:
Acton, *Sir Harold Mario*
Aesop
Albee, *Edward (Franklin)*
Auden, *W(ystan) H(ugh)*
Ayres, *Noreen*
Banks, *Lynne Reid*
Bates, *H(erbert) E(rnest)*
Blake, *William*

Blume, *Judy*
Burke, *Edmund*
Caine, *Sir (Thomas Henry) Hall*
Camus, *Albert*
Corvo, *Baron*
Crane, *Stephen*
Defoe, *Daniel*
Digby, *Anne*
Doyle, *Arthur Conan*
Dumas, *Alexandre*
Eliot, *T(homas) S(tearns)*
Ellis, *(Henry) Havelock*
Genet, *Jean*
Gogol, *Nikolai Vasilievich*
Gorky, *Maxim*
Gosse, *Sir Edmund (William)*
Greer, *Germaine*
Grimm, *Wilhelm Carl*
Hardy, *Thomas*
Henry, *O (William Sydney Porter)*
Henty, *G(eorge) A(lfred)*
Hesse, *Hermann*
Heyer, *Georgette*
Homer
Ibsen, *Henrik*
Innes, *(Ralph) Hammond*
James, *Henry*
Jones, *Diana Wynne*
Joyce, *James (Augustine Aloysius)*
Kafka, *Franz*
Kempe, *Margery*
Lewis, *C(live) S(taples)*
Lodge, *David (John)*
Lorca, *Federico García*
Mason, *Alfred Edward Woodley*
Milne, *A(lan) A(lexander)*
Munro, *H(ector) H(ugh)*
Musil, *Robert*
Nashe, *Thomas*
Ouida
Paine, *Tom*
Pater, *Walter Horatio*
Paton, *Alan (Stewart)*
Pepys, *Samuel*
Pliny
Pound, *Ezra (Loomis)*
Powys, *John Cowper*
Reade, *Charles*

Writers

Renan, *(Joseph) Ernest*
Rilke, *Rainer Maria*
Sagan, *Françoise*
Scott, *Sir Walter*
Seuss, *Dr (Theodor Seuss Geisel)*
Shute, *Nevil*
Smith, *Dick King*
Spark, *Dame Muriel (Sarah)*
Stark, *Dame Freya Madeline*
Stein, *Gertrude*
Swift, *Jonathan*
Synge, *(Edmund) J(ohn)*
  M(illington)
Twain, *Mark (Samuel L Clemens)*
Verne, *Jules*
Waugh, *Evelyn (Arthur St John)*
Wells, *H(erbert) G(eorge)*
Wilde, *Oscar (Fingal O'Flahertie*
  Wills)
Woolf, *(Adeline) Virginia*
Yates, *Dornford*
Yonge, *Charlotte Mary*

6 letters:

Alcott, *Louisa May*
Ambler, *Eric*
Arnold, *Matthew*
Artaud, *Antonin Marie Joseph*
Ascham, *Roger*
Asimov, *Isaac*
Austen, *Jane*
Balzac, *Honoré de*
Baring, *Maurice*
Barrie, *J(ames) M(atthew)*
Belloc, *(Joseph) Hilaire (Pierre)*
Bellow, *Saul*
Blyton, *Enid (Mary)*
Borges, *Jorge Luis*
Borrow, *George Henry*
Braine, *John (Gerard)*
Brecht, *Bertolt (Eugen Friedrich)*
Bronte, *Emily Jane (Ellis Bell)*
Buchan, *John*
Bunyan, *John*
Butler, *Samuel*
Capote, *Truman*
Cicero, *Marcus Tullius*
Colfer, *Eoin*
Conrad, *Joseph*
Cowper, *William*
Cronin, *A(rchibald) J(oseph)*

Daudet, *Alphonse*
Dryden, *John*
Durrel, *Laurence George*
Engels, *Friedrich*
Fowles, *John (Robert)*
France, *Anatole*
Gibbon, *Edward*
Godwin, *William*
Goethe, *Johann Wolfgang von*
Graves, *Robert (Ranke)*
Greene, *(Henry) Graham*
Harris, *Joel Chandler*
Heller, *Joseph*
Hobbes, *Thomas*
Hughes, *Thomas*
Hutton, *R(ichard) H(olt)*
Huxley, *Aldous (Leonard)*
Inkpen, *Mike*
Irving, *Washington*
Jarvis, *Robin*
Jerome, *Jerome K(lapka)*
Jonson, *Ben(jamin)*
Le Fanu, *(Joseph) Sheridan*
London, *Jack*
Lucian
Lytton, *Bulwer*
Mailer, *Norman (Kingsley)*
Malory, *Thomas*
Mannin, *Ethel*
Miller, *Henry (Valentine)*
Milton, *John*
Morgan, *Edwin (George)*
Murphy, *Jill*
Nerval, *Gérard de*
Nesbit, *E(dith)*
Onions, *Charles Talbut*
Orwell, *George*
Parker, *Dorothy*
Proust, *Marcel*
Racine, *Jean (Baptiste)*
Runyon, *Damon*
Ruskin, *John*
Sachar, *Louis*
Sapper *(H C McNeile)*
Sayers, *Dorothy L(eigh)*
Sewell, *Anna*
Smiles, *Samuel*
Steele, *Richard*
Sterne, *Laurence*
Storey, *David (Malcolm)*
Thomas, *Dylan (Marlais)*

Writers

Updike, *John (Hoyer)*
Virgil
Walton, *Izaac*
Wilder, *Laura Ingalls*
Wilson, *Jacqueline*

7 letters:

Addison, *Joseph*
Aldrich, *Thomas Bailey*
Aretino, *Pietro*
Beckett, *Samuel (Barclay)*
Bennett, *(Enoch) Arnold*
Bentley, *Edmund Clerihew*
Boileau, *Nicholas (Despréaux)*
Boswell, *James*
Burgess, *Anthony*
Carlyle, *Thomas*
Carroll, *Lewis (Charles Lutwidge Dodgson)*
Chaucer, *Geoffrey*
Chekhov, *Anton Pavlovich*
Cobbett, *William*
Colette, *(Sidonie-Gabrielle)*
Collins, *Wilkie (William)*
Coppard, *A(lfred) E(dgar)*
Corelli, *Marie*
Cranmer, *Thomas*
Cushman, *Karen*
Deeping, *(George) Warwick*
Dickens, *Charles (John Huffam)*
Drabble, *Margaret*
Dreiser, *Theodore Herman Albert*
Durrell, *Gerald (Malcolm)*
Emerson, *Ralph Waldo*
Erasmus, *Desiderius*
Fénelon, *François de Salignac de la Mothe*
Forster, *Margaret*
Gissing, *George (Robert)*
Golding, *Sir William (Gerald)*
Grahame, *Kenneth*
Haggard, *Sir H(enry) Rider*
Hazlitt, *William*
Herbert, *George*
Hichens, *Robert Smythe*
Johnson, *Samuel*
Kipling, *(Joseph) Rudyard*
Lardner, *Ring(gold Wilmer)*
Marryat, *(Captain) Frederick*
Maugham, *W(illiam) Somerset*
Mauriac, *François*

Mérimée, *Prosper*
Mitford, *Jessica Lucy*
Moravia, *Alberto*
Murdoch, *Dame (Jean) Iris*
Nabokov, *Vladimir (Vladimirovich)*
Naipaul, *Sir V(idiadhar) S(urajprasad)*
Peacock, *Thomas Love*
Pullman, *Philip*
Pushkin, *Aleksander Sergeyevich*
Ransome, *Arthur Mitchell*
Riddell, *Chris*
Rostand, *Edmond*
Rowling, *J(oanne) K(athleen)*
Saroyan, *William*
Sassoon, *Siegfried (Louvain)*
Shelley, *Mary (Wollstonecraft)*
Simenon, *Georges (Joseph Christian)*
Sitwell, *Sir (Francis) Osbert*
Stephen, *Leslie*
Stewart, *Paul*
Surtees, *Robert Smith*
Terence
Thoreau, *Henry David*
Tolkien, *J(ohn) R(onald) R(euel)*
Tolstoy, *Count Leo (Nikolayevich)*
Travers, *Ben(jamin)*
Wallace, *(Richard Horatio) Edgar*
Walpole, *Sir Hugh Seymour*
Wharton, *Edith (Newbold)*
Whitman, *Walt(er)*

8 letters:

Andersen, *Hans Christian*
Beaumont, *Sir John*
Browning, *Robert*
Caldwell, *Erskine*
Chandler, *Raymond*
Childers, *(Robert) Erskine*
Christie, *Dame Agatha (Mary Clarissa)*
Constant, *Benjamin*
Coolidge, *Susan*
De la Mare, *Walter (John)*
Disraeli, *Benjamin*
Faulkner, *William*
Fielding, *Henry*
Flaubert, *Gustave*
Forester, *C(ecil) S(cott)*
Goncourt, *Jules*

Writers

Ishiguro, *Kazuo*
Kingsley, *Mary St Leger*
Lawrence, *T(homas) E(dward)*
Mannheim, *Baron Carl Gustav Emil*
Melville, *Herman*
Meredith, *George*
Morpurgo, *Michael*
Perrault, *Charles*
Plutarch
Rabelais, *François*
Rattigan, *Sir Terence (Mervyn)*
Remarque, *Erich Maria*
Rousseau, *Jean-Jacques*
Salinger, *J(erome) D(avid)*
Schiller, *(Johann Christoph) Friedrich von*
Smollett, *Tobias George*
Stendhal *(Marie-Henri Beyle)*
Taffrail *(Henry Taprell Dorling)*
Traherne, *Thomas*
Trollope, *Joanna*
Turgenev, *Ivan Sergeyevich*
Voltaire *(François Marie Arouet)*
Williams, *Tennessee*

9 letters:
Aeschylus
Ainsworth, *William Harrison*
Blackmore, *R(ichard) D(oddridge)*
Boccaccio, *Giovanni*
Brent-Dyer, *Elinor M(ary)*
Burroughs, *Edgar Rice*
Dos Passos, *John Roderigo*
Du Maurier, *Dame Daphne*
Edgeworth, *Maria*
Goldsmith, *Oliver*
Hawthorne, *Nathaniel*
Hemingway, *Ernest (Millar)*
Isherwood, *Christopher (William Bradshaw)*
Jefferson, *Thomas*
Lermontov, *Mikhail Yurievich*
Linklater, *Eric*
Mackenzie, *Sir (Edward Montague) Compton*
Madariaga, *Salvador de*
Mansfield, *Katherine*

McCullers, *Carson*
Oppenheim, *Edward Phillips*
Pasternak, *Boris Leonidovich*
Pratchett, *Terry*
Priestley, *J(ohn) B(oynton)*
Santayana, *George*
Sholokhov, *Mikhail Aleksandrovich*
Steinbeck, *John (Ernest)*
Stevenson, *Robert Louis (Balfour)*
Thackeray, *William Makepeace*
Wodehouse, *Sir P(elham) G(renville)*

10 letters:
Ballantyne, *R(obert) M(ichael)*
Chesterton, *G(ilbert) K(eith)*
Dostoevsky, *Fyodor Mikhailovich*
Fitzgerald, *F(rancis) Scott (Key)*
Galsworthy, *John*
Richardson, *H(enry) H(andel)*

11 letters:
De Cervantes (Saavedra), *Miguel*
De Montaigne, *Michel Eyquem*
Machiavelli, *Niccolò*
Maeterlinck, *Count Maurice*
Shakespeare, *William*
Streatfield, *Noel*

12 letters:
Aristophanes
Chesterfield, *Lord*
De Mandeville, *Sir Jehan (or John)*
De Maupassant, *(Henri René Albert) Guy*
Solzhenitsyn, *Alexander Isayevich*

13 letters:
Sackville-West, *Vita (Victoria Mary)*

14 letters:
Wollstonecraft, *Mary*

15 letters:
De Chateaubriand, *Vicomte (François René)*

24 letters:
APH *(Sir Alan Patrick Herbert)*

See also:
➤ **Diarists** ➤ **Dramatists** ➤ **Novelists** ➤ **Poets**
➤ **Shakespeare**

Yellow, shades of

4 letters:
Buff
Ecru
Gold

5 letters:
Amber
Beige
Lemon
Maize
Ochre
Straw
Topaz

6 letters:
Almond
Bisque

Bistre
Citron
Golden

7 letters:
Gamboge
Jasmine
Mustard
Nankeen
Oatmeal
Old gold
Saffron
Tea rose

8 letters:
Cinnamon
Daffodil

Eau de nil
Eggshell
Magnolia
Primrose

9 letters:
Butternut
Champagne

12 letters:
Canary yellow

13 letters:
Tortoiseshell

Z

Zodiac

SIGNS OF THE ZODIAC

Name	Symbol
Aquarius	the Water Carrier
Aries	the Ram
Cancer	the Crab
Capricorn	the Goat
Gemini	the Twins
Leo	the Lion
Libra	the Scales
Pisces	the Fishes
Sagittarius	the Archer
Scorpio	the Scorpion
Taurus	the Bull
Virgo	the Virgin

CHINESE ANIMAL YEARS

Chinese	English	Years				
Shu	Rat	1960	1972	1984	1996	2008
Niu	Ox	1961	1973	1985	1997	2009
Hu	Tiger	1962	1974	1986	1998	2010
Tu	Hare	1963	1975	1987	1999	2011
Long	Dragon	1964	1976	1988	2000	2012
She	Serpent	1965	1977	1989	2001	2013
Ma	Horse	1966	1978	1990	2002	2014
Yang	Sheep	1967	1979	1991	2003	2015
Hou	Monkey	1968	1980	1992	2004	2016
Ji	Cock	1969	1981	1993	2005	2017
Gou	Dog	1970	1982	1994	2006	2018
Zhu	Boar	1971	1983	1995	2007	2019

Zoology

BRANCHES OF ZOOLOGY

3 letters:
Shu

7 letters:
Zootomy

8 letters:
Cetology
Ethology
Zoometry

9 letters:
Mammalogy

Ophiology
Zoography

10 letters:
Entomology
Malacology

11 letters:
Arachnology
Herpetology
Ichthyology
Myrmecology

Ornithology
Primatology

12 letters:
Protozoology
Zoogeography

13 letters:
Palaeozoology

14 letters:
Archaeozoology

ZOOLOGY TERMS

3 letters:
Fin

4 letters:
Gill
Prey
Pupa

5 letters:
Biped
Imago
Larva
Spawn
Spine

6 letters:
Caudal
Cocoon
Coelom
Colony
Dorsal
Raptor
Rodent
Sucker
Thorax

7 letters:
Abdomen

Antenna
Bivalve
Decapod
Primate
Reptile
Segment
Ventral

8 letters:
Anterior
Arachnid
Chordate
Dipteran
Edentate
Omnivore
Pectoral
Placenta
Predator
Ruminant
Skeleton

9 letters:
Amphibian
Appendage
Arthropod
Carnivore
Chrysalis

Gastropod
Herbivore
Marsupial
Migration
Passerine
Posterior
Protozoan
Quadruped

10 letters:
Crustacean
Echinoderm
Gasteropod
Parenchyma
Vertebrate

11 letters:
Aestivation
Hibernation
Insectivore

12 letters:
Coelenterate
Invertebrate
Lepidopteran

13 letters:
Metamorphosis

Zoology

Index

A

abuse *see* Insults and terms of abuse

academia *see* Colleges →Degrees →Education terms →Ivy League universities

accommodation *see* Homes

accountancy *see* Economics →Trade terms

aeronautics *see* Aircraft →Aviation terms

aeroplane *see* Aircraft →Airline Flight Codes →Aviation terms

afflictions *see* Diseases →Skin, afflictions of

agronomy *see* Agriculturalists →Agricultural terms

air *see* Atmosphere, layers of

alliances *see* European Union

American football *see* Football: Terms used in American football

American universities *see* Ivy League universities

amusements *see* Entertainment

anatomy *see* Blood cells →Body, parts of →Bones →Brain, parts of →Ear, parts of →Eye →Glands →Heart, parts of →Humours of the body →Membranes →Muscles →Nerves →Organs →Teeth →Veins

Ancient Greece *see* Gods and Goddesses →Gorgons →Graces →Greeks →Harpies →Hercules, Labours of →Muses

ancient languages *see* Languages

Ancient Rome *see* Emperors →Festivals →Furies →Gods and Goddesses →Muses

animal years *see* Zodiac: Chinese animal years

animation *see* Cartoon characters →Dwarfs

anthropology *see* Inhabitants →Peoples

antiques *see* Chinaware →Furniture

Apocrypha *see* Bible

apparel *see* Caps →Clothing →Coats and cloaks →Dresses →Hats →Hoods →Jackets →Scarves →Shirts →Shoes and Boots →Skirts →Socks and Tights →Suits →Sweaters →Ties and cravats →Trousers and shorts →Underwear

apparitions *see* Supernatural

arachnids *see* Spiders and other arachnids

archaeology *see* Fossils

aristocracy *see* Nobility

arithmetic *see* Mathematics

army *see* Aircraft →British Forces →Crosses →History →Military ranks →Regimental nicknames

aromatherapy *see* Medicine: Branches of alternative medicine →Oils

artillery *see* Guns →Warfare terms →Weapons

Association football *see* Football: Terms used in (association) football

astrophysicists *see* Astronomers

attire *see* Caps →Clothing →Coats and cloaks →Dresses →Hats →Hoods →Jackets →Scarves →Shirts →Shoes and boots →Skirts →Socks and tights →Suits →Sweaters →Ties and cravats →Trousers and shorts →Underwear

Australia *see* Marsupials →Prime Ministers: Australian Prime Ministers

Australian football *see* Football: Terms used in Australian Rules Football

authors *see* Novelists →Poetry: Poets →Writers

automobiles *see* Cars

awards *see* Cups →Film and television →Medals

Aztec *see* Emperors →Gods and Goddesses

B

bathroom *see* Household items

battle *see* Armour →Battles →Guns →Warfare terms →Weapons

beasts *see* →Giants and giantesses →Gorgons →Harpies →Hercules, labours of →Monsters →Mythology: Characters in classical mythology, Mythological creatures

bedroom *see* Beds →Household items

beliefs *see* Religion: Religions, Religious books

beverages *see* Alcohols →Drinks →Wines

Biblical figures *see* Angels →Apocalypse, Four Horsemen of →Giants and giantesses →Lovers

billiards *see* Snooker and billiards terms

biography *see* Diarists

birds of prey *see* Prey, birds of

birthstones *see* Birthstones →Gemstones →Stones

board games *see* Games

boas *see* Snakes

boats *see* Boats and ships →Ships, parts of

boiled sweets *see* Confectionary

bombs *see* Explosives

books *see* Books →Religion: Religious books →Works of literature and music

boots *see* Shoes and boots

boroughs *see* London, boroughs of

bovine *see* Cattle, breeds of →Cows

breeds *see* Cats →Cattle, breeds of →Dogs →Horses →Pigs →Rabbits and hares →Sheep

Britain *see* Counties →Prime Ministers: British Prime Ministers

British Empire, former colonies *see* Commonwealth members

broadcasting *see* Cinema and television →Film and television

Broadway *see* Theatre terms

Buddhism *see* Buddhism →Monastic orders →Monks →Religion

buildings *see* Arches →Architecture →Castles →Cathedrals →Entertainment: Places of entertainment →Homes →Religion: Religious buildings →Roofing

business *see* Business people →Economics

C

cabins *see* Huts

calculus *see* Mathematics

Cambridge *see* Oxbridge Colleges

Canada *see* Prime Ministers: Canadian Prime Ministers →Provinces of Canada

cancers *see* Tumours

canine *see* Dogs

cantons *see* Swiss cantons

Capitoline *see* Rome, the seven hills of

cash *see* Coins →Currencies

catalysts *see* Enzymes

Catholicism *see* Christian denominations and sects →Monks →Popes →Saints

Caucasus *see* Russian federal republics

celestial bodies *see* Angels →Comets →Planets →Satellites →Stars and constellations

Celtic *see* Gods and Goddesses: Celtic →Languages

ceramics *see* Crafts →Pottery

cereals *see* Rice and other cereals

characters *see* History: Historical characters →Literature: Literary characters →Musketeers →Shakespeare: Characters in Shakespeare

Charities *see* Graces

chemicals *see* Acids →Alcohols →Alkalis →Compounds

children's games *see* Games

China *see* Emperors →Zodiac: Chinese animal years

Christianity *see* Angels →Arthurian legend →Cathedrals →Christian denominations and sects →Crosses →Devils and Demons →Disciples →Ecclesiastical terms →Festivals →Monastic orders →Monks →Popes →Religion →Saints

Christian names *see* First names

churches *see* Cathedrals →Christian denominations and sects →Religion: Religious buildings

cinema *see* Actors →Cinema and television →Film and television

circuits *see* Electronics terms

civilisation *see* Ancient Cities →Archaeology

class *see* Nobility

classical music *see* Orchestral instruments

classics *see* Actaeon's Hounds →Ancient Cities →Devils and demons →Emperors →Fates →Furies →Giants and giantesses →Gods and Goddesses →Gorgons →Graces →Greeks →Harpies →Hercules, labours of →Lovers →Seven against Thebes

cleaning *see* Household items

climate *see* Atmosphere, layers of →Clouds →Weather

cloths *see* Fabrics →Fibres →Materials

coastal regions *see* Capes →Ports

coats of arms *see* Heraldry terms

cobras *see* Snakes

colours →Blue, shades of →Brown, shades of →Green, shades of →Orange, shades of →Purple, shades of →Red, shades of →Yellow, shades of

combat *see* Clubs and bats →Fencing terms →Martial arts →Military ranks →Missiles →Warfare terms →Weapons

design *see* Art →Engineering →Furniture

desks *see* Tables and desks

digital *see* Communications →Computer games →Computers →Internet domain names →Programming languages

dignitaries *see* Officials

directions *see* Compass and cardinal points

disinfectant *see* Alcohols

Disney *see* Cartoon characters →Cats: Famous cats →Dwarfs

distillation *see* Alcohols →Whiskies

doctors *see* Medicine: Medical practitioners and specialists

doctrines *see* Philosophy

dogs *see* Carnivores →Dogs

double-acts *see* Comedians

drama *see* Actors →Shakespeare

drawing *see* Art

dressings *see* Sauces

dwellers *see* Inhabitants →Peoples

dyes *see* Colours →Dyes →Pigments

E

earthenware *see* Pottery

educational establishments *see* Colleges →Oxbridge Colleges

eels *see* Fish

Egyptian *see* Gods and Goddesses

elected officials *see* Officials →Parliaments

epochs *see* Geology

equations *see* Mathematics

equipment *see* Apparatus →Cutting tools

equitation *see* Equestrianism →Horses

energy *see* Electronics terms

England *see* Counties

entertainers *see* Comedians →Jazz: Jazz musicians

eras *see* Geology

ethereal *see* Supernatural

ethnic minorities *see* Inhabitants →Peoples

events *see* Festivals →History

Everest *see* Mountains

executive *see* Officials

F

fanatics *see* Collectors and enthusiasts →Mania

farm(ing) *see* Agriculturalists →Agricultural terms →Cattle and other artiodactyls →Cattle, breeds of →Cheeses →Pigs

fashion *see* Caps →Clothing →Coats and cloaks →Dresses →Hats →Hoods →Jackets →Scarves →Shirts →Shoes and boots →Skirts →Socks and tights →Suits →Sweaters →Ties and cravats →Trousers and shorts →Underwear

fears *see* Phobias

feast days *see* Religion: Religious festivals

federal republics of Russia *see* Russian federal republics

feline *see* Cats

felonies *see* Crime terms

fences *see* Agricultural terms

fermentation *see* Alcohols

fiction *see* Diarists →Dramatists

grammar *see* Figures of speech
  →Grammatical cases

Great Britain *see* Counties

Greek *see* Alphabets →Ancient cities
  →Foreign words and phrases
  →Gods and Goddesses →Gorgons
  →Graces →Greek figures →Harpies
  →Hercules, Labours of →Muses

Gregorian *see* Time: Gregorian
  calendar

groups *see* Collective nouns

growths *see* Skin, afflictions of
  →Tumours

guilds *see* Clubs

gulls *see* Sea birds

gums *see* Resins

H

habits *see* Eating habits

Hades *see* Rivers of Hell

handiwork *see* Crafts

hardware *see* Communications
  →Computers: Computer parts,
  Computer terms →Cutting tools

hares *see* Rabbits and hares

headwear *see* Caps →Hats →Hoods

hearing *see* Ear, parts of

Heaven *see* Angels

Hell *see* Rivers of Hell

Hellenism *see* Actaeon's Hounds

herbivores *see* Cattle →Dinosaurs

Hinduism *see* Gods and Goddesses
  →Religion

hobbies *see* Crafts →Embroidery
  stitches →Knitting stitches

holidays *see* Airline flight codes
  →Airports →Festivals

hollywood *see* Actors →Film and
  television

homeware *see* Carpets and rugs
  →Chinaware →Cupboards and
  cabinets →Furniture →Household
  items

hominids *see* Mammals, extinct

honour *see* Medals

horoscope *see* Astrology →Zodiac

horse racing *see* Racing

horticulture *see* Flowers →Plants

hosiery *see* Underwear

houses *see* Homes →Huts

hyde *see* Leather

I

ideology *see* Philosophy

idioms *see* American and British
  Equivalents

Iliad *see* Graces

illnesses *see* Diseases →Parasites

Incan *see* Gods and Goddesses

industry *see* Electronics terms
  →Engineering →Fabrics

infantry *see* Regimental nicknames

infections *see* Diseases

information *see* Newspapers and
  magazines

Information Technology *see*
  Communications →Computers
  →Internet domain names
  →Programming languages

institutions *see* Schools

instruments, musical *see* Music:
  Musical instruments →Orchestral
  instruments

Internet *see* Communications
  →Internet domain names

Islam *see* Festivals →Muslim denominations and sects →Time: Muslim calendar

isles *see* Islands and island groups

Italian *see* Foreign words and phrases

Italy *see* Regions, administrative

J

jewellery *see* Gemstones

jobs *see* Occupations

Judaism *see* Festivals →Religion →Time: Jewish calendar

K

Kilimanjaro *see* Mountains

killers *see* Murderers

King Arthur *see* Arthurian legend →Knights

kitchen *see* Household items

knives *see* Household items →Swords and other weapons with blades

L

landscape *see* Deserts →Geography →Hills →Mountains →Peninsulas →Volcanoes

language *see* Alphabets →American and British Equivalents >Dialects →Figures of speech →Foreign words and phrases →Grammatical cases →Homophones

Latin *see* Foreign words and phrases

leaders *see* Generals →Presidents of the U.S. →Prime Ministers

leagues *see* American football teams

leaves *see* Palms →Plants

legend *see* Actaeon's Hounds →Ancient cities →Arthurian legend →Fates →Furies →Giants and giantesses →Gods and Goddesses →Gorgons →Graces →Greeks →Harpies →Hercules, Labours of →Heroes →Monsters →Muses →Rivers of Hell →Seven against Thebes →Wonders of the ancient world

legislation *see* Law

leisure *see* Entertainment

letters *see* Alphabets

lexicography *see* Alphabets

lingerie *see* Underwear

lochs *see* Lakes, lochs and loughs

loughs *see* Lakes, lochs and loughs

love *see* Affection, terms of

M

machinery *see* Agricultural terms →Aircraft parts →Apparatus →Cutting tools

mammals *see* Animals →Anteaters →Antelopes →Carnivores →Cats →Cattle →Cows →Dinosaurs →Dogs →Horses →Mammals, extinct →Marsupials →Rabbits and hares →Rodents →Shrews and other insectivores →Seals

mapping *see* Compass →Continents →Counties →Countries →Geography

marinade *see* Cookery →Sauces

marine life *see* Algae →Crustaceans →Fish →Seals →Sea mammals

→Seaweeds →Sharks →Shellfish →Whales and dolphins

marriage *see* Anniversaries

masonry *see* Arches →Architecture →Stone

maths *see* Mathematics →Units

Mayan *see* Gods and Goddesses

meals *see* Cookery →Dishes →Meals

measurements *see* Units →Weather: weather measuring instruments →Weights and measures

mechanics *see* Aircraft parts →Engineering

media *see* Communications →Newspapers and magazines

medication *see* Drugs and drug terms

medieval *see* Armour →Arthurian legend →Heraldry terms →Knights

menswear *see* Ties and cravats

mental health *see* Mania →Phobias →Psychology

mental illness *see* Mania →Phobias →Psychology

Mesopotamia *see* Ancient Cities

metamorphoses *see* Actaeon's Hounds →Artemis

meteorology *see* Weather: Meteorological terms

metric *see* Weights and measures: Metric system

mice *see* Rodents

military *see* Aircraft →British Forces →Crosses →History →Military ranks →Regimental nicknames

modes *see* Music: Musical modes

monarchy *see* Castles →Emperors →History →Kings →Queens

money *see* Coins →Currencies →Economics

moons *see* Satellites

motor racing *see* Grand Prix circuits →Racing

movements *see* Poetry: Poetry movements and groupings →Religion: Religious buildings

movies *see* Actors →Cinema and television →Directors →Dwarfs →Film and television

mugs *see* Cups and other drinking vessels

mushrooms *see* Fungi →Mushrooms and other edible fungi

music(ians) *see* Composers →Jazz Musicians →Jazz terms →Works of literature and music

N

names *see* First names

nations *see* Countries →Flags →Republics

natural history *see* Fossils →Mammals, extinct →Time

nature *see* Flowers

nautical terms *see* Ropes →Ships, parts of

navy *see* Military ranks →Regimental nicknames

nebula *see* Galaxies →Stars and constellations

New Testament *see* Bible

New Zealand *see* Prime Ministers: New Zealand Prime Ministers →Territories of New Zealand

nicknames *see* Places and their nicknames →Regimental nicknames

nobility *see* Emperors →Kings →Nobility →Queens →Rulers

non-contact sports *see* Sports

norse *see* Gods and Goddesses

Northern Ireland *see* Counties

notes *see* Notes and rests

novels *see* Literature →Works of literature and music

numbers *see* Roman numerals

numerals *see* Roman numerals

O

ocean *see* Algae →Channels →Crustaceans →Fish

offences *see* Crime terms

offensive *see* Insults

ointments *see* Resins

Old Testament *see* Bible

Olympics *see* Athletic events

operations *see* Surgical operations

orchestra *see* Composers →Orchestral instruments

organs *see* Heart, parts of

orienteering *see* Compass

ornaments *see* Chinaware

outfits *see* Clothing

outhouses *see* Huts

Ovid *see* Actaeon's Hounds

ovine *see* Sheep

Oxford *see* Oxbridge Colleges

P

Pagan *see* Festivals

painters *see* Artists

painting *see* Art →Colours →Pigments

palaeontology *see* Mammals, extinct

Palatine *see* Rome, the seven hills of

pants *see* Underwear

Paradise *see* Angels

particles *see* Subatomic particles

party games *see* Games

pastimes *see* Crafts →Embroidery stitches

people *see* Inhabitants →Peoples

periodicals *see* Newspapers and magazines

periods *see* Geology →Time

pharmaceuticals *see* Alcohols →Drugs and drug terms

phenomena *see* Weather: Weather phenomena

philosophers *see* Greeks →Philosophy

phonetics *see* Homophones

photography *see* Cameras →Photography

phrases *see* Foreign words and phrases

physicists *see* Astronomers →Physics: Physicists

physics *see* Astronomy →Comets →Electronics terms →Engineering

pictures *see* Photography

pigments *see* Colours →Dyes

pills *see* Drugs and drug terms

piscine *see* Fish

place names *see* Capes →Capitals →Cities →Places and their nicknames

plankton *see* Algae →Plants

plays *see* Shakespeare: Plays of Shakespeare →Theatre terms

pleasure *see* Entertainment

poems *see* Poetry →Shakespeare: Poems of Shakespeare

police *see* Crime terms

politics *see* European Union →Government →Parliaments

→Political parties →Presidents of the U.S. →Prime Ministers →Swiss cantons

popular music *see* Music: Popular music types

ports *see* Capes

poultry *see* Fowl

power *see* Electronics terms →Emperors →Kings →Political parties →Presidents of the U.S. →Prime Ministers →Queens →Rulers

precious stones *see* Gemstones →Stones

prehistoric *see* Dinosaurs →Fossils →Mammals, extinct

print *see* Newspapers and magazines →Papers →Typefaces

production *see* Drama →Theatre terms

profession *see* Occupations

programmes *see* Cinema and television

programs see Computers →Programming languages

prosody *see* Poetry: Poetry and prosody terms

Protestantism *see* Christian denominations and sects

psychiatry *see* Mania →Medicine →Phobias →Psychology

publishing *see* Newspapers and magazines →Typefaces

puddings *see* Cakes and Pastries →Desserts

puzzles *see* Games

pythons *see* Snakes

Q

qualifications *see* Degrees

R

racing *see* Bets and betting systems →Equestrianism →Racing

ranks *see* British Forces →Military ranks

rashes *see* Skin, afflictions of the

rats *see* Rodents

rays *see* Fish

reconstructive surgery *see* Surgical operations

recreation *see* Entertainment

Regents *see* Rulers

regions *see* Places and their nicknames →Provinces of Canada →Provinces of South Africa →Regions, administrative →Wine: Wine-producing areas

republics of Russia *see* Russian federal republics

Republic of Ireland *see* Counties

revolution *see* History →Time: French Revolutionary calendar

rigging *see* Knots →Ropes

Roman *see* Emperors →Festivals →Furies →Gods and Goddesses

rope *see* Knots →Ropes

Round Table *see* Arthurian legend →Knights

rowing *see* Racing

royalty *see* History

rulers *see* Government →Kings →Queens →Rulers

rules *see* Law

S

sailing *see* Knots →Pirates →Ports →Ships, parts of

schools *see* Colleges →Degrees →Education terms →Ivy League universities →Oxbridge colleges

science *see* Archaeology →Asteroids →Astronomers →Astronomy terms →Biology →Botany →Geography →Geology →Mathematics →Medicine →Physics →Psychology →Zoology

Scotland *see* Counties

Scottish law *see* Law: Scots law terms

scriptures *see* Ecclesiastical terms

sculptors *see* Artists

sculpture *see* Art

seating *see* Chairs →Furniture →Household items

sects *see* Christian denominations and sects →Hindu denominations and sects →Muslim denominations and sects

serial killers *see* Murderers

serials *see* Detectives

seven hills of Rome *see* Rome, the seven hills of

seven wonders of the world *see* Wonders of the ancient world

sewing *see* Embroidery stitches

shades *see* Blue, shades of →Brown, shades of →Colours →Green, shades of →Orange, shades of →Purple, shades of →Red, shades of →Yellow, shades of

shooting stars *see* Meteor showers

shows *see* Entertainment: Types of entertainment

Siberia *see* Russian federal republics

sight *see* Eye: Afflictions of the eye →Eye: Parts of the eye

Sikhism *see* Religion

simian *see* Monkeys, apes and other primates

skins *see* Leather →Skin, afflictions of

slander *see* Insults

slugs *see* Snails, slugs and other gastropods

snacks *see* Confectionary

Socialism *see* Political parties

societies *see* Clubs

software *see* Communications →Computer games →Computers: Computer terms

soldiers *see* Military ranks

South Africa *see* Provinces of South Africa

space *see* Asteroids →Astronomy →Comets →Galaxies →Meteor showers

Spain *see* Regions, administrative

Spanish *see* Foreign words and phrases

speech *see* Dialects

spirits *see* Supernatural

sportsmen and women *see* Cricketers →Footballers →Golfers →Mountaineers →Tennis players

stage *see* Entertainment →Theatre terms

staples *see* Rice and other cereals

star signs *see* Astrology

states *see* Regions, administrative →Republics

stimulants *see* Drugs and drug terms

sting rays *see* Fish

stockings *see* Socks and tights

stock market *see* Economics →Trade terms

V

valves *see* Heart, parts of

vegetation *see* Flowers →Plants →Shrubs

vehicles *see* Aircraft →Carriages and carts →Cars →Locomotives →Vehicles

vermin *see* Insects →Rodents →Shrews and other insectivores

vernacular *see* Alphabets →Dialects →Languages

vertebrates *see* Amphibians →Animals →Anteaters and other edentates →Antelopes →Bats →Birds →Carnivores →Cats →Cattle and other artiodactyls →Cattle, breeds of →Dinosaurs →Dogs →Ducks →Hawks →Horses →Lizards →Mammals, extinct →Marsupials →Monkeys, apes and other primates →Pigs →Prey, birds of →Rabbits and hares →Reptiles →Rodents →Sea birds →Seals →Sea mammals →Sharks →Sheep →Shrews and other insectivores →Snakes →Whales and dolphins

vessels *see* Cases →Containers for liquids →Ships, parts of

vipers *see* Snakes

virology *see* Diseases →Eye: Afflictions of the eye

vocations *see* Occupations

volga *see* Russian federal republics

volume *see* Units

W

Wales *see* Counties

war *see* Aircraft →Apocalypse, Four Horsemen of →Armour →Battles →Clubs and bats →Generals →Heroes →History →Knights →Martial arts →Military ranks →Missiles →Models →Seven against Thebes →Swords and other weapons with blades →Warfare terms →Weapons

Warner Brothers *see* Cartoon characters

water *see* Lakes, lochs and loughs →Sounds →Straits

waterways *see* Canals →Dams →Rivers

weapons *see* Clubs and bats →Guns →Missiles →Swords and other weapons with blades

witches *see* Supernatural

wizards *see* Supernatural

work *see* Occupations

writing *see* Alphabets →Crime writers →Critics →Diarists →Dramatists →Greek figures →Novelists →Papers →Poets →Shakespeare →Works of literature and music

Z

zip codes *see* States

zones *see* Time: Time zones